Rebirth
of
Feminism

REBIRTH
OF
FEMINISM

Judith Hole and Ellen Levine

Quadrangle/The New York Times Book Co.

Contents

Preface   ix

Acronyms   xiv

Preface to the Paperback Edition   xv

Introduction: Historical Precedent   1

I   ORIGINS AND DEVELOPMENT OF THE NEW
WOMEN'S MOVEMENT   15

    1   Women's Rights   17

        Federal Policy and Law   17
        Equal Rights Amendment   54
        National Women's Rights Organizations   77

    2   Women's Liberation   108

        Historical Background   109
        Early Groups   114
        A National Movement   123
        Organizational Development   135
        State of the Movement   157

II   FEMINIST ANALYSIS: IDEAS AND ISSUES   167

    3   "Biological Differences" Argument   171

        Science   172
        Morality   184
        Technology   186
        The Politics of Biological Differences   192

4 Feminist Social Critique   194

      Sex-Role Stereotyping   197
      Self-Image   200
      The Public Self-Image   202
      Social Role and Function   203
      Chivalry   216
      The "Sexual Revolution"   218
      The Politics of Language   222

5 Resistance to the Women's Movement   226

      Ridicule   228
      Accusations of Deviance   232

III AREAS OF ACTION   243

6 Media   247

      Image of Women   247
      Professional Status of Women in the Media 252
      Media Coverage of the Women's Movement   266
      Feminist Media   270

7 Abortion   278

      History of Abortion Laws   279
      Development of the Reform/Repeal
        Movement   282
      Feminist Activities   294

8 Child Care   303

      Feminist Analysis and Action   305
      Government and Industry Activity   312

9 Education   318

      Pending Legislation   319
      College and University Campuses   322
      High Schools   329
      Elementary Education   333

10 Professions   338

      Academic Disciplines   342
      Law   349
      Medicine   355
      Municipal Government   362
      The Arts   365

11 The Church   372
      Origins of Feminist Activity   373
      Feminist Issues   377
      Women's Rights Organizations
        Within the Church   390

CONCLUSION   397

CHRONOLOGY   401

      Addenda   427

APPENDICES, BIBLIOGRAPHY AND INDEX   429

      Historical Documents   429
        1848—Seneca Falls Declaration of
              Sentiments and Resolutions   429
        1963—President's Commission on the
              Status of Women   433
        1968—National Organization for Women
              (NOW) Bill of Rights   439
        1969—Politics of the Ego: A Manifesto
              for New York Radical Feminists   440

      Charts and Tables   444

      Bibliography   450

      Index   472

Preface

THIS BOOK is a study of the resurgence of feminism in the United States—a history and analysis of the origins, organizational development, philosophical thinking, issues and activities of the new women's movement. It begins with a brief discussion of the first feminist movement in America in the 19th and early 20th centuries. This introduction is not meant to offer a detailed description of the earlier movement, but rather to serve as an indication that the contemporary women's movement has a much-ignored historical predecessor.

At the outset, it is necessary to define descriptive terms as they are used in this book:

Women's rights—the term women's rights is used to describe the branch of the women's movement primarily active in attempting to bring about legislative, economic, and educational reforms to eradicate sex discrimination in social institutions. The women most often work through traditional political and legal channels. Women's rights groups are for the most part organized on a national basis, and by and large are composed of moderate and conservative feminists. Some of the groups deliberately avoid "controversial" issues in an attempt to reach as many women as possible.

Women's liberation—the term women's liberation is frequently used as a catch-all expression to describe the entire women's movement. In this book its use is restricted

to the branch of the movement that had its origins in the
student activism of the early 1960's. These women, primarily radical feminists, have thus far been primarily
concerned with analyzing the origins, nature, and extent
of women's subservient role in society, with an emphasis
on the "psychology of oppression." For the most part they
have engaged in activities to educate themselves and
others about these issues. The structure most common to
this branch of the movement is the small locally-based
"consciousness raising" group.

Women's movement—the phrase women's movement is used
to describe the entire spectrum of women's group from
moderate to radical.

The book is divided into three major sections. Part I traces the
growth of both the women's rights and women's liberation
branches of the movement. It begins with a discussion of the
President's Commission on the Status of Women established in
1961, which marked the first time since the ratification of the
women's suffrage Amendment in 1920 that the United States
government formally addressed itself to "women's issues." This
section also outlines the changes in federal policy and law with
regard to women, and includes a discussion of the emergence and
development of the major national women's rights organizations.
The second half of Part I explores the beginnings of the women's
liberation movement. The discussion combines both a chronological overview of the development of this radical branch of the
women's movement with a description and analysis of the organizational and conceptual problems with which the women have
grappled.

The mass media, with complex systems of communication,
provide instant and potentially extensive news coverage of political phenomena; nevertheless, information is often transmitted in
slogan phrases. Part II is an attempt to enlarge the area of knowledge about the women's movement by delineating in some detail
the philosophical basis and social critique of feminists today.

From the mid-1960's, the women's movement has grown at
an extraordinary rate. It is almost impossible to estimate the
numbers of women involved since, as feminists note, the movement is at present almost as much a state of mind as it is a movement. Nevertheless, it is probably safe to say that by 1971

hundreds of thousands of women had, since the movement's inception, participated in women's rights or women's liberation groups, supported various activities, and participated in different actions. Part III is a discussion of the areas in which the most significant feminist actions have taken place.

The book concludes with a chronology from 1961 to 1971 of representative events and activities concerning women's issues. Not only does such a listing graphically illustrate the rapid growth of the movement, but it also indicates the broad spectrum of feminist concerns, tactics and goals.

The appendices include four historical documents of interest: one from the first feminist movement of the 19th century; a federal government report that can serve to date the beginnings of the contemporary movement; and two papers from the movement today that represent both moderate and radical feminist thinking.

It is important to note that much of the material included in this book had never been systematically compiled. It was possible to gather this information only through many hours of interviews with women throughout the country, some of whom have been involved in the movement since its inception. Many of the women (both moderate and radical feminists) were willing to be interviewed as long as it was understood that their comments were not for attribution. In order to respect their wishes and yet convey with some degree of accuracy the tone of their thinking, we have included some quotations for which we can give no specific citation.

We are exceedingly grateful to all the women across the country who were willing to talk with us. We are particularly indebted to the following women who both provided us with background information and research materials, and generously shared with us their time, their thinking, and their ideas about the women's movement: Dr. Elizabeth Boyer, Catherine East, Mary Eastwood, Shulamith Firestone, Jo Freeman, Dr. Jo-Ann Evans Gardner, Anne Koedt, Dr. Bernice Sandler.

The idea for this book grew out of a brief background report on the women's movement prepared within the CBS News Broadcast Research unit for CBS radio and television coverage of the August 26, 1970, Women's Strike Day demonstration. At CBS News, we are grateful to Samuel T. Suratt, Archivist, and Joseph P. Bellon, Director, Resources Development and Production, who gave us the opportunity to write this book, and whose time and effort contributed to its completion; we would also like to thank Edward Hamlin, Coordinator, Broadcast Research; Virginia Huber, staff member, Broadcast Research, and Barbara Laschinger, Resources Development and Production; in the CBS Special Projects Library, Susan Mills, Evelyn Hisz, Virginia Gerhart, and Alice Wilkins. In addition, we would like to thank Herbert Nagourney and Lee Foster of *The New York Times* for their encouragement and support throughout; and a special word of appreciation to Ronald Hudson of Browning Editorial Services, for his careful reading of the manuscript and his many valuable suggestions; to Bente Hamann and Joan Lamm for expediting every phase of production; and to Lucinda Cisler for compiling and annotating such an extensive bibliography.

We would like to acknowledge the following authors and publishers for permission to quote from copyright material: Lucinda Cisler ("Unfinished Business: Birth Control and Women's Liberation," reprinted in *Sisterhood Is Powerful*, Random House, Inc., 1970), Ruth Herschberger (*Adam's Rib*, Harper & Row, 1970), Joreen ("Bitch Manifesto," reprinted in *Notes From The Second Year: Women's Liberation*, 1970), Leo Kanowitz (*Women and the Law: The Unfinished Revolution*, University of New Mexico Press, 1969), Anne Koedt ("The Myth of the Vaginal Orgasm," and "Politics of the Ego: A Manifesto for New York Radical Feminists," reprinted in *Notes From The Second Year: Women's Liberation*, 1970), Naomi Weisstein (" 'Kinder, Küche, Kirche' As Scientific Law: Psychology Constructs the Female," reprinted in *Sisterhood Is Powerful*, Random House, Inc., 1970), Ellen Willis c/o International Famous Agency ("Up From Radicalism: A Feminist Journal," *US* #2, Bantam, 1969). Association Press (*Women's Liberation and the Church*, ed. Sarah Bentley Doely, 1970), Brooks/Cole Publishing Co. (*Beliefs, Attitudes, and Human Affairs*, S. L. Bem and D. J. Bem, 1970), Doubleday & Co., Inc. (*Sexual Politics*, Kate Millett, 1969, 1970), Feminists on Children's Media (*Report on Sexism in Children's Literature*, 1970), *McCall's* Magazine ("Five Passionate Feminists," July, 1970), William Morrow & Co., Inc. (*The Dialectic of Sex: The Case for Feminist Revolution*, Shulamith Firestone, 1970), *New York* Magazine ("The March of *Time*'s Women," Lilla Lyon, February 22, 1971), *Psychology Today*, Communications/Research/Machines, Inc. ("Fail: Bright Women," Matina Horner, November, 1969), Alfred A. Knopf, Inc. (*The Second Sex*,

Simone de Beauvoir, 1952, 1968), *Variety* ("CBS Tips Hat to Women's Lib," August 26, 1970), *The YWCA Magazine* ("Racism and Sexism," January, 1971).

New York City   J. H., E. L.
July, 1971

Acronyms

ALI	American Law Institute
ARAL	Association to Repeal Abortion Laws
ASA	Association for the Study of Abortion
BFOQ	Bona Fide Occupational Qualification
BPW	National Federation of Business and Professional Women's Clubs
EEOC	Equal Employment Opportunity Commission
EO	Executive Order
ERA	Equal Rights Amendment
FEW	Federally Employed Women
HRW	Human Rights for Women, Inc.
NCNP	National Conference for a New Politics
NOW	National Organization for Women
NYALR	New Yorkers for Abortion Law Repeal
OFCC	Office of Federal Contract Compliance
PWC	Professional Women's Caucus
SDS	Students for a Democratic Society
SNCC	Student Non-Violent Coordinating Committee
SWP	Socialist Workers' Party
WEAL	Women's Equity Action League
YSA	Young Socialist Alliance
YWCA	Young Women's Christian Association

Preface to the Paperback Edition

A YEAR AGO when we completed *Rebirth of Feminism* hundreds of thousands of women had directly participated in movement activities as well as felt the impact of feminist ideas. Nonetheless, women's issues were not yet viewed as serious by most traditional political analysts, right, left, or center.

In the intervening year, although the critics remain, the movement has expanded so dramatically that even the most established institutions have been forced to recognize women's issues. To cite only the most visible examples: In 1972, after a 49-year struggle, the Equal Rights Amendment was passed; for the first time a woman was a candidate for a party presidential nomination; in that same election year, 21 other women campaigned for congressional seats; almost daily the press reported the election, appointment, or hiring of women to jobs previously held only by men; consciousness-raising groups proliferated and became almost as accepted in their communities as the PTA; and dozens of books and periodicals on feminism were published and widely read.

Since feminism challenges the most basic assumptions about the "natures" of men and women, it is not surprising to find that the most organized resistance to it has centered primarily around the issues of reproduction and child care. Two examples: the President vetoed the most comprehensive and widely supported child care bill ever passed by Congress; a militant anti-abortion campaign by "right-to-lifers" threatened the efforts of feminists and other activists to repeal the many restrictive state abortion laws.

Some of the changes in law and custom that have taken place during the past year have been noted in an addendum to the chronology. Since the issues and strategies of the women's movement, as well as the resistance to it, have for the most part remained as described, the text proper has not been revised.

New York City   J. H., E. L.
August, 1972

Introduction:
Historical Precedent

THE CONTEMPORARY women's movement is not the first such movement in American history to offer a wide-ranging feminist critique of society. In fact, much of what seems "radical" in contemporary feminist analysis parallels the critique made by the feminists of the 19th century. Both the early and the contemporary feminists have engaged in a fundamental re-examination of the role of women in all spheres of life, and of the relationships of men and women in all social, political, economic and cultural institutions. Both have defined women as an oppressed group and have traced the origin of women's subjugation to male-defined and male-dominated social institutions and value-systems.

When the early feminist movement emerged in the 19th century, the "woman issue" was extensively debated in the national press, in political gatherings, and from Church pulpits. The women's groups, their platforms, and their leaders, although not always well received or understood, were extremely well known. Until recently, however, that early feminist movement has been only cursorily discussed in American history textbooks, and then only in terms of the drive for suffrage. Even a brief reading of early feminist writings and of the few histories that have dealt specifically with the woman's movement (as it was

called then) reveals that the drive for suffrage became the single
focus of the movement only after several decades of a more multi-
issued campaign for women's equality.

The woman's movement emerged during the 1800's. It was a
time of geographic expansion, industrial development, growth of
social reform movements, and a general intellectual ferment with
a philosophical emphasis on individual freedom, the "rights of
man" and universal education. In fact, some of the earliest efforts
to extend opportunities to women were made in the field of education. In 1833, Oberlin became the first college to open its doors
to both men and women. Although female education at Oberlin
was regarded as necessary to ensure the development of good and
proper wives and mothers, the open admission policy paved the
way for the founding of other schools, some devoted entirely to
women's education.[1] Much of the ground-breaking work in education was done by Emma Willard, who had campaigned vigorously
for educational facilities for women beginning in the early 1820's.
Frances Wright, one of the first women orators, was also a strong
advocate of education for women. She viewed women as an
oppressed group and argued that, "Until women assume the place
in society which good sense and good feeling alike assign to them,
human improvement must advance but feebly."[2] Central to her
discussion of the inequalities between the sexes was a particular
concern with the need for equal educational training for women.

It was in the abolition movement of the 1830's, however, that
the woman's rights movement as such had its political origins.
When women began working in earnest for the abolition of
slavery, they quickly learned that they could not function as
political equals with their male abolitionist friends. Not only were
they barred from membership in some organizations, but they
had to wage an uphill battle for the right simply to speak in
public. Sarah and Angelina Grimké, daughters of a South Carolina slaveholding family, were among the first to fight this battle.
Early in their lives the sisters left South Carolina, moved north,
and began to speak out publicly on the abolition issue. Within a
short time they drew the wrath of different sectors of society. A

---

[1] Mount Holyoke opened in 1837; Vassar, 1865; Smith and Wellesley, 1875;
Radcliffe, 1879; Bryn Mawr, 1885.
[2] Quoted in Eleanor Flexner, *Century of Struggle: The Woman's Rights
Movement in the United States* (Cambridge, Mass.: The Belknap Press of
Harvard University Press, 1959), p. 27.

Pastoral letter from the Council of the Congregationalist Ministers of Massachusetts typified the attack:

> The appropriate duties and influence of woman are clearly stated in the New Testament. . . . The power of woman is her dependence, flowing from the consciousness of that weakness which God has given her for her protection. . . . When she assumes the place and tone of man as a public reformer . . . she yields the power which God has given her . . . and her character becomes unnatural.[3]

The brutal and unceasing attacks (sometimes physical) on the women convinced the Grimkés that the issues of freedom for slaves and freedom for women were inextricably linked. The women began to speak about both issues, but because of the objections from male abolitionists who were afraid that discussions of woman's rights would "muddy the waters," they often spoke about the "woman question" as a separate issue. (In fact, Lucy Stone, an early feminist and abolitionist, lectured on abolition on Saturdays and Sundays and on women's rights during the week.)

In an 1837 letter to the President of the Boston Female Anti-Slavery Society—by that time many female anti-slavery societies had been established in response to the exclusionary policy of the male abolitionist groups—Sarah Grimké addressed herself directly to the question of woman's status:

> All history attests that man has subjugated woman to his will, used her as a means to promote his selfish gratification, to minister to his sensual pleasures, to be instrumental in promoting his comfort; but never has he desired to elevate her to that rank she was created to fill. He has done all he could to debase and enslave her mind; and now he looks triumphantly on the ruin he has wrought, and says, the being he has thus deeply injured is his inferior. . . . But I ask no favors for my sex. . . . All I ask of

---

[3] *History of Woman Suffrage* (Republished by Arno Press and *The New York Times*, New York, 1969). Vol. I, p. 81. Hereafter cited as *HWS*. Volumes I to III were edited by Elizabeth Cady Stanton, Susan B. Anthony and Matilda Joslyn Gage. The first two volumes were published in 1881, the third in 1886. Volume IV was edited by Susan B. Anthony and Ida Husted Harper and was published in 1902. Volumes V and VI were edited by Ida Husted Harper and published in 1922.

our brethren is, that they will take their feet from off our
necks and permit us to stand upright on that ground
which God designed us to occupy.[4]

The Grimkés challenged both the assumption of the "natural
superiority of man" and the social institutions predicated on that
assumption. For example, in her "Letters on the Equality of the
Sexes," Sarah Grimké argued against both religious dogma and
the institution of marriage. Two brief examples are indicative:

. . . Adam's ready acquiescence with his wife's proposal,
does not savor much of that superiority *in strength of
mind,* which is arrogated by man.[5]

. . . man has exercised the most unlimited and brutal
power over woman, in the peculiar character of husband
—a word in most countries synonymous with tyrant. . . .
Woman, instead of being elevated by her union with man,
which might be expected from an alliance with a superior
being, is in reality lowered. She generally loses her individuality, her independent character, her moral being.
She becomes absorbed into him, and henceforth is looked
at, and acts through the medium of her husband.[6]

They attacked as well the manifestations of "male superiority" in
the employment market. In a letter "On the Condition of Women
in the United States" Sarah Grimké wrote of:

. . . the disproportionate value set on the time and labor
of men and of women. A man who is engaged in teaching,
can always, I believe, command a higher price for tuition
than a woman—even when he teaches the same branches,
and is not in any respect superior to the woman. . . . [Or]
for example, in tailoring, a man has twice, or three times
as much for making a waistcoat or pantaloons as a
woman, although the work done by each may be equally
good.[7]

---

[4] Sarah M. Grimké, *Letters on the Equality of the Sexes and the Condition
of Woman* (Boston: Isaac Kanapp, 1838, reprinted by Source Book Press,
New York, 1970), p. 10 ff.
[5] *Ibid.*, pp. 9–10.
[6] *Ibid.*, pp. 85–86.
[7] *Ibid.*, p. 51.

The abolition movement continued to expand, and in 1840 a World Anti-Slavery Convention was held in London. The American delegation included a group of women, among them Lucretia Mott and Elizabeth Cady Stanton. In Volume I of the *History of Woman Suffrage*, written and edited by Stanton, Susan B. Anthony and Matilda Joslyn Gage, the authors note that the mere presence of women delegates produced an ". . . excitement and vehemence of protest and denunciation [that] could not have been greater, if the news had come that the French were about to invade England."[8] The women were relegated to the galleries and prohibited from participating in any of the proceedings. That society at large frowned upon women participating in political activities was one thing; that the leading male radicals, those most concerned with social inequalities, should also discriminate against women was quite another. The events at the world conference reinforced the women's growing awareness that the battle for the abolition of Negro slavery could never be won without a battle for the abolition of woman's slavery:

> As Lucretia Mott and Elizabeth Cady Stanton wended their way arm in arm down Great Queen Street that night, reviewing the exciting scenes of the day, they agreed to hold a woman's rights convention on their return to America, as the men to whom they had just listened had manifested their great need of some education on that question.[9]

Mott and Stanton returned to America and continued their abolitionist work as well as pressing for state legislative reforms on woman's property and family rights. Although the women had discussed the idea of calling a public meeting on woman's rights, the possibility did not materialize until eight years after the London Convention. On July 14, 1848, they placed a small notice in the *Seneca* (New York) *County Courier* announcing a "Woman's Rights Convention." Five days later, on July 19 and 20, some three hundred interested women and men, coming from as far as fifty miles, crowded into the small Wesleyan Chapel (now a gas station) and approved a Declaration of Sentiments (modeled on the Declaration of Independence) and twelve Resolutions. The delineation of issues in the Declaration bears a startling resem-

---

[8] *HWS*, p. 54.
[9] *Ibid.*, p. 61.

blance to contemporary feminist writings. Some excerpts are illustrative[1]:

> We hold these truths to be self-evident: that all men and women are created equal; that they are endowed by their Creator with certain inalienable rights; that among these are life, liberty, and the pursuit of happiness;
>
> . . . . The history of mankind is a history of repeated injuries and usurpations on the part of man toward woman, having in direct object the establishment of an absolute tyranny over her. To prove this, let facts be submitted to a candid world. . . .
>
> He has compelled her to submit to laws, in the formation of which she has no voice. . . .
> He has made her, if married, in the eye of the law, civilly dead. . . .
> He has monopolized nearly all the profitable employments, and from those she is permitted to follow, she receives but a scanty remuneration. He closes against her all the avenues to wealth and distinction which he considers most honorable to himself. As a teacher of theology, medicine, or law, she is not known.
> He allows her in Church, as well as State, but a subordinate position, claiming Apostolic authority for her exclusion from the ministry, and, with some exceptions, from any public participation in the affairs of the Church.
> He has created a false public sentiment by giving to the world a different code of morals for men and women, by which moral delinquencies which exclude women from society, are not only tolerated, but deemed of little account in man.
> He has usurped the prerogative of Jehovah himself, claiming it as his right to assign for her a sphere of action, when that belongs to her conscience and to her God.
> He has endeavored, in every way that he could, to destroy her confidence in her own powers, to lessen her self-respect, and to make her willing to lead a dependent and abject life.

[1] Both the Declaration of Sentiments and the Resolutions are reprinted in full in the appendix.

Included in the list of twelve resolutions was one which read: "*Resolved,* That it is the duty of the women of this country to secure to themselves their sacred right to the elective franchise."

Although the Seneca Falls Convention is considered the official beginning of the woman's suffrage movement, it is important to reiterate that the goal of the early woman's rights movement was not limited to the demand for suffrage. In fact, the suffrage resolution was included only after lengthy debate, and was the only resolution not accepted unanimously. Those participants at the Convention who actively opposed the inclusion of the suffrage resolution:

> . . . feared a demand for the right to vote would defeat others they deemed more rational, and make the whole movement ridiculous. But Mrs. Stanton and Frederick Douglass seeing that the power to choose rulers and make laws, was the right by which all others could be secured, persistently advocated the resolution. . . .[2]

Far more important to most of the women at the Convention was their desire to gain control of their property and earnings, guardianship of their children, rights to divorce, etc. Notwithstanding the disagreements at the Convention, the Seneca Falls meeting was of great historical significance. As Flexner has noted:

> . . . [The women] themselves were fully aware of the nature of the step they were taking; today's debt to them has been inadequately acknowledged. . . . Beginning in 1848 it was possible for women who rebelled against the circumstances of their lives, to know that they were not alone—although often the news reached them only through a vitriolic sermon or an abusive newspaper editorial. But a movement had been launched which they could either join, or ignore, that would leave its imprint on the lives of their daughters and of women throughout the world.[3]

From 1848 until the beginning of the Civil War, Woman's Rights Conventions were held nearly every year in different cities in the East and Midwest. The 1850 Convention in Salem, Ohio:

---

[2] *HWS,* p. 73.
[3] Flexner, p. 77.

. . . had one peculiar characteristic. It was officered entirely by women; not a man was allowed to sit on the platform, to speak, or vote. *Never did men so suffer.* They
implored just to say a word; but no; the President was in-
flexible—no man should be heard. If one meekly arose to
make a suggestion he was at once ruled out of order. For
the first time in the world's history, men learned how it
felt to sit in silence when questions in which they were
interested were under discussion.[4]

As the woman's movement gained in strength, attacks upon
it became more vitriolic. In newspaper editorials and church
sermons anti-feminists argued vociferously that the public arena
was not the proper place for women. In response to such criticism, Stanton wrote in an article in the Rochester, New York
National Reformer:

If God has assigned a sphere to man and one to woman,
we claim the right to judge ourselves of His design in reference to *us,* and we accord to man the same privilege.
. . . We have all seen a man making a jackass of himself
in the pulpit, at the bar, or in our legislative halls. . . .
Now, is it to be wondered at that woman has some doubts
about the present position assigned her being the true one,
when her every-day experience shows her that man makes
such fatal mistakes in regard to himself?[5]

It was abundantly clear to the women that they could not
rely on the pulpit or the "establishment" press for either factual
or sympathetic reportage; nor could they use the press as a means
to disseminate their ideas. As a result they depended on the abolitionist papers of the day, and in addition founded a number of
independent women's journals including *The Lily, The Una,
Woman's Advocate, Pittsburgh Visiter* [sic], etc.
One of the many issues with which the women activists were
concerned was dress reform. Some began to wear the "bloomer"
costume (a misnomer since Amelia Bloomer, although an advocate of the loose-fitting dress, was neither its originator nor the
first to wear it) in protest against the tight-fitting and singularly
uncomfortable cinched-waisted stays and layers of petticoats.

---

[4] *HWS,* p. 110.
[5] *Ibid.,* p. 806.

However, as Flexner has noted, "The attempt at dress reform, although badly needed, was not only unsuccessful, but boomeranged and had to be abandoned."[6] Women's rights advocates became known as "bloomers" and the movement for equal rights as well as the individual women were subjected to increasing ridicule. Elizabeth Cady Stanton, one of the earliest to wear the more comfortable outfit, was one of the first to suggest its rejection. In a letter to Susan B. Anthony she wrote:

> We put the dress on for greater freedom, but what is physical freedom compared with mental bondage? . . . It is not wise, Susan, to use up so much energy and feeling that way. You can put them to better use. I speak from experience.[7]

When the Civil War began in 1861, woman's rights advocates were urged to abandon their cause and support the war effort. Although Anthony and Stanton continued arguing that any battle for freedom must include woman's freedom, the woman's movement activities essentially stopped for the duration of the War. After the War and the ratification of the 13th Amendment abolishing slavery (for which the women activists had campaigned vigorously), the abolitionists began to press for passage of a 14th Amendment to secure the rights, privileges and immunities of citizens (the new freedmen) under the law. In the second section of the proposed Amendment, however, the word "male" appeared, introducing a sex distinction into the Constitution for the first time. Shocked and enraged by the introduction of the word "male," the women activists mounted an extensive campaign to eliminate it. They were dismayed to find no one, neither the Republican Administration nor their old abolitionists allies, had any intention of "complicating" the campaign for Negroes' rights by advocating women's rights as well. Over and over again the women were told, "This is the Negroes' hour." The authors of *History of Woman Suffrage* analyzed the women's situation:

> During the six years they held their own claims in abeyance to the slaves of the South, and labored to inspire the people with enthusiasm for the great measures of the Republican party, they were highly honored as "wise,

---

[6] Flexner, p. 83.
[7] *Ibid.*, p. 84.

loyal, and clear-sighted." But again when the slaves were emancipated and they asked that women should be recognized in the reconstruction as citizens of the Republic, equal before the law, all these transcendent virtues vanished like dew before the morning sun. And thus it ever is so long as woman labors to second man's endeavors and exalt *his sex* above her own, her virtues pass unquestioned; but when she dares to demand rights and privileges for herself, her motives, manners, dress, personal appearance, character, are subjects for ridicule and detraction.[8]

The women met with the same response when they campaigned to get the word "sex" added to the proposed 15th Amendment which would prohibit the denial of suffrage on account of race.[9]

As a result of these setbacks, the woman's movement assumed as its first priority the drive for woman's suffrage. It must be noted, however, that while nearly all the women activists agreed on the need for suffrage, in 1869 the movement split into two major factions over ideological and tactical questions. In May of that year, Susan B. Anthony and Elizabeth Cady Stanton organized the National Woman Suffrage Association. Six months later, Lucy Stone and others organized the American Woman Suffrage Association. The American, in an attempt to make the idea of woman's suffrage "respectable," limited its activities to that issue, and refused to address itself to any of the more "controversial" subjects such as marriage or the Church. The National, on the other hand, embraced the broad cause of woman's rights of which the vote was seen primarily as a *means* of achieving those rights. During this time Anthony and Stanton founded *The Revolution* which became one of the best known of the independent women's newspapers. The weekly journal began in January, 1868, and took as its motto, "Men, their rights and nothing more; women, their rights and nothing less." In addition to discussions of suffrage, *The Revolution* examined the institutions of marriage, the law, organized religion, etc. Moreover, the newspaper touched on ". . . such incendiary topics as the double standard and prostitution."[1] Flexner describes the paper:

---

[8] *HWS*, Vol. 2, p. 51.
[9] The 13th Amendment was ratified in 1865; the 14th in 1868; the 15th in 1870.
[1] Flexner, p. 151.

> . . . [It] made a contribution to the women's cause out of
> all proportion to either its size, brief lifespan, or modest
> circulation. . . . Here was news not to be found elsewhere—
> of the organization of women typesetters, tailoresses, and
> laundry workers, of the first women's clubs, of pioneers in
> the professions, of women abroad. But *The Revolution* did
> more than just carry news, or set a new standard of pro-
> fessionalism for papers edited by and for women. It gave
> their movement a forum, focus, and direction. It pointed,
> it led, and it fought, with vigor and vehemence.[2]

The two suffrage organizations coexisted for over twenty
years and used some of the same tactics in their campaigns for
suffrage: lecture tours, lobbying activities, petition campaigns,
etc. The American, however, focused exclusively on state-by-state
action, while the National in addition pushed for a woman suffrage Amendment to the federal Constitution. Susan B. Anthony
and others also attempted to gain the vote through court decisions. The Supreme Court, however, held in 1875[3] that suffrage
was not necessarily one of the privileges and immunities of citizens protected by the 14th Amendment. Thus, although women
were *citizens* it was nonetheless permissible, according to the
Court, to constitutionally limit the right to vote to males.

During this same period, a strong temperance movement had
also emerged. Large numbers of women, including some suffragists, became actively involved in the temperance cause. It is
important to note that one of the main reasons women became
involved in pressing for laws restricting the sale and consumption of alcohol was that their legal status as married women
offered them no protection under the law against either physical
abuse or abandonment by a drunken husband. It might be added
that the reason separate women's temperance organizations were
formed was that women were not permitted to participate in the
men's groups. In spite of the fact that temperance was in "women's
interests," the growth of the women's temperance movement solidi-
fied the liquor and brewing industries' opposition to woman suffrage. As a result, suffrage leaders became convinced of the
necessity of keeping the two issues separate.

As the campaign for woman suffrage grew, more and more
sympathizers were attracted to the conservative and "respectable"

---

[2] *Loc. cit.*

[3] *Minor v. Happersett,* 21 Wall. 162, 22 L. Ed. 627 (1875).

American Association which, as noted above, deliberately limited
its work to the single issue of suffrage. After two decades "respectability" won out, and the broad-ranging issues of the earlier
movement had been largely subsumed by suffrage. (Even the
Stanton-Anthony forces had somewhat redefined their goals and
were focusing primarily on suffrage.) By 1890, when the American and the National merged to become the National American
Woman Suffrage Association, the woman's movement had, in
fact, been transformed into the single-issue suffrage movement.
Moreover, although Elizabeth Cady Stanton, NAWSA's first president, was succeeded two years later by Susan B. Anthony, the
first women activists with their catholic range of concerns were
slowly being replaced by a second group far more limited in their
political analysis. It should be noted that Stanton herself, after
her two-year term as president of the new organization, withdrew
from active work in the suffrage campaign. Although one of the
earliest feminist leaders to understand the need for woman
suffrage, by this time Stanton believed that the main obstacle to
woman's equality was the church and organized religion.

During the entire development of the woman's movement
perhaps the argument most often used by anti-feminists was that
the subjugation of women was divinely ordained as written in the
Bible. Stanton attacked the argument head-on. She and a group
of twenty-three women, including three ordained ministers, produced *The Woman's Bible*,[4] which presented a systematic feminist critique of woman's role and image in the Bible. Some
Biblical chapters were presented as proof that the Scripture itself
was the source of woman's subjugation; others to show that, if
reinterpreted, men and women were indeed equals in the Bible,
not superior and inferior beings. "We have made a fetish [sic] of
the Bible long enough. The time has come to read it as we do all
other books, accepting the good and rejecting the evil it teaches."[5]
Dismissing the "rib story" as a "petty surgical operation," Stanton
argued further that the entire structure of the Bible was predicated on the notion of Eve's (woman's) corruption:

> Take the snake, the fruit-tree and the woman from the
> tableau, and we have no fall, nor frowning Judge, no In-
> ferno, no everlasting punishment,—hence no need of a
> Savior. Thus the bottom falls out of the whole Christian

---

[4] New York, European Publishing Company, 1895 and 1898, Two Parts.
[5] *Ibid.*, II, pp. 7–8.

theology. Here is the reason why in all the Biblical re-
searches and higher criticisms, the scholars never touch
the position of women.[6]

Not surprisingly, *The Woman's Bible* was considered by most
scandalous and sacrilegious. The Suffrage Association members
themselves, with the exception of Anthony and a few others,
publicly disavowed Stanton and her work. They feared that the
image of the already controversial suffrage movement would be
irreparably damaged if the public were to associate it with Stanton's radical tract.

Shortly after the turn of the century, the second generation of
woman suffragists came of age and new leaders replaced the old.
Carrie Chapman Catt is perhaps the best known; she succeeded
Anthony as president of the National American Woman Suffrage
Association, which by then had become a large and somewhat unwieldy organization. Although limited gains were achieved (a
number of western states had enfranchised women) no major
progress was made in the campaign for suffrage until Alice Paul,
a young and extremely militant suffragist, became active in the
movement. In April, 1913, she formed a small radical group
known as the Congressional Union (later reorganized as the
Woman's Party[7]) to work exclusively on a campaign for a *federal*
woman's suffrage Amendment using any tactical means necessary no matter how unorthodox. Her group organized parades,
mass demonstrations, hunger strikes, and its members were on
several occasions arrested and jailed.[8] Although many suffragists
rejected both the militant style and tactics of the Congressional
Union, they nonetheless did consider Paul and her followers in
large part responsible for "shocking" the languishing movement
into actively pressuring for the federal Amendment. The woman
suffrage Amendment (known as the "Anthony Amendment"),
introduced into every session of Congress from 1878 on, was
finally ratified on August 26, 1920.

Nearly three-quarters of a century had passed since the demand for woman suffrage had first been made at the Seneca Falls
Convention. By 1920, so much energy had been expended in

[6] Stanton, letter to the editor of *The Critic* (New York), March 28, 1896,
quoted from Aileen S. Kraditor, *The Ideas of the Woman Suffrage Movement, 1890–1920* (New York: Columbia University Press, 1965), n. 11, p. 81.
[7] See Chapter 2, National Women's Rights Organizations.
[8] A total of 218 women from 26 states were arrested during the first session
of the 65th Congress (1917). Ninety-seven went to prison.

achieving the right to vote, that the woman's movement virtually collapsed from exhaustion. To achieve the vote alone, as Carrie Chapman Catt had computed, took:

> . . . fifty-two years of pauseless campaign. . . . fifty-six campaigns of referenda to male voters; 480 campaigns to get Legislatures to submit suffrage amendments to voters; 47 campaigns to get State constitutional conventions to write woman suffrage into state constitutions; 277 campaigns to get State party conventions to include woman suffrage planks; 30 campaigns to get presidential party conventions to adopt woman suffrage planks in party platforms, and 19 campaigns with 19 successive Congresses.[9]

With the passage of the 19th Amendment the majority of women activists as well as the public at large assumed that having gained the vote woman's complete equality had been virtually obtained.

It must be remembered, however, that for most of the period that the woman's movement existed, suffrage had not been seen as an all-inclusive goal, but as a means of achieving equality— suffrage was only one element in the wide-ranging feminist critique questioning the fundamental organization of society. Historians, however, have for the most part ignored this radical critique and focused exclusively on the suffrage campaign. By virtue of this omission they have, to all intents and purposes, denied the political significance of the early feminist analysis. Moreover, the summary treatment by historians of the 19th and 20th century drive for woman's suffrage has made that campaign almost a footnote to the abolitionist movement and the campaign for Negro suffrage. In addition, the traditional textbook image of the early feminists—if not wild-eyed women waving placards for the vote, then wild-eyed women swinging axes at saloon doors—has further demeaned the importance of their philosophical analysis.

The woman's movement virtually died in 1920 and, with the exception of a few organizations, feminism was to lie dormant for forty years.

---

[9] Carrie Chapman Catt and Nettie Rogers Shuler, *Woman Suffrage and Politics* (New York, 1923), p. 107. Quoted from Flexner, p. 173.

I

Origins and
Development
of the
New Women's
Movement

1

Women's Rights

Federal Policy and Law

THE FIRST DRIVE for women's equality ended in 1920 with the ratification of the 19th Amendment. It was another forty years before the United States Government again formally addressed itself to the "woman question," and even somewhat longer before another women's movement emerged.

Between 1920 and 1960 public interest in women's rights to all intents and purposes had vanished. In fact, by the late 1940's there was a renewed public articulation (via advertising, women's magazines, psychologists, etc.) of the "feminine mystique" as Betty Friedan called it in her bestselling book of the same title. By 1960, the assumption that woman by nature was destined to be a full-time homemaker and mother was so widely believed to be true that it was as if there had never been a feminist movement in this country which had questioned that assumption.

This prevailing image of woman had two main effects. On the one hand, many women fully believed that their destiny was indeed the home. Any discontent they felt (as described and analyzed in *The Feminine Mystique*) was believed to have resulted from individual maladjustments. On the other hand, because of the Depression, World War II, the development of labor-saving devices for the home, the widespread use of contraceptives, etc., many women were in fact working. However, the existence of these millions of women in the labor force was virtually ignored because according to the prevailing social ethic women who worked were only marking time until they would marry and "settle down." The statistics tell quite a different story. By 1960 women made up more than one-third of the nation's workers; 54 percent of these working women were married (with husbands present) and 33 percent were mothers. In fact, the percentage of married women and mothers in the work force had grown steadily since World War II. In addition, because of the prevailing assumptions about woman's proper social role, the uniformly low status of women workers was accepted without question.

Only a handful of indefatigable activists believed the low status of women workers to be a result of discrimination, but they were unable to effect any enduring legislative reforms to alter the status quo. They did marshal enough support, however, to have an Equal Rights Amendment[1] introduced into nearly every session of Congress beginning in 1923. Such an Amendment would require absolute equality of men and women under the law and would affect thousands of state and local laws expressly designed to treat the sexes differently. Amendment advocates[2] were also forceful enough to succeed in having a recommendation for the Amendment included in the platforms of both political parties in nearly every election campaign from 1940 to 1960.

THE PRESIDENT'S COMMISSION ON THE STATUS OF WOMEN

On December 14, 1961, John F. Kennedy signed an Executive Order establishing the President's Commission on the Status of Women. Its mandate was to examine and recommend remedies to combat the ". . . prejudices and outmoded customs [that] act as barriers to the full realization of women's basic rights. . . ."[3] It is difficult to say whether the Commission's Report, *American Women*, released on October 11, 1963, actually changed anyone's basic assumptions about the nature of women and their proper role. The Commission also appears to have accepted without question at least a portion of the "feminine mystique"—particu-

---

[1] For a detailed discussion of the Equal Rights Amendment see separate entry in this chapter.
[2] The most active lobby groups were the National Woman's Party and the National Federation of Business and Professional Women's Clubs. See "National Women's Rights Organizations" in this chapter.
[3] Executive Order 10980, establishing the President's Commission on the Status of Women, December 14, 1961. Reprinted in *American Women* (GPO: 1963), p. 76.

larly the assumption that the responsibility of homemaking and child rearing belongs uniquely to women whether or not they work outside the home. There is no doubt, however, that the Commission created the atmosphere, fashioned many of the tools, and engendered the momentum that has enabled many of today's feminists to challenge head-on those basic assumptions and popular images of women.

The President's Commission was the first official body ever to examine the status of women in the United States, although the idea for such a commission was not a new one. In 1946 and in January, 1961, Rep. Emanuel Celler (D., N.Y.), chairman of the House Judiciary Committee, made a similar proposal; in 1957 the National Manpower Council, as a result of its study *Womanpower*, suggested such a commission. It is not known whether political considerations were part of the Manpower Council recommendation; however, it is generally agreed that Rep. Celler, a strong opponent of the Equal Rights Amendment, wanted his proposed "Commission on the Legal Status of Women" established for the express purpose of killing the Amendment once and for all.

The precise combination of politics and altruism that was responsible for the creation of the Kennedy Commission will, of course, never be known. However, many observers speculate that the elimination of "prejudices and outmoded customs [that] act as barriers to the full realization of women's basic rights," was at least not the central motive. Kennedy had appointed Esther Peterson, a member of his campaign staff, and a long-time labor lobbyist, to head the Women's Bureau. It was she who originated the idea for a President's Commission, and it was she who convinced Kennedy to set it up. Some of the suggested "political" reasons for establishing such a Commission are: it would allow Kennedy to discharge political obligations to women who had worked hard for his election in 1960 (none of whom, with the exception of Peterson, had been appointed to policy-making positions in his administration); it would result in the creation of a strong political block (women) to campaign for Kennedy in 1964; it could be used to get his administration "off the hook" on the Equal Rights Amendment which, as in the past, had been included in the Democratic Party platform. Even Peterson remarked ten years after the Commission disbanded, "We were up against that awful Equal Rights Amendment situation."[4] In

---

[4] Interview, March, 1971.

addition proponents of the Amendment have subsequently argued that since Kennedy was beholden to labor for electoral support and labor was dead set against the Amendment, the Commission was clearly not being set up simply to gather data about the status of women, but rather to marshal those facts which would support the anti-Amendment bias of the Administration.

Notwithstanding the "politics" involved in the creation of the Commission, its authority was virtually unlimited, with instructions to study the status of women in all phases of their lives and to recommend measures to make women's rights a reality. Eleanor Roosevelt, not an enthusiastic supporter of the Kennedys, but a close friend of Esther Peterson, agreed to chair the Commission and she served until her death on November 7, 1962. Peterson, who in fact did the bulk of the work even before Eleanor Roosevelt's death, was made executive vice-chairman. The Commission members included thirteen women and eleven men from public and private life.[5]

The Commission's Report, *American Women,* was based in great part on the in-depth analysis and recommendations of seven Committees—Civil and Political Rights, Education, Federal Employment, Private Employment, Home and Community, Social Security and Taxes, and Protective Labor Legislation. The individual reports and recommendations of these Committees were also released publicly. In addition to the Committees, the Commission consulted with outside individuals and groups about four of its areas of concern: Private Employment Opportunity, New Patterns of Volunteer Work, Portrayal of Women by the Mass Media, and the Problems of Negro Women. In all, well over one hundred men and women were involved in the preparation of *American Women.*

Recommendations:[5a]   Although the Commission relied heavily on the advice and information of the study Committees, in a number of cases it rejected or changed Committee recommendations. The net result was a Commission Report that was moderate in tone and one that limited itself to compilations of data and concrete recommendations. There are charts and statistics throughout *American Women* that document the fact that most women work to earn a living, that the status of women in the labor market is uniformly low, that their educational level is also low, and that many laws exist which discriminate against women. However, the Commission chose to let the data stand by itself

---

[5] See Appendix for full list of members.
[5a] Recommendations reprinted in full in Appendix.

rather than set it in an extensive framework of sociological and psychological analysis. Frequently, the individual Committee reports were more analytical, more strongly worded, and their recommendations more incisive, than the overall Commission Report. According to some members, the Commission Report was deliberately moderate in tone to make it more acceptable. In fact, they argue that even a slightly more "radical" *American Women* would have been ridiculed and rejected out-of-hand by Administration policy-makers. They surmise that by keeping the *official* Report temperate, but also publicly releasing the Committee reports, the politically shrewd Commission members were able to have the best of both worlds.

Perhaps the most concrete recommendations made by the Commission involved employment and labor standards. Although acknowledging the deep-seated bias against granting women equal employment opportunities, many of these recommendations were extremely moderate. For example, the Commission urged passage of an Executive Order embodying the principle of equal employment opportunity, but the Order would have left enforcement of that principle to voluntary compliance. In addition, the Commission rejected a suggestion to add "sex" to an existing order that barred racial discrimination by federal contractors because ". . . discrimination based on sex . . . involves problems sufficiently different from discrimination based on the other factors listed to make separate treatment preferable."[6] It has been suggested that the reluctance of the Commission to treat race and sex discrimination in the same way was due to its conception of women as an under-utilized *resource,* rather than a *class* that was being discriminated against. (Sex and race were not linked as similar forms of discrimination until the passage of the 1964 Civil Rights Act—and even then somewhat inadvertently.[7])

Although moderate in some of its recommendations on employment issues, in two areas of "equal opportunity" the Commission recommendations were enacted even before that body was disbanded: in 1962 a Presidential directive was issued reversing the long-held interpretation of an 1870 law used to bar women from high-level federal employment; in 1963 the Equal Pay Act was passed.[8]

The other labor standards discussed fell primarily under the

---

[6] *American Women,* p. 30.
[7] See separate entry (Title VII) this chapter.
[8] See separate entries (Equal Pay Act and Executive Order 11375) this chapter.

rubric of protective legislation—state laws setting minimum wage requirements, maximum hours and weight-lifting limits, etc., for female workers—the concept of which the Commission endorsed. If, as suggested above, defeat of the Equal Rights Amendment was one of the purposes of establishing the Commission, its endorsement of these protective laws (which would be eliminated by the Amendment, at least on the basis of sex) was inevitable from the outset.

The civil and political rights of women were extensively reviewed and resulted in the most in-depth and broad-reaching examination and analysis of the laws (state and federal) affecting women ever undertaken by the federal government. Almost all laws pertaining to women were studied: labor, social security, jury service, marriage, child custody, property rights, etc. Since women at that time were still unable to serve on juries in three states, the Commission recommended that legislation be passed to remove these exemptions. In the field of marriage and property rights the Commission recommended that all the legal restrictions be removed which prohibited married women from owning property, entering into business, contracting, controlling their own earnings, etc. (It should be noted that many of these restrictions still exist in state laws.) In an attempt to equalize the structure of marriage, the Commission established the principle that "Marriage . . . [is] a partnership in which each spouse makes a different but equally important contribution."[9] Thus, according to the Commission, women's work of homemaking and child rearing should be viewed as a financial contribution to the marriage.[1]

Constitutional recognition (or the absence thereof) of women's rights and the degree to which the Constitution had been used to grant or deny women equal legal status became the most controversial issue undertaken by the Commission because it centered on debate of the Equal Rights Amendment. (The Committee on Civil and Political Rights whose area of responsibility this was has often been described as the most "battle-fatigued" of all the Commission study committees.) The Commission recommendation in this area was based in large part on a thorough analysis of the history of Supreme Court decisions regarding women's rights. Notwithstanding the great majority of "unfavor-

---

[9] *American Women,* p. 47.
[1] This principle was adopted in 1970 by the generally conservative Commission on Uniform State Laws in a proposed Uniform Marriage and Divorce Act.

able" decisions handed down by the Court, the Commission argued that the principle of women's equality was already embodied in the 5th and 14th Amendments; hence there was no need to pass an Equal Rights Amendment. Moreover, the existing Amendments would allow more latitude of interpretation regarding women's rights than would an Equal Rights Amendment. The recommendation did concede, however, that:

> Early and definitive court pronouncement, particularly by the U.S. Supreme Court, is urgently needed with regard to the validity under the 5th and 14th amendments of laws and official practices discriminating against women, to the end that the principle of equality become firmly established in constitutional doctrine.[2]

To proponents of the Amendment, this "latitude of interpretation" merely meant the retention of protective legislation and other laws that were discriminatory against women.

The only Commission member, frequently described as the only "real feminist" on the Commission, who fought for the Equal Rights Amendment, was lawyer Marguerite Rawalt. She has subsequently noted that it was an uphill battle to persuade the Commission even to mention that the Equal Rights Amendment approach to women's legal equality existed. Rawalt did manage to accomplish what she felt was "a small coup" just before the full Commission report went to press. She was able to insert one word in the section discussing the Amendment so that the Commission's opposition did not appear to be immutable: ". . . we conclude that a constitutional amendment need not *now* be sought in order to establish this principle"[3] (emphasis added).

As noted above the President's Commission made recommendations regarding many areas of women's lives—particularly those affecting their social roles. Thus, a good portion of the Report centered on education and counseling and women's contribution to home and community life. It is in these areas that the Commission's ambivalence about the "proper" role for women was most visibly manifested. On the one hand, the Commission strongly urged that "imaginative counseling" for girls be available to ". . . lift [their] aspirations beyond stubbornly persistent

---

[2] *American Women*, p. 45.
[3] *Loc. Cit.*

assumptions about 'women's roles' and 'women's interests,' and [to] result in choices that have inner authenticity for their makers."[4] Moreover, it recommended that day care services be available for all children regardless of family income, and that there be tax deductions for child care expenses of working mothers. On the other hand, the Commission endorsed ". . . the fundamental responsibility of mothers and homemakers and society's stake in strong family life."[5]

Taken as a whole, the Commission's entire inquiry, Report, and its many broad-reaching recommendations appear to have been based on several implicitly (sometimes explicitly) stated assumptions. The most fundamental of them presupposed that the nuclear family unit was vital to the stability of American society and that women have a unique and immutable role in that family unit; accordingly, women who work, and who are also married and possibly mothers, play a dual role in society to a much greater degree than do men who work and are also married and fathers. Another fundamental assumption of the Report was that, notwithstanding women's dual role, every obstacle to their full participation in society must be removed. Today's feminists would argue that in fact these two assumptions are contradictory: the barriers against women's *full* participation in society cannot be removed until and unless men (and society at large) share equally with women the responsibilities of homemaking and child rearing.

To many women active in today's movement the greatest impact of the President's Commission on the Status of Women was made not by its Report, *American Women*, but by the very *fact* of the Commission's existence, which in their view generated for the first time in nearly a half-century a general interest in women's issues. That interest spread rapidly and as early as 1963, when the Commission itself was disbanded, a number of individual State Commissions on the Status of Women had been established. By 1967 all fifty states had such Commissions, every one of which was pressuring for women's equality.

Citizen's Advisory Council on the Status of Women: When President Kennedy received the Commission Report, he enacted almost immediately two of the recommendations. The Report was transmitted to him October 11, 1963, and on November 1

---

[4] *Ibid.*, p. 13.
[5] *Ibid.*, p. 18.

he established the Interdepartmental Committee on the Status of Women, composed of the Secretaries of those Departments concerned with women's interests, and other government officials, and the Citizens' Advisory Council on the Status of Women, made up of twenty private citizens appointed by the President. By the end of 1971, these two groups had co-sponsored four national conferences of State Commissions on the Status of Women and co-published a series of updated progress reports on the status of women.

The most original work and most "radical" analysis, however, has been done consistently by the Council on its own. The President's Commission in its Report had anticipated that this would be the case:

> We consider the establishment of such a citizens' committee to be of real import. Many of our recommendations can be made effective only through private, nongovernmental initiative . . .[6]

Indeed, there are many in today's women's movement who believe that the Citizens' Advisory Council represents the most far-reaching "official" result of the Commission's two years of work. The Council's first project under its Johnson-appointed chairman, Margaret Hickey,[7] was the preparation of a policy paper on the section of Title VII of the 1964 Civil Rights Act dealing with sex discrimination. The paper was presented on October 1, 1965, to the Equal Employment Opportunity Commission (EEOC), administrator of Title VII, and recommended a narrow interpretation of the Title VII provisions which would allow exceptions to the general rule that all jobs should be open to both men and women. The Council argued that exceptions should not be allowed ". . . based on stereotypes of characteristics of the sexes; the preferences of the employer, coworkers, clients, or customers; or assumptions of the comparative characteristics of women (or men) in general."[8] EEOC accepted this recommendation but re-

---

[6] *Ibid.*, p. 54.
[7] Hickey was a Commission member, co-chairman of the Committee on Federal Employment, and at the time public affairs editor of the *Ladies' Home Journal*. Kennedy had named all the Council members before his death, but not the chairman.
[8] "Report on Progress in 1965 on the Status of Women," *Second Annual Report of Interdepartmental Committee and Citizens' Advisory Council on the Status of the Women,* December 31, 1965, p. 25.

jected the Council's additional suggestion that sex-segregated "want-ad" columns be outlawed. The "want-ad" controversy later developed into a major women's rights issue.[9]

When Hickey resigned her chairmanship, President Johnson appointed (in June, 1966) former Senator Maurine Neuberger to chair the Council. Under Neuberger the Council expanded its paid staff and broke some new ground. Task Forces were established to update and study in greater depth four areas touched upon by the President's Commission: Health and Welfare, Social Security and Taxes, Labor Standards, and Family Law and Policy. Released in April, 1968, the recommendations of the first three Task Forces were more detailed, but basically the same as those of the Commission. The recommendations set forth by the Family Law and Policy Task Force, however, represented what was considered at that time a radical and extremely feminist position for a government-sponsored study. The Task Force, which included lawyers Marguerite Rawalt and Mary Eastwood and sociologist Alice Rossi, argued that the right of a woman to control her own reproductive life was a basic civil right. Its Report called for the *repeal* of all laws which make abortion a criminal offense, and all laws which restrict access to contraceptive devices and information. In 1968, most lobby groups were still working on the state level for abortion law *reform*.[1] In other areas of family law the Task Force further developed the idea, originally introduced by the President's Commission, that marriage is an economic partnership. It recommended that support and alimony laws be based on need and ability to pay, not on the sex of the spouse, and that married women should have the same property rights as their husbands. In addition, the Task Force declared that illegitimate children should be accorded the same legal rights as legitimate children.

Under the Nixon Administration, new Citizens' Advisory Council members were appointed, with the exception of the original staff executive secretary, Catherine East, who remained in that position. President Nixon waited until August, 1969, to select his Council and it was rumored that he would not have appointed one at all had it not been for the pressure he received from women's rights activists. The new chairman was Jacqueline Gutwillig, a retired lieutenant colonel of the Women's Army Corps.

---

[9] See "Title VII."
[1] See Chapter 7 for detailed discussion.

As is customary, the twenty new members came from all parts of the country and all occupations. According to one of the women, the new Council's frame of reference "is considerably more feminist than that of the original group, mostly because the organizations and industries which are the worst offenders of sex discrimination are not represented on this Council."[2] Another member was amused at the thought that a group of Republican women could be more "radical" in any area than their Democratic counterparts.

The first policy paper under Gutwillig was a memorandum on the Equal Rights Amendment released in March, 1970. The paper thoroughly analyzed the issues and strongly endorsed the Amendment's passage. The Administration, however, for whom the paper was primarily intended, did not address itself to the issue at that time. In November, 1970, the Council issued a second position paper on job-related maternity benefits. The paper stated:

> Childbirth and complications of pregnancy are, for all *job-related purposes*, temporary disabilities and should be treated as such under any health insurance, temporary disability insurance, or sick leave plan of an employer, union, or fraternal society. . . . Economically it makes no difference whether an employee is unable to work at his regular job because of pregnancy or because of hernia, ulcers, or any other illness or accident; in any case he or she suffers loss of pay and has extra medical expenses.[3]

The Council noted that women and men lose about the same amount of time from work because of acute disabilities, including childbirth and pregnancy complications. It recommended further that no additional benefits be extended because of maternity since ". . . men and other women who are suffering from disabilities other than pregnancy will have less benefits than pregnant women. This is not sociologically or economically justified and would be divisive."[4] The Council's paper was perhaps the first time maternity leave was defined as a temporary disability.

---

[2] The reader is reminded that many of the women were interviewed with the understanding that their comments were not for attribution. To respect their position, quotations from such women have no citations.
[3] *Memorandum—Job Related Maternity Benefits* (Citizens' Advisory Council, November, 1970), pp. 1 & 3.
[4] *Ibid.*, p. 4.

The strong tone of the many reports issued by the Citizens' Advisory Council since its creation in 1963 has caused women's rights activitists, both within the government and without, to suggest that it is the Council's "civilian" status that has allowed it to produce what is to all intents and purposes "feminist propaganda": what might be deemed controversial from a government agency such as the Women's Bureau, can come from the Council with impunity. On the other hand, activitists are equally well aware that such a council exists only by an executive order, which can be repealed at any time by the President.

As noted earlier, the President's Commission on the Status of Women made a number of legislative recommendations that would enable women to achieve a more equitable status in the labor market. Some of the recommendations were enacted into law. Moreover, enough interest in women's rights had been generated by the Commission to create an atmosphere conducive to the passage of other federal laws barring sex discrimination. Each such law has become a political issue in its own right, and its passage and enforcement procedures have contributed uniquely to the growth of the women's movement.

1963 EQUAL PAY ACT

On June 10, 1963, President Kennedy signed the Equal Pay Act (effective June 11, 1964), the first piece of federal legislation prohibiting discrimination on the basis of sex. It remains the only federal law that deals only with sex. The law amended the Fair Labor Standards Act of 1938 to require that men and women receive equal pay for equal work performed under equal conditions, and culminated a drive to obtain such legislation that had begun during World War I. The common assumptions that women neither deserve nor need the same salaries as men have been difficult to erase, however, despite passage of the Act. The most frequent reasons given for paying women less for the same work include: women have a higher absentee and turnover rate; nonwage costs of hiring women are more than they are for men; single women do not need as much money as single men; and married women do not need as much money as married men. Statistical data have proved each of the assumptions false.

The originally proposed Equal Pay Bill did not exempt executive, professional, or administrative employees, nor were these exemptions introduced at any point during the Bill's legislative history. However, when the Bill was passed as an amendment to the Fair Labor Standards Act, the exemptions written into that Act were automatically extended to the Equal Pay provisions. Several subsequent bills have been introduced since 1963 to remove the executive, professional and administrative exemptions from the equal pay provisions.[5] Statistics have documented an extreme salary gap between men and women holding identical positions in these areas. In starting salaries, for example, women graduating from college in 1970 in six technical and professional fields were being offered from three to ten percent less than were men in the same fields.

Although basically a private sector law, the entire Fair Labor Standards Act was extended in 1966 to cover some employees in state hospitals, transportation systems, schools and universities. Pressure is being brought by women's groups to broaden the Act's coverage even further to include such fields as agriculture and domestic labor, in which the majority of workers are women.

The Equal Pay Act is administered and enforced by the Wage and Hour and Public Contracts Divisions of the U.S. Department of Labor, which has regional field offices throughout the United States. The enforcement machinery was set up in 1938 with the passage of the original law, and the equal pay amendment did not alter it. Indeed, some activists consider the Equal Pay Act the only law dealing with sex discrimination that is anywhere near properly enforced. Routine compliance investigations of working establishments are made continuously—over 70,000 every year. When a violation is found during one of these investigations, the local compliance officer can require a settlement without waiting for a complaint to be filed on behalf of the employees discriminated against. If an independent complaint is filed, however, and a settlement cannot be reached, the Wage and Hour Divisions have the additional authority to bring suit, taking that burden of litigation off the aggrieved employee.

The number of equal pay complaints is continually rising. In 1965 complaints against 351 establishments were received; in 1970, against well over 700 establishments. Part of the increase is credited to the publicity the women's movement has given to the laws prohibiting sex discrimination. The Wage and Hour Di-

---

[5] These categories are covered under the equal employment section, Title VII, of the 1964 Civil Rights Act. However, Title VII does not permit a complainant to remain anonymous as can be done under the Fair Labor Standards Act.

visions have also publicized the Equal Pay Act by disseminating literature to employers and conducting regional conferences to explain the provisions of the Act.

At the end of the fiscal year 1970, three years after the Equal Pay Act went into effect, more than $17 million in back wages had been awarded to over 50,000 employees, nearly all of whom were women.

TITLE VII—1964 CIVIL RIGHTS ACT

Title VII, the Equal Employment Opportunity section of the 1964 Civil Rights Act (effective July 2, 1965), prohibits discrimination based on race, color, religion, national origin or sex by private employers, employment agencies and unions. Exempted from the Act's coverage are federal, state and local governments (except for the U.S. Employment Service and state and local employment services receiving federal assistance), and educational institutions (teachers and administrative personnel).

Title VII, which has the legislative potential for profoundly altering the sex pattern of employment, allegedly was not intended to cover sex discrimination at all. After nearly two weeks of floor debate in the House, on February 8, 1964, Rep. Howard Smith (D., Va.), an opponent of the Civil Rights bill, offered an amendment to add "sex" as a prohibited basis for discrimination in employment. Smith kept referring to his proposal as "my little amendment" and, although he repeatedly insisted "I am very serious about this amendment, and I do not think it can do any harm to this legislation—maybe it can do some good," many Washington observers felt that the "sex" amendment was a calculated political maneuver designed to do a great deal of harm. Specifically, they believed his aim was to bring so much controversy to the bill as to kill it entirely.[6] Many liberals in Congress, long advocates of the Civil Rights bill, registered their opposition to the Smith amendment for precisely that reason. Rep. Edith Green (D., Ore. and a co-sponsor of the Equal Pay Act) was the only woman to oppose the addition and she argued that the amendment "will clutter up the bill and it may later—very well— be used to help destroy this section of the bill by some of the very

---

[6] A detailed account of the "sex" amendment controversy can be found in *Born Female*, by Caroline Bird (New York: David McKay Company, Inc., 1968; rev. 1970), pp. 1ff.

people who today support it."[7] The controversy notwithstanding,
the sex amendment was passed on the same afternoon by a vote
of 168 to 133. Caroline Bird reports that when the final vote was
announced, a female voice in the gallery shouted, "We made it!
God bless America!" The entire Civil Rights bill passed the House
the next day, February 9, and on July 2 of that year was enacted
by Congress.

Procedure: The Equal Employment Opportunity Commission (EEOC), composed of five members appointed by the President, was established to administer Title VII. EEOC was given no
enforcement power, however, which made Title VII, in the view
of many, little more than a pronouncement of national policy.
One of the original EEOC Commissioners, Aileen Hernandez,
noted, "It's the kind of law that raises the hopes of a lot of people,
but doesn't provide any means of realizing those hopes."[8] When
charges of alleged discrimination are brought to EEOC, the Commission has the authority to investigate the charges and then
issue decisions as to whether or not reasonable cause exists. If,
according to the Commission's findings, discrimination does exist,
EEOC's role is to attempt conciliation. It does not have cease and
desist power.[9] If EEOC is unable to obtain voluntary compliance
with its decision, the Commission can recommend that the Attorney General of the United States institute a lawsuit on behalf of
the aggrieved party. That office is not bound, however, to follow
EEOC's recommendations. The only other means of enforcement
requires the individual complainant to institute legal proceedings
against the alleged discriminatory employer.

Bona Fide Occupational Qualification: Whereas Title VII
recognizes no difference under the law for hiring and promotion
purposes among racial groups, it does recognize sex differences.
Therefore, while prohibiting sex discrimination in employment,
Title VII does permit an employer to hire only one sex when it is
considered reasonably necessary to the functioning of a particular

---

[7] 110 Congressional Record 2581 (1964). It should be noted that long-time
women's rights advocate, Rep. Martha Griffiths (D., Mich.) had planned
herself to propose the addition of "sex" to Title VII. She held off, believing
that Smith could obtain the votes of Southern Congressmen which she
could not.

[8] Interview, March, 1971. Hernandez later became President of the National Organization for Women.

[9] At nearly every session of Congress since Title's VII's passage, a bill has
been introduced to give EEOC cease and desist authority. (As of June,
1971, no such bill had been passed.)

business enterprise. For example, it is not discriminatory for an employer to hire only women for the job of actress, model for women's clothes, attendant for a women's restroom, etc. In such cases, sex is considered a "bona fide occupational qualification" (*bfoq*), and as such, an exception to the prohibition against sex discrimination in employment.[1] Exactly what is or is not a *bfoq*, however, almost immediately became, and still remains, the major point of contention under the sex provisions of Title VII.

State Protective Legislation: During the late nineteenth and early twentieth centuries, many states passed laws restricting the employment of women to certain occupations, establishing maximum hours, minimum wages, maximum weights to be lifted, etc. These laws were designed to protect women from exploitation and the hazards of industrial life; indeed, some of the earliest ones were enacted during the days of "sweatshop" conditions, and they represented the *only* labor laws on the books for men or women. In 1920 the Women's Bureau was established and, among other things, became central in the continuing drive during the subsequent decades for protective laws for women. The Women's Bureau and the organized labor movement worked in concert around this issue.

Originally these laws were enacted to protect all workers regardless of sex, and early in the century the Supreme Court considered whether they were constitutional. According to the Court, these kinds of labor restrictions could *not* be imposed on men because they violated men's constitutional rights of personal liberty and the liberty of contract[2]; this was not held to be true for women, however. In 1908 the Supreme Court upheld an Oregon State law limiting working hours of female factory employees arguing that:

> . . . history discloses the fact that woman has always been dependent upon man. He established his control at the outset by superior physical strength, and this control in various forms, with diminishing intensity, has continued to the present. As minors, though not to the same extent, she has been looked upon in the courts as needing especial care that her rights may be preserved. . . . Though limitations upon personal and contractual rights may be removed by legislation, there is that in her disposition and

---

[1] *bfoq* exceptions also pertain to religion and national origin.
[2] *Lochner v. New York*, 198 U.S. 45.

habits of life which will operate against a full assertion of those rights. . . . *Differentiated by these matters from the other sex, she is properly placed in a class by herself, and legislation designed for her protection may be sustained, even when like legislation is not necessary for men, and could not be sustained.*[3]

Based on the language of *Muller v. Oregon*, sex became a valid basis for legal distinctions and, for the most part, the courts have upheld these state laws as necessary for the protection of the female, the happiness of the home and the progress of the commonweal.

Women workers opposing and supporting these laws today argue just these points. So-called "protection", opponents say, is both unrealistic and discriminatory. It is unrealistic, for example, to place a limitation of thirty pounds (often less) on the weight a female is permitted to lift on a job; three-year-old children often weigh more than thirty pounds and mothers lift them often and without hesitation. Moreover, they argue that it is discriminatory to establish maximum hours and minimum wage laws because such laws keep women from applying for certain jobs, earning overtime pay and advancing in a company, i.e., competing with men in the job market. They also point out that this legislation was passed in the context of Victorian views of woman, her role, function and place in society. These notions are outmoded, unrealistic, and in the words of many, represent "male chauvinism."

Supporters of protective legislation, on the other hand, argue that women fought many years to have maximum hour and minimum wage regulations established. They acknowledge that some laws are indeed discriminatory; these pieces of legislation, however, should in their view be dealt with on a case-by-case basis. For the most part, they argue, only through a difference in treatment of men and women workers will a semblance of equality be achieved: women play a double role in our society; if they are expected to continue to function as wives and mothers, as well as workers, they cannot be forced to work long overtime hours, lift heavy weights, etc.

Both opponents and supporters of protective legislation do agree that the "progress of the commonweal" would be furthered if laws which truly protect workers from exploitation and the

---

[3] *Muller v. Oregon*, 208 U.S. 412, quoted from *Report of the Committee on Civil and Political Rights* (GPO: 1963), pp. 61–62 (emphasis added).

hazards of industry were to apply to all persons regardless of sex. Proponents of protective legislation argue, however, that it would indeed be an empty equality to wipe out all pieces of enlightened legislation simply because legislators were not enlightened enough to extend certain protections to both sexes.

Title VII and State Protective Legislation: Title VII expressly prohibits *discrimination* in employment on the basis of sex; state protective laws expressly establish *legal distinctions* on the basis of sex. The question immediately apparent is whether the states' *legal distinctions* constitute *discrimination* (prohibited), or a valid exception (*bfoq*). EEOC, charged with the responsibility of resolving this conflict, had no precedents to follow. Both proponents and opponents of protective legislation pressured EEOC for resolution of this conflict. Often, and to the outrage of women's rights advocates, the *bfoq* provision was treated as a joke. At a White House Conference on Equal Opportunity in August, 1965, one person wondered if the law required Playboy Clubs to hire male bunnies. Almost immediately the *bfoq* section became known as the "bunny law." A *New York Times* front page story on the Conference was headlined "For Instance, Can She Pitch for the Mets?"; the "bunny problem" was referred to throughout. The next day *The Times* published an editorial: "De-Sexing the Job Market." Carrying the frivolity of the "bunny problem" to an extreme, *The Times* noted:

> Federal officials . . . may find it would have been better if Congress had just abolished sex itself. . . . [The problem] demands a wholesale rewriting of the language, for one thing. Everything has to be neuterized. Housemaid becomes a dirty word; it is, of course, discriminatory. Handyman must disappear from the language; he was pretty much a goner anyway, if you ever started looking for one in desperation. No more milkman, iceman, serviceman, foreman or pressman. . . . The Rockettes may become bi-sexual, and a pity, too. . . . Bunny problem, indeed! This is revolution, chaos. You can't even safely advertise for a wife any more.[4]

Even EEOC director Herman Edelsberg publicly stated that the sex provision was a "fluke . . . conceived out of wedlock."[5]

---

[4] *New York Times* editorial, August 21, 1965.
[5] Bird, p. 15.

As shown below, various sets of EEOC guidelines issued between 1965 and 1969 reveal how the Commission itself wavered in its attempts to deal with the sex provision:

—EEOC's December 2, 1965, guidelines stated that state laws could be interpreted as a *bfoq* exception provided that the employer acted in good faith and that the laws effectively protected rather than discriminated against women. (EEOC did not define what constituted "protection" or "discrimination.")

—In guidelines issued August 19, 1966, EEOC disclaimed authority to determine whether or not Title VII superseded state laws, and stated that the courts would have to resolve the conflict.

—Public hearings were held by EEOC in May, 1967, on this issue, convened in large part because of the pressure brought by women's rights advocates. Those favoring state protective legislation argued that women "needed these laws which they fought so hard to get"; and that it was the intent of Congress to prohibit only those laws which denied women equality of job opportunity. Opponents of the state laws argued that any law that restricts or grants benefits to one sex and not the other is inherently discriminatory. Sex-segregated "want-ads" were also discussed.

—On February 21, 1968, new guidelines were issued, which stated that EEOC itself would determine on a case-by-case basis whether state legislation which appeared to be discriminatory rather than protective was superseded by Title VII.

—On August 19, 1969, EEOC issued revised guidelines on "Discrimination Because of Sex," which stated that "state laws and regulations, although originally promulgated for the purpose of protecting females, have ceased to be relevant to our technology or to the expanding role of the female worker in our economy." The Commission concluded that such laws and regulations were in conflict with and therefore superseded by Title VII, and did not qualify under the *bfoq* exception section of the Act.[6]

Court Cases: As of mid-1971 there was no one authoritative resolution of the conflict between Title VII and state protective legislation. A number of lawsuits have dealt with this conflict and a summary listing of some of the significant cases follows. These

---

[6] Both before and after the issuance of the August 19, 1969, guidelines, several State Attorneys-General issued opinions on their respective state laws and regulations. Some held that Title VII superseded state legislation; some, that state legislation would stand until a Federal Court ruling to the contrary.

cases indicate a strong court trend toward the invalidation of state protective legislation. It should be noted also that substantial financial and legal assistance, which enabled the women workers to appeal lower court decisions, was supplied by the National Organization for Women and Human Rights for Women.[7]

In the case of *Rosenfeld v. Southern Pacific*,[8] a woman was denied a position with Southern Pacific on the grounds that the job required overtime and the lifting of weights in excess of California's legal limitations for women. The District Court ruled that Title VII superseded California's protective laws. The case is being appealed by Southern Pacific.

In the case of *Weeks v. Southern Bell Telephone and Telegraph Co.*,[9] Southern Bell refused to promote a woman because of a state law which limited weights women could lift. The District Court upheld the state law. Before the case came to the Appeals Court, the Georgia legislature repealed the law. The issue therefore was no longer one of a possible conflict between Title VII and a state law, but whether the company rule limiting weights women could lift would qualify as a *bfoq* exception. The Appellate Court reversed the lower court and held that Southern Bell had failed to prove sex as a *bfoq* for the job in question. The Court set forth the following principle with regard to *bfoq* exceptions:

> . . . the employer has the burden of proving that he has reasonable cause to believe, that is a factual basis for believing, that all or substantially all women would be unable to perform safely and efficiently the duties of the job involved.

Moreover, the Court gave a broad interpretation of Title VII:

> Title VII rejects just this type of romantic paternalism as unduly Victorian and instead vests individual women with the power to decide whether or not to take on unromantic tasks. Men have always had the right to determine whether the increase in remuneration for strenuous, dan-

---

[7] See separate entries, this chapter.
[8] *Rosenfeld v. Southern Pacific Co.* (C.D. Calif. 11-22-68) 293 F. Supp. 1219, on appeal in Ca-9.
[9] *Weeks v. Southern Tel. & Tel. Co.* (CA-5, 3-4-69) 408 F. 2d, rev. & rem. S.D. Ga. 277 F. Supp. 117.

gerous, obnoxious, boring or unromantic tasks is worth the candle. The promise of Title VII is that women are now to be on equal footing.

Although the Weeks decision did not invalidate a state law (as noted earlier Georgia had repealed the law prior to the decision), by establishing a test for *bfoq* exceptions the court decision could well be an important precedent for overruling other states' protective legislation. Opponents of protective legislation considered the Weeks decision a landmark. It was not until April, 1971, however, three years after the decision, and after an extensive pressure campaign by women's rights organizations, that Southern Bell finally promoted Lorena Weeks to the job for which she had originally applied in 1966. Southern Bell was also required to award her back pay, travel and premium pay for that period which totaled nearly $31,000.

In the case of *Bowe et. al. v. Colgate-Palmolive Co. et. al.*,[1] at issue was a company, not state, regulation that excluded women from jobs requiring the lifting of certain weights. A lower court held that Title VII did not prohibit a company from establishing such a restriction. On September 26, 1969, the U.S. Court of Appeals (7th Circuit, Chicago) reversed the lower court decision and held that the weight-lifting restriction for women did not constitute a *bfoq* exception. Moreover, the Appellate Court stated that the weight requirement is invalid if applied only to women; the company therefore could retain the weight requirement only if it were to be applied to all employees.

Three other cases are noteworthy. They are somewhat distinguished from the above-discussed cases because factors other than the Title VII-state legislation conflict are present.

1) In the case of *Phillips v. Martin-Marietta Corporation*,[2] state legislation was not at issue. The Martin-Marietta Corporation had refused to hire Ida Phillips for a trainee job on the basis that female applicants with pre-school age children were not considered for such positions. The Federal District Court (M.D. Fla.) upheld the company's position that its policy was not in violation of Title VII. The U.S. Court of Appeals for the Fifth Circuit upheld the ruling against Phillips, reasoning that:

---

[1] *Bowe et al. v. Colgate-Palmolive Co. et. al.* (CA-7, 9-26-69) 416 F. 2d 711 rev. S.D. Ind. 272 F. Supp. 332.
[2] *Phillips v. Martin-Marietta*, 400 U.S. 542.

> The discrimination was based on a two-pronged qualifica-
> tion, i.e. a woman with pre-school age children. Ida Phil-
> lips was not refused employment because she was a
> woman nor because she had pre-school age children. It
> is the coalescence of these two elements that denied her
> the position she desired.

Lower court rulings such as this had become known as the "sex-
plus" theory: a woman could not be barred from a job because of
her sex, but she could be barred because of her sex plus another
factor—in the Phillips case, as the mother of small children. On
March 2, 1970, the Supreme Court agreed to hear the case, after
EEOC and the Department of Justice had filed an *amicus curiae*
brief in behalf of Phillips. The Phillips case was the first Title VII
case involving sex discrimination before the Supreme Court. On
January 25, 1971, the Court unanimously struck down the "sex-
plus" theory of employment, ruling that the company could not
have "one hiring policy for women and another for men" because
another distinction had been added to the sex of a person. (This
might be applied, for example, to forbid a common airline policy
of requiring female stewardesses to retire when they marry or
reach 35 unless the same ruling applies to male personnel.) In
the Phillips case the Court ruled that the company could not bar
mothers with small children from jobs unless it also barred fathers
with small children.

However, while wiping out the "sex-plus" theory, the Court
suggested that motherhood might come under a *bfoq* exception.
The unsigned opinion read that parenthood, "if demonstrably
more relevant to job performance for a woman than for a man,
could arguably be a basis" for excluding women from jobs. The
Supreme Court returned the case to the lower court to see if such
a *bfoq* condition existed. Women's rights advocates who favor an
extremely narrow definition of *bfoq* were angered by the Court's
ruling, arguing that such a broad interpretation of the exception
could easily be used in a discriminatory manner. They were
pleased, however, by Justice Thurgood Marshall's opinion which,
although concurring, disagreed that a *bfoq* exception might be
based on motherhood rather than parenthood:

> I fear that in this case . . . the Court has fallen into the
> trap of assuming that the Act [Title VII] permits ancient

canards about the proper role of women to be a basis for discrimination. . . . When performance characteristics of an individual are involved, even when parental roles are concerned, employment opportunity may be limited only by employment criteria that are neutral as to the sex of the applicant.[3]

2) The case *U.S. v. Libbey-Owens, United Glass and Ceramic Workers of North America, AFL-CIO, Local No. 9* was the first sex discrimination suit brought by the Justice Department under Title VII. Libbey-Owens and the union were charged with hiring women for only one of the five glass plants in Toledo, Ohio and, in that one plant, assigning them only to the less-desirable and lower-paying jobs. The Justice Department, which filed the suit on July 20, 1970, sought not only a change in policy but also back pay to compensate those women discriminated against by that policy. Libbey-Owens responded that Ohio's state laws requiring special treatment of women—in particular the weight-lifting limitation and the maximum hours law—prevented the company from fully complying with Title VII. The case was settled by a consent agreement on December 7, 1970, in which Libbey-Owens agreed, among other things, to open more departments to women employees, to undertake an educational campaign to acquaint women with all the available job opportunities, and to promote some women to supervisory positions almost immediately. The company also agreed to uphold its continuing obligation not to discriminate on the basis of sex. Back pay was not part of the agreement.

Some women's rights advocates look upon the settlement as a "sellout" by the Justice Department. They argue that when the Department institutes a lawsuit it should take the responsibility to settle legal points that go beyond the scope of the specific issue and specific defendant. In this case, the women hoped for an authoritative clarification of the Title VII-protective law conflict. An EEOC staff member agreed that the outcome of the case was a "travesty" but for different reasons. He sees the responsibility of the Justice Department in these kinds of cases as not necessarily to settle legal points, but to open up jobs for the aggrieved class, and to obtain full relief for the particular defendants. By

---

[3] *Phillips v. Martin-Marietta*, No. 73, October Term, 1970. Justice Marshall, concurring opinion.

not insisting that back pay be part of the consent agreement, argued this staff member, "the Justice Department sold out the whole class of women."

3) As noted above, the *Muller v. Oregon* decision established the precedent that women's constitutional rights are not violated by laws which distinguish them on the basis of sex. A case currently pending has the *potential* of reversing that interpretation and becoming the new landmark decision regarding women's rights under the constitution.

The case in question is *Mengelkoch v. Industrial Welfare Commission of California.*[4] Velma Mengelkoch in a class action suit argued that California's hours laws deprived women of job opportunities (women were not considered for the higher-paying supervisory positions that might require longer hours, and were also denied opportunity to earn overtime wages) and therefore were in violation of the 14th Amendment to the Constitution and of Title VII of the Civil Rights Act. The District Court held in 1968 that the women could not raise the constitutional issue regarding the working hours restrictions because those laws had been upheld as constitutional by the Supreme Court in 1908 (*Muller v. Oregon*) and 1912 (*Miller v. Wilson*). In other words, the case could be argued only on the grounds that the laws violated Title VII. Mengelkoch appealed, and on January 11, 1971, the U.S. Court of Appeals for the 9th circuit (the court that originally decided *Muller v. Oregon*), reversed the District Court decision. It ruled that previous Supreme Court decisions notwithstanding, whether state hours laws for women but not for men violated the rights of women under the 14th Amendment did indeed present a "substantial constitutional issue." The case has been remanded to the District Court (in this instance a three-judge court), which will determine whether women's constitutional rights have been violated or whether the laws in question only violate Title VII. A decision is expected in late 1971 or early 1972. In many ways the Mengelkoch case has become *the* test case for women's rights advocates. Human Rights for Women, a legal aid organization set up expressly to take on potentially landmark sex discrimination cases, has represented Mengelkoch.

Title VII and Help-Wanted Advertisements: The removal from newspapers of sex-segregated "want-ads" has been an ongo-

---

[4] *Mengelkoch v. Industrial Welfare Commission of California,* 437 F. 2d. 563.

ing battle for the women's movement, and one which had not been fully settled by mid-1971.

Section 704.b of Title VII states that it is unlawful

> For employers, labor organizations, or employment agencies to print, publish, or cause to be printed or published advertisements indicating preference, limitation, specification or discrimination on the basis of sex.[5]

Although newspaper publishers are not specifically mentioned in the language of the section, on August 18, 1965, EEOC issued guidelines expressly forbidding them from carrying separate *racial* headings for "want-ads." The question arose whether newspapers could maintain their separate sex headings—Help Wanted Male and Help Wanted Female.

On October 1, 1965, the Citizens' Advisory Council sent a memorandum to EEOC urging the Commission to make it clear that sex-segregated "want-ads" on the part of newspaper publishers were in violation of Title VII. The memorandum was also approved by the Interdepartmental Committee on the Status of Women, which consisted of the Attorney General, the Secretaries of State, Defense, Labor, Agriculture, Commerce, Health Education and Welfare, and the Civil Service Commissioner. On April 22, 1966, EEOC issued guidelines regarding sex-segregated advertising:

> Advertisers covered by the Civil Rights Act of 1964 may place advertisements for jobs open to both sexes in columns classified by publishers under "Male" or "Female" headings to indicate that some occupations are considered more attractive to persons of one sex than the other. In such cases the Commission will consider only the advertising of the covered employer and not the headings used by publisher[6] [i.e., the advertisement itself cannot express a sexual preference unless the job is a *bfoq* exception].

On June 20, on the floor of Congress, Rep. Martha Griffiths expressed her contempt for EEOC's "specious, negative and arrogant" attitude toward sex discrimination. "I would remind them

---

[5] *Laws on Sex Discrimination in Employment* (Women's Bureau, Wage and Labor Standards Administration, U.S. Department of Labor, 1970), p. 1.
[6] *Congressional Record,* June 20, 1966, p. 13055.

that they took an oath to uphold the law, not just the part of it that they are interested in."[7] EEOC's rationale for its guidelines was that separate male and female listings did not discriminate but merely helped the advertiser "obtain the maximum reader response." Moreover, "these column headlines do not prevent persons of either sex from scanning the area of the 'jobs available' page."[8] In some newspapers a disclaimer expressing that sentiment was placed at the head of the entire Help Wanted section. Noting the psychological barriers presented by separate listings, Rep. Griffiths remarked, "I have never entered a door labeled 'men' and I doubt that [a man] has frequently entered the women's room. . . . The same principle operates in the job-seeking process."[9] She called for EEOC to issue new guidelines expressly forbidding such labeling by newspaper publishers.

This issue of newspaper "want-ads" was one of the catalysts that caused the formation of the National Organization for Women ten days after Griffiths' speech (June 30). After NOW was formally incorporated in October, 1966, it led the campaign to end sex-segregated "want-ads." (It should be noted that a few newspapers had already ended such listings because they interpreted Title VII as forbidding separate headings, or because local laws passed shortly after Title VII was passed expressly forbid them.) In December, 1966, NOW petitioned EEOC to hold hearings on all the sex guidelines and in the succeeding months used various lobbying tactics to bring them about. In May, 1967, EEOC did hold hearings and women's rights advocates testified to the fact that "merely the repetition of Help Wanted Male; Help Wanted Female, plays a role-conditioning part in continuing myths that rely on false assumptions about sex in relation to work."[1] Publishers countered that their revenue dropped and advertisers that the response to the advertisements dropped. In addition to pressuring EEOC in Washington, NOW had filed a formal complaint against *The New York Times*, followed by picketing and conferences with *The Times* staff. On December 14, NOW organized a National Day of Demonstration Against EEOC

---

[7] Griffiths, statement on floor of Congress, June 20, 1966 (*Congressional Record*, p. 13054).
[8] *Congressional Record*, June 20, 1966, p. 13056. Quoting from letter written by EEOC Commissioner.
[9] *Congressional Record*, p. 13056.
[1] NOW mimeographed pamphlet, *Special Edition #2: NOW vs. Segregated Help-Wanted Ads*. Unpaginated.

with picket lines set up in various cities. It marked one of the earliest national demonstrations of the current movement regarding a women's rights issue. By this time the women's protest had broadened to include all aspects of sex discrimination under Title VII, although "want-ads" remained the most often discussed issue. On February 15, 1968, NOW filed a suit against EEOC to "force it to comply with its own governmental rules, [i.e., Title VII]." The succeeding months were filled with more letters and lobbying on the part of NOW members, members of other women's organizations, and various individual women.

On August 9, 1968, EEOC issued new guidelines (effective December 1, 1968) expressly prohibiting newspaper publishers from carrying separate columns for men and women. The controversy was not over, however; on September 20, 1968, the American Newspaper Publishers Association instituted a suit against EEOC arguing that the guidelines did not have the force of law and EEOC should be enjoined from enforcing them. The court's decision and an appeal by ANPA that was finally dropped in 1970 delayed the effective date of the guidelines until January 25, 1969.[2]

A number of suits have also been brought against individual newspaper publishers across the country, some of which have resulted in the demise of sex-segregated advertisements. One federal case is pending which women's rights advocates hope will decide the issue once and for all. In *Brush v. San Francisco Newspaper Printing Company*[3] the plaintiff is trying to establish the principle that in the area of employment advertising a newspaper functions as an employment agency. If the court establishes that principle then newspapers would be obliged to follow the language of Title VII itself which prohibits employment agencies from classifying or referring "for employment any individual on the basis of sex." EEOC has filed an *amicus* brief on behalf of the plaintiff. Women's Equity Action League has also filed a brief. A decision is expected in the fall of 1971. Many women's rights advocates argue that the prohibition of sex-segregated "want-ads" in newspapers will eliminate one psychological barrier which

---

[2] The ANPA case continued for many months. By this time another women's rights group, Women's Equity Action League, had formed. One of its first formal actions was an attempt to intervene in the ANPA suit as representatives of the working women who were to benefit from the EEOC guidelines. The court turned down WEAL's request in the summer of 1970.
[3] *Brush v. San Francisco Printing Company* (315 F. Supp. 577, N.D. Cal. 1970).

prevented women from seeking to elevate their status and salaries in the employment world.

EXECUTIVE ORDER 11375

Executive Order 11375 is divided into two sections: one concerns federal contractors and subcontractors; the other, federal employment.

Federal Contractors and Sub-Contractors: On September 24, 1965, President Lyndon B. Johnson signed Executive Order 11246 which prohibited discrimination by federal contractors and sub-contractors because of race, color, religion and national origin.[4] Although sex discrimination was already prohibited in private employment by Title VII, it was not until two years later that "sex" was added to the discriminatory bans in the Executive Order. During those two years women's groups lobbied extensively for the addition. Executive Order 11375 (sometimes referred to as "Executive Order 11246 as amended"), which officially prohibits sex discrimination by contractors and sub-contractors, was finally signed on October 13, 1967, and went into effect one year later.

The Order is administered under the Department of Labor by the Office of Federal Contract Compliance which was set up in 1965 when the original Order was passed. OFCC issues rules and regulations to guide employers in compliance as well as actual enforcement of the Order. Routine compliance checks of contractors and potential contractors are carried out by federal agencies such as the Department of Defense, and Health, Education and Welfare before and after a contract is awarded. If the company in question is not complying with OFCC guidelines, OFCC can terminate the contract, prohibit its being awarded to the company, or hold it up until the company complies with the Order. Individual or class action complaints against contractors can also be filed directly with OFCC. OFCC has actively enforced the Executive Order to combat *racial* discrimination. It has been severely criticized, however, for its seeming lack of concern about *sex* discrimination and particularly for its "unwillingness" to issue strict guidelines for the sex provisions of the Executive Order.

A set of *proposed* guidelines on sex discrimination was issued

---

[4] An Executive Order prohibiting federal contractors from discriminating on the basis of race, color, religion or national origin existed prior to 11246, but the enforcement procedure was different.

by OFCC on January 17, 1969, and public hearings on them were held on August 4, 5, and 6. Members of women's rights organizations testified strongly in favor of them. The proposed guidelines almost paralleled those already issued to combat racial discrimination. The women argued that as a result of strict guidelines for minority hiring and promotion, OFCC had been able to actively enforce the Executive Order; by the same token, equally strict guidelines were needed to combat sex discrimination. The proposed guidelines would have required that recruiters include in their recruiting trips women's colleges, female students at co-educational colleges, technical institutions, and high schools; that in the few instances where a valid reason existed to exclude all men or all women from a job category (*bona fide* occupational qualification) "the contractor would have the burden of proving the justification for this exception"; that "affirmative action" must be taken to eliminate "ghetto departments," (i.e., where women and men do similar work but are segregated into all-female and all-male departments, and the women are paid less). After the public hearings little more was heard about these guidelines purportedly because of the hostility engendered by them in the business and industrial communities.

One year later, on February 5, 1970, the Labor Department issued Order No. 4, which outlined the requirements for affirmative action programs for all federal contractors and sub-contractors. The Order stipulated that specific goals and timetables be incorporated into those plans. The Order called for an ". . . analysis of the racial composition of the work force and applicant flow, but made no mention of the need for an analysis by sex."[5] Considerable disagreement ensued as to whether or not Order No. 4 applied to women. Although not officially stated, the general consensus was that it did not. Women's groups mounted a strong campaign to get Order 4 officially extended to include women and at the same time pressured the Department of Labor to release the sex discrimination guidelines. (One of the recommendations of the President's Task Force on the Status of Women, transmitted to the President in December, 1969, urged "immediate issuance by the Secretary of Labor of guidelines to carry out the prohibitions against sex discrimination by government contractors."[6]

---

[5] *Background on Federal Action Toward Equal Opportunity for Women* (National Organization for Women, June, 1970). Unpaginated.
[6] *A Matter of Simple Justice*, The Report of The President's Task Force on Women's Rights and Responsibilities, April, 1970. The report was not officially released until June, 1970.

On June 9, 1970, nearly seventeen months after the *proposed* guidelines were first issued, the Department of Labor finally made public an official set of sex discrimination guidelines. They were released at the time of the Women's Bureau 50th anniversary conference. These guidelines were substantially weaker than the proposed set: recruiter trips to women's colleges were *suggested*, not required; in the *bona fide* occupational qualification section, the contractor was no longer required to *prove* his justification for refusing to hire women for a particular job; no mention was made of the need to eliminate "ghetto departments." Moreover, in NOW's view, ". . . they create a huge loophole by allowing employers to refuse to hire women if they don't have space to build new restrooms."[7] The major weakness, according to women's groups, was the continued lack of mention of specific goals and timetables applicable to women. "The guidelines do not speak of affirmative action *programs* in regard to sex, just of affirmative action; therefore, the exclusion of women from affirmative action programs under Order No. 4 would not make a bid 'unawardable.' "[8] Women's rights groups called the guidelines "useless." Nonetheless on June 25, the National Organization for Women filed a formal blanket complaint charging more than 1300 corporations receiving federal funds with sex discrimination. A month later, Secretary of Labor James D. Hodgson made his now famous but impolitic remark that he had "no intention of applying literally exactly the same approach for women,"[9] in carrying out the Executive Order as had been applied to eliminate discrimination against minority groups. Women's groups were predictably outraged at Hodgson's statement. On July 31 he revised his stand and said that amended guidelines containing "some kinds of goals and timetables applying to some kinds of federal contractors" would be issued.[1] He stated further that he would set up an advisory committee including representatives of women's rights groups to study different proposals. The committee was established in February, 1971, but new guidelines were not expected for months.

Even without strict guidelines, women's groups are filing sex discrimination charges against recipients of federal funds. The greatest activity along these lines has been in the area of educa-

[7] *Background on Federal Action.*
[8] *Ibid.*
[9] *New York Times,* July 26, 1970.
[1] *New York Times,* July 31, 1970.

tion. Colleges and universities receive over $3 billion in federal funds every year, and in January, 1970, the first formal sex discrimination complaint against an educational institution was filed against the University of Maryland by Women's Equity Action League.[2] Since that time women's rights groups have filed formal charges against more than 300 colleges and universities (over ten percent of the national total) plus some elementary and secondary schools. The Department of Health, Education and Welfare is the compliance agency for complaints in the area of education, and it has begun investigating the charges. In some cases contracts have been held up pending proper compliance with the Executive Order and/or the issuance of an acceptable affirmative action program regarding the hiring and promotion of women in educational institutions.[3] According to a number of women activists, HEW's "zealousness" is the result of Congressional pressure put on that agency combined with an already existing commitment on the part of some HEW officials to combat sex discrimination.[4]

Federal Employment: The other part of Executive Order 11375 prohibits discrimination on the basis of race, color, religion, national origin or sex in federal employment (as distinct from employment by federal contractors).[5] This portion of the Order is administered by the Civil Service Commission which set up the procedures by which sex discrimination complaints would be heard.

The Civil Service Commission created the Federal Women's Program to coordinate the enforcement effort. A coordinator of the Federal Women's Program is in each federal agency and is charged not only with enforcing the ban against sex discrimination (in accordance with Civil Service guidelines), but also with creating an agency plan to actively recruit and promote women

---

[2] See separate entry (WEAL), this chapter.

[3] See chapter 9 for detailed discussion.

[4] In February, 1971, HEW became the first government agency to launch its own internal women's rights program. Xandra Kayden was hired to survey the status of women in HEW and recommend ways to upgrade them. Dr. Bernice Sandler was named associate director. Each HEW agency will have a representative to the new Women's Action Program.

[5] The Order superseded and strengthened a directive to that effect issued by President John F. Kennedy in 1962. The 1962 directive, requested by Attorney General Robert F. Kennedy, reversed the interpretation of an 1870 law regarding government employment, which had been used for years as legal authority to keep women from higher level government jobs. The 1870 law itself was repealed in 1965.

to top level jobs. Women's rights activists have accused the Federal Women's Program of paying little more than "bureaucratic lip service."[6]

On August 8, 1969, President Richard M. Nixon issued Executive Order 11478, which superseded the federal employment section of 11375, but did not substantially change its aims or provisions.

PRESIDENT'S TASK FORCE ON WOMEN'S RIGHTS AND RESPONSIBILITIES

Pressure on the Nixon Administration to elevate the status of women began almost immediately upon the President's inauguration. In January, 1969, Rep. Florence Dwyer (R., N.J.) proposed to the President that he establish in the Executive branch a new organizational structure to deal solely with the elimination of sex discrimination. In February, 1969, at a press conference, Washington columnist Vera Glaser asked Nixon directly why he had not appointed more women to policy-making positions. Six months later when no action had taken place, Rep. Dwyer and her three Republican women colleagues, Reps. Catherine May (Wash.), Charlotte Reid (Ill.), and Margaret Heckler (Mass.), drew up a lengthy memorandum detailing the problems of discrimination against women and proposing a set of recommendations to combat them. The four women met with the President on July 9 to urge action. At about the same time reporter Glaser requested and was granted a meeting with presidential counselor Arthur Burns to discuss the "woman question."

In August, 1969, the Administration finally acted. That month Nixon appointed the new members of the Citizens' Advisory Council on the Status of Women. In September the President set up fourteen task forces on a wide range of subjects to produce ideas for his State of the Union message the following January. The Task Force on Women's Rights and Responsibilities was one of them, and its establishment was formally announced on October 1. According to Glaser and her colleague, Malvina Stephenson:

> When the task forces were named . . . some White House staffers pooh-poohed inclusion of the "woman question."

---

[6] See separate entry (Federally Employed Women), this chapter.

The group came into being largely because Dr. Arthur Burns, then counselor to the President, regarded the subject as important.[7]

At the convening meeting of the Task Force, Burns credited its existence in large part to the meeting he had had with Glaser.

The Task Force, chaired by Virginia Allan, executive vice-president of a Michigan drug store chain and former president of the National Federation of Business and Professional Women's Clubs, was made up of ten prominent women and two men.[8] The group met in secret for the next three months (a common procedure for Presidential task forces) and transmitted its Report, *A Matter of Simple Justice,* to the White House on December 15, 1969. However, none of its recommendations, nor indeed even the subject of women, was mentioned in the State of the Union address. Activists both within the Administration and without vigorously protested the omission and began to campaign for the public release of the Task Force Report. Weeks turned into months and conflicting views developed on why the Report had not been released. Bootleg copies were being circulated widely, and women's groups argued that the Report was being "suppressed" because of its militant tone and far-reaching recommendations. Official sources insisted that the delay (not only of the release of the women's report but of the other task forces as well) was due solely to bureaucratic red-tape, printing and distribution problems. The *Miami Herald* reprinted in full a bootleg copy of the report, the first installment of which appeared on April 22. A number of other newspapers followed suit producing even more accusations of "administration cover-up."

A Matter of Simple Justice was finally released on June 9, 1970, during the Women's Bureau Fiftieth Anniversary Conference. The long-awaited sex discrimination guidelines for federal contractors were also issued at that time by the Department of Labor. Rumor continued, however, that had it not been for the public outcry on the part of women's groups and the direct pressure brought on the White House by Elizabeth Koontz, head of the Women's Bureau, the Report would never have been officially released. Notwithstanding a continued lack of official enthusiasm since the Report's release, by mid-1971 well over 30,000 copies

---

[7] *Miami Herald,* March 8, 1970.
[8] See Appendix for list of Task Force members.

had been distributed to individuals and groups and the demand
for copies was continuing.

In essence, the content of *A Matter of Simple Justice* breaks
no new ground on women's issues, but its language and tone are
considerably stronger and more urgent than that of any past
federally-sponsored report. The letter to the President accompanying the Report reads in part:

> As President of the United States, committed to the prin-
> ciple of equal rights for all, your leadership can be crucial
> to the more than half our citizens who are women and
> who are now denied their full constitutional and legal
> rights. . . . The research and deliberation of this Task
> Force reveal that the United States, as it approaches its
> 200th anniversary, lags behind other enlightened, and in-
> deed some newly emerging, countries in the role ascribed
> to women. . . . So widespread and pervasive are discrim-
> inatory practices against women they have come to be
> regarded, more often than not, as normal. . . . American
> women are increasingly aware and restive over the denial
> of equal opportunity, equal responsibility, even equal pro-
> tection of the law. An abiding concern for home and chil-
> dren should not, in their view, cut them off from the
> freedom to choose the role in society to which their in-
> terest, education, and training entitle them. . . . Equality
> for women is unalterably linked to many broader ques-
> tions of social justice. Inequities within our society serve
> to restrict the contribution of both sexes. We have wit-
> nessed a decade of rebellion during which black Ameri-
> cans fought for true equality. The battle still rages. Noth-
> ing could demonstrate more dramatically the explosive
> potential of denying fulfillment as human beings to any
> segment of our society. What this Task Force recommends
> is a national commitment to basic changes that will bring
> women into the mainstream of American life. . . . Without
> such [a commitment] . . . there is danger of accelerating
> militancy or the kind of deadening apathy that stills prog-
> ress and inhibits creativity.[9]

Some of the Task Force recommendations called for

---

[9] *A Matter of Simple Justice: The Report of the President's Task Force on
Women's Rights and Responsibilities*, April, 1970.

—the establishment of an Office of Women's Rights and Responsibilities whose director would report directly to the President.

—a White House conference on women's rights and responsibilities to be called by the President in 1970, the 50th anniversary of the ratification of the suffrage amendment.

—a Presidential message to Congress proposing legislation to combat the widespread discrimination against women.

—initiation by the Attorney General of legal actions in cases of sex discrimination brought under Title VII, and intervention or filing of *amicus* briefs by the Attorney General in pending cases challenging the validity of sex-based laws under the 5th and 14th Amendments.

—the appointment of more women to high-level positions within the Administration.

—the passage of the Equal Rights Amendment.

—immediate issuance by the Secretary of Labor of guidelines to implement Executive Order 11375.

Although only one of the Task Force recommendations had been carried out by mid-1971—the issuance of sex discrimination guidelines to implement Executive Order 11375—the mere existence of the Task Force and the militant tone of its Report appear to have sensitized at least a few Administration officials and some members of Congress to women's issues.

A record number of bills dealing with women's rights were introduced in the 91st and 92nd Congresses. One, the Women's Equity Act, sponsored by Rep. Abner Mikva (D., Ill.), proposed that nearly all the Task Force recommendations be enacted. Others, often covering the same areas of legislation as the Equity Act, have been introduced individually and range from revamping the Social Security and tax laws, to giving EEOC cease and desist powers, to including all categories of employees under the Equal Pay Act, and to setting up a national network of child care centers. By mid-1971 no significant bill dealing with women's rights had been passed. President Nixon's proposed 1971 budget, however, appeared to have acknowledged indirectly the growing pressure in this area. Although it made no distinction between sex and other forms of discrimination, the budget proposed additional funds be allocated to HEW ($2.4 million) to assure non-bias compliance in contracts awarded by that agency; to the Labor Department ($32.6 million) to permit doubling of on-site reviews of contract compliance; to EEOC ($11.1 million) to double its staff from 780 to 1570. It must also be noted, however, that the President's 1971 State of the Union message again made no mention of women's issues.

WOMEN'S BUREAU

One quite significant change in the Government's position on women's rights occurred during the first year of the Nixon Administration—a different (some would say radically different) philosophical orientation of the Women's Bureau. As noted previously, the Bureau, established in 1920, had always been oriented toward the needs of working women in industry; indeed, to a large extent it grew out of the trade union movement. Although the Bureau always advocated equal pay for equal work and supported non-discriminatory hiring and promotion practices, it traditionally defended protective legislation for women because of their dual social role—homemaker and worker. A Bureau publication, reprinted from a 1964 seminar paper, articulated its underlying rationale.

> It is not the policy of the Women's Bureau to encourage married women and mothers of young children to seek employment outside the home. Home and children are considered married women's most important responsibilities. But the fact is that married women *are* working outside their homes in increasing numbers . . . most often to add to the family income.[1]

Feminists over the years have accused the Bureau of impeding women's employment opportunities rather than furthering them because of its philosophy that mothers and married women should not work unless absolutely necessary. Feminists, even the most conservative, have also argued that the Women's Bureau, because of its origins in the trade union movement, has always been strongly influenced by that movement—a movement which traditionally has been male-oriented, male-dominated and, in the view of women's rights activists, not in the least interested in opening industrial opportunities to women on an equal basis with men.

[1] *To Benefit Women at Work,* U.S. Department of Labor, Wage and Labor Standards Administration, April, 1969, pp. 5–6.

A shift in attitude began to occur within the Bureau when Title VII was finally interpreted to supersede most state protective legislation. A more dramatic shift occurred when Elizabeth B. Koontz was appointed by President Nixon in January, 1969, to head the Bureau, the first Negro to be so appointed. Koontz, a former teacher and president of the National Education Association, brought a non-governmental approach to the Bureau's work, and perhaps because of it, she has guided the Bureau into the mainstream of the women's rights movement. The first major event sponsored under the new directorship was a conference on June 10–12, 1970, commemorating the Bureau's fiftieth anniversary. According to Koontz, "The Bureau had not been close enough to the disparate philosophies of the women's movement."[2] To remedy that situation, she invited more than 1000 women whose views ranged from conservative-reformist to radical feminist to attend the conference. The two-day meeting consisted primarily of workshops, most of which have been described as "brainstorming" sessions. Out of the workshops came a group of strong resolutions, which in large part echoed the Task Force recommendations. The Conference also supported the Equal Rights Amendment. As a result of considerable pressure from Koontz on the Department of Labor before the Conference, the Department reversed its traditional opposition to the Amendment and announced its new stand during the Conference proceedings.

The original mandate of the Women's Bureau was to "investigate and report upon all matters pertaining to the welfare of women in industry."[3] Within this framework Director Koontz believes the Bureau's central job should be "to keep abreast of and disseminate information on social changes in the labor market making particular note of the changing *aspirations* of women."[4] Over the decades the Bureau has produced a constant stream of reports and statistics about women workers, and it is continuing to do so at an increasing rate. Indeed, the Bureau is the only government agency that compiles, analyzes and publishes statistics about women. Consequently, the *1969 Handbook on Women Workers* with more than 300 pages of comparative data has become the bible, of sorts, of the current movement. It

---

[2] Interview, October, 1970.
[3] "An Act to establish in the Department of Labor a Bureau to be known as The Women's Bureau," June 5, 1920. Reprinted in the *1969 Handbook of Women Workers,* Women's Bureau Bulletin 294 (GPO, 1969).
[4] Interview, October, 1970.

prompted one radical feminist to remark, "It's the only book of graphs and statistics guaranteed to raise a woman reader's blood pressure."[5]

•   •   •

The traditionally accepted discriminatory biases against women found in federal policy and law are under attack from all sides, and the pressure for change, which began in 1961 with the establishment of the President's Commission on the Status of Women, has become increasingly militant with each year. Although women's rights activists acknowledge that some progress has been made, they are pressing for more radical and rapid change. They now argue that great strides can be made legislatively if women will begin to vote as a bloc to remove unsympathetic politicians from office.

Equal Rights Amendment

"EQUALITY OF RIGHTS under the law shall not be denied or abridged by the United States or by any State on account of sex."

HISTORY

The Equal Rights Amendment was first introduced in Congress in 1923 (three years after the ratification of the 19th Amendment) by Sen. Charles Curtis and Rep. Daniel Anthony (Susan B. Anthony's nephew), both Republicans from Kansas. The idea for an Equal Rights Amendment was suggested earlier that year by the National Woman's Party[6] at the 75th anniversary conference of the Seneca Falls Convention. The Amendment has since been introduced in both the House and the Senate in every session of Congress, primarily because of the continued pressure of the National Woman's Party.

A number of hearings have been held over the years by the Senate, and the Amendment always has been reported out of Committee favorably. In addition, in 1950 and 1953 the Senate

---

[5] Joreen, "The 51 Percent Minority: A Statistical Essay," *Sisterhood Is Powerful*, ed. Robin Morgan (New York: Random House, 1970), p. 41. Anthology hereafter referred to as *Sisterhood*.
[6] See separate entry, this chapter.

passed the Amendment; however, both times the "Hayden rider" was attached. The Hayden rider was a floor amendment proposed by Sen. Carl Hayden (D., Ariz.) which in effect kept all the state protective legislation intact. Each time the rider accomplished its purpose of killing the bill's intent, a primary aim of which was to nullify protective legislation. The House Judiciary Committee held hearings once in 1948, but between that time and 1971 no hearings were held because Rep. Emanuel D. Celler (D., N.Y.), Chairman of the Committee, refused to schedule them. Twice however, in 1948 and 1961, he introduced a counterproposal—the establishment of a Commission on the Legal Status of Women "to study and review the nature and extent of discrimination based on sex."[7] It is generally agreed that his proposed Commission was meant to kill the Amendment.

Since 1944 both political parties have traditionally included recommendations for an Equal Rights Amendment in their platforms, except in the most recent campaigns of 1964 and 1968. Many feel that formal party support was withdrawn because the Commission on the Status of Women, set up by President Kennedy in 1961, opposed passage of the Amendment. In October, 1967, President Lyndon B. Johnson reiterated his personal support for the Amendment, and in July, 1968, during his presidential campaign, Richard Nixon voiced his support. President Nixon has made no formal statement about the Amendment since his election, but Mrs. Nixon, when she spoke to the participants of the 50th anniversary conference of the Women's Bureau in June, 1970, said her husband supported it.

After over forty years of public apathy (and virtual ignorance) about the Amendment, the growth of the new women's movement has caused a resurgence of interest in it. In December, 1969, President Nixon's Task Force on the Status of Women supported passage of the Amendment (although the Report was not publicly released until June), and in March, 1970, the Citizens' Advisory Council on the Status of Women issued a memorandum on the Amendment strongly recommending passage. In May, 1970, the Subcommittee on Constitutional Amendments of the Senate Judiciary Committee held hearings, the first since 1956. Sen. Birch Bayh (D., Ind.), chairman of the subcommittee, ad-

---

[7] Cited in testimony of Marguerite Rawalt at Equal Rights Amendment hearings before Committee on the Judiciary, Subcommittee No. 4, U.S. House of Representatives, March 25, 1971, p. 19. Hereafter referred to as *ERA Hearings 3.*

mits that those May hearings were the direct result of an earlier confrontation between his subcommittee and a group of ERA advocates: on February 17, 1970, during hearings on a constitutional amendment to enfranchise eighteen-year-olds, Wilma Scott Heide, chairman of the board of directors of NOW, and about twenty women disrupted the proceedings and demanded that hearings be scheduled on the Equal Rights Amendment.

The resulting hearings were held the following May and most of the forty-two witnesses testified in favor of the Amendment. They included leaders of nearly every women's rights organization in the country, well-known lawyers and a number of Senators and Representatives. For the first time in its history, the Department of Labor supported the Amendment's passage; some labor unions also voiced support. On July 28 the Amendment was reported favorably out of the Subcommittee.

Perhaps the most noteworthy development in the history of the Amendment occurred in the House in 1970. On June 11, Rep. Martha Griffiths (D., Mich.), a long-time advocate of women's rights and the Equal Rights Amendment, introduced a rarely used parliamentary tactic, the discharge petition, to force the Amendment out of the House Judiciary Committee. With the lobbying aid and letter-writing campaigns of women's rights groups, Rep. Griffiths forced the Amendment onto the floor of the House for a vote on August 10. After an hour of debate, it was passed by an overwhelming, and surprising, majority of 352 to 15.[8] Thus, the full House acted on the Amendment for the first time since it was first introduced in 1923.

With the House passage, the controversy reopened. On August 17, Sen. Sam J. Ervin, Jr. (D., N.C.), member of the Senate Committee on the Judiciary, proposed a substitute amendment which, like the Hayden rider, kept intact all the state protective legislation, and also prohibited women from being drafted. In addition, Sen. Ervin's substitute amendment read, "This article shall not impair the validity of any law . . . which is reasonably designed to promote the health, safety, privacy, education, or economic welfare of women, or to enable them to perform their duties as homemakers or mothers."[9] Sen. Ervin held full Judiciary

---

[8] The most commonly used figures are 350–15. The 352 figure includes absentee additions to the pro column. (Source, *Congressional Quarterly.*)
[9] Hearings before the Senate Judiciary Committee, September, 1970, p. 8. Hereafter referred to as *ERA Hearings 2.*

Committee hearings on his substitute proposal in September, 1970. Whereas the Senate May hearings had been weighted heavily in favor of passage of the original Equal Rights Amendment, many of the witnesses testifying at Ervin's hearings were, for the most part, opposed to the original wording and favored instead his substitute Amendment, which would ensure at least partial retention of protective legislation, as well as other laws designed to "protect" women.

On October 7, the debate reached the floor of the Senate, where unrelated riders were introduced[1] in the hope of weighting the bill with so much controversy that it would die. It did. Some political observers noted the ironic position in which the Senate found itself in the 91st Congress: "Eighty senators—much more than the required two-thirds—had signed their names as sponsors of the Amendment. But that was back when no one in the Senate thought the Amendment would ever get through the House."[2] Thus in 1970, for the first time in history, the Senate was in the position to veto the Equal Rights Amendment; and accordingly, for the first time in history each Senator was required to take stock of exactly what a *pro* or *con* vote would mean to him or her *politically.*

The Amendment was introduced in the 92nd Congress in both the House and Senate in January, 1971, and hearings were held by a House Subcommittee on the Judiciary in March. For the first time in ten years the Administration voiced its support of the Amendment. The ERA was reported favorably out of the Subcommittee in April.

Lobbying pressure for and against the Amendment began anew, and the fragile coalitions on both sides bore out the cliché —"politics make strange bedfellows." Those supporting the Amendment ranged from the most conservative Republican women, some of whom find "feminism a dirty word," to the most radical feminists who challenge the institutions of marriage, the family, and in fact define sexual relationships as a political institution to be restructured. Those opposing the Amendment included conservative (often Southern) male politicians; much of organized labor; and most recently, some radical women involved in new left politics whose positions on most other issues

---

[1] One had to do with jurisdiction of public schools, another with prayer in schools.

[2] Eileen Shanahan, *New York Times,* September 13, 1970.

are totally antithetical to those of labor and conservatives in general.

AREAS OF LAW POTENTIALLY AFFECTED
BY THE EQUAL RIGHTS AMENDMENT

The core of the *legal* debate over women's rights is embodied in the ERA controversy, for what is being questioned, is the very definition of female equality under the law.

Although the arguments *pro* and *con* have become lost in the morass of political rhetoric and the specifics of the myriad laws potentially affected—marriage and divorce laws, property rights, draft laws, jury service laws, etc.—through it all, there is only one question to be considered: is it valid for *legal* distinctions to be made on the basis of sex; and if they are made on that basis, is the principle of equality under the law being subverted. The debate has remained essentially unchanged since the Amendment was originally introduced nearly half a century ago.

Opponents of the Equal Rights Amendment (which include men and women) without exception admit that laws exist which grievously discriminate against women, particularly in the area of employment. Nonetheless, they argue that in view of woman's dual role as homemaker and worker, legal distinctions between men and women are not only valid in some cases, but necessary "to protect the best interest of women and the highest interest of society."[3] To them the law cannot and should not be "sexblind" as it has become "colorblind."

Conversely, proponents of the Amendment (also including men and women) argue that in the eyes of the law, distinctions based on sex should not be made because they serve not to "protect" and "support" the best interests of women, but to restrict their rights, downgrade their status, and legally force them to accept a dual role whether or not they desire it. In addition, the existing laws which distinguish one sex from the other are based on now-outmoded concepts of the roles of men and women in society. Moreover, it is argued that:

> Classifications that treat persons differently simply because they were born into a class [i.e., race, religion, national origin, sex] are antithetical to democracy because the individual is permanently condemned to legal restric-

---

[3] Sen. Sam J. Ervin, Jr., testimony, *ERA Hearings 2*, p. 7.

tions by virtue of a status over which he or she has no control.[4]

There are a number of laws (mostly enacted by state or lesser jurisdictions) that treat men and women differently and would be affected by the passage of the Equal Rights Amendment. It is within the above frame of reference—should or should not sex be a reasonable legal classification of persons— that these laws and the arguments over the potential impact of the ERA can be best discussed and understood. With few exceptions the laws in question fall into one of six areas: jury selection, criminal punishment, public education, selective service, family law, and protective legislation.

Jury Selection: Although all states now stipulate that women are eligible to be jurors,[5] women are not always required to be automatically selected for jury service as are men. In some states women (but not men) must pre-register to be considered eligible; in others, there are specific exemptions and excuses for women simply because they are women. In 1961, the Supreme Court upheld the constitutionality of these kinds of special qualifications:

> Despite the enlightened emancipation of women from the restrictions and protections of bygone years, and their entry into many parts of community life formerly considered to be reserved to men, woman is still regarded as the center of home and family life. We cannot say that it is constitutionally impermissible for a State, acting in pursuit of the general welfare, to conclude that a woman should be relieved from the civic duty of jury service unless she herself determines that such service is consistent with her own special responsibilities.[6]

Proponents argue that the Amendment would make unconstitutional any statute which treats men and women differently in the

---

[4] Mary Eastwood, "The Double Standard of Justice: Women's Rights Under the Constitution," *Valparaiso Law Review,* Symposium Issue: "Women and the Law," Vol. 5:2, 1971, p. 296.
[5] The Civil Service Act of 1957 made women eligible to sit on all federal juries. In 1966, a three-judge Federal Court declared an Alabama law excluding women from state juries unconstitutional as a denial of equal protection under the 14th Amendment. *White v. Crook,* 251 F. Supp. 401, 408 (M.D. Ala., 2-7-66).
[6] *Hoyt v. Florida,* 368 U.S. 57 (1961).

jury selection process. In addition, since present statutory provisions disqualify certain professions, for example attorneys, and since jurors are consistently excused for hardship cases, supporters of the Amendment see no legal problems in exempting women who have small children in their care in the same manner that men would also be exempted. All these exemptions, however, should be viewed as individual privilege and not determined by sex. There is little disagreement from opponents to the Amendment in the area of jury selection, but they see no need for a constitutional amendment to rectify the inequities in these state laws.

Criminal laws: The Amendment would make unconstitutional different penalties for men and women who commit identical offenses. Some states still carry statutes requiring longer prison sentences for women than men for the same crime, or convict women on a more serious charge for the same misdeed committed by a man. Apparently, many of these laws were originally enacted on the legislative rationale that "it required longer to rehabilitate a female criminal than a male criminal."[7] ERA opponents agree that such inequitable criminal laws must be changed, but again they see no need to resort to a constitutional amendment to accomplish this goal. They argue further that the legislative machinery already exists to repeal these old laws and, furthermore, that legal precedents have already been set in this area.[8]

Public Education: Proponents argue that state educational institutions discriminate against women by not admitting them as students, not hiring them as teachers, not awarding them public scholarships on an equal basis with men, and not paying them salaries equal to those of their male counterparts. They argue further that there is no federal legislation prohibiting these practices, and they cite examples of the effects of the lack of anti-sex discrimination legislation in this area: the University of North Carolina, a publicly-supported institution, openly declares,

---

[7] Marguerite Rawalt, testimony at hearings before the Senate Subcommittee on Constitutional Amendments of the Committee on the Judiciary, May, 1970, p. 128. Hereafter referred to as *ERA Hearings 1.*
[8] In 1968 the Supreme Court of Pennsylvania voided that state's Muncy Act in a case in which a woman convicted of robbery was sentenced to a prison term of 10 years instead of the 1–4 year term required for a man committing the same offense. (*Commonwealth v. Jane Daniels,* 430 Pa. 642, 243A 2d 400 1968). A Federal District Court in Connecticut struck down a similar statute (*U.S. ex rel. Robinson v. York,* 281 F. Supp. 8 (D. Conn. 2-28-68)).

"admission of women on the freshman level will be restricted to those who are especially well qualified";[9] the University of Virginia turned down 21,000 women applicants, but during the same period of time did not reject one male applicant; the numbers of public high schools which offer specialized technical and scientific training restricted to boys; and, finally, high schools which refuse attendance to pregnant or married girls, but not to unwed fathers or married boys. Recent court decisions offer little hope of changing these practices, argue ERA proponents, because they have upheld exclusionary practices or have refused to rule on them at all.[1] Proponents seek to declare all forms of sex discrimination in public education unconstitutional and believe that "the Equal Rights Amendment will state loudly and clearly that the time has come for sex discrimination to end in America's colleges and universities."[2] The only question that appears to trouble most opponents of the Amendment in this particular area is the possibility that West Point, Annapolis and the thirteen other publicly-supported military schools would have to admit women on an equal basis. The Amendment would not affect private educational institutions.

Selective Service laws: The emotional level of the ERA debate rises sharply over the issue of the draft, particularly on the part of the Amendment's opponents. Indeed, a large part of the case against the Amendment is based on the grounds that if it were passed women would be subjected to the draft on the same basis as men:

> . . . perhaps the most distasteful thing of all, is that, as long as we keep selective service on the books, or, if it is repealed, then at any time when we may reinstate it, women, along with men, must be equally subject to military conscription. Conscription is objectionable enough, many think, where men are concerned but I can think of

---

[9] Publication by Office of Undergraduate Admissions, University of North Carolina. Cited in *ERA Hearings 1*.
[1] In 1960 the Texas Court of Appeals upheld the exclusion of women from Texas A&M (*Allred v. Heaton* 336 S.W. 2d 251 1960). See also *Heaton v. Bristol* (317 S.W. 2d 86 1958). The Supreme Court denied *certiori* in both cases. In March 1971 the Supreme Court affirmed without a hearing a lower court decision (*Williams v. McNair* 316 F. Supp. 134) that a single sex admissions policy of a state supported college, in this case all-female Winthrop College (South Carolina), was not in violation of the 14th Amendment.
[2] Dr. Bernice Sandler, testimony, *ERA Hearings 1*, p. 427.

no more far reaching social change, nothing more likely
to destroy the family unit, nothing so likely to threaten to
transform us into a national socialistic type of state, than
to conscript American women into the Armed Forces.[3]

The Federal Courts apparently agree with this view. In a case involving a violation of the Military Selective Service Act of 1967,
the defendant raised the issue of sex discrimination, arguing that
his rights to due process of law under the 5th Amendment were
violated because men, but not women, are compelled to serve in
the Armed Forces. The Court disagreed:

> In the Act and its predecessors, Congress made a legisla-
> tive judgment that men should be subject to involuntary
> induction but that women, presumably because they are
> "still regarded as the center of home and family life"
> (*Hoyt v. State of Florida* . . .) should not. Women may
> constitutionally be afforded "special recognition" (cf.
> *Gruenwald v. Gardner* . . .) particularly since women are
> not excluded from service in the Armed Forces. . . .

> In providing for involuntary service for men and volun-
> tary service for women, Congress followed the teachings
> of history that if a nation is to survive, men must provide
> the first line of defense while women keep the home fires
> burning.[4]

Proponents of the ERA agree with the defendant in the above-
mentioned case that the Selective Service laws do in such instances discriminate against men. They also agree that passage
of the Equal Rights Amendment would subject women to the
draft as well as men. Exactly how women would be conscripted,
however, is a matter of opinion. Some argue that the idea of
drafting women is a good idea in its own right, ERA notwithstanding. They feel that all young people should serve their
country in some way, either in the armed forces or some other
kind of national service. Others, troubled by the idea of women

---

[3] Rep. Dennis, House floor debate on ERA, August 10, 1970. *Congressional
Record*, H7960.
[4] *U.S. v. St. Clair*, 291 F. Supp. 122 (S.D. N.Y., 1968). Quoted from Citizens' Advisory Council *Memorandum on the Equal Rights Amendment*,
p. 8.

"bearing arms," nonetheless support the Amendment arguing that the majority of draftees do not bear arms as it is; instead, they perform the same kinds of jobs they might have done in civilian life—running stores, driving trucks, doing office work. Undoubtedly, the same would be true of women, and they would not be required to partake of combat duty at all, ". . . where they are not fitted, any more than men are required to so serve."[5] Sen. Marlow C. Cook (D., Kan.) accused ERA opponents of turning the draft issue into a "good red herring," by implying that suddenly every young American woman would be on the front lines. Those who feel strongly that the draft itself is wrong, argue that if women were required to be drafted, the anti-draft movement would become even stronger than it is presently and might more quickly precipitate an all-volunteer army:

> If some do object to people, male or female, being drafted, then it is up to those of us who object to the draft to change the world so that the draft can become a part of our primitive history. Until that time, women and men must share equal responsibility in being subjected to the draft.[6]

Noting that women are conscripted in other countries, supporters of the Amendment believe that much of the emotional reaction against the thought of drafting women comes primarily from middle-aged and older people simply ". . . because it was something they never considered for themselves when they were of draft age."[7] Indeed, at the March, 1971, House hearings on the Amendment, NOW president Aileen Hernandez assailed the Subcommittee for not inviting as witnesses some young women to testify on the draft issue since it would be they, "not the middle-aged, male Committee members who would be affected by any such change in the law."[8]

It should also be noted that the Intercollegiate Association of Women Students, a national organization of undergraduates, passed a resolution in March, 1971, endorsing the draft for women if the draft itself remained in existence.

Another reason against drafting women appears to be fear for

---

[5] *Ibid.*, p. 11.
[6] National Organization for Women statement in *ERA Hearings 1,* p. 75.
[7] *Ibid.*, p. 74.
[8] Interview, March, 1971.

the country's "manhood" if women are in uniform. Author Caroline Bird doubts, however,

> ... that working alongside a woman draftee in a Pentagon office would do any more damage to American manhood than working beside a woman civilian on Madison Avenue or Michigan Boulevard. For that matter, I doubt that the American man is in such a precarious state of manhood that a woman's draft would destroy him.[9]

Family law: All the state laws which fall under the general rubric of family law—minimum marriage age, support, divorce, alimony, child custody, property rights, etc.—would be greatly affected by the passage of the Equal Rights Amendment.

In the vast majority of states the laws affecting married men and married women are rooted in the tradition of common law in which the husband was regarded as the head of the family and the guardian of his wife.[1] Under common law the woman completely lost her identity upon marriage, since the husband and wife legally became one person, i.e., the person of the husband. Because of this legal assumption, most states require the wife to assume her husband's name and his place of domicile. In some states it can be grounds for divorce if a wife sets up a separate legal domicile for the purposes of running for public office, voting, or to serve on a jury. In addition, in several states the wife has no right to make contract and, if she wishes to go into business for herself, she must often go through a lengthy court procedure to prove her fitness. In the realm of property rights, the husband often has exclusive ownership and control of his earnings and property acquired during the marriage. Although he is legally required to support his wife he may dispose of his property and earnings without her consent. If the wife works during the marriage, she usually retains ownership and control of those earnings. It has been noted, however, that the case is rare when a wife's earnings equal or exceed her husband's. In a handful of states community property laws are in effect. Under this system earnings and property acquired by either husband or wife during the marriage are owned jointly by both spouses. However,

---

[9] Caroline Bird, "Let's Draft Women Too," *Saturday Evening Post,* June 18, 1966. Read into testimony, *ERA Hearings 1,* p. 340.
[1] In contract and property rights, the laws affecting single persons, male and female, are generally the same.

though the ownership is joint, the control and management of these earnings and property frequently rests solely with the husband. In a 1944 opinion, the Florida Supreme Court commented on the inequities within the property rights laws:

> . . . a woman's responsibilities and faculties remain intact from age of maturity until she finds her mate; whereupon, incompetency seizes her and she needs protection in an extreme degree. Upon the advent of widowhood she is reinvested with all her capabilities which had been dormant during her marriage, only to lose them again upon remarriage. Intermittently, she is protected and benefitted accordingly as she is married or single.[2]

There are also many inequities in the laws governing marriageable age, support, divorce, alimony and child custody. According to Leo Kanowitz, who has written a comprehensive study of women and the law, the generally lower marriage age for women is based on two sociological presumptions:

> One is that the married state is the only proper goal of womanhood. The other is that the male, and only the male, while not to be denied the benefits of marriage, should also be encouraged to engage in bigger, better and more useful pursuits. Recognizing that early marriage impedes preparation for meaningful extra-family activities, society has decreed that males should not be permitted this digression from life's important business at too early an age.[3]

After marriage, because the laws are based on the premise that the husband is the breadwinner and head of household, the legal obligations of family support rest on him, regardless of his wife's financial status. (A few states stipulate that the wife must support the husband if he is disabled.) Kanowitz notes, however, that "the precise nature of the husband's legal duty to support his wife is . . . rarely ever articulated while the marriage is in progress and the spouses are living together. In fact, its exact details are normally spelled out by the law only in cases of

---

[2] Cited by Rawalt, *ERA Hearings 1*, p. 126.
[3] Leo Kanowitz, *Women and the Law: The Unfinished Revolution* (Albuquerque: University of New Mexico Press, 1968), p. 11.

marital breakdown."[4] In the event of divorce the obligation of support most often rests with the husband and alimony is almost automatically awarded to the wife. A few states stipulate also that the husband may be awarded alimony. Proponents of the Equal Rights Amendment argue that the legal obligation for support should rest on both spouses, ". . . with due regard to financial conditions, earning capacities and other circumstances of either spouse that bear upon the discharge of this obligation."[5]

The primary fear of Amendment opponents is that its passage would impose an undesired fundamental change in the role of the husband as breadwinner and the wife as householder. Sen. Ervin commented:

> The common law and statutory law of the various States recognize the reality that many women are homemakers and mothers, and by reason of the duties imposed upon them in these capacities, are largely precluded from pursuing gainful occupations or making any provision for their financial security during their declining years. To enable women to do these things and thereby make the existence and development of the race possible, these State laws impose upon husbands the primary responsibility to provide homes and livelihoods for their wives and children, and make them criminally responsible to society and civilly responsible to their wives if they fail to perform this primary responsibility. . . . If the . . . equal rights amendment should be interpreted by the Supreme Court to forbid any legal distinctions between men and women, it would nullify all existing and all future laws of this kind.[6]

Thus, opponents of the Amendment fear that the millions of non-working wives and mothers would have no legal guarantee of support if it were passed. Proponents of the Amendment counter that objection by arguing that the role of wife and mother would neither disappear nor be threatened but rather reconceived in a more equitable manner:

> The argument of some opponents of the Equal Rights Amendment that it would allow a man to escape from

---

[4] *Ibid.,* p. 71.
[5] Association of Women Lawyers testimony, *ERA Hearings 1,* p. 512.
[6] Sen. Ervin, *Congressional Digest,* January 19, 1971, p. 15.

his obligation of support is not a valid argument. So long
as the wife contributes in services to the family, in the
duties of homemaking, of rearing children, of being a
social hostess for her husband, etc., she is contributing
equally to the marriage, and with each year that she
makes such contribution to the marriage her ability to
earn an independent income from the outside world
diminishes while her contribution to the marriage increases. It is conceivable that there may be a few cases
where the spouse contributing the services to the home or
caring for small children would be the husband. . . . The
Equal Rights Amendment should result in State Legislation making the support of one spouse by the other dependent upon the circumstances of those spouses, and
their respective contributions to the marriage (the
contribution of home-making and related duties being as
vitally important a contribution as that of earning the
family income).[7]

They argue further that the ownership and control of earnings and property should be held jointly by both spouses regardless of whether one or both work. By the same token the legal
obligations of alimony, child support and child custody should
not be based automatically on sex, but on the individual circumstances and need of the respective partners. Moreover, ERA
proponents point out that in reality the courts already interpret
most alimony and child support laws on a case-by-case basis.
The National Conference of Commissioners on Uniform State
Laws, a conservative and generally respected body, drafted in
August, 1970, a proposed Uniform Marriage and Divorce Act
which eliminates all references to sex and substitutes the word
"spouse" wherever "husband" or "wife" would traditionally have
appeared. ERA advocates argue that the Amendment would do
no more than this.[8]

Protective legislation: The most heated debates in the ERA
controversy are over the potential effect of the Amendment on
protective legislation. Again, the central point is: can sex be
considered a valid classification for making legal distinctions be-

[7] Association of Women Lawyers testimony, *ERA Hearings 1*, p. 512.
[8] As noted previously, the concept that marriage is an economic partnership was first endorsed by the President's Commission on the Status of
Women (1963) and then further developed by the Citizens' Advisory
Council Task Force on Family Law and Policy (1968).

tween men and women. Whereas family law covers a sphere of
life in which historically men and women have had separate and
distinct roles, i.e., breadwinner and homemaker, the protective
labor laws operate in a sphere where men and women have the
same role, i.e., employee/worker. Thus, in the employment area,
whether laws that treat women differently from men "protect"
them or "discriminate" against them has become the primary
issue of the debate.

Since Title VII of the Civil Rights Act was passed which in
theory strikes down many of the protective laws, the Equal Rights
Amendment controversy regarding this particular area has somewhat shifted emphasis. Prior to Title VII, the arguments were
strictly on the basis of *pro* or *con* protective legislation for women.
Now ERA opponents, while admitting that some of the laws indeed may be discriminatory, argue that the validity of each one
should be tested individually in the courts. By testing each law
separately, sex might, in some of them, remain a *bona fide* occupational qualification. The Equal Rights Amendment ". . . however, permits no negotiation or compromise no matter what the
circumstance";[9] *all* such laws would be deemed unconstitutional.
Conversely, advocates of the Amendment maintain that protective legislation will not necessarily be wiped off the books; it will
merely cease to be based on sex. Moreover, they point out that
laws which truly "protect" women by extending benefits such as
minimum wage would be extended to men. Only those laws that
"restrict" in the name of "protection"—weightlifting, maximum
hours, etc., will be nullified, at least on the basis of sex.

Since battle lines over the Equal Rights Amendment are most
clearly drawn on the issue of protective legislation, the major
organized opposition to the Amendment centers around this
point. A good portion of the labor movement (primarily the AFL-
CIO) and many radical women involved in new left politics have
joined forces to block passage of the Amendment. These opponents
accuse ERA advocates, i.e., both moderate and radical feminists,
of being white, middle-class, college-oriented women with no
experience of economic "hardship" and no understanding of working-class women. They argue further that most working women
are not covered by union contracts and are therefore even more
dependent on state protective laws to avoid being exploited by
their employers. Proponents counter both points: 1) it is not only
"lady lawyers" supporting the Amendment; their ranks have been

---

[9] Myra Wolfgang testimony, *ERA Hearings 2*, p. 41.

joined by the United Auto Workers and a number of other unions. In addition, all the court actions filed under Title VII charging that various protective laws *are* discriminatory have been brought by blue-collar workers; 2) there may be great numbers of non-union women covered by protective laws, but those laws are at best spotty and exempt entire employment categories, such as domestic help, night cleaning people and agricultural workers.

THE CONSTITUTION AND WOMEN

There is little disagreement between proponents and opponents that discrimination against women exists to a greater or lesser degree in all the above-mentioned areas of law. However, because of the *fundamental* disagreement about what constitutes discrimination, the debate becomes in part a tactical one of what is the best method of achieving "equality." As noted earlier, one method is to push to reform the laws in question in the various state legislatures. Another is to challenge these laws in the lower courts and if necessary carry an appeal under the 5th or 14th Amendment up to the Supreme Court. In both of these approaches each law would have to be reformed or tested individually. A third method is to pass the Equal Rights Amendment which would establish at the outset a national policy of equal treatment under the law, which would ". . . restrain the courts from applying different rules to women under the Constitution."[1] Since this method involves amending the Constitution, it becomes necessary to look at the definitions of women's rights in Constitutional law: Are the rights of women protected under the Constitution as it presently stands? How has the Supreme Court traditionally interpreted the Constitution with regard to women's rights?

Proponents of the Equal Rights Amendment argue that while the *potential* for complete equality exists within the framework of the Constitution and its amendments, and in the long run the Supreme Court might indeed interpret them in a manner very close to the concept of the Equal Rights Amendment, there is no guarantee of that eventuality. One constitutional lawyer argues:

> . . . the Supreme Court has been subjected over a period of time to powerful attack for moving too fast and too far into frontier areas of the law. The Court may conse-

---

[1] Eastwood, p. 282.

quently be somewhat reluctant to take the lead in bringing about another major social reform, regardless of how
constitutionally justified that reform may appear to be.[2]

ERA advocates argue further that a radical departure by the
Court in its interpretation of women's constitutional rights appears even less likely when one analyses the Constitution, its
amendments, and the legal precedents based on those amendments handed down by the Supreme Court over the last century.
To the proponents, such an analysis highlights even more clearly
the need for an amendment which expressly guarantees the legal
equality of women. Often their analysis begins by placing the
Constitution itself in its historical framework:

> When the Constitution was written, a Negro man was
> considered three-fifths of a person and no woman was
> legally considered any fraction of a person. Only men
> wrote the Constitution; women were expressly excluded
> in intent and content.[3]

In addition, they note that the 14th and 15th Amendments were
passed (1868 and 1870 respectively) to protect the rights of
newly freed Negroes, and when advocates of women's equality
attempted to get women's rights written into those Amendments
they were rebuffed with "this is the Negroes' hour."
Advocates argue further that although the 14th Amendment
has since been interpreted to give "equal protection" to many
groups besides Negroes, including corporations, in the cases involving alleged sex discrimination the Supreme Court has never
handed down a decision that found sex as a legal classification to
be unreasonable, and therefore unconstitutional. This means to
women's rights advocates that women are not considered "persons" under the Constitution or in the eyes of the Court. Lawyer
Marguerite Rawalt describes the dilemma:

> [Women] are the one remaining "class" and category not
> yet adjudged to come under the legal umbrella of the
> Constitution, except for their right to vote. Constitutional
> guarantees may not be denied on account of race, religion,
> or national origin (even aliens). Yet, that one-half of each

---

[2] Thomas Emerson, testimony, *ERA Hearings* 2, p. 301.
[3] Wilma Scott Heide, testimony, *ERA Hearings* 2, p. 289.

race, or origin, born female, is still outside the ambit of such legal protection. For example, shall the Negro woman be employed because race discrimination is illegal, or be denied such employment because she is female subject to restrictive laws?[4]

A number of Supreme Court decisions are cited to support the view that, as traditionally interpreted, the Constitution restricts the rights of women, but not those of men. Almost without exception the decisions have been based on two presumptions (often given the stamp of Divine Sanction): 1) women first and foremost belong at home; 2) women are physically weaker than men.

The first decision was handed down in 1872 and involved an Illinois statute barring women from practicing law. The Court upheld the statute, and the decision reads in part:

> Man is, or should be, woman's protector and defender. The natural and proper timidity and delicacy which belongs to the female sex evidently unfits it for many of the occupations of civil life. The constitution of the family organization, which is founded in the divine ordinance, as well as in the nature of things, indicates the domestic sphere as that which properly belongs to the domain and functions of womanhood. The harmony, not to say identity, of interests and views, which belong, or should belong, to the family institution is repugnant to the idea of a woman adopting a distinct and independent career from that of her husband. . . . The paramount destiny and mission of woman are to fulfill the noble and benign offices of wife and mother. This is the law of the Creator. And the rules of civil society must be adapted to the general constitution of things, and cannot be based upon exceptional cases.[5]

ERA advocates point to three later Supreme Court decisions all involving the "right" to earn a living, in which the Court extended the protection of the 14th Amendment to aliens. In 1886, the Court overturned a San Francisco ordinance which barred

---

[4] *Congressional Record,* June 10, 1970, p. E5452.
[5] *Bradwell v. the State,* 16 Wall. 130 (U.S. 1972).

Chinese aliens from operating laundries.[6] In 1915, the Court in-
validated an Arizona statute which required employers to hire
eighty percent native-born citizens. The decision held that this
law violated an Austrian cook's 14th Amendment rights.

> It requires no argument to show that the right to work for
> a living in the common occupation of the country is the
> very essence of the personal freedom and opportunity that
> it was the purpose of the amendment to secure.[7]

In 1948, a California statute barring aliens from acquiring commercial fishing licenses was struck down on nearly the same
grounds.[8] Conversely, in 1948, the Supreme Court upheld a
Michigan statute prohibiting women from obtaining licenses to
act as bartenders unless they were the wives or daughters of a
male owner.[9] Although all states eventually admitted women to
the legal profession, they are still barred from being bartenders
in some states as well as from various other occupations.

As noted earlier the landmark case from which has been
extracted the legal *principle* that "sex is a valid basis for classification," was *Muller v. Oregon.* The 1908 decision, which contained a discussion of the general physical differences between
the sexes, upheld a statute limiting the number of hours women
could work in a day or week. The general physical differences
mentioned in the Muller decision have been cited in cases uphold-
ing the whole structure of protective labor laws which treat men
and women differently. The Muller ruling reads in part:

> . . . history discloses the fact that woman has always been
> dependent upon man. He established his control at the
> outset by superior physical strength, and this control in
> various forms, with diminishing intensity, has continued
> to the present. . . . Though limitations upon personal and
> contractual rights may be removed by legislation, there is
> that in her disposition and habits of life which will oper-
> ate against a full assertion of those rights.

The Muller decision has also been cited in cases that uphold the

---

6 *Yick Wo v. Hopkins*, 118 U.S. 356 (1886).
7 *Truax v. Raich*, 239 U.S. 33 (1915).
8 *Takahashi v. Fish and Game Commission*, 334 U.S. 410 (1948).
9 *Goesaert v. Cleary*, 335 U.S. 464 (1948).

exclusion of women from juries and state supported universities, and bar them from various occupations. Kanowitz argues that:

> The subsequent reliance in judicial decision upon the *Muller* language is a classic example of the misuse of precedent, of latter courts being mesmerized by what an earlier court had *said* rather than what it had *done*.[1]

Consistent with their analysis, opponents to the Equal Rights Amendment view some of the above Court decisions in a different light:

> The Supreme Court has not held, as is sometimes loosely stated, that women are not "persons" within the meaning of [the 14th] amendment. Rather the Court has found in the past that certain laws do not discriminate unfairly against women.[2]

It is precisely this latitude of application allowed by the 14th Amendment (and the 5th Amendment as well) that appeals to the ERA opponents and forms the basis of their case against it. They believe the Court is moving in a more liberal direction regarding the equal status of women and will soon judge unconstitutional those laws which truly discriminate against them. However, by keeping women's rights within the meaning of the 5th and 14th Amendments, it would still be possible for sex to remain a reasonable legal classification under certain circumstances —in particular, in labor laws, family and draft laws. That the Court has already taken a more progressive stand is evident, according to opponents of the Amendment, by its most recent decision involving women's rights in the *Phillips v. Martin-Marietta* case. Although the case was not brought under the 14th Amendment, but under Title VII, the decision is indicative of the current Court's psychological framework. In January, 1971, the Court ruled that an employer could not refuse to hire a mother with small children unless the same policy also applied to a father with small children. Ironically, advocates of the Equal Rights Amendment cite the same case, but a different section of the decision, to support their contention that without a specifically worded amendment to the contrary, the Court will continue to

---

[1] Kanowitz, p. 154.
[2] Paul Freund, testimony, *ERA Hearings 2*, p. 74.

consider sex, although perhaps more narrowly applied, a reasonable legal classification of persons. The portion of the decision to which they refer declared that the obligations of motherhood (it did not say parenthood) might be found by the lower courts to be a justified exception under Title VII for not hiring a woman employee.

There are three final, but central, points of disagreement between the opposing factions in the Equal Rights Amendment debate.

1) Opponents argue that if it is passed and men and women are treated identically under the law, then separate facilities such as prisons, restrooms, and dormitories would be rendered unconstitutional. Proponents view these discussions as so many more "red herrings," but nonetheless counter with the argument that such an eventuality is unlikely: the Supreme Court ruling that recognized a constitutional "right to privacy"[3] would justify separate facilities in public buildings. After one such discussion of "facilities" during Senate hearings, one ERA advocate remarked that she wondered "if the people who are horrified at the thought of common restrooms have ever traveled in an airplane, stayed at a hotel in Europe, or for that matter, been in a private home."

2) If passed, opponents argue that the Amendment will create mass judicial confusion and tie up the already overburdened courts with years of litigation. The *Salisbury* (North Carolina) *Evening Post* reports on this issue; and quotes Freund:

> "It will open a Pandora's box of legal complications. . . .
> The amendment expresses noble sentiments, but I'm
> afraid it will work much mischief in actual application."
> What kind of mischief? Every provision in the law which
> has a sexual basis, every statute dealing with the manifold relations of men and women in society, would be
> transformed into a constitutional issue . . . says Freund.[4]

Proponents of the Amendment counter that it is within the power of the courts to set down rules for a transitional period to avoid confusion and disruption. They see no more potential judicial disruption in passing the Equal Rights Amendment than when-

---

[3] *Griswold v. Connecticut* (381 U.S. 479, 1965).
[4] August 17, 1970. Article reprinted in *ERA Hearings* 2, p. 19.

ever the courts declare a part of a statute unconstitutional. Moreover:

> When [the 14th] amendment was passed no one could have predicted the ways it would affect life in the United States or the amount of litigation and the difficulties of interpretation that would ensue, many of which we still face today. . . . Yet, it surely was no mistake to pass that amendment because of these difficulties. Could the Nation have shirked the responsibility of guaranteeing in our basic charter of Government the equal protection of the laws because of difficulties of interpretation?[5]

3) If passed, opponents argue that the Equal Rights Amendment will not eliminate discrimination against women. Sen. Ervin, a strong opponent, has stated:

> It is the better part of wisdom to recognize that discriminations not created by law cannot be abolished by law. They must be abolished by changed attitudes in the society which imposes them. . . . I am convinced that many of [the women's] just grievances are founded upon discriminations not created by law, and that for this reason the equal rights amendment will have no effect whatsoever in respect to them.[6]

Congresswoman Shirley Chisholm (D., N.Y.) articulated the counter-argument:

> The argument that this amendment will not solve the problem of sex discrimination is not relevant. If the argument were used against a civil rights bill—as it has been used in the past—the prejudice that lies behind it would be embarrassing. Of course laws will not eliminate prejudice from the hearts of human beings. But that is no reason to allow prejudice to continue to be enshrined in our laws—to perpetuate injustice through inaction.[7]

---

[5] Professor Norman Dorson, testimony, *ERA Hearings* 2, p. 314.
[6] Sen. Ervin, speech made on floor of Senate, cited in *ERA Hearings* 2, p. 2.
[7] House floor debate on Equal Rights Amendment, August 10, 1970. *Congressional Record*, H 7977.

In conclusion, all the arguments for and against the Equal
Rights Amendment, and indeed for and against all the laws that
treat men and women differently, rest on opposing interpretations
of what might be termed the "biological differences" argument.[8]
Opponents to equal treatment under the law contend:

> The physiological and functional differences between men
> and women constitute earth's most important reality.
> Without them human life could not exist. For this reason,
> any country which ignores these differences when it
> fashions its institutions and makes its law is woefully
> lacking in rationality.[9] . . . Keep the law responsible where
> the good Lord put it—on the man to bear the burdens of
> support and the women to bear the children.[1]

Wilma Scott Heide, chairwoman of the board of directors of the
National Organization for Women, stated at the Senate Judiciary
Committee hearings on the Amendment the position of proponents
of absolute legal equality of men and women:

> . . . social roles are learned phenomena. Parenthood is a
> social role after birth, legislator is a social role, teacher
> is a social role, soldier is a social role, nurse and physician
> are social roles. . . . With several crucial exceptions, all
> social roles can be fulfilled by some men or some women.
> Therefore, there are only two roles or jobs no man is or
> could be qualified to perform: Human incubator and wet
> nurse; likewise, there is only one role or job which no
> woman is or could be qualified to perform: Sperm donor.
> . . . And so it is with other women and men as classes of
> people. Homemaking and child care are learned social
> roles without biological imperatives as to who performs
> them. . . . Any law addressed to our duties as homemakers
> and mothers would be a gross invasion of our privacy. . . .
> We will define our own life styles and whatever duties
> thereof to combine parenthood, career, marriage, friend-
> ship, recreation, citizen action. We don't need the State
> to invade our private pursuit of happiness.[2]

---

[8] For detailed discussion of the "biological differences" argument, see
Chapter 3.
[9] Sen. Ervin, testimony, *ERA Hearings* 2, p. 4.
[1] *Ibid.*, p. 114.
[2] Heide, testimony, *ERA Hearings* 2, pp. 290 and 292.

Leo Kanowitz extends the analysis even further and describes his view of the impact on society of embodying sex differences, real or imagined, into law:

> Rules of law that treat of the sexes *per se* inevitably pro-
> duce far-reaching effects upon social, psychological and
> economic aspects of male-female relationships beyond the
> limited confines of legislative chambers and courtrooms.
> As long as organized legal systems, at once the most
> respected and most feared of social institutions, continue
> to differentiate sharply, in treatment or in words, be-
> tween men and women on the basis of irrelevant and arti-
> ficially created distinctions, the likelihood of men and
> women coming to regard one another primarily as fellow
> human beings and only secondarily as representatives of
> another sex will continue to be remote. When men and
> women are prevented from recognizing one another's
> essential humanity by sexual prejudices, nourished by
> legal as well as social institutions, society as a whole re-
> mains less than it could otherwise become.[3]

All the arguments of the Equal Rights Amendment advocates are perhaps most succintly summed up by Rep. Edith Green:

> It has been said that if this amendment is passed it will
> create profound social changes. May I say to you, it is
> high time some profound social changes were made in
> our society.[4]

National Women's Rights Organizations

As NOTED PREVIOUSLY the first wave of feminism culminated in (or, according to some historians, was submerged by) the cam-paign for suffrage. The public at large assumed that the goals of

---

[3] Kanowitz, p. 4.
[4] Edith Green, statement during House floor debate, August 10, 1970. *Con-gressional Record,* H7963.

women's rights and feminism had been achieved with the 19th Amendment. Although the many and varied women's clubs and organizations passed resolutions during the subsequent decades supporting non-discriminatory legislation including the Equal Rights Amendment, only two groups—the National Woman's Party and the National Federation of Business and Professional Women's Clubs—made women's rights a substantial part, or all, of their agendas. Since these were the only two groups active in a major way between 1920 and the early sixties when the current women's movement began, it is useful to discuss them in some detail.

NATIONAL WOMAN'S PARTY

This is the oldest existing women's rights organization in the country and was founded in 1913 by Alice Paul as part of the suffrage movement. A temporary but extremely militant group formed to secure the vote for women, the organization considered disbanding when the 19th Amendment was ratified on August 26, 1920. After a series of meetings with an organization called Wage Earning Women, however, the Woman's Party became convinced that the 19th Amendment, limited to voting rights, was not sufficient to correct the social and economic inequalities between men and women written into the law. Therefore, in 1921, the group reorganized as a permanent body to work for the removal of all legal distinctions based on sex.

The group directed its initial political efforts to the state level, pressuring legislatures to change what the Woman's Party regarded as discriminatory legislation. However, the time and expense involved in a state-by-state campaign were prohibitive. Moreover, the group encountered enormous opposition, primarily from women who were not interested in changing the *status quo*, or who felt that the most direct way of achieving a semblance of "equality" between men and women was to press for legislation specifically designed for the protection of women workers.

In 1923, at the 75th anniversary conference of the Seneca Falls Convention, the Woman's Party decided to turn its efforts to the national level and lobby for constitutional reform. The group drafted an equal rights amendment (the wording of which is substantially the same as that of the Amendment on the floor of Congress today), and arranged to have it introduced into the 68th session of Congress that same year. At nearly every subsequent session of Congress, the Woman's Party has arranged for the Amendment's introduction, secured a chief sponsor in each house, appeared at hearings and lobbied vigorously for its passage. In fact some feminists argue that the Woman's Party alone kept the Amendment alive during the years between 1923 and the emergence of the new Women's movement.

Shortly after the Amendment was first introduced, the Woman's Party locked horns with the Women's Bureau (established under the Department of Labor in 1920), primarily over the Amendment's potential impact on protective legislation. For over forty years the Woman's Party and the Bureau fought bitterly over the validity of these laws—the Bureau accusing Alice Paul and her organization of embracing "a kind of hysterical feminism with a slogan for a program."[5]

Undaunted by the years of opposition, the Woman's Party has continued its campaign. It has remained a one-issue party, single-minded in its conviction that the principle of equality between men and women can only be established by an amendment to the constitution.

NATIONAL FEDERATION OF BUSINESS AND PROFESSIONAL WOMEN'S CLUBS (BPW)

BPW was formed in 1919 as an outgrowth of a federal drive, organized through the YWCA, to help recruit women for office work during World War I. When the war was over BPW became primarily a service organization to "elevate the standards and promote the interests of business and professional women." Since its formation, one of BPW's major purposes has been to support and press for legislation which would provide equal rights for women. At its first convention in 1919 it urged the opening of Civil Service examinations to women as well as men; this initial concern with federal policy has not changed. Over the fifty years of its existence, BPW has urged passage of minimum wage laws, more equitable social security benefits, an equal pay bill, etc. A legislative platform incorporating these goals has been adopted and updated every two years.

In 1937, BPW went on record in support of the Equal Rights Amendment and has campaigned vigorously for its passage ever

---

[5] Mary Anderson, *Woman at Work* (Minneapolis: The University of Minnesota Press, 1951), p. 168. Anderson was the first director of the Women's Bureau.

since. BPW members have often worked closely with Congressional sponsors of the Amendment, researching the various issues involved and suggesting possible witnesses for hearings. In 1947, a separate office was set up in Washington to work exclusively on the Amendment.

In 1944, BPW was instrumental in getting the word "women" included in the language of the Preamble to the United Nations Charter. In that same year Eleanor Roosevelt joined a conference called by BPW to discuss the placement of more women in policy-making positions in the government. Ever since that time BPW has kept a roster of women across the country qualified for high echelon jobs and has urged each administration to appoint more women. When appointments are to be made BPW frequently submits résumés of available candidates. Through all this activity the organization has developed working relationships with the different administrations. In 1961, several BPW members were appointed to the President's Commission on the Status of Women and Marguerite Rawalt, a lawyer and president of BPW, co-chaired the Committee on Civil and Political Rights. As a result of the interest engendered by the Commission, BPW took on as its national project for 1962–63 a campaign to get State Commissions on the Status of Women established. In 1970, BPW members also served on President Nixon's Task Force on Women's Rights and Responsibilities which was chaired by Virginia Allan, another former president of the organization.

Business and Professional Women has also been active in the field of education. In 1956, the Business and Professional Women's Foundation was set up "to expand educational opportunities for *all working women* and to advance the frontiers of knowledge about women."[6] To that end the Foundation gives research grants, small scholarships and maintains a large library on the subject of women. In 1970, the Foundation funded research papers on the dual career family and on discrimination against women graduate students, a book on the woman executive, and preliminary research for a book on the legal rights of women in Europe.

Currently BPW members number approximately 170,000 (any working woman is eligible) in some 3400 clubs across the country. Although for years the organization has pressed for legislative changes to achieve women's equality, and although a number of its members consider themselves feminists, the organ-

---

[6] Business and Professional Women's Foundation, *Annual Report, 1969–70,* unpaginated.

ization has not taken a feminist position in defining its goals or tactics. Indeed, in 1966 BPW rejected a number of suggestions that it redefine those goals and tactics and become a kind of "NAACP for women." The membership refused, allegedly out of fear of being labeled "feminist." It should be noted as well that only as a result of the growth of the current women's movement has BPW even begun to consider itself primarily a women's rights organization.

Although the National Woman's Party and Business and Professional Women pressed over the years for legislation to end discrimination against women, their activities to all intents and purposes were carried out in a political vacuum. Neither a dramatic issue around which to rally, nor anything resembling public support for women's rights existed to aid the efforts of these two organizations.

This complacent atmosphere changed considerably with the formation of the President's Commission on the Status of Women, which, from 1961 to 1963, produced reams of new data about women, and resulted in the formation of the Citizens' Advisory Council, various State Commissions on the Status of Women, and the passage of the Equal Pay Act. The passage of Title VII in 1964 added a sense of excitement and reality to the issue of "women's equality" and precipitated a psychological shift of emphasis from the idea of "women as an untapped resource" to "women as a discriminated-against class." After Title VII went into effect in 1965, the lack of strict enforcement of the sex provision added another element: anger—perhaps the most important element in the creation of any social movement. Betty Friedan has written:

> The absolute necessity for a civil rights movement for women had reached such a point of subterranean explosive urgency by 1966, that it only took a few of us to get together to ignite the spark—and it spread like a nuclear chain-reaction.[7]

NATIONAL ORGANIZATION FOR WOMEN

The "spark" to which Friedan referred was the formation of the National Organization for Women (NOW), the first militant

---

[7] Betty Friedan, "N.O.W.—How It Began," *Women Speaking* (London, April 1967), p. 4.

feminist group in the twentieth century to combat sex discrimination in all spheres of life: social, political, economic, psychological.

NOW's direct origins can be traced to a series of interrelated
and overlapping events which occurred between 1965 and 1966.
Betty Friedan, whose book *The Feminine Mystique* had made her
an extremely controversial figure, began commuting to Washington to research material for a second book. In the process she
talked with many people about sex discrimination and the best
means to combat it. Those with whom she discussed the subject
at greatest length included: Rep. Martha Griffiths; lawyers Pauli
Murray and Mary Eastwood, who had worked on the Civil and
Political Rights Committee of the President's Commission, and
who subsequently co-authored "Jane Crow and the Law," a law
review article which delineated the ways in which Title VII and the
14th Amendment could be interpreted to afford women equal
rights; and Catherine East, executive secretary of the Citizens' Advisory Council, who was able to supply Friedan with data documenting the low status of women. During this same period "pro-
women" EEOC Commissioners, Richard Graham and Aileen Hernandez, were privately suggesting the need for an organization to
speak on behalf of women in the way civil rights groups had done
for blacks. Only that kind of pressure, they felt, would force EEOC
and the government to take sex discrimination as seriously as
race discrimination. At some point during those same months
both BPW and the League of Women Voters, the two largest
"politically" oriented organizations of women, had rejected suggestions that they pick up the anti-sex discrimination banner,
reportedly because they feared being labeled "feminist" and
"militant."

In addition, by the spring of 1966 sex-segregated newspaper
"want-ads" had become an issue. The Washington, D.C. chapter
of BPW had passed a resolution in May stating that the EEOC
guidelines which permitted separate male and female listings
". . . violate the intent of Congress . . . and are recognized by
thinking women as a deliberate disregard of their interests."[8] The
Citizens' Advisory Council reprinted the resolution and sent it to
members of the various State Commissions on the Status of
Women to draw their attention to the controversy. (The third
National Conference of these State Commissions was to convene

---

[8] BPW resolution, reprinted *Congressional Record,* June 20, 1966, p. 13060.

in Washington the last weekend in June.) On June 20, 1966, Rep. Griffiths spoke on the floor of the House for one hour and "laid out in forty shades of lavender"[9] EEOC's lack of interest in women's rights and its poor performance regarding help-wanted advertisements. Those remarks were reprinted and distributed to the participants of the National Conference when it opened on June 28.

All during this period prior to the Conference, Friedan was being urged to organize a *new* action group. She was extremely interested, but thought that the "want-ads" controversy and the need to pressure for the reappointment of Richard Graham to EEOC[1] were not dramatic enough issues around which to organize. Thus, although no thought was given to actually forming a new organization at that time, it was decided to sound out other potentially interested people when they came to Washington for the Conference.

After the second day's proceedings an informal meeting was held in Friedan's hotel room. Attending it were some of those people already enthusiastic about the possibility of a new action group, some UAW union women, and the heads of a few of the State Commissions on the Status of Women.[2] Little was accomplished that night because a split over tactics occurred at the outset. The State Commission women argued strongly that the machinery to combat sex discrimination already existed within the framework of the State Commissions; others argued equally strongly that the time had come to think about pressure and action *outside* the realm of government commissions. Ultimately, they all agreed that at least a start could be made with a strongly worded anti-sex discrimination resolution to be passed by the entire Conference at the final luncheon the next day. Dr. Kathryn Clarenbach, head of the Wisconsin Commission, framed the resolution. When she learned, however, that the Conference was not allowed to pass resolutions or take action, she and the other State Commission women also became convinced of the need for a new organization to be set up immediately. One participant recalls that Clarenbach's sudden reversal to a position advocating a new organization "took us by surprise. We couldn't figure out what had really happened overnight. The Conference problem

---

[9] Bird, p. 268.

[1] Graham's appointment was due to expire in July, 1966.

[2] Some of those attending included: Pauli Murray, Kathryn Clarenbach, Dorothy Haener, Catherine Conroy, Mary Eastwood.

didn't seem enough of an explanation. But we figured, 'O.K., why not?' " Friedan described what happened next:

> [We] cornered a large table at the luncheon, so that we could start organizing [the new organization], before we had to rush for planes. We all chipped in $5.00, began to discuss names. I dreamed up N.O.W. on the spur of the moment, which everybody seemed to like, and Kay [Clarenbach] agreed to be temporary Chairman since she had the facilities to get the clerical work done during the first months. We all agreed, that noon, on our main purpose—"to take action to bring women into full participation in the mainstream of American society now, assuming all the privileges and responsibilities thereof in truly equal partnership with men."[3]

Even before the luncheon meeting was over, the women had taken their first action: telegrams signed by twenty-eight women were sent to each EEOC Commissioner urging that EEOC rescind its guidelines permitting sex-segregated "want-ads" in newspapers, and that it replace those guidelines with others expressly forbidding "help wanted—male," "help wanted—female" columns.

In spite of the general agreement on the "main purpose" of NOW, it should be remembered that at this point in time Friedan's avowed feminist position coupled with her flamboyant and combative personal style had made her extremely controversial and, in some corners, greatly feared. Several observers have interpreted the sudden urgency to organize the new action group "on the spot," even before the Conference had adjourned, as an attempt to circumvent Friedan, and keep control of any new women's group in less militant hands. Apparently the endeavor to keep NOW firmly within the "establishment" continued over the summer as charter members were being recruited. While Friedan and the "east coast contingent" tried to interest feminists and potential feminists in joining, the "mid-western and western contingents" strove to attract more conservative members, reportedly through the recruiting efforts of Women's Bureau staff members in the midwest. In addition, it was only after a certain amount of haggling between the east and midwest factions that the formal organizing conference was scheduled to be held in the east.

---

[3] Friedan, *Women Speaking*, p. 4.

With 300 charter members, male and female, NOW announced its incorporation at a press conference in Washington, D.C., on October 29, 1966. Betty Friedan was elected the first president; Dr. Kathryn Clarenbach, chairman of the board; and Richard Graham, treasurer.[4] The statement of purpose reiterated the original goal:

> . . . to take action to bring women into full participation in the mainstream of American society *now*, exercising all the privileges and responsibilities thereof in truly equal partnership with men.

And continued in a strong feminist perspective:

> . . . it is nc longer either necessary or possible for women to devote the greater part of their lives to child-rearing; yet childbearing and rearing which continues to be a most important part of most women's lives—still is used to justify barring women from equal professional and economic participation and advance. . . . Until now, too few women's organizations and official spokesmen have been willing to speak out against these dangers facing women. Too many women have been restrained by the fear of being called "feminist". . . .

> We do not accept the traditional assumption that a woman has to choose between marriage and motherhood, on the one hand, and serious participation in industry or the professions on the other. . . .

> We believe that a true partnership between the sexes demands a different concept of marriage, an equitable sharing of the responsibilities of home and children and of the economic burdens of their support. We believe that proper recognition should be given to the economic and social value of homemaking and child-care. . . .

> We will protest, and endeavor to change, the false image of women now prevalent in the mass media, and in the

---

[4] Graham's appointment to EEOC had not been renewed. Aileen Hernandez resigned her EEOC appointment in November, 1966, feeling that EEOC was not seriously enforcing any of the Title VII provisions—sex or race. In February, 1967, she became NOW's western regional vice-president.

texts, ceremonies, laws, and practices of our major social
institutions. Such images perpetuate contempt for women
by society and by women for themselves. We are similarly
opposed to all policies and practices—in church, state,
college, factory, or office—which, in the guise of protec-
tiveness, not only deny opportunities but also foster in
women self-denigration, dependence, and evasion of responsibility, undermine their confidence in their own
abilities and foster contempt for women. . . .

Above all, we reject the assumption that these problems
are the unique responsibility of each individual woman,
rather than a basic social dilemma which society must
solve.[5]

NOW wasted no time in the drive toward its stated goals. At
the organizing conference a legal committee, chaired by Marguerite Rawalt, was authorized to arrange for appeals in two
pending sex discrimination cases involving the Title VII-state
protective laws conflict,[6] and also to take action on behalf of a
group of airline stewardesses who were fighting a company policy
forcing their retirement when they married or reached the age
of 32; male stewards were not restricted by this policy. Also at
the organizing conference seven task forces were set up to study
and recommend action regarding discrimination against women
in education, employment, religion, the particular problems
of poor women, women's image in the mass media, women's
political rights and responsibilities, the family. In December,
1966, NOW formally petitioned EEOC to hold hearings on the
"want-ads" guidelines. (They were finally held the following
May.) In the succeeding months after NOW announced its existence, Friedan accompanied by other members conducted lengthy
face-to-face interviews with all the EEOC Commissioners; all the
members of the Civil Service Commission and its chairman, John
Macy, Jr.; and Attorney General Ramsey Clark. In addition, a
strongly-worded and lengthy letter was sent to President Johnson
detailing the major areas of discrimination against women and
suggesting possible immediate actions to combat it; e.g., the
President was urged to appoint women to the two Commissioner

---

[5] Excerpts from NOW Statement of Purpose. Adopted at Organizational
Conference, October 29, 1966.
[6] *Bowe v. Colgate-Palmolive; Mengelkoch v. State of California.*

vacancies in EEOC. The impact of NOW during those initial months was enormous, largely because nothing like it had ever happened before. "NOW scared the wits out of the government," according to one founding member. In an interview shortly after its formation, Friedan said that NOW would use every political tactic available to it to end sex discrimination: "We don't even exclude the possibility of a mass march on Washington."[7]

In the subsequent years NOW became involved in almost every area of feminist activity. The group organized what was perhaps the first national demonstration on a women's rights issue (since the suffrage campaign) in December, 1967, when picket lines were set up at EEOC offices in cities across the country. The following February, NOW filed formal suit against EEOC "to force it to comply with its own governmental rules [i.e., Title VII]." A questionnaire regarding women's rights issues was drawn up and presented to the major presidential candidates in the 1968 election. At the hearings in 1970 regarding the qualifications of Supreme Court nominee G. Harrold Carswell, Betty Friedan testified against his being appointed to the Court because of his "anti-woman" position in a 1969 court case.[8] NOW also filed formal charges against the nation's 1300 largest corporations for sex discrimination. Its members have testified at federal and local hearings on sex discrimination in education, employment, welfare payments, and public accommodations. They have picketed and desegregated "all-male" bars and restaurants; campaigned via their "barefoot and pregnant in the kitchen" award against advertising agencies that present an insulting image of women; lobbied for federal and local funds for child care centers, and in a few cases sponsored private NOW nurseries. Also, although nearly every women's group in the country from conservative to radical participated in some way in the August 26th Women's Strike, the preliminary work and the strike activities in most cities were coordinated by NOW chapters.

NOW and the Women's Movement: NOW had been founded to fill an organizational need for a strong political lobby for women's rights as well as a philosophical need for a forum for new feminist ideas. Thus, it functioned initially as an umbrella group for women from extremely diverse backgrounds and with extremely diverse expectations for the organization. Not sur-

---

[7] *National Observer*, December 26, 1966.
[8] As one of the Federal Judges in the *Phillips v. Martin-Marietta* case Carswell ruled in favor of the defendant.

prisingly, disagreements developed during the first years of its existence, which led, at least indirectly, to the formation of splinter groups—some more conservative than NOW and some considerably more radical.

The first conflict within NOW arose at the second national conference held in Washington in November, 1967. At that conference the organization drew up a Bill of Rights for Women for 1968 to be presented to the platform committees of both political parties as well as major candidates running for all national offices in the 1968 election. The Bill of Rights called for:

I. Equal Rights Constitutional Amendment
II. Enforcement of Laws Banning Sex Discrimination in Employment
III. Maternity Leave Rights in Employment and in Social Security Benefits
IV. Tax Deduction for Home and Child Care Expenses for Working Parents
V. Child Care Centers
VI. Equal and Unsegregated Education
VII. Equal Job Training Opportunities and Allowance for Women in Poverty
VIII. The Right of Women to Control Their Reproductive Lives[9]

The first and last "rights" were included only after long and bitter debate. The membership had not been given advance notice that these two issues would be presented for discussion, so that many argued simply for "more time to think." Proponents of both points insisted, however, that the organization take a position on those issues immediately.

The controversy over the Equal Rights Amendment was more one of tactics than of philosophy. Some dissenters felt it was a dead issue and not worth bothering with, and that pressure to reform specific legislation would be more useful. In addition, the union women (United Auto Workers), while not themselves opposed to the Amendment, argued that they could not vote for it because their union was still on record in opposition. They threatened to leave NOW if the organization insisted on taking a vote at that time. The vote was taken and the Amendment supported. The union women did not resign, but the clerical services that their offices had supplied NOW were stopped. This action threw NOW into administrative chaos for months.

---

[9] Bill of Rights reprinted in full in Appendix.

The "right" of women to control their reproductive lives called for the repeal of all laws that restricted access to birth control information and devices; and in particular the abortion laws. The debate on this question centered around whether or not abortion was a women's rights issue, and what a position on such a controversial subject would do to NOW's image. The opposition argued that NOW was already open to much derision and ridicule. Again, dissenters threatened to leave the organization if the resolution was passed. The resolution was passed and a number of women did resign. NOW's position made it the first women's rights organization to put the civil libertarian argument for abortion into clear feminist terms—the right of a woman to control her body. Moreover, by making abortion an issue of the fledgling women's movement, NOW contributed considerably to a more rapid growth of the already existing but limited anti-abortion law movement.[1]

At that same conference, Friedan argued that economic equality was not at the core of sex discrimination, and therefore the organization had to begin:

> . . . a major national dialogue on the sexual implications of full equality between women and men. . . . The sex-role debate . . . cannot be avoided if equal opportunity in employment, education and civil rights are ever to mean more than paper rights.[2]

She went on to say that women in many of the communist countries enjoyed full equality in terms of employment, education and political rights, but that they worked:

> . . . 80 and 90 hours [a week] carrying the full burden of housework. . . . They had never really confronted the question of full equality between men and women with all its implications of equal responsibility in relation to children and home as well as equal opportunity in work and politics.[3]

During the following year NOW's membership continued to expand as well as become more and more eclectic—it was still

---

[1] For further discussion of NOW's involvement with the abortion issue, see Chapter 7.
[2] Report of the President, Second National Conference, Washington, D.C., November 18, 1967, p. 6.
[3] *Ibid.*, p. 7.

the only existing feminist membership organization. The members from New York City tended to be much more radical than those from other locales, both in their feminist thinking and in their tactical approach to solving problems. Thus, by the time of the 1968 annual meeting, it was not the conservative faction that rebelled and resigned but a small radical group led by Ti-Grace Atkinson, president of the New York chapter. At the board meeting held prior to the third national conference, Atkinson proposed rewriting the bylaws in order to replace NOW's organizational structure—president, vice-president, etc.—with the more egalitarian approach of a "participatory democracy." Decision-making positions would be chosen by lot and rotated frequently. To Atkinson, NOW's basic premise—"full partnership with men"— combined with its hierarchical organization would never result in equality; it would ultimately merely replace one power structure with another—similarly oppressive. "We want to destroy the positions of powers, not get into these positions."[4] Her plan was rejected out of hand by the national board and a later attempt to rewrite the New York chapter bylaws to incorporate her scheme locally was equally unsuccessful. Atkinson left NOW and on October 17 organized the extremely radical group, "The October 17th Movement," later called "The Feminists."[5]

Although the main reason for her resignation appeared to be Atkinson's quarrel with NOW over structure, their ideological positions on other issues had become equally divergent. For example, Atkinson believed that NOW's position on abortion was basically reformist, whereas she advocated total repeal of all laws. Moreover, she argued that the Catholic Church should be directly attacked for its position on abortion and contraception. She criticized NOW's refusal to take a stand on the Church arguing, "They're kidding themselves. If you've got a position on abortion, you've got one on the church."[6]

Events outside the organization also contributed to the Atkinson-NOW split. By the fall of 1968 the younger branch of the women's movement—women's liberation—had begun to burgeon and become more vociferous.[7] Manifestos began to appear with increasing frequency, many of them demanding that feminists identify with and support all women as a *class*,

[4] Janine Sade, "History of the Equality Issue in the Contemporary Women's Movement," p. 2. The Feminists' literature packet.
[5] See separate entry (The Feminists), Chapter 2.
[6] Interview, April, 1971.
[7] See Chapter 2.

and oppose all men as a *class*. Conservative and moderate feminists, whose ideology was firmly based on achieving equality by working together *with* men, were concerned that they would be associated with these manifestos and the terms used to describe their authors—most often "lesbian" and "man-hating."[8] One particularly extreme statement was Valerie Solanas' SCUM (Society for Cutting Up Men) Manifesto which not only blamed men for the state of the world but argued for their annihilation. Hers was an individual tract and not a working paper of any radical group; nevertheless, the NOW board was extremely concerned that their organization would be linked in the public's mind with Solanas because Atkinson, publicly identified as the New York NOW president, had appeared at the widely reported hearing at which Solanas was charged with the attempted murder of "Pop" artist Andy Warhol.[9] Atkinson's reply was that she had not gone as a representative from NOW. "Valerie Solanas was a woman in trouble. For that reason and that reason alone I had to support her."[1] One NOW lawyer suggested that the organization issue a statement supporting Solanas' right to a fair trial. The NOW board rejected this idea on the grounds that the organization should not support a woman who had advocated and used violence.

By the end of 1969, NOW appeared to have allayed some of its fears about the younger women and attempted to define its own relationship to "women's liberation." In a memorandum to NOW Board Members and Chapter Presidents, president Friedan wrote:

> Keep in mind that there is far more response and support for our program among the under-40 than the over-40 age groups, and be especially careful to bring in on the planning, from the very beginning, the young leadership from which the main troops are going to have to come in our continuing battle. . . .

She urged that NOW:

> . . . form a power bloc or alliance with groups whose style, origins, structure and general ambience may be quite different from ours, but who have come from various

---

[8] For detailed discussion see Chapter 5.
[9] Solanas shot Warhol on June 3, 1968 and was arraigned on June 4.
[1] Interview, April, 1971.

directions to understand the need for concerted action to give women a decision-making and self-determining voice in our society. . . . As a rule of thumb, those people who already think NOW is too activist may be less important in the future than the youth, who only need a little more experience to understand that the gut issues of this revolution involve employment and education and new social institutions and not sexual fantasy.[2]

NOW's attempts to form a liaison with the younger women of the new movement were for the most part unsuccessful. Some of the younger women viewed NOW (and still do) as part of the "capitalist establishment" attempting to gain privileges only for middle-class white women. Others argued that NOW's analysis of male-female relationships was superficial; indeed, it was NOW, *not* the radical feminist groups, that did not understand "the gut issues of this revolution." Even so, a number of them who had joined more radical groups also joined NOW, appreciating the need for such organizations. One of them remarked, "The more we talk about test-tube babies, the more NOW can demand child care centers and abortion repeal."

By the spring of 1970 it had become clear that any kind of permanent alliance between NOW and other factions of the women's movement was impossible and, according to many, undesirable as well. "It takes much too much valuable time and energy to try to solve every difference," noted one feminist lawyer. The gap has been bridged from time to time, however, and NOW has forged some broadly-based *ad hoc* coalitions. The largest was the August 26, 1970, Women's Strike for Equality. According to Betty Friedan, a national women's strike was the best and most dramatic way to commemorate the fiftieth anniversary of women's suffrage. Plans for the Women's Strike were announced March 21 during a NOW conference in Des Plaines, Illinois. At a press conference, Friedan urged that:

> . . . the women who are doing menial chores in the offices as secretaries put the covers on their typewriters and close their notebooks and the telephone operators unplug their switchboards, the waitresses stop waiting, cleaning women stop cleaning and everyone who is doing a job for which a man would be paid more stop . . .[3]

---

[2] National Organization for Women, Memorandum, September 22, 1969.
[3] *New York Times*, March 22, 1970.

Strike committees were set up in cities and towns across the country; most often these committees were local NOW chapters. Three central demands were drawn up—24-hour child care centers, abortion on demand, and equal opportunity in employment and education. Factional differences within the women's movement about these and other issues were laid aside for one day. On Strike Day women all over the country, including some veterans of the suffrage movement, marched, picketed, protested, held teach-ins, staged rallies, presented guerrilla theater skits, and often took the day off from work or housework (one frequently seen picket sign read, "Don't Cook Dinner—Starve a Rat Today"). In addition, the mayors of some cities officially dedicated the day to women's equality.

August 26 marked the largest demonstration ever held for women's rights, and many people both within the movement and without were startled and thrilled both at the number of women who participated and the wide range of backgrounds from which they came. In some feminist circles it was considered a personal triumph for Friedan and an organizational triumph for NOW; in others, not surprisingly, the strike was considered a false show of unity within a movement which tactically and ideologically was anything but unified. Accordingly, when the exhilaration of the day receded, many of the coalitions formed prior to and during the strike collapsed, despite efforts on the part of NOW and others to keep them intact.

A new issue emerged in 1970 that also affected NOW. A Gay Liberation Movement had developed and homosexuality and lesbianism became publicly discussed issues. Lesbians working within women's rights organizations began refusing to hide the fact of their lesbianism; moreover, they began demanding open acceptance and public support from those organizations.[4] The issue received extensive press coverage, and a handful of NOW members spoke out individually in support of civil rights for homosexuals. As a result, other members feared that NOW would be considered a lesbian organization. Some of the arguments against open support of lesbians were the same as those made against support of abortion law repeal three years earlier: the issue is not a women's rights issue; taking an affirmative stand on such a controversial issue will damage NOW's image and credibility. In December, 1970, NOW president Aileen Hernandez (elected that year as Friedan's successor) issued a statement:

---

[4] For a more detailed discussion of lesbianism and the women's movement, see Chapter 5.

[NOW does] not prescribe a sexual preference test for
applicants. We ask only that those who join NOW commit
themselves to work for full equality for women and that
they do so in the context that the struggle in which we are
engaged is part of the total struggle to free *all* persons to
develop their full humanity.

She accused those, particularly the media, who discredited the
women's movement by calling it lesbian of employing a kind of
"sexual McCarthyism":

It attempts to turn us away from the real business of the
movement and towards endless and fruitless discussions
on matters which are *not* at issue. . . . We need to free *all*
our sisters from the shackles of a society which insists on
viewing us in terms of sex.[5]

The statement came under attack from conservative NOW
members who argued that the issue should not have been given
official recognition by NOW at all. On the other hand, militant
lesbians in the organization attacked NOW for issuing such a
weak statement. In their view, by not confronting the issue of
lesbianism itself, the statement implied that self-avowed lesbians were not welcome in NOW, nor would their goals receive
any support from the organization. The fears and anger of both
factions almost caused the demise of the New York chapter in
the spring of 1971. Hernandez subsequently remarked that as far
as the national organization was concerned, she thought that
the issue would evolve into one of legislative reform. "If the issue
of lesbianism were put on the basis of a legal right to sexual
privacy, I think even conservative NOW members would work
for the repeal of laws that denied people that right."[6] One of
the California NOW chapters planned to frame a resolution to
that effect for presentation at the fifth national conference in
September, 1971.

                    •   •   •

When NOW was founded in 1966, in many ways it was the
vanguard of the new wave of feminism. It quickly chose, however, to define itself as a kind of baseline of the women's move-

---

[5] Statement issued at a press conference, December 17, 1970. Reprinted in
K.N.O.W. Inc. News Service, February 14, 1971.
[6] Interview, April, 1971.

ment and to work solidly for reform within the "establishment." Although some have derided the organization for its moderate stand on certain issues, most feminists (and non-feminists) believe that NOW's activities have helped to give women's issues credibility. One NOW member has commented, "We have forced the government to take sex discrimination seriously, to enforce the laws already banning it, and we made it and the public aware of the need for many more such laws. With NOW working hard on those kinds of legal issues, it's difficult for people to say the women's movement is full of kooks."

NOW's major actions for the next year or two will center primarily around the Equal Rights Amendment and child care centers. Both are considered by the organization not only important practical issues, but also excellent vehicles by which to educate people about feminism. In NOW's view both these issues form a natural springboard to more general discussions about the nature of work, the institution of marriage, the pattern of child rearing; in addition, these issues are relevant to *all* women regardless of economic status.

Over the first five years of its existence NOW grew from a handful of chapters and a charter membership of 300 to more than 150 chapters throughout the country and a membership numbering somewhere between five and ten thousand. Also during that period other nationally organized women's rights groups were established. Following are descriptions of some of the organizations that came into being after NOW, their origins and particular goals. Included also are discussions of some traditional women's groups whose original goals have been redefined as a result of the emergence of a women's movement.

Women's Equity Action League (WEAL)

WEAL was incorporated in Cleveland, Ohio on December 1, 1968, and by 1971 had representation in well over forty states. According to some of the founding members of NOW, the formation of WEAL was a direct result of the early controversy in NOW over the abortion issue. Opponents to NOW's call for abortion law repeal argued that a stand on such a controversial issue would damage the organization's image and deter great numbers of potential sympathizers from actively working for women's rights.

WEAL was founded by Dr. Elizabeth Boyer, an Ohio lawyer,

who felt a strong women's organization was needed which would channel all its efforts into three areas of sex discrimination—employment, education and *de facto* tax inequities. "Give a woman a decent education, a decent paycheck and don't clobber her with unfair taxes, and she can survive pretty well."[7] Because WEAL's field of action is deliberately limited, and its many behind-the-scenes projects are carried out with "smiling faces and combed hair," the organization has been able to attract many women who might ordinarily shy away from joining a campaign for women's equality. Dr. Boyer noted that "one of WEAL's most active chapters is in Iowa of all places, where you couldn't sell 'women's liberation' if you gold plated it. But the women there are acutely conscious of the economic inequities operating against females, and around that issue they have organized and are using every political tactic in the book to change the economic *status quo*. Our 'League of Women Voters' type members and our image of decorum are always causing people to describe WEAL as the far right wing of the women's Mafia."[8]

WEAL has also made a concerted effort to attract members with an already established degree of power and respect who can use that power to lobby in high places for legislative and judicial change. For example, the membership of the Washington, D.C. group includes Congresswomen and high government officials. In addition, deans of women, career counselors, judges and lawyers are active in nearly all chapters of the organization.

In the first year and a half of WEAL's existence nearly half of its correspondence and inquiries dealt with sex discrimination in higher education and how best to combat it—a difficult undertaking since there is no federal legislation prohibiting such discrimination. In late 1969, WEAL made a study of the University of Maryland and found evidence of serious discrimination in the University's hiring and promotion policies. Having learned that the university receives federal funds, WEAL filed a formal complaint against it with the Office of Federal Contract Compliance on January 31, 1970. It was the first time Executive Order 11375 had ever been used as the basis of a sex discrimination complaint against an educational institution. On the same date, WEAL requested Secretary of Labor George P.

---

[7] Boyer, interview, July, 1970.
[8] Interview, February, 1971.

Shultz to begin a class action and compliance review of *all* colleges and universities receiving federal funds. Since January 31, 1970, WEAL has filed complaints with OFCC against more than 300 colleges and universities including the entire State University System of California (June 1, 1970), MIT (April 26), and a class action against every medical school in the country (October 5). Dr. Bernice Sandler, Chairperson of WEAL's Action Committee for Federal Control Compliance in Education, and described by a Washington reporter as "the scourge of the universities," commented: "If nothing else we have been enormously successful in legitimizing the issue of sex discrimination in the academic world. And if we are successful, colleges and universities will not only have to end discriminatory practices but will also have to develop plans for affirmative action to remedy the effects of past discrimination in admission and employment practices."[9] To end this WEAL has been active in pressuring the Department of Labor to issue strong sex discrimination guidelines for the Executive Order. Notwithstanding the potential effectiveness of the Executive Order, WEAL strongly supports the passage of federal legislation banning sex discrimination in education, and WEAL members have testified at government hearings on such proposed legislation. WEAL has also acted to aid future women graduates in their search for employment. In the spring of 1970, WEAL designed a poster encouraging them to seek "appropriate high-level jobs and equal pay." The poster was mailed to 1900 deans of women. Included with each WEAL poster was an official Labor Department equal opportunity poster which the Department had revised to include sex, and to alert women to the threat of discrimination in the employment world.

Although WEAL's activities in the area of higher education are the most visible manifestations of its work, the group by no means limits itself to this field. WEAL is one of the most active organizations in pressing for passage of the Equal Rights Amendment and played a central role in Rep. Martha Griffiths' campaign to force the Amendment out of the House Judiciary Committee in August, 1970. WEAL members also have testified at all the ERA hearings. In addition, WEAL members have also campaigned for reform of all laws, federal and local, which discriminate against women in the employment market.

WEAL is also investigating sex discrimination in labor

---

[9] Interview, January, 1971.

unions. The group has received a considerable number of complaints from union women which taken together appear to indicate that "a woman's union can be her worst enemy."[1] One case against a union, the Communications Workers Union, has already been filed in Louisiana.

Perhaps the greatest amount of unpublicized work being done by WEAL involves the gathering of data about sex discrimination in all areas for lawyers who will argue sex discrimination cases. WEAL strongly believes that women's rights, like civil rights, should be a law specialty.[2] This it might be noted is the primary goal of women's rights groups on law school campuses and many of these groups have become liaison members of WEAL to work toward this shared aim.

Finally, there is a growing demand from corporations and educational institutions for speakers on women's rights and sex discrimination. WEAL has set up a speakers' bureau to help meet the need, and looks upon it as a major breakthrough in getting the business community at least to listen to the issues being raised by the women's movement. One WEAL member noted further, "women in high positions in corporations are beginning to relay information to us about their company's discriminatory policies. In times past the women would have considered that an act of grave disloyalty. Now they consider it an act of retribution."

FEDERALLY EMPLOYED WOMEN (FEW)

FEW was founded in September, 1968, and is the only organization devoted specifically to achieving legal equality and equal employment opportunity for women who are federally employed. Daisy Fields, a founder of FEW, explains that the idea for a women's rights "lobby group" within the Federal Government was inspired by a series of government-sponsored executive training sessions held in April, 1968. She and some of the women attending the sessions discussed the futility of executive training when the opportunities for women to advance within the Government were practically non-existent. FEW was the outgrowth of that meeting and was established to combat sex discrimination in the Government. Although the organization is Washington-

---

[1] Boyer, interview, November, 1970.
[2] See separate entry (Law), Chapter 10.

based, by the spring of 1971 fifteen chapters had been formed in cities all across the country. According to Fields, "sex discrimination is particularly noticeable in the one company towns where the Federal Government is the one company."[3]

FEW's campaign for equal rights for women under federal employ has legal support: one section of Executive Order 11375, passed in 1967 and strengthened in 1969, prohibits sex discrimination in federal employment. The Civil Service Commission administers the Order and is responsible for compliance. According to the Commission's own employment figures, it would appear that the need for elevating the status of women is great indeed. In 1968,[4] women made up 34 percent of the federal workforce, which totals nearly 2 million employees. However, 78.7 percent of the women were employed in the lowest grades GS–1 through GS–6; 1.0 percent were in grades 13 and above and only .02 percent in grade 16 and above. (.02 percent represents 147 women, a drop from 161 in 1966.)

The primary focus of FEW's attack is the Civil Service Commission, whose equal employment responsibilities include enforcing the Executive Order, appointing a director of the Federal Women's Program within each agency, and outlining the procedures by which employees can file discrimination complaints. The Federal Women's Program was set up to carry out the sections of the Executive Order which require each agency to actively search for and promote qualified women. According to FEW, the Program merely pays lip service to women's equality, primarily because the Civil Service Commission and personnel and management executives are not as intent about pursuing equal opportunity for women as they are for blacks:

> Whenever we discuss the problems of minority groups, it is always in a serious vein. As soon as the subject changes to equal employment opportunity for women, the condescending smiles appear, a few jokes are made about women's socially acceptable role in our society; and I am assured they have some women on their respective staffs in the middle or upper grades and that they are performing their jobs admirably—as though surprised that

---

[3] Interview, February, 1971.
[4] Latest figures available. Subsequent figures expected to change only slightly.

women could indeed be good workers. I am never told
how well the men on the staff perform their jobs. This
is taken for granted, of course.[5]

The theme for FEW's second national conference in June, 1971,
is "Federal Women's Program—Fact or Fiction?"

FEW criticizes the established complaint procedures, arguing
that they should be removed from the authority of the Commission and placed under some independent agency not reporting to the Commission; at present the Commission is responsible for combating discrimination within its own ranks, as
well as judging its own accomplishments in this area. This
situation, according to FEW, intimidates employees from seeking
legal redress. Moreover, sometimes when complaints have been
filed:

> . . . [Women] have suffered reprisals in the form of having
> their jobs abolished and being reduced to lower grades on
> the pretext of reorganization or reductions in force; or
> have been reassigned to some degrading position far be-
> low their capabilities in anticipation they might resign;
> or they have been order transferred to a different geo-
> graphic area, allegedly "for the good of the service," on the
> assumption they would refuse the transfer and could
> therefore be separated.[6]

As a result of these reported "intimidation tactics," much
of FEW's behind-the-scenes work is to reassure government
women both in Washington and in the field that FEW and its
goals are absolutely legal, and that no woman can be fired for
filing a complaint or participating in FEW activities; indeed if
she files a complaint the organization is behind her. The organization's openness in some cases has made FEW members *personae
non gratae* in their respective agencies, but the same openness
has begun to make sex discrimination a legitimate issue among
government workers.

Since a woman's ability to work and be promoted is often

---

[5] Daisy Fields, testimony, Hearings on discrimination against women before the House Special Subcommittee on Education of the Committee on
Education and Labor, June–July, 1970, p. 465. Hereafter referred to as
Green Hearings.
[6] *Ibid.,* p. 463.

related to her ability to find proper care for her children, FEW is campaiging to get the Federal Government to take the responsibility of setting up child care facilities for its employees inside or within walking distance of federal establishments. Outside the province of federal employment, FEW members have testified at Government hearings on women's rights, petitioned Congressmen urging them to press for legislative reforms, and cooperated with other women's groups toward these ends. Its major drives have been to push for passage of the Equal Rights Amendment and for the implementation of the Nixon Task Force recommendations. Like a number of the women's rights groups, FEW has a speakers' bureau which has sent representatives to corporation meetings, college and university campuses, etc., to talk about careers for women in the federal service and to alert them to the ways in which discrimination can be combatted.

HUMAN RIGHTS FOR WOMEN, INC. (HRW)

Human Rights for Women was incorporated in Washington, D.C., in December, 1968, as a research, education and legal aid service. The founders were three lawyers: Mary Eastwood, Sylvia Ellison, Caruthers Berger; and Ti-Grace Atkinson. At the time of their incorporation, they argued that what the women's movement needed was not another feminist-action-membership group, but a non-profit, tax-exempt corporation devoted to women's rights and feminist projects. To date, the group's work has been limited to the legal aid area.

HRW has acted as a kind of ACLU in the area of sex discrimination. In 1969, it furnished legal counsel for some of the plaintiffs in the *Bowe v. Colgate-Palmolive* appeal and did the same for the plaintiff in the *Mengelkoch v. State of California* appeal. It also presented an *amicus* brief for the plaintiff in the *Phillips v. Martin-Marietta* case when it was submitted for Supreme Court consideration; for the plaintiff in *Rosenfeld v. Southern Pacific* when it was appealed; and for the defendant in *U.S. v. Vuitch* (a District of Columbia abortion case) when it was presented to the Supreme Court.

Human Rights for Women plans to give free legal aid to any woman involved in a sex discrimination suit, but its small size and budget has limited its work thus far to those cases it considers potentially landmark. Its mere existence, however, has already interested other young women lawyers in taking on sex discrimination cases.

Professional Women's Caucus (PWC)

The Professional Women's Caucus was founded April 11, 1970, the outcome of a conference held that day in New York City. The seventeen-hour meeting was attended by over 300 women (and some men) from the various academic and professional fields. The Conference was planned by Dr. Jo-Ann Evans Gardner, a behavioral scientist, and Doris Sassower, a New York attorney, who had met the previous November at the Congress to Unite Women.[7]

At that time the two women had discussed the possibility of a future conference "to bring together leading women from different academic and professional fields interested in upgrading the status of women, and their ideas on how to do it."[8] They wanted also to unite into a single national coalition the isolated splinter caucuses that women had been conducting for the previous two years within their respective professional organizations.[9] Moreover, they hoped that such a group would attract women who could not identify with any of the consciousness-raising kinds of groups because "many professional women are not caught up in the 'mystique' of feminism, but they are interested in 'action' projects aimed at upgrading women's salaries and status."[1]

The April 11 Conference was devoted to a series of reports and workshops on the status of women in various professional fields. Kate Millett presented a paper on women in academia; Lucinda Cisler, on architecture and city planning; Sonia Pressman, on federal employment; Doris Sassower, on law. There were additional reports on the role of women in professional schools and in the fields of engineering, library science, general science, social work, and the arts.

Professional Women's Caucus was perhaps the first nationally organized women's rights group to have been influenced by the organizational ideology of radical feminist groups: it has eschewed the traditional hierarchical slate of officers, and is

---

[7] For detailed discussion of the Congress to Unite Women, see Chapter 2.
[8] Gardner, interview, November, 1970.
[9] See Chapter 10.
[1] Gardner, interview, November, 1970.

Women's Rights

instead run by a thirty-member steering committee. The long range aim of PWC is to change both the status of women in the professions (caused by discrimination in job opportunities and low pay) and the underlying assumption which has created the discriminatory attitudes—i.e., that women do not belong in professional life at all. To this end PWC has set up eleven task forces to research these issues and recommend action. For example, the Political Task Force is attempting to line up a coordinator in every Congressional district throughout the country to keep each Congressman and Congresswoman apprized of women's issues; the Legal Task Force, in March, 1971, filed a class action suit charging sex discrimination against every law school in the country receiving federal funds. In addition, PWC members have continued to work for reforms within their respective professional organizations.

Young Women's Christian Association (YWCA)

The YWCA was formed in 1867 to provide meeting places and centers of activities, both educational and recreational, for young women. Its stated purpose was to "labor for the temporal, moral, and spiritual welfare of self-supporting young women." Although the YWCA's membership and scope of activities have altered considerably over the years, the group has been unable to shake its image of a non-political organization of prim and polite working girls.

The turmoil of the sixties has, however, had its effect on the organization. A statement issued at its 1970 National Convention in Houston, Texas, could almost be interchanged with one from a radical feminist group: "It is essential that women move beyond being sexual playthings of the male to an affirmation of their role as human beings, with capacity for leadership and contribution in varied ways. . . . They need an identity of their own." During the summer of 1970 the organization conducted a survey of 400 of the more than 4000 delegates to teenage conferences throughout the country. According to one of the directors the results of the survey "show that we're dealing with young people who are activists and agree with many of the platforms of adult contemporary feminists."[2] The Y. has a membership of more than 2.5 million women of all ages in 7800

[2] YWCA press release, Helen Southard, September 17, 1970.

local chapters. With a membership of this size, geographically distributed throughout the country, the Y. is potentially a strong ally of the women's liberation movement. In fact in some smaller cities the Y. offices are at present being used by women's liberation groups.

At the 1970 Convention, the Y. announced the formation of a National Women's Resource Center, to realize an organizational priority of mobilizing "our full power as a movement to revolutionize society's expectations of women and their own self-perception."[3] The Center will serve as a "data bank" of films, tapes, literature, survey materials, research information for seminars, etc. An "Input" questionnaire was sent to all Y. chapters and leaders requesting various kinds of information for the Center—books or articles of interest, names of persons who would work with groups on the concerns of women, locations and descriptions of women's centers, names of television programs, books with "good role models" of men and women, descriptions of actions which have reversed sex discrimination, etc. The primary purpose of the Center is to enable the Y. to reach "the poorer young girls throughout the country and educate them about the options available to them besides marriage."[4]

In some ways the YWCA and its Women's Resource Center are more part of the minority group movement than of the women's movement. A special issue of *The YWCA Magazine* devoted entirely to women carried an editorial entitled "Racism and Sexism," which read in part:

> Both racism and sexism are systemic evils that must be eliminated. These systemic oppressions have been much compared recently, particularly by some members of the newer women's movements who are quick to point out the similarities of oppression. . . . However, most members of this women's movement are white and middle class. Why is this when there are women of minority groups who would seem to be doubly oppressed? Perhaps this is true because the articulated values so far are basically white. . . . In its struggle to "revolutionize society's expectation of women" the YWCA must clearly recognize that its top

---

[3] *Ibid.*
[4] Helen F. Southard, Director of the National Women's Resource Center of the YWCA, interview, July, 1970.

priority is the elimination of racism which is a more pervasive and deadly oppression than that of women. For example, white women, though victims, are also perpetrators of racism through their individual actions and their support and encouragement of a system that oppresses minority people. Therefore, women must set out to eliminate racism before they can effectively combat sexism.[5]

The YWCA has been in existence for more than one hundred years. During much of its history, it has not participated actively in movements for social change. Although the ultimate impact of the contemporary women's movement on the Y.'s activities cannot be known, its 1970 platform indicates that a significant step has been taken in a new direction.

UNITED AUTO WORKERS WOMEN'S DEPARTMENT

The UAW formally organized a separate Women's Department in 1944 to deal with the problems presented by the large numbers of women coming into industry during World War II. That department has since been described by staff members as UAW's "agitator" in the field of women's rights. Over the years it has conducted all manner of research projects, the results of which have helped to form UAW policy with regard to women. Women's Department pressure has also resulted in the passage of strong women's rights resolutions at all the UAW national conventions, and has often put the union in the vanguard of working women's rights.

UAW has traditionally added "sex" to its discriminatory clauses and has been on record since 1941 (when issues concerning women were still under UAW's Fair Practices Department) urging the Federal Government to do the same regarding its federal contract discriminatory clauses. In 1949, the union supported a national equal pay law, and in the same year went on record opposing eight-hour laws affecting *only* women workers. From 1961 to 1963 Caroline Davis, director of the Women's Department, served on the Private Employment Committee of the President's Commission on the Status of Women. In response

---

[5] Mary Abbott Waite, "Racism and Sexism," *The YWCA Magazine*, January, 1971, p. 2.

to one of the Committee's recommendations to ban sex discrimination on the part of employers, Davis filed a dissent urging a much stronger enforcement procedure than the Committee had outlined.

When Title VII was passed in 1964, the UAW, a long-time supporter of state protective legislation, reversed its stand and interpreted the Act as superseding protective legislation. The new position was a result of its Women's Department studies which found those laws, more often than not, to be discriminatory rather than "protective." Caroline Davis stated this position at the 1965 White House Conference on Equal Employment Opportunity when she served as a panelist on the workshop "Discrimination Because of Sex."

In June, 1966, while attending the third National Conference of the State Commissions on the Status of Women, she and Women's Department staff member Dorothy Haener helped to found the National Organization for Women. Haener was part of the temporary steering committee, and Davis was elected the first secretary-treasurer when NOW was incorporated the following October.

In 1967, at the EEOC public hearings on protective legislation, UAW General Counsel, Stephen Schlossberg, urged strict enforcement of Title VII and assailed EEOC's "performance in this area of the law"[6] The union also urged EEOC to issue strong guidelines clearly indicating that Title VII superseded state protective legislation. UAW was the first large labor union to take this stand. (Indeed, the national AFL-CIO still supports state protective laws for women.) In March, 1969, UAW filed an *amicus* brief on behalf of the plaintiff in the *Bowe v. Colgate-Palmolive* case, arguing that Title VII contravened and superseded any state protective legislation.

On April 25, 1970, at its national convention, the UAW adopted a strong resolution about women's rights, including a call for the repeal or reform of abortion laws and the establishment of a network of child care centers. For the first time their resolution also included support of the Equal Rights Amendment. Olga Madar, vice president of the UAW International Union, testified two weeks later at the May, 1970, Senate Subcommittee hearings because ". . . people were getting the impression that

---

[6] Statement to Equal Employment Opportunity Commission, May 2, 1967. Included in *ERA Hearings 1*, p. 603.

all unionized workers were opposed to the Equal Rights Amendment, and I am here to tell you that is not so."[7]

.   .   .

The foregoing descriptions of the nationally-organized groups reveal both the historical and ideological development of what is generally termed the "women's rights" branch of the contemporary women's movement. As is evident, these groups for the most part have clearly defined their parameters both in terms of their tactics and in terms of their feminist goals. Moreover, there exists among them a shared desire "to work within the system," toward reform of existing social institutions. Notwithstanding this common frame of reference, however, the emphasis of each organization is sufficiently distinct from that of the others so that no one of them could ever be *the* voice for all moderate and conservative feminists.[8] As the movement continues to grow, undoubtedly new national groups will be formed. Moreover, as new issues arise coalition organizations will probably be established to concentrate on them. One such coalition group, Women United, announced its formation in the spring of 1971; its purpose, to be a clearing house for any and all matters concerning the Equal Rights Amendment, both on the Congressional level and, assuming it soon passes the House and Senate, on the state level when the ratification process begins. One woman involved in the formation of Women United commented on the fragility of political coalitions, and in the case of this organization noted, "The absolutely only feminist issue we all agree on is the Amendment, and were conversation to stray from that subject for more than thirty seconds, the group might well disintegrate into a not-too-pleasant free-for-all."

Since the beginning years of the new movement, women's rights groups have transformed themselves into a sufficiently strong and vital pressure block that legislators, educators, union officials, and business and industry leaders have begun to accept them as a permanent part of the political scene and a part with which they must all begin to reckon.

---

[7] Testimony, *Ibid.*, p. 592.
[8] Needless to say, even though the organizations themselves take a moderate "official" stand on most issues, many individual members consider themselves radical feminists.

2

Women's Liberation

ALTHOUGH THERE HAS BEEN cross-fertilization between the women's liberation and women's rights branches of the feminist movement, until 1970–1971 there existed to all intents and purposes two movements distinct in their origins, politics, tactics and general "style." As previously noted, most of the moderate and conservative feminists (the "rights" branch) came from traditional political and social backgrounds: government work, State Commissions on the Status of Women, women's business and professional groups. The women initially involved in the "liberation" movement were generally younger than the moderate and conservative feminists, and came from a more radical political background that had its roots in the student activism of the early nineteen-sixties. Some of the women in the "liberation" branch had been involved in the civil rights movement; some, new left politics; some, the peace movement. These varied political allegiances of the women, in retrospect, seem to have influenced both the politics of their feminism and the growth of the women's liberation movement.

From the beginning of the women's liberation movement, in fact from the first meetings of groups of women before one could speak of "a movement," some women viewed "women's issues" as part of the larger struggle for socialist change; others saw "women's issues" as in fact *the* issue, arguing that the measure of oppression in any society is the oppression of women.[1] These con-

---

[1] The term *oppression* is one commonly used in the movement. "The con-

flicting political positions, called *politico-feminist* respectively, have had many variations in theme and emphasis during the short history of the movement. As the movement grew it became more and more clear that at the core of the dispute was a profound disagreement about the source of women's subjugation. Politicos accept for the most part the Marx-Engels critique of society which locates the source of oppression in the family, the first institution of private property and the division of labor, and by extension, in capitalism. Feminists, on the other hand, although most of them are also critical of capitalism, argue that the male-defined social institutions and value structure, both of which stereotype people on the basis of sex roles, are responsible for women's status. This politico/feminist division has influenced the organizational development, characterized much of the literature, provided the basis for conflicting theoretical formulations, and caused internal dissension within the movement, the long-range effects of which can only be speculated upon. This distinction, implicit in the origins of the movement, became explicit during the movement's growth and development.

It is important, however, to keep in mind the fact that many women forming new small groups in 1971 have either no knowledge of, or are confused by, references to these divisions within the movement. That despite this ignorance small groups continue to form may well be a testament to the fact that the *idea* of women's liberation apparently touches a raw-nerve sensitivity in women regardless of their political orientation or lack of one.

Historical Background

THE SO-CALLED "SILENT FIFTIES" came to an abrupt end with the beginnings of confrontation politics in the early 1960's—marches, pickets, sit-ins. College and university students began to participate in political activities. They were fired with an

cept of oppression brings into use a term which has long been avoided out of a feeling that it was too rhetorical. But . . . discrimination was inadequate to describe what happens to women . . ." Jo Freeman, *The Women's Liberation Movement: Its Origins, Structures and Ideas*, p. 13. Hereafter referred to as Freeman, *Origins*.

idealism that was coupled with a wariness of traditional (old) left political rhetoric and tactics. Their new politics was one of total involvement in and commitment to changing through direct participation what they considered to be unjust and inequitable social realities.

In 1960, the Student Non-Violent Coordinating Committee (SNCC)[2] was formed by a group of Southern black college students who sought to end segregation in the South through voter registration drives, marches and sit-ins. In the North, college students, mostly white, also began to organize. They too marched, protested, and picketed stores whose Southern branches had segregated facilities.

In the early sixties, large numbers of students, both men and women, spent their summers working in the new activist civil rights movement (SNCC and CORE as opposed to the more traditional groups such as the NAACP) in the South. Women had gone to the South to work alongside men in the fight for equality only to find that they were second-class citizens in a movement purportedly determined to wipe out all discrimination. Rarely permitted to participate in policy-making, they found themselves relegated to kitchen-work, mimeographing, typing and serving "as a sexual supply for their male comrades after hours."[3]

In 1964, a small group of SNCC women began to meet and talk about their role in the organization. At a SNCC staff meeting that year, Ruby Doris Smith Robinson presented a paper that had resulted from the talks and analysis of the small group. Titled, "The Position of Women in SNCC," it elicited the comment from Stokely Carmichael, "the only position for women in SNCC is prone."[4]

Women in the civil rights movement continued to meet and talk with each other. They discussed the irony of the fact that the price for participating in a battle for someone else's equality

---

[2] On July 29, 1969, the organization changed its name to the Student National Coordinating Committee, still SNCC.

[3] Anne Koedt, "Women in the Radical Movement." Speech given at a New York City-wide meeting of radical women's groups, February 17, 1968. Reprinted in *Notes from The First Year*, June, 1968, unpaginated. Hereafter referred to as *Notes 1*. (Out of print.)

[4] One radical feminist in New York who had worked in the civil rights movement in the early sixties noted that perhaps Carmichael has been too much singled out for that thoughtless comment when many other men in the movement had made similar statements. Moreover, she pointed out, Carmichael was one of the few men in the organization who shared kitchen "drudge" work.

was the loss of one's own equality.[5] In 1965, Casey Hayden and Mary King, women active in SNCC, wrote a paper on the role of women in the movement.[6] The paper provoked both scorn and fury from male radicals. Nonetheless, women remained in the movement, either believing in the importance of the "larger" battle, or simply clinging to their new "activist" style of life.

By the mid-sixties, tension was growing between black and white workers in the civil rights movement and more and more whites left the movement. In 1966, SNCC formally banned white members. Even prior to this ban student political activity had begun to move in other directions. New left politics groups formed, some on an *ad hoc* basis around particular issues or events, some long-term, e.g., Students for a Democratic Society. These groups were concerned with a broad range of issues: military expenditures and the arms race, abrogation of civil liberties, problems of newly developing nations (in 1970 the term is "third world"), capitalism and economic injustice, and corruption in universities. New waves of college students filled these ranks. Although some ex-civil rights movement women joined, others dropped out of active politics altogether.

Women in the new left movement found themselves being treated in the same way as their counterparts in the civil rights movement:

> This kind of desperate attempt by men to defend their power by refusing to participate in open public discussion with women would be amusing if it were not so effective. And one sees the beginnings of it even now, while still students, in SDS meetings. You are allowed to participate and to speak, only the men stop listening when you do. How many times have you seen a woman enter the discussion only to have it resume at the exact point from which she made her departure, as though she had never said anything at all? How many times have you seen men get up and actually walk out of a room while a woman speaks, or begin to whisper to each other as she starts?[7]

---

[5] This directly parallels the experience of the first feminist movement in the United States, which had had its roots in the movement to free the slaves.

[6] Later published. Casey Hayden, Mary King, *et. al.*, "Sex and Caste," *Liberation*, Part I April 1966; Part II December 1966.

[7] Beverly Jones and Judith Brown, *Toward a Female Liberation Movement* (Boston: New England Free Press, 1968), p. 6. Hereafter referred to as *The Florida Paper*.

At an SDS conference in December, 1965, a discussion of the "women's issue" elicited "catcalls, storms of ridicule and verbal abuse, 'She just needs a good screw', or (the all-time favorite) 'She's a castrating female.' "[8] At a 1966 SDS convention women demanding a plank on women's liberation "were pelted with tomatoes and thrown out of the convention."[9]

Women in newly-formed draft resistance groups had yet again the same experiences. In the resistance movement the male rationale for inequality was to many women brutally ironic: the draft by definition was a male issue. "Men could resist the draft. Women could only counsel resistance."[1] Many women, nonetheless, continued to participate in new left activities. Some began to form small women's caucuses within new left groups and attempted to define their role within the movement.

New left political groups had planned the first nationwide gathering of the different groups to meet in Chicago the first week in September, 1967. In retrospect this National Conference for a New Politics (NCNP) was the first event which indicated that the conflict between "women's issues" and "new left politics" might indeed be sufficiently great to cause a split between what was to become the women's liberation movement and the new left political movement.

The previous spring, Heather Booth and Naomi Weisstein had conducted a seminar on women's issues at the Center for Radical Research, a free university program at the University of Chicago. As a result of these sessions a small group of women began meeting in the late summer of 1967 to discuss the possibility of presenting a list of demands to the New Politics Conference. This small group was the first known independent radical women's group, i.e., not a women's caucus within another political organization.

NCNP received mass media attention when a black caucus presented a list of twelve demands, one of which was for 50% representation on all committees, and had them accepted. Riddled by what many observers called "white guilt," the conference accepted various resolutions which both revealed the dissension and furthered the destruction of any cohesion that had existed in the new left movement.

[8] Marlene Dixon, "On Women's Liberation," *Radical America*, February, 1970, p. 27.
[9] "Introduction: The Women's Revolution," *Sisterhood*, p. xxi.
[1] Freeman, *Origins*, p. 4.

In the new left's own reportage of the events of the conference, the presence of an *ad hoc* women's caucus and its
resolutions received no attention. However, the presence of the
radical women's caucus at the conference was very significant
inasmuch as the event sparked the first serious, although small,
efforts to organize women. Although the Chicago women's group had decided not to
attend the conference as a group, some of its members did
participate. They joined with other women at the conference to
form an *ad hoc* radical women's caucus. The caucus planned to
present for general debate a resolution embracing a civil rights
plank for women, i.e., equal pay for equal work, unrestricted
abortion, etc. The resolution also included a demand for 51%
representation on all committees of the conference. Although the
women did not expect this demand to be accepted, they felt it
was as reasonable as the black demand for 50% representation,
if not more so: women constitute 51 percent of the population.
Through a series of political maneuverings, however, a much
more traditional "women for peace" plank was substituted for
the original civil rights one and approved by the resolutions
committee. At a general meeting, after most of the resolutions
had been debated, the chair announced that there was only time
for discussion of ten planks, none of which was the women's
resolution. In a brief meeting with the conference chairman, Jo
Freeman, one of the founders of the independent Chicago
women's group and proponent of the stronger women's plank at
the conference, threatened: "If you don't debate the women's
plank, we have enough women here to tie up this convention
for at least an hour on procedural motions alone." Although
only a handful of women were part of the caucus, the threat
appeared to work. The chairman, however, quickly read the
peace plank, permitted no discussion (though several of the
women had planned to offer the stronger plank as a substitute
motion), and brought the motion to a vote. At this point, when
no more resolutions were to be introduced, a young man rose
to speak about what he called "the forgotten minority, the
American Indians." When the women realized that the convention was willing to listen to a new set of resolutions as long
as they had nothing to do with women's issues, that women's
issues were not considered political, Freeman and Shulamith
Firestone, another member of the *ad hoc* women's caucus, went
up to the platform to demand a hearing. They were told in no
uncertain terms that their "trivial" business was not going to

stop the conference from dealing with the important issues of
the world. Reportedly, one of them was literally patted on the
head and told, "Calm down, little girl." Both subsequently became founders of the first women's groups of the movement
in Chicago and New York respectively.

Early Groups

THE CHICAGO WOMEN left the NCNP conference and began meeting with others on a regular basis. One commented, "rage at what
had happened at the convention kept us going for at least three
months."[2] At its largest, the group consisted of about thirty
women; most often, a core of seven attended. The group discussions often centered around the issues of male-exclusion from
the group, and the relationship of a women's group to the radical
movement. The idea of male-exclusion was often heatedly argued
because the radical women were being pressured by their male
co-participants in new left political groups. Discussions notwithstanding, male-exclusion in fact happened naturally: when the
women were with new left men they did not discuss women's
issues.[3] The real split was to come over the problem of whether
or not a women's group, and by extension, movement, was to be
independent and autonomous or part of the new left movement.
    Although the words *politico* and *feminist* were not yet used,
the seeds of this split were apparent in this first Chicago group.
In the beginning women with a background in radical politics
dominated. Thus, although separate from other political organizations, the Chicago women limited their discussions for the most
part to analyses of women's roles in traditional political leftist

---

[2] It is perhaps necessary to repeat that many of the women were interviewed with the understanding that their comments were not for attribution. Thus, in instances of quotations from such women, there are no
citations.
[3] Many radical women today are both amused and angered that white
liberal-radical men claim to understand, appreciate and endorse the need
of blacks to meet alone to analyze and define their needs and plan action;
if blacks prohibit whites from meetings, it is seen as political necessity; if
women prohibit men from their meetings, it is perceived as man-hating,
counter-revolutionary, and, in the most benign of criticisms, as yet another
example of the trivial nature of women's business.

contexts: women as a consumer class, women in Cuba and Vietnam, women in new left politics, etc.

The Chicago group expanded, changed composition (more politicos joined) and spun off two groups, one of which was Women's Radical Action Project which later took part in the sit-in at the University of Chicago in January, 1969.[4] After these splits, the remaining women called themselves the Westside group. In March, 1968, the Westside group began the first attempt at some kind of formal communication with women in different parts of the country. Jo Freeman, one of the founders, wrote and circulated a newsletter, *Voice of the Women's Liberation Movement*. *Voice* was published for more than a year. It contained articles on the role of women in socialist countries, in America's new left movement, and in American society as a whole. The newsletter was distributed in Chicago and sent to individuals around the country. At this point women's liberation, if it was at all a movement, was a movement of friends. The first issue of *Voice* consisted of three mimeographed pages and had a "press" run of approximately 200 copies, thirty of which were mailed out. The last issue had twenty-four pages of offset printing. One thousand copies were distributed in Chicago and another 1000 mailed out.

At the end of October, 1967, Shulamith Firestone left Chicago and went to New York where she and Pam Allen organized that city's first women's group, Radical Women (subsequently called New York Radical Women). Firestone and Allen attended political meetings to find new people, and contacted women they knew or knew of. Most of the women they met were in new left political groups and expressed either indifference to or scorn about the idea of a women's political group focusing on "women's issues." The first successful contacts were made at an SDS convention in Princeton in the late fall of 1967. Some of the participants in a "workshop on women" returned to New York and with Firestone and Allen formed the first group. The New York group began to experience the same political conflicts that the Chicago group was undergoing. Most of the women who attended meetings (at the early meetings they numbered from fifteen to thirty) had had some involvement with left politics. It might be noted that women who had been involved in the civil rights movement tended to become feminists more often and more quickly than women in the peace movement and new left political organizations. One

---

[4] See separate entry (College and University Campus), Chapter 9.

explanation frequently suggested is that witnessing another's subjugation can make one more conscious of one's own. Women in the civil rights movement responded to and identified with the situation of a powerless group—the second-class status of blacks. One woman who had participated in the civil rights movement has written:

> I had spent a year in Mississippi in 1965–66, and I had watched the problems of racism that blacks ran into with movement whites long before Black Power became the proud cry of the Meredith March. I had watched white movement workers telling black people what to do. (I probably would have, too, except I didn't *know* what they should do, and besides, I was relegated to the research library and the mimeograph machine.) I was amazed that these white radicals seemed to have so many answers that were in conflict with those of the beautiful, plain-speaking black people who taught me so much about how they were oppressed by Senator Eastland, the local sheriff, the liberals, and ME. I learned from them more concretely how I wasn't so free myself, and I began to worry about that.[5]

Unlike the politicos, the women who would later be called *feminists* did not have a language or theory with which to distinguish themselves and their ideas from the other radical women. They talked somewhat vaguely about women's oppression while the other radical women talked about capitalism and the war. In these beginning days, the disagreement was somewhat loosely defined as feminists seeing "man as the enemy," politicos, "the system." In fact, one feminist recalled, "in the beginning, it wasn't considered 'good taste' to talk about men at all." At times the discussions became acrimonious, with the politicos carrying the argument by accusing the feminists of "man-hating," a charge both confusing and distressing to feminists who had not yet developed a sufficiently sophisticated analysis with which to respond.[6]

In order to assert their political identity the women in the New York group wanted to undertake "actions." They were, how-

---

[5] Carol Hanisch, "Hard Knocks: Working in a Mixed (Male-Female) Movement Group," *Notes From the Second Year: Women's Liberation—Major Writings of the Radical Feminists*, p. 60. Hereafter referred to as *Notes 2*.
[6] See separate entry (Man-hating), Chapter 5.

ever, unable to agree on what kind of action since traditional radical activities—anti-war and anti-capitalism protests—seemed not to include the "women's issues." The ensuing brief period of inactivity was ended with the group's participation in an anti-war demonstration in Washington, D.C. In January, 1968, a coalition of women's peace groups had planned to go to Washington to demonstrate against the Vietnam War at the opening of Congress. They called themselves the Jeanette Rankin Brigade.[7] Five thousand women participated in the march for peace.

Members of the New York group, Radical Women, attended some of the planning sessions for the Jeanette Rankin Brigade action. Although these radical women were politically opposed to the war in Vietnam, they saw the planned actions as useless, for to them it was predicated on traditional views of womankind: women as mothers, wives, sisters, lovers protesting the war on the grounds that "their men" were being killed. Radical Women planned a demonstration during the Brigade protest—"The Burial of Traditional Womanhood" in a torchlight parade at Arlington Cemetery. Their pamphlet distributed to the peace group women read:

> You have refused to hanky-wave boys off to war with admonitions to save the American Mom and Apple Pie. You have resisted your roles of supportive girl friends and tearful widows, receivers of regretful telegrams and worthless medals of honor. And now you must resist approaching Congress playing these same roles that are synonymous with powerlessness. We must not come as passive supplicants begging for favors, for power cooperates only with power. . . . Until we have united into a force to be reckoned with, we will be patronized and ridiculed into total political ineffectiveness. So if you are really sincere about *ending* this war, join us tonight and in the future.[8]

Some three to five hundred women split off from the main Brigade and met with Radical Women. One participant commented on this large defection: "although predictable . . . never-

---

[7] Jeanette Rankin was the first woman in the United States to serve in Congress, 1917–1919. She was also elected to the House in 1941 for a two-year term. A pacifist, she voted against the declaration of war against Germany in 1917 and cast the only vote in the House in 1941 against the United States entering World War II.

[8] Shulamith Firestone, "The Jeanette Rankin Brigade: Woman Power?" *Notes 1.*

theless it was unexpected. We were not really prepared to re-channel this disgust, to provide the direction that was so badly needed. There was chaos. . . . It was a great moment. But we lost it. . . . I think one good guiding speech at the crisis point which illustrated the *real* causes underlying the massive dis-content and impotence felt in that room then, would have been worth ten dummies and three months of careful and elaborate planning."[9]

"The Burial of Traditional Womanhood" was based on the idea that women must begin to deal with their own subjugation, or they will remain powerless. Kathie Amatniek, a member of the New York group, delivered a speech at the "Burial" ceremony and addressed herself to the question,—why bother with women's issues when thousands of people are being killed in Vietnam in the name of American Democracy? :

> Sisters who ask a question like this are failing to see that they really do have a problem as women in America . . . that their problem is social, not merely personal . . . and that their problem is so closely related and interlocked with the other problems in our country, the very problem of war itself . . . that we cannot hope to move toward a better world or even a truly democratic society at home until we begin to solve our own problems.[1]

"The Burial of Traditional Womanhood" at the Jeanette Rankin demonstration was the first public action radical women under-took to "raise the consciousness" of other women. It was at this protest that the slogan "Sisterhood Is Powerful" was first used—in a leaflet written by Amatniek.

The political differences among the women were sharpened during the Jeanette Rankin demonstration. Radical women (politicos) in Washington had opposed the New York group's counter-demonstration as irrelevant and non-political. The fem-inists on the other hand defined the demonstration as extremely relevant and distinctly political. In addition, The New York fem-inists became more acutely aware of their conflicts with the politico women, not only in Washington, but within their own group as well. "We learned a lot. We found out where women,

[9] *Loc. cit.*
[1] Kathie Amatniek, "Funeral Oration for the Burial of Traditional Woman-hood," *Notes 1.*

even the so-called 'women radicals' were *really* at. We confirmed our worst suspicions, that the job ahead, of developing even a minimal consciousness among women will be staggering, but we also confirmed our belief that a real women's movement in this country will come, if only out of the sheer and urgent and immediate necessity for one."[2]

Although increasing numbers of women were coming to the New York meetings, the group was still sufficiently small for it to continue despite intensified political differences. In June, 1968, after eight months of meeting, talking, and participating in several public actions, New York Radical Women put together a mimeographed journal, *Notes from the First Year. Notes* included articles reviewing the Jeanette Rankin Brigade action, a "new view of the Women's Rights Movement in the United States," and a short essay soon to be one of the most talked about articles of the women's liberation movement, "The Myth of the Vaginal Orgasm."[3] The magazine also included several pages of notes of conversations between men and women, and a four page dialogue called "Women Rap about Sex." This style of description, explanation and analysis from discussions of personal experiences became not only a technique used within women's groups, but also a frequent form used in the literature emerging from the movement—books, journals, newspapers, and even radio programs. *Notes* was the first instance of its use in a publicly issued journal. Although the issue was distributed primarily in New York, $0.50 to women, $1.00 to men, copies managed to make their way across country. Through the journal many young women outside New York, as well as in the city, read about "women's liberation" for the first time. In 1968, women's groups began to form throughout the country although there was no women's liberation movement as such; in fact, the term *women's liberation* was not yet known. In some instances, women who had met in Chicago, New York, or Washington moved to other cities and spurred organizational growth. In other cases, with little or no knowledge of what was happening elsewhere, women began to feel the need to meet together, separate from men, and talk about the "women's issue."

Seattle, for example, was one of the first cities after Chicago

[2] Firestone, *Notes 1.*

[3] See separate entry (Science), Chapter 3; (The "Sexual Revolution"), Chapter 4.

and New York to form a women's group independent of any other political organization. A specific incident in Seattle had sparked the formation of this first women's group. In the early part of 1968, an SDS speaker came to the University of Washington campus to talk about SDS organizational tactics. In the course of explaining the development of feelings of brotherhood between SDS workers and poor whites, he noted that sometimes after analyzing societal ills, the men shared leisure time by "balling a chick together." He pointed out that such activities did much to enhance the political consciousness of the poor white youth. A woman in the University of Washington audience asked, "and what did it do for the consciousness of the chick?" After the meeting, a handful of women got together and formed Seattle's first group. Some of the participants were members of the old left organizations, (e.g., Socialist Workers Party) and had been concerned for years with women's issues; some were students at the University. None had any knowledge of activities in any other part of the country. Although initially Seattle's Radical Women was separate from other political groups, the tie to new left organizations was sufficiently strong for some of the women to leave the group and become a women's committee of Seattle's Peace and Freedom Party, and later a women's caucus in SDS. When the women disrupted the University of Washington's Men's Day program[4] many of the other SDS members opposed the action as not sufficiently militant and anti-imperialist—if not apolitical, then a case of bad politics. In May, 1969, some of the women left SDS to form Women's Liberation Seattle. One has noted, "We more or less came to the position that we must, again, become an organization independent of all other organizations." Although the group is autonomous, its feminist analysis is in large part based on socialist theory.

Although in Seattle a specific incident had triggered the formation of the first women's group, a growing *general* disenchantment with new left political organizations spurred the formation of groups in other cities. In San Francisco, for example, women "dropouts" from new left politics formed that city's first group in September, 1968. Their disenchantment with new left political organization was, however, so strong, that for a while the women resisted defining themselves as a political entity. After several months of talking and writing they took the name, Sudsofloppen.

[4] See separate entry (College and University Campuses), chapter 9.

"One of our members had used the name in her paper and we all felt that the concept of a nonsensical name was good because it would leave us plenty of room to grow and develop. No notion of who or what we were could be derived from the name separate from the work and ideas we produced."[5]

In an essay, "Why We Came Together," Pat Hansen, one of the original members, discussed the group's origins:

> Some of us had been friends before the group began. We had discussed the problems we had as women—problems with men, chauvinistic things they did and said, pressures to do things to please them, envy at times that they seemed more free to act, to go out into the world, to be independent. . . . But as much as we talked about men even then we had begun to talk about ourselves as women, as separate from men—about sex and about our bodies— the shame, pride, fear and pain and probably above all, of course, the lack of ownership. . . . We realized, married or not, our bodies had ownership by many: men, doctors, clothes and cosmetic manufacturers, advertizers, churches, schools—everyone but ourselves. . . . At this time we had heard about women's groups being formed in other parts of the country, but our experience in the 'movement' had burned us so badly that anything that hinted of organizing, meetings or objectivity was synonymous with manipulation, rhetoric, and ego-trips, so for a long time we didn't seriously consider meeting in any kind of formal way. But finally we did decide to meet. Since one of us was involved in the Resistance (because her man was active there) we approached the other women who were there also. Thus we met together with about half the group strangers to the other half.[6]

Since the formation of Sudsofloppen, San Francisco and the East Bay (Berkeley and Oakland), have witnessed the growth of myriad groups. Some are strongly politico in orientation; others are strongly feminist, and still others have sufficiently eclectic politics to defy labeling. It might well be noted here that while

---

[5] Pam Allen, *Free Space: A Perspective On The Small Groups in Women's Liberation* (first published by Women's Liberation Basement Press, Albany, California, January, 1970; subsequently, Times Change Press), p. 9.
[6] Pat Hansen, "Why We Came Together," *Free Space*, p. 49.

the distinction between feminists and politicos is both clearly observable today as well as an historically accurate description of movement politics, politicos tend to belittle the distinction whereas feminist˜ assert it. The politicos often accuse the feminists of not being really political. The latter, they argue, do not have a *radical* politics: it is counterrevolutionary to try to alter the system (e.g., demand equal pay for equal work); rather, one must overthrow the system. By denying feminism as political in its own right, politicos subsume feminism under the socialist rubric, thus virtually denying the distinction between politicos and feminists. Most politicos, in fact, rarely if ever call themselves as such; rather, they speak of themselves as feminists or feminist-socialists. Feminists, on the other hand, always call themselves feminists. As one has noted, "the distinction is very useful to us, less so for politicos." Feminists focus on the difference because, apart from the fact that the division exists, this political/philosophical/ideological differentiation serves the tactical function of sharpening and refining that which is singular to feminist thought: the recognition that the core of women's oppression rests in the sex-role segregation system. In their analysis, it is this system of male-female differentiation which must be eliminated. Thus, although many feminists are in fact liberal or left in their politics, they argue that an attack on the capitalist system alone will not eradicate women's status of subjugation, cf. China, USSR, Cuba.

In August 1968, a meeting of women's groups was held in Sandy Springs, Maryland. Approximately thirty women from Florida, Washington, D.C., Massachusetts, New York and Illinois met to talk about their different groups. This was the first attempt to bring together radical women from different parts of the country. The women discussed goals and priorities for a women's movement; argued, often heatedly, about political commitments and ideological assumptions; and talked about possible specific action projects for the future. The idea of a national movement was novel and still very much a future possibility. The women returned to their respective cities to organize groups locally. When in September of that year "women's liberation" made national headlines and the media spoke of a "movement," in actuality no such movement existed.

A National Movement

ONE EVENT brought mass media attention to women's liberation: the Miss America Contest demonstration. At one of the meetings of Radical Women in New York, the group had decided to protest the Miss America Contest in Atlantic City, N.J., on Saturday, September 7, 1968. The New York women joined with women from Washington, D.C., New Jersey and Florida for this action. Carol Hanisch, one of the organizers of the protest, wrote: "We all agreed that our main point in the demonstration would be that all women were hurt by beauty competition—Miss America as well as ourselves. We opposed the pageant in our own self-interest, e.g., the self-interest of all women."[7] The Miss America protest was the first time the mass media gave head-line coverage to the new feminist movement. The *Daily News*, with a Sunday circulation of over three million, reported: ". . . some women who think the whole idea of such contests is degrading to femininity, took their case to the people. . . . During boardwalk protest, gals say they're not anti-beauty, just anti-beauty contests."[8] The American public learned for the first time that there was a new thing called the women's liberation movement.

The tactics of protest that the radical women used were very much in the hippy style of street theater. A live sheep was crowned Miss America, and a freedom trashcan was set up in which women could discard items symbolic of traditional ideas of femininity. The leaflet distributed for the event told women to "bring old bras, girdles, high-heeled shoes, women's magazines, curlers, and other instruments of torture to women!" From this last action came the media misrepresentation of bra-burning. No bras were in fact burned. The image, however, stuck, and women in the movement have since then often been ridiculed as "bra-burners."[9]

The radical women were fairly critical of their own actions and fearful of the effects on non-involved women:

---

[7] Carol Hanisch, "A Critique of the Miss America Protest," *Notes 2*, p. 87.
[8] *Daily News*, September 8, 1968.
[9] For more detailed discussion, see Chapter 5.

One of the reasons we came off anti-woman . . . was our
lack of clarity. We didn't say clearly enough that we
women are all *forced* to play the Miss America role—not
by beautiful women but by men who we have to act that
way for, and by a system that has so well institutionalized
male supremacy for its own ends.[1]

The protest action was an example of an *ad hoc* action designed to deal with a specific issue, single event, often symbolic
in nature. Women in the movement often speak of this kind of
activity as a "zap action." These actions:

. . . are using our presence as a group and/or the media to
make women's oppression into social issues. In such actions we speak to men as a group as well as to women. It
is a rare opportunity to talk to men in a situation where
they can't talk back. (Men must begin to learn to listen.)
Our power of solidarity, not our individual intellectual ex-
changes will change men.[2]

The Miss America protest was the first indication that the
new women's movement was not going to limit itself to statements of principles or traditional actions of political protest.
Targets of what radical women considered "sexism" were everywhere, and susceptible to attack. Moreover, by such a demonstration as the Miss America protest, feminists were trying to explain to the public at large that beauty contests were as much an
expression of social/political oppression as the more obvious
manifestations of discrimination such as job and wage inequities.
    By virtue of the national television and press coverage of the
demonstration, women in different parts of the country became
aware that there was "a movement." The effects of media exposure are hard to assess. On the one hand, coverage by the
media has brought new women into the movement; on the other,
the image portrayed has more often than not been sufficiently
flippant and derogatory that many women have felt both alien-
ated from and antagonistic to the movement. Nonetheless, for
women who were ready to form groups, the Miss America protest
and the issues it raised were yet another impetus.
    In New Orleans, for example, a women's group independent

---

[1] Hanisch, p. 87.
[2] *Ibid.,* p. 88.

of any political affiliations was formed in the fall of 1968, although formal discussions of "the women's issue" began in the city much earlier. Two years before, in the summer of 1966, a Free School had been established by students from Tulane and civil rights community organizers. Two women had conducted a seminar on the sociology of women which became a reading and discussion group in which suburban housewives, wives of students and faculty, students, and civil rights "drop-outs" talked about their experiences as women. The Free School ended when the University year began in the fall, and with it, the women's group stopped meeting. Two years later a group of women, some from the Free School summer, some new, began to meet. They had read the Casey Hayden-Mary King paper, and knew of the experiences of the SDS women's caucus. The final impetus was the Miss America demonstration. The women met somewhat hesitantly, trying to figure out why they were getting together, but according to one participant they realized as they told of men's strong reactions against their meetings that, "there must be something going on if its upsetting them so." The women's initial hesitation and resistance prevailed three years later in 1971. According to women in the movement such resistance indicates that the stereotypical image of the triviality of "women's meetings" and "woman-talk" is deeply ingrained in and accepted by many women.

Shortly after the Miss America protest demonstration developments took place within New York Radical Women which have affected the nature and growth of the entire movement. The differences between feminists and politicos, still not yet clearly articulated, were beginning to be argued as differences in tactics. In their meetings the women had begun to "rap" about themselves, recalling their individual experiences, relating personal problems, and focusing on their personal feelings. They were slowly and hesitantly beginning to conclude that what seemed to be a woman's idiosyncratic pattern of behavior was in fact a prescribed social role, and ". . . that what was thought to be a personal problem has a social cause and probably a political solution."[3] This process of relating the personal to the political later became the formalized intra-group method of discussion called consciousness raising, an educational process used throughout the country in women's groups. Moreover, since con-

---

[3] Freeman, *Origins,* p. 8.

sciousness raising works best with a limited number of women (seven to fifteen), the small group has become the most widespread organizational unit of the movement. Consciousness raising has thus come to define both the form and content of much of the activity of the women's movement. In this respect, it is not limited to radical feminists. Suburban housewives, who might well hesitate to call themselves "feminists," are among the most frequent employers of the small group technique.

At the end of 1968, however, the basic assumption of consciousness raising, that women's personal experiences are political in content, was by no means a generally accepted idea. In fact, "The political background of many of the early feminists . . . predisposed them against the rap group as 'unpolitical' and they would condemn discussion meetings which 'degenerated' into 'bitch sessions.' "[4] Within New York Radical Women several members formed a small separate group to do "a different kind of rapping" (the term "consciousness raising" was not yet in use). Rather than talk about "feelings," they preferred what they called a more "political" analysis. Moreover, they wanted to plan public actions. The new group, WITCH, became a byword of the whole movement. On Halloween 1968, the first WITCH coven appeared. Women, dressed up as witches, hexed and spooked the New York Stock Exchange. The new group's differences with the larger group resulted from personality conflicts as well as the theoretical differences of analysis and action v. "bitching." That the split was, however, in large measure along politico-feminist lines, is apparent from a number of factors. The "hexing" of the Stock Exchange had certainly less to do with women than with capitalism. In addition, before WITCH emerged as a distinct group, the women who were to organize it had participated as a group in an action in the New York spring 1968 march against the war in Vietnam. They had dressed as Vietnamese, carried anti-war signs, and wailed the Algerian women's high-pitched, eerie cry. Some of the women in the larger group had criticized this activity as directed toward a political effort the central issue of which was not feminist. Moreover, the action emphasized theatrical style and rhetoric similar to yippie guerrilla theater tactics.

The idea of WITCH had resulted from discussions in the small group about female power—did it exist and was there an

---

[4] *Ibid.,* p. 10.

historical basis for discussing the concept? The answer for the women was witchcraft. Some of the members of the group had had prior interest in theater and magic and WITCH was the natural outgrowth. One of the early members commented:

> Street theater gave us a place to put ourselves out publicly in a different way, to say what we wanted to say. What was so good was the concept of working in a small group of people who were supporting you. Speaking alone is really hard whether or not you have a hostile audience. The theatrical thing was a group thing, and we could be outrageous.

WITCH has no permanent organization. Covens exist in cities across the country, each one autonomous. They reveal their existence by "zap" actions; in some cases a coven may form for an *ad hoc* action. The acronym WITCH first stood for Women's International Terrorist Conspiracy from Hell, but has changed with the different targets under attack: telephone company workers protesting working conditions became Women Incensed at Telephone Company Harassment; a group working for an insurance corporation became Women Indentured to Traveler's Corporate Hell; on Mother's Day, a coven announced its identity as Women Infuriated at Taking Care of Hoodlums, and another as Women Interested in Toppling Consumption Holidays; at a protest against high consumer prices, one group called itself Women's Independent Taxpayers, Consumers and Homemakers. The permutations are as limitless as the possible targets.

A statement from the New York covens illustrates the style and theatrical flair of the group:

> WITCH is an all-women Everything. It's theater, revolution, magic, terror, joy, garlic flowers, spells. It's an awareness that witches and gypsies were the original guerrillas and resistance fighters against oppression— particularly the oppression of women—down through the ages.

> WITCH lives and laughs in every woman. She is the free part of each of us, beneath the shy smiles, the acquiescence to absurd male domination, the make-up or flesh-suffocating clothing our sick society demands. There is no

"joining" WITCH. If you are a woman and dare to look
within yourself, you are a Witch.

. . . Whatever is repressive, solely male-oriented, greedy,
puritanical, authoritarian—those are your targets. Your
weapons are theater, satire, explosions, magic, herbs,
music, costumes, cameras, masks, chants, stickers, sten-
cils and paint, films, tambourines, bricks, brooms, guns,
voodoo dolls, cats, candles, bells, chalk, nail clippings,
hand grenades, poison rings, fuses, tape recorders, in-
cense—your own boundless beautiful imagination. Your
power comes from your own self as a woman, and it is
activated by working in concert with your sisters.

. . . You are pledged to free our brothers from oppression
and stereotyped sexual roles (whether they like it or not)
as well as ourselves.[5]

For a time there were purportedly three WITCH covens in
New York. The last major public appearance of WITCH was at
the Bridal Fair exposition on Valentine's Day 1969. There was a
simultaneous Bridal Fair demonstration in San Francisco. The
protest was meant to be an attack on an industry which makes its
profits from reinforcing generally accepted romantic myths about
marriage:

The whole purpose of the booths, exhibits and fashion
shows at the fair is to romanticize and embellish the marriage ceremony as the most important day in a woman's
life: The purchase of a wedding gown is the creation of a
memory and the wedding itself an elevation into the ec-
stasy and acceptability of wifehood. They sell and sell and
sell, and the mothers and daughters buy eagerly, focused
as they are on proving how much they are worth on the
marriage market.[6]

The action at the New York Fair was not only unsuccessful with
the "mothers and daughters" who attended, but it also provoked
sharp criticism from feminists who had refused to join the protest. The latter felt that the demonstration had only succeeded

---

[5] Leaflet reprinted in *Sisterhood*, pp. 539–40.
[6] Cellestine Ware, *Woman Power: The Movement For Women's Liberation*
(New York: Tower Publications, Inc., 1970), p. 47.

in alienating women by attacking them personally; thus, it failed to communicate the political issues involved. One woman commented:

> The WITCH group was extraordinarily insensitive to the women at the fair. They made them feel like pieces of meat because they were getting married. Then when they [WITCH] turned loose a whole lot of mice in the Coliseum —my God, talk about stereotyping the women, let alone the cruelty to the mice!

In California the same disagreements on tactics existed. Some women picketed the Bridal Fair and staged guerrilla theater skits. Others used a "soft-sell" of leafleting but finally decided that the fair "was not really a good recruiting place."

The effect of WITCH on the internal development of the women's liberation movement in New York was twofold. On the one hand, the split within New York Radical Women deepened. On the other, many women, previously uninvolved in the movement, became curious about "women's liberation" and joined groups. In retrospect, the emergence of WITCH within New York Radical Women represented not so much a clear confrontation between politicos and feminists as an interim attempt by the WITCH women to bridge the gap between the feminist movement and new left politics. By defining witchcraft as political the women were declaring that witches had been a *politically* oppressed group: they were women who had been persecuted. The "up against the wall" attitude that WITCH "zap" actions seemed to imply did in fact make the group acceptable to new left men, who applauded WITCH's emergence and chose to define WITCH as synonymous with the women's movement. Thus in some new left circles feminism by association with WITCH became for a time fashionable. In addition, women who were members of new left organizations (some in women's caucuses, some not) as well as separate women's groups which were avowedly politico in orientation, on occasion donned witches costumes to leaflet or picket at political demonstrations.

On the other hand, some of the feminists in New York Radical Women viewed the smaller group's *raison d'être* as a "cop-out. They're hiding behind masks and in the safety and security of history. What about persecution today?" These feminists noted that it was easy for new left political men to accept the idea that witches as women had been politically persecuted: it relieved them of the necessity of recognizing and analyzing the ways in which men today oppress women generally, as well as specifically in new left groups. Moreover, the feminists argued that by turning the "women's issue" into an arty, gimmicky, game-playing phenomenon—"see we're not so grim and humorless as you think we are"—the group was doing the worst kind of pandering to male taste. In the last analysis, perhaps WITCH's major contribution may well be the fact that women involved in the movement today smile in recognition at the idea that "WITCH lives and laughs in every woman."

By the end of 1968, a sufficient number of women's liberation groups had formed throughout the country for the women themselves to think that the movement was indeed national. On Thanksgiving weekend 1968, over 200 women from 37 states and Canada convened in Chicago for the first national women's liberation conference. The conference had been planned and organized by Chicago women, some of whom had participated in the Sandy Springs meeting in August where the possibility of a large conference had been suggested, although no definite plans had been made. Some of the women who came to the Thanksgiving conference were already involved in groups in their own cities; for some the meeting was their first exposure to the movement.

The division between politicos and feminists was quite apparent at the conference. Long and intense debates about the necessity of women's participation or non-participation in left political groups confused and bewildered many women new to the movement. The politicos, secure in a pre-existing analysis, argued that women's liberation could only be understood as part of the revolutionary struggles throughout the world. These women, although they considered themselves feminists, defined feminism as an analytic tool with which to explain and interpret the anger of women; socialism was the tool to eradicate women's oppression. The feminists, on the other hand, were not as sharply defined in their theoretical analysis. There had never been a feminist political movement with a comprehensive social analysis of all the ways in which women are oppressed—social, political, cultural, economic, psychological. Their analysis was, therefore, and still is, an evolving one, refining and extending itself almost daily. Two papers, "The Myth of the Vaginal Orgasm" and "A

Program for Feminist 'Consciousness Raising,' "[7] were prepared specifically for the conference and indicated the new directions in which feminists were moving. "The Myth of the Vaginal Orgasm" by Anne Koedt was distributed for a Workshop on Sex. The thesis of the paper was that woman's sexuality had always been defined by men and had little or no relation to woman's actual physiological makeup. Thus, the standards by which women were being judged sexually "inadequate" were themselves inadequate. Although it was easy enough to understand that women suffered economic and political discrimination, this was the first time anyone had suggested that assumptions about the nature of heterosexual intercourse were oppressive to women.

The paper "A Program for Feminist 'Consciousness Raising' " was an attempt to formalize the process that the New York women had been using in their meetings. Although the paper had been written primarily as a defensive tactic against the politico arguments which belittled the idea of women "rapping" together, it can be read as an early formulation of the concept central to feminist analysis that women are a political group and that women's issues are political in content. To counter the idea that discussions and analyses of feelings were non-political and therefore trivial if not irrelevant, it was argued:

> We always stay in touch with our feelings. . . . We assume that our feelings . . . mean something worth analyzing . . . that our feelings are saying something *political*. . . . In our groups, let's share our feelings and pool them. Let's let ourselves go and see where our feelings lead us. Our feelings will lead us to ideas and then to actions. Our feelings will lead us to our theory, our theory to our action, our feelings about that action to new theory and then to new action.[8]

The paper then explored in outline form the technique of consciousness raising, the forms and reasons for resistance to it, the process of developing radical feminist theory, and the kinds of actions and organizing that could be undertaken. Kathie Sarachild, author of the paper, described the outline as based ". . . on

---

[7] Both papers are reprinted in *Notes 2*.
[8] Kathie Sarachild, "A Program for Feminist 'Consciousness Raising,' " *Notes 2*, p. 78.

the assumption that a mass liberation movement will develop as more and more women begin to perceive their situation correctly and that, therefore, our primary task right now is to awaken 'class' consciousness in ourselves and others on a mass scale."[9]

As has been noted earlier, consciousness raising has since become both the technique for analyzing women's role as well as the primary organizational unit of much of the movement. At the time of the Thanksgiving Conference, however, the value of consciousness raising was by no means generally accepted. There were heated debates between those who argued that "feelings" were a legitimate basis for political analysis, and those who insisted on a more traditional analytic approach. One observer has described both factions. She wrote of:

> . . . the impassioned messianic prophecy of the New York women committed to 'consciousness raising' . . . that calls up women to recognize at the deepest emotional level their own contained resentment flowing from frustrated aspirations, their loneliness as the givers of understanding who are themselves not understood.[1]

In contrast, the author described the women involved in new left politics:

> The strategy that the leftist women had adopted . . . was to develop a 'politics' with sufficient analytical merit to force the men to recognize the legitimacy of the women's movement. . . .[2]

As an overall assessment of the conference she wrote:

> The character of Women's Liberation as a powerful and politically original movement appeared in workshops, while the defensive, [left] Movement-trained quality of women's liberation dominated plenary sessions. The workshops often left one elated, while the plenary sessions left one depressed. The conference ended in the atmosphere in which it had begun . . . [with] the sure knowledge that

---

[9] *Ibid.*, p. 79.
[1] Dixon, p. 26.
[2] *Ibid.*, p. 27.

one's consciousness raising or one's socialist ideology was the single truth.[3]

Other participants, much more sanguine in their observations, acknowledged the existence of sharp divisions, but felt that the most significant aspect of the conference was the discovery that women all over the country had begun to organize and discuss the issues. In spite of the differences, confusions and tensions, in their view the conference was "an extraordinarily exhilarating experience." One of the participants has written that the women ". . . returned to their cities turned on by the idea of women's liberation and since then the movement has expanded at an exponential pace."[4]

After Richard Nixon's election to the presidency, Mobilization for Peace, a coalition of organizations opposed to the Vietnam War, planned to stage counter-inaugural activities in Washington, D.C., in January, 1969. New York Radical Women had split into three groups after the Thanksgiving Conference. Not only had the original group become large and unwieldy, but some of the feminists felt that consciousness raising, while valuable, was not enough. These women, now in Group I, planned to participate in the counter-inaugural ceremonies with an action of their own: the tearing up of voter registration cards as a feminist action to dramatize the fact that in their view the extension of the vote to women had accomplished little or nothing toward the eradication of the oppression of women. A group of Washington, D.C. women, more committed than the New York group to the left movement, asked the men to join the women in the destruction of the cards, thereby changing the action from a specifically feminist protest to a more general new left rejection of electoral politics. Regardless of the political differences among the women, their attempt to take any kind of a stand *as women* was both jeered at and ignored by the men. The following quote is one of the most detailed descriptions of the event:

> Our moment comes. M. from the Washington group gets up to speak. This isn't the protest against movement men, which is second on the agenda, just fairly innocuous

---

[3] *Ibid.*, p. 26.
[4] Jo Freeman, "The Revolution is Happening in Our Minds," *College and University Business*, February, 1970, p. 65.

radical rhetoric—except that it's a good-looking woman talking about women. The men go crazy. 'Take it off!' 'Take her off the stage and fuck her!' They yell and boo and guffaw at unwitting double entendres like 'We must take to the streets.' When S., who is representing the New York group, comes to the mike and announces that women will no longer participate in any so-called revolution that does not include the abolition of male privilege, it sounds like a spontaneous outburst of rage.

By the time we get to the voter card business, I am shaking. If radical men can be so easily provoked into acting like rednecks, what can we expect from others? What have we gotten ourselves into?

Meanwhile [David] Dellinger has been pleading with us to get off the stage, 'for your own good.' Why isn't he telling *them* to shut up?

Just yesterday many of the women present were arguing against S.'s statement on the grounds that in spite of their chauvinism movement men are basically our allies, and we shouldn't embarrass them in front of the straight press! As it turns out, none of the above ground papers so much as mentions the women's action. Even the *Guardian* mysteriously neglects to report the second speech.[5]

Many of the women in the New York group determined as a result of the counter-inaugural experience to cut all ties with new left groups. They argued that it was anti-feminist to see women as a constituency to be organized for other purposes:

Many of us now reject this view of our purpose as anti-woman. We have come to see women's liberation as an independent revolutionary movement, potentially representing half the population. We intend to make our own analysis of the system and put our interests first, whether or not it is convenient for the (male-dominated) Left.[6]

---

[5] Ellen Willis, "Up From Radicalism: A Feminist Journal," *US* #2 (Bantam, October, 1969), p. 114.
[6] Ellen Willis, "Women and the Left," originally published in the *Guardian* (radical newspaper published in N.Y.), February, 1969, reprinted in *Notes 2*, p. 55.

Moreover, in their view, women had always subsumed their own interests to the broader male-defined goals of social change and thereby lost sight of their own needs.

> It is . . . clear that a genuine alliance with male radicals will not be possible until sexism sickens them as much as racism. This will not be accomplished through persuasion, conciliation, or love, but through independence and solidarity: radical men will stop oppressing us and make our fight their own when they can't get us to join them on any other terms.[7]

Organizational Development

AFTER THE COUNTER-INAUGURAL demonstration and for the remainder of 1969, the radical women's movement in New York underwent important changes that have both influenced the development of the movement throughout the country and indicated the kinds of organizational and theoretical problems implicit in the creation of a radical feminist movement. Precisely because the movement in New York is so varied and protean in character it can in some sense serve as a microcosm of the movement as a whole. Moreover, although other cities may not have experienced these problems and transitions, it is most often the case that the changes and growth patterns in New York only precede similar changes elsewhere.

For any political movement to survive and grow, both its political analysis and organizational structure must change, adapt to, or be sufficiently flexible to respond to new circumstances and needs. By the beginning of 1969, the women's liberation movement had during its short history changed in several important ways. First, it was publicly recognized as a movement despite the fact that many did not take its existence seriously. Perhaps more important, it had begun to take itself seriously. Prior to 1969, the statements that women's liberation is "an independent revolutionary movement" and that no alliance with male radicals was possible "until sexism sickens them as much as

---

[7] Willis, "Up From Radicalism," p. 115.

racism" could not have been made. By 1969, the women were insisting that feminism was political, that their movement was political, and that they would only entertain changes that were political in content.

From mid-1969 through much of 1970, "women's liberation" might well have seemed to the public at large to have abandoned its earlier "zap" tactics and yielded in its "radicalism" to more generally acceptable kinds of public demonstrations. Much of the news about the women's movement reported during this period focused on the debate over the Equal Rights Amendment and the large mass demonstration for women's rights on August 26, 1970. Although the Amendment debate and the Strike march received widespread media coverage, neither provoked the kind of hostility the so-called "bra-burners" had evoked. Despite this seemingly more moderate public face, however, it would be incorrect to assume that "radical" feminism was on the decline. On the contrary, the growth of the movement had been sufficiently rapid that a new plateau, albeit an awkward one, had been reached: women's liberation was a political movement, but one that did not yet have a clearly defined politics. Three groups that formed in New York in 1969 attempted to define a feminist politics to answer the ideological, structural and tactical needs of the growing movement: Redstockings, The Feminists, New York Radical Feminists. The manifestos and position papers of each group are a clear indication of the direction in which each thought the movement should develop.

REDSTOCKINGS

Two members of New York Radical Women, after their participation in the counter-inaugural demonstration in January, formed the group called Redstockings. The founders, Ellen Willis and Shulamith Firestone, conceived of the group as a militant, activist, feminist organization, and indeed the group became nationally known in the women's movement for its disruption of a public abortion hearing in New York City and the holding of its own abortion hearings.[8] Shortly thereafter, several of the members from New York Radical Women who had most forcefully advocated consciousness raising in that group joined Redstockings. The activist stance the founders had envisioned for the

---

[8] For a more detailed discussion of these actions, see Chapter 7.

group was soon replaced by a complete commitment to the idea and practice of small group consciousness raising.

Although consciousness raising had evolved out of meetings of New York Radical Women, its widespread use as both an organizing and an educational tool for the new movement must be credited to Redstockings, the first group to clearly articulate its function, purpose, and process, and to advocate its use. The group is also to be credited with the first articulation of what has become known as the "pro-woman" line—the idea that women are in no way responsible for their oppression, and that men, not women, must change their behavior.

Consciousness Raising: The small consciousness raising group fills certain needs. It is a structured way of overcoming the individual "ghettoization" of women from one another. The "Redstockings Manifesto" dated July 7, 1969, reads in part:

> Because we have lived so intimately with our oppressors, in isolation from each other, we have been kept from seeing our personal suffering as a political condition. This creates the illusion that a woman's relationship with her man is a matter of interplay between two unique personalities, and can be worked out individually. In reality, every such relationship is a *class* relationship, and the conflicts between individual men and women are *political* conflicts that can only be solved collectively.[9]

The recognition that women are a political group, a "class," is the first step toward the realization that women, as a class, can exercise political power. As one political scientist has written, "It is when social development creates natural structures in which people can interact with each other and compare their common concerns that social movements take place."[1] No "natural" structures existed for women. Just as innovations always occur to meet new needs, the consciousness raising group evolved to fill the gap for women. The small group was, however, more than just a structural innovation to overcome the physical isolation of individual women. The very process of consciousness raising worked to overcome the psychological isolation of women by the recognition that what had always been viewed as an individual

---

[9] "Redstockings Manifesto," reprinted in *Notes* 2, pp. 112–113.
[1] Freeman, *Origins*, p. 6.

woman's "neurotic" problem was in fact shared in its different manifestations by all other women. Feminists often point to the fact that it is revered revolutionary style for the Chinese to "speak pains to recall pains," and for blacks to "tell it like it is." When women, however, use this technique, it is considered a hen *qua* therapy party. Women in the movement argue strongly that consciousness raising is not therapy. In therapy a person learns to recognize and understand his/her individual problems and to work to change "neurotic" patterns of behavior. In consciousness raising, although the process may be in part similar, the goal is antithetical to therapy. The "Redstockings Manifesto" addresses itself to this point:

> We regard our personal experience, and our feelings about that experience, as the basis for an analysis of our common situation. . . . Our chief task at present is to develop female class consciousness through sharing experience and publicly exposing the sexist foundation of all our institutions. Consciousness-raising is not 'therapy,' which implies the existence of individual solutions and falsely assumes that the male-female relationship is purely personal, but the only method by which we can ensure that our program for liberation is based on the concrete realities of our lives.[2]

A leaflet which outlined topics for consciousness raising began by explaining that the emphasis on personal experiences was to "clean out our heads—uncork and redirect our anger politically—learn to understand other women—learn that our 'personal' problems are not ours alone."[3] A list of the kinds of topics discussed at consciousness raising meetings is illustrative of the process of relating the personal to the societal, or political:

> How do you learn as a little girl what 'feminine' meant? Do you worry about being 'truly feminine'? What does 'femininity' mean to you in terms of your own life? What did you do as a little girl that was different from what little boys did? Why? Did you ever want to do anything else? What is a 'nice girl'? Were you a 'nice girl'? Do you pretend to have an orgasm? What hopes do you have for

---

[2] *Notes 2*, p. 113.
[3] New York Radical Feminists leaflet.

your daughter? For your son? Why are these hopes different?[4]

The emphasis on the recognition of the 'personal as political' is
rooted in the idea that change can only come about through a
recognition of the need for change. As one feminist succinctly
noted, "the goal of consciousness raising is to raise consciousness."

The Pro-Woman Line: Traditionally there have been two
kinds of general explanations for female behavior:

1) If a woman's behavior is deemed appropriate—the gamut
   from "sexy" to "motherly"—it is understood as "natural";
   that is, "women are that way."
2) If a woman's behavior is deemed inappropriate—"unwomanly" or "unfeminine"—she is believed to be neurotic or maladjusted as an individual.

In both cases, the reasoning is based on assumptions about the
psychological nature of women.

Through their discussions about the nature of women's oppression, feminists began to analyze the ways in which women,
from earliest childhood, had been "programmed" to accept certain roles and values. They argued that women's behavior was
not in fact inherent ("women are that way"), but rather the result
of socially-imposed values. Redstockings took a third position,
which has become called the pro-woman or "anti-brainwashing"
line. These women rejected the traditional explanations for female behavior, agreeing with other feminists that women's behavior is not the result of inherent psychological characteristics.
However, the Redstockings women also rejected the notion that
women had been "programmed" to play certain social roles. They
argued that "programming" or "brainwashing" implied that
women were stupid, that they had let "the wool be pulled over
their eyes." The "Redstockings Manifesto" contained the first
articulation of this pro-woman line. It reads in part:

We . . . reject the idea that women consent to or are to
blame for their own oppression. Women's submission is
not the result of brainwashing, stupidity, or mental illness

---

[4] *Ladies' Home Journal,* August, 1970, p. 71.

but of continual, daily pressure from men. We do not
need to change ourselves, but to change men.[5]

This "pro-woman" position was important for several reasons. It
was the first time the argument had been made that there was a
rational basis for women's actions. In "Brainwashing and
Women," a Redstockings paper which elaborated on the Manifesto clause, the argument is made that "There are real consequences a woman must suffer every time she steps out of line."
For example:

> There is a frequent putdown of women who wear makeup
> and bleach their hair. According to the brainwashing
> theorists such a woman has blindly accepted the ad men's
> image of what she should look like. She must 'liberate
> herself' by learning to accept her natural beauty. Com-
> pletely left out of the picture is the fact that a woman's
> appearance is her work uniform. If she shows up to work
> without the proper uniform her boss (or husband) can
> harass her or find a replacement.[6]

Thus the fact that women are concerned about their appearance
is not a sign of their vacuousness or the triviality of their concerns. Women, Redstockings was asserting, are not stupid or
neurotic, just realistic.

Although its contribution to "movement thinking" was important, Redstockings as a group fell victim to the extremes to which
it took its positions on both consciousness raising and "anti-
brainwashing." It is important to keep in mind the fact that the
women's movement was breaking new ground in every direction
it went. No one knew, from either history or personal experience,
what all the implications of a new organizational form or theory
might be. Although consciousness raising has come to be understood as a means to the development of a politics, not an end in
itself, for Redstockings, consciousness raising became an end.
The group turned completely inward, and in the name of
"politics" in fact focused almost exclusively on "the personal."
Although their papers continue to be published in most antholo-

---

[5] *Notes 2*, p. 113.
[6] "Brainwashing and Women: The Psychological Attack," by A Redstockings Sister, mimeographed leaflet, reprinted in *The Radical Therapist*,
Special Issue: Women, Aug.–Sept., 1970.

gies, the group is defunct.[7] One feminist analyzed the collapse in the following way: "When you stop looking out, and turn exclusively inward, at some point you begin to feed on each other. If you don't direct your anger externally—politically—you turn it against yourselves."

The same problem emerged with the Redstockings "antibrainwashing" position. What began as a positive idea of standing up for "women who are down," of "refusing to blame the oppressed for their oppression," became a glorification of the victim. The more the scars of oppression one could show—a bad marriage, for example, the more "real" one's confrontation with sexism, the more support one deserved from the movement. One non-Redstockings member described the process:

> If a woman had a very bad marriage situation, or with a boyfriend, and you tried to suggest that maybe she should get out, they called you a 'traitor' to the movement for not really understanding her problem.

Most feminists argue that the anti-brainwashing position is in fact a "half-truth"—there are indeed social reinforcements for proper behavior and women are conscious of many of them. However, these feminists argue that without an analysis and critique of the ways in which women *have* internalized and accepted these reinforcements, the depth and pervasiveness of sexism will never be perceived. In addition, "brainwashing" was never assumed to be the primary cause of women's submission, or a question of women's "stupidity," but rather a manifestation of the oppressiveness of the sex-role system as a whole.

Finally, they argue that both consciousness raising and the "anti-brainwashing" position can lead to the same state of inaction: consciousness raising, while important for the understanding of problems and formulation of analysis, effects no external change unless accompanied by action. One group in a paper on its origins and development has written, "We've found a total emphasis on the personal a dead end. We don't want to lose the personal emphasis. . . . But again work, reaching out, is essential."[8]

The "anti-brainwashing" line also leads to inaction: Red-

---

[7] Although other groups have used the name "Redstockings," the original group no longer exists.

[8] *Free Space,* "Sudsofloppen Paper," p. 44.

stockings' refusal to accept the idea of "brainwashing" or internalization has led to an ironic defense of the *status quo*. In an editorial to the special issue on women of *The Radical Therapist*, one feminist, advocating the "anti-brainwashing"/pro-woman line, argued, for example, that "The current trend toward unisex . . . is not a sign of female liberation. In Unisex the male is co-opting the few ornaments women have to make themselves more attractive in the necessary race for a man."[9] Other feminists argue that such a statement is harmful to the movement because the rational explanation of women's behavior becomes in fact a rationalization of that behavior, and often leads to the paradoxical situation of the glorification of "feminine" behavior. Precisely because of this, the pro-woman position is also referred to as a politics of female "cultural nationalism." As one feminist commented, "It's one thing to recognize how we're all caught up in the roles. It's another thing to justify them. In fact, it's a betrayal of feminism because we've got to eliminate the roles, not play them." Another feminist noted that the unisex argument seems at first a clever insight, but in fact it reveals a poverty of political imagination. "What it's telling us is that sexism is a 'no-exit' system—there's nothing we can do to change our lives."

In the view of many feminists the "anti-brainwashing"/pro-woman position leads not only to a paralysis of action—what external changes in behavior can a woman effect if her behavior is understood only as a rational response to the social system—but also to a paralysis of thought. Although Redstockings' rejection of traditionally-accepted psychological explanations of women's behavior does offer new insights, one former member of the group has argued, "When you begin to believe the pro-woman line it distorts your perceptions of reality. It's too simplistic." Redstockings in fact reached the extreme point of eschewing any psychological explanations not only in theory but in its group process as well. It attempted to prohibit the use of all psychological terminology by its members, with specific avoidance of the words "internalization," "socialization," "masochism," and, of course, "brainwashing."

The Feminists

At the same time that Redstockings had been formed and was developing its *raison d'être*, another group had formed which was

---

[9] Judith Brown, editorial, *The Radical Therapist, Special Issue: Women*, p. 2.

to have an influence far beyond its numbers. On October 17, 1968, Ti-Grace Atkinson, president of the New York chapter of the National Organization for Women left NOW with several other members and formed "The October 17th Movement" later to be called The Feminists. Within a few months of its existence, most of the original NOW members left "October 17th." New women, some former members of New York Radical Women, some with no prior group affiliations (and later, some Redstockings "dropouts") joined.

From the outset the women defined themselves as a theory-action group. On January 22, 1969, "October 17th" undertook its first public action—a demonstration at New York City Criminal Court to show support for Dr. Nathan Rappaport, an abortionist,[1] and to demand the repeal of abortion laws. Several new members joined as a result of the demonstration.

The two most important contributions of the group were their attempts at rigorous theoretical analysis of women's social role and their attempts at developing an egalitarian structure within the group.

Analysis: The Feminists (the name was changed in June, 1969) rejected the Redstockings consciousness raising approach and instead began to analyze the nature and source of women's oppression in theoretical terms. The titles of some of the papers the group wrote and distributed indicate the wide range of topics covered: The Archetypal Woman, Radical Feminism, The Rise of Man, Marriage, Man-hating, The Institution of Sexual Intercourse, Radical Feminism and Love, History of the Equality Issue in the Contemporary Women's Movement. Although feminists had been countering politico women's arguments by asserting that feminism in and of itself was political, the group, The Feminists, was the first to formulate this concept in detailed analytical and theoretical arguments. They used the term *radical feminism* and defined it as the annihilation of sex roles, a definition now widely accepted in the movement. In their analysis, women's oppression is the result of the role system which ". . . distorts the humanity of the Oppressor and denies the humanity of the Oppressed."[2] Women are a political class ". . . sep-

---

[1] The women were protesting court proceedings concerning charges of homicide against Rappaport, who was accused of responsibility in an abortion death.

[2] All quotations, unless otherwise noted, are from the paper, "The Feminists: A Political Organization to Annihilate Sex Roles," a mimeographed statement of principles and purposes reprinted in *Notes 2*, pp. 114–118.

arated out from humanity and thus denied their humanity. While men performed this expulsion, it is the male role or the role of the Oppressor that must be annihilated—not necessarily those individuals who presently claim the role." Since the source of women's oppression lies in the male-female role division, "The sex roles themselves must be destroyed. If any part of these role definitions is left, the disease of oppression remains and will reassert itself again in new, or the same old, variations throughout society." The Feminists began to analyze those social institutions which are rooted in the sex-role system and thus reflect and reinforce women's subjugation: the institutions of marriage, love, motherhood, heterosexual sex.[3] The underlying assumption of the attack was that women have been denied their individual humanity, their right to grow and develop as self-sustaining and fulfilling human beings.

Committed to theory *plus* action, The Feminists took their politics "into the street." On September 23, 1969, the group picketed and distributed leaflets at the New York City Municipal Building Marriage License Bureau to protest the institution of marriage. Their leaflet, "Women—Do You Know the Facts About Marriage?" detailed several points:

DO YOU KNOW THAT RAPE IS LEGAL IN MARRIAGE? According to law, *sex* is the purpose of marriage. You have to have sexual intercourse in order to have a valid marriage. DO YOU KNOW THAT LOVE AND AFFECTION ARE NOT REQUIRED IN MARRIAGE? If you can't have sex with your husband, he can get a divorce or annulment. If he doesn't love you, that's *not* grounds for divorce. DO YOU KNOW THAT YOU ARE YOUR HUSBAND'S PRISONER? You have to live with him wherever *he* pleases. If he decides to move someplace else, either you go with him or he can charge you with desertion. . . . DO YOU KNOW THAT, ACCORDING TO THE UNITED NATIONS, MARRIAGE IS A "SLAVERY-LIKE PRACTICE"? According to the marriage contract, your husband is entitled to more household services from you than he would be from a live-in maid. SO, WHY AREN'T *YOU* GETTING PAID? Under law, you're entitled only to "bed

---

[3] For more detailed discussion of the generally prevailing feminist critique of these institutions, see Chapter 4.

and board". . . . DO YOU RESENT THIS FRAUD? All the discriminatory practices against women are patterned and rationalized by this slavery-like practice. We can't destroy the inequities between men and women until we destroy marriage.

Structure: One of the reasons, as noted earlier, that the split with NOW had occurred, was because of the hierarchical structure of that organization. In resigning her offices Atkinson had said:

I realize that by holding these offices I am participating in oppression itself. You cannot destroy oppression by filling the position of the oppressor. I don't think you can fight oppression from the inside. Since I have failed to get rid of these power positions I hold, I have no choice but to step out of them.[4]

Other women's liberation groups had also rejected formal organizational patterns. Without any substitute form, however, they were floundering in an amorphous state. The Feminists were committed to the idea of equal participation and attempted to structure their group accordingly. They devised a lot system "to develop knowledge and skills in all members and prevent any one member or small group from hoarding information or abilities." Work assignments generally fell into two categories, creative and menial. By distributing work equally, there might be:

. . . an initial loss of efficiency but [it] fosters equality and allows all members to acquire the skills necessary for revolutionary work. When a member draws a task beyond her experience she may call on the knowledge of other members, but her own input and development are of primary importance.

Whether or not new groups use the lot system, the idea of breaking down traditional leadership (power) roles is a central tenet of the radical sector of the women's movement.[5]

Although its contributions to feminist analysis were impor-

---

[4] Sade, p. 2.
[5] For further discussion of this issue, see separate entry (State of the Movement), this chapter.

tant, The Feminists declined in much the same way as Redstockings—through a rigid adherence to its own propositions.[6]
During the summer of 1969, while several members of the group
were out of New York, The Feminists passed a series of resolutions. One of the new regulations read:

> Membership must be a primary commitment and respon-
> sibility; no other activity may supersede work for the
> group. . . . Outside study, participation in discussions,
> completion of individual assignments *and* attendance at
> actions are all equally important and compulsory.

If a woman missed a certain number of meetings she would
forfeit voting privileges and, without an acceptable excuse, she
could lose her membership in the group. The most well-known
of the new regulations was the one that read:

> We have a membership quota: that no more than one-
> third of our membership can be participants in either a
> formal (with legal contract) or informal (e.g., living
> with a man) instance of the institution of marriage.

From a group with a self-defined stance of discipline and commitment to feminism, it became a group structured to dominate its
members' lives.

At the end of the summer several of the members left the
group. Although the passage of the new regulations had been the
"final straw," internal tensions had been building over theoretical
issues as well. According to several former members, when papers
were prepared and read to the group as a whole, often those
who disagreed with a certain line of reasoning were accused of
"not being radical enough." Whereas in Redstockings the challenge was to show the scars of oppression, in The Feminists the
challenge, as one member commented, was "how farout you were
willing to go. You really felt pressured to be a super-radical and
you had nothing to do with defining what radical meant." There
were those who felt the new regulations were cause enough to
leave the group, arguing that the rules were "authoritarian if not
fascistic." Moreover, although the group had formulated strict

---

[6] Although the group still exists, its impact on the movement has not, for
the most part, extended beyond its early contributions. It is still, however,
a theory-action group.

membership rules from the beginning, the hurried passage of the new regulations, while some members were away for the summer, was seen as an internal struggle for control of the group—a power-play. After the dissenters left the group, The Feminists became the most vociferously anti-male of all groups in the movement. One former member noted, "It was all very negative. And they made the lot system into a religion, lotting each other to death. The principle of equality was distorted into an anti-individualist mania." By the spring of 1970, the "anti-leader" ethic of The Feminists was turned against the founder of the group, Ti-Grace Atkinson. In a paper reprinted in the June 5-19 issue of the underground politico women's newspaper, *Rat*, the group declared:

> The Feminists has always paraded itself as a leaderless group—that is, a group of equals. Despite this the media has consistently portrayed Ti-Grace Atkinson as the group's "leader," "spokeswoman" and "theorist." How could this happen in a group that professes to use the lot system for everything?

The paper answered the question by arguing that "The media needs stars; the movement does not. The important thing for us is getting our *ideas* across as free of individual personalities as possible." To avoid "star-making" the group passed an "April The Fifth Resolution" which stipulated that all contact with the media by a Feminist member be approved by the group and a spokeswoman (to be identified, if at all, only as a member of The Feminists) to be chosen by lot. "Anyone who violates this rule will be held accountable to the group. Anyone who flagrantly or consistently violates this rule will no longer be a member of The Feminists." Two days later Atkinson left the group. According to the paper, her reason was that the resolution was "wrong on principle."

By mid-1969, the women's liberation movement had reached another stage. Women with similar job interests, or who lived in the same apartment building, or who sent their children to the same preschool group, or who were simply friends, were beginning to meet in small groups to talk about "women's liberation." In addition, serious and intensive analysis of woman's social role had started, and organizational structures were being devised to serve a dual purpose: re-educating women and providing them with an organizational base for political action. Everything was, however, so new and untested that the search for new forms led to intense intra-movement conflicts. By the end of 1969 and through much of 1970, this dissension was not limited to New York. Throughout the country, most particularly in large cities, groups were forming, splitting over ideological and structural disagreements, regrouping and re-splitting.

Moreover, the politico-feminist antagonism had by no means abated. Politicos remained committed to the position that the socialist revolution was primary, although women were to be a vanguard in it. They attacked feminists as being predominantly white middle-class women who were "selling their Third-World Sisters down the river." Whereas radical feminists were beginning to realize that they often had a great deal more in common with women's rights groups and moderate feminists than with politicos, the latter denounced the women's rights groups as insidiously destructive of the whole movement.[7] Moreover, some politicos insisted that the third-world and working-class women were more oppressed than their white middle-class "sisters" and therefore the women's movement must look for leadership from them.[8] One politico woman working with a collective argued further that:

> Feminism is subject to racial and class issues and therefore the idea that we're all sisters, we all have the same problems, is bullshit. Don't tell me that there's no difference between a woman who can hardly feed her kids and that comfortable suburban housewife with her maid.

Feminists acknowledged the different problems women face and that black women have borne the double burden of racism

---

[7] There was also a middle-ground position: "An ecumenical view (which I hold on alternate Tuesdays and Fridays) would see that such an organization [NOW] is extremely valid and important; it reaches a certain constituency that is never going to be reached by, say, a group called WITCH. . . . On certain Mondays and Thursdays, however, I fear for the women's movement's falling into precisely the same trap as did our foremothers, the suffragists: creating a bourgeois feminist movement that never quite dared enough. . . ." *Sisterhood*, p. xxii.

[8] Cf. "Bread & Roses," Kathy McAfee & Myrna Wood. Paper reprinted from *Leviathan*, distributed separately—a clear statement of the politico position that women's liberation is part of the larger socialist revolution; and that it can only be working-class women who "will develop a revolutionary women's liberation movement."

and sexism, nevertheless, as one woman argued, "Weighing one oppression against another is obscene. The class and race issues are used to divide us and give the politicos the rhetoric to get women back into the new left movement." Feminists argued further that sexism runs deeper than class or race divisions: "They [politicos] are blind if they think sexism will disappear when everybody's eating three meals a day." They also pointed to what they considered the blatant sexism of militant black groups, which were asserting that for black men to rebuild the egos that a racist society had destroyed, black women had to march behind their men.

Although an ideological issue, the problem of third-world women has not been a major organizational one in the movement. Black and other minority group women have participated in limited numbers and primarily on an individual basis. Notwithstanding the fact that there are several women's caucuses in black militant groups as well as a few independent black women's liberation groups, for the most part activist minority women have defined the elimination of racism as their primary concern.[9]

Although some black activist women have accepted the idea that they must take a second-place role until the black man's battle is won, many are very aware of the sexist problems in the black movement which defines its goal as freeing blacks as a class, with little or no recognition of the special problems of women. On the other hand, these black women argue that although the women's liberation movement views women as an oppressed class there is no room for black participation since the movement is composed mostly of white women. As one black woman author has written: "Are women after all simply women? I don't know that our priorities are the same, that our concerns and methods are the same, or even similar enough so that we can afford to depend on this new field of experts (white, female). It is rather obvious that we do not. It is obvious that we are turning to each other."[1] Feminists reject the implication of this argument —that white women have *excluded* blacks from the women's liberation movement. Rather, they argue black women have *chosen* not to participate in the movement. As one feminist com-

---

[9] For a more detailed analysis of the relationship of black women and the women's liberation movement, see Cellestine Ware, *Woman Power: The Movement for Women's Liberation*, Chapter 2.

[1] Toni Cade, ed., *The Black Woman: An Anthology* (New York: The New American Library, Inc., 1970), p. 9.

mented: "We were all there together at the beginning. Most black women just weren't interested."

Despite the "growing pains" of the women's movement, a regional conference, the Congress to Unite Women, was held November 21–23, 1969, in New York City. The Congress was the first large-scale structured meeting of the various women's groups. Over 500 women, representing organizations from Massachusetts to Maryland, met for three days to discuss feminist issues, ideas, and activities. The Thanksgiving conference in Chicago a year earlier had indicated to the women themselves that there was a national movement. At the Congress to Unite Women in 1969, the groups in effect presented the movement to the outside world. Although the media were barred from attending the general meetings and workshops, a press conference was held at the end of the Congress ". . . to announce this meeting to the public and announce women's unity."[2]

The groups participating in the Congress covered the spectrum of feminist thought and politics: NOW (National and several east coast city chapters), Boston Female Liberation, New Yorkers for Abortion Law Repeal, Redstockings, Stanton-Anthony Brigade, WITCH Resurrectus, Women's Liberation Club-Bronx High School of Science, Women Lawyers-Boston, Daughters of Bilitis, etc. The reports from the workshops and the conference resolutions thus represented a fusion of the interests and positions of moderate and radical feminists. The Congress resolutions covered a wide range of issues, including demands for total repeal of all abortion laws, the passage of the Equal Rights Amendment, free nationwide twenty-four-hour child care centers, development of women's studies programs, etc. These resolutions grew out of twelve discussion workshops which ran throughout the second day of the Congress. Workshop meetings also focused on such topics as the Feminine Image, Love and Sex, Family Structure, the Nature and Function of a Feminist Group, and the Sex-Role System.

In one of the reports, the workshop on the Nature and Function of a Feminist Group stated:

We are united here because each of us as a woman is oppressed within this society. Regardless of political, eco-

---

[2] "Congress to Unite Women—Northeast Region: Report from the New York City Meeting of November 21–23, 1969," published March, 1970, p. 5.

nomic, social, cultural, religious, or age differences we share and agree upon basic issues of women's oppression where action must be taken.[3]

Agreement on issues, most often an ideal, was to a large extent a reality at the Congress. According to many of the women who attended, the Congress was extraordinarily free of the divisiveness that had begun to surface within the movement. There are at least two possible reasons for this: 1) many politico women had gone to New Haven for the weekend to participate in a demonstration to free Panther Party member Joan Bird; 2) when The Feminists' demands for strict use of the lot system went unheeded, the group left the conference. Thus the two potentially volatile areas of conflict—politics and structure—were to all intents and purposes diffused from the outset.

One event at the Congress indicated that, notwithstanding the absence of politico women, there was indeed a wide range of analytic and tactical definitions of feminism among feminists themselves. A dramatic example of this occurred the first evening of the Congress, when a group of approximately ten women from Boston's Female Liberation stood on stage in a semi-circle around one woman while a member of the group cut off the woman's long hair. Each then spoke about why she had short hair. Although the "testimonials" were individual and personal, they all offered a feminist explanation: the rejection of the traditionally-accepted "feminine" self-image. According to Congress participants, the "hair-cutting" action was electric in effect. When it began one woman in the audience shouted, "Oh, no, don't!" After the short speeches were over, some argued strongly against the action, others agreed wholeheartedly with it; still others were troubled by it. Although a heated debate followed the hair-cutting, there was no atmosphere of internecine warfare, a feeling often predominant when politicos and feminists would meet in debate.

The Congress established a Continuing Committee to carry out its resolutions and build a coalition of women's groups to counteract the amorphous and random growth of the movement. Although a coalition of different political groups can be a powerful force for change, the idea of a coalition was premature at this point in the development of the women's movement. There were too many internal problems over structure and theory to be

---

[3] *Ibid.*, p. 40.

worked out. Although a second Congress to Unite Women was held in mid-1970, it was nowhere near as successful as the first.[4]

New York Radical Feminists

Shortly after the first Congress to Unite Women, New York Radical Feminists was founded. A number of women had been meeting together for close to two months. Two of the women, Anne Koedt, who had been a member of The Feminists, and Shulamith Firestone, of Redstockings, were particularly dissatisfied with their prior group affiliations and wanted to form a citywide organization that would combine consciousness raising, theory and analysis, and action. On December 5, 1969, Koedt and Firestone presented to a group of about forty women a manifesto and set of organizing principles which they had written respectively. The principles incorporated in these papers attempted to grapple with the political/theoretical and organizational problems that were foremost in the movement. Both the Manifesto, "Politics of the Ego," and the Organizing Principles attempted to incorporate the best of the theory and form of other groups as well as to specifically reject those positions the new group deemed destructive of the growth of a strong women's movement. The politics and organizational structure of New York Radical Feminists warrant a fairly detailed discussion because they indicate, both explicitly and implicitly, the growth process of the radical sector of the movement. In addition, the group was one of the first to clearly delineate the problems and attempt solutions.

The Manifesto presented a clear statement of the politics of the group: *radical feminism*, the goal of which was the elimination of the sex-class system, the "fundamental political oppression wherein women are categorized as an inferior class based upon their sex.[5] Divided into four sections, "Politics of the Ego" outlined a broad theoretical statement on the nature and source of women's oppression; a brief outline of the sexual institutions— marriage, motherhood, love, and sexual intercourse which ". . . keep women in their place"; a description of the process of "Learning to Become Feminine"; and a concluding section, "Internalization," which in essence defined the need for a radical feminist movement so that women could ". . . help each other to trans-

---

[4] See separate entry (State of the Movement), this chapter.
[5] All quotations are taken from the Manifesto which is reprinted in full in the appendix.

fer the ultimate power of judgment about the value of our lives from men to ourselves."

Although a general statement of principles, the Manifesto was very specific in its rejection of the politico argument, the Redstockings pro-woman line, and the rigidity of The Feminists' theory and structure. The purpose of specifically rejecting these positions was not only ideological, but tactical as well. Although group splittings were often marked by enmity, "they can be fine and healthy—you have to do what you think is right. Everyone moves at her own speed, in her own direction. And this was our direction."[6]

The politics of New York Radical Feminists was clearly not in the politico camp. According to the Manifesto:

> We believe that the purpose of male chauvinism is primarily to obtain psychological ego satisfaction, and that only secondarily does this manifest itself in economic relationships. For this reason we do not believe that capitalism, or any other economic system, is the cause of female oppression, nor do we believe that female oppression will disappear as a result of a purely economic revolution.

The Manifesto rejected the "anti-brainwashing" argument in two places. It included a brief description of the socialization process by which women are trained from birth for their "female role," and concluded with a statement which recognized the "half-truth" of the Redstockings position:

> By the time she is of marrying age she has been prepared on two levels. One, she will realize that alternatives to the traditional female role are prohibitive; and two, she will herself have accepted on some levels the assumptions about her female role.

The final subsection entitled, "Internalization" made the argument even more specific:

> It is politically necessary for any oppressive group to convince the oppressed that they are in fact inferior, and

---

[6] Koedt, interview, March, 1971.

therefore deserve their situation. For it is precisely
through the destruction of women's egos that they are
robbed of their ability to resist. For the sake of our own
liberation, we must learn to overcome this damage to ourselves through internalization.

In the Organizing Principles, as well as the Manifesto, the new
group rejected the pro-woman position that women do not have
to change, only men. The Principles read in part: "We have all,
in order to adjust to our condition, had to develop elaborate
blinders. It is our purpose here to remove these blinders, and to
uncork our anger and frustration in order to rechannel it in the
right direction. Before we can remove the structures of oppression, we must remove our own accommodations to them."[7]

The new group, although firm in its delineation of the source
of woman's subservient status—". . . the agent of our oppression
is man insofar as he identifies with and carries out the supremacy
privileges of the male role"—eschewed the extreme "anti-male"
position of other groups. In a position paper of The Feminists,
"Radical Feminism and Love,"[8] *love* had been defined as a
". . . psycho-pathological state of fantasy" akin to hysteria:
". . . anxiety converted into functional symptoms of illness, am-
nesia, fugue, multiple personality," and it was stated that "There's
no such thing as a 'loving' way out of the feminist dilemma . . ."
In the New York Radical Feminists Manifesto, it was argued that
love as a social institution which justifies "the dominant-submissive relationship" must be eliminated. Nevertheless, the Manifesto offered a definition of a "healthy" love because, as the
author commented, "What, after all, are we talking about if not
building a new world."[9] According to the Manifesto, "non-oppres-
sive" relationships will be possible when ". . . the need to *control*
the growth of another is replaced by the love *for* the growth of
another."

The Organizing Principles of New York Radical Feminists
were an attempt to overcome structural problems groups had
previously experienced, as well as to anticipate possible future
problems. There were three main areas of concern: incorporating

---

[7] "Organizing Principles of the New York Radical Feminists," *Notes 2,* p.
120.
[8] Paper included in The Feminists' packet. Written by Ti-Grace Atkinson,
April 12, 1969.
[9] Koedt, interview, April, 1971.

women new to the movement, providing a flexible enough framework for individual growth, and building a mass women's movement. The three-stage procedure established for membership in New York Radical Feminists was so structured as to meet these concerns.

New Members: The combined effect of word-of-mouth from friend to friend and media coverage of "women's liberation" had brought many new women into the movement. Their different ages, backgrounds and experiences, and levels of "consciousness" made it extremely difficult to assimilate them into already existing groups without disrupting the workings of the group. To deal with this, the Principles had set up a three-stage process for new groups of women. In the first stage a group of women, from five to fifteen, would spend a minimum of three months doing consciousness raising, and then a minimum of three months of reading and discussing literature from both the current women's movement and movements of the past. In this way they would undergo the educational process of consciousness raising with one group of women from beginning to end, developing over the six-month period a sense of "trust" and "unity" with each other.

Flexibility: In the Organizing Principles it was explicitly stated that New York Radical Feminists was "a group in which people will become radicalized feminists of their own accord and at their own pace . . ."[1]; that there would be no "official line" imposed from above, no "external rules and regulations" to force attendance from fear of reprisals, or to create an artificial cohesion. At the end of the first stage, the new brigade (as new groups were called) would have the option of joining, with minimal approval requirements, the larger New York Radical Feminists group, or of continuing in its own direction. Once part of the larger group, the brigade was to have full autonomy to ". . . begin the serious work of an experienced brigade, attacking the problem of women's liberation in whatever aspect and by whatever method they shall decide. . . ."[2]

Mass Organization: The founding members of New York Radical Feminists were firmly committed to the idea that only through a "mass-based radical feminist movement" could women

---

[1] *Notes 2,* p. 119.
[2] *Ibid.,* p. 121.

overcome the problems in their individual lives as well as eliminate or drastically change the social structures which had made
women "the second sex." Since there was no limit on the number
of brigades that might join the larger group, potentially New York
Radical Feminists could become the mass-based women's group
in the New York area and a model for other parts of the country.
The three-stage structure was also designed to ensure that the
mass group would be radical feminist. First, the tactics of a radical feminist movement, incorporating consciousness raising,
analysis and action, were provided for; in addition, the main
criterion for acceptance of the beginning brigade into the larger
group was the expressed commitment by each woman to the
principles of radical feminism as outlined in the Manifesto.

Although the unofficial estimate of membership of the larger
group at the beginning of 1971 was over 400 women, New York
Radical Feminists was unsuccessful in overcoming the problems
of internal dissension. By mid-1970, the Stanton-Anthony Brigade
(the founding group of New York Radical Feminists) had disbanded and the three-stage structure eliminated. The structure
was, in retrospect, probably less the cause of the problem than
the fact that it was premature: the radical feminist movement
was not yet capable of building or supporting such a structured
organization, however loosely defined. The group had been
founded at the height of movement dissension and was unable to
survive attack. Although couched in terms specific to New York
Radical Feminists, the issue which brought about the disbanding
of the Stanton-Anthony Brigade and the collapse of the three-
stage structure in large part was a reflection of a crisis in the
whole movement throughout the country: the issue of "elitism"
and "leadership."

One of the brigades charged Stanton-Anthony with "elitism."
These women argued that they had left structured organizations
—both radical and moderate—precisely because such groups encouraged elitism and power hierarchies. Others, however, have
noted that this "theoretical" argument about "elitism" was in fact
not what was at issue. As one early member who remained in the
organization commented:

> It really boiled down to jealousy. Stanton-Anthony had
> founded the organization and was functioning as a com-
> plete brigade. When these women couldn't be part of the
> Stanton-Anthony brigade, they started hollering "elitism."

It sounded a little like protesting too much—like *they* wanted to be "leaders."

Two meetings of the larger group were held in the late spring and early summer of 1970. Charges of elitism were once again leveled at Stanton-Anthony and some of its members were attacked on personal grounds as well. At the second meeting a vote was taken with the result that the structure of New York Radical Feminists was abandoned. The motion had been passed with the support of many new members who, as another observed, "didn't know what the hell was going on. The charge of 'elitism,' although unproved, sounded real—after all, we all know we're against elitists."

New groups continued to form and consider themselves part of New York Radical Feminists; others remained in the consciousness raising stage sometimes for more than a year, periodically questioning their purpose and raising the possibility of disbanding; still others broke up. Without any formal structure through which to measure their growth, define and refine their politics, and initiate actions, most of the groups lost any sense of the larger organization. "Nothing was asked of anybody so why should there be any feeling of being part of a big group," one member noted. The larger group, however, continues to exist, its activities, planned on an *ad hoc* basis. Two in 1971 are of particular interest. On January 24 the group held a "Speak-out on Rape." Women testified about their experiences with assailants, and analyzed traditionally-accepted social, legal, and psychological assumptions about rape. As a follow-up to the meeting, on April 17 the group sponsored a full day conference of workshops on rape. One of the discussions centered around the need to change the laws regarding that crime because in the women's view the existing rape laws protect the rapist rather than the victim.

State of the Movement

THE TWO-YEAR PERIOD, 1969 through 1970, was a time of extraordinary growth in the women's liberation movement. Knowledge of the movement was by no means limited to large urban areas; women's groups were forming in small towns and suburbs throughout the country. In mid-1970, *Notes From the Second Year,* the largest and most comprehensive feminist journal to date, was published. The journal, which sold over 40,000 copies, contained 126 pages of articles, tracts, personal testimonials, theoretical analyses of feminist issues and movement politics. Although *Notes* was specifically a radical feminist publication, there were also politico journals, movement newsletters and newspapers, books, songs, films, all produced by women in the movement.

As distinct from women's rights groups, this part of the movement has grown without form or structure. In fact, for the most part this ". . . branch of the movement prides itself on its lack of organization. Eschewing structure and damning the idea of leadership, it has carried the concept of 'everyone doing her own thing' almost to its logical extreme."[3] On the one hand, this has led to experimentation and innovation in both form and thinking. One of the most characteristic aspects of the women's liberation movement is the enthusiasm and doggedness with which any and every preconceived notion, pattern of behavior, theory or analysis, is questioned. On the other hand, because of both the rejection of the traditional and the very nature of innovation itself, there is a lack of direction, and often an inability to clearly define goals, and plan and execute the actions necessary to achieve them. Actions and activities are for the most part on an *ad hoc* basis. Often they are effective as educational tactics (e.g., speak-outs on abortion, rape, etc.) but do little to effect visible changes in the social institutions.

As a result of its lack of direction, the radical branch of the movement is currently in a state of organizational disorder. "This is necessitating a good deal of retrenchment and rethinking; cities undergoing this process often give the impression of inactivity and only time will tell what will be the result."[4] Certain specific problems, tensions, and ideological issues within the movement both reveal and perpetuate this state of organizational flux: the question of leaders and elitism; the pro-woman/"anti-brainwashing" position; the problem of infiltration by tightly-organized left politics groups attempting to take over control of the movement in different cities.

---

[3] Freeman, *Origins,* p. 4.
[4] *Ibid.,* p. 11.

LEADERSHIP

The anti-leadership ethic of the women's movement had in its origin been a constructive idea—an egalitarian ideal. In a report on the Miss America demonstration in 1968, one feminist wrote:

> We didn't want leaders or spokesmen. It makes the movement not only *seem* stronger and larger if everyone is a leader, but it actually *is* stronger if not dependent on a few. It also guards against the time when such leaders could be isolated and picked off one way or another. And of course many voices are more powerful than one.[5]

The anti-leadership ethic, was considered valuable for several reasons. Women, traditionally unaccustomed to working together, organizing together, thinking of themselves as a political group, began to learn that despite differences in education and previously acquired skills, there was much they shared in common. Moreover, since skills are in fact acquired, it was imperative that women without them be encouraged to grow in new directions. To avoid the structuring of power relationships to them inherent in formally organized groups, the women were forced to search for new forms of organization. Communes were one; the lot system another. Both were partially successful but neither could be sustained. Many communes or groups which worked on projects communally ("everyone makes all the decisions") began to fall apart; several newspapers attempted communal decision-making and abandoned it. In addition, through much of 1969 and 1970 the injustices if not absurdities of an extreme commitment to the lot system became increasingly apparent. At the second Congress to Unite Women, held May 1–3, 1970, in New York City, many women recognized the tyranny and cruelty of the system. At one general meeting, a volunteer for chairwoman was turned down with shouts of "elitist" and several women were vociferous in their insistence that lots be drawn. Since there were too many women to draw by name, the lot was based on birth date. As one participant described the event,

> It was extraordinarily painful and infuriating to watch. At first nobody claimed the date. Then finally one poor

---

[5] Hanisch, *Notes 2*, pp. 87–88.

woman timidly raised her hand. She clearly didn't want to chair the meeting but she got up to do it anyway. It was a disorderly and argumentative group and they really made it rough for her. Finally, quivering with rage and on the verge of tears she told the lot-maniacs off. She said she hadn't wanted the job, and by God she wasn't going to do it anymore. It was really beautiful to watch her end it, but what an awful thing to have been put through.

The period 1969–1971 has been sometimes described as "the movement's McCarthy era." Although by no means accurate as the *sole* description of the state of the movement during this time, in cities throughout the country charges of "elitist," and "power-seeker" were leveled against individual women and groups. Women who wrote books or articles were accused of making a name for themselves "off the suffering of their sisters." At the Second Congress, a group called the Class Workshop, which included some members of The Feminists and Redstockings, had, according to participants, used "bullying tactics" in several workshop sessions. The Class Workshop women denounced others not only for elitism but racism as well. One feminist explained the attacks ". . . as the logical result of the worst kind of consciousness raising and 'theorizing.' If that's all you do, to the exclusion of anything else, then the enemy becomes the enemy within. First they attack leaders, then lifestyles, then racism. They're rallying around negatives." The group interrupted a general meeting and insisted on presenting a paper denouncing elitism. The paper outlined rules for the movement about dealing with the press and the media in general. One woman was attacked by name and accused of making a career out of the oppression of other women. According to the Class Workshop paper, collective action was the only possible and "true" way: there was no such thing as an "individual thought" or idea. Written material, if signed at all, could only bear the name of the group. The paper concluded with the assertion that any woman who did not comply with the regulations was no longer in the movement. Most of the women at the session were enraged at the Class Workshop's disruption of an on-going meeting, at the presumption of anyone claiming authority to set rules for "the movement," at the idea of a "line" at all, and at the personal attacks on individuals. As one commented, "In the name of anti-elitism, they were trying to pull off the most elitist thing possible. The meeting ended with charges and counter-charges and a distinct lack of a feeling of 'sister-hood.' "

As a result of the charges of elitism, so frequent during this period, some individual women felt forced to leave groups and withdraw from all activity in the movement. In the early summer of 1970, in New York, a group of women from cities throughout the country (some of them had founded the first groups in their respective cities) met to talk about the "purges." With mixed degrees of bitterness and humor they called themselves "feminist refugees." Although nothing came of their plan to write a series of position papers on the state of the movement, the very fact of their meeting was an indication of the depth of internal dissension in the movement.

Some groups and individuals began to realize that what was needed was a redefinition, not abandonment, of the idea of leadership; that it was necessary to make a distinction between "strong" women and "power-seeking" individuals; that unless there was recognition of the strengths, talents, and skills of individuals the movement could well head in the direction of a glorification of weaknesses; that the idea of "sisterhood" was farcical if it was used to oppress some sisters; that it was an illusion to think that, as one commented, "you can lose individuals in a collective or group."

PRO-WOMAN LINE

As with the anti-leadership ethic, the pro-woman/"anti-brainwashing" position did offer some new insights into the nature of women's situation. The emphasis on the commonality of women's experiences and the idea that female behavior had, at least in part, a rational explanation, were considered necessary for the development of a feminist consciousness. As noted earlier, however, this position led to a rejection of any criticism of women; a justification of all female behavior; and, for some, the extreme position of the glorification of female behavior, of "female culture." This female chauvinism, or cultural nationalism, led to the same organizational impasse as the anti-leadership ethic: an attack on "strong women," and by logical extension, attacks on specific individuals. As one feminist noted, "If the victim is heroine, the non-victim or woman who simply keeps her head above water, is clearly the devil." Some feminists suggest that the reason the formulation is so negative is because it has a negative source: fear and envy of the "strong" woman. In any group or movement there are those individuals who are indeed "power-hungry" and attempt to manipulate others for their own purposes. Often, however, the women singled out for attack had done little more than speak articulately, write or produce work in any other form, or assume organizational responsibilities when others failed to do so. Sometimes the attacks were stated in explicitly personal terms, sometimes couched in the rhetoric of anti-elitism. Whatever the form, the most frequent formulation was "you're oppressing me."

As noted earlier, the movement was caught up in the throes of this internal dissension at the time of the second Congress to Unite Women. As part of the program of the first evening of the Congress, Anselma dell'Olio, founder of the New Feminist Theater,[6] delivered a speech entitled, "Divisiveness and Self-Destruction in the Women's Movement: A Letter of Resignation." The speech might well be described as an enraged outcry against the direction in which the movement seemed to be going. In it she described the different kinds of attacks on individuals, examined some of the reasons for the attacks, and concluded with suggestions for overcoming the problem. The speech read in part:

> I learned three and a half years ago that women had always been divided against one another, were self-destructive and filled with impotent rage. I thought the movement would change all that. I never dreamed that I would see the day when this rage, masquerading as a pseudo-egalitarian radicalism under the "pro-woman" banner, would turn into frighteningly vicious anti-intellectual fascism of the left. . . .
>
> Before we got it from men; now we're getting it from our sisters—and often from those who espouse the pro-woman line most strongly. . . . Do anything . . . that every other woman secretly or otherwise feels she could do just as well—and baby, watch out, because you're in for it. . . .
> If, in short, you do not fit the conventional stereotype of a "feminine" woman . . . it's all over, unless you have the patience of Penelope, the shell of an armadillo and the perennial optimism of Voltaire's Candide—in which case

---

[6] See separate entry (The Arts), Chapter 10.

what the hell do you need the women's movement for any-way?

. . . Women with aggressive-assertive personalities have been getting flak all their lives for not being "lady-like" or feminine enough. They didn't join the movement to get the same shit from their sisters just because the words have changed from "unlady-like" to "male-identifier." A desire for power is no more an automatic consequence of a forceful personality than it is of a non-forceful one. "STRONG" women do not necessarily want power. "WEAK" women do not necessarily NOT want power.

. . . One last plea: If we women are ever to pull ourselves out of the morass of self-pity, self-destruction and im-potence which has been our heritage for as long as we can remember, then it is perhaps even more important that we be as supportive of each other's achievements and suc-cesses and strengths, than it is for us to be compassionate and understanding of each other's failures and weak-nesses.

The speech hit a responsive chord. There was extensive applause, and many women expressed personal "gratitude" to dell'Olio for having delivered it.

INFILTRATION

Women are often asked, "are you a member of women's libera-tion?" or "do you belong to the movement?" The fact that there is no direct answer to these questions is indicative of the nature of the movement: there is no such thing as "membership" in the movement. There are mostly small groups, some larger organiza-tions, all different in their definitions of and extent of commitment to feminism. Precisely because the movement is so formless and some groups are often self-consciously structureless, it seemed to be relatively easy for a tightly-knit organized group to infiltrate. The pattern of attempted take-overs can be seen as an extension and refinement of the politico-feminist split. In almost every case in cities around the country, the infiltrating group has been the Socialist Workers Party (SWP) and/or its youth affiliate, the Young Socialist Alliance (YSA). There is little reason to assume from the evidence so far that SWP/YSA will be successful in co-opting the women's movement as a whole. First, their efforts at control have been limited to the radical branch of the movement where they expected to find more fertile ground for entry than in the women's rights branch. However, many of the radical feminist groups, despite their initial political naivete about such maneuverings, have learned relatively quickly to "play the game" and quickly disassociate themselves from SWP/YSA. Nonetheless, since infiltration was a "problem" in the movement during 1969–1970, it warrants at least brief discussion.

SWP/YSA views itself as the vanguard of social change. Women are a constituency to be organized and led, since the feminist movement is not in and of itself a revolutionary force for change. Given SWP's political commitment to lead the masses, the masses of newly organized women are, for them, potential political material. SWP/YSA has maneuvered for control in several ways. In some cities it has attempted to take over the women's centers. The process can be particularly insidious because SWP/YSA members volunteer to do menial paperwork. By controlling what appears to be administrative/trivial detail they put themselves in a position of knowing all about a city's various groups and activities, assuming an important role in the organizing of new groups, and preparing and distributing written material and dispensing information. In New York City for example, they were at first successful in taking over the Women's Center. However, within a short period of time the women, realizing what was happening, voted to bar anyone who was affiliated with SWP/YSA from working on administrative and policy-making committees.

Within the radical movement perhaps the most widely known co-optation challenge was SWP/YSA's attempted control of the radical feminist publication *A Journal of Female Liberation* (*No More Fun and Games*), produced by Cell 16 in Boston. Cell 16's own statements are the best description of its politics:

> Because we were a small group and in political agreement, our democracy was spontaneous. When political disagreement arose with one or two of our original members, we disbanded the group as a formal entity rather than to either impose the majority will on those who disagreed or waste time in conflict with each other.[7]

[7] All quotations are from Cell 16's mimeographed newsletter detailing the attempted takeover by YSA.

The women reconstituted themselves as a Committee to put out the journal. They rented an office which was turned into a women's center by new women and some old Cell 16 members who had joined YSA. At first the journal women refused to take action against the YSAers because they felt ". . . that until there was an overt attempt to take control of the *Journal* or office we were not justified in purging people with whom we had worked comfortably in the past." Within a short period of time there was ample justification. By mid-November 1970, a series of melodramas ensued with YSA attempting, in part successfully, to appropriate *Journal* funds, files and mailing lists. Cell 16 reformed under its original name and, in a three-page newsletter mailed to subscribers of the *Journal*, friends, women's newspapers, and groups around the country, described in detail the attempted takeover by YSA.

SWP/YSA infiltration tactics have not been limited to radical feminist groups or centers. In Chicago, for example, the politico-oriented women's liberation movement has had problems with SWP. Politico women's groups espouse the position that feminism has no revolutionary potentiality separate from the socialist revolution, and that the feminist movement can in fact be counterrevolutionary precisely because it insists on a separate definition and existence. This view is to all intents and purposes shared by SWP/YSA. There are important differences between the two, however. Politico women's groups, while part of the new left movement, are nonetheless often independent of new left organizations and value their autonomy as such. SWP and YSA are part of the "old left" and as such are highly structured and firmly committed to a political "line." With groups such as Cell 16, the conflict with SWP was not simply a question of political maneuverings—power politics—and the disruption of work, but a profound disagreement about politics: the definition and goals of feminism. With politico groups, the conflict with SWP is primarily twofold: although the goal for both is the socialist revolution, the "generation gap" has produced a partial difference in rhetoric and a profound difference in style.

• • •

The women's liberation branch of the movement has undergone since its inception an extraordinary rate of growth. Having rejected traditional analyses and organizational patterns, its chronological evolution has, much more than that of the women's rights branch, been marked by important conceptual and structural changes. Although the movement has been described as being in a state of organizational flux, it is well to keep in mind the fact that the very freshness and newness of its approach to both thought and structure, which produce problems, is likely to provide the creativity to solve those problems.

II

Feminist Analysis:
Ideas and Issues

ALTHOUGH FEMINISM has a long history, the contemporary feminist movement is sufficiently new that there is no systematically-organized body of the new feminist thought. Books, journals, magazines, newsletters, newspapers, and mimeographed essays are being written and distributed at an extraordinary rate. Although pieces have been written that are already considered "classics" within the movement, there is no single recognized theoretician or theory of the movement. Instead, the theoretical formulations are scattered throughout the multitude of feminist writings. One can, however, abstract from these writings and construct the main outlines of feminist thought.

The subsequent discussion has been drawn in large part from radical feminist writings for several reasons. The women's movement, encompassing as it does such a diversity of individuals and groups, has adherents who represent almost every shade of political opinion regarding both women's issues as well as traditional political concerns—"We . . . have our right wing and left wing, our separatists, gradualists, and Uncle Toms. But we are changing our own consciousness, and that of the country."[1] Since radical feminists are the ones most concerned with raising consciousness, they tend to formulate the theory and analysis. In addition, by understanding the "pure" feminist critique, all the

---

[1] Gloria Steinem, testimony, *ERA Hearings 1,* p. 334.

variations of thought in the movement are cast into sharp relief. It is, moreover, radical feminist thought that is new or "revolutionary." Indeed, the very attack upon the social manifestations of discrimination against women in large part rests on the new feminist understanding of the psychological oppression of women. Moderate feminists, while subscribing to much of the analysis, have for the most part directed their energies toward actions largely within the traditional framework of political activity. Politico feminist analysis, on the other hand, is in large measure formulated in the language of socialism which is not necessarily feminist; moreover, the specifically socialist critique can be found elsewhere. When moderate and politico feminist analyses differ significantly from the radical feminist framework, the differences will be noted.

The ideas and issues explored in almost all of the new feminist writings fall into two major areas of concern:

—Analysis of the "biological differences" argument: the single most important assumption of feminist analysis is that there are no inherent emotional, intellectual, or psychological differences between men and women. All differences that are considered to be rooted in "nature" are, according to feminists, a reflection of socially-imposed values.

—Feminist social critique: feminists describe the social values which distinguish male from female (on the basis of psychological characteristics and social roles) as a system of sex-role stereotyping. They are examining the ways in which the sex-role system, based on the unquestioned acceptance of the asserted differences between men and women, has in fact "created" those very differences. Thus, much of feminist writing is concerned with analyzing social institutions and values which reflect and reinforce the sex-role system: the family, the educational system, marriage, social expectations, etc.

In addition to these two major areas of concern, feminists are also writing about and analyzing the kinds of resistance the women's movement has encountered. Since feminist thought addresses itself to the "biological differences" argument, a critique of society, and resistances to feminism, an examination of feminist thought can best be understood by a detailed discussion of these three areas of concern. The remainder of the section is divided accordingly.

3

"Biological Differences" Argument

ALL SOCIAL ANALYSIS begins with assumptions about the basic nature—the inherent characteristics—of human beings. Generally-accepted social analysis assumes that the differences between the sexes (psychological, emotional, etc.) are inherent because they reflect the biological differences between male and female.

Feminist analysis, on the other hand, begins with the assumption of the absolute equality of men and women notwithstanding biological differences. Humanness and not anatomy is the irreducible component that both men and women share. This analysis holds that the socially unequal position of women throughout history is not the result of biology, but rather the result of the value society has placed, at any given time, on the biological differences between the sexes.

Thus feminist and generally-accepted social analyses are to all intents and purposes irreconcilable precisely because the underlying assumptions about the basic nature of human beings are diametrically opposed. Perhaps the only observation both feminist and anti-feminist thought accept in common is that social roles and social institutions have been structured and defined on the basis of biological (translated into emotional and psychological) differences.

Theories of biological determinism underlying the projection of social roles and characteristics onto racial, ethnic and religious groups have been recognized as inherently discriminatory and oppressive. Only in the realm of sex is such determinism still deemed valid. Feminists view biological determinism with regard to sex-role differentiation as equally discriminatory and oppressive. As noted above, feminist analysis holds that the facts of biology take on the values society imposes on them. These values are not neutral; they are social judgments which, according to feminists, consign women in the name of "the natural" to inferior status.[2]

Feminists attack the social interpretations of biological distinctions on scientific, moral, and technological grounds.

Science

TWO BRANCHES of science are most often used to describe and interpret woman's nature: biology and psychology. Feminists argue that observation and analysis in both fields are marked by bias and distortion. In the field of biology there are several approaches to the question of woman's nature. One is the study of primate behavior from which are deduced characteristic role and behavioral patterns for humans; another is the study of the ways in which the sex hormones purportedly effect differences between male and female behavior.

PRIMATE STUDIES

The title of a paper presented at a recent Anthropological Association convention is indicative of the problem of relating primate to human behavior: "Role incompatibility of mother-son incest among tree-ranging rhesus monkeys." Language used to describe human relationships is applied to primate behavior, and from that behavior in turn are "deduced" patterns which describe human relationships. Naomi Weisstein in an article, " 'Kinder, Kuche, Kirche' As Scientific Law: Psychology Constructs the Female," briefly notes this problem of bias in primate studies:

> After observing differences between male and female rhesus monkeys, Harlow quotes Lawrence Sterne to the

---

[2] Ruth Herschberger, in *Adam's Rib* (originally published New York: Pellegrini & Cudahy, 1948; New York: Harper & Row, 1970) describes "Mankind" as "the erector of tyrannous Norms," p. 2.

effect that women are silly and trivial, and concludes that "men and women have differed in the past and they will differ in the future."[3]

Human beings, as distinct from primates, to some extent control the "natural" conditions of their social environment and alter social groupings accordingly. Weisstein argues that one cannot draw conclusions about human behavior from primate behavior since primates lacking human inventiveness are restricted by their social environment. What she calls "the crucial experiment" has not been attempted. It

> . . . would manipulate or change the social organization of these groups, and watch the subsequent behavior. Until then, we must conclude that, since primates are at present too stupid to change their social conditions by themselves the "innateness" and fixedness of their behavior is simply not known. As applied to humans, the argument becomes patently irrelevant, since the most salient feature of human social organization is its variety; and there are a number of cultures where there is at least a rough equality between men and women.[4]

The problem of preconceptions marring the validity of "scientific" observation is thrown into sharp relief by Ruth Herschberger when she writes a fictional account (based on an actual study) of an interview with a female chimpanzee whose behavioral patterns, *vis-à-vis* a male chimpanzee, had been duly observed and recorded by a scientist. The lady chimpanzee exclaims at one point:

> When Jack takes over the food chute, the report calls it his "natural dominance." When *I* do, it's "privilege"—conferred by him. . . . While I'm up there lording it over the food chute, the investigator writes down "the male temporarily defers to her and allows her to act as if dominant over him." Can't I get any satisfaction out of life that isn't *allowed* me by some male chimp? Damn it![5]

---

[3] Naomi Weisstein, " 'Kinder, Kuche, Kirche' As Scientific Law: Psychology Constructs the Female," *Sisterhood*, p. 218, n.16. Originally a paper read at Davis, University of California American Studies Association meeting, October 26, 1968.
[4] *Ibid.*, p. 218.
[5] Herschberger, p. 10.

The female chimpanzee's conclusion is that:

> It all comes from there being so few women scientists.
> Some woman scientist ought to start passing it around
> that males must be unnatural because they don't have
> cyclical changes during the month. Then see the furor
> start. Maybe they'll see how much fun it is being deviants
> half your life.[6]

SEX HORMONES

Another biological argument supporting sex-role differentiation
rests on theories about the nature, functioning and social implications of male and female sex hormones. The political import
of the debate gained national attention when Dr. Edgar Berman,
physician and advisor to former Vice President Hubert Humphrey
and member of the Democratic Party's Committee on National
Priorities, exchanged words with Patsy Mink, Congresswoman
from Hawaii. On April 30, 1970, Rep. Mink brought up the issue
of women's rights for discussion at a Democratic Committee
meeting. Berman denied the importance of the issue by arguing
that women's physiological and hormonal characteristics, in particular the menstrual cycle and menopause, limited her capacity
for leadership. He cited two examples: "If you had an investment
in a bank, you wouldn't want the president of your bank making
a loan under these raging hormonal influences at that particular
period."[7] In a more detailed hypothesis, Berman argued:

> Suppose we had a President in the White House, a meno-
> pausal woman president who had to make the decision of
> the Bay of Pigs, or the Russian contretemps with Cuba at
> time? All things being equal, I would still rather have had
> a male J.F.K. make the Cuban missile crisis decisions
> than a female of similar age who could possibly be subject
> to the curious mental aberrations of that age group.[8]

---

[6] *Ibid.*, p. 9.
[7] Nancy L. Ross, *Washington Post*, July 29, 1970.
[8] *New York Post*, August 3, 1970. Clayton Fritchey in a column, "The Good
Doctor," speculated, "Mrs. Mink might have called the doctor's attention to
the fact that the highest officials in government (no doubt going through
the male menopause) recently wanted to lend the bankrupt Penn Central
railroad $200 million of the taxpayers' money, and had to be forcibly
restrained by Congress."

In a *Washington Post* feature story, writers Lloyd Shearer and Carol Dunlap responded:

> ... John F. Kennedy's Bay of Pigs fiasco hardly constitutes exemplary proof of superior male ability in either decision-making or crisis diplomacy. Moreover, the people of this nation now know that during his incumbency Kennedy suffered from Addison's disease, treatment for which involves the administering of cortisone, a drug which has potentially a greater disruptive effect on behavior and judgment than the periodical hormonal changes in the female.[9]

The argument from the feminist point of view does not rest on the question of John Kennedy's hormonal condition, but rather on the reality of women's consignment to her "place" on the basis of her hormonal condition.

In feminist analysis Dr. Berman and others who propound such theories are in the name of science merely reflecting the age-old fear of woman's menstrual cycle. "Menstruation and the menopause cannot by any stretch of masculine logic be regarded as evolution's answer to man's immediate pleasure. These two natural phenomena have therefore assumed an exaggerated role of tragedy in sex literature."[1] Simone de Beauvoir, author of *The Second Sex*, consistent with her thesis that the meaning attached to the differences between the sexes reflects not inherent characteristics but rather social judgments, has analyzed this "tragedy" of menstruation:

> Just as the penis derives its privileged evaluation from the social context, so it is the social context that makes menstruation a curse. The one symbolizes manhood, the other femininity; and it is because femininity signifies alterity and inferiority that its manifestation is met with shame.[2]

The hormonal changes that take place in women during menstruation are, however, only part of the whole class of sex

---

[9] *Washington Post*, February 7, 1971.
[1] Herschberger, p. 47.
[2] Simone de Beauvoir, *The Second Sex* (originally published in America, New York: Alfred A. Knopf, 1953; New York: Bantam Book, 1970), p. 295.

hormones which scientists summon to make their case for psychological and emotional differences based on biology. Feminists argue that seemingly "neutral" scientific formulations on hormonal differences obscure the fact that such evidence is used to restrict women from the full exercise of their intellectual capabilities. In this context S. L. Bem and D. J. Bem, in a paper on the socialization of women, comment, "One difficulty with this argument, of course, is that female hormones would have to be different in the Soviet Union, where one-third of the engineers and 75% of the physicians are women."[3] In addition, Weisstein in "Kinder, Kuche, Kirche" refutes studies that define emotional differences based on body chemistry with counter-studies that indicate that when changes in body chemistry are artificially induced, individuals continue to behave on the basis of what they perceive are the social expectations in any given situation.[4]

In addition to their critique of the biological sciences, feminists attack the field of psychology. Their discussion covers at least three main areas: Freudian theories of female sexuality, clinical and experimental methods, and the therapeutic process.

FREUDIAN THEORIES OF FEMALE SEXUALITY

The feminist attack on psychology is often construed as an attack on Sigmund Freud alone. Such an understanding of feminist thinking misses the central point of the argument which is that all psychological theories are in the main anti-feminist. In view of the fact that Freud's formulations are the basis of most psychoanalytic thought, and that those formulations have had an enormous impact on twentieth century thinking, Freud, in the feminist perspective, can be considered ". . . the strongest individual counterrevolutionary force in the ideology of sexual politics during the [1930–1960] period."[5]

Shulamith Firestone, in *The Dialectic of Sex: The Case for Feminist Revolution*, argues that "Freud captured the imagina-

---

[3] S. L. and D. J. Bem, "Case Study of a Nonconscious Ideology: Training the Woman to Know Her Place," *Beliefs, Attitudes and Human Affairs* (Belmont, California: Brooks/Cole, 1970), reprinted in *Green Hearings*, pp. 1042ff. See p. 1045.
[4] Weisstein, pp. 217ff.
[5] Kate Millet, *Sexual Politics* (New York: Doubleday and Co., Inc., 1970), p. 178. The period referred to, 1930–1960, was, according to Millett, a time of the reshoring of anti-feminist ideologies.

tion of a whole continent and civilization for a good reason. . . .
*Freudianism is so charged, so impossible to repudiate because
Freud grasped the crucial problem of modern life: Sexuality.*"[6]
The feminist attack on Freud, then, is in fact an attack on his
analysis of sexuality, an analysis rooted in preconceptions about
the quintessential nature of male and female, but articulated in
terms of biology:

> Although generally accepted as a prototype of the liberal
> urge toward sexual freedom, and a signal contributor to-
> ward softening traditional puritanical inhibitions upon
> sexuality, the effect of Freud's work, that of his followers,
> and still more that of his popularizers, was to rationalize
> the invidious relationship between the sexes, to ratify tradi-
> tional roles, and to validate temperamental differences.[7]

It is by no means original with feminism to examine
Freud's ideas and theories in their historical context. There have
been, for example, serious studies of Freud by non-feminists,
which have described the world in which he lived and thought,
analyzed his biases and prejudices and how they influenced his
theories, rejected or significantly altered key Freudian concepts
of sexuality precisely because they had been formulated in the
context of his times and therefore are not applicable today. These
same components of Freud's theories of sexuality—penis envy,
castration, Oedipal and Electra complexes, narcissism and masochism, etc.—come under feminist review as well. What is significant in feminist analysis and qualitatively different from
"break-away" schools of psychology is the feminist perception that
the entire construct of psychology is based on the male "nature"
as the norm. Thus even when specific Freudian theories about
women and their sexuality have been questioned and rejected by
non-feminists, the *implications* of these theories—women are
passive; receivers and nurturers—have remained largely unchal-
lenged.

On these grounds Erik Erikson's theories, for example, come
under feminist attack. In his essay "Inner and Outer Space: Re-

---

[6] Shulamith Firestone, *The Dialectic of Sex: The Case for Feminist Revolution* (New York: William Morrow and Co., Inc., 1970), pp. 48–49. Hereafter referred to as *Dialectic*.
[7] Millett, p. 178.

flections on Womanhood,"[8] Erikson rejects the idea of "genital trauma," or penis envy. However, despair for lack of the male organ is replaced by the joy of "inner space." Feminists argue that such a theory of biological destiny is as overtly oppressive and covertly pernicious as race-based justifications of the doctrine of "separate but equal." In contrast to the theory of penis envy, Millett describes Erikson's theories of "uterine glorification [as] . . . a gentler form of persuasion."[9]

One concept central to Freudian theories of female sexuality deserves special attention[1] because it sparked the contemporary feminist examination of all of psychological thought and has drawn the greatest public attention; that is, the Freudian theory of the double, or vaginal, orgasm. According to Freud the transition of the young girl into womanhood was accompanied by a corresponding transition from clitoral to vaginal orgasm. Although a woman did not lose the capacity for clitoral orgasm, in Freudian theory chronological and psychological growth into maturity required that she experience the vaginal orgasm. By this standard, subscribers to the theory could argue:

> . . . whenever a woman is incapable of achieving an orgasm via coitus, provided the husband is an adequate partner, and prefers clitoral stimulation to any other form of sexual activity, she can be regarded as suffering from frigidity and requires psychiatric assistance.[2]

Large numbers of women with this "problem" were subsequently diagnosed as frigid and subject for treatment. The sensitivity of the clitoris had long been known. Kinsey's studies of human sexuality in the late forties and early fifties not only supported such knowledge but indicated as well the lack of evidence for the vaginal orgasm. In 1948 (pre-Kinsey) Herschberger had written, in a chapter entitled "A Minor Mystery," "One finds in the annals of love the leading vision of woman as a harp upon which the

---

[8] Erik H. Erikson, "Inner and Outer Space: Reflections on Womanhood," *Daedalus*, The Journal of the American Academy of Arts and Sciences (Spring, 1964).
[9] Millett, p. 213.
[1] For detailed feminist analyses of psychological and sociological theories which root personality (psychological) differences in male-female biological differentiation, see de Beauvoir, Firestone, Millett.
[2] Frank S. Caprio, M.D., *The Sexually Adequate Female* (Greenwich, Conn.: Fawcett Publications, Inc., 1953, 1966), p. 64.

husband plays a melody. . . . In the symphony of love, the lost chord is a small organ lying somewhat north of the vagina."[3] With their publication of *Human Sexual Response* in 1966, Masters and Johnson clinically disproved the existence of a vaginal orgasm. Yet it remained for the new feminist movement to put the idea of the vaginal orgasm in a political context. In 1968–69 feminists began to discuss both the scientific data and their social implications.[4]

The first new feminist article on the vaginal orgasm was written by Anne Koedt and appeared in the June, 1968, publication *Notes From the First Year* as a short essay entitled "The Myth of the Vaginal Orgasm." These brief notes were later expanded into an article with the same name in *Notes From the Second Year.* In this by now "classic" in movement literature, Koedt pointed to the crucial distinction between areas of arousal and area of response and noted that "Because of the lack of knowledge of their own anatomy, some women accept the idea that an orgasm felt during 'normal' intercourse was vaginally caused."[5]

In the essay, she reviewed the data and analyzed the reasons "Why Men Maintain the Myth," concluding:

> All this leads to some interesting questions about conventional sex and our role in it. Men have orgasms essentially by friction with the vagina, not the clitoral area, which is external and not able to cause friction the way penetration does. Women have thus been defined sexually in terms of what pleases men; our own biology has not been properly analyzed. Instead, we are fed the myth of the liberated woman and her vaginal orgasm—an orgasm which in fact does not exist.

> What we must do is redefine our sexuality. We must discard the "normal" concepts of sex and create new guidelines which take into account mutual sexual enjoyment.[6]

---

[3] Herschberger, p. 30.
[4] Until that time, only Ruth Herschberger had examined the social implications of the data in a feminist context. In a report by Susan Brownmiller, "Sisterhood is Powerful" (*New York Times Magazine,* March 15, 1970), p. 130, Herschberger is quoted, "When I wrote *Adam's Rib,* I was writing for readers who wouldn't accept the first premise. Now there was a whole roomful of people and a whole new vocabulary."
[5] *Notes 2,* pp. 39–40.
[6] *Ibid.,* pp. 37–38. In the early days of the movement, there was a great

Clinical and Experimental Psychology

Most feminists would not deny that there *may* be inherent psychological and emotional differences between men and women. They argue, however, that male-female behavior has never been studied in a value-free atmosphere. It is, in fact, quite possible that there are more differences among individuals than between the sexes. In this light, Samuel Johnson, who was once asked, "which is more intelligent, man or woman?" replied "which man and which woman?"

Thus feminists are questioning not only psychological theories but the evidence used to support them. In her paper, "Kinder, Kuche, Kirche," Weisstein examines the biases implicit in both clinical practice and academic psychologcal research. "Psychology has nothing to say about what women are really like, what they need and what they want, essentially, because psychology does not know,"[7] precisely because the criteria for gathering and evaluating information are invalid. She argues that analysis and evaluation on the basis of "clinical experience" is a process of fitting evidence to existing theories. For example:

> . . . those who claim that fifty years of psychoanalytic experience constitute evidence enough of the essential truths of Freud's theory should ponder the robust health of the double orgasm. Did women, until Masters and Johnson, believe they were having two different kinds of orgasm? Did their psychiatrists cow them into reporting something that was not true? If so, were there other things they reported that were also not true? Did psychiatrists ever learn anything different than their theories had led them to believe? If clinical experience means anything at all, surely we should have been done with the double orgasm myth long before the Masters and Johnson studies.[8]

Moreover, clinical experience resting as it does on "insight" and "intuition" cannot be empirically validated. Weisstein cites

---

deal of resistance among some of the women to the idea that the vaginal orgasm was a myth. For more detailed discussion, see separate entry (The "Sexual Revolution"), Chapter 4.

[7] Weisstein, p. 208.

[8] *Ibid.*, p. 210.

studies that demonstrate that psychological testers, specifically chosen on the basis of their clinical experience:

> . . . do no better than chance in identifying which of a certain set of stories were written by men and which by women; which of a whole battery of clinical test results are the products of homosexuals and which are the prodducts of heterosexuals. . . .[9]

She also examines personality and behavior testing procedures and argues that built into testing methods are biases which reflect the testers' assumptions about the basic patterns of human behavior. Among the studies she reviews is the Rosenthal and Jacobson series of tests revealing experimenter bias in expectations of student achievement which influenced the actual performance of students.[1] She concludes that any examination of psychological and behavior patterns without regard for the social context in which they occur will reflect not "reality" but prejudice:

> In some extremely important ways, people are what you expect them to be, or at least they behave as you expect them to behave. Thus, if women, according to Bruno Bettelheim, want first and foremost to be good wives and mothers, it is extremely likely that that is what Bruno Bettelheim (and the rest of society) want them to be.[2]

THE THERAPEUTIC PROCESS

The feminist critique of psychology extends beyond the attack on the definitions of female sexuality and the questionable validity of psychology's empirical method. Feminists are also arguing that the popularization of psychology, to the point where almost anything is subject for "analysis," has made psychology:

> . . . our modern Church. We attack it only uneasily, for you never know, on the day of final judgment, whether they *might be right*. Who can be sure that he is as a

---

[9] *Ibid.*, p. 211.
[1] R. Rosenthal and L. Jacobson, *Pygmalion in the Classroom: Teacher Expectation and Pupil's Intellectual Development* (New York: Holt, Rinehart & Winston, 1968).
[2] Weisstein, pp. 215ff.

healthy as he can get? Who is functioning at his highest
capacity? And who not scared out of his wits? Who
doesn't hate his mother and father? Who doesn't compete
with his brother? What girl at some time did not wish she
were a boy? And for those hardy souls who persist in their
skepticism, there is always that dreadful word *resistance*.
They are the ones who are sickest: it's obvious, they fight
it so much.[3]

Yet it is precisely on these grounds that feminists attack the
therapeutic situation. Apparent to critics of psychology in general is the inherent contradiction in the psychoanalytic process:
if one recognizes that there are inequities, if not ills, in society
in general, how can one justify a process through which the
individual learns to adjust to a "sick society"? Certainly, in feminist analysis, society in all its manifestations is marked by
sexism. Thus the psychoanalytic process for women has meant
that women's neuroses, "hysteria" and "sickness," are often
measured by the yardstick which defines "health" for women as
the recognition and acceptance of their feminine role. Therapy
for women is thus potentially harmful because it attempts
". . . the resolution of a problem within the environment that
created it."[4]

Feminists attack the "scientific case" for biological differences
on semantic grounds as well. For implicit in scientific analysis is
the assumption that biological and psychological data are by
definition unbiased, a mere recording of observation. Herschberger's book, *Adam's Rib,* is in large part a semantic analysis of
woman's secondary status. In one of the more pointed discussions, she writes a typical textbook description of embryonic
genital development and sperm-egg contact and suggests that this
traditionally-accepted description is in fact a "patriarchal" account. She then compares it to what might be called a "matriarchal" account, equally unacceptable. The contrast, however,
highlights the biases implicit in what is assumed to be "objective"
description. Several examples suffice to illustrate the point:
The "patriarchal" account:

> The female, we find, does not develop in any important
> way from the asexual or early embryonic state. Her sexual

[3] Firestone, *Dialectic,* p. 47.
[4] *Ibid.,* p. 52.

organs remain in an infantile condition, displaying an early arrest of development.

Whereas in the male the genital tubercle progresses rapidly toward the mature penis form, the genital tubercle in the female embryo slowly regresses until it forms the clitoris, or vestigial penis, a minute glans hidden in an upper depression of the vulva.

The female egg is incapable of self-motion. It is dependent on mechanical means for transportation from the ovary to the fallopian tube, where it is fertilized by the male sperm. It is significant that only one egg is provided each month in the female, while billions of active sperm are produced in the male for the purposes of reproduction.

The "matriarchal" account, obvious in its satire, throws the "patri archal" description into sharp relief:

The male, we find, does not develop in any important way from the asexual or early embryonic state. His sexual organs remain in an infantile condition, displaying an early arrest of development.

Whereas in the female the genital tubercle becomes the complex and highly differentiated organ, the clitoris, in the male the infantile genital projection remains, merely thickening and growing larger. The penis is best described as a vestigial clitoris which has lost much of its sensitivity.

In the complex tissues of the ovary one egg each month attains maturity. The ovum is composed of very rich and highly specialized material. By the active pressure of its growth, it produces a slit in the wall of the ovary and escapes into the abdominal cavity. From here it works its way into the fallopian tube aided by active cilia and moisture.

The sperm are provided with a continuous enclosed passageway from the testes to the penis, thus making their conveyance as simple as possible. For the female, how-

ever, there is a remarkable gap between ovary and tube, a
gap which the egg must traverse alone. When we consider
that an egg never gets lost on its route, we realize the
striking efficiency of the female sexual mechanism.[5]

As noted earlier, feminists rebut the "biological differences"
argument not only on scientific but on moral and technological
grounds as well.

Morality

However articulated, the one proposition that all feminists
agree with is that women are an oppressed, dominated, discriminated against group. That this secondary status is interpreted as a logical extension of woman's biology is to feminists
morally untenable. The moral argument is simple and clear-cut:
domination of one group by another is immoral. Moreover, in
accordance with feminist analysis, to deny that women are "the
second sex" by calling them a "separate sex," is to deny both
historical reality and libertarian traditions.

Nearly one hundred years ago early American feminists wrote
in the introduction to the six-volume *History of Woman Suffrage:*

> It is often asserted that as woman has always been man's
> slave—subject—inferior—dependent, under all forms of
> government and religion, slavery must be her normal con-
> dition. This might have some weight had not the vast
> majority of men also been enslaved for centuries to kings
> and popes, and orders of nobility, who, in the progress of
> civilization, have reached complete equality. . . . Woman's
> steady march onward, and her growing desire for a broader
> outlook, prove that she has not reached her normal con-
> dition, and that society has not yet conceded all that is
> necessary for its attainment.

Moreover, feminists argue that society has still "not yet conceded
all that is necessary" for woman to attain her "normal condition." In February, 1971, ninety years after the publication of the

---
[5] All quotations, Herschberger, pp. 74–83.

first two volumes of *History of Woman Suffrage, McCall's* magazine printed a study based on six months' research listing hundreds of state-by-state laws that still discriminate against women.[6]

In addition, feminists argue that the idea of separate but equal status is antithetical to generally-accepted social traditions that deem respect for the identity and liberty of the individual to be central to democratic civilization:

> . . . suppose that it *could* be demonstrated that black Americans, on the *average*, did possess an inborn better sense of rhythm than white Americans. Would *that* justify ignoring the unique characteristics of a *particular* black youngster from the very beginning and specifically socializing him to become a musician? We don't think so. Similarly, as long as a woman's socialization does not nurture her uniqueness, but treats her only as a member of a group on the basis of some assumed *average* characteristic, she will not be prepared to realize her own potential in the way that the values of individuality and self-fulfillment imply she should.[7]

The moral issue becomes crucial in feminist analysis with regard to the generally-accepted belief that since women give birth to children, motherhood is their most important, if not their only acceptable, social role. Women have the capacity to bear children; but they have, according to feminists, however, the choice to do so or not. The distinction between capacity and choice or desire has been obscured by the idea of need:

> Women don't need to be mothers any more than they need spaghetti. . . . But if you're in a world where everyone is eating spaghetti, thinking they need it and want it, you will think so too. Romance has really contaminated science. So-called instincts have to do with stimulation. They are not things that well up inside of you.[8]

Thus feminists claim as an unassailable moral right a woman's complete control of her reproductive capacity.

---

[6] "Women's Legal Rights in 50 States: The Geography of Inequality," *McCall's*, February, 1971, pp. 90–95.
[7] Bems, p. 1045.
[8] Dr. Richard Rabkin, psychiatrist, quoted in "Motherhood—Who Needs It?" by Betty Rollin, *Look* magazine, September 22, 1970, p. 15.

The libertarian response to the feminist position is twofold and, feminists note, contradictory. On the one hand, history is perceived as a slow process of change bringing about the gradual elimination of social inequality: women in time will achieve their rights. In the second argument, the idea of woman's *rights* is transformed in'o the idea of woman's *rightful place:* although political, social and economic inequalities are indeed unjust, woman's true happiness lies not in the "active life," but in the home. To take this argument to its logical conclusion one would have to assert that all women in every century who have fought for, or simply desired, something more than motherhood were, and are today, maladjusted and neurotic. Joseph Rheingold, a Harvard Medical School psychiatrist, virtually does so in a book published in 1964:

> Anatomy decrees the life of a woman. . . . When women grow up without dread of their biological functions and without subversion by feminist doctrine, and therefore enter upon motherhood with a sense of fulfillment and altruistic sentiment, we shall attain the goal of a good life and a secure world in which to live it.[9]

To deny psychologically what is acknowledged politically is to highlight the moral dilemma implicit in the social meanings attached to woman's anatomy. Thus, according to feminists, arguments about "woman's place" in the world are in fact rationalizations about women's subservient social status. Feminists deem this not only immoral but particularly repugnant in light of our ignorance of the true implications, if any, of woman's biology.

Technology

THE TECHNOLOGICAL BASIS on which feminists refute the traditionally accepted social implications of woman's biology is particularly interesting because it would seem to be a natural out-

---

[9] Joseph Rheingold, *The Fear of Being a Woman* (New York: Grune & Stratton, 1964), p. 714.

growth of the *traditionally* accepted understanding of the progress of civilization. Yet it is the argument which most horrifies its opponents.

The history of civilization can be seen as the steadily increasing refinement of tools with which to challenge if not control the exigencies and overcome the limitations of nature. Man has transcended the limitations of his anatomy: he has clothed himself to cover his nakedness; built shelters against the cold; fashioned tools and implements to grow, gather, manufacture and exchange goods; invented and mass-produced vast machines to transport himself and his goods over the face of the earth. Yet the idea of woman transcending the limitations of her anatomy has met with resistance at every step of the way. Perhaps most important, woman has been rooted to the biological family, her function, reproduction. Our technology is sufficiently advanced for women to control with some degree of success this anatomical destiny through contraception and abortion. Yet there is still widespread resistance to the free and readily available dissemination of birth control information, and even more resistance to changing/eliminating the restrictive abortion laws that exist in almost every state of the Union.

In refuting the ideology and institutions of male supremacy some feminists are involved in tortuous attempts to deny biological differences between men and women (e.g., "the only reason men are physically stronger is that they are trained to be," etc.), excepting, of course, genital differences. Foregoing all these attempts, Firestone in *The Dialectic of Sex* argues that man's domination over woman does originate in biological differentiation. She points out, however, that it is the reproductive functions of these differences, not the differences as such, that lie at the root of male domination. Woman bound by her biology, her "nature," to undergo the physical disruptions of menstruation, childbirth and nurture was originally dependent upon man for protection and the production of other services necessary for survival. But, ". . . the 'natural' is not necessarily a 'human' value. Humanity has begun to outgrow nature: we can no longer justify the maintenance of a discriminatory sex class system on grounds of its origin in Nature."[1]

Although scientific experimentation in test-tube fertilization and artificial placentas is already being undertaken, there still

---

[1] Firestone, *Dialectic*, p. 10.

exists an enormous cultural bias that has inhibited extensive research and experimentation:

> Are people, even scientists themselves, culturally prepared for any of this? Decidedly not. . . . The money allocated for specific kinds of research, the kinds of research done are only incidentally in the interests of women when at all. For example, work on the development of an artificial placenta still has to be excused on the grounds that it might save babies born prematurely.[2]

Not all women in the women's movement are prepared to raise these questions either. For some, the fear of being labeled "unnatural" persists. This resistance might be assumed to lessen somewhat as the women's movement grows not only in size but in the security of its analysis. It is important to point out, however, that for other feminists, as radical in their thinking as Firestone, technological changes in the reproductive process are less central to their analysis of oppression than other issues. Although they are in complete agreement with the call for repeal of all abortion restrictions (for a woman has the absolute right to control her body), they argue that the development of technological devices to change the process of reproduction does not *necessarily* get to the root of the problem. In their analysis, the very idea that women are limited by their biology is a function of the psychology of oppression. That is, "When the power men exercise over women, which is a product of the *psychological* needs of the male ego, is eliminated, the belief that the childbearing process is necessarily oppressive will also be eliminated."[3]

There is, however, some resistance within the women's movement itself to arguments for technological control of reproduction. It has been noted earlier that there exists an ideological division between radical and politico feminists. Some of the women are divided along these lines on the issue of abortion. The black liberation movement has charged that birth control in general and abortion in particular are government programs for the planned genocide of black people. Militant blacks argue that the importance of expanding the black population as a bedrock for gaining political power increases in direct proportion to govern-

---

[2] *Ibid.*, p. 225.
[3] Anne Koedt, "Some Views on the Institution of Motherhood," unpublished paper.

mental zeal in fostering birth control programs in poor and black communities. In an article, "Genocide? Women Re-Examine Abortion Demands," the author questions one of the basic aims of the women's movement—the right of all women to control their own bodies. She argues that birth control:

> . . . is an international strategy . . . in application throughout the world; in Vietnam population control of uncontrollables takes the form of outright genocide, but in Latin America, India, here, and in American colonies birth control is the favored method.[4]

This politico argument is centered around the belief that significant differences exist between black and white women's experiences and until the women's liberation movement, predominantly white and middle-class, begins to understand the black experience, it may be expending its energies in fruitless directions. She raises the possibility that if there is any truth to the idea of a genocide campaign against black and other minority women, ". . . our sisterly concern for abortion victims begins to look like a blind."[5]

Feminists, on the other hand, argue that whether or not a woman chooses to have an abortion, she must have the right to make that choice. Moreover, they point to the fact that poor, black and other minority group women are victims along with white women of repressive abortion laws. Thus the case might be made that abortion restrictions, and not the lack of them, constitute a "genocide" program particularly for all poor women who constitute the largest percentage of illegal abortion cases (and fatalities).

In *The Dialectic of Sex*, Firestone acknowledges the fact that governments seem almost too willing to dispense "birth control devices to the Third World or to Blacks and the poor in the U.S. . . . ."[6] But she argues that although the fear is well-founded:

> . . . it is also responsible for a general failure of vision on the Left to see beneath the evil effects of birth control to a genuine ecological problem, which no number of fancy

---

[4] Lynn Phillips, *Everywoman*, January 22, 1971, p. 17. Reprinted from *Liberated Guardian*, December 14, 1970.
[5] *Ibid.*, p. 18.
[6] Firestone, *Dialectic*, p. 223.

arguments and bogey statistics can erase. . . . Once again
radicals have failed to think radically enough: capitalism
is not the *only* enemy, redistribution of wealth and resources are not the *only* solution, attempts to control
population are not *only* Third World Suppression in dis-
guise.[7]

In this light she asks ". . . do the black militants who advocate
unchecked fertility for black women allow *themselves* to become
burdened with heavy bellies and too many mouths to feed? One
gathers that they find contraception of some help in maintaining
their active preaching schedules."[8]

A number of black activist women, who are committed to the
battle for black liberation and either explicitly or implicitly de-
nounce what they perceive as "genocidal" policies, nonetheless
argue that abortion and contraceptive methods are essential. In
an essay, "The Pill: Genocide or Liberation?" Toni Cade wrote:

I agree it is a sinister thing for the state to tell anyone not
to have a child. And I know it's not for nothing, certainly
not for love, that b.c. clinics have been mushrooming in
our communities. . . . But. . . . Seems to me the Brother
does us all a great disservice by telling her to fight the
man with the womb. Better to fight with the gun and the
mind. . . . The all too breezy no-pill/have-kids/mess-up-
the-man's-plan notion these comic-book-loving Sisters find
so exciting is very seductive because it's a clear-cut and
easy thing for her to do for the cause since it nourishes
her sense of martyrdom. If the thing is numbers merely,
what the hell. But if we are talking about revolution, creating an army for today and tomorrow, I think the Brothers who've been screaming these past years had better go
do their homework.[9]

It should be noted that both moderate and radical feminists
reject "genocide" as an argument for not supporting abortion law
repeal. The demand for total control of a woman's own reproduction functions thus remains a central issue for most of the women
in the movement. With the technology available, there is no

---

[7] *Ibid.*, pp. 223–224.
[8] *Ibid.*, p. 224.
[9] Cade, *The Black Woman*, pp. 167–168.

longer any reason, they argue, for the continuance of restrictions.

Apart from the question of reproduction, the secondary sex characteristics of musculature are often invoked to justify a socially-acceptable sex-role differentiation: the physical frailty of woman prohibits her participation in the outside-the-home work of society. In 1851, well in advance of significant labor-saving technological developments, Sojourner Truth, an ex-slave, questioned this proposition. In a speech before a woman's rights convention in Akron, Ohio, she said:

> The man over there says women need to be helped into carriages and lifted over ditches, and to have the best place everywhere. Nobody ever helps me into carriages or over puddles, or gives me the best place—and ain't I a woman? . . . Look at my arm! I have ploughed and planted and gathered into barns, and no man could head me—and ain't I a woman? I could work as much and eat as much as a man—when I could get it—and bear the lash as well! And ain't I a woman? I have born thirteen children, and seen most of 'em sold into slavery, and when I cried out with my mother's grief, none but Jesus heard me—and ain't I a woman?[1]

Even if one were to argue that women had been dependent in the past on men's physical strength for protection and provision, technological developments have sufficiently altered the nature of human labor so that most work today requires if anything physical dexterity rather than strength. Nonetheless, the bias of "men's work" persists. Indeed, feminists point out that "Women's weaker physical constitution has never exempted them from hard physical labor in the United States in the home, in factories, in the fields." Rather, women have been excluded from "the most valued forms of human achievement"[2]—intellectual—which are not dependent upon physical strength.

---

[1] Reprinted in Flexner, *Century of Struggle*, pp. 90–91.
[2] Dr. Ann Sutherland Harris, testimony, *Green Hearings*, p. 239.

The Politics of Biological Differences

FROM THE FOREGOING DISCUSSION it is apparent that the scientific disciplines are antithetical to feminism. Whether defined in chemical, psychological or sociological terms the common base of all the theories is that there is an irreducible natural component in woman that can be characterized as passive, receiving, unassertive, submissive, and by implication, non-intellectual, illogical and emotional. Women who are assertive and intellectual are, therefore, not "natural" women; for woman, given her natural characteristics finds her only real fulfillment in the home and motherhood. For feminists, this projection of social roles on the basis of physiological function takes an interesting twist: man biologically implants his seed in woman. This act is then translated metaphorically to define his social function as one of planting his seed in the world. Man is to create and build in the world. Woman biologically is the receiver of the seed which she nurtures within her body. There is, however, no metaphorical translation: her social function is to nurture man's seed first in the womb and then in the home. A man's social role is determined by whatever he does with his human potential; a woman's social role is motherhood. A man needs the world to be "fulfilled"; a woman needs a man.

The question "Where is it written that a uterus uniquely qualifies a woman to wield dust mops and wash dishes?"[3] is to women in the movement a question of politics. For according to feminist analysis, hidden in the language of scientific fact is a political fiction, or myth, of male supremacy. Feminists argue that the cultural articulation of male supremacy has taken varied forms throughout history, its single purpose, however, to maintain control over the other half of humanity. When and wherever feminism has arisen, new and more sophisticated political fictions are developed. Thus in their analysis the intensification of the ideology of male supremacy has been in direct proportion to the growth of feminism.[4]

Simone de Beauvoir's description of the status of women in the period of the Roman Empire is applicable:

[3] Lucy Komisar, testimony, *Green Hearings*, p. 423.
[4] See particularly Millett, pp. 157–235.

Thus it was just when woman was most fully emancipated that the inferiority of her sex was asserted, affording a remarkable example of the process of male justification of which I have spoken: when women's rights as daughter, wife, or sister are no longer limited, it is her equality with man, as a sex, that is denied her; "the imbecility, the weakness of the sex" is alleged, in domineering fashion.[5]

According to feminists, to attempt to root male supremacy in nature is to define the position of dominance as both inherent and irrevocable, for power explicable in biological-physiological terms gives ". . . patriarchy logical as well as historical origin."[6] It provides male society with "evidence" that its position is the correct one, always has been and always will be.

Feminists argue further that there is a self-fulfilling prophecy component: when one group dominates another, the group with power is, at best, reluctant to relinquish its control. Thus in order to keep woman in "her place" theories are propounded which presume that her place is defined by nature.

---

[5] DeBeauvoir, pp. 87–88.
[6] Millet, p. 27.

4

Feminist Social Critique

FEMINIST WRITINGS in journals, newspapers, newsletters and books for the most part describe and analyze the prescribed image and roles of women in society. Some women are writing essays and compiling reports about the status of women in their respective professions. Others make much the same critique in different ways. Their writings tend to be either personal testaments or theoretical abstractions, sometimes combining both. In the personal statements women write about their childhood, school experiences, jobs, lives with husbands or lovers, housework, sex, experiences with psychologists, doctors, etc.; almost every human encounter is considered illustrative of the role of women in society. The theoretical abstractions are the transformations of the personal stories into political statements: the recognition that the individual woman's story contains generalizable truths about the ways in which women are perceived and treated by men.

From all of the written material—essays, reports, studies, personal statements, theoretical abstractions—it is clear that central to the feminist critique is the understanding that oppression has a dual manifestation: the social, i.e., social institutions; and the psychological. It is the emphasis on the psychology of oppression that most clearly distinguishes the new feminist movement from the earlier one. In the age of psychology, this emphasis is perhaps only to be expected. Yet feminists have added a unique dimension: they have politicized psychology, insisting that the "personal" is the "political."

In the July, 1970, issue of *Esquire* magazine, one woman wrote: "It is hard to fight an enemy who has outposts in your head."[1] Another speaks of "interior colonization" and says that it:

> . . . tends moreover to be sturdier than any form of segregation, and more rigorous than class stratification, more uniform, certainly more enduring. However muted its present appearance may be, sexual dominion obtains nevertheless as perhaps the most pervasive ideology of our culture and provides its most fundamental concept of power.[2]

Feminists maintain that this "pervasive ideology" cuts across all class and caste lines, is manifested in the economic, political, social-cultural spheres of life, and is reflected in language, media, laws, literature; but it is found ". . . within human consciousness even more pre-eminently than it is within human institutions."[3] Still a third feminist has described anti-feminism as a ". . . cultural iceberg: for every one-tenth which is overt, or showing, the other nine-tenths are covert—submerged in a largely unquestioned tradition of women as inferiors."[4] This "interior colonization," "cultural iceberg," "outposts in your head," is the ideology of sexism.

One can substitute sexism for racism in the dictionary definition and the meaning is apparent:

> n.l. a belief that human races [sexes] have distinctive characteristics that determine their respective cultures, usually involving the idea that one's own race [one's own sex] is superior and has the right to rule others. 2. a policy of enforcing such asserted right. 3. a system of government and society based upon it.[5]

As with racism, however, sexism has not manifested itself in society as neutrally as in a dictionary definition. Just as the white race historically has deemed itself superior, so too, according to feminists has the male sex:

---

[1] Sally Kempton, "Cutting Loose," *Esquire*, July, 1970, p. 57.
[2] Millett, p. 25.
[3] *Ibid.*, p. 63.
[4] Ann Scott, testimony, *Green Hearings*, p. 213.
[5] *The Random House Dictionary of the English Language*, Unabridged Edition (New York: Random House, 1967), p. 1184.

Radical feminism recognizes the oppression of women as a fundamental political oppression wherein women are categorized as an inferior class based upon their sex. It is the aim of radical feminism to organize politically to destroy this sex class system.[6]

It is crucial to an understanding of feminist analysis to recognize that the stated goal of feminism is freedom; and feminists argue that freedom can be achieved only by the elimination of sexism—sex-role stereotyping. For, role-typing is built on a power structure of male dominance, and the exercise of power by definition destroys freedom. The process of the destruction of freedom has been called by one feminist "metaphysical cannibalism"[7]—the consumption of another's self. The phrase "Politics of the Ego," though less vivid an image, also makes the point:

Man establishes his "manhood" in direct proportion to his ability to have his ego override woman's, and derives his strength and self-esteem through this process. This male need, though destructive, is in that sense impersonal. It is not out of a desire to hurt the woman that he dominates and destroys her; it is out of a need for a sense of power that he necessarily must destroy her ego and make it subservient to his. . . . We [women] do not choose to perform these ego services, but instead assert ourselves as primary to ourselves . . .[8]

It is upon their perception of sexism as the underlying ideology of society, molding both social institutions, social relationships, and individual psyches, that feminists base their analysis, define their goals, and undertake activities to effectuate those goals. Whatever the tactics employed and language used, the goal for feminists is a sexual revolution, not simply in the traditional usage of that phrase—an easing of moral strictures on sexual relations—but rather a revolution to eliminate sexism in all its manifestations.

It is both despair and anger about the systematic and all-pervasive denial of freedom to women that informs the feminist critique:

---

[6] "Politics of the Ego: A Manifesto for N. Y. Radical Feminists." (See Appendix.)
[7] Ti-Grace Atkinson, "Radical Feminism," *Notes 2*, p. 35.
[8] "Politics of the Ego."

No matter how many levels of consciousness one reaches, the problem always goes deeper. It is everywhere. The division Yin and Yang pervades all culture, history, economics, nature itself; modern Western versions of sex discrimination are only the most recent layer. To so heighten one's sensitivity to sexism presents problems far worse than the black militant's new awareness of racism: Feminists have to question, not just all of *Western* culture, but the organization of culture itself, and further, even the very organization of nature. Many women give up in despair: if *that's* how deep it goes they don't want to know. Others continue strengthening and enlarging the movement, their painful sensitivity to female oppression existing for a purpose: eventually to eliminate it.[9]

Sex-Role Stereotyping

IN FEMINIST ANALYSIS, the core of sexism is that a woman's identity is dependent upon her relationship with a man. The key words are *identity* and *relationship*. As de Beauvoir has written, "man is defined as a human being and woman as a female— whenever she behaves as a human being she is said to imitate the male."[1] Thus the formulation that a woman finds happiness and fulfillment as mother and homemaker is understood as an outgrowth of the more basic identity definition—that she finds happiness and fulfillment not only through her man's life but by virtue of having a man. Thus it is expected that career women, women with "lives of their own," will demonstrate signs of their womanhood. U.S. Rep. Edith Green has noted:

> When I first came to Washington, there were four women who entered the Congress that year and all the papers called up and said "We would like to take a picture of you." Every single time they wanted me to be whipping up pancakes or a cake. Finally, I just said, the congressional job is not making a cake perfectly. I will not have any

[9] Firestone, *Dialectic*, p. 2.
[1] De Beauvoir, p. 47.

more such pictures! I asked: When you ask a new male
Member of Congress to have his picture taken, do you
say, "We want a picture of you painting the window or
driving some nails to prove that you are a man?" This is
again exemplary of the psychological warfare.[2]

In an advertisement for a movie released in 1971,[3] of the
nine characters listed, six are women described as The Girlfriend,
The Nymph, Tough Lady, The Party Girl, Earth Mother, The
Mother, all of which are definitions *vis-à-vis* men. The leading
character, a man, is called The Hero. The extent to which films,
however crudely articulated, mirror basic socially-accepted values
and stereotypes, is reflected in this list of characters. Feminists
argue that however simplistic the above characterizations may
appear, they are directly expressive of the fact that a man is
measured by what he does, a woman by what she is:

> With man there is no break between public and private
> life: the more he confirms his grasp on the world in
> action and in work, the more virile he seems to be; human
> and vital values are combined in him. Whereas woman's
> independent successes are in contradiction with her
> femininity, since the "true woman" is required to make
> herself object, to be the Other.[4]

Socialization and social control are processes subtle in and of
themselves, for they are manifested most often in covert, un-
articulated ways. Not only are they difficult processes to study
and define, but they seem inherently antithetical if not antagonistic to notions of a free society operating on the basis of free
choice. In an essay "The Building of the Gilded Cage," Jo Freeman
analyses the process of the socialization of women. Introducing
the discussion, she notes:

> We have so thoroughly absorbed our national ideology
> about living in a "free society" that whatever else we may
> question . . . we are reluctant to admit that all societies,
> ours included, do an awful lot of controlling of *everyone's*

---

2 Rep. Edith Green, testimony, *Green Hearings*, p. 269.
3 Advertisement for "Pigeons," *New York Times*, February 4, 1971.
4 De Beauvoir, p. 246.

lives. We are even more reluctant to face the often subtle ways that our own attitudes and our own lives are being controlled by that same society.[5]

The socialization of role differentiation based on sex begins before the birth of the child when the "twinkle in the eye" often registers hope for a male child. When born the child is immediately put into pink or blue blankets and clothes—symbolic representations and as such informative. Among other things they are badges that tell the stranger that he/she is looking at a boy or girl. The appropriate comments follow: "Isn't he an active little one!"/"Isn't she pretty!"

From the outset of child rearing, studies on the behavior of parents reveal differences in treatment of girls and boys:

> . . . parents begin to raise their children in accord with the popular stereotypes from the very first. Boys are encouraged to be aggressive, competitive, and independent, whereas girls are rewarded for being passive and dependent. . . . In one study, six-month-old infant girls were already being touched and spoken to more by their mothers while they were playing than were infant boys. . . . No one knows to what extent . . . sex differences at the age of thirteen months can be attributed to the mothers' behavior at the age of six months, but it is hard to believe that the two are unconnected.[6]

After infancy sex-role stereotyping is much more sharply defined. Children's toys reflect the patterning: doctor kits and chemistry sets are for boys; nurse kits and "little homemaker" sets are for girls. Feminists counter the arguments that boys and girls "naturally" gravitate to separate kinds of toys and activities by arguing that preference grows out of conditioning: boys will indeed prefer trucks and girls, dolls, since these are the toys given to them.

Children's books reinforce the stereotypical roles of boys as aggressive and active, girls as passive and receiving. In an essay

---

[5] Jo Freeman, "The Building of the Gilded Cage," reprinted in *Green Hearings*, p. 273.
[6] Bems, p. 1044. Feminists challenge studies that claim to find observable behavioral differences between boys and girls shortly after birth with counter studies arguing that a "sexist bias" is built into the very process of defining observations.

on the subject, Elizabeth Fisher reported the findings of her survey of children's literature:

> I found an almost incredible conspiracy of conditioning. Boys' achievement drive is encouraged; girls' is cut off. Boys are brought up to express themselves; girls to please. The general image of the female ranges from dull to degrading to invisible.[7]

She also found that despite the fact that women are fifty-one percent of the population, they constituted only 20–30 percent of both human and animal representations. One of the most popular children's books is Richard Scarry's *Best Word Book Ever*. The two-page spread called "Things We Do" is particularly instructive of sex-role distinctions: boys dig, push, build, break, pull, eat, drink, cry, laugh, smile, jump, etc. Several words are paired or in groups of three and four: the boy *shouts*—the girl *whispers*, the boy *talks*—the girl *listens*, the boy *reads, draws*—the girl *watches* television, the boy *walks, runs, stands*—the girl *sits*.

Self-Image

ALTHOUGH YOUNG GIRLS when they begin schooling do as well if not better academically than boys, they learn rather quickly that social acceptance for a girl is not related to her intelligence, in fact can work negatively to isolate her as "a brainy one."

> Here were these bright girls, and as soon as there were boys around, they'd get babyish and dependent. That's what flirting is, for women: making yourself dependent. They'd play baseball with the boys and purposely miss the ball, or hit it and run slow, so that they'd be out. Think about that: Girls have to pretend they can't perform to impress boys. Boys have to perform *well* to impress girls. Right there is where it's all at.[8]

---

[7] Elizabeth Fisher, "The Second Sex, Junior Division," *New York Times Book Review*, May 24, 1970.
[8] Anne Koedt, as told to Martha Weinman Lear, "Five Passionate Feminists," *McCall's*, July, 1970, p. 114.

The results of Matina Horner's study of a group of under-graduate students at the University of Michigan support the conclusions Koedt drew from her personal school experience. In an article, "Fail: Bright Women," Horner calls the process the "motive to avoid success."

> . . . consciously or unconsciously the girl equates intellectual achievement with loss of femininity. A bright woman is caught in a double bind. In testing and other achievement-oriented situations she worries not only about failure, but also about success. If she fails, she is not living up to her own standards of performance; if she succeeds she is not living up to societal expectations about the female role. Men in our society do not experience this kind of ambivalence, because they are not only permitted but actively encouraged to do well.[9]

The results of her study showed that more than 65 percent of the women, as opposed to less than 10 percent of the men, were motivated to avoid success.

Women are not only motivated to avoid success for themselves, but they often perceive the achievements of other women as inherently inferior to those of men. A cyclical response pattern is set in motion in which the socially-accepted image forms the self-image and in turn reinforces the social image. Psychologist Philip Goldberg tested college women by giving them sets of professional articles from six fields. Although the articles were identical, the names of the authors in the different sets were changed. For example, in the one set an article would be authored by "John T. McKay," the same article in another set by "Joan T. McKay." Each article was to be evaluated on the basis of the expertise of the author in writing style, persuasiveness, profundity, etc. The male authors were uniformly rated superior. In his conclusion Goldberg argued that, "Women are prejudiced against female professionals and, regardless of the actual accomplishments of these professionals, will firmly refuse to recognize them as the equals of their male colleagues."[1]

---

[9] Matina Horner, "Fail: Bright Women," *Psychology Today, November,* 1969, pp. 36–37. (Reprinted in *Green Hearings.*)
[1] Philip Goldberg, "Are Women Prejudiced Against Women?" *Transaction,* April, 1968, pp. 28–30.

The Public Self-Image

SINCE A WOMAN'S IDENTITY is dependent not upon her own human accomplishments, but rather on her relationships to a man, her *success* as a woman is dependent not upon her own intelligence, but on the extent to which she satisfies the criteria of femininity. In order to be "feminine" a woman must carefully attend to her physical appearance:

> The self-consciousness we are filled with! It is so painful, so physical. We are taught to feel that our only asset is our physical presence, that that is all other people notice about us. The most minute blemish on a total person—a pimple, excess weight, a funny nose, larger than average breasts—can ruin a day, or years, with the agonies of constant awareness of it. The whole world is looking only at that pimple![2]

Thus, a woman must make herself into a sexual-erotic object to gain men's attention. The obvious accoutrements are make-up and clothes. "Ninety percent of the women in this country have an inferiority complex because they do not have turned-up noses, wear a size ten or under dress, have 'good legs,' flat stomachs, and fall within a certain age bracket."[3] These are not according to feminists frivolous concerns of women. "When you have been told all of your life that the right pair of shoes, or the right hairdo, can determine your whole destiny, it is difficult to make such decisions casually."[4] Women have become exceedingly skilled at the objectification of their bodies. Acceptance by peers, family, educators, society in general, depends upon that skill.

---

[2] Meredith Tax, "Woman and Her Mind: The Story of Everyday Life," *Notes 2*, p. 11.
[3] *The Florida Paper*, p. 17.
[4] Tax, *loc. cit.*

Social Role and Function

FEMINISTS MAINTAIN that the end result of the development, refinement and exposure of a woman's femininity is marriage,
woman's "only socially rewarded achievement."[5] If the reward is
marriage, the palliative is love. Feminists do not deny either the
need for or the potential pleasures of love. They argue, however,
that:

> Love, in the context of an oppressive male-female rela-
> tionship, becomes an emotional cement to justify the
> dominant-submissive relationship. The man "loves" the
> woman who fulfills her submissive ego-boosting role. The
> woman "loves" the man she is submitting to—that is,
> after all, why she "lives for him." LOVE, magical and sys-
> tematically unanalyzed, becomes the emotional rationale
> for the submission of one ego to the other. And it is
> deemed every woman's natural function to love.[6]

The song "Down With Love" might well express the feminist rejection of the romanticization of love:

> You, sons of Adam, you, daughters of Eve, the time has come
> To take your love-torn hearts off your sleeve.
> Look, look about you, what, what do you see?
> Love-sick, love-lorn, love-wrecked, love-worn boo hoo-manity.
> There'll be no peace on earth until this curse
> Is wiped off from this love-mad universe.
> . . .
> Down with love, the flowers, and rice and shoes,
> Down with love, the root of all midnight blues,
> Down with things that give you that well known pain.
> Take that moon and wrap it in cellophane . . .[7]

---

[5] Freeman, "The Building of the Gilded Cage," p. 284.
[6] "Politics of the Ego."
[7] Copyright © 1937 by Chappell & Co., Inc. Copyright renewed. Used by
permission.

It is precisely the romanticization of love that feminists object to, for, according to them, it serves to:

1) Obscure the fact that a woman's ". . . whole identity hangs in the balance of her love life. She is allowed to love herself only if a man finds her worthy of love."[8]

2) Mask the brutalities of the search for a mate:

From the day she learns to understand signals, all a woman hears is a series of contradictory instructions and conflicting descriptions of the way she is to look and behave. She must be sexy and a virgin at once. She must be appreciative, yet challenging. She must be strong, yet weak. Vulnerable, yet able to protect herself. Smart enough to get a man, but not smart enough to threaten him, or, rather, smart enough to conceal her intelligence and act manipulatively. Desired by all, but interested only in one. Sophisticated, yet naive at heart. And so on down the line.[9]

3) Veil the economics of marriage. Both a woman's identity and security depend upon marriage. "In reality a woman is never free to choose love without external motivations. For her at the present time, the two things, love and status, must remain inextricably intertwined."[1] Once married, it is the generally accepted belief that man not woman is the breadwinner. Thus it is interesting that, despite Department of Labor statistics which show that two-thirds of the women who work do so out of economic necessity, it is assumed that if a woman works it is for psychic pleasure and/or "pin money"; or, if economic necessity is too blatant to be denied, she is perceived as having been forced by circumstances to do man's work, i.e., work for a living. In either case, work is not her "true" or "natural" role. Moreover, most women are quite literally dependent upon men for economic sustenance,[2] if for no other reason than that most working women hold the poorest paying jobs, are paid less than men for

---

[8] Firestone, *Dialectic*, p. 149.
[9] Tax, pp. 15–16.
[1] Firestone, *Dialectic*, p. 156.
[2] It is in this light that feminists argue that sexism cuts across class lines; for, a woman's "class" status is determined by that of her husband.

the same jobs, and have little or often no access to the highest paying jobs. Thus it is generally believed by both men and women that the single woman who works is only "marking time" until she is married.

The following fictional description of a young woman's thoughts upon just having accepted a proposal of marriage makes the feminist point that women often marry for reasons of economic necessity:

> Mr. Collins, to be sure, was neither sensible nor agreeable; his society was irksome, and his attachment to her must be imaginary. But still he would be her husband. Without thinking highly either of men or of matrimony, marriage had always been her object; it was the only honorable provision for well-educated young women of small fortune, and however uncertain of giving happiness, must be their pleasantest preservative from want.[3]

If marriage is a woman's goal, homemaking is her role and motherhood her destiny. The feminist response to the argument that women are happiest when they are in the home is twofold. On the one hand, as the Bems point out, the issue is not that housework is or is not an inferior job:

> Rather, the point is that our society is managing to consign a large segment of its population to the role of homemaker solely on the basis of sex just as inexorably as it has in the past consigned the individual with a black skin to the role of janitor or domestic. It is not the quality of the role itself which is at issue here, but the fact that in spite of their unique identities, the majority of America's women end up in the *same* role.[4]

Thus, by the inexorable rules of logic, if man is the breadwinner, woman is the caretaker of the home. Although some women, if not most, claim to prefer the role of homemaker to any other, there is no reason, feminists argue, that all women should be consigned to that role, and that the woman who refuses the categorization be subject to ridicule and social opprobrium.

---

[3] Jane Austen, *Pride and Prejudice,* originally published 1813; (New York: MacMillan, 1962), pp. 122–123.
[4] Bems, p. 1045.

On the other hand, feminists do attack the almost lyrical descriptions of the joys of housework, descriptions which they argue are rationalizations for the tedium and monotony of the daily routine. They readily acknowledge the drudgery and mindlessness of most jobs in the "work-a-day" world. However, the drudgery of most men's jobs has not been romanticized; moreover, women have so fewer options than men. Thus, although there may be women who would rather stay home, few women are in a position to choose.

Moreover, feminists argue that it is a measure of the low significance attached to housework that men do so little of it. If homemaking were in fact ". . . as glamorous as the women's magazines and television commercials portray it, then men, too, should have that option."[5] In one of the tersest descriptions of the nature of housework de Beauvoir has written:

> Few tasks are more like the torture of Sisyphus than housework, with its endless repetition: the clean becomes soiled, the soiled is made clean, over and over, day after day. The housewife wears herself out marking time: she makes nothing, simply perpetuates the present.[6]

In "The Politics of Housework," an article widely circulated in the women's movement, Pat Mainardi analyzes men's responses to the suggestion that they participate in housework. The structure of the essay is clear-cut: the man's statement is followed by an analysis of its real "meaning." For example:

> "I've got nothing against sharing the housework, but you can't make me do it on your schedule." MEANING: Passive resistance. I'll do it when I damned well please, if at all. If my job is doing dishes, it's easier to do them once a week. If taking out laundry, once a month. If washing the floors, once a year. If you don't like it, do it yourself oftener, and then I won't do it at all.[7]

Feminists argue that men refuse to really share housework because they recognize its essential nature: repetition and drudgery.

---

[5] Bems, p. 1047.
[6] De Beauvoir, p. 425. Betty Friedan also examines and analyzes the frustrations of "housewifery" in detail in *The Feminine Mystique*.
[7] Pat Mainardi, "The Politics of Housework," *Notes* 2, p. 29. (Also read into *Green Hearings*, pp. 265ff.)

On the other hand, feminists argue that women have been "brainwashed" to believe that newly waxed floors, spotless china, sparkling ovens, and the absence of "ring around the collar," equal fulfillment.

The use of the phrase "politics of housework" is an indication of the nature of feminist analysis: the individual role definition applied to a woman serves a *social-political* function. A necessary job in society has been delegated to a group of people and rationalized on the basis of inherent personality (biologically-derived) traits: ". . . 'political' classes are *artificial; they define persons with certain capacities by that capacity, changing the contingent to the necessary, thereby appropriating the capacity of an individual as a function* of society."[8]

The same analysis is applied to the role of motherhood. A woman's reproductive capacity is transformed by the "myth of motherhood" into her existential-social destiny. That feminists reject the argument of biological determinism has been noted elsewhere. Suffice it to repeat that to feminists biological capacity is distinct from socially determined destiny. "To choose not to use the equipment is no more blocking what is instinctive than it is for a man who, muscles or no, chooses not to be a weight lifter."[9] Thus, as with housework, it is for feminists a question of options. If motherhood is woman's destiny, any other choice she makes is "unnatural." For example, in the academic world, according to Dr. Ann Harris, women are admonished that:

> . . . the "difficulties of combining the career (sic) of marriage and motherhood with a career as a scholar and teacher" will be beyond the physical and mental energies of all but the "exceptional woman" (but never, of course, of men, who are presumed to spend no time at all being husbands, and fathers). Women are told that they are welcome first and foremost as decoration for the male academic turf. Even in academe, women are sex objects.[1]

There is nothing inherently wrong with motherhood in feminist analysis except the idea that motherhood itself is inherent:

> If there were genuine alternatives, I would like to have a child. Children are great, and I think there is something

---

[8] Atkinson, *Notes 2*, p. 34.
[9] Rollin, p. 15.
[1] Harris, *Green Hearings*, p. 247.

incredibly beautiful about seeing a person develop from the beginning. But the choices simply aren't there for a woman. A man can choose to have both children and a life of his own. A woman can't. If she tries, she's not being a "good mother."[2]

The "myth of motherhood" once again defines women in a service capacity. It is for the very characteristics of service to others that psychologist Erik Erikson urges the necessity for women's participation in the public life; and, exactly for this reason that feminists discount his argument. Erikson asserts that women will bring to the world at large those virtues which distinguish their private service: ". . . realism of householding, responsibility of upbringing, resourcefulness in peacekeeping, and devotion to healing . . ."[3] Millett responds:

> One cannot but note in passing that the force of this rec-
> ommendation is to urge that women participate in politi-
> cal power not because such is their human right, but
> because an extension of their proper feminine sphere into
> the public domain would be a social good. This is to argue
> from expediency rather than justice.[4]

Feminists also point to a statement by Charles de Carlo, President of Sarah Lawrence College as illustrating the same point: "Feminine instincts are characterized by caring qualities, concern for beauty and form, reverence for life, empathy in human relations, and a demand that men be better than they are." The quote was read into the transcript of the Green hearings by Dr. Ann Harris, Assistant Professor of Art History of the Graduate Faculties of Columbia University, who commented, "What is a man who does not think that women are people, doing as president of a women's college?"[5]

Since woman's identity depends upon her relationship to a man, her fulfillment through motherhood is equally dependent upon a man. Thus, it is generally accepted that a single woman should not have a child, a married woman without a child is to be pitied, and a married woman who does not want a child is

---

[2] Koedt, *McCall's*, p. 114.
[3] Erikson, p. 583.
[4] Millett, p. 210.
[5] *Green Hearings*, p. 239.

"unnatural." It is precisely on this understanding that Firestone argues for the "humanness" of artificial reproduction:

> At very least, development of an option should make possible an honest reexamination of the ancient value of motherhood. At the present time, for a woman to come out openly against motherhood on principle is physically dangerous. She can get away with it only if she adds that she is neurotic, abnormal, childhating and therefore "unfit." . . . This is hardly a free atmosphere of inquiry. Until the taboo is lifted, until the decision not to have children or not to have them "naturally" is at least as legitimate as traditional childbearing, women are being forced into their female roles.[6]

With motherhood, a woman is not only fulfilling her purpose in life, but precisely because it is her purpose, to fulfill it is to secure happiness.[7] "From infancy woman is told over and over that she is made for childbearing, and the splendors of maternity are forever being sung to her."[8] Paradoxically, according to feminists, although motherhood is "woman's destiny" (and if destiny is happiness, then motherhood is happiness) explicit in the myth of motherhood is the idea that there are good mothers and bad mothers. The annals of psychology, sociology and literature are replete with studies and stories documenting the cruelties of the "bad mother." According to feminist argument, if motherhood were indeed natural, there would be no such thing as a bad mother. As de Beauvoir has written: "There is no such thing as an 'unnatural mother,' to be sure, since there is nothing natural about maternal love; but, precisely for that reason, there are bad mothers."[9] Thus, for feminists it is the institution of motherhood and not the woman-mother herself that is the root of the problem.

---

[6] Firestone, *Dialectic*, pp. 227–228.
[7] Unpublished letter from a thirty-one-year-old woman with three children aged six months, eighteen months, and three years: "I don't know about women's lib, but let me tell you, before it you didn't dare say kids weren't truly blissful. Do you know what three means? . . . who eats breakfast—I hope one of them left over some juice and a half slice of toast. I never wanted them to watch t.v. and friends told me I was crazy. Now I know. The real horror people tell me is when they get older. But don't get me wrong. I wouldn't trade it for anything in the world. Like I mean I wouldn't give them up for adoption . . . loan, maybe . . ."
[8] De Beauvoir, p. 463.
[9] *Ibid.*, p. 493.

"A mother who whips her child is not beating the child alone; in a sense she is not beating it at all: she is taking her vengeance on a man, on the world, or on herself."[1]

If motherhood were not a political fiction, feminists argue, women would not have to be both trained and exhorted to fulfill the role. In a word: "That the child is the supreme aim of woman is a statement having precisely the value of an advertising slogan."[2]

Despite the high rate of divorce, the rate of alcoholism and dependency on tranquilizing drugs by married women,[3] marriage continues to be the anticipated source of fulfillment for women. In the feminist view, in order for women to truly have options, they must be free not to marry without incurring society's disapproval, ridicule, or extended condolences. "Our society made women into slaves and then condemned them for acting like slaves. Those who refused to act like slaves they disparaged for not being true women."[4]

All feminists agree that education and early childhood training must be radically altered if women are to be able and available to equally participate in society. The Director of Women in the Air Force, Col. Jeanne M. Holm, has written:

> It is high time we stop telling children that girls don't have the aptitudes for mathematics, engineering, science, etc.; besides "it's unladylike." We raise a little boy to believe that plans for his life's work are his number 1 priority when he grows up. Boys are forced to face up to this reality at an early age. Most girls, on the other hand, are still raised with a romantic image of life—school, marriage, family—and they lived happily ever after. *But Cinderella is dead!*[5]

Feminists perceive the institution of marriage as it presently exists as constituting the legalization of women's subservient

---

[1] *Ibid.*, p. 484.
[2] De Beauvoir, p. 493.
[3] Susan Kennedy Calhoun, "The Mental Health of American Women: Programmed for Breakdown," *The New Broadside*, pp. 8–9. (Ceased publication.)
[4] Joreen, "The Bitch Manifesto," *Notes 2*, p. 6.
[5] Col. Jeanne M. Holm, "Women and Future Manpower Needs," originally published in *Defense Management Journal*, Winter, 1970. Read into *Green Hearings*, p. 993.

social status under the guise of the Cinderella role. Built into the very structure of marriage, the body of law defining the nature and responsibilities inherent in the institution, is the sex-role polarization which feminists argue is at the heart of sexism. Leo Kanowitz, in *Women and the Law: The Unfinished Revolution,* documents the ways in which law both mirrors and perpetuates the prevailing social value of "natural male dominance."[6] The original legal basis for the married woman's loss of rights rests in the feudal idea of coverture, formulated by Blackstone and the cornerstone of common law prescriptions on marriage:

> By marriage, the husband and wife are one person in law; that is, the very being or legal existence of the woman is suspended during the marriage, or at least is incorporated and consolidated.[7]

Thus, husband and wife are one and that one is the husband, and:

> Because the "one" was always the husband, the dominance of the male was assured. Above all, the position of married women at common law both resulted from and contributed to a failure of men and women to see themselves essentially as human beings rather than as representatives of another sex.[8]

Under common law and case law built thereon, married women have suffered legal disabilities with regard to their property rights, contractual abilities, domicile preferences, etc. In attempts to alleviate these legal disabilities, laws adjusting women's property rights have been passed to grant her the right to sign contracts, bring lawsuits, manage and control her real property. Not only do disabilities, however, still exist in the law, but it seems clear to Kanowitz, by no means a radical feminist, that until there is a change in the role definitions of husband and wife (man and woman) the legal disabilities of married women will remain, however reformed. This role differentiation is clearly seen in the context of laws of domicile which, notwithstanding adjustments of necessity permitted by law, rest on the assump-

---

6 Kanowitz, pp. 37 ff.
7 *Ibid.,* p. 35.
8 *Ibid.,* p. 38.

tion that a woman lives where her husband chooses. Thus, a court decision held:

> Parties marrying contract to live together. The husband obligates himself to furnish a proper home for his wife and to maintain her there in a degree of comfort authorized by his circumstances, and they mutually agreed to live together. It is a matter of great public concern that this should be so. In this association there can be no majority vote, and the law leaves the ultimate decision to the husband.[9]

And in another court decision:

> The law imposes upon the husband the burden and obligation of the support, maintenance and care of the family and almost of necessity he must have the right of choice of the situs of the home. . . . The principle is not based on the common law theory of the merger of the personality of the wife with that of the husband; it is based on the theory that one domicile for the family home is still an essential way of life.[1]

Feminists argue that another indication of a woman's loss of her own identity through marriage is to be found in the prevailing legal requirement, supported by social custom, that a woman assume the name of her husband upon marriage. Although legally a married woman's surname is that of her husband, she can use her own name for professional reasons, only as long as her husband does not object:

> The probable effects of this unilateral name change upon the relations between the sexes, though subtle in character, are profound. In a very real sense, the loss of a woman's surname represents the destruction of an important part of her personality and its submersion in that of her husband.[2]

---

[9] California Supreme Court ruling in *Estate of Wickes*, cited in Kanowitz, p. 49.
[1] Arizona Supreme Court ruling in *Carlson v. Carlson*, cited in Kanowitz, p. 50.
[2] Kanowitz, p. 41. For feminists, although the battle is just beginning, a small skirmish has been won, as reported in the *New York Post*, December

Although the descriptive language may vary, both radical and moderate feminists concur in their analyses of the social institution of marriage. The differences lie in their respective prescriptions for change. Whereas moderate feminists describe marriage as an unequal partnership, radicals define it as oppressive. In consequence, the moderates want to restructure the institution, the radicals to abandon it. Simone de Beauvoir's definitions can serve both. For the reform-oriented feminists: "The tragedy of marriage is not that it fails to assure woman the promised happiness—there is no such thing as assurance in regard to happiness—but that it mutilates her; it dooms her to repetition and routine."[3] The Action Resolutions of the National Organization for Women passed March 20–22, 1970, list thirteen changes in the institution of marriage to eliminate the machinery of mutilation.[4] The resolutions proposed an absolute equality in household, economic and child rearing responsibilities. If, for example, "only one partner works outside the home, half the income should by law belong to the other partner."[5] The underlying assumption is that home maintenance constitutes work equivalent to "outside the home" work warranting therefore not merely social approval but monetary recompense as well. The insistence on equality in the NOW resolutions is stated in a language of neutrality: partner, spouse (independent and dependent), parenthood. The partners are distinguished by sex in the resolutions only where it is urged that the woman's title should be "Ms."[6] and that:

. . . the wife should be able to keep her own name or the husband should be able to take his wife's name, and/or there should be the option of both partners choosing a neutral second name to be used also by the children, or the children should use both the wife's and husband's name.[7]

The resolutions include alterations in the social security law to ensure equal coverage for the dependent spouse and children,

11, 1970: "Seattle (AP)—A Kirkland, Wash., wife had her maiden name restored in Superior Court this week because she said her married name 'implies possession by another human being.'"
[3] De Beauvoir, p. 451.
[4] Paper submitted in testimony, *Green Hearings*, p. 145.
[5] Resolution 3, p. 145.
[6] Resolution 13, p. 145.
[7] Resolution 12, p. 145.

guaranteed health and accident insurance upon the dissolution of a marriage, and government-sponsored child care centers.

Radical feminists support most if not all of these reforms, but acknowledge them as adjustments rather than more central redefinitions. The fact, for example, that a woman is forced by law to assume her husband's surname is not simply a problem of changing the law, but rather, a symbolic manifestation of woman's oppression necessary to change, reflective of a more deep-rooted sexism.

At another point in her analysis, de Beauvoir speaks more in the spirit of today's radical feminists:

> Marriage is obscene in principle in so far as it transforms into rights and duties those mutual relations which should be founded on a spontaneous urge; it gives an instrumental and therefore degrading character to the two bodies in dooming them to know each other in their general aspect *as* bodies, not as persons. The husband is often chilled by the idea that he is doing a duty, and the wife is ashamed to find herself given to someone who is exercising a right over her.[8]

Thus, radical feminists define marriage as the ". . . atomization of a sex so as to render it politically powerless."[9] To them marriage is a social contract which by legal means institutionalizes woman's subservient roles as housewife and mother—roles from which men derive economic and psychic benefits. Moreover, the institution of marriage perpetuates woman's subservient position by functioning as a domestic model of sex-role relationships for children. In this light, marriage is not simply a social institution whose purpose is to ensure the perpetuation of the race. For if that were the case the legal stamp would not be necessary, and the idea of legitimacy irrelevant if not nonexistent. Thus radical feminists argue marriage is the social institution whose purpose is to ensure the perpetuation of the family.

> It is a potent instrument for maintaining the status quo in American Society. It is in the family that children learn so well the dominance-submission game, by observation and participation. Each family, reflecting the perversities

---

[8] De Beauvoir, pp. 418–419.
[9] *The Florida Paper*, p. 24.

of the larger order and split off from the others, is power-less to force change on other institutions, let alone attack or transform its own. And this serves the Savage Society well.[1]

One writer has made the argument in another way: "The point is that Women's Liberation is not destroying the American family. It is trying to build a human, compassionate alternative out of its ruins."[2]

In the feminist perspective, the social values explicit and implicit in prevailing cultural ideology and social institutions narrowly define women as sexual beings designed to serve others in whatever capacity (e.g., sexual pleasure, propagation of the race, etc.). The feminist position is succinctly stated in the April 28, 1970, issue of the California women's newspaper, *It Ain't Me Babe.*[3] The center-fold spread is entitled, "In Memoriam: Avenge Norma Jean Baker!" It reads in part:

> In a society where a woman's entire identity rests on her success at being wife, mother and sexual object, Marilyn Monroe was a miserable failure: Each of her attempts at marriage and childbearing ended in disaster. In the end, even her success as the embodiment of the female ideal was bankrupt. At thirty-six, her media-manufactured sexual identity was deteriorating with age. The inhuman mythology which murdered Marilyn Monroe is the same one which maims and kills the spirits of all women daily.

As is evident from their writings, feminists are questioning all social institutions, patterns of interpersonal relations, generally accepted cultural as well as more refined academic "ideologies" about male-female behavior. Suffice it to outline briefly the feminist critique of two patterns of culturally prescribed social behavior and one "institution": chivalry, the "sexual revolution," and the institution of language.

---

[1] *Ibid.,* p. 23. For detailed discussions of the nature and implications of the family in patriarchal society, see Millett, Firestone, de Beauvoir.

[2] Gloria Steinem, "Women Freeing the Men, Too," *Washington Post,* June 7, 1970. Consistent with their analysis that the source of women's exploitation is economic, politico feminists argue that ". . . the family as the basic unit of society constitutes a permanent source of proletarian conservatism and a basis for further super exploitation." Seattle, *The Woman Question,* undated, unpaginated.

[3] Ceased publication.

Chivalry

ACCORDING TO FEMINISTS, in return for the stultification of a woman's personality, the result of the channeling of the bulk of her psychic as well as physical energies toward the primary goal of pleasing a man, society offers a woman chivalry—the mark of true respect for a woman. "Every political action has its special ritual,"[4] and chivalrous acts are the rituals performed in the service of sex differentiation. In its most neutral formulation chivalry might well be defined by Emily Post's explanation of etiquette, ". . . merely a collection of forms by which all personal contacts in life are made smooth."[5] This "collection of forms" or patterns of behavior while applying to both men and women differentiate the "proper" behavior of each. Proper behavior for a man demands that one show especial courtesy and consideration to women. Anti-feminists seem particularly irked by the feminist rejection of the so-called "niceties." They argue that questioning these forms of common courtesy indicates how unimportant the women's movement is. In feminist analysis, however, it is quite clear that the application of a double standard, and chivalry is its politest formulation, is both an expression of and reinforcement for sex-role stereotyping, the core of sexism:

> In comparison with the candor of "machismo" or oriental behavior, one realizes how much of a concession traditional chivalrous behavior represents—a sporting kind of reparation to allow the subordinate female certain means of saving face. While a palliative to the injustice of woman's social position, chivalry is also a technique for disguising it.[6]

Although men appear to be "servicing" women with acts of chivalry, it is, in feminist analysis, the kindness a master shows his servant. For women, "proper" behavior serves a different

---

[4] Ernst Cassirer, *Myth of the State* (New Haven: Yale University, 1946; issued as a Yale Paperbound, January, 1961), p. 284.
[5] Emily Post, *Etiquette: "The Blue Book of Social Usage"* (New York & London: Funk & Wagnalls Co., 1927), p. 545.
[6] Millett, p. 37.

function. By regulating women's behavior according to what is considered "ladylike," women are relegated into service occupations and activities in which ladylike behavior is both warranted and functional. Feminists cite as a typical example the announcement by John Volpe, Secretary of Transportation in the Nixon Administration, in which he urged women to perform a political service by uniting to lobby against drunken drivers.[7] The extent to which this service role is accepted by women can be measured by the response reported in the news story: "Most of the leaders of the women's organizations, which say they have a combined membership of 40 million, needed no such exhortation. The Administration's blessing on what many of them were already doing would have been enough."

Sylvia Roberts, attorney and southern regional director of NOW, noted in her testimony before a House Subcommittee on Education that the "reparation" of chivalry was unacceptable:

> We have in our literature in the National Organization for Women a sheet called *Vive la Différence,* with a question at the end and we show just how costly this difference is. I am speaking in terms of the differential in wages, and the fact that only 3 percent of all lawyers are women, only 1 percent of all women make over $10,000 a year whereas 28 percent of all men do, so that these differences, and such courtly manners as opening doors and lighting cigarettes are just too expensive. We can't afford them. They just cost us so much, and the doors that are opened don't represent the millions of doors that are closed.[8]

Feminists also note that if decorum and respect for others are to be socially-valued behavioral patterns, then courtesy, i.e., opening of doors, should be extended to all regardless of sex.

Another aspect of chivalry—putting woman on a pedestal— in feminist analysis once again denies her human status and instead turns her into an object to be admired and protected. Objects serve a function for others; they are not human beings unto themselves. Thus feminists argue that when a man puts a woman on a pedestal, he does not have to look her in the eye.

---

[7] Felix Belair, Jr., "Women Are Asked to Lobby Against Drunken Drivers," *New York Times,* January 13, 1971.
[8] Roberts, testimony, *Green Hearings,* p. 414.

Author John Seelye in an article, "The Persistence of the Suffering Woman," makes the same point in a different way: "Perhaps
the chief disadvantage to a woman on a pedestal is that the nasty
little boys can see up her skirts, thus reassuring themselves that
she doesn't have what they do have."[9]

The "Sexual Revolution"

THE SEXUAL REVOLUTION has been understood to mean the relaxation of social taboos and restrictions on the sexual behavior
of women. Most would agree that the relaxation of restriction
does indeed constitute a freedom. It is precisely on this point that
some critics of the women's movement seem to throw up their
hands in exasperation: "The sexual revolution which oppresses
her ('the liberated woman') is a revolution made in her behalf by
other women, wrested from men and assented to by them . . . in
the face of the power of the revolutionaries, and not from some
notion of particular advantage to themselves."[1] In feminist analysis, however, the new freedom for a woman to not only have
sexual relations with a man before marriage, but to have them
quite apart from the idea of marriage, is only an illusion of freedom for several reasons. They argue, for example, "What used to
be a 'wifely obligation' is now a 'revolutionary duty.' "[2] Whereas in
the past a woman was inhibited in expressing her sexuality by
accepted social standards of behavior, it was the price she had to
pay to attain her goal of marriage. Marriage, as has been noted
earlier, was necessary not only for social approval, but for economic security as well. According to feminists this restricted
sexual activity, while limiting behavior, was functional.

The elimination of social restrictions, however, has changed
the oppression from a behavioral one to a psychological one:

> Women today dare not make the old demands for fear of
> having a whole new vocabulary, designed just for this pur-
> pose, hurled at them: "fucked up," "ballbreaker," "cock-

---

[9] *New York* magazine, February 15, 1971, p. 43.
[1] Midge Decter, "The Liberated Woman," *Commentary*, October, 1970, p.
43.
[2] Virginia Blaisdell, "Freedom is a Long Time Comin'," reprinted from
View From the Bottom.

teaser," "a real drag," "a bad trip,"—to be a "groovy chick" is the ideal.[3]

Although the emphasis shifted from the question "will you?" to "how did it go?" many feminists maintain that the essential power relationship between men and women still obtains:

> Coitus can scarcely be said to take place in a vacuum; although of itself it appears a biological and physical activity, it is set so deeply within the larger context of human affairs that it serves as a charged microcosm of the variety of attitudes and values to which culture subscribes. Among other things, it may serve as a model of sexual politics on an individual or personal plane.[4]

Thus, radical feminists began to talk about the act of sexual intercourse itself. The "liberated woman" was not only free to have sexual intercourse, but was expected to have orgasms.[5]

In *Notes From the First Year* an article, "Women Rap About Sex" reconstructs the following dialogue among women:

> "You know, just asking your partner when it's over, 'Did you come?' isn't the same as being concerned all along."
> "Yeah, it's that old 'did you come, did you come, did you come,' until you could scream!"
> "Or until you lie."
> "Oh, so you lie too?"
> "I really think we ought to examine what's going on. He asks you when it's all over if you came. Well, what good will that do you by then? If you did come, the question is crude; if you didn't, it makes you feel guilty. What's really happening is that responsibility for the failure is being subtly shifted to you so that you'll blame yourself for being frigid instead of blaming him for a bad trip."

---

[3] Firestone, *Dialectic*, p. 161.
[4] Millett, p. 23.
[5] In 1947, Mary McCarthy wrote an essay-review, "The Tyranny of the Orgasm," of *Modern Woman, The Lost Sex*, by Lundberg and Farnham. The authors had, among other things, equated higher education with frigidity in women, thus urging women to return to the home in order to find sexual fulfillment. McCarthy posed a question that ". . . is really one for the medieval schoolmen: that is, if by the abortion of a single Spinoza, Bacon, Descartes, et cetera, every housewife in Iowa could have an orgasm, should it be done?" Essay reprinted in *On the Contrary: Articles of Belief, 1946–1961* (New York: Farrar, Straus and Cudahy, 1961), p. 171.

De Beauvoir puts the question in more theoretical terms:

> . . . the very fact of asking such questions emphasizes the
> separation, changes the act of love into a mechanical oper-
> ation directed by the male. And that is, indeed, why he
> asks them. He really seeks domination much more than
> fusion. . . . He likes to have the woman feel humiliated,
> possessed, in spite of herself; he always wants to take her
> a little more than she gives herself. Woman would be
> spared many difficulties if man did not carry in his train
> the many complexes that make him regard the act of love
> as a battle; then she could cease to view the bed as an
> arena.[6]

Not only was the "liberated woman" expected to have sexual
intercourse and orgasms, but her orgasms were to be vaginal.
When the short essay, "The Myth of the Vaginal Orgasm," was
first published there was some resistance within the women's
movement itself. One might have expected that the reaction to
the article would have been a sense of psychological liberation
for women who had hitherto been told, and believed, that full
maturity into womanhood depended on moving from clitoral to
vaginal orgasms. That reaction was not forthcoming. The political implications of the article were that freedom of behavior
did not necessarily constitute freedom at all. The restraint on
female sexuality, previously in the name of "modesty," only had a
new name, "vaginal orgasm." Once it was apparent that there
was no such thing as a vaginal orgasm, its conceptualization to
radical feminists was clearly another form of bondage. In the
longer essay[7] analyzing "Why men maintain the myth," Koedt
had suggested as one possibility:

> Men fear that they will become sexually expendable if the
> clitoris is substituted for the vagina as the center of pleas-
> ure for women. Actually this has a great deal of validity if
> one considers *only* the anatomy. The position of the penis
> inside the vagina, while perfect for reproduction, does not
> necessarily stimulate an orgasm in women because the
> clitoris is located externally and higher up. . . . It forces us
> as well to discard many "physical" arguments explaining

---

[6] De Beauvoir, p. 373.
[7] The longer essay was written and distributed in November, 1968, prior
to its 1970 publication in *Notes 2*.

why women go to bed with men. What is left, it seems to me, are primarily psychological reasons why women select men at the exclusion of women as sexual partners.[8]

Women who believed that they were defining their own sexuality, by virtue of their freedom to have sexual relations whenever they chose, resisted the notion that their sexuality was still defined by men. At first there were attempts to dismiss the evidence of the lack of vaginal orgasm.[9] Then the argument shifted to refusal to accept the suggestion that the male was sexually expendable "if one considers *only* the anatomy." Koedt had not argued that women should necessarily choose to reject sexual relationships with men, although that option existed; rather, that the choice of a male sexual partner be understood as based on psychological rather than physical reasons. The "only" was overlooked in the defense of heterosexuality.

Although much of the intra-movement dissension has abated,[1] both moderate and politico feminists, from different vantage points, often argue that radical feminists place too much emphasis on sex. The moderate feminist argument is that "The real sexual revolution is the emergence of women from passivity, from thingness, from the point where they can be the easiest victim and the channel, if you will, for all the seductions."[2] The sexual revolution will liberate sex from being a "dirty joke." Any more specific discussion of sex, however, is often considered as an indication of the age difference that frequently exists between the moderate and radical feminists. In this light, Betty Friedan commented that the young women ". . . only need a little more experience to understand that the gut issues of this revolution involve employment and education and new social institutions and not sexual fantasy."[3]

---

[8] Koedt, *Notes 2*, p. 41.

[9] Cf. Elizabeth Fisher, "Anything You Can Do . . .", *N. Y. Free Press*, November 21, 1968.

[1] When Koedt's article was first published the women's liberation movement was to a large extent underground. Thus it was more than two years before the controversy surfaced into "establishment" circles. It is interesting, though not unexpected, to note that Norman Mailer in a magazine article, "Prisoner of Sex" (*Harper's*, March, 1971), in much more dramatic prose, resisted the Koedt argument in much the same fashion as some of the women had earlier.

[2] Betty Friedan, Keynote Speech, First National Conference for Repeal of Abortion Laws, Chicago, Illinois, February 14, 1969.

[3] National Organization for Women, memorandum from president to board members, chapter presidents and governors, September 22, 1969.

On the other hand, women's sexuality is analyzed in politico
literature primarily as it concerns another aspect of her more
general social and economic exploitation by capitalism: women
are defined by the needs of an oppressive economic system. A
written response to the Koedt piece on the vaginal orgasm, while
accepting its non-existence, stressed the fact that both men and
women have emotional problems caused by capitalist society that
they bring to sexual relations:

> I'm sure it's no coincidence that so many people in this
> country have bad sex. It goes along with the general disre-
> gard for human pleasures in favor of the logic of making
> profit. Obviously people have real control over and respon-
> sibility for their actions in sex. But for women to blame it
> all on men (or men to blame it all on women) is bad
> politics. . . . Sex, work, love, morality, the sense of com-
> munity—the things that have the greatest potential for
> being satisfying to us are undermined and exploited by
> our social organization. That's what we've got to fight. If
> you can't get along with your lover you can get out of bed.
> But what do you do when your country's fucking you
> over?[4]

Radical feminists maintain, however, that sex is central to feminist analysis, for women are not defined as human beings, but as
females—a sex-role (not economic) categorization. Thus they
argue that sexual relationships between men and women must be
recognized as not simply personal but political, i.e., power, relationships.

The Politics of Language

IN FEMINIST ANALYSIS sexism in all its manifestations—cultural,
political, social—is subject to examination. Insofar as language
reflects and reinforces this sex-role polarization, it too is to be
analyzed. Language transforms perceptions into symbols—words

---

[4] Nancy Mann, "Fucked-Up in America," *New England Free Press*, November, 1968.

—which serve as a form of communication. Although words and their usage appear to be "objective" because they define objects, the very process of articulation implies value, suggests "meaning." Language and social or political myth are interrelated. Studies of language and society and the social implications of linguistic analysis have in general analyzed language and its uses in a clearly defined and limited context. For example, Joseph Bram in *Language and Society* discusses the relationship of language to the political construct of nationalism; William Labov, in *Sociolinguistics*, with regard to class and ethnicity. The problem for feminists is that the political myth of sexism has not its own language, but all language. One need not search further than the example that the word used to describe humanity is "mankind," and that the singular pronoun to designate human being is "he." A few examples will illustrate the direction of feminist analysis of words and their usage.

The belief central to feminist analysis that woman is defined by her relationship to man is illustrated by the words used for formal address: a man is always "Mr."; a woman is "Miss" or "Mrs." The words "spinster" and "bachelor" which ostensibly refer to precisely the same social situation—unmarried—in fact imply different things:

> . . . there has somehow always been attached an individual social stigma to a woman if she does not marry. The old spinster term was a word of derision. It has most often meant she was rejected. It isn't, you know, in terms of the man. The "bachelor" is referred to as the "eligible bachelor."[5]

Herschberger makes this point when she notes that apart from general language usage, biologists in particular use the term:

> . . . *erection* in regard to male organs and *congestion* for female. Erection of tissue is equivalent to the filling of local blood vessels, or congestion; but erection is too aggressive-sounding for women. Congestion, being associated with the rushing of blood to areas that have been infected or injured, appears to scientists to be a more adequate characterization of female response.[6]

---

[5] Rep. Green, *Green Hearings*, p. 247.
[6] Herschberger, p. 72.

Most often the same word is applied to both men and women but, just as the characteristics of men and women are assumed to be different, so too are the meanings implicit in the word usage. For example, if a man is said to be *assertive* most generally there is the suggestion of a person with will and determination saying "I am, and I think . . ." When a woman is called *assertive* it is generally understood that she is doing something not quite "feminine" and at worst "castrating"—a sexual allusion the social inference of which is that she is taking over, moving into a world not her own.

In an article, entitled "Manglish,"[7] author Varda One notes that the words *virtue, virile* and *virago* all stem from the same Latin root *vir* which means man. In *Webster's Academic Dictionary* published in 1895, the first meaning of *virago* is "a woman of extraordinary stature, strength, and courage; female warrior." This definition is now "archaic" and in general usage the word means "a turbulent, quarrelsome woman; a termagant."[8] In Varda One's analysis, "Probably it was considered a compliment once for a woman to have such qualities and then they became threatening to men so the word degenerated into an insult."[9] She briefly considers the problem of slang usage: "Testicles are also used to express praise—he's got balls, he's a ballsy guy, that's ball-busting work."[1] Since the feminist emphasis on the psychology of oppression is basic to their understanding that the personal is political, slang terms can be understood in terms of power:

The penis has been called weapon, dagger, pistol, sword, nail, needle, rod, sting, tool, knife. The female organs are referred to as wound, gash, sheath, hole. The man overpowers the woman and many verbs relating to intercourse have violent elements in them, i.e., to violate.[2]

---

[7] *Everywoman*, January 22, 1971.
[8] *Webster's New Collegiate Dictionary*, 1953.
[9] Varda One, p. 14.
[1] *Loc. cit.* The application of such slang expressions to women connotes something other than courage or strength or endurance. Women are irreducibly women: they do not have "balls." Thus, when Norman Mailer writing in Harper's magazine is "shocked" by the new feminist writing, its tension, directness, tautness, he concludes: "Some of the women were writing like very tough faggots. It was a good style." (*Harper's*, p. 48.)
[2] *Loc. cit.*

Feminists are also examining the "politics" of language usage. They have become particularly alert to the fact that when women are written about, for example in the news media, their "femininity," or lack of it, has to be clearly established: "Women in the news are constantly described in physical terms. When was the last time the *Washington Post* referred to 'the vivacious Robert Finch'?"[3] An interview with a woman, whether she is a political figure, opera star, or housewife, will nevertheless describe her as "the petite Mrs. ——, who still wears a size 6 dress."

Insofar as language reflects sexism it must be changed: "Nigerians have only one pronoun for him and her and I think this is the direction we'll go someday. Ultimately people won't be distinguished by sex or gender with anymore import than we give eye color."[4]

---

[3] Komisar, testimony, *Green Hearings*, p. 423.
[4] Varda One, *loc. cit.*

5

Resistance to the
Women's Movement

FEMINISM BY DEFINITION challenges the *status quo*. It questions
political, social and cultural institutions, ways of thinking and
the very articulation of those thoughts. Challenges to the *status
quo* always incur resistance; and resistance to feminism has
taken many forms.

Resistance from men is perhaps most understandable, and
feminists had no illusions that it would not be forthcoming, for
those in positions of leadership and power are reluctant to relinquish them. Resistance from women has other sources. According to feminists, women's entire emotional and social existence is defined by their relationship to men. Unlike other minority
groups, women do not live in a physical ghetto, but rather a
ghetto of the mind. "No other minority lives in the same household with its master, separated totally from its peers and urged
to compete with them for the privilege of serving the majority
group."[1] Thus to analyze, for example, the nature of the institution of marriage is to question women's socially accepted goal as
well as threaten one of the few positions of security and "authority," however limited, that she has.

A woman is judged and judges herself in comparison with
other women. Her efforts in order to secure a man are to indi-
vidualize herself, not to find common ground with other women.
Thus, feminists point out that women have little or no history of

---

[1] Freeman, "The Building of the Gilded Cage," p. 280.

thinking of themselves as a group, an interest group, in political terms. Moreover, as noted earlier, the history book treatment of the first feminist movement in the United States most often has been limited to a discussion of suffrage, and minimized in importance when not virtually ignored:

> More than most they have been denied any history. Their tradition of subjection is so long that the most dedicated feminist scholars cannot unearth a past era worthy of emulation. For the most part even this tradition is purged from the history books so women cannot compare the similarities of their current condition with that of the past. In a not-so-subtle way both men and women are told that only men make history and women are not important enough to study.[2]

Perhaps one of the most difficult problems for the women's movement is that "most women have refused to recognize their own oppression."[3] The leaders of the feminist movement of the 19th century were faced with this problem. In the late 1800's Susan B. Anthony wrote:

> It is the disheartening part of my life that so very few women will work for the emancipation of their own half of the race. . . . Very few are capable of seeing that the cause of nine-tenths of all the misfortunes which come to women, and to men also, lies in the subjection of women, and therefore the important thing is to lay the ax at the root.[4]

Contemporary feminists make the same point when they argue:

> . . . how can we be surprised that this woman has chosen to stay at home today? . . . How can we now expect that she be here, when that life-long intimidation in her is so deep-rooted that even if you put her in solitary for twenty years she wouldn't dare to *think* un-kosher thoughts or to question her position in this society. For she has internal-

---

[2] *Loc. cit.*
[3] *Loc. cit.*
[4] Alma Lutz, *Susan B. Anthony: Rebel, Crusader, Humanitarian* (Boston: Beacon Press, 1959), p. 283.

ized its values, she has accepted, and indeed in many cases she has *become,* its low estimate of her human worth.[5]

Feminists maintain that the first line of resistance to feminism is found in the argument that women *are* happiest in the home. The typical approach taken on this point is illustrated by an article in the January, 1971, issue of *Esquire* magazine, "The Feminine Mistake."[6] The import of the article is that women do indeed like to bake cakes. The feminist case, however, does not rest on a denial of that fact. Rather, as has been noted earlier:

A lot of women who may say they just want to play the traditional roles are simply fearful—or unable to imagine other ways of being. Old roles can seem to offer a certain security. Freedom can seem frightening—especially if one has learned how to achieve a certain degree of power inside the prison. Maybe they are just afraid of choices. We don't seek to impose anything on women but merely to open up all possible alternatives; we do seek choice, as one of the functions which makes people human beings. We want to be full people, crippled neither by law or custom or our own chained minds. If there is no room for that in nature, then nature must be changed.[7]

The "happy homemaker" argument is perhaps most fully analyzed and answered from the feminist perspective by Friedan in *The Feminine Mystique,* the title of which clearly served as the source for the title of the *Esquire* piece.

Ridicule

ANOTHER FORM resistance to feminism often takes is the disparagement of the movement by ridicule or humor. As Pauli

[5] Shulamith Firestone, Speech given at an abortion law repeal rally in New York, March, 1968, reprinted in *Notes 1.*
[6] Helen Lawrenson.
[7] Carol Hanisch, Elizabeth Sutherland, "Women of the World Unite—We Have Nothing To Lose But Our Men," *Notes 1.*

Murray has noted, violence has generally been "the ultimate weapon of resistance to racial desegregation, its psychic counterpart, ridicule, has been used to resist sex equality."[8] Ridicule and humor can clarify by comic juxtaposition; they can also relieve the tension and nervousness which result from confrontation with new and disturbing ideas. Both are also used to belittle a movement by denying significance and worth to the ideas of its proponents. Moreover, ridicule and humor can function to obfuscate an issue by distraction from the point at hand. For example, writer Gloria Steinem was interviewed on an evening television talk-show in January, 1971. She described a recent tour of various parts of the United States, during which time she spoke about the women's movement. When she noted that she planned to write about the lecture tour, moderator Dick Cavett asked if the title of her article would be "Bra-less in Boise." The more common expression is "bra-burning," or "bra-burner." A brief discussion of the term is illustrative of both the confusion about and attack upon the women's movement.

All political movements develop their own language and set of symbols for several reasons. A group or movement language serves as a way of articulating a new social and political perspective as well as defining the analytic construct itself; for example, the word and concept "sexism." A group language also functions as a shorthand both to identify as quickly as possible the "outsider," in this case, the "male-chauvinist" or "sexist"; and to identify and reinforce intra-movement bonds. As such, a group language is functional to a movement. It can, however, become dysfunctional when those outside the group employ the shorthand and symbols, and, by attaching meanings to them quite different from the original intra-group intent, use them to denigrate or belittle the movement and its philosophy.

The label "bra-burner," an historically inaccurate one as has been noted earlier, is a case in point. The term originated with media coverage of the Miss America Contest protest demonstration in 1968. The organizers of that demonstration had set up a trashcan in which articles symbolically representative of femininity were to be discarded. Brassieres were one of the suggested items. As one of several articles of clothing which "restrict," the act of discarding them was meant to serve as a political metaphor for the rejection of all restrictions and limitations implicit in the

---

[8] Quoted by Sonia Pressman, *Green Hearings*, p. 343.

traditionally accepted definitions of "the feminine woman." Needless to say, there are feminists who wear bras and those who do not, just as there are non-feminist women who do both. The reasons for confusion, however, were several. Quite apart from the women's movement, the "bra-less look" had indeed become the fashion in some circles. Originating with young women, as part of their new "life-style," it had moved from the commune to the cabaret, from "hippy" to "chic." As fashion, the style was yet another "woman's look." When some women defined it as a *political* issue, politics, "life-style" and chic femininity became hopelessly confused. If the issue had been only one of a new style in fashion, there is little reason to doubt that public discussion would have abated if not ended entirely. There had been, however, a political gesture and it drew a mixed response. On an individual level, it became apparent to some feminists that, their personal sense of physical freedom notwithstanding, the very thing they opposed—sex-objectification—was being reinforced. Other feminists treated the raising of the issue as just another manifestation of sexism, perhaps one of least importance. On a political level, just as the world of fashion belongs to women and politics does not, some critics argued that the transformation of fashion into politics was indicative of both the trivial nature of the movement, and the "unnaturalness" or "unwomanliness" of the women. The phrase "bra-burner" was sufficiently provocative to make headlines, and, with steady usage by the media—television, radio, magazines, newspapers—it even assumed an historical reality. In all cases, its usage, ostensibly as a statement of "fact" or description, served to ridicule.

The problem of humor and ridicule was touched on during the House Subcommittee hearings on sex discrimination in an exchange between lawyer Sylvia Roberts and chairwoman Rep. Edith Green:

> *Mrs. Roberts:* As soon as Mrs. Kuck started questioning the witness there was a wave of laughter throughout this courtroom. . . . Apparently discrimination against women is a very funny matter, and that everything to do with women's condition and fight to try to obtain equal opportunity is the most humorous subject imaginable, and we don't know why. Of course it is better than being spat upon, but we always wonder why this invokes this reaction.

Mrs. Green: They are not mutually exclusive, though.
Mrs. Roberts: Yes; I realize that. I realize that it may be
a cover for the other, but we find that this not taking us
seriously, it is like putting us on a pedestal. If you are on
a pedestal you are not looking eye-to-eye. You are away
and you do keep insulating yourself from the subject by
putting this wall of humor into the thing.[9]

The converse of ridicule *of* the movement is the accusation
that women *in* the movement "have no sense of humor." It is
quite true that women in the movement do not find traditional
jokes about women "funny." They see "witticisms" about mothers,
mother-in-laws, wives, ex-wives, sex, etc., as merely another cultural expression reflecting the sex-role stereotyping of women.
Nor can they accept attacks on the movement in the guise of
humor, for the women's intent is serious and their analysis not
in the slightest capricious. Thus, when advertising campaigns
are based around the "women's lib" issue, according to feminists
the effect is to depoliticize the import of the movement: for example, in an advertising campaign for Ballantine's Scotch which
features a picture of three women each with her foot on a bar
rail, the caption reads, "Why should men get all the Ballantine's
Scotch? Talk it up! Liberty, Equality, Ballantines!" The "hu-
morous" commercialization of a social-political idea is for feminists the belittling of that idea.

Some feminists argue further that the reason men accuse
women in the movement of humorlessness is that, as one noted,
"when women stop smiling (pleasing men) and start taking
themselves seriously, men get uptight (and therefore accuse us
of no humor)—we are no longer reassuring them with our acqui-
escent smiles."

Finally, feminists find the accusation of humorlessness inaccurate; as with ethnic minority groups, their humor is intra-
group: just as there is "Jewish humor," "black humor," so too
there is "feminist humor."

Ridicule as a weapon of resistance is ultimately all-inclusive,
a closed system that allows no answer; for it functions as both
a style and content: the *description* of feminism as a trivial issue
is also the underlying *assumption* of the attack. Thus, by definition, feminism, dared to prove its importance, cannot possibly
meet the challenge.

---

[9] *Green Hearings*, p. 413.

Accusations of Deviance

PERHAPS the most common way to resist a movement and ideology is to define the adherents and proponents as social pariahs. Ostracism, unlike its ancient Greek form of physical exile, while still serving a political function operates today by socially isolating the unacceptable individual or group. There is a peculiar symmetry to the argument. The women are met, if not on their own ground, indeed in their own terms: because feminists reject the definitions of the "natural" or "real" woman, they are in consequence attacked as being "unnatural" women.

Psychology, which is used to tell women what they are, is quite logically employed to define their "deviance." The most frequent charges brought against the women are that they are emotionally and sexually frustrated, man-hating, castrating, and when all else fails, lesbians. The act of labeling (castrator, lesbian, etc.) presupposes that there is a single movement ideology, that this ideology reflects the personality characteristics of all women committed to women's liberation, and by derivation, that all the women in the movement have this same personality structure. None of these presumptions is true of the women's movement today. While feminists reject these labels, more important than this general rejection is the variety of ways in which the charges are answered. By briefly outlining the women's responses, the wide-range of thought within the movement comes into perspective, and variation in "feminist analysis" previously unexplored can be noted.

EMOTIONALLY AND SEXUALLY FRUSTRATED

Responses run the gamut from dismissal as both irrelevant and silly, to outrage at what is perceived as a "cheap" and "base" attack. Two brief and temperate comments are suggested in an article, "Questions I Should Have Answered Better: A Guide to Women Who Dare to Speak Publicly" by Sally Medora Wood. She poses the question and then the answer:

> *Are you bitter because you're unloved?* Yes. If you felt that half of the country was trying to put you down, wouldn't you feel unloved too?

*Why don't you go home (where you belong) and solve
your own sexual hang-ups?* I don't live in a vacuum. I
don't think any individual living in this society can avoid
having sexual hang-ups. So if everybody has them, we
may as well solve them together.[1]

A more ideological response is that this accusation is a logical
corollary of sex-role characterization which presumes that a
woman is by definition "satisfied" intellectually when "satisfied"
sexually; that is, when she has a man.

Often implicit, sometimes explicit, in the accusation of frustration is the idea that any woman "involved in women's liberation" must be unattractive. Again, some feminists ignore this
charge for it is so clearly a reflection, in their analysis, of sex-
role polarization that defines the attractive or beautiful woman
as satisfied with her feminine self, at peace with the world, con-
comitantly apolitical, and by implication, non-thinking. It is
with no small degree of resentment that they sometimes find
themselves defensively asserting that many of the women in the
movement are "attractive"; that it is precisely because of their
"attractiveness," and the roles in which it immediately traps them,
that they became feminists. Again, a temperate response:

*Well, you're attractive enough. Why don't you just relax
and enjoy it?* I enjoy having people think me attractive,
myself included. But most of the men who look at me
aren't concerned with my attractiveness, or lack of it.
They see me only as a collection of sexual parts walking
down the street for their amusement. This enrages me
and makes me want to kill them, which is not quite the
sentiment for effective relaxation.[2]

"The Bitch Manifesto"[3] by Joreen, represents an entirely different approach. Not measured by the need of formulating a
"reasonable" response to an audience question, it is by no means
"temperate." It fairly blasts the myths of femininity by describing the personality, physicality, values, life-style, and torments
of being a woman society has deemed unwomanly. The Manifesto
is the Bitch Declaration of Independence from those value judg-

---

[1] Reprinted in *Voices From Women's Liberation*, ed. Leslie B. Tanner (New
York: New American Library, 1970), p. 150.
[2] *Ibid.*, pp. 150–151.
[3] *Notes* 2, pp. 5–9.

ments. Of the many definitions of Bitch the most complimentary, it is asserted, is a female dog:

> A true Bitch is self-determined, but the term "bitch" is usually applied with less discrimination. It is a popular derogation to put down uppity women that was created by man and adopted by women. Like the term "nigger," "bitch" serves the social function of isolating and discrediting a class of people who do not conform to the socially accepted patterns of behavior.

Defying discreditation, to qualify as a Bitch one must fulfill at least two of the three essential characteristics:

> *Personality:* Bitches are aggressive, assertive, domineering, overbearing, strong-minded . . . ambitious, tough, brassy, masculine, boisterous, and turbulent. . . . A Bitch occupies a lot of psychological space. You always know she is around. A Bitch takes shit from no one. You may not like her, but you cannot ignore her.

> *Physical:* Bitches are big, tall, strong, large, loud, brash, harsh, awkward, clumsy, sprawling, strident, ugly. Bitches move their bodies freely rather than restrain, refine and confine their motions in the proper feminine manner. They clomp up stairs, stride when they walk and don't worry about where they put their legs when they sit. They have loud voices and often use them. Bitches are not pretty.

> *Orientation:* Bitches seek their identity strictly through themselves and what they do. They are subjects, not objects. They may have a relationship with a person or organization, but they never *marry* anyone or anything; man, mansion, or movement. . . . Often they do dominate other people when roles are not available to them which more creatively sublimate their energies and utilize their capabilities. More often they are accused of domineering when doing what would be considered natural by a man.

BITCH does not use this word in the negative sense. A woman should be proud to declare she is a Bitch, because Bitch is Beautiful. . . . If a woman qualifies in all three, at least partially, she is a Bitch's Bitch. Only Superbitches qualify totally in all three categories and there are very few of those. Most don't last long in this society.[4]

MAN-HATING

The term "man-hating" is often used by critics of the women's movement ostensibly in response to the male-exclusionary policy of many groups. More often it is a shorthand way of questioning the psychological "normality" of the women in the movement. On this level the charge is dismissed by the women as a functional equivalent of "red-baiting." Within the movement itself, however, the issue has been debated on ideological grounds. Although no longer the divisive issue it was in 1968–69, a delineation of the positions reveals the variety and extent of feminist thinking.

In moderate feminist organizations men are most often a part, albeit small, of the membership. The inclusion of men is for both philosophical and tactical reasons. On ideological grounds moderate feminists argue that the relationship between men and women is the source of oppression: "I want people to recognize that there are tremendous positive aspects in both men and women; that both men and women have been seriously hurt by the sex roles they've been required to play in our society. . . ."[5]

Tactically, moderate feminists argue, male-exclusion and certainly "man-hating" are impractical:

. . . If man is characterized as the main enemy, women will wallow around in self-pity and man-hatred and never really be moved to political action. . . . A random hatred of men, a hatred that can lead nowhere, with no allies, will produce no significant changes; but it can serve as the soil for a fascist appeal, which I think is an enormous danger in America today.[6]

Most, if not all, radical feminist groups do have a male-exclusionary policy and justify it, as moderate feminists justify their

---

[4] *Notes 2*, pp. 5ff.
[5] "Critique of Sexual Politics: An Interview with Betty Friedan," *Social Policy*, November/December, 1970, p. 40.
[6] *Ibid.*, pp. 38–39.

inclusion policy, on both ideological and tactical grounds. The ideological position outlined in "Politics of the Ego," although an organizing manifesto for a particular group, is representative of the argument:

> As radical feminists we recognize that we are engaged in a power struggle with men, and that the agent of our oppression is man insofar as he identifies with and carries out the supremacy privileges of the male role.

Thus a movement is necessary to help women ". . . effectively direct their energy to the obliteration of the structures which create those problems."[7] In the recognition that the social institutions of sex-role polarization are at the core of female oppression, both moderate and radical feminists agree.[8] Radical feminists go an ideological step further, however, arguing that since social institutions are man-made, men are the "class" enemy. "Man-hating" in this context does not mean that an individual woman who is a feminist greets every man with hatred. However, there is a political function in "man-hating." An understanding of the origins of the intra-movement debate clarifies this distinction. As noted elsewhere, in the early days of the women's liberation movement, women with different political orientations remained in tenuous alliance, too few in numbers to split, and too unsure of their analyses to make strong ideological distinctions. The new left influence was very strong at the time. Many radical women were fearful of any charge of "oppression" leveled at men (as opposed to capitalism), for their radicalism was dependent on their political involvement with movement men. As the women's movement grew, the differences sharpened and the splits took place. Feminists, in their analysis, came to the conclusion that the sex-role system, predating capitalism and not necessarily vanishing with the end of capitalism, was the source of oppression. But, as political truths are learned from an examination of personal experience, abstractions alone, in their view, could be misleading. In an article, "Them and Me" the author describes a meeting where she was the lone feminist among politicos:

---

[7] "Organizing Principles of the N.Y. Radical Feminists," *Notes* 2, p. 119.
[8] Politico feminists do not accept this analysis. They argue that sex-role institutions are the outgrowth of an oppressive economic system; therefore the latter is the source of oppression.

> I said that their analysis was a more comfortable one because it hurts less to be oppressed by economics than by your man . . . . No woman is oppressed by an abstract capitalism and any attempt to convince her of same is foolish. She is oppressed by her *employer* or her *husband,* etc., and for her to fully realize this she has to examine her personal experiences.[9]

Thus, the phrase "men are the enemy," a feminist slogan which is potentially misleading to outsiders, does serve a political purpose. Many radical feminists make a distinction between hate, which can be a paralyzing emotion, and anger. They argue that the recognition of oppression does indeed provoke anger and only by acknowledging this anger will women mobilize their energies to bring about change. Thus, the recognition of men as the "class" enemy is in their analysis not only ideologically correct but tactically necessary.

The male-exclusionary policy of radical feminist groups is the logical extension of this analysis. Friedan argues that both men and women have a stake in the revolution and thus must work together, "but we've got to take the lead in fighting it as any other oppressed group has had to."[1] Radical feminists agree that both men and women have a "stake in the revolution," but at this point in time, when women are just beginning to recognize their oppression, it is neither practical nor possible to raise women's consciousness by working with men. They argue that to break through the definitions of *woman* that society has spent so many years instilling and reinforcing is a difficult and painful process when women are alone with each other. It would be impossible with men present. Moreover, when men have been included in consciousness raising sessions, more often than not they have tended or attempted to run the meetings. Radical feminists argue further that precisely because at this time female consciousness of oppression is generally so low, male support should not necessarily be solicited since it would tend to reinforce the traditional sex-role pattern of women needing and seeking men's approval.

It is quite possible that with sufficient resistance to the fem-

---

[9] *Notes 2,* pp. 64–65.
[1] "Tokenism and the Pseudo-Radical Cop-out: Ideological Traps for New Feminists to Avoid," Speech, Cornell University Conference on Women, January 22/25, 1969.

inist movement exclusion may become real separatism: that is, completely an ideological rather than partly a tactical position for many radical feminists. The absence of any perceivable changes in the social structure may have the same effect. In this light, Rep. Green commented:

> It is my judgment that if our society, which is run by men, in the National Congress, State legislatures, et cetera, does not put more attention to ending the discrimination against women, I think we are going to have an increased polarization in this country. I think we are going to have more and more militant women who will not be willing to tolerate this slow progress. . . .[2]

This extreme position already exists within the women's movement. Those who advocate it argue that hatred exists and should be expressed; ". . . the realization of our past and continued subjugation has most likely aroused in us some sentiment resembling hatred."[3] Women, however, are supposed to be "understanding," "loving," "giving" and:

> . . . congenitally incapable of hatred. . . . Oh, I know we ought to hate the sin and love the sinner. But too often we end up loving the sinner and hating his victim (as when one woman seeing another put down or hearing about her unhappy affair calls it masochism and that's the end of it). If hatred exists (and we know it does) let it be of a robust variety. If it is a choice between woman-hating and man-hating, let it be the latter.[4]

This ideological position was institutionalized in the group, The Feminists. The group argues that the male-female role system is at the core of all social institutions of oppression and must be destroyed. However, the process of freeing the individual from the role system is interpreted by them to mean the freeing of women from men since men are ". . . the only possible embodiment of the male role and . . . are the enemies and the Oppressors of women."[5] With this analysis male-exclusion from the

---

[2] *Green Hearings*, p. 432.
[3] Pamela Kearon, "Man-Hating," p.1. The Feminists' literature packet.
[4] *Ibid.*, pp, 2–3.
[5] Manifesto of The Feminists, *Notes 2*, p. 114.

group organization becomes male-exclusion from the individual's life. As noted earlier, one of the membership rules of The Feminists reads:

> . . . no more than one-third of our membership can be participants in either a formal (with legal contract) or informal (e.g., living with a man) instance of the institution of marriage.[6]

Thus for The Feminists their analysis rests on the personal *as* the political, rather than the belief that the personal *is* the political.

CASTRATING

Feminists regard this charge as indicative of male paranoia, a fear common to oppressors who anticipate the outcome of an uprising of the oppressed as simply a reversal of the power roles.

> Men have told me I want to be a man. Good lord, I don't. Men are nothing I want to emulate in this society. And men have told me that I want to castrate them. This is something they never understand: the idea of a female-dominated society is as repugnant to me as the idea of a male-dominated society. What I do want to cut off is the power men exercise over women. And if a man associates that power with his genitalia, that's his problem.[7]

Moreover, some feminists note that one cannot deny that sex is political when the word *castrate,* meaning the removal of the testicles, is used to mean the removal of social power.

LESBIANISM

The charge of "lesbian" is frequently leveled against women in the movement. In the early days of the movement, women either dismissed it or defensively denied it. The issue, has, however, become important within the movement itself. It did not fully surface within the movement until 1970 at the second Congress to Unite Women, May 1–3, in New York City, when a group of

---

[6] *Ibid.,* p. 117.
[7] Koedt, *McCall's,* July, 1970, p. 114.

women wearing T-shirts with the label "lavender menace" interrupted the first evening meeting. The phrase "lavender menace" was a twist on the comment "lavender herring" Betty Friedan is alleged to have murmured when the issue of lesbianism and the women's movement were first connected. The lesbian issue had, however, been brewing under the surface. The intra-movement reaction to the article "The Myth of the Vaginal Orgasm" was indicative of the sensitivity to the question. Since women are not necessarily sexually satisfied through heterosexual-coital-relations, ". . . heterosexuality [is] not an absolute, but an option. . . . The establishment of clitoral orgasm as fact . . . would thus open up the whole question of *human* sexual relationships beyond the confines of the present male-female role system."[8] The defense of heterosexuality by critics of the Koedt essay was in part a fear of raising the lesbian issue: already ridiculed as a "bunch of dykes" and "unnatural women" the movement might be thoroughly discredited.

The issue nonetheless could not be avoided. On ideological grounds, some feminists argued if women were rebelling against social roles predetermined by sex, sexual preference should be equally irrelevant. In addition, a gay liberation political consciousness had developed, and homosexuals, male and female, were beginning to publicly demand their civil rights. Gay women pressured the women's movement for support as "sisters," and also because: "As you might expect, the organizations open to both male and female homosexuals practice the same sort of sexual denigration of women as does the heterosexual society at large."[9]

The women's movement has adherents who were lesbians before the existence of a women's liberation movement, and those who have become lesbians since their involvement with the movement. For some of the latter, lesbianism is a form of political protest—"Lesbianism is one road to freedom—freedom from oppression by men."[1] Many radical feminists, while respecting the rights of lesbians, as well as believing that in a world without restraints and oppression sexual preference will be optional, nevertheless are wary of certain pressures from lesbians. One radical feminist noted that "In some circles in the movement

---

[8] Koedt, *Notes 2*, p. 41.
[9] Gene Damon, "The Least of These: The Minority Whose Screams Haven't Yet Been Heard," *Sisterhood*, p. 305.
[1] Martha Shelley, "Notes of a Radical Lesbian," *ibid.*, p. 306.

you're out if you're not a lesbian. At a recent conference your political commitment was measured by whether or not you were a lesbian." Another feminist commented drily, "we've heard that before—when it's not men asking for our bedroom credentials, it's women." Some radical feminists are also wary of lesbianism because often the power relationship between man and woman is mirrored in the woman-woman relationship.

Although an issue within the women's movement, the connection of lesbianism and the movement did not enter public discussion until the end of 1970. In the December 14 issue of *Time* magazine, an article in the "Behavior" section reviewed recent attacks on the women's movement and added:

> Ironically, Kate Millett herself contributed to the growing skepticism about the movement by acknowledging at a recent meeting that she is bisexual. The disclosure is bound to discredit her as a spokeswoman for her cause, cast further doubt on her theories, and reinforce the views of those skeptics who routinely dismiss all liberationists as lesbians.[2]

Several days after the appearance of the article, on December 18, a press conference was held at the Washington Square Methodist Church in New York City. It had been planned by a group of women some of whom represented such groups as NOW, Radicalesbians, Daughters of Bilitis (a lesbian organization founded in 1955), and Columbia Women's Liberation. Millett read a statement prepared at a prior meeting. It read in part:

> Women's liberation and homosexual liberation are both struggling towards a common goal: A society free from defining and categorizing people by virtue of gender and/or sexual preference. "Lesbian" is a label used as a psychic weapon to keep women locked into their male-defined "feminine role." The essence of that role is that a woman is defined in terms of her relationship to men.[3]

The intra-movement response to the *Time* article and the press conference statement was varied. Among feminists some

---

[2] *Time*, p. 50.
[3] "The Lesbian Issue and Women's Lib," *New York Times*, December 18, 1970.

argued that the attempt to smear the movement and Millett had demanded a response. Moreover, the raising of the issue was ultimately beneficial because it opened up the question of the variety of human options with regard to sexuality. Others, agreeing with the need to counter the smear as well as accepting the ideological position, argued nonetheless that extended public discussion was tactically harmful because the movement was too young and too vulnerable to outside criticism.

The vast majority of feminists, whatever their views of the press conference, argue that lesbianism is not and should not be made a central issue of the women's movement. The primary attack must be on the sex-role system, for by its elimination the *issue* of lesbianism becomes irrelevant.

· · ·

The one universal answer women in the movement give to all accusations of deviance is that they constitute the "sexist" equivalent to "red-baiting." As in all such "baiting," not only the movement but individuals are attacked. Feminists argue that for women this distinction is a particularly crucial one, for it serves to reinforce the isolation of women from one another: precisely the social condition that is responsible for women's continued subjugation. For this very reason feminist analysis begins with the belief that the personal is the political.

Members of NOW interrupt Senate hearings on lowering the voting age to demand Senate hearings on Equal Rights Amendment, Feb. 17, 1970.

Women in publisher John Mack Carter's office during Ladies' Home Journal *sit-in, March 18, 1970.*

New York women demonstrate for child care centers Dec. 12, 1970, (Betty Friedan, right).

Washington, D.C., feminists stage Mother Day march at White House for child care centers, May 9, 1971.

Syracuse, N.Y., women "deposit" children on Mayor Lee Alexander's desk to dramatize need for child care centers, Aug. 26, 1970.

Statue of Liberty demonstration, Aug. 10, 1970.

Demonstration for abortion law repeal, Feb. 29, 1968. (Kate Millett).

Demonstration at NY Playboy Club to "liberate" bunnies, June 9, 1970.

EMPLOYERS
TYPECAST
→WOMEN←
INTO
LOW-PAYING
JOBS

EQUAL
PAY
FOR
EQUAL
WORK

STATE
PAY
FOR
HOUSEWORK

Florence Luscomb, suffragist, addresses Boston Rally.

Representative picket signs.

WOMEN'S STRIKE FOR EQUALITY, AUGUST 26, 1970

Strike Day demonstrator supports Equal Rights Amendment.

TIMES

Goucher College, Md., course for women in auto-repair, electronics, etc., Jan., 1971.

Exchange between protester and onlooker during feminist demonstration, June 9, 1970.

Abortion demonstration, New York City, March 28, 1970.

NOW meeting discussion on marriage, Feb. 22, 1968.

Strike Day demonstration, Indianapolis, Ind., Aug. 26, 1970.

Consciousness-raising session.

Below: Confrontation between feminist and onlooker at Strike Day rally, New York City, Aug. 26, 1970.

NY TIMES

Right: Feminists picket San Francisco Press Club protesting restrictions against female members, Nov. 17, 1970.

NY TIMES

UP

Left: Protest accusing advertisers of exploiting women, Aug. 26, 1970.

AI

Above: Airline stewardesses in Washington, D.C., protest industry policy barring mothers from stewardess jobs, Aug. 26, 1970.

III

Areas of Action

WITHIN THE FIRST YEARS of the women's movement feminists have directly challenged social policies and institutions. Their actions have been both group-sponsored and individual, and reflect the entire range of feminist thinking, tactics and style. For example women have filed suits against employers for sex discrimination, organized retreats, established feminist theaters, set up all-women rock bands. Some have opened feminist bookstores, others have organized reprint/distribution services of feminist articles. Groups have desegregated all-male restaurants and bars, and forced changes in local public accommodations ordinances to legally ban sex segregation; feminist studies programs have been incorporated into college and university curriculums, and many professional associations have commissioned studies on the status of women in their particular fields. In addition, groups of feminists have commandeered condemned buildings to set them up as child care centers, co-op food stores, medical clinics; other groups have sponsored "speak-outs" on rape and abortion, "teach-ins" on auto and plumbing repair.

To an individual woman a feminist "action" may be writing Members of Congress urging their support of the Equal Rights Amendment; asking for a raise or promotion on her job; joining a consciousness raising session or a karate class; getting her husband to do the dishes; or, as in the case of one California housewife, picketing her own house in an "unfair to wife strike."

It is not likely that these kinds of actions will abate, but rather they are likely to increase in both intensity and scope. The following chapters will outline those areas in which *major* feminist activity has taken place to date: Media, Abortion, Child care, Education, Professions and the Church.

6

Media

BECAUSE of their pervasive and powerful impact on contemporary life, the mass media (advertising, magazines, television, newspapers and books) became one of the earliest focal points of attack for the new women's movement. Four primary issues regarding the media form the springboard of feminist activity in this area: 1) the image of women portrayed by the media; 2) the professional status of women working within the media; 3) the media coverage of the women's movement; 4) the creation of independent feminist media.

Image of Women

IN THE FEMINIST VIEW, the mass media over the last quarter of a century have reflected and reinforced (some would say "created") an image of the role of women in American society that is both unfair and distorted. Feminists point to the leaders of the media, note that the majority are male, and accuse them of simply re-presenting in modern dress all the ancient "myths" about women. Thus, women are portrayed almost exclusively as housewives, mothers or sex symbols. (This despite the fact that 42 percent of all women are in the labor force.)

Feminists point to the myriad "housewife/mother" commercials in which the high point of a woman's day is her "whiter than white wash," a visit from "the white tornado," or the appear-

ance of her "vitamin enriched" children. They also point to
women's magazines (with a combined circulation of more than
50 million[1]) which "deify" the role of homemaker, both in advertisements and in editorial content; and to television programming, particularly daytime, in which "Women are almost always
pictured as housewives and mothers (an occasional interior
decorator or nurse may be thrown in to take care of the divorcée
category) . . . [but] there is rarely any mention of a woman who
has work outside the home."[2]

Moreover, according to feminists, women in the media are
not portrayed simply as housewives; they are almost always de-
picted as silly, scatter-brained or melodramatic housewives.
Franchellie Cadwell, former president of Cadwell Davis advertising agency, has written, "When over 55 per cent of the women in
the country are high school graduates and 25 per cent have attended college . . . aren't they beyond 'hous-i-tosis'? At the very
least women deserve recognition as being in full possession of
their faculties."[3] In 1970 NOW created a "Barefoot and Pregnant
in the Kitchen" award which it sent to "offending" advertising
agencies.[4]

Betty Friedan speculated about the media's role in the perpetuation of the "feminine mystique" and asked "Why is it never
said that the really crucial function, the really important role
that women serve as housewives is *to buy more things for the
house*. In all the talk of femininity and woman's role, one forgets
that the real business of America is business."[5] Feminists point
to an event in 1966 which they argue supports the Friedan thesis.
On February 10 of that year, the Senate Foreign Relations Committee was holding hearings on the war in Vietnam. However:

CBS broadcast an "I Love Lucy" rerun instead of the Senate hearings—not because the rerun was part of television
folklore, but because the commercials surrounding it involved money. [Fred] Friendly, [then president of CBS

---

[1] 1971 Ayre **Directory** of Newspapers, Magazines and Trade Publications
(Philadelphia: Ayre Press).
[2] Alice Embree, "Media Images I: Madison Avenue Brainwashing—The
Facts," *Sisterhood*, p. 182.
[3] *TV Guide*, August 8, 1970, p. 9.
[4] It should be noted that one of the first task forces established by NOW
in 1966 concerned women's image as portrayed by the mass media.
[5] Betty Friedan, *The Feminine Mystique* (New York: W. W. Norton, 1963;
Dell, 1970), p. 197.

News] reports in his book, *Due to Circumstances Beyond Our Control,* that one of the unpublicized reasons for the CBS decision was the fact that housewives, not "opinion leaders," were tuned in at that hour, and housewives weren't interested in Vietnam. Housewives were thus summarily disenfranchised, and the soap operas went on uninterrupted.[6]

If the media image of women as little more than wives and mothers piques feminists, then the media image of women as "sex objects" infuriates them. Feminists resent the media's use of sex and the female body to sell products. They see this as an advertising tactic created by men for the delight and titillation of other men. Advertisers are accused of using women's bodies draped and undraped to sell everything from shaving cream to cars to cigarettes to airplane tickets. In order to dramatize their displeasure the women devised stickers—"This ad *exploits* women"—that were pasted on advertisements in subways, buses, and on billboards across the country.

Not only are women's bodies used to sell products to men, feminists argue, but a majority of the consumer products aimed at women have only one goal: to make women's bodies attractive to men. In addition, there is an implicit corollary: if you do not use *this* deodorant or *that* hair conditioner, no man will want you, i.e., you will never get married without the aid of nationally advertised products.

"Blondes have more fun."

"Ultra-brite toothpaste gives your mouth sex appeal."

"Wear a Playtex bra if you have an average figure, but don't want to look average."

"Camay keeps the girls different from the boys."

"Want him to be more of a man? Try being more of a woman" (Emeraude perfume).

Thus, according to feminists, the media-created woman is 1) wife, mother and housekeeper for men, 2) a sex object used to sell products to men, 3) a person trying to be beautiful for men. One of the August 26 Strike demands was the call for a boycott of what feminists felt were representative "products"—Ivory soap, because of its solid identity with motherhood; Pristeen, a

---

[6] Embree, *Sisterhood,* p. 183. See also Fred Friendly, *Due to Circumstances Beyond Our Control* (New York: Random House, 1967), Chapter 9.

feminine hygiene spray for "women's problems,"[7] and *Cosmopolitan* magazine, whose *raison d'être* is to teach women how to "trap" men by being sexy.

Feminists have also been highly critical of the field of journalism, both print and broadcast. Activist women contend that the mere existence of a "woman's page" in newspapers implies that women's interests are restricted to recipes, hemlines, "human interest" stories, and child development, and assumes that women are not bright enough to understand the rest of the paper. They argue further that by implication men are not expected to be interested in so-called "women's issues." The same criticism holds for "women's segments" of many radio and television news broadcasts.

At the same time, feminists maintain that "News departments don't consider women news. News equals the male government, the male war machine, the male world. There are fantastic women, women of great achievement in this country of whom people have never heard because the networks [and papers] don't cover them."[8] When stories *are* carried about women achievers, feminists accuse reporters of writing in a condescending manner —the tone being, "that's pretty good for a woman." In a similar vein, newspapers have been attacked for presenting too many stories about the *wives* of famous men. These articles, feminists argue, merely reinforce the idea that a woman has no identity apart from her husband. In October, 1969, two *New York Post* reporters, Lindsy Van Gelder and Bryna Taubman, refused by-lines on stories they wrote about wives of famous men.

The image of women portrayed in children's media has also been criticized by feminists. In September, 1969, Dr. Jo-Ann Evans Gardner, a behavioral psychologist, directed a sharply-worded analysis of the highly-acclaimed children's program "Sesame Street" to the executive producer of the program, Joan Cooney. (In total the program has received about 200 complaints from feminists.) The letter stated in part:

The sexrole stereotype portrayed by the production . . . is extreme. . . . Virtually all [the programs] emphasized that

---

[7] In an effort to show the absurdity of the marketing campaigns for feminine hygiene sprays, one women's liberation newspaper ran a centerfold ad for "Butterballs," a male genital spray in four scents: "meat and potatoes," "locker-room," "seamen," and "gunsmoke." *Off Our Backs*, November 8, 1970.

[8] Shulamith Firestone, quoted by Edith Efron, "Is Television Making a Mockery of the American Woman?" *TV Guide*, August 8, 1970, p. 8.

there is men's work and then there is women's work—that men's work is outside the home and women's work is in the home. (This in spite of the fact that 17 *million* children under eighteen have mothers who are employed outside the home; of these 4.5 million are under six.) . . . A consequence of promoting "femininity," motherhood and homemaking as the most desirable and only appropriate roles for females is that it virtually guarantees that every female child will grow up singlemindedly determined to marry and have children. . . . [The media must begin to represent] women as people first, females second. (We do not represent males first and foremost as fathers, do we?)

Joan Cooney apparently took the feminist criticism seriously for she met at length with Dr. Gardner and two other feminist psychologists. Since that time "Sesame Street" has portrayed women in roles other than wives and mothers; most often, however, working women are in "female" occupations such as nursing. According to a "Sesame Street" staff member, the program's rationale for *not* having a great many "active" roles for women is that "our target audience—ghetto and culturally deprived children—needs strong male figures with which to identify."[9] Feminists have also objected to the sex-role stereotyping on another lauded children's program, "Mister Rogers' Neighborhood." "Mister Rogers" is accused of treating little girls as "incipient ladies." Dr. Gardner claims that the program encourages little girls to "grow up to roles that won't exist by the time they're adults."[1]

Feminists criticize magazines directed at teenage girls in much the same way as they criticize magazines such as *Cosmopolitan:* each to its own audience reinforces the notion that girls/women are dependent on boys/men for their self image. A particularly blatant example, according to feminists, was a lengthy article in the March, 1971, issue of *Seventeen* entitled "The Male Mystique—500 boys rate you, your clothes, your looks. . . . Do they want to show you off or keep you to themselves?" According to *Seventeen*'s survey, 93.6% of the boys "say girls' legs should be seen and not hid (and the more they can see, the better they like it). Boys go on record to urge that minis are the most." On the other hand "4.8% (a pretty ho-hum number) applaud the causes of the women's lib movement. Why

[9] Jay Levine, interview, January, 1971.
[1] Interview, February, 1971.

aren't boys moved? They like more traditional roles: men in charge, girls in minis!"[2]

Although to a lesser degree thus far, films have also come under feminist attack. Some women's journals and newspapers regularly review films; in addition, feminists on occasion review films for the "establishment" press. In the fall of 1970, the American Film Institute of Washington, D.C. sponsored a program on "Women's Liberation and the Cinema," which invited moviegoers to look at a series of films in the light of the new consciousness about women and their role in society. According to Michael Webb, the director of the Institute, "Women are beginning to realize that they have been just as much the victims of stereotyped Hollywood thinking as minority groups like Negroes and American Indians. . . . Women in Hollywood films . . . are either docile and domesticated wives and mothers like Myrna Loy [in 'Cheaper by the Dozen'] or successful career women who get bested by the male, like [Katharine] Hepburn in 'Woman of the Year' or sex objects like Marilyn Monroe and James Bond's girls."[3] Ten films, plus a number of short excerpts, were selected as representative of these stereotypes and shown throughout November. The movies spanned Hollywood film-making from the early days of the 20th century to the present, and in many cases were some of America's most popular and most famous films.

Professional Status of Women in the Media

A MAJOR FACTOR contributing to the "unacceptable" media image of women, according to feminists, is the lack of women in decision-making positions within the professional ranks of the media.

An informal survey was taken in the spring of 1970 of women working in all areas of the media—television, radio, wire services, newspapers, magazines, advertising and publishing.[4] As in most

---

[2] Pp. 110–127.
[3] *Washington Post*, November 1, 1970.
[4] Lucy Komisar, *Women in the Media*. Report given at Professional Women's Conference, April 11, 1970, New York City.

surveys examining employment levels, the number of women in high-ranking media jobs was found to be exceedingly small. In the field of journalism there were no women news managers, and very few writers, producers, reporters or announcers. The survey's findings were supported by 1968 EEOC figures indicating that women comprise only 10 percent of the officials and managers in radio and television, and under 5 percent in newspapers. They make up just 10 percent of the professionals[5] in those three areas. Women seeking jobs as writers, reporters or news producers say the reasons given for *not* hiring females cover a wide range: "it's our policy to have a quota on women"; "women are a distraction in the city room"; "how can we send a woman to cover riots?"; "women's voices (for newscasting) don't have 'credibility.'" One woman applying for a summer journalism training program recalled ". . . the director regarded me sadly and told me that I just didn't *look* like a newspaperman."[6] In the field of women's magazines the survey found that women do hold a majority of the editorial positions—55 percent—but that men almost always have the top jobs. Feminists argue that the reason women are not promoted to high-level jobs on at least one magazine (*Ladies' Home Journal*) is that the male editor-publisher ". . . believes them to be essentially incompetent, emotionally driven, and neither desiring nor deserving equality with men."[7]

In the field of publishing, the survey statistics are similar to those of the women's magazines—large numbers of women make up the ranks of managers and professionals, but few hold the prestigious editorial jobs or run publishing houses. Moreover, most of the women are concentrated in the areas of publicity, children's books and textbooks.

Although many women in the field of publishing are part of the women's movement, it should be noted that (at least until 1971) most *organized* feminist activity within the publishing industry had been very closely allied with a drive to unionize. Publishing is one of the last remaining industries whose professional employees are not unionized, a situation, according to union advocates, that enables publishing houses to hire college grad-

---

[5] Included in the "professional" category are research jobs which are traditionally held by women.

[6] Lindsy Van Gelder, "The Trials of Lois Lane: Women in Journalism," *Sisterhood*, p. 82.

[7] Media Women press release, March 18, 1970. Distributed on the day of the *Ladies' Home Journal* sit-in.

uates as "editorial assistants," etc., at salaries well below $100 a week. (One of the union demands in 1970 was a $100/week minimum.) Feminists claim that nearly all these low-paying editorial jobs are held by women. The union/feminist activities reached a peak in the spring of 1970, the union issue taking priority in some houses, the women's issue in others. The unionization attempt failed however; feminist activity within publishing also abated, although individual women have remained active in the women's movement.

By the fall of 1969 a number of women working in the establishment and underground media had become interested in the women's movement (in fact some were members of organized feminist groups) and ideas for public actions began to be formulated. Some of these early rumblings would ultimately result in intra-company actions organized internally by staff personnel; others, in more general anti-media actions. The most publicized of the general actions, the *Ladies' Home Journal* sit-in, grew out of the meetings of a group of women representing all phases of the media.

Called Media Women, the group had its formal beginnings in the previously-organized Media Projects, a cross-industry but primarily "underground" activist group (male and female) concerned with the media's attitude and response to contemporary political problems. Many of the women members felt, however, that they were cast into a "ladies-auxiliary-but-occasionally-useful-as-a-political-issue" role, and that the only way to attack what they felt were the unique problems facing women in the media— the image presented by, and the professional status within—was to organize themselves independently.

In the first few months of its existence, Media Women was a large (50–75 women at every meeting) but fluid and amorphous group unable to decide on a course of action. Battles over political ideology and priorities often divided the group along politico-feminist lines. The politicos, usually women from the underground newspapers, wanted the group to concentrate on non-media issues such as a defense fund for Black Panther women and anti-war projects; the feminists, largely from the establishment media, wanted to make "women" the issue. Accordingly, they wanted the group to atack job discrimination against women within the professional ranks of the media, and change the image of women presented by the media. The feminists also wanted the meetings to be run in a systematic fashion, the politicos in a non-structured manner. "We would waste hours battling over who could and should be allowed to vote," recalled one early member, "and nothing would get accomplished."

In the late fall of that year Sandie North, a freelance writer who had spent three years working at the *Ladies' Home Journal,* conceived the idea for the now-famous *Ladies' Home Journal* sit-in. "We couldn't unite on a philosophy, but I thought perhaps we could around an action."[8] Many of the women saw the project not only as a way of unifying the group but also, if they were successful, as a way "to scare the whole magazine business into seeing the seriousness of the women's movement." The months of planning included surveying the editorial content of the previous fifteen months' issues of the *Journal;* preparing alternate article suggestions, for example, "Prostitution and the Law," "Can Marriage Survive Women's Liberation," and even creating a dummy cover of a "liberated issue" showing a pregnant woman holding up a placard saying "Unpaid Labor." In addition, the organizers enlisted the aid of various non-media feminist organizations throughout the city, including NOW, The Feminists, and Redstockings.

For eleven hours on March 18, 1970, approximately 100 women occupied the offices of editor-in-chief and publisher John Mack Carter (sometimes called the "dean" of women's magazine editors[9]) "raising his consciousness" and negotiating a long list of demands. In a press release written for the occasion, the women stated:

> The editorial message driven home by the *Ladies' Home Journal* to date is that women are meant to be totally passive, ever-suffering second class citizens whose greatest fulfillment in life is having our collective psyche divined by the out-of-touch men, the editors and advertisers, who determine the content of this magazine. . . . "The Magazine Women Believe In" deals superficially, unrealistically, or not at all with the real problems of today's women: job opportunity, day care, abortion. Though one out of every three adult women in America is single, divorced, or widowed, the *Journal* depicts no life style alternative for the American woman, aside from marriage and family.[1]

---

[8] Interview, January, 1971.
[9] *Newsweek,* February 8, 1971, p. 102.
[1] Media Women, press release, March 18, 1970, unpaginated.

The women pointed out that three of the four top editors at the *Journal* were men (also noting that a similar ratio existed at the other women's magazines). Moreover, in the previous fifteen months' issues, the majority of bylined articles were by men.

The demands presented to Carter included: replacing him with a woman—"We . . . challenge his right to hold that job . . . for he admittedly sees women through male eyes";[2] establishing a company-financed day care center for pre-school children of employees; setting a minimum wage of $125 a week and revamping the magazine hierarchy so that all employees would have a chance to contribute to the editorial decisions of the magazine; allowing the protesters to put out a "liberated issue" in which to present their views and attitudes. This last demand, after eleven hours of negotiating, was granted in the form of a supplement to a regular issue for which the *Journal* paid the women $10,000.[3]

The supplement "The New Feminism" appeared in the August, 1970, issue and was written collectively and anonymously. Of it, editor Carter wrote,

> We have deliberately chosen to be more permissive then [sic] usual in our editing standards, in order to permit these women to express in their own terms exactly how they feel. We do not agree with many of the assumptions their arguments rest on. But having decided to give them a hearing in our pages, we felt it should be one that they considered accurate. . . . As a magazine that for 87 years has served as an emotional and intellectual forum for American women, we can do no less than devote part of one issue to an explanation of Women's Liberation.[4]

The August supplement may well represent the first time millions of women in "middle America" were exposed to an explanation of feminism written by feminists themselves. The articles included "Women and Work," "Your Daughter's Education," "Should This Marriage Be Saved?" "How Appearance Divides Women," and a "Housewives' Bill of Rights." "The New Feminism" apparently made an impact on the readers of the *Journal*. According to the magazine's public relations department,

---

[2] *Loc. cit.*
[3] Much of that money went to set up New York City's first Women's Center.
[4] John Mack Carter, "Why You Find the New Eight Pages in the Ladies' Home Journal," *Ladies' Home Journal*, August, 1970, p. 63.

the response was 34 percent *pro,* 46 percent *con,* and 20 percent *mixed* ("cheering equal pay, etc., but condemning 'far-out antics' "[5]). The women involved in the protest rejected these figures and accused the *Journal* of lowering the number of favorable responses by creating the third "mixed" category.

During the demonstration itself, the underlying tension between the "planners" of the action and the "rank and file supporters" emerged at various times. Some of the women resented the "elitism" they felt was implicit in the "self-appointed" committee negotiating with Carter. At one point, one of these dissenters allegedly said to Carter that she had not come to talk "but to Destroy." She "leapt on [Carter's] desk, intent on [his] forcible eviction. 'We can do it,' she urged, 'he's small.' "[6] The other women joined to evict her from the room. After the sit-in there were differing assessments of the success of the action. According to Sandie North, the action and the resulting supplement represented a real "victory" for the women's liberation movement. "We knew we could make an impact on the entire women's magazine business, and we did."[7] Another felt they had brought "one of the heaviest men in the industry to his knees." Still another believed that the agreement to carry the feminist supplement was "more victory than was strictly needed to get rid of us."[8] Most of those who felt the demonstration was a success, however, believed also that John Mack Carter had carefully calculated the publicity *he* and the *Journal* would get out of the "take-over." A number of the politico women felt the action was not a success at all:

> We thought "taking over" meant a shift of power—like the students taking over the Columbia University president's office, like the two sailors taking over the shipful of bombs and waylaying it to Cambodia, like the women taking over RAT. The old occupants would be ousted.[9] . . . [But] by the end of the day the self-appointed negotiators had succeeded only in "winning" an eight-page supplement on Women's Rights. How this is any different from

---

[5] *Ladies' Home Journal*, press release, October 20, 1970.
[6] Vivian Leone, "Ladies Felt at Home at the Journal," *Manhattan Tribune*, March 28, 1970, p. 15.
[7] Interview, January, 1971.
[8] Leone, p. 15.
[9] Verna Tomasson, "Ladies' Home Journal 2," *Rat*, April 4–18, 1970, p. 5.

> *Mademoiselle, Atlantic Monthly,* or any other Establish-
> ment Press's special climb-on-the-bandwagon issues, is
> still unclear to me. . . . The Ladies Home Journal action
> was effective as publicity. As a radical action (that which
> effects changes in the existing structure) it did not suc-
> ceed.[1]

These women argued further that too much emphasis was placed on elevating the status of women already working professionally in the media, and not enough on issues such as day care, minority hiring and the lack of opportunities for non-professional writers. The manner in which the supplement was put together also came under attack. Although most of the articles were written by non-professional writers, a small collective of professional writers did the final editing, eliciting complaints of "elitism."

After the appearance of the August *Journal* supplement, Media Women as any kind of on-going feminist group disbanded. However, interest in continuing pressure against the media persisted, and in January, 1971, another group of women working in media was formed. Organized by some members from the original Media Women, the second group was more feminist in orientation. The first project of the new group was the publication of a pamphlet, "Women's Guide to the Media," rating each media outlet in New York City on its "sexism quotient"—the number of women in top jobs, secretaries promoted, secretaries with college degrees, the salary differential between men and women with the same qualifications doing the same job, and the criteria used in hiring—are women job seekers asked about their marital status, number of children, plans for having children, etc. The purpose of the pamphlet was twofold: to "embarrass" the various magazines, networks, and publishing houses sufficiently so they would begin to change discriminatory practices; and to be distributed on college campuses so that graduating women interested in careers in some phase of the media would know what to expect, what questions to ask, and what their legal rights were if they encountered sex discrimination.

The first intra-company "public" action concerning women in the media occurred the same week as, but independently of, the *Ladies' Home Journal* demonstration. On March 16, 1970, 46 women (virtually every woman in an editorial capacity) at

---

[1] *Ibid.,* p. 22.

Newsweek magazine filed formal charges with EEOC against the magazine for sex discrimination in hiring and promotion. Unlike the *Journal* action which encompassed a number of issues and was organized by women outside the magazine, the *Newsweek* suit was completely internal and dealt only with the issue of the professional status of the women employees. Plans to file charges against the magazine had been brewing for months, but a *specific* issue around which to rally support did not seem to exist. The catalyst was finally provided when the women learned that the editors had hired a freelance woman to rewrite the in-progress cover story on women's liberation.[2] The activists then timed the filing of their complaint with the appearance of that week's issue.[3] On the day it appeared on the newsstands, the women called a formal press conference, announced they were filing charges and noted among other things the statistical count of women at *Newsweek* on the editorial level: one woman writer out of 52; 12 women reporters out of 76; one male researcher out of 35. The core of the complaint was that women were hired only to be researchers, and never promoted out of that category. *Newsweek* denied discrimination, stating:

> The fact that most researchers at *Newsweek* are women and that virtually all writers are men stems from a news magazine tradition going back almost 50 years. A change in that tradition has been under active consideration by *Newsweek* and the magazine intends to pursue its plans to expand opportunities for qualified women.[4]

The women said they filed charges against *Newsweek,* not so much to bring the magazine to court, but rather to create enough publicity so that the magazine could no longer ignore the problem of the low status of its women employees. Negotiations between a representative panel of the women and *Newsweek* management began almost immediately. A settlement was reached and a "Memorandum of Understanding" was signed on August 26, 1970. The Memorandum, which is primarily a statement of management's "good intentions," covers the usual issues of hiring

---

[2] The freelance writer was Helen Dudar, staff writer for the *New York Post,* and wife of a *Newsweek* senior editor, Peter Goldman. Hiring an outside writer to do a cover story was almost unprecedented.
[3] March 23, 1970.
[4] Cited by Komisar, in "Women in the Media," unpaginated.

and promotion but stipulates also that a panel of women will meet with management every two months for progress checks. Since the original charges were filed, some staff women have been promoted, although the activists felt that the promotions represented nothing more than tokenism. Six months after the agreement was signed, one woman noted that what had *not* changed in her opinion was the overall attitude toward the women employees. "I don't see any guilt on the part of the men regarding the lack of women writers, etc., that exists *vis-à-vis* the lack of black writers. And guilt is important because it means you think you're doing something wrong. They obviously don't think discriminating against women is wrong."

The action at *Newsweek* prompted a group of women at Time, Inc., none of whom were previously involved in the women's movement, to file similar charges against that corporation. On May 4, 1970, 147 women, possibly the largest group of women ever to charge an employer with sex discrimination, complained to the New York State Attorney General's Office and charged Time, Inc.'s four magazines, *Time, Life, Fortune,* and *Sports Illustrated,* with sex discrimination.[5] The State Division of Human Rights investigated and found "probable cause" that "the nation's largest publisher had discriminated against its employees on the basis of sex."[6] The Attorney General filed a formal complaint charging that the women employed at the four magazines ". . . had been confined principally to research and clerical positions despite often impressive backgrounds in journalism and degrees from the nation's most prestigious colleges and universities."[7] A former *Time* researcher described the research job in detail:

> Wife-like, the researcher mediates between the writer and the public. Soft-voiced, tenacious, she gets on the phone to wheedle some nugget of information from someone the writer doesn't want to talk to. In his windowed office, the writer gazes out at the construction workers on the new building going up next door, stares at the typewriter,

---

[5] A lengthy account of the Time, Inc. action can be found in *New York* magazine, February 22, 1971, pp. 26–30.
[6] Office of Attorney General Louis J. Lefkowitz, New York, "Lefkowitz gets Agreement from Time, Inc. on Alleged Discrimination Against Women," News Release (February 6, 1971).
[7] *Loc. cit.*

thinks of lunch. Later he may call the researcher in to show her a particularly pleasing sunset or some questionable activity going on in the Americana [hotel].

Researchers work in doorless and windowless cubicles laid out along the inside of the building. Writers and editors have windows, doors, more space. No matter how hard she is working, a researcher has no way to shut herself off from the lost visitor looking for the way out, the writer asking her to make an appointment or type up a cable (in *his* words), the murmur of gossip at the next desk, or the insistent buzz of an unanswered telephone down the row.[8]

While the negotiations were in progress between the women and management, some changes took place regarding the status of women at the four magazines. Various women researchers were promoted, and for the first time in *Time* magazine history, men were hired as researchers. The January 25, 1971, issue of *Time* changed its masthead category of Researchers to Reporter-Researchers. The change was accompanied by "A Letter from the Publisher" which stated:

For many years, a sizeable part of *Time*'s editorial staff has been identified as RESEARCHERS. Their duties have gradually outgrown that title, and henceforth those staffers will be known as REPORTER-RESEARCHERS. . . . When *Time* started out, the research staff consisted of a single puzzled but mightily determined young woman, who clipped newspaper articles and mined whatever information she could from a bookshelf that held a dictionary, a thesaurus, an almanac and a world history book. As *Time*'s research efforts became more sophisticated, so did the girls—and their titles. At first they were titled "secretarial assistants"—but known less formally as "checkers." Eventually, *Time*'s founders, Henry Luce and Briton Hadden, decided that they were "researchers."[9]

Although pleased to see the *Time* women getting credit for their contributions to the magazine's production, a number of feminists

---

[8] Lilla Lyon, "The March of Time's Women," *New York* magazine, February 22, 1971, p. 28.
[9] "A Letter from the Publisher," *Time*, January 25, 1971.

felt the letter was distressingly patronizing. After nine months of negotiation, a final settlement between the management of Time, Inc. and the women filing suit was reached on February 6, 1971. The agreement provided that all jobs would be open to qualified candidates regardless of sex or marital status, and that the State Human Rights Division would make periodic compliance reviews. Thus the burden was shifted from the women's having to prove discrimination to the magazine's having to prove non-discrimination.

A number of other "public" actions involving women and the media should also be noted. In almost all cases the two overriding issues—the image of women portrayed by the media and the professional status of women working in the media—were emphasized.

On April 15, 1970, nine members of the Women's Liberation Front in San Francisco broke into the CBS stockholders' annual meeting charging CBS, and the media in general, with downgrading and distorting the role of women in commercials and programming. One of the nine shouted:

> CBS abuses women. . . . You tell us to be happy housewives. We don't want to be slaves of any kind. You use our bodies to sell products. We don't want to be put out on the market. You blackmail us with the fear of being unloved if we do not buy. We will no longer pay your extortion. [We demand] . . . an end to derogatory images of women in programming and commercials.[1]

The women also demanded that CBS begin producing a one-hour daily program, created and produced by the Front, as well as structuring a new employment policy requirement that women make up 50 percent of every employee category. CBS chairman William S. Paley denied the charges of exploitation. Stockholders present found the interruption irrelevant to the proceedings, and began to out-shout the women. The women were escorted out by eight plainclothesmen, and the meeting was recessed briefly.

The front page of the August 26 issue of the trade publication *Variety* reported on a subsequent event within CBS. The *Variety* story was allegedly touched off by a high-level internal memorandum attached to a detailed report on the women's liberation move-

---

[1] *Advertising Age*, April 27, 1970, p. 8.

ment prepared for news coverage of the August 26 Strike. *Variety* quoted the memorandum:

> Television must show a new image of a woman as a doer, as an educated serious-minded individual person. Not just a kitchen slave or a single swinger. Acceptance of advertising hostile to women's dignity denigrates and causes the existent ridicule. It has been suggested that the television industry become as sensitive about women in program content and advertising, as they are concerning blacks. . . . One thing is certain: the movement is definite and it is not going to go away. . . . Regardless of the forms the protests take or the manner in which the demands are made, representatives for equal rights and for an end to discrimination are serious business and deserve calm, respectful and understanding attention.[2]

On June 3, 1970 Benjamin Bradlee, editor of the *Washington Post*, issued a staff memorandum regarding the newspaper's policy on women. The memorandum reportedly stated that henceforth reporters should not use words like "brunette," "divorcee," "cute," "grandmother," to describe women unless the same kinds of words were also applied to men. Further, he stated that when a story was written about a woman achiever it should not be done in a patronizing, "pretty good for a girl" tone. Bradlee is also said to have reiterated the *Post*'s policy to hire and upgrade women at the same rate as men. The memorandum allegedly was issued in response to rumors that female reporters on the *Post* and *Washington Evening Star* were planning to start women's liberation groups.

The *San Francisco Chronicle* was invaded on June 4, 1970, by 50 feminists who presented a list of demands to the publisher and employees. The women met with the executive publisher and then proceeded to the city room where they tore down the pin-up pictures from the walls and distributed examples of the *Chronicle*'s "sexist" writings.

A number of actions against the media took place across the country as part of the August 26 Strike. Suffice it to describe one such action against *The New York Times*. A group of feminists went to the office of A. M. Rosenthal, managing editor, to protest

---

[2] *Variety*, August 26, 1970.

the tone of *The Times* editorial of August 11 against the Equal
Rights Amendment. The editorial, carried the day after the
Amendment had passed the House of Representatives, was headlined "Henpecked House" and described the "tactics" used by
women's groups to "push" the Amendment through the House.
The women said they did not object to *The Times*'s opposition to
the Amendment, only to the condescending tone used to describe
the House activity:

> Do you really think that it's proper for the *New York
> Times* to use this sort of terminology—"The Henpecked
> House?" Would you call something the "Nigger-loving
> House?"[3]

The next *New York Times* editorial on the Amendment appeared
on October 10. It still firmly opposed passage of the Amendment
as the best way to achieve women's rights; the editorial, however,
was headlined simply "Equal Rights."

One of the most ambitious projects involving feminists and
the media was begun in the spring of 1971. The National Organization for Women employed the resources and membership of
its nearly 100 local chapters and launched a nationwide campaign monitoring the television networks and local stations. NOW
members filled in lengthy survey forms rating stations on the
basis of the image of women portrayed; the quantity and quality
of the coverage of news events about women, e.g., Supreme Court
decisions, Equal Rights Amendment progress; the orientation of
women's programs, amount of time devoted to household hints
and fashion, to day care and job opportunities. The survey form
was reprinted in *Woman's Day* to encourage non-NOW members
to participate in the monitoring effort. The end goal of the project
was to collect data about the stations and to challenge the license
of any station with a "bad record" when it came up for renewal
before the Federal Communications Commission. Challenges are
to be based upon an FCC policy statement of July 1, 1968, which
states that "discrimination in violation of the Civil Rights Act of
1964 by broadcast licensees could be the basis for a complaint
against individual licensees based upon the overall obligation of
broadcasters to serve the public interest."[4] It should also be

---

3 *The New Broadside*, October, 1970, p. 3.
4 "NOW Takes on the Networks," *The Spokeswoman*, October 30, 1970,
p. 3.

noted that NOW filed a petition with FCC requesting that the word "sex" be added to a September, 1970, ruling, which required all broadcasters to have an affirmative action program in the hiring and promotion of *minorities*.

The direct pressure by feminists on the media and the indirect pressure created by the growth of the women's movement have caused some changes in the image of women in the media, the most visible of which can be seen in the women's magazines. Although still primarily concerned with the "traditional" women's concerns, more and more of them include pieces on abortion, child care, higher education for women, and profiles of women who have careers outside of the home. For example the February, 1971, issue of *McCall's* carried a state-by-state guide to women's legal rights, "The Geography of Inequality"; in addition, the magazine hired Betty Friedan to write a monthly column; *Cosmopolitan* reprinted excerpts from Kate Millett's *Sexual Politics; Family Circle* of March, 1971, discussed "sexism" in children's books. Pat Carbine, managing editor of *McCall's,* commented on what may be a change of direction for these magazines: "A magazine that will matter with women must fulfill its commitment to services [cooking, etc.] as well as enlarging its scope by becoming a little more contemporary. The key word is balance."[5] Similarly, newspapers around the country began to carry slightly more news about women's rights issues.

Two events in Washington, D.C. involving the press corps were a direct result of the growing pressure of the women's movement. On December 8, 1970, the Women's National Press Club changed its name to the Press Club of Washington and voted to admit male members. On January 14, 1971, the National Press Club, a 62-year-old "male stronghold" voted to admit women members.

The television industry also began to reflect "new images" of women. In one series, a war widow works as a nurse to support her son; smart and attractive women lawyers appear in a few others; in another a woman is a television producer. Although feminists support the industry's attempts at portraying women "as people," at the same time they are quick to point out that these "new women" are *still* assigned to the "woman's work" of their respective professions; moreover, the plots frequently revolve around the woman's love life rather than her professional

---

[5] *Newsweek,* February 8, 1971, p. 102.

life. Author Caroline Bird noted in the February 27, 1971, issue
of *TV Guide:*

> None of the independent women is head of the firm, head
> of the hospital, the chief of police, the city editor. Worse,
> many of them seem shadowy, token characters who never
> take the initiative and sometimes don't appear at all for
> several shows at a time. Scriptwriters don't seem to know
> what to do with the "serious-minded, individual woman."
> . . . [Moreover] none of these shows recognizes the new
> ground women's liberation has broken. None of these
> women is challenging the family system, demanding a
> new kind of sexual relationship or a new division of labor
> in the home. If they are television's sop to feminism, it is
> a timid, old-fashioned and already obsolete version of fem-
> inism.[6]

Media Coverage of the
Women's Liberation Movement

RAGE would not be too strong a word to describe the emotion felt
by large numbers of feminists about the media's coverage of the
women's movement, particularly in the movement's early days.
The women feel their activities were either ignored entirely, reported with amused condescension, or reported only for the purpose of exploitation. The media are directly accused of creating
a false image of women in the women's movement simply to "sell
newspapers." "The media-created woman is . . . a total weirdo—
a bra-burner, man-hater, lesbian, sickie!"[7] Feminists point out
continuously that bras were never burned; furthermore, they
argue that discussion of the marital and sexual status of feminists is the media's way of ridiculing and obfuscating the real
issues. It must be noted, however, that the acrimonious reactions
are not always solely directed at the media. Although rarely publicly stated, some of the moderate feminists blame not only the

---

[6] "What's Television Doing for 50.9% of Americans," *TV Guide*, p. 7.
[7] Marilyn Salzman-Webb, "Media Strategy," *Women: A Journal of Liberation*, Summer, 1970, p. 58.

press but some of the more radical women in the movement as well for giving a "bad" image to the movement by their use of guerrilla tactics and obscene language. These moderates feel that such actions provide the media with "instant" headlines thereby detracting from coverage of the serious activities of the establishment groups. The radical women, on the other hand, accuse both the press and the moderate women of not understanding that, in part, "the medium *is* the message": eschewing the traditional polite, ladylike demeanor is precisely the issue of women's liberation.

Many of the younger women had a strong anti-media bias before they joined the women's movement; this bias was caused in part, they say, by press coverage of radical activities during the sixties. They argue that marches, demonstrations, sit-ins and all similar actions were either ignored by the media or inaccurately reported in terms of the number of demonstrators present, the atmosphere of the event, and the character of the participants. Additionally, in ideological terms many of them have come to look upon the media as little more than the handmaiden and voice of the establishment power structure, the very thing they are trying to tear down.

One of the earliest feminist statements protesting media coverage of a feminist event was a Letter to the Editor sent in 1968 to the "radical" publication *Ramparts*. The February, 1968, issue of the magazine had carried a cover story entitled "Woman Power," and included a lengthy report on the radical women within the Jeanette Rankin Brigade. The *Ramparts* coverage did not meet with feminist approval. According to an article in *Notes from the First Year*, *Ramparts* was flooded with angry letters from radical women's groups. "But *Ramparts* just chuckled, patted the little women on the cheek, published a few (out of context) and went on [with] its more important radical business."[8] One of the letters to *Ramparts* was included in *Notes from the First Year:*

> I take offense and serious objection to the tone of your article on "Woman Power." . . . Your attitude was condescending throughout, and your analysis of radical women's groups [within the Jeanette Rankin Brigade] . . . amounted to a movement fashion report.

[8] Shulamith Firestone, "The Jeanette Rankin Brigade: Woman Power?" *Notes 1.*

"The Miniskirt Caucus," the section describing the younger women radicals, treated them with the same approach that a society columnist might. Emphasizing clothes, personalities throughout, the authors never dealt with thought, action, or political content. . . .

Your glorification of the Establishment ideal is completely bewildering. "Besides having a sense of Establishment chic and style, the Brigade ladies are frighteningly businesslike." The term "frighteningly" here reveals the threat posed by women breaking out of pre-established social roles, even though doing something as mild-mannered as appearing businesslike. The duty of a radical publication, far from encouraging establishment behavior, is to promote the shattering of social molds, and the substitution of new liberating thought, action, and life-styles.[9]

The cumulative effect of patronizing coverage from "their own" media, the false image of the women's movement that they felt had been created by the mass media, and the traditional radical distrust of the establishment media, resulted in early attempts on the part of the radical women to establish some kind of criterion for dealing with the press. (The majority of the women acknowledged the need to cooperate with the media in some way in order to reach a large number of women.)

Perhaps the first "guideline" to be established was the policy of talking only to women journalists[1]; men were summarily barred from women's liberation functions. From its earliest use this tactic was not simply an attempt to avoid "bad" reporting. It was also intended in part to be a "shock" tactic to make the media take the movement more seriously, and also in part to force the media to give more reporting and writing jobs to women. It should be noted that radical feminists, more often than politicos were willing to cooperate with the press:

. . . We are not adverse to the (cautious) use of mass media, though we are not blind to its corruptions. . . . We will work only with women reporters but will inform and penalize in an appropriate manner any reporter and me-

---

[9] Letter to *Ramparts,* by Lynn Piartney.
[1] It should be noted that most moderate and conservative feminists will cooperate with both female and male journalists.

dium that, for whatever reason, in tone or substance, presents distorted or partial information about our group. We will also seek to form a strong coalition with other women's rights groups in order to deal more effectively with the problems and potential of the media.[2]

Some politicos, on the other hand, took the extreme position of boycotting the establishment press entirely—"no news is better than bad news." Radical feminists countered that policy, arguing, "Ignorance based on purist aversion results most often, not in no coverage, but in an even sloppier one. . . . We don't have to be revolutionaries for the hell of it."[3] Even most politicos rejected the extreme position of total boycott, but nevertheless were generally much more hostile to the media than were feminists. Hence, the "guidelines" drawn up by politico groups often detailed quite specifically how members were to deal with the press. The "guidelines" usually included one or more of the following:

—One woman should never conduct an individual interview. At least two or more members from the group should be present. (This policy has grown out of the "anti-elitism" ethic, and the general distrust by a group of any one woman who might become "famous off the backs of her sisters." Some radical feminist groups also adopted this policy.)

—The group should be allowed to tape all interviews.

—The group should retain some degree of final editing control.

Despite the policy of limited cooperation, by the spring of 1970 cover stories on women's liberation had appeared in nearly every major magazine, and their broadcasting counterparts carried on the television networks. Moreover, after the August 26 Strike, which was extensively covered, one survey concluded that four out of every five people over eighteen had "read or heard about women's liberation."[4] The transformation of "women's liberation"

---

[2] Organizing Principles of the New York Radical Feminists, *Notes* 2, pp. 119, 122.
[3] *Ibid.*, p. 120.
[4] CBS News Poll conducted September 4–5, 1970.

into a "household word" caused one radical feminist, involved in the movement since its inception, to remark, "The media have won the first round. They're going to write and broadcast stories about women's liberation whether we talk to them or not. That being the case we might as well give in and talk to them. That way at least there's a chance they'll write accurate stories since their information will be from reliable first-hand sources."[5] Another factor also appears to have contributed to the visible easing of feminist/media acrimony: as the number of women journalists sympathetic to the movement began to increase, so the "bad" reporting of the movement began to decrease; hence, more feminists were willing to talk to more reporters.

Notwithstanding an easing of tension, both feminists and politicos have always felt the need for independent women's media. They argue that such independent media are indispensable to building a solid political movement.

Feminist Media

ONE REASON the women's liberation movement was able to expand so quickly during its early days was that it had ready access to an existing underground communications network. One feminist noted:

> What took the black and student movements so long to get off the ground was all that time spent figuring out how to communicate nationally. They had decided early on against using the mass media, and it was a long time before a network of underground papers emerged. But by 1967–68, when women began organizing for themselves, putting out newspapers and knowing where to distribute them was second nature.[6]

The first feminist publication was started by Jo Freeman and the nascent Chicago women's liberation group in March 1968

---

[5] Kathie Sarachild, interview, November, 1970.
[6] Jo Freeman, interview, December, 1970. (In 1964 there were four underground newspapers; by 1968 there were 150 with an estimated combined circulation of between one and two million.)

It was called *Voice of the Women's Liberation Movement,* and for more than a year was the only means of national communication among the handful of radical women around the country who were interested in "women's issues." Small as the newsletter was in size and distribution (six mimeographed pages distributed to approximately 200 women), it accomplished three things: it created a forum in which to discuss women's issues; it served as a grapevine of information for radical women around the country; it turned the name "women's liberation" into a national, albeit underground term.[7] By the time *Voice* stopped publishing in 1969 its circulation was up to two thousand, and two or three other women's liberation publications had either started or were in the formative stages. One, *Women: A Journal of Liberation* (Baltimore), grew out of the August, 1968, Sandy Springs conference where the concept of independent women's media was discussed at length. Another, *A Journal of Female Liberation (No More Fun and Games),* was (and continues to be) published by Cell 16, a feminist group in Boston. It should be noted that most of the early publications were politico in orientation. *No More Fun and Games, Notes From the First Year* (published in New York) and *Lilith* (published in Seattle) were the first distinctly radical feminist journals.

By the beginning of 1971 there were over one hundred women's liberation journals and newspapers being published. Moreover, by that time a number of them were coming from the moderate and conservative branch of the movement. These journals and newspapers run the gamut from the extremely amateur and local to the highly professional and nationally distributed. Articles cover every conceivable aspect of women's liberation—biographies of historical feminists; position papers on the Equal Rights Amendment; discussions of women revolutionaries in other countries; original poetry and artwork; personal testaments from women who have had abortions, bad experiences with psychiatrists, employers or boyfriends; theoretical discussions of stereotyped sex-roles and their psychological implications; practical information—how to change a flat tire, or fix plumbing, as well as suggestions on how to relate to the mass-circulation press.

---

[7] A year after *Voice* began, a feminist group in Boston called itself Female Liberation arguing that the word *female* included minors as well as adults and was therefore preferable. The group hoped that the term "female liberation" would replace "women's liberation," but by that time the latter phrase was firmly entrenched.

Frequently the publications reprint each other's articles (K.N.O.W. Inc., which owns its own press, functions primarily as a reprint service). In addition, almost all carry a "movement news" section, e.g., an abortion demonstration held in Detroit; a day care center formed at Buffalo State University; a sex discrimination case won by women employees, etc. The publications also carry notices of new women's groups being formed around the country. This kind of diverse coverage has turned these newspapers into a crucial communications link within the women's movement, many factions of which eschew any national organizational structure. Taken together, the publications seem to combine all the functions of regular newspapers and magazines, traditional industry newsletters, company directories and calendars of events.

Unlike establishment newspapers and magazines, however, some of the women's publications are run collectively. To produce a publication in this manner, editorial decisions are made collectively, and each woman works in every area of production: writing, lay-out, editing, advertising, distribution, typing and keeping the books. Sometimes an editorial will carry a discussion of the collective experience, what it has meant to the group, how the paper has changed because of it, and what kinds of problems collectivity causes. An example of such a discussion was reported in the Albany, California women's paper, *It Ain't Me, Babe:*

> Since we began publication in January [1970], we have experimented with various kinds of organization on our staff. . . . We originally tried to keep editorial decisions "open." For the first two issues, we called open meetings for women in the community to look over all articles that had been submitted and collectively decide on the content of the paper. This was a disastrous failure. . . . The meetings were simply too large . . . [and full of] haggling discussions over moot points in various articles. . . . By issue #9, a group of three or four women were making all editorial decisions. We felt that we needed a change.
>
> So with issue #10 we revolutionized our structure. . . . Each collective member is in charge of one page. She has full editorial control of this page and is responsible for getting the material typed and laid out. . . . We realize that

the highest form of autonomy can only exist in a group. . . . We . . . believe that cooperative groups can do things far better than individuals. . . . Defining ourselves in this manner has been a process and it is far from completed. At this point, the membership of our collective is tentative and uncertain. . . . If the paper looks motley and un-unified it is because each page is the expression of a different woman.[8]

In many ways the women's movement has changed the complexion of the "traditional" underground press. One of the most dramatic changes was the women's *coup d'état* of *Rat,* a New York based underground paper that mixed radical politics with large doses of pornography. On January 26, 1970, a women's liberation coalition took over *Rat,* and has kept it a collectively run women's newspaper since. Many feminists, however, criticize the paper for not being *feminist* at all. One woman involved in the "coup" expressed disappointment: "It's now just a radical paper that happens to be run by women." Notwithstanding the differing opinions about the new character of the paper, at the time the takeover was looked upon as a "breakthrough" in the political relationship between radical women and radical men. Robin Morgan, one of the leaders of the takeover, wrote a long and angry piece about that relationship. "Goodbye to All That" is now somewhat of a classic among feminist writings.

Rat . . . has always tried to be a really radical *cum* life-style paper. . . . It's the liberal co-optative masks on the face of sexist hate and fear, worn by real nice guys we all know and like, right? We have met the enemy and he's our friend. And dangerous. "What the hell, let the chicks do an issue; maybe it'll satisfy 'em for a while, it's a good controversy, and it'll maybe sell papers"—runs an unheard conversation that I'm sure took place at some point last week. And that's what I wanted to write about—the friends, brothers, lovers in the counterfeit male-dominated Left. The good guys who think they know what "Women's Lib," as they so chummily call it, is all about—and who then proceed to degrade and destroy women by almost everything they say and do: The [pornographic] cover on

---

[8] August 6–20, 1970.

the last issue of Rat. . . . The token "pussy power" or "clit militancy" articles. The snide descriptions of women staffers on the masthead. The little jokes, the personal ads, the smile, the snarl. No more, brothers. No more well-meaning ignorance, no more co-optation, no more assuming that this thing we are all fighting for is the same: one revolution under *man*, with liberty and justice for all. No more. . . . Goodbye to the "straight" male-dominated Left . . . who will allow that some workers are women, but won't see all women (say, housewives) as workers (just like the System itself); to all the old Left-over parties who offer their "Women's Liberation cau-cuses" to us as if that were not a contradiction in terms; to the individual anti-leadership leaders who hand-pick certain women to be leaders and then relate only to them, either in the male Left or in Women's Liberation—bring-ing their hang-ups about power-dominance and manipula-tion to everything they touch. . . . Goodbye, goodbye for-ever, counterfeit Left, counterleft, male-dominated cracked-glass-mirror reflection of the Amerikan Night-mare.[9]

By less dramatic means than the *Rat* takeover, many of the radical papers have undergone certain changes attributed to direct pres-sure from the women's liberation movement: many of the papers no longer accept pornographic advertising—either "personals" or advertisements for "sex-ploitation" movies and books; nearly all the underground papers now have women's columns; and most of them have turned at least one entire issue over to women, in content and editorship. In addition, Liberation News Service, established in October, 1967, as a wire service for the under-ground papers, now has a woman's caucus collecting and dis-tributing women's movement news items.

Another example of feminist-created "media" are the feminist speakers' bureaus. Most have been set up locally and, like pro-fessional lecture bureaus, supply speakers to business groups, women's clubs, high school panel dicussions, church groups, etc. Some of these bureaus are run independently; others, by the local chapter of a nationally organized women's rights group. Unlike professional lecture bureaus, however, they will supply speakers for little or no fee. If a fee is involved often it will be

---

[9] *Rat*, February 7, 1970.

split among the speaker, the bureau and another local feminist project. According to the women who run the bureaus, this "little or no fee" policy not only enables groups with limited budgets to learn about the women's movement, but also affords non-professional women with opportunity to learn to speak in public. Although the bureaus are sometimes criticized for being run in an "unprofessional" manner, most feminists agree that they serve a crucial function by meeting the growing demand for information about feminism and the women's movement.

Since the fall of 1969, FM radio stations have become another outlet for feminist ideas. Since these stations are licensed by the federal government, they cannot operate as freely or as informally as underground newspapers. However, there are several which could be considered broadcasting counterparts of the underground press. With the advent of the women's liberation movement, many of their program producers, announcers and engineers were criticized by feminists as chauvinistic and sexist. In a few instances confrontations were staged, with demands ranging from the inclusion of regularly scheduled women's liberation-produced programs to the hiring of more women disc jockeys. In other cases, the stations opened their doors to the women before a confrontation took place. Following are some examples of the early feminists actions *vis-à-vis* FM radio stations.

WBAI-FM (the New York outlet of Pacifica Foundation, Inc., which also runs listener-sponsored stations in Houston, Los Angeles, and Berkeley) carried the first and apparently only continuing feminist radio program in the country. Since the fall of 1969, WBAI has produced "Womankind: Discussion and Commentary from the Feminist Community." Nanette Rainone moderates the half-hour program which includes reports of women's movement events such as strikes, protests, etc., as well as discussions of feminist issues (e.g., equal pay, child care, abortion, etc.). In October, 1970, WBAI began another type of women's program called "Electra Rewired." Although not always feminist in content, the all-night once-a-week talk show is put together and broadcast entirely by women. Later in the fall a third feminist program was added to WBAI's schedule. Entitled "Consciousness Raising," the program presents a 45-minute pre-taped consciousness raising session. During the second half of the program listeners are invited to call the station and participate in an on-air consciousness raising session.

WEAW-FM—Evanston, Illinois. Every night from 12 a.m. to

5 a.m. WEAW broadcasts "Radio Free Chicago," a catch-all title
for the seven music/talk programs sponsored by the local radical
community. Two nights a week, "Radio Free Chicago" is turned
over to the "Suzie Cream Cheese Collective," a women's liberation group organized in July, 1970, which puts together the broadcasts. Although music makes up much of the five-hour program,
the talk part is devoted to feminist issues. (It is interesting to note
that WEAW's *daytime* programming is conservative to the point
of being radically right-wing.)

KSAN-FM—San Francisco, California. KSAN is an FM rock
music station, somewhat anti-establishment in outlook. In the
spring of 1970, a coalition of feminist groups disrupted a station
staff meeting demanding that the group be allowed to produce and
broadcast its own programs. Although the women knew nothing
about putting together a radio program, the station agreed to
train them in all aspects of production and allow them to produce three half-hour programs.

WBCN—Boston, Massachusetts. WBCN is a hard rock music
station. In the spring of 1970, Bread and Roses, a politico group
in Boston, picketed the station, objecting to the sexist content of
rock music lyrics.[1] A few months later, the group produced an
hour program on the subject which WBCN broadcast. It might
be noted that WBCN is one of the few rock stations that has a
woman disc jockey.

WEEI—Boston, Massachusetts. WEEI is an all-talk station.
On June 2, 1970, the station devoted its entire programming day
to the women's movement. Women representing the spectrum of
the movement from NOW to radical feminist and politico groups
appeared on the show to discuss various feminist issues and to
answer telephone queries.

•   •   •

Most feminists agree that since the advent of the women's
movement the image of women portrayed by the media has become slightly more realistic; that the coverage of movement activities and issues is, if not serious, at least somewhat less
ridiculing and condescending; that the status of women working
in the media has improved a little (at least those women con-

---

[1] It should be noted that rock lyrics have been widely criticized by feminists
throughout the country.

cerned have begun to demand that it improve). Not surprisingly, however, nothing resembling a radical change has occurred in any of these areas. Thus, the primary result of women's movement pressure appears to be a slightly "raised consciousness" on the part of the media to feminism and feminist issues. On the other hand, the rapid growth of independent women's media, in the view of most feminists, does constitute a significant change in the relationship between women and the media—the existence of women's newspapers, journals and magazines has freed feminists from dependence on the mass media for dissemination of information about feminist issues and activities.

7

Abortion

THE FEMINIST BELIEF that it is a woman's right to choose whether or not to be a mother has involved the women's movement in a long-range (although not always co-ordinated) campaign to re-educate the public about sex, contraception, abortion and health care in general. Much of the activity is directed at repealing laws or changing long-accepted beliefs and practices which restrict access to birth control information and methods, including sterilization and abortion. Since the bulk of existing laws and practices concern abortion, it is around that issue that feminists are waging their most visible and active campaigns.

The women's movement is not the first to argue against the existence of abortion laws. Indeed, there has been an anti-abortion law movement in this country for a number of years. Feminists, however, articulate the issue in distinctly "feminist terms" and therefore draw sharp distinctions between abortion law reform and abortion law repeal. In pure feminist analysis (to which all feminists do not necessarily subscribe) true abortion law repeal can be likened to a blank piece of paper[1]: there should be no qualifications that restrict any woman who so desires from having an abortion at any time.

In addition to casting the abortion issue in a feminist perspective, the women's movement is also credited with bringing the issue itself into widespread public debate. What might be

---

[1] New Yorkers for Abortion Law Repeal, a state-wide feminist political action group, uses a blank sheet of paper with "Model Abortion Law" printed on the top as part of their campaign. They distribute their materials in New York State and around the country in an effort to gain support for the abortion law repeal movement.

considered the first "official" involvement of the women's movement with the abortion issue occurred in November, 1967, at the second national convention of the National Organization for Women (NOW). The organization wrote a Bill of Rights for Women, the last of which read: "The right of women to control their reproductive lives by removing from the penal code laws limiting access to contraceptive information and devices and by repealing penal laws governing abortion." The statement was adopted, however, only after lengthy and emotional debate. Ironically, few NOW members disagreed privately with the premise that abortion laws should be repealed; the opposition was based rather on the fear of what such a stand would do to the public image of the organization, an image already too controversial in the view of some members. Several dissenters argued further that abortion law repeal had nothing to do with civil rights for women and therefore was not an issue on which NOW should take a stand. Moreover, such a radical stand might deter potential allies from joining the cause for women's rights. "After a very painful confrontation with our own conflicts on abortion,"[2] the organization voted approval, and the statement was passed.[3] Its passage caused the resignation of some of the opposition from NOW and indirectly caused the formation of other women's rights organizations. The conflicting opinions within the nascent women's movement on the abortion issue are best understood against the complex history of the abortion laws themselves and the development of the abortion reform/repeal movement.

History of Abortion Laws

WHEN THE UNITED STATES CONSTITUTION was ratified in 1787, a woman's right to an abortion before "quickening"[4] was recog-

---

[2] Excerpts from three speeches by Betty Friedan, "Our Revolution Is Unique," President's report to the National Conference of NOW, Atlanta, Georgia, December 6, 1968.

[3] In April, 1968, the Citizens' Advisory Council issued a task force report, *Family Law and Policy*, which recommended repeal of the abortion laws. Some of the members of the Advisory Council who prepared the report were the same NOW members who had prepared the original NOW proposal for repeal.

[4] "Quickening" is the first movement of the fetus within the body, usually at about four months. It has been used traditionally as the demarcation

nized at common law and not punishable as a crime, unless the woman died during the operation. The move away from hundreds of years of this common law approach to the prohibitive framework of current legislation did not begin until the mid-19th century and was due to a confluence of disparate ideas and influences—medical, socio-economic, moral, religious and legal. (Feminists would add—"All conceived, framed and put into practice by men.")

To many who treat abortion laws ". . . as if they were as permanent a part of the social fabric as the Ten Commandments, it seems startling that [they] . . . are a comparatively recent innovation."[5] The first abortion laws in this country were passed in the 1820's, purportedly for the humanitarian reason of protecting women from the hazards of surgery, particularly by unskilled abortionists. The 19th century was not a time of advanced medical techniques, and any kind of operation was avoided if at all possible. Abortion historians also point to the socio-economic conditions of the early 19th century to suggest another reason for the development of restrictive abortion laws: to increase population, in order to fulfill the growing labor needs. "Woman, to a great extent, was prized only as a breeder and child-rearer. . . . Right through the era of America's expanding frontiers in the nineteenth century, the pioneer expected his wife to breed until exhaustion, and often replaced her after an early death with more wives to continue the procreative process."[6] One 1850 court decision branded abortion as "a flagrant crime because it interferes with and violates the mysteries of nature by which the human race is propagated and continued."[7] By the mid-1800's a number of states had passed laws which made abortion a crime except to save the life of the woman. Many of the laws, however, retained the concept of legal abortion before quickening. It was not until after the Civil War that legal restrictions on abortion became enshrouded in a morality of sexual repression. By then Puritanism, with its repressive sexual code, had grown into full flower. In an obsessive attempt to legislate morality and to "stamp out sin," a number of omnibus

---

line establishing "personhood" since Thomas Aquinas expounded the theory that it was at that moment that the "rational soul" entered the fetus. Before Aquinas, most theologians and laymen accepted the Aristotelian view that the soul entered the fetus forty days after conception for a male and eighty to ninety days for a female.

[5] Lawrence Lader, *Abortion* (Indianapolis: Bobbs-Merrill, 1966), p. 75.
[6] *Ibid.*, p. 167.
[7] *Ibid.*, p. 88. (*Mills v. Commonwealth of Pennsylvania.*)

federal laws were passed banning anything and everything having to do with sex (including talking about it), except for the purpose of procreation. "Marital choice in family planning and timing became a subordinate interest . . . [to] the interests of community elders in compelling uniform adherence to specific moral norms."[8] Following the federal lead, state laws were revised and in the process many of them outlawed abortion from the moment of conception on. According to one lawyer, "An incidental effect of the abolition of legal abortion before 'quickening' was to confer on the tiny developing fetus a legal status in many ways equivalent to that of human beings who had already developed and been born. . . ."[1] Exactly when a fetus becomes a "person" entitled to full protection of the laws is still a major legal stumbling block to repeal. Since there are no scientific data which irrevocably prove when that instant might be, the law often incorporates and reflects theological and metaphysical arguments. There has been, however, no single theological position, since each of the three major religions subscribes to a different set of beliefs: Catholics believe a "person" is created at conception; most Protestant denominations, at "quickening"; Jews, at birth. The Catholic Church has always spoken the loudest, however, and so their belief that abortion from the moment of conception on constitutes "murder" has had a profound influence on legislators and the public.

Thus, over the last hundred years the abortion issue has been surrounded by an aura of almost obsessive emotionalism; legal, theological and medical restrictions; and a moral code which has rendered the entire subject taboo. ". . . abortion? The word itself sets off shudders of distaste."[2] Nevertheless there has always been at least a handful of people committed to doing away with the abortion laws for one or more of the following reasons:

—Parents are the only ones who should decide when and if to have a child and, indeed, the final choice must be the woman's alone.

---

[8] Roy Lucas, "Federal Constitutional Limitations on the Enforcement and Administration of State Abortion Statutes," *The North Carolina Law Reviews* (June, 1968), p. 732.
[1] *Loc. cit.*
[2] Marya Mannes, Address presented at the Second Annual Forum of the Association for the Study of Abortion, Inc., New York Academy of Medicine, March 30, 1966. Reprinted by Association for the Study of Abortion. Despite the intense emotionalism surrounding public discussion of the issue, in recent years it has been estimated that more than a million women a year break both the law and the taboo to have abortions.

—The illegality of abortion forces doctors to pit the health of a woman against the future of their careers.

—One set of religious dogma should not be incorporated into the legal code of a country which expressly separates church and state.

—Practically, morality cannot be legislated; to wit, the fact that more than a million women break the law each year and have abortions.

—The socio-economic reasons contributing to the passage of the original laws no longer exist. Moreover, present ecological conditions impel a concern for population growth control. Abortion is one such method.

—Abortion laws are unconstitutional because they violate individual rights.

Advocates for change have always lamented, however, that the attendant aura of "self-righteousness" and "mysticism" has prevented anyone—woman, lawyer, legislator, doctor, clergyman, sociologist—from extracting the purely rational arguments from the emotional and theological ones in order to determine whether or not any is currently applicable. Whenever such intellectual abstraction is made, they contend, it is amidst cries of "murder" and/or "sin."

Development of the Reform/Repeal Movement

THE EARLIEST anti-abortion law advocates maintain that their aim at the outset was to eliminate the restrictive laws entirely. However, anticipating strong resistance from both the public and the legislators, they took what they saw as the politically expedient route of reform, i.e., creating more justifications for legal abortion within the framework of the existing 19th century laws (which prohibited abortion at any time except when the woman's life was at stake).

In 1959, the nascent "reform" movement was given a legislative push when the American Law Institute drafted its Model Penal Code, which included a section on abortion reform. This was the first time a formal proposal had been made in this country to change the abortion laws. ALI recommended that the restrictive laws should stand, but that in addition to saving the woman's life, abortion should be justified when there was "substantial risk" that continuation of pregnancy would "gravely impair the physical or mental health of the mother"; that the child would be born "with grave physical or mental defects"; or if the pregnancy "resulted from rape or incest."[3] The Code also recommended that the operation be performed by a licensed physician with the written concurrence of two other physicians, a concept retained from the old laws. One critic of the ALI Code commented:

> The complete legalization of abortion is the one just and inevitable answer to the quest for feminine freedom. All other solutions are compromises. The American Law Institute code offers a practical plan that might eventually be accepted by a few state legislatures. But it evades the real problem, touching only a fraction of essential cases, and leaving the average woman chained to a tenuous and possibly unmanageable law, and the medical profession still struggling to decide what cases can be accepted under the vague definition of "health."[4]

Legalistic discussions notwithstanding, to the public at large abortion was still a dirty word and a taboo subject. It was not until 1962, as a result of the front-page publicity surrounding the thalidomide scare, that any degree of public debate took place. This drug, used as a tranquilizer and frequently given to pregnant women, was found to produce extreme birth defects.[5]

Once the thalidomide scare was no longer headline news, public discussion abated and was not reactivated until two years later after a German measles epidemic which, because of the illegality of abortion, resulted in the birth of over 20,000 se-

---

[3] For a discussion of the Code, see Lader, pp. 144ff.
[4] *Ibid.*, p. 169.
[5] The most publicized case involved Sherri Finkbine who, in the early stages of pregnancy, took substantial amounts of thalidomide in the form of tranquilizers. Upon learning that thalidomide had caused deformities in scores of children born in Europe, she tried to get an abortion. She met with unalterable opposition in her native state of Arizona and was also subjected to a great deal of public harassment. She and her husband finally went to Sweden where she had an abortion.

verely deformed children in the U.S. Yet there was still little
community support for reform.

In 1964, the tax exempt Association for the Study of Abortion
was founded on the premise that public apathy was in large part
due to the lack of available factual information about the issue
of abortion. Doctors, theologians, social welfare aides and lawyers contributed time and expertise to compile data on the subject to fill this void. (ASA still exists and has a nationwide membership. One of its services, and the one considered most valuable
by many anti-abortion law advocates, is to compile and distribute
to its members summaries of all the court decisions regarding
abortion.) That same year, long-time birth control advocate Bill
Baird established Parents' Aid Society in New York to help women
find qualified abortionists and access to contraceptive information and methods. Parents' Aid was perhaps the first such "above-
ground" abortion referral service.

Legislative action did not occur until 1967, when Colorado
became the first state to reform its original 19th-century law.
Between 1967 and 1970 eleven other states (Arkansas, California, Delaware, Georgia, Kansas, Maryland, New Mexico,
North Carolina, Oregon, South Carolina and Virginia) followed
suit. The new laws were all closely modeled on the ALI Code.

As the idea of legislative reform began to acquire a degree of
respectability, other "above-ground" counseling-referral services
were organized to help women find qualified and humane abortionists. These services, by operating openly and thereby inviting
arrest and conviction, also served as a means to test the laws. In
addition to Parents' Aid Society, the earliest and best known of
these services were the Association to Repeal Abortion Laws in
California, formed by medical technologist Patricia Maginnis in
July, 1966, and the Clergy Consultation Service, founded in the
spring of 1967 by New York's Reverend Howard Moody of the
Judson Memorial Church.[6]

The reform movement continued to gather steam. By 1968
it had been joined by feminists, increasing numbers of constitutional lawyers, a sizeable segment of the clergy, population control advocates and welfare rights groups. It became politically
acceptable to publicly confront the laws head-on, questioning
their very existence, rather than simply making a case for reform
under the old laws. "Repeal" bills began to be introduced into a

---

[6] All these services are still in operation as of the spring of 1971.

few state legislatures (the first was in N.Y. in 1969) and, in addition, the existing laws began to be challenged on constitutional grounds. Cases were (and still are) being brought both under the 5th and 14th Amendments based on the argument that women's civil rights, rights to equal protection, and rights to privacy are being violated by restricting access to abortion. The distinction between reform and repeal also began to be clearly articulated:

> . . . "reform" and repeal are actually fundamentally incompatible ideas. . . . Proposals for "reform" are based on the notion that abortions must be regulated, meted out to deserving women under an elaborate set of rules designed to provide "safeguards against abuse." . . . Repeal is based on the quaint idea of *justice:* that abortion is a woman's right and that no one can veto her decision and compel her to bear a child against her will.[7]

By 1970, the "repeal" forces appeared to be gaining strength. In that year three states—Hawaii, Alaska and New York[8] rejected the ALI approach and based their new laws on repeal arguments, the core of which is "abortion on request." Bills subsequently introduced in other states followed suit. Moreover, for the first time in history, a bill was introduced in Congress to extensively liberalize the country's restrictive abortion laws.[9] The repeal pressure was growing at the judicial level as well. By 1971 some seventy civil and criminal cases were pending in more than twenty states, causing many anti-abortion law advocates to feel that court decisions might change the abortion laws before legislators do. Almost all the cases are based to a greater or lesser degree on the constitutional grounds that abortion laws violate a woman's civil rights. In May 1971 the Supreme Court agreed to hear two such cases (*Roe v. Wade* and *Doe v. Bolton*, from Texas and Georgia respectively).[1]

[7] Lucinda Cisler, "Unfinished Business: Birth Control and Women's Liberation," *Sisterhood*, p. 276.

[8] Hawaii's new law took effect on March 11; Alaska's on April 30; New York's on July 1. (It should be noted that New York's law, the most liberal of the three, had hardly taken effect when conservative pressure to reinstate the old law began to build.)

[9] In April, 1970, Sen. Robert Packwood (R., Ore.) introduced the "National Abortion Act" as part of a legislative package to stabilize population growth.

[1] In April, 1971 the Supreme Court handed down its first decision on the abortion issue. The case challenging the Washington, D.C. law (*U.S. v.*

Although nearly all anti-abortion law advocates now speak of "repeal," the meaning of the word "repeal" varies from person to person in the abortion movement and from feminist to feminist in the women's movement. The first three "repeal" laws (Hawaii, Alaska, New York), as well as bills introduced later in other states, attached some qualifications to the basic premise of abortion on request. Most often the qualifications include one or more of the following:

—the woman must be a resident of the state;
—a married woman needs the permission of her husband; a minor, as with any medical procedure, needs the permission of a parent or guardian;
—the operation may be performed only in a licensed hospital;
—the operation may be performed only by a licensed physician;
—the operation may not be performed beyond a certain date in the pregnancy.

The acceptance or rejection of these restrictions divides activists into what might be termed "liberal reformers" and "total repealers." Since radical feminists are most often the advocates of "total repeal," the objections to the above-mentioned restrictions will be discussed from their perspective.

1. *The woman must be a resident of the state* (length of time varies in each instance). Proponents of the residency requirement argue in the main that because of the illegality of abortion in other states "quality" medical care will have to be sacrificed for "quantity" care and thus their states will be turned into "abortion mills." Feminists argue (and are supported by many nonfeminist lawyers) that since a residency requirement is not a qualification for any other medical procedure, it should not be for abortion. On this basis they feel that this qualification may be the easiest to challenge on constitutional grounds.

Vuitch, October term, 1970, No. 84) charged that it was "unconstitutionally vague." Although the Court upheld the law as *not* unconstitutionally vague, abortion law repeal advocates argue that the Court passed only on the question of the vagueness of the criminal statute and not on its constitutionality. Thus, the ruling was sufficiently ambiguous to allow doctors to continue performing abortions in states with similar laws. Since the question of women's civil rights was not at issue in the Vuitch case, both abortion law repeal advocates and opponents agree that the decision will have only limited legal effect on the existing laws.

2. *A married woman needs the permission of her husband; a minor, the permission of a parent or guardian.* The feminist objection to this qualification is simple: no one but the woman herself should be able to decide whether or not to have a child. Specifically in the case of a minor, she "may be compelled by her parents to bear an unwanted child."[2]

3. *The operation must be performed in a licensed hospital.* Great debate has ensued over this issue. "Liberal reformers," including many doctors, argue that abortion is "not as simple as a tooth extraction,"[3] and severe complications can be prevented only by having the patient in a hospital. From the feminist perspective (and agreed to by many other doctors) the above attitude ignores new medical technology that has rendered abortion "one of the safest medical procedures,"[4] easily able to be carried out in a clinic or doctor's office. They argue further that "hospital boards are extremely conservative and have always wanted to minimize the number of abortions performed within their walls."[5] Moreover, overcrowding in public hospitals creates lengthy and unnecessary delays forcing poor women to continue to seek out "back alley abortionists." In these cases, activists argue, the "severe complications" factor is substantially higher than if the operation were performed in a clinic or a doctor's office.

4. *The operation must be performed by a licensed physician.* "This restriction sounds almost reasonable to most women who have always been fairly healthy and fairly prosperous. . . . But it is one of the most insidious restrictions of all, and is most oppressive to poor women."[6] The opposition to this qualification is again based on the argument that new medical techniques have made the operation simple enough to be performed by trained paramedicals. According to one doctor, the medical profession should

[2] *New York's Abortion Law: What About It,* New Yorkers For Abortion Law Repeal leaflet, May, 1970.

[3] Robert E. Hall, "Realities of Abortion," *New York Times,* January 13, 1971.

[4] June Finer, M.D., part of statement at an April 7, 1970, press conference, New York City.

[5] Lucinda Cisler, "On Abortion and Abortion Law—Abortion Law Repeal (Sort Of): A Warning to Women," *Notes* 2, p. 91. Reprinted in *From Feminism to Liberation,* ed. Edith Hoshino Altbach (Cambridge, Mass.: Schenckman, 1971).

[6] *Loc. cit.*

> . . . help in the training of a new profession of qualified
> abortionists working in registered abortion clinics. . . . It
> will not take much more time than it does to teach nurses
> how to save lives in a coronary care unit or medical corps-
> men how to treat shock. An abortion, as thousands of
> years have taught us, does not require extensive anatomic
> or physiologic knowledge. Abortion is the field for the
> medical assistant, involving only one diagnostic option, a
> limited anatomic area, a single treatment.[7]

Feminists argue further that "only if paramedicals are allowed
to do abortions can we expect to have truly inexpensive (and
eventually free) abortions available to all women . . . . The general crisis in the medical delivery system in fact demands that
paramedical people be trained to do a great many things that
physicians do now."[8]

5. *The operation may not be performed after a certain date
in the pregnancy, unless the woman's life is at stake.* The "time
limit" is perhaps the most controversial of all the restrictions
because the issue becomes encumbered not only with medical
and legal rationales, but also with those based on theology and
morality. Most doctors, though by no means all, argue that the
risks of complication from abortion increase in the later stages
of pregnancy; and legislators, following suit, incorporate the
"protective" time limit restriction into the laws. Other time limit
restrictions are based on the principle of "viability," i.e., the point
after conception at which doctors think the fetus can sustain
life outside the womb. Radical feminists note, "Significantly
enough, the magic time varies from bill to bill, from court decision to court decision. . . ."[9] They argue further that many doctors feel that abortion is not unduly risky in the later stages, and
that the point of "viability" is impossible to determine accurately.
Moreover, any woman who wishes to terminate a late pregnancy
undoubtedly has a very good reason and should have the right to
do so. In addition, they argue that the concepts of "quickening"
and "viability" are based on religious doctrine and ancient myths
about when "life" begins. Any woman who believes in them will
not seek an abortion beyond the time dictated by her beliefs. All
women, however, should not be required to follow one doctrine.
    Within the women's movement itself there is disagreement

---

[7] Michael T. Halberstam, M.D., *Redbook*, April, 1970, p. 138.
[8] Cisler, *Notes* 2, pp. 91, 92.
[9] *Ibid.*, p. 92.

on a number of these questions. Radical feminists maintain that many moderate feminists work for and support less than total repeal because, according to the radicals, they ". . . haven't informed themselves about the complexities of the abortion situation or developed a feminist critique of abortion that goes beyond 'it's our right.' "[1] Some moderate and conservative feminists disagree with the radical position for personal and/or other reasons. Others counter the radical criticism of their position by arguing that their activities are based on realistic political tactics, not an undeveloped "feminist critique."

On the other hand, a large portion of public opinion, including that of legislators and doctors, rejects out of hand any feminist analysis of the abortion issue. One feminist has suggested a reason:

> All the excellent supporting reasons—improved health, lower birth and death rates, freer medical practice, the separation of church and state, happier families, sexual privacy, lower welfare expenditures—are only embroidery on the basic fabric: *woman's right to limit her own reproduction*. It is *this* rationale that the new woman's movement has done so much to bring to the fore. Those who caution us to play down the women's-rights argument are only trying to put off the inevitable day when the society must face and eradicate the misogynistic roots of the present situation. And anyone who has spoken publicly about abortion from the feminist point of view knows all too well that it is *feminism*—not abortion—that is the really disturbing idea.[2]

Others argue that a major barrier (perhaps *the* major barrier) to complete repeal is not a fear of feminism but the lingering aura of Puritanism which equates abortion with sex and implies both should be repressed. All anti-abortion law advocates state that their aim is to make abortion like any other medical procedure. "Total repealers" argue, however: "By legislating abortion as a *separate* medical procedure, the concept remains that abortion, in itself, is wrong. One does not speak of a 'legal' tooth extraction . . . then why a 'legal' abortion?"[3]

Notwithstanding the differing positions, the ranks of the

---

[1] *Ibid.*, p. 90.
[2] Cisler, *Sisterhood*, p. 276.
[3] *Toward Human Abortion*, Society for Humane Abortion paper, no date.

anti-abortion law movement are expanding and more and more individuals and organizations are taking public stands against the existence of abortion laws. In ignorance of, or in spite of, the radical feminist analysis of the true meaning of "repeal," the word "repeal" is used by nearly all activists in the field and describes almost any new bill more liberal than one based on the ALI code. Thus, when organizations recommend "repeal," it is difficult to ascertain exactly what is meant, without a close reading of their statements.

The snowballing of "repeal" recommendations began in earnest in 1970. In March, Planned Parenthood, an organization long associated with parental choice in family planning, recommended repeal. The group is also distributing a booklet to help women in the United States obtain legal abortions. The booklet contains over 200 sources for consultation and referral. Also in March, the Board of Managers of Church Women United issued a resolution calling for repeal, noting also: "Whereas there are a variety of opinions about when life becomes human, laws of the state should not bind all women to one view."[4] In June, during its annual convention, the Board of Trustees of the American Medical Association recommended that abortion become a completely private matter between patient and doctor. In addition, a number of the delegates to the convention urged that the AMA go on record favoring repeal of all abortion laws. The official position finally taken by the entire organization, however, was a compromise between liberal and conservative (primarily Catholic) doctors. It states that a physician may perform an abortion in accordance with state laws, for other than medical reasons with due consideration of the patient's welfare, but not "in mere acquiescence to the patient's demands."[5] The operation must be performed in an accredited hospital and only after consultation with two other physicians. Many doctors feel the statement is vague enough to be interpreted however an individual doctor sees fit. Some feminists argue that the position represented "one step forward and two steps back."[6] One woman places most of the blame for the continuing existence of abortion laws on the medical community:

---

[4] *Resolution on Abortion*, Board of Managers, Church Women United, St. Louis, Missouri, March 19, 1970.
[5] "AMA Abortion Position Liberalized," *American Medical News* (July 6, 1970), p. 1.
[6] Society for Humane Abortion, Inc., *Newsletter* (Summer, 1970), unpaginated.

Every abortion law in the United States would fall tomorrow if doctors would rise in indignation and demand that
lawyers and theologians confine themselves to the fields
in which they profess competency. When will doctors
also confine themselves to the practice of medicine, and
leave morality to the theologians and individual con-
sciences of the people, to be practiced in churches and
homes, and not in hospitals by abortion committees![7]

At its August, 1970, convention the YWCA recommended
the repeal of abortion laws, and also in August the Commission
on Uniform State Laws, considered a very conservative body,
drafted a uniform abortion law based on the concept of elective
abortion.

It should be noted that two phrases added by some feminists
to the general call for repeal often distress the more establish-
ment-oriented groups: one, that abortion be "free," and two, that
it be granted "on demand." The more conservative elements insist that the militant rhetoric does more harm than good to the
common goal of repeal. They feel that legislators and doctors
who might be sympathetic to the basic feminist argument for
repeal are repelled by the notion of granting anything "on demand." Most often those who use the phrase "on demand" merely
mean that no restrictions whatsoever should prevent a woman
from having an abortion. Some feminists also argue that abortion
be "free." In their opinion only a small gain would be made by
merely legalizing abortions within the existing system of medical
care. They believe that only women who can already afford
illegal abortions would benefit. The only way *not* to discriminate
against the poor would be to make abortions and all other medical services free.[8]

The sole major organized body opposing *all* reforms has been
the Catholic Church, which has succeeded in exerting enough
political pressure in many states to defeat proposed reform/re-
peal bills. In 1967, when reform bills first began being introduced with any frequency, the National Conference of Catholic
Bishops authorized a first year budget of $50,000 to combat re-

[7] Lana Clarke Phelan, "Abortion Laws: The Cruel Fraud," Speech presented
at the California Conference on Abortion in Santa Barbara (February 10,
1968), p. 4.
[8] For some of these women, the abortion issue is part and parcel of a growing challenge to the entire U.S. health care system rather than a distinctly
feminist issue.

form efforts. State assemblymen have been deluged with letters from their Catholic constituents, including influential members of the Catholic hierarchy; advertising campaigns have been mounted; Catholic doctors have threatened to resign from the AMA if that organization takes a liberal stand on the issue; and pastoral letters have been read to Catholics from pulpits across the country. An unusually emotional example of such a letter was read to New York Catholics on a Sunday in December, 1970. The letter denounced the liberalized New York law, stating that ". . . each day [abortionists] grow wealthier from the killing of unborn children—some of whom have been heard to cry as they were dropped into surgical trash cans."[9] Anti-abortion law advocates have consistently argued that the theological doctrine of one church should not be incorporated into civil law. "This is no more valid than if the legislature were asked to outlaw pork because of Jewish beliefs or imposing the Christian Scientists's view on medicine or the Jehovah's Witnesses' objections to blood transfusions on everyone."[1] Feminists argue, in addition, that the Catholic opposition has been created not simply by men, but by *celibate* men who have no understanding of women, particularly one who is pregnant with a child she does not want. Perhaps the first legal challenge to the Church was announced in April, 1971. A coalition of organizations and individual women led by feminist lawyers Florynce Kennedy and Diane Schulder stated at that time that they planned to bring formal suit against the Catholic Church for using its tax exempt funds for lobbying purposes.

Also in the spring of 1971, the abortion law repeal movement received, if not an actual, then a psychological setback when President Richard Nixon, Sen. Edmund Muskie (D., Me.) and New York Governor Nelson Rockefeller took public stands on the abortion issue. On April 3, Nixon reversed an armed forces liberal abortion regulation and declared that army personnel would be subject to the laws of the states in which they were based. Nixon did not limit his statement to the regulation change, however; he elaborated on his personal beliefs about the issue as well:

---

[9] *New York Times*, December 6, 1970.
[1] Lader, *Abortion*, pp. 148–149. It is interesting to note that the late archbishop of Boston, Richard Cardinal Cushing, stated in a letter in 1963: "There is nothing in Catholic teaching which suggests that Catholics should write into civil law the prescriptions of church law, or in any way force the observance of Catholic doctrine on others." Cited in Lucas, p. 737.

From personal and religious beliefs I consider abortion an unacceptable form of population control. Further, unrestricted abortion policies, or abortion on demand, I cannot square with my personal belief in the sanctity of human life—including the life of the yet unborn. . . . Ours is a nation . . . with serious social problems—problems of malnutrition, of broken homes, of poverty and of delinquency. But none of these problems justifies such a solution. A good and generous people will not opt, in my view, for this kind of alternative to its social dilemmas. Rather, it will open its hearts and homes to the unwanted children of its own, as it has done for the unwanted millions of other lands.[2]

A *New York Times* editorial the following day stated:

. . . that any actions at the Federal or state level to make it [the statement] the basis for public policy would be both cruel and regressive. Issues affecting the "sanctity of human life" are far more involved in the Vietnam war than they are in the removal of legal obstacles to abortion.[3]

In a television interview a few days earlier, Senator Muskie, a Catholic and declared Presidential candidate, also stated his personal beliefs on the issue. While he supported contraception and believed the government should help dispense information about contraceptive methods, the question of abortion "troubled" him:

I suppose it's related to my religious training, or my church training. . . . I'm concerned about diluting in any way the concept of the sanctity of life. . . . First of all, we're not entirely sure of the psychological impact upon mothers themselves who become free or indiscriminate in the use of this way of avoiding the consequences of sexual relations. . . . [Besides] a life has been taken away from them, and it's the very nature of motherhood, you know, to shield and protect that life, not to destroy it.[4]

---

[2] *New York Times*, April 3, 1971.
[3] *New York Times*, April 4, 1971.
[4] Transcript, *The David Frost Show*, Westinghouse Broadcasting Company, March 31, 1971.

On April 1, Governor Rockefeller of New York announced during
the state legislative budget controversy that he was prepared to
drop Medicaid coverage of abortion costs allegedly to obtain
conservative votes for his entire budget. (On May 18 the State
Supreme Court voided the directive ruling that it discriminated
against the poor and violated their rights of equal protection
and due process.) These statements and actions by the President
of the United States and two important government representatives may well make the abortion debate a major issue in the
1972 Presidential campaign.

Not surprisingly, feminists reacted to what they considered
"shocking" and "regressive" positions. A statement issued on
April 8 by a spokeswoman for the Women's Strike Coalition of
New York concluded:

> If Mr. Nixon is so concerned about the "sanctity of human
> life," let him begin *now* to heed the voices of living women
> —who are from time to time thought to be human—
> when we say we no longer want to sacrifice *our* physical
> lives and our mental health and well-being for the sake
> of other people's consciences. We say instead: we will
> grant Mr. Nixon the freedom to take care of *his* uterus, if
> he will let us take care of *ours*.[5]

Feminist Activities

ALMOST ALL of the feminist activities on the abortion issue fall
into two categories—political action and referral. The different
approaches reflect the range of opinion within the women's
movement.

POLITICAL ACTION

There are several kinds of political action. Some feminists prefer
to set up on-going political action groups designed to attain
repeal by going through established channels, using traditional

[5] Press conference, Washington, D.C.

lobbying techniques to influence legislators and traditional legal moves to force judicial action. Others prefer *ad hoc* "zap" actions designed to educate the public, "raising its consciousness" to the issue of abortion and the need for repeal. Which approach is most effective is a matter of continuous debate.

Since most of the on-going repeal groups operate at the state level it would be impossible to describe them all.[6] Some are representative, however, and can serve to illustrate the kinds of groups being formed. It should first be noted that the National Organization for Women has a National Task Force on Reproduction and Its Control, which serves as a communications link between the repeal projects within local NOW chapters, as well as a distribution source for educational materials on the abortion issue.

The *Association to Repeal Abortion Laws in California* (now named *Association to Repeal Abortion Laws*) was perhaps the first "total repeal" political action group. Founded in July, 1966, in San Francisco, by Patricia Maginnis, it predated the formal existence of the women's movement by more than a year. The word "feminist" was not used at the time, but the group advocated *total* repeal of abortion laws. ARAL had its origins in the tax-exempt research and educational organization Society for Humane Abortion, founded in 1961, also by Patricia Maginnis. The Society, which still exists, conducts debates, discussion groups, symposia and research projects to educate the public to the fact that abortion is a surgical procedure and should not be a criminal offense; therefore, it concludes, laws governing abortion are unnecessary. In 1966 when the decision was made to test California's abortion laws via civil disobedience, the political action group ARAL was formed. The first acts of civil disobedience included compiling and dispensing lists of abortionists, along with public announcements that any woman desiring an abortion could receive help from ARAL. Classes in self-abortion techniques were also given, less to encourage self-abortion than as another means of testing various sections of the law. General lobbying tactics were and still are employed. Maginnis and other members of

---

[6] The one nationally-organized group committed to abortion law repeal is the New York-based National Association for Repeal of Abortion Laws. The group was founded in 1969 as an outgrowth of the abortion reform movement. Although NARAL and feminist groups often cooperate in repeal actions, in practice NARAL does not always campaign for the elimination of *all* restrictions to abortion laws.

ARAL have lectured throughout the country in an attempt to create other "total repeal" groups. Although ARAL is California-based its membership and scope are now nationwide.

In January, 1969, the Abortion Committee of the New York Chapter of NOW founded an independent statewide organization, *New Yorkers for Abortion Law Repeal.* NYALR was the first abortion law repeal group whose philosophy was based entirely on a radical feminist analysis of the abortion issue. In addition, it was perhaps the first feminist group that limited its activities solely to the issues of abortion and contraception. Like ARAL, the group is state-based, but membership is nationwide. In addition, members lecture across the country to try to organize similar groups in other states. NYALR (like ARAL) campaigns vigorously against any restrictions to a woman's access to abortion or any other form of birth control. The organization also campaigns against the passage of "reformed" abortion laws, encouraging anti-abortion law advocates to press for "total repeal" bills. When New York's abortion law was liberalized in July, 1970, NYALR continued its drive to remove the restrictions that still existed in the law.

In addition to the activities of ongoing repeal groups, feminists have organized many *ad hoc* actions around the abortion issue. One of the first and now most famous of the *ad hoc* actions occurred in New York City in the spring of 1969. A state legislative hearing on abortion reform was held on February 13 and was picketed by a large number of people who favored repeal. A group of women, many of whom subsequently formed Redstockings, left the demonstration and invaded the hearing itself demanding that the meeting be turned over to them since women are the only "real experts" on abortion. The women argued vociferously for repeal of the law, "instead of wasting more time talking about these stupid reforms."[7] They also questioned the make-up of the assembled panel of witnesses: "Why are fourteen men and only one woman on your list of speakers—and she a nun?"[8] The women were not allowed to testify. The hearing was moved to another room where it continued, closed to the public. One month later, Redstockings held its own "public hearings." A member of Redstockings described the plan leading up to the hearings:

---

[7] *New York Times*, February 14, 1969.
[8] *Loc. cit.*

One problem in setting up the hearing is to make sure it's understood as politics rather than soap opera. A poor man can tell how it feels to go hungry, and everyone will take for granted the political context. But if a woman speaks frankly about her sexual/reproductive life—which is as central to her oppression as the poor man's economic life —the standard response is pornographic enjoyment of what are considered highly intimate revelations. As a result we are inhibited about discussing sex with each other, let alone in public. At one meeting we got into men's attitudes towards women's sexual pleasure and a woman said "Let's get serious" (by which she meant let's discuss capitalism). . . . The very idea of male-female relations as a political question confounds most people; politics takes place between groups of men, in the "world." . . . There are two ways to get over this obstacle: to confront the audience with the spurious personal-political distinction and to have at our disposal a thorough knowledge of the politics of abortion. . . . We agree that although the witnesses will have this context in mind, they will not talk theory. They will talk about themselves.[9]

The counter-hearings took place on March 21, 1969, at the Washington Square Methodist Church. The meeting had been advertised and drew an audience of some 300 men and women. Twelve Redstockings women addressed them:

It works. In fact it's more effective than we had hoped. The testimony is honest and powerful and evokes strong reactions from the audience—empathy, anger, pain. Women stand up to give their own testimony. One woman decries "the atmosphere of hostility toward men." A man yells "Lesbians!" another remarks that women talk too much, and another sneers at "sob stories." A hint of defensiveness creeps into the women's replies. But then a feminist in the audience walks up to the mike and speaks, controlling but not concealing her rage: "Yes, I have to admit I'm hostile to men. Men have exploited us; why shouldn't we be hostile? Is an oppressed group supposed to love its oppressors?"

---

[9] Ellen Willis, *Up From Radicalism*, pp. 117–118.

Afterward a Black guy says he's never been to such a supercharged meeting except where Blacks were speaking to white people.

We're hoping the idea will catch on and become the equivalent, for the women's movement, of the Vietnam teach-ins.[1]

Although the Redstockings hearings may be remembered as one of the most dramatic *ad hoc* actions *vis-à-vis* the abortion issue, similar examples of confrontation politics have taken place in other parts of the country. Among them:

In January, 1970, in the state of Washington a massive abortion rally was staged by anti-abortion law advocates. A small group of radical women invaded the rally with picket signs depicting the instruments and the methods used by illegal abortionists—pictures of coat-hangers were the most prevalent. The women argued for complete repeal of the law instead of limited reform.

On March 7, 1970, while the Michigan legislature debated a reform bill, the Detroit Women's Liberation Coalition staged a funeral march, mourning the death of women "murdered by back-alley abortionists." Fifty women and five men dressed in black with veils covering their faces marched to the city morgue because "thousands of our sisters have been taken here, victims of those who oppose a woman's right to control her own body." They spent one minute "wailing and displaying coat-hangers, safety pins and other means of self-abortion" and then proceeded to the office of the county prosecutor, William Cahalan, to deliver a "hex":

> Cahalan for you we made this hex.
> The souls of our sisters called forth the moon,
> To cover the sun and bring on your doom.[2]

From June 21 to June 25, 1970, as part of the AMA convention in Chicago, dissenting groups were allowed to present their views to the whole convention. Among the many radical groups protesting the AMA's generally conservative medical stance, Chicago feminists staged several skits about medical treatment of women, including one on the AMA position on abortion.

---

[1] *Ibid.*, pp. 118–119.
[2] *Detroit Free Press,* March 8, 1970.

On strike day, August 26, 1970, demonstrations on the abortion issue were held all over the country. In Minneapolis about twenty women took part in a guerrilla theater skit. Each woman dressed up to represent a different "character" in the abortion drama. A *pregnant* woman was followed by ten small children. A *state legislator* carried a sign saying "have your baby for the state." A *clergyman* carried a sign "have your baby for the church." The *doctor's* placard read "I won't give you an abortion unless you give me $500." The *figure of death* followed the entire procession carrying a coat-hanger. The group wandered through the downtown area leafleting and talking to passers-by about the need for abortion law repeal.

REFERRAL SERVICES

Although the repeal of abortions laws is the ultimate goal, feminists are also involved in "stop-gap" and "first aid" abortion activities helping women find abortionists. It is estimated that a referral service exists every place a women's liberation group exists. Most often the services are run by younger women who have organized themselves independently of any formal feminist group, local or national. It should be noted, however, that many local chapters of NOW make referrals as do a number of YWCA chapters. NOW also distributes a general fact sheet on abortion counseling information.

As noted earlier, the first abortion referral services were organized prior to the emergence of the women's movement and, in fact preceded feminist involvement in the abortion issue. The Association to Repeal Abortion Laws in California, founded by Patricia Maginnis; Parents' Aid Society, founded by Bill Baird; and Clergy Consultation Service, founded by Reverend Howard Moody, were all in operation by the spring of 1967.

A degree of antagonism has developed between Clergy Consultation Service and some women's liberation referral groups. The Clergy service now operates publicly in eighteen states and involves about 700 clergy and lay people. In many places they and the local women's liberation service work closely together; in others they operate independently amidst less than charitable feelings. Staff members of Clergy say the militant attitude of feminists offends local doctors who tend to be conservative. Some feminists, on the other hand, accuse Clergy of operating with a self-righteous, patronizing "Lord Bountiful" attitude which they feel offends and oppresses women:

The term "counseling" is a flattering, patronizing term; flattering to the counselor, patronizing to the counselee. . . . The "counseling" approach comes with a not-so-new prepackaged image of the woman (who is never, never referred to as "woman" but is always "girl") portrayed in the proper penitent, crumpled way, with her head flopped down on her chest and her long hair covering her face. Her pregnancy is referred to as a "problem pregnancy," which somehow puts into one's mind the image of the "problem girl."[3]

Women's liberation referral services, on the other hand, are accused by Clergy Counseling groups of being haphazardly and unsystematically organized. Feminists resent this criticism; as one commented: "Sure we could be much more thorough if we had the operating budget Clergy has to fly all over this country and abroad to personally check out every doctor they use."

Dissension notwithstanding, there are certain generally accepted aims of any abortion referral service. The purpose of a referral service is to maintain an up-to-date list of doctors who will perform medically sound, albeit (in most cases) illegal abortions for reasonable fees. In states where abortion has been legalized (with different restrictions in different states), referral services exist to help women find the most efficient and least expensive places to go. Some services have found that they have a certain degree of bargaining power and have been able, in a few cases, to force doctors to lower their fees considerably. (Currently, fees run between $100–600, excluding transportation expenses. The fee charged is not the only standard used in finding a qualified abortionist. The services also seek out doctors who treat women humanely, who do not themselves make sexual advances (an apparently common practice) and who refrain from including a "morality lecture" with the operation. These qualifications require most services to make an arduous search for individual doctors, though in some large cities women's liberation services have been helped by radical medical groups.[4]

---

[3] Patricia T. Maginnis, "Verbal Systems and Women's Status," speech given at the San Francisco Women's Rally, August 26, 1970.
[4] Radical medical groups have grown up over the last few years to dispense inexpensive and sympathetic medical aid to the growing numbers of hippies, "street people" or radicals, for drug use, riot injuries, venereal disease, and unwanted pregnancies.

It must also be noted that referral services run by women's groups, Planned Parenthood, Parents' Aid, and Clergy Counseling rarely charge fees. In states where legal abortions are obtainable, however, a new industry has developed—referral services run on a profit-making basis. The non-profit services strongly criticize what they consider to be the "outrageous and extortionist" policies and fees of these new business groups. In May, 1971, the New York State Supreme Court barred from operation that state's largest such commercial service. Legal authorities argue that the decision could be interpreted to outlaw *all* the profit-making referral services in the state. The ruling reads in part:

> The law which sought to emancipate women from servitude as unwilling breeders did not intend to deliver them as helpless victims of commercial operators for the exploitation of their misery.[5]

Many women's liberation services around the country operate publicly with the aim of testing the restrictive laws; others run on a *sub rosa* basis to avoid legal harassment. Referrals to out-of-state doctors are considered safest from a legal point of view. If the service, the woman, and the doctor are not all in the same state, arrest and prosecution of any of the involved parties is much more difficult. Getting to another state, or a foreign country, is expensive, however, and many of the women in need of abortions are students, "street people" or poor women with little or no money for transportation costs. Therefore, much referral work takes place quietly within the service's own community.

All the referral services are vitally dependent on "feed-back"—their only means of keeping up-to-date and accurate information on their list of recommended doctors: Were their fees as listed? Were they still "on tap" or "on vacation"? Was their treatment humane? Many services complain of not being able to get women to report back on their experiences. The reasons most often cited are that many women simply want to forget the event as soon as possible, and that others expect a horrible experience and accept a bad one without question or comment.

Since many services around the country operate "overground," it is now almost possible to piece together a "national

---

[5] *New York Times,* May 16, 1971.

abortion referral network." Feminists argue strongly, however, that this does not mean that getting an abortion is easy. Finding an abortionist, legal or not, is still extremely expensive, difficult, and more often than not on a someone-who-knows-someone-who-knows-someone basis.

Politically, the import of the abortion issue varies among the different factions of the women's movement. Some see the legalization of abortion as an end in itself. Their job will essentially be done when the abortion laws are repealed or substantially reformed. Others do not limit their activities to abortion law repeal, for they see the issue as only one of the many legal inequities to be rectified in the area of sex and procreation. They argue, for example, that all restrictions must be lifted, not only from abortion laws, but also from laws governing contraception, so that devices can be publicly advertised and available "over the counter" to any woman regardless of her age or marital status, and purchasable without a doctor's prescription. (Laws exist in more than half the states in the Union limiting in one or more ways such open access.) There are still other feminists who see the abortion/contraception issue as only the most visible manifestation of an entire health care system that is "anti-women" in both theory and practice.[6] Regardless of the political significance they attach to the abortion issue, however, all feminists would agree that it is a woman's basic and inalienable right to limit her reproduction.

---

[6] See separate entry (Medicine), Chapter 10.

8

Child Care

For various historical and sociological reasons a limited number of day care facilities have existed in the United States for the last quarter century. The first massive effort to set up child care centers came during World War II, when six million additional women joined the labor force to fill the gap created by the men who were overseas. The Lanham Act was passed in 1941 to provide federal funds for the children of mothers working for the war effort, and approximately 3100 day care centers were set up. They serviced primarily the children of white collar and blue collar workers. When the war ended, however, no further funds were appropriated.

More recently "developing the country's manpower" has been one of the primary rationales for establishing child care facilities. With this approach, day care has become the support system of work-training programs designed to get welfare recipients off welfare rolls and into productive jobs. Day care services were made available so that mothers of pre-school children could enroll in these work-training programs. In other cases, facilities have been established to enable working mothers (with family incomes below a certain level) to continue working.

Day care advocates include the "Head Start" program as still another approach to the issue. However, in this instance the focus is on raising the educational level of economically deprived children rather than on the mother's needs. In similar fashion, new educational theories have contributed to the desire for better day care facilities regardless of the parental economic status. Many child development experts maintain that children attain fifty percent of their intellectual development before the age of four. Therefore, they argue, there is great need for formal educational experience before the first grade.

For the above reasons, public and private money has been allocated over the years to establish day care facilities. At present, these funds provide for approximately 640,000 "places" in licensed day care centers. The current need is estimated at somewhere over four million places. The gap between availability and need is generally understood as a problem of funding. Feminists, however, argue that it is the enormous psychological resistance to the idea of out-of-home care for children that has impeded both government and industry from dealing with the issue at all realistically. Caroline Bird notes in *Born Female:*

> State-supported centers are taken for granted abroad . . .
> [but in the United States] except for a small group of
> social workers, most Americans deplored public day-care
> for children as one of the sadder devices of the Soviet
> Union to extract labor from mothers at the expense of
> their little children. . . . [The money appropriated during
> World War II] was withdrawn at the end of the war on
> the ground that mothers ought to be at home. Welfare
> workers under the influence of Freudian doctrine on the
> importance of mothering became so worried about the
> large numbers of mothers who wanted to continue earn-
> ing that they mounted long-term studies to "prove" that a
> mother's outside employment hurt her children. The
> studies, when they trickled in during the 1950s, proved
> no such thing, but the reassurance was not reported in the
> popular magazines and newspapers.[1]

Stated in a slightly different way, "The assumption was that at any and all times, mother knew best and mother *was* best. Mother and child were locked in an internal embrace."[2] Thus, despite the fact that the number of working mothers has increased nearly eight-fold since 1940, day care, according to feminists, has always (and only) been looked upon as an emergency stop-gap, a temporary measure until mothers can return to their homes to care for their children themselves.

---

[1] Bird, p. 207.
[2] Susan Edmiston, "The Psychology of Day Care," *New York* Magazine, April 5, 1971, p. 39.

Feminist Analysis
and Action

BY 1969–70, due in large part to the emergence of the women's movement, child care had become a "hot issue." Indeed, the demand for child care facilities linked otherwise disparate groups of people: conservatives, liberals, middle and lower class families, early education experts and feminists. Of all the different arguments for increased child care facilities, however, it is the feminist analysis that is most often attacked.

The feminist demand for child care[3] springs from a deliberate rejection of the traditional view that it is the woman's responsibility, and only hers, to take care of children. Thus, feminists view child care as crucial to woman's emancipation:

> A basic cause of the second-class status of women in America and the world for thousands of years has been the notion that . . . because women bear children, it is primarily their responsibility to care for them and even that this ought to be the chief function of a mother's existence. Women will never have full opportunities to participate in our economic, political, cultural life as long as they bear this responsibility almost entirely alone and isolated from the larger world. . . . [We believe] that the care and welfare of children is incumbent on society and parents. We reject the idea that mothers have a special child care role that is not to be shared equally by fathers.[4]

Feminists are most frequently accused of being willing to sacrifice the welfare of their children to attain their own "liberation." They respond to the criticism directly, arguing that a woman must have her own identity as a person (not merely as a mother) and she must not be made to feel guilty about her desire or need to work or pursue other interests. They argue

---

[3] Feminists make a distinction between *child* care and *day* care. The words *day* care imply that facilities are needed only during the daytime. Feminists, noting the numbers of women who work at night, talk about *child* care centers, ideally operating on a 24-hour basis.
[4] NOW, "Why Feminists Want Child Care," press release, December, 1970.

further that such a woman will be a better parent than one who
is chained to her home and her family.

> Anyone who believes that the best environment for chil-
> dren is being locked up in a small area with a person who
> is . . . becoming ill out of frustration and lack of stimula-
> tion, who sees no way out of her entrapment, is deluding
> himself. I do not believe that any woman, no matter how
> educated or creative, can cope lovingly with a small child
> when she is isolated and dependent. . . . [Women are] so
> stunted as whole people . . . that they must find their
> identities through their children and husbands. Conse-
> quently the growth of those children and their eventual
> independence is extremely threatening. The terrible ma-
> ternal grasping, the real fight almost to the death that is
> waged by teenagers in order to get away from these
> mothers, grows out of women's realization that when
> these children are gone, they are no one.[5]

Like so much of the current feminist activity, the child care
issue involves short-term and long-term goals. The short-term
goals are simply to get child care facilities from whatever source
possible to serve whoever might need them. The long-range goal
is, not surprisingly, the implementation of radically different
theories of child rearing and pre-school education. Stated briefly,
a child care center based on feminist thinking is one in which
"sexism," i.e., male and female sex-role categorization, is absent.
Teachers, ideally men as well as women, do not present to the
children the traditional male-female roles—"mommy's job is
always to take care of the house; daddy's is always to go to work"
—as the only roles acceptable for men and women. When anti-
feminists object that these methods will make it difficult for the
young child to accept his/her sexual identity, feminists argue
that critics are confusing sexual identity with sex roles. Roles,
according to feminists, must be eliminated; as for sexual identity,
"acceptance is irrelevant; it's an almost immutable fact, like
saying acceptance of the location of one's head."[6]

---

[5] Melody Kilian, "Children Are Only Little People," *Women's Liberation
Notes on Child Care* (New York City), p. 10. (Hereafter referred to as
Notes on Child Care.)
[6] Carol Burris, Wilma Scott Heide, *Critique of Reports—White House Conference on Children: Cluster on Individuality*, December, 1970, unpaginated.

Although feminists believe that both men and women should be equally responsible for child rearing, there have been several problems in recruiting and utilizing men in child care center work. "Men just won't work for the salaries we can afford to pay," according to Betty Foloway, one of the organizers of a nursery established jointly by the Central New Jersey chapter of NOW and Princeton University. She added, "It's a shame women are still willing to work for so little."[7]

One women's liberation child care center staffed by volunteer workers was run on a Saturday-only basis in an effort to involve men. (On university campuses where student and faculty schedules are more flexible, the scheduling problem is alleviated somewhat.) Organizing around work/study schedules, and/or raising salaries, however, do not appear to be the only difficulties in attracting men to child care centers. A woman involved in the Saturday Center wrote:

> Our problems recruiting men include their fear of taking care of children; not considering it a radical or masculine activity, in fact considering it trivial. . . . Few of the men had previous experience with children, and were curious about them. . . . Only one man needs to be confronted about his refusal to diaper. Another man enjoys it, finding satisfaction in this very personal encounter in which he knows he has been able to meet a concrete need. One of the men finds himself more protective of the little children.

> . . . At first one man feared he would hurt a child, not understand or know how to meet their demands, not know what to do in emergencies. . . . [But] those who initially experience fear and impotence in the face of infants, feel more comfortable with them. . . . Some women feel the men will have to learn about child care as they did. . . . The men think they need to know more about taking care of children. There was talk of setting up a course at Alternate U. but the men don't yet seem to want to spend too much of their time on this. One man suggested they meet an hour or two earlier on Saturdays to talk some issues out. There isn't much discussion among staff and the more experienced are reluctant to take leadership . . .

---

[7] Interview, March, 1971.

[but] as one man said, if we are developing a model for an
alternative institution, we should think more systematically about it.[8]

Books chosen for feminist child care centers do not reinforce
the traditional views of men and women; nor do toys. In one
center run by feminists, the group "scraped together" $22 for a
Petit Frère doll with male genitals, so that the children wouldn't
think that all dolls are female. Ironically, though perhaps not
surprisingly, "parents seemed to be the only ones to take notice of
the stressedly male doll."[9] The traditional "housekeeping corner"
or "doll corner" does not exist as a segregated area in feminist
centers; nor are the building blocks and trains kept separately
from the other toys. Neither boys nor girls are discouraged from
"rough-housing," building things, playing with dolls or "cooking."
Some of the most concentrated campaigns by women's movement activists for these kinds of child care centers can be found
on college and university campuses. Feminists and other members of the academic community are demanding that there be
university-financed parentally-controlled child care centers available to student, faculty and employee parents. In addition, nearly
every official and unofficial report on the status of women at a
particular university places the provision of child care facilities
as central to elevating the status of women in academia. One
of the earliest demands for university-financed child care was
sparked by the women's liberation (and other radical) groups'
protest of the firing of sociologist Marlene Dixon from the University of Chicago in January, 1969. Women students demanded
and won from the administration a pledge of support for child
care facilities. By mid-1971, nothing had materialized, although
a group of students and parents had been meeting on a regular
basis and had prepared a formal proposal for a $200,000 center
with a 100-child capacity. Other universities where similar formal proposals have been made include Buffalo State in New
York, Harvard University, University of Pittsburgh (the city's
largest employer), Temple University in Philadelphia, University
of California at Berkeley, Columbia University, and the University of Washington in Seattle.

On many campuses—in the absence of administration sup-

---

[8] Bette Freed, "It's Not Only Up to Mom: The Beginnings of Child Care
Service Staffed by Men and Childless Women," *Notes on Child Care*, pp.
23ff.

[9] Rosalyn Baxandall, "Cooperative Nurseries," *Notes on Child Care*, p. 19.

port, or pending administration studies of licensing requirements, financing, space allocation, professional personnel, etc.—
"bootleg" child care centers have been organized and run on a
volunteer basis by students and faculty parents themselves.
Some have met with harassment from the universities, others
have been more or less "left alone." Some of the earliest University centers grew "spontaneously" out of student strikes of the
late 1960's; some of these centers are still operating, although
illegally and on shoestring budgets. One student described the
origins of the San Francisco University center:

> The SFU Co-op Family grew out of the Board of Governors' meeting room sit-in in the spring of 1968. The
> Board Room was occupied by students during the . . .
> censure crisis. They decided somewhat satirically to use
> the space to fill a student need. The idea of a nursery was
> hit upon and some students and faculty who agreed with
> the sit-in brought their children for a number of days.
> When the sit-in ended the nursery also ended, but the
> idea of an on-campus nursery was born.[1]

An on-campus nursery has also been in operation on the Columbia University campus since the spring of 1968. During the strike
there, a building was commandeered for child care. After the
strike, the cooperatively run center moved to another location
and continued to operate.

Women's liberation child care centers have also opened in
storefronts and abandoned buildings in cities across the country.
It should be noted that these "liberation" centers are almost exclusively run by radical or politico feminists; moderate feminists
are more apt to press for licensed and professionally-operated
centers. The first known women's liberation child care center
was started in New York in April 1967; by mid-1971 estimates of
parentally-controlled centers ranged from forty to sixty.[2] Although they are all operating extra-legally, there has been little
effort by the city to close them.[3]

If the problems of financing and licensing a *legal* child care

---

[1] Kilian, p. 11.
[2] Not all are run by feminists.
[3] In fact, by July 1970 enough pressure had been brought by feminists and
other child care activists that the city eased licensing requirements, and
many of these "bootleg" centers qualified for licenses and thus became
eligible for city funds. In addition, some city money was extended to some
of the centers despite their unlicensed status.

center are enormous, then those of organizing a cooperatively-run, non-funded, extra-legal center are said to be "horrendous." Rosalyn Baxandall, one of the organizers of New York's first center has described some of the initial problems:

> Dues were paid in accordance with the number of days worked [in the center] by a mother. Those who couldn't work at all paid $20.00 a month, those who worked once a week paid $12.50, and those who worked twice weekly paid $5.00. . . . When the nursery first started most women had much free time and their schedules were flexible. As people began to count on the free time and found work or activities to be involved in, it became harder for them to adapt their schedules in cases of sickness or other crises, and a continued shortage of people to work has developed. Much time is spent, on the phone, changing and hassling with the schedule: who can work on which day in replacement of somebody else, who had been scheduled to work, etc. . . . The majority felt that all should equally contribute, although I feel that ideally, a cooperative could work if everyone puts in what they are able to and takes out what is needed. . . .

> As these nurseries operated, we discriminated against the most needy, those who were so disorganized generally as to have trouble in participating in this project. Another example of this discrimination appeared when the group decided that a mother of an extremely disruptive child, who would have tantrums throughout a session would have to withdraw. Certainly this mother and child had greater need of the nursery than the average woman.

> . . . Money has always been a tremendous hassle. Many women can't afford anything, and others can't afford very much. We are always behind in our rent, gas and electricity and our telephone was shut off because we were behind in paying the bill.[4]

Once the centers are functioning, however, the participants for the most part are pleased with the freewheeling approach and, in some cases, are uninterested in attempting to gain licensed status.

---

[4] Baxandall, pp. 18ff.

A number of the radical women involved in child care activities have attempted to put into practice some of the philosophical and organizational ideas of the women's movement. In some centers, for example, a non-authoritarian structure is part of their concerted effort to break down the traditional nuclear family pattern:

The fact that we have no supervisor or coordinator, no person in fact, who has any role different from that of any other parent, has meant that there is no one authority figure for the children to become dependent on. We began to see the [SFU Co-op] Family as an experiment in the formation of a new type of extended or communal Family wherein a number of parents take real responsibility for each others' children. . . . At first, we thought that the children might be "insecure" or "confused" by having twenty parents during the week plus numerous other students who come in to play. . . .

Each child in the Family now regularly sees at least fifty other people each week—twenty parents and about twenty-five other children and various student friends. His or her universe is greatly expanded—in fact, exploded, compared to a nuclear home. . . . They do not look to any one adult for direction or protection. They have very strong friendships among themselves and with students and they all have good friends that their biological parents may not even know. They do not view people other than their parents as enemies or threats, but rather they tend to view others as real parts of their world.[5]

Of equal importance to some of the women is their wish to cut across class lines and attract lower class and poor women to these centers. To this end, a number of the "liberation" centers have been located in ghetto communities and a conscious effort has been made to publicize them among community residents. In some instances the attempt has worked; in others, cutting across class lines has not always been so easily accomplished:

Most of the group were white middle-class hippy or radical type women, a third of whom had Black children. There were no Black mothers, and most efforts to recruit Black

---

[5] Kilian, pp. 12–13.

or Puerto Rican mothers failed. The objection seemed to
be that our nursery was non-institutional: dirty and
sloppy, and emphasis was placed on free play rather than
structured learning. One Black mother did join the group
but left because she didn't feel at ease with the other
mothers who seemed like hippies to her.[6]

Government and Industry Activity

AS NOTED EARLIER the short-term goal of establishing as many
child care centers as possible—as quickly as possible—has united
women's movement activists with other child care advocates into
a sizeable political lobby group. They are bringing pressure on
the federal, state and municipal levels and on private industry to
establish these facilities. It is important to note, however, that
women's movement activists are by no means united on the
issue of how the centers should be funded or run. For example,
some accept the idea of federal, state, municipal or industry
financing, while others reject some or all of these approaches arguing instead for parental or community control of the centers.

On the public level, countless legislative proposals have been
circulated (and some enacted) within federal, state and local
government departments. Activists have demanded not only financial assistance, but also an easing of what they feel are
bureaucratic and needlessly strict licensing requirements. They
have demanded further that everything concerning child care
be centralized in one government department. New York, Berkeley and Chicago were among the first cities to put this principle
into practice. In addition, activists demand a change in the tax
laws (federal and state) to permit the deduction of child care
expenses for working parents.

By 1970 enough interest in child care had built on the federal
level[7] that five separate bills authorizing funds for day care were
introduced in Congress. Most of them, however, linked funds for

---

[6] Baxandall, p. 18.
[7] It should be noted that since 1968 both the Departments of Labor and
Agriculture have operated small-scale experimental centers for children of
employees.

day care with various poverty programs. Consistent with their view, feminists have strenuously argued that the rationale for child care facilities must be divorced from public assistance programs. "They must be developed not in order to lessen public assistance roles but rather as a basic right."[8]

In December, 1970, more than 4000 delegates assembled in Washington, D.C. for the once-a-decade White House Conference on Children. Among the many recommendations (dealing with every conceivable aspect of children's lives) sent to the President at the end of the week-long conference, the most widely supported was a proposal for a federally financed national child care network. A comprehensive bill introduced into Congress after the White House Conference would authorize up to $6 billion annually to support such a network of centers.[9] Clearly the existence of this kind of facility would constitute a radical change in child rearing practices in this country.

Although a White House Conference on Children has been held every ten years since 1909, it is probably safe to say that the 1970 Conference was the first one at which a strong feminist voice was heard. The National Organization for Women organized a women's caucus in order to introduce feminist thinking into discussions of child care practices and early childhood education. For instance, NOW's critique of several of the prepared task force reports often assailed the many proposed "children's commissions," "task forces," and "long-range recommendations" on child development, for excluding children, feminists, and "average mothers" from their planning committees; and also for ignoring almost entirely the question of sex-role stereotyping in child development theories and practices. For example, the women criticized the highly acclaimed "Sesame Street" program, arguing that, excellent as it is, the program reinforces sex-role stereotypes. In another critique, NOW members took sharp exception to the language used in the prepared reports, in particular the use of the pronoun "he" whenever "person" was meant:

> We advocate you read every report, all literature, and all written material for the rest of your life in the following way: When person is the reference, simply substitute she

---

[8] Women's Caucus of the White House Conference on Children, "Resolutions Passed," press release, December, 1970.

[9] The government usually spends about $500 million a year on a number of child care programs—all, however, linked to other pieces of legislation.

and her for he, his, and him, and [we] guarantee you'll
shortly worry about the exclusion of the male from
thought and language, let alone the behavioral reality.[1]

A strong interest in child care facilities has also emerged in
the private sector, and hundreds of reports and proposals have
been prepared on the subject. Many child care advocates believe
that industries should take at least partial responsibility for the
child care needs of their employees' children. For example, one
of the central demands of the *Ladies' Home Journal* sit-in in
March, 1970, was for a company-financed, employee-controlled
day care center. The protesters stated:

> It occurred to us . . . that the *Journal*, a magazine for
> wives and mothers, would do well to take the lead in child
> care by establishing on its premises a day care center for
> the pre-school-age children of its employees.[2]

It should be noted that a number of corporations have been
experimenting with on-premises day care for several years[3]
(some, prior to the emergence of the women's movement). According to these companies, the provision of child care facilities
not only attracts more women workers, but also appears to cut
down on absenteeism and turnover by about 25 percent. Some
of the women child care activists fear, however, that unless these
centers are under complete parental (or community) control,
employees will be merely "controlled" by their companies. For
example, if child care centers were treated as a "fringe benefit,"
some feminists argue that employee-parents might hesitate to
criticize company policy or working conditions, be reluctant to
jeopardize their jobs by pressing for raises and/or promotions,
etc. It should be noted further that some child care advocates
maintain that any company-sponsored center should serve community children as well as employee children. In a number of the
existing company centers this is already the case.

In the above "private sector approach," child care facilities

---

[1] Burris and Heide.
[2] *Ladies' Home Journal*, August, 1970, p. 64.
[3] Tioga Sportswear (Fall River, Mass.), KLH Research and Development
Corp. (Cambridge, Mass.), Avco Economic Corp. (Roxbury, Mass.), Sky-
land Texture Co. (Morgantown, N.C.), and Illinois Bell Telephone were
some of the earliest to establish these facilities.

serve a particular company or industry. There are, however, other businessmen who see child care itself as an industry. These businessmen are said to "package and sell franchises for day care centers in much the same way others have sold franchises for fried chicken, hamburgers and root beer."[4] It is precisely this "chicken delight" concept that has created tremendous controversy over these centers among feminists and non-feminists alike. Formula production methods are a key to successful franchising, they argue, but while "you can train anyone to produce a hamburger that tastes the same in California and New York . . . there isn't any rule book for running a day-care center. It's too complex."[5] The core of the controversy is not whether these centers should exist, but what will be their priority—profit or children. Controversy notwithstanding, by the end of 1970 over one hundred franchised centers were already in operation in twenty-one states, and the companies were predicting that by the end of 1971 they would be serving over 200,000 children.

. . .

There are now many advocates of out-of-home child care facilities and their number is growing steadily and rapidly, primarily because of the expansion of the women's movement. Without a complete reordering of national priorities, however, which in this instance involves the acceptance of a radically different attitude about the responsibility of child rearing, significant change will not occur. The projected child care need in 1980 is 5.3 million places. If child care facilities, both public and private, grow at a rate of ten percent a year,[6] by 1980 the gap between need and existing places will have widened, not lessened. To the many feminists who view the child care issue as central to the emancipation of women, these figures and estimates paint a pessimistic picture.

---

[4] *New York Times*, December 27, 1969.
[5] Alice Lake, "The Day Care Business," *McCall's*, November, 1970, p. 96, quoting a business consultant.
[6] The "educated guess" of the Day Care and Child Development Council of America.

9

Education

FEMINISTS ARGUE that the entire U.S. educational system, public and private, from kindergarten to graduate school, will have to undergo radical transformation before the status of women will visibly improve. There are feminists active at every level of the system challenging educational assumptions, practices and laws which, they say, perpetuate the image and reinforce the reality of woman as wife and mother and, in fact, discourage her from seeking any other roles. They argue that females who perceive themselves as scholars are simply not taken seriously by their peers, their professors or their employers; hence, furthering educational or career aims becomes almost impossible. Finally, they point to the fact that there is no federal law which prohibits sex discrimination in education.

In June and July, 1970, the House Special Subcommittee on Education held hearings on sex discrimination in education. The 1250 pages of testimony that resulted from the seven days of hearings constitute the most extensive compilation of feminist arguments against the educational system ever gathered in one place. The hearings were in conjunction with anti-sex discrimination legislation proposed by Rep. Edith Green (D., Ore.) and marked the first time in U.S. history that hearings had ever been held on the subject. The testimony touched on every aspect of the educational process: picture books for nursery school children; reading books for elementary school children; the effect of sex segregated classes on high school boys and girls; the status of female students in undergraduate and graduate schools; the status of female teachers in elementary, secondary, undergraduate and graduate schools; the status of females in corresponding administrative ranks; the effect of career counseling on women; the sociology of education; the psychology of education; minority women and education; and the need for strong federal legislation banning sex discrimination from the educational process.

The feminist critique of the status of women in the educational system can be summarized in five major points:

1. Non-college teaching is the single largest profession for women (in 1968, 42 percent of all professional women were teachers), but very few women rise to the highest-level jobs. A 1969 National Education Association study found: Elementary Schools: 86 percent of teachers are women; 78 percent of principals are men. Secondary Schools: 47 percent of teachers are women; 95 percent of principals are men. Public School system: Of the 13,000 school superintendents, two are women.

2. Women teaching in colleges and universities are in the lower professional ranks, and are not promoted as quickly as their male counterparts. A 1969 study by the American Council on Education found:

34.8 percent of instructors are women
28.7 percent of assistant professors are women
15.7 percent of associate professors are women
9.4 percent of full professors are women.

Studies made at individual universities or of individual disciplines show substantially the same results. Concurrently, it has been found that 90 percent of the men with doctorates and twenty years' experience will be full professors; for women with the same qualifications barely half will be full professors.[1] In a 1969 study of graduate sociology departments across the country another inverse ratio was found: the more prestigious the university, or the particular sociology department, the lower the percentage of women faculty and of women doctoral candidates.[2] Feminists have carried the "prestige" argument one step further, noting the lack of women faculty at the high status "Seven Sisters" colleges, as well as the trend in the last few years of replacing the retiring female presidents of these institutions with males.

3. The salaries of women teaching at the college level are

---

[1] "WEAL Fact Sheet on Sex Discrimination in Universities and Colleges." Included in *Green Hearings*, pp. 310ff.
[2] Alice Rossi, "Status of Women in Graduate Departments of Sociology, 1968–1969." Reprinted in *The American Sociologist*, February, 1970.

almost always less than those of their male counterparts. A 1965 National Education Association survey (the most recent available) reveals that the median annual income of female faculty members was 16.6 percent lower than that of males. Again, studies made of individual colleges reflect the same statistics. Although some of the inequity is due to the generally lower rank women hold, often there are pay differences between men and women with the same academic positions and qualifications and even sometimes within the same institutions. Citing Department of Labor figures on the general earnings gap between men and women, one witness at the hearings noted that ". . . education does not appear to enhance [women's] earning capacity to the same degree as is true for men."[3]

4. Women are often required to have higher academic qualifications than men for admission to college. The American Council on Education's annual survey of college freshmen shows that for the class of 1968 over 40 percent of the girls admitted to four-year colleges had B+ or better averages in high school, whereas only 18 percent of the boys had such grades. The same point is made at the graduate school level, where it has been found that women almost uniformly have higher I.Q.'s and better grades than their male counterparts. Feminists also cite numerous examples, including publicly supported universities, where a quota system restricts the admission of women to only the most highly qualified.

5. According to feminists, women students are unable to receive decent career counseling at both the high school and college levels, and are continually discouraged from entering "non-feminine" occupations. Most of this discouragement, they say, comes from teachers, professors, and professional career counselors, all of whom preach the "feminine mystique." In its fact sheet on counseling WEAL argues that the "feminine mystique" career advice is due primarily to the fact that education departments which train future counselors are headed and staffed by men. Of the 343 departments, 209 (61 percent) have no women at all; 82 (25 percent) have one woman; and 52 (15 percent) have two or more women.[4]

---

[3] Jean Ross, Chairman, Legislative Program Committee American Association of University Women, testimony, *Green Hearings*, p. 26.
[4] WEAL Fact Sheet, "Some Good Reasons Why It is Difficult For Girls to Get Good Counseling." Included in *Green Hearings*, pp. 314ff.

Pending Legislation

As of 1971 every federal law specifically dealing with sex discrimination exempts the field of education, and no federal law dealing with education includes "sex" among its discriminatory bans:

—Title VII of the 1964 Civil Rights Act, which addresses itself to equal employment opportunity, does not cover employment in educational institutions, public or private.

—Title VI of the 1964 Civil Rights Act, which deals with programs and activities receiving federal assistance (including educational institutions), does not include "sex" among its discriminatory bans of race, color, religion or national origin.

—The 1963 Equal Pay Act does not cover executive, administrative or professional employees (in this case most teachers, professors and administrators).

—The U.S. Civil Rights Commission's jurisdiction does not include sex discrimination.

Neither does any federal or state law prohibit exclusion of women from public colleges or universities.

In February, 1970, Rep. Edith Green introduced the Omnibus Post-Secondary Education Act, which included four anti-sex discrimination proposals. The above-mentioned hearings were held to debate these proposals:

—Amend Title VII to include educational institutions.

—Amend Title VI to include sex in its discriminatory bans.

—Extend the Equal Pay Act to cover executive, administrative and professional employees.

—Direct the Civil Rights Commission to investigate discrimination against women.

Although the majority of witnesses were in favor of all the proposals (the only criticism had to do with the proposals' effect on private all-male or all-female schools), during the 91st Congress the bill never got out of committee. Rep. Green will reintroduce some or all of her proposals in the 92nd Congress, depending on the extent to which anti-sex discrimination bans are included in the Administration's 1971 education bill.

In the meantime, feminists have invoked Executive Order

11375 to combat sex discrimination in education. Although the Order does not have the status of law, it does prohibit sex discrimination on the part of government contractors. It is estimated that over 2,000 colleges and universities receive approximately $3.3 billion in federal contracts each year.

Since January 31, 1970, Women's Equity Action League and other women's rights groups have brought nearly three hundred complaints of "patterns of discrimination" against colleges and universities; among them, the University of Maryland (the first university against which a complaint was filed), the entire State University and College systems of Florida, California, New Jersey and New York, Columbia University, Harvard University, and the University of Michigan. WEAL also filed a class action against all the medical schools in the country, based on testimony given at the Green hearings. A similar charge was filed by Professional Women's Caucus against all the law schools. By the end of the year, compliance investigations (carried out by HEW) had begun at 120 of the charged schools, and in at least two cases federal contracts were delayed until the institutions complied with the Order.[5] At Harvard, more than three million dollars in pending contracts was held up for two weeks, until the University agreed to disclose to an HEW investigator certain personnel information regarding its women employees and students. Following a complaint filed against the University of Michigan by FOCUS, a Michigan women's rights group, over $400,000 in contracts was withheld until the University presented a satisfactory affirmative action program to improve the status of women. "In tight times like these we can't afford to have any contracts held up," Fedele Fauri, Michigan's vice-president, commented. "We just want to get those bastards at HEW off our backs."[6]

Of all the investigations, the one at Michigan constituted what activists felt was the first, albeit limited, "breakthrough" in serious compliance with the Order because Michigan's affirmative action plan incorporated specific numerical goals and timetables. The announcement of the Michigan plan in March, 1971, marked the first time the concept of goals and timetables had

---

[5] According to HEW, twenty-one institutions had had contracts delayed over the issues of racial, ethnic, religious or sex discrimination. According to WEAL, most of these were over sex discrimination.
[6] Daniel Zwerdling, "The Womanpower Problem," *The New Republic,* March 20, 1971, p. 12.

been included in an agreement dealing with sex discrimination. The total Michigan plan was considered by HEW to be the "most comprehensive" of any to date and has since been used as a model for other universities. The university committed itself to equal pay for men and women employees having the same qualifications and doing the same work (this provision included the awarding of back pay to any woman employee who lost wages because of sex discrimination by the university); "vigorous" recruitment of females for academic positions; equal treatment for "tandem teams," i.e., husband and wife both working at the same university; giving priority to "all present female employees occupying clerical or other non-academic positions who seek promotion and who possess qualifications equivalent to those of higher-level male employees."[7] The Michigan president's assistant, Barbara Newell, viewed the "historic" plan less optimistically and remarked that the goals and timetables regarding increased hiring and promotion would merely serve to make sure "women aren't the first to be squeezed out."[8]

Charges of sex discrimination have also been filed against school systems on the elementary and secondary levels. Perhaps the earliest formal complaint was filed in October, 1970, against Montgomery County Schools, Montgomery County, Maryland. The charges were based on several allegations:

> Of the 23 Senior High Schools in the county, *not one* has a woman principal. Of the 24 Junior High Schools, *only one* has a woman principal. . . . Yet nationally, women are approximately two thirds of the teaching force . . . and it is from the teaching force that principals are drawn.[9]

The complaint also charged that the Montgomery County maternity leave policy was in direct violation of the June, 1970, sex discrimination guidelines accompanying Executive Order 11375.

The vast majority of feminist activists want strong legisla-

---

[7] *Chronicle of Higher Education*, January 11, 1971. It should be noted as well that one of the first women to apply for back pay on the grounds that she was equally if not better qualified than her male counterpart was refused by the University. The University contended that she was not underpaid, but the man was overpaid. The man did not receive a salary cut.
[8] Zwerdling, p. 12.
[9] Letter to the Secretary of Health, Education and Welfare, from Women's Equity Action League, October 13, 1970.

tion prohibiting sex discrimination in education, such as that proposed by Rep. Green. Nonetheless, ". . . by filing charges under the Executive Order we have been able to 'legitimize' the issue and confirm the suspicion that there really *is* discrimination," according to Dr. Bernice Sandler, WEAL's Action Committee Chairman for Federal Contract Compliance in Education. "The very possibility of being able to be formally charged with sex discrimination with resultant loss of contract monies has spurred administrators to examine the status of women on their campus and to develop affirmative action programs for women. As always, money talks! And, in this respect—potential loss of money—the Executive Order is even more persuasive than a law."[1] It is quickly pointed out, however, that without strong legislation there is nothing to stop a university from discriminating against women if it chooses to give up its federal support.

College and University Campuses

IN MANY RESPECTS the entire women's movement, its issues and activities, can be seen in microcosm on a college or university campus. The degree of feminist activity, quite naturally, varies from campus to campus, although it can be safely assumed that every U.S. campus has been exposed to women's liberation either directly or indirectly. On one campus there may be only a handful of women students at a tentative once-a-week consciousness raising session; on another, a faculty/student-run child care center; on still another, an abortion counseling service. On a number of campuses women's groups are sufficiently organized to have set up a women's center and a number of women's studies courses; to have produced an in-depth task force report on the status of women at that university; and to have brought formal charges against the university because of sex discrimination.

It is difficult to pinpoint exactly when the women's movement emerged on college campuses. When NOW was formed in 1966, some of its founders and charter members were women in academia who undoubtedly carried the broad issues of equal employment and equal education back to their respective cam-

---

[1] Interview, June, 1971.

puses. Moreover, many campus women had read and discussed de Beauvoir's *The Second Sex* and Friedan's *The Feminine Mystique*. In addition, some of the women students involved in radical campus politics had begun to talk about the "woman issue." Included below are some examples of early "visible" actions directly involving academic women with feminist issues. These are not necessarily the only, or the first, events of their kind. They do, however, indicate the geographic spread of the movement and the variety of issues discussed and activities undertaken.

—April 29, 1968: At the University of Washington's annual Men's Day, the appearance of a Playboy bunny was protested by a small group of radical women as "an exhibition of womanhood just as body." The protesters caused enough disruption to be physically removed from the ballroom where the Playboy bunny was answering questions from students.

—Summer, 1968: After the Columbia strike which closed the university down, various undergraduate and graduate students organized a "free university" to continue classes. Included in the "liberation" classes was one on women's liberation that reportedly lasted longer than any of the others, and had the largest and most consistent attendance.

—January, 1969: Dr. Marlene Dixon, a politically radical assistant professor of sociology at the University of Chicago was refused reappointment. The reason given was her failure to meet the academic standards of the university. The radical students and faculty members believed her firing was due to the radical political emphasis she brought to her classes, and the fact that she was female. The firing sparked a two-week series of protests involving numerous campus issues and as many factions of radical students. The occasion marked the first public appearance of the campus women's liberation group. Among other actions, the women issued a policy paper which delineated what the students saw as ". . . the University of Chicago's consistent policy of discrimination and exploitation of women."[2] The paper touched on the issues of

2 "Position paper on the Woman Question," University of Chicago, unpaginated.

salary discrepancies between male and female faculty members; the lack of courses (except for Professor Dixon's) on women's history or socialization
process; the nepotism rule forbidding two members of
the same family from teaching at the same level ("for
example, Marie Meyer, Nobel Prizewinner in Physics,
was refused a position on the faculty, whereas her
husband worked as a full professor");[3] the hours restrictions placed on women undergraduates but not on
men; the lack of day care centers and paid pregnancy
leaves; the discouragement given women who aspire to
academic careers. These issues have since become the
basis of many feminist activities on the university
level.

—February 5, 1969: At Grinnell College, Grinnell, Iowa
ten students (six women and four men) staged a
"nude-in" to protest *Playboy* magazine as demeaning to
women. A *Playboy* representative had come to Grinnell
to deliver a series of talks on the *Playboy* "philosophy"
as part of the college's Sex Education Series. When he
entered the room the ten students disrobed while supporters carried signs and handed out leaflets explaining the protest. The demonstration was sponsored by
Grinnell's women's liberation group which called *Playboy* "a money changer in the temple of the body."[4] One
woman added that "most Grinnell males had previously
thought very little about what *Playboy* was actually
about, so this was a real eye opener for them."[5]

—Spring, 1969: The first "official" women's studies
course offered for credit was included in the spring
curriculum of Cornell University. The course grew out
of the Cornell Conference on Women (a conference
the previous January which drew over 2000 people),
and began as a small informal colloquium on the nature of the female personality from the behavioral
science perspective. (By the 1970 spring semester the

---

[3] *Ibid.*
[4] *Grinnell Herald Register*, February 6, 1969.
[5] "Playboy Fucked Up," *Women: A Journal of Liberation*, Fall, 1969, p. 53.

course had been formally titled "Evolution of the Female Personality," had incorporated other disciplines, and had enrolled over 200 students and 100 auditors.)

Also during the Spring, 1969, semester the first women's law course was given (on a non-credit basis) at the University of Pennsylvania. The following fall the course, "Women and the Law," was offered for credit at New York University Law School.

By the late spring of 1969 the college and university community in general was well aware of the existence of a new women's movement. Several reports documenting the status of women at individual campuses had been written; others were in the process of being compiled. In May, 1969, the first two administration-appointed task forces on the status of women were set up in response to feminist pressure—at the University of California at Berkeley and at the University of Chicago. Each was given a year to prepare an in-depth report on women at its respective university.[6] Also, plans were being discussed for the formation of women's caucuses or official committees within some of the academic disciplines.[7] Moreover, the National Organization for Women had begun to actively recruit members from the college community. Two national organizations within the academic community also responded to the growth of the women's movement. In the spring of 1970, the American Association of University Professors, a policy-making and watchdog organization of academia, reactivated its Committee W after a forty-year hiatus,[8] with the aim of encouraging policy changes regarding employment of women at universities. A national student organization, Intercollegiate Association of Women Students, reordered its priorities somewhat and began working at the grassroots level educating women students about women's issues.

By the end of 1970, the "visible" results of this growing pressure could be seen in the some 75 official and unofficial reports on the status of women on individual campuses, as well as in

---

[6] A ten-volume study on education at Stanford University was published in March, 1969, and included a lengthy appendix on the status of women. The report on women, however, was not compiled in the context of women's rights although it has since been viewed from that standpoint.
[7] See separate entry (Academic Disciplines), Chapter 10.
[8] Committee W was formed in 1919 during the first movement for women's rights. It was deactivated in 1928 after the demise of that movement.

the existence of formal complaints of sex discrimination filed against some 300 colleges and universities.[9]

There is one expression of feminism unique to the college campus: the women's studies courses. The first such courses appeared in the "alternate U's" or "free universities" organized by radical students during the mid-to-late sixties. The women's courses that were included were so freewheeling and informal as to have constituted little more than consciousness raising groups with reading lists. As noted above, the first formally-taught course on the subject was at Cornell in the spring semester of 1969. Sheila Tobias, who set up that course, has written about the need for women's studies programs at every college and university in the country, noting that the feminist demand for these courses is similar to that of blacks for Black Studies programs:

> A female (or male) undergraduate learns little of the history of Woman as a class; almost nothing of the history of individual women. Nor is it even deemed worthy of explanation as to why women are so absent from history, economics, politics and the arts. By implication, they were "different"; and by omitting any analysis, the "difference" appears to be natural, inevitable, unalterable. . . . And how much does the average college graduate, male or female, find out about suffragism, the Marxist analysis of the condition of women, and J. S. Mill's book on the subject? . . . [Regarding the Cornell course] as instructors, we found that there was material in abundance, but that we put it together in a different way. We looked at Mary McCarthy's *The Group,* for example, as a social history of female college grads in the 1930's. We looked at "masculinity" and "femininity" as categories of acceptable behavior, and not as givens. We looked at motherhood and child-rearing practices in other societies and in our own as culturally determined. We asked whether male-female relations (in the aggregate at least) can and ought to be defined in political terms. . . . And we looked at the consumer society, the suburbs, at marriage, at the Oneida Community [Cornell's location], at

---

[9] A summary and analysis of many of these reports was published April, 1971: "The Status of Academic Women," Eric Clearing House on Higher Education, Washington, D.C.

the Flapper, and at *Playboy* in new ways. . . . Eventually, perhaps, Female Studies, like Black Studies, may not be necessary. When the ordinary curriculum has incorporated these points of view . . . [and critically looks at the role of women in society] then Female Studies can be retired.[1]

By mid-1971, close to one hundred colleges, including Harvard and MIT, offered one or more credit courses on women. The courses cover a wide spectrum of academic disciplines: "Images of Women in Literature," "Woman as Hero," "The Women's Rights Movement in America," "Images of Woman in German Literature," "A Contradiction in the Status of Women in Old English Society," "Women in the American Economy."

In the fall of 1970, San Diego State College became the first college in the country to structure a complete Women's Studies Program. The women at San Diego have proposed that the Program be the academic component of an entire Women's Studies Center, which would include research, publications, community, child care and cultural centers. The Studies Program, the only component thus far approved, consists of ten elective courses under the College of Arts and Letters. Among the courses are: "Socialization Process of Women," "Women in Comparative Cultures," "Human Sexuality" and "Woman and Education."

Although feminists are by and large united in their enthusiasm about women's studies, much of the academic community is not. When a questionnaire was distributed to the Cornell faculty in the spring of 1970, half of the 185 who responded opposed setting up women's studies. An informal *New York Times* survey on women's studies documented some of the objections of academicians around the country. One humanities professor called the idea "a disaster," and said, "black studies is divisive enough, female studies would inevitably be aimed toward political goals, which I am far from sharing."[2] Skeptical educators questioned the objectivity of the courses and "warned of the risks of fragmenting the curriculum into services for special interest groups. Such concern implies that there might eventually be demands for 'old people's studies' or 'Italian-American stud-

[1] *Female Studies I*, July, 1970. At the time Tobias was assistant to the vice-president for academic affairs. Unpaginated; reprinted by K.N.O.W., Inc., Pittsburgh, Pa.
[2] *New York Times*, January 7, 1971.

ies.' "[3] The objections seem to be less about the courses themselves than about the need to integrate them into the framework of traditional scholarship instead of separating them out. According to Goucher sociologist Dr. Alice Rossi, the women's studies courses will in fact be "transitional" in nature. "They will receive special attention for a few years and then will be incorporated into a basic curriculum that will be revised to fit student's needs."[4]

The first "practical" feminist course was offered in 1971 at Goucher College during its one-month January term. Two male chemistry professors created and taught, "Nuts and Bolts in Contemporary Society" to show women (no men allowed; "a guy would walk in here and feel impelled to show off"[5]) the techniques of simple electronic and mechanical repairs—rewiring a lamp, repairing a television set, automobile, toaster. Of all the four-week courses offered, including trips to study in Europe, "Nuts and Bolts" had the greatest student response, receiving applications from one-quarter of Goucher's 1000 undergraduates. Alumnae and faculty and staff members, including men, requested that a similar course be set up on an evening basis. The only criticism came from some faculty who insisted the course was "anti-intellectual" and therefore had no place in a scholastically-oriented liberal arts college. The instructors countered ". . . you mustn't confuse a change of approach with being anti-intellectual. Because it's simply practical doesn't mean it's academically unimportant."[6]

However women's studies courses are structured, their very existence may well mean that young people (male and female) will begin to perceive men and women and their roles in history and society quite differently from their predecessors.

College alumnae and alumni associations have also been criticized for their biases about women. For the most part, in association bulletins, women graduates are identified primarily, if not only, by their marital status. A recent biographical questionnaire from Connecticut College provoked a response from one alumna who has worked since her graduation in 1966 as a film producer:

---

[3] *New York Times,* January 10, 1971.
[4] Quoted from *The Spokeswoman,* October 30, 1970, p. 4.
[5] *New York Times,* February 1, 1971.
[6] *Loc. cit.*

First, I find it curious that [the questionnaire] . . . assumed that my husband has an occupation (which gets top billing on this form) while I am only expected to have "worked after graduation." I gather by the use of the past tense in the question "Did you work after graduation?" that I am only expected to work *until I get married.* Then, of course, it is my husband's "occupation" and my reproductive organs which are important to the Alumnae Association. *But what about the single or married woman who has an occupation equally as valid as that of any man, including her husband?*[7]

It has been observed that "women's liberation" is as much a state of mind as it is a formal movement. Although the author of the letter had never directly participated in any feminist activities, she concluded her remarks by noting: "[This questionnaire] . . . is truly an example of what the Women's Liberation Movement is all about."

High Schools

THERE IS a growing awareness of the women's liberation movement among teenage girls, and a number of high school women's liberation groups, devoted primarily to consciousness raising, have formed in schools across the country. Editorials about women's rights and feminism have appeared in high school newspapers, the women's liberation movement has been a topic for high school debating teams, and projects about famous women in history have been undertaken in history and English classes.

If the ideas of feminism gain a strong foothold among high school girls (and boys) the implications are far reaching, for it is at this age level that so much of social behavior is formalized. A YWCA survey of 400 teenagers conducted in the summer of 1970 indicated that teenage girls have already begun to discard some of the traditional views about the roles of men and women:

---

[7] Letter from Patt Dale to Connecticut College President, Charles E. Shain, February 22, 1971.

—61 percent of those surveyed said priority should not be given a husband's identity at the wife's expense.

—39 percent did not think it necessary that a wife earn less than her husband, "a common assumption some years ago."

—25 percent did not think it necessary for a woman to relinquish her maiden name at marriage.

—60 percent felt men should help with household chores.[8]

A 1970 national survey by *Seventeen* magazine found that 23 percent of girls aged sixteen and under believe to some degree that the institution of marriage is becoming obsolete.[9]

High School Women's Liberation Coalition in New York City drew up a questionnaire entitled "What Every Young Girl Should Ask," and distributed it to all interested high school students. Following is a partial list of the questions, which indicate the range of topics discussed in high school consciousness raising sessions:

—Can you play basketball, soccer, football?

—Did you ever pretend to be dumb?

—Are your brothers asked to help clean house?

—Did you discuss masturbation and lesbianism in your sex education class? Did you discuss intercourse? Orgasm? Abortion?

—How many famous women do you know about (not counting Presidents' wives or movie stars)?

—How are women portrayed in the books you read?

—How do your classes react to "ugly" women teachers?

—In extracurricular coed organizations, do girls make decisions? Or do they take minutes?

—Are girls with boyfriends winners? What did they win?

—Do you ask boys out? If not, why not?

—Do you believe boys get sexually aroused fast, at a younger age, and more often than girls? Who told you *that*?

—Do you ever hug or kiss your girl friend?

—Do you like your body?

—How much time and money do you spend on your makeup? Why?

---

8 YWCA Press release, September 17, 1970.
9 *Dating, Mating and Sex: Seventeen In Depth Study, 1970*, Triangle Publications, Inc.

—Do you think of unmarried women as "bachelor girls" or "old maids"?

—Is your mother an oppressed woman?

According to many feminists, it is in high school that boys and girls are irrevocably "tracked" into traditional life-roles. Boys are encouraged to think about careers and their life's work; girls, about marriage and children. Boys are encouraged to take math and science; girls, typing. Boys are required to take shop; girls, home economics. Boys are encouraged to partake in physical activity and have well-equipped gymnasiums for that purpose; girls get "hand-me-down" equipment. Some isolated events beginning in 1969 indicate that the days of these "segregated" areas of high school education may be drawing to a close.

—Spring, 1969: In New York City there are three public high schools that specialize in science—Stuyvesant, Brooklyn Technical, and Bronx Science. Until 1969, only Bronx Science admitted girls and then on a very limited basis. Alice de Rivera, a high school girl, wanted to study biology at Stuyvesant because of its proximity to her home. While attempting to get a court decision establishing the illegality of using public funds to support a sex-segregated public institution, the New York Board of Education admitted her to Stuyvesant. She entered in the spring, and although pleased with the decision, looked upon her victory as limited since no legal precedent was set.

—December, 1969: A New York City junior high school girl sued the Board of Education on the grounds that she was deprived of the opportunity to take a shop course because of her sex. She was subsequently allowed to take the course, but rather than dropping the individual complaint, her attorneys turned it into a class action complaint against New York City schools for following a pattern of sex discrimination in this area of study. The converse charge was brought against the Washington State Board of Education in September, 1970. A Seattle High School girl sued the Board for discriminating against girls by requiring them to take home economics in order to graduate, but not requiring boys to do so.

—April, 1970: A high school girl in Asbury Park, New
Jersey sued the local Board of Education for not allow-
lowing her to be a member of the boys' tennis team.

—February, 1971: New York City Board of Education
voted to allow girls to compete with boys on high school
athletic teams in non-contact sports. The decision resulted from an experiment in coeducational sports
conducted by one hundred high schools throughout the
state the previous year. The issue was first raised by
sixteen-year-old Phyllis Graber, who sought a place on
the boys' tennis team of her high school (there was no
girls' team) and was turned down because of her sex.

Before the advent of "women's liberation" there had been
several court cases on the issue of high school dress and appearance codes. Most often the central issue was the length of a boy's
hair, but frequently the question concerned the permissibility of
girls wearing slacks to school. On July 28, 1969, a New York
State Commissioner of Education ruled that high school principals could not suspend or discipline students for wearing what
the school might consider improper dress. A Westchester county
high school girl, active in women's liberation, described how the
decision affected her:

> . . . I heard about the momentous decision . . . that prin-
> cipals could no longer tell girls what to wear, and I went
> up to my principal; he said he couldn't stop me, but he
> thought slacks "were in bad taste." Anyway, since that,
> I've worn dresses or skirts about five times—one time it
> was to the Passover Sedar. Since I began wearing pants I
> have discovered two things: 1) I feel more equal with
> boys, and 2) I no longer have to worry as to how my legs
> are placed and all that bullshit as I had to when I wore
> skirts. I no longer feel myself fighting other girls for the
> attention of boys, and am generally much more at ease
> with the world.[1]

In early 1970, after a history teacher had pointed out the
dearth of women mentioned in textbooks, two Baltimore high
school girls drew up a petition and had it signed by 74 of their

---

[1] Connie Dvorkin, "The Suburban Scene," *Sisterhood*, pp. 363–4.

classmates. The petition was sent to the school board and the *Baltimore Sun.* It noted that of the 643 people mentioned in the school's American history book, only 26 were women:

> And most of these women make the scene as queens (e.g., Elizabeth I), domestics (e.g., Betsy Ross), writers (e.g., Louisa May Alcott), or humanitarians (e.g., Jane Addams) doing their social bit in a man's world. If we are to accept the view of our society presented by our history text, ours is a society without women.[2]

The students concluded their petition "demanding the amelioration of this condition."

On the "official" level, at the August, 1970, convention of the American Federation of Teachers, a resolution was passed to launch a major investigation into the history textbook field to determined how the early feminist and suffragist movement is portrayed. The Federation also planned to draw up lesson plans on women's history.

Elementary Education

CHILDREN'S BOOKS, which most educators agree contribute greatly to the perceptions of sex roles, are getting a highly critical look from feminists. They say that the vast majority of children's books show "women as mothers, nurses, mothers, teachers, mothers, mothers, mothers—mothers in an endless round of baking, dusting, ironing, and waving good-by."[3] A children's book reviewer surveyed the picture-book market and noted:

> [In picture books] there were five times as many males in the titles as there were females, four times as many boys, men, or male animals pictured as there were females. . . . Only in Noah's Ark does Biblical authority enforce equal representation for males and females. Except for Random House's "Pop-up Noah," which has eliminated Mrs. Noah

and does not show the animals in equal distribution on the cover. . . . [When women do appear in picture books] what they do is highly limited. . . . They do not drive cars. Though children see their mothers driving all the time, not a single description or picture of a woman driver could I find. In the world today women are executives, jockeys, stockbrokers, taxidrivers, steelworkers, in picture books these are non-existent.[4]

Two groups of feminists, one in New Jersey and one in New York City, combined forces in June, 1970, to create Feminists On Children's Media. The collective, which includes teachers, children's book editors, mothers and housewives, adopted as its long-range aim to rid the children's book market of "sexist" books. The collective's first step was to prepare an in-depth study on that market. The study was presented on October 15, 1970, to a joint meeting of the Authors' Guild and the Children's Book Council. The study, *Sexism in Children's Books,* was divided into three parts. One part, sponsored by the New Jersey chapter of NOW, surveyed the reader series used in elementary schools. The second dealt with trade books. Part three was a study of picture books.

For the textbook portion of the survey, 144 readers representing the fifteen major publishers were read, categorized and coded. The women found that 881 stories centered around boys and 344 centered around girls. Similarly, 282 stories were about adult males and 127 about adult females. One hundred thirty-one biographies of famous men were included and twenty-three of famous women. The report described the "boy story line" in one of the series of readers:

Boy finds policeman's button and returns it. Father mends boy's sled and they go off together to ride on it (leaving Mother at home). Boy wins race with renovated sled. Boy helps to deliver groceries. Boy waits for postman, longs for letter, learns of new boy on block and makes friends. Boy on farm befriends pony.[5]

---

[4] Fisher, "The Second Sex, Junior Division."
[5] *Sex Role Stereotyping in Elementary School Readers,* November 29, 1970. A report compiled by the Central New Jersey Chapter of National Organization for Women, p. 2.

The "girl's story line" of the same series:

> Girls boast of new dresses, find they are identical. Girl goes shopping for mother and forgets where her pocketbook is. Girl goes shopping, drops apples, forgets eggs. Girl loses bunny, boy finds it for her. Girl longs for her own telephone call, finally gets one from mother, calling the children home. Girls make corn patties, chickens eat them.[6]

Feminists on Children's Media sent the reader portion of their study to many of the state buying committees who are responsible for the selection of reader series to be used by that state's elementary schools. One woman in the collective fears, however, that substantial change is in the far distant future. "After all, many textbook publishers still carry two versions of the same series—one showing only white people and one showing a more normal mixture of races. Moreover, one of the all-white versions is used in a wealthy New Jersey suburb. How will those kinds of people ever understand about the insidiousness of how boys and girls are portrayed in books?"[7]

For the trade book portion of the survey, more than 1000 books were read, chosen from the recommended lists of the American Library Association, the Children's Book Council, the Newbery Award winners, as well as suggestions from librarians across the country. The report opened with the question "Is the portrayal of females in children's books sexist? That is, are girls and women assigned only traditional female roles and personalities?"[8] Out of the 1000 books read, the group found only 200 which they felt offered child readers a positive image of women's "physical, emotional and intellectual potential." In outlining these criteria for good children's literature, Feminists on Children's Media stated:

> We want to see girl readers encouraged to develop physical confidence and strength without the need to fear any corresponding loss of "femininity." We would like to see

---

[6] *Loc. cit.*
[7] Joan Bartl, interview, January, 1971.
[8] *Report on Sexism in Children's Literature,* Feminists on Children's Media, unpaginated.

the elimination of all those tiresome references to "tom-
boys." Why can't a girl who prefers baseball to ballet
simply be a girl who prefers baseball to ballet? . . . Can't
we encourage girls to find satisfaction and fulfillment in
work, and lay forever to rest the suspicion that work outside the home for a *woman* is primarily proof of her inability to love a man, or to land a sufficiently lucrative
one? . . . Words like "sissy"—and "hero," too—should be
dissected and exposed for the inhuman demands they
make on growing boys. Children's books could help. . . .
How about books showing more divorced and single-par-
ent families? And, for heaven's sake, every divorced or
widowed mother does not solve her problems through re-
marriage—or even wish to do so. . . . Despite our criticism
of socially assigned roles, we don't mean to diminish or
ignore the mother or housewife. She is often a strong,
wonderfully rich human being . . . and sometimes she
finds satisfaction in it. But let's not insist on that as *her*
role. Men can also cope skillfully with household tasks—
and not necessarily look for a woman or daughter to take
them off the hook.[9]

The 200 "good" children's books were compiled in April, 1970,
into a well-annotated bibliography and sold to publishers,
authors, libraries and women's groups as well as individuals.[1]
Interest in the bibliography was high from the outset: there
were over 4000 *pre*-publication orders filled. A similar in-depth
study was carried out in 1970 by the New York Task Force on
the Status of Women in the Church. Entitled "Sex-role Stereotyping in the United Methodist Nursery School Curriculum," the
survey found the same portrayal of women in the books used in
their nursery schools: women and girls were passive and un-
creative, men and boys, the opposite. In addition, various State
Commissions on the Status of Women have begun to conduct
studies of children's educational tools.

An independent non-profit venture to produce "non-sexist"
children's books and educational materials got under way in the
winter of 1971. Lollipop Power, a feminist children's publishing
company in Chapel Hill, North Carolina, formed a "cooperative

---

[9] *Ibid.*
[1] *Little Miss Muffet Fights Back: Recommended Non-Sexist Books About
Girls for Young Readers.* See Bibliography, Section 8.

alliance" with the Feminist Press in Baltimore which publishes biographies of women. Lollipop Power will publish books suitable for readers from pre-school to teens; the Feminist Press, from teens upward. Feminists who are also professionally involved in the field of children's education, fear two things—one, an enormous resistance to the feminist concept of children's literature; and two, a sudden rush of books written by feminists who are not writers, but who think anyone can create a children's book.

In still another area of children's education—toys—feminists feel changes are needed and have begun to pressure toy manufacturers. One step toward de-emphasizing stereotyped sex-roles, they argue, is not to direct little girls to dolls and stoves and little boys to building blocks and footballs. A well-known manufacturer of toy cars and trucks, Tonka Toys, has as its slogan—"You can't raise boys without Tonka Toys." In December, 1970, Joan Levine Roth, whose daughter plays with Tonka Toys, wrote the company suggesting they revise their slogan to "Girls and boys love Tonka Toys," so that girls would not be discouraged from playing with Tonka products. The company replied:

> . . . there is a psychological factor involved in that little boys don't want toys that girls can also play with. We and our advertising people decided we had to "give in" to the boys, as they were the majority—more boys than girls actually ask for and receive Tonka Toys. Thankfully girls aren't so fussy![2]

[2] Letter from Lorna Shevlin, Sales Department, Tonka Toys, December 14, 1970.

10

Professions

EQUAL PAY for equal work and equal job opportunity are perhaps the only demands of the women's movement the validity and justness of which no one disputes, at least not openly. Statistics about working women clearly illustrate that salary scales and job opportunities are not the same for men and women. Thus, despite the fact that 38 percent of the labor force is composed of women and at least two-thirds of these women work out of economic necessity:

—the median salary of women is about 58 percent of men's (only 3 percent of working women make over $10,000 compared to 24 percent of men);
—the majority of women who work are in the lower status and lower paying jobs (34 percent alone are clerical workers);
—women make up only 37 percent of all professional and technical workers (in 1945 they made up 45 percent).[1]

It is not surprising, then, that an enormous amount of feminist activity is devoted to occupational issues, particularly upgrading the status of working women. As noted previously, federal and local legislation exists which protects certain groups of working women from sex discrimination, and a major goal of the national women's rights organizations and their local chap-

---

[1] For further information about women workers see Charts and Tables.

ters is to push for the vigorous enforcement of these laws. These organizations are also lobbying to have the word "sex" added to the discriminatory bans (race, religion, etc.) of other laws. At the same time, they are pressing for the removal of the executive, administrative and professional job category exemptions from laws which do prohibit sex discrimination.[2]

In addition, groups of women have organized within their respective occupational fields to combat sex discrimination from the "inside." The feminists who make up these groups are for the most part well-educated, white, middle- or upper-middle-class, and have already established, or are interested in, professional careers. It is these women who are most often criticized by politico feminists as being little more than privileged women demanding more privileges. For example, one contends that this "elitism" will discourage potentially sympathetic women from joining the movement. "More women will support social transformation than will support self-interested women wheeling and dealing within women's caucuses to advance their own careers."[3] Feminists reject this view. As one noted, "There has never been a movement in history that was not led by the middle class. They are the ones with education, money, power, access to laws, and time. You can't call it elitist. Because these women most clearly articulate the concerns, all classes of women will benefit from the women's movement."[4] Feminists argue further that it is the college-educated middle-class women, entering the labor force and attacking the traditional forms of sex and minority discrimination, who are precisely the ones supporting and publicizing sex-discrimination complaints filed by white and blue collar workers.

Moreover, in the last analysis feminists argue that all women *as women* are oppressed, notwithstanding their socio-economic status. Thus, central to their analysis is the idea that, although a woman factory worker and a woman professor have to contend with different environments, to define one oppression as worse than the other is "obscene" and nothing more than a functional counterpart of the idea, "all people are equal, only some are more equal than others."

---

[2] The Equal Pay Act and certain sections of the Civil Rights Act exempt these categories from coverage.
[3] Marlene Dixon (sociologist), Associated Press story, September 2, 1970.
[4] Elizabeth D. Koontz, Director, Women's Bureau, interview, September, 1970.

Another response to the "elitist" criticism is on a more personal basis—women who have graduated with honors from college and universities resent being told that they need secretarial skills in order to find employment. Moreover, they are angered by the fact that they are often passed over for promotion in favor of younger, less-experienced, yet better paid men. While these particular complaints pertain to the business world, their counterparts exist for almost all professional fields. The oft-repeated statistics bear out the arguments—women make up considerably less than ten percent of the nation's doctors, business executives, college professors and presidents, artists, lawyers, editors-in-chief, chemists, musicians, municipal and state officials, television producers, stockbrokers, architects, etc., etc. When women do enter these professions, they are consistently offered from three to ten percent lower starting salaries, and usually in the less prestigious and lower-paying echelons. One woman writer noted, ". . . no matter what sphere of work women are hired for or select, like sediment in a wine bottle they seem to settle to the bottom."[5]

The first and most obvious goal of the occupationally-organized feminists is to increase the percentage of women in "upper-level" jobs, and to confront directly the assumption that only men are suited to enter the professions.[6] The best means by which to accomplish this goal within a given profession is, however, a matter of continuous and considerable debate. The women who have already "made it" professionally tend to prefer the traditional and "polite" women's rights approach, while the radical activist women see much more value in the "startling" *zap* actions. Not surprisingly, these debates result in a certain amount of tension as well as a variety of tactical approaches. In fact, a single group sometimes employs several different kinds of tactics. At the 1970 convention of the American Psychological Association, for example, the Association for Women Psychologists presented scholarly panel discussions about women, as well as staging an *ad hoc* action in which $1 million reparations were demanded from the nation's "sexist" psychologists.

---

[5] Cynthia Fuchs Epstein, *Woman's Place* (Berkeley and Los Angeles: University of California Press, 1970) p. 2.
[6] A 1970 CBS News survey indicated how ingrained that assumption is. Of those men and women questioned, seven out of ten would trust a man more than a woman doctor or lawyer; over half, a male accountant over a female accountant. It might be noted that women were somewhat more likely than men to say sex made a difference.

Tactical differences notwithstanding, there is probably greater convergence and cross-pollination of radical and moderate feminist analyses in groups concerned with occupational issues than in any other area of feminist activity. The moderates, who have traditionally attacked occupational barriers against women *via external* means (pressuring for legislative and institutional reforms) have been profoundly influenced by the radicals who believe that the primary way to attack these barriers is *internally*—that is by raising the consciousness of women so that they are able to redefine their self-image. Rita Block, a Wall Street stockbroker, analyzed the interrelationship between the two approaches:

> Getting men used to the idea of women leaders and decision makers isn't really the hard part. The really hard part is getting women to raise their *own* level of aspirations. In professional terms women must learn to think of themselves as executives, not "assistants to"; as doctors, not nurses; as lawyers, not legal secretaries; as artists and musicians, not high school art and music teachers; as registered stockbrokers, not research analysts; and as political columnists not fashion columnists. That's the most important and profound thing women's liberation can do, and until that happens women won't go through doors that reformed laws and practices have opened to them.[7]

On the other hand, most radical feminists have come to believe that the external approach is vital as well, and they have joined the moderates in pushing for legislative change and institutional reform.

Feminists strongly believe that all the professions would benefit from the presence of women. Women lawyers point to the plethora of laws that profoundly affect women—abortion, contraception, property rights, child custody—which might have been quite different had there been women legislators and judges contributing over the years to their formulation; women psychiatrists note the endless series of psychiatric theories about women, particularly about female sexuality, and suggest that some of these "accepted" theories might not be so "accepted" had

---

[7] Interview, January, 1971.

there been more women working in the field of psychiatry; women historians point out that a great deal more would be known about Mary Wollstonecraft, Susan B. Anthony, Elizabeth Cady Stanton, Lucy Stone, the Grimké sisters, Charlotte Perkins Gilman, Elizabeth Blackwell, etc., had more women been writing history books; and women working in government suggest that had there been more high-ranking women officials, more publicly-financed child care centers might now exist.

Since the fall of 1969, when the first handful of occupationally-oriented groups were formed, women in nearly every professional field have organized themselves. Although many groups continue to exist, some disbanded after a few months, some after only a few meetings. Indeed, some of the groups seemed to have formed on an *ad hoc* basis merely to organize one particular action. Thus, the groups and professional organizations described below should be considered as representative and *not* as all-inclusive.[8]

Academic Disciplines

THE FIRST THREE occupationally-oriented feminist groups were formed in September, 1969, although their simultaneous appearance was coincidental. That they were all organized within the professional associations of related disciplines was also coincidental. Thus, Sociology, Psychology, and Political Science became the first professional fields to be confronted directly with feminist issues and feminist pressure.

The women's caucus of the *American Sociological Association* was formed by Dr. Alice Rossi, a sociologist (and one of the founders of NOW) whose scholarly writings over the years have focused on discrimination against women. During the 1968–69 academic year, Dr. Rossi noticed a sharp upturn in the number of letters she was receiving from women graduate students in sociology who were concerned about their future careers in that field. The young women appeared particularly distressed about

---

[8] In April, 1970, many of these groups banded together in a national association—Professional Women's Caucus. Each group has remained autonomous, however, and continues to work within its own field.

the lack of support and encouragement from their faculty advisors and professors. According to Dr. Rossi, many of the letters said in effect, "Women in sociology suffer a new double disadvantage these days—we are not male and we are not black."[9] Others asked whether something should not be done within the profession itself to combat discrimination against women sociologists. In preparation for the 1969 annual meeting of the American Sociological Association, at which Dr. Rossi planned to bring up the issue of the status of women within the profession, she conducted a nationwide survey on the "Status of Women in Graduate Departments of Sociology, 1968–1969." In brief, the data revealed that women comprised thirty-three percent of the graduate students in sociology, but only four percent of the professors; none of the four percent was in a prestige university or department.

Women in the sociology departments at Berkeley and Johns Hopkins University helped with the preparation of the survey which was presented at the September, 1969, ASA meeting. Dr. Rossi recalled, "Since no professional association had a women's caucus, we had no idea how to proceed. But we thought the best method was to merely put 'a finger to the wind' and see which way it was blowing."[1] The activist women asked the convention to vote informally on the "spirit" of a series of resolutions, rather than formally on each separate statement. To their great surprise, there was no dissent in the convention's endorsement of the "general sense" of the resolutions. The prepared statement was a strongly-worded one which focused on two areas—the utter lack of scholarly sociological research on women; and the low status of women in the professional ranks. The statement read in part:

> Sociological research and scholarship is rife with a complacent, conventional acceptance of the "what is-ought to be" variety, nowhere more apparent than in theory and research on women, marriage and the family. There is a great and pressing need for critical reassessment of many psychological and sociological assumptions in the area of sex role and family structure. . . . [In addition we seek] a concerted commitment to the hiring and promotion of

[9] Alice S. Rossi, "Status of Women in Graduate Departments of Sociology, 1968–1969," *The American Sociologist,* February, 1970, p. 1.
[1] Interview, January, 1971.

women sociologists to right the imbalance that is represented by the current situation, in which 67 percent of
the women graduate students in this country do not
have a single woman sociology professor of senior rank
during the course of their graduate training, and when
we participate in an association of sociologists in which
NO woman will sit on the 1970 Council, NO woman is
included among the associate editors of the *American
Sociological Review* or the Advisory Board of the *American Journal of Sociology,* and NO woman sits on the 13-
member Committees on Publications and Nominations.[2]

By the 1970 convention a women's caucus was well organized
and considerably bolder than in the previous year. The women
demanded the establishment of an official ASA Committee on the
Status of Women in Sociology, an official session during the
1970 convention on the Sociology of Sex Roles, and a free child
care center during the convention. All the demands were met.
The Caucus also sponsored a series of small workshops during
the convention. To some, the progress of the Women's Caucus
during the first years of its existence was not dramatic enough.
Nonetheless, Dr. Rossi and other women activists feel that in
the long run the greatest strides are to be made by working "within
the system," in this case, framing resolutions and demands
acceptable to the parent organization. Moreover, only in this way
do they feel that the Caucus' position will be attractive to the
women members of ASA. On the theory that their power base
and sense of sex-solidarity will be much stronger if they are a
separate group, the Caucus dissolved itself and reorganized in the
winter of 1971 as an independent organization—*Sociologists for
Women in Society.* The new group admits men and women and
works both from within ASA and independently of it.

The *Women's Caucus for Political Science* was formed in
September, 1969, at the annual meeting of the American Political Science Association. The Caucus had its origins in the 1968
annual meeting during which a petition requesting an investigation into the status of women in the profession was signed by 82
political scientists and presented to the Association. The action
prompted APSA to create an official Committee on the Status of

[2] Statement and Resolutions of the Women's Caucus, *The American Sociologist,* February, 1970, pp. 63–64.

Women. When the five Committee members reported at the 1969 convention that their course of action would be to undertake an in-depth study on the status of women in the field of political science, "it became apparent this Committee was set up to 'study and recommend' and *not* to take any action. And many of us felt that we needed an action group."[3] Consequently, by the end of the 1969 meeting, there were two groups in APSA concerned with "women's issues"—an officially-appointed study group (Committee on the Status of Women), and a dues-paying independent activist group (Women's Caucus for Political Science). The two groups hammered out several compromise resolutions that were presented to and passed by the entire Association. The resolutions covered several points: they expressed APSA disapproval of the overall pattern of sex discrimination against women in the field, promised support for active recruitment of women students and teachers, and agreed to elevate women members of APSA to decision-making positions within the organization itself.

During the following year, both the study Committee and the Women's Caucus continued their work. The Caucus concentrated on broadening its power base by raising money and recruiting members; by the 1970 convention more than 300 women and some men belonged to the group. The Committee continued its research and delivered an interim report at the 1970 meeting. The final report was due in June, 1971. The study reportedly cost approximately $30,000 and was the most elaborate survey on the status of women commissioned by any of the professional associations.

Although the activist Caucus concerns itself primarily with the practical problems of women's status in the field, members have also begun research to determine what kinds of political science studies about women could be undertaken. For example, do the voting patterns of women in America disclose anything relevant about the role of women in America; why have women historically never organized as a political "interest group," and what would be the implications of such a self-definition. To find out what had been already written about women by political scientists, a survey was made of the articles in the *American Political Science Review* since that journal's inception in 1903. Of

[3] Kay Klotzburger, one of the organizers of the Women's Caucus, interview, February, 1971.

the more than 2800 articles only five were about women, four of which dealt with women in Europe.

The *Association for Women in Psychology* (originally called Association for Women Psychologists) was formed during the September, 1969, meeting of the American Psychological Association by Dr. Jo-Ann Evans Gardner. With no prior thoughts of organizing a caucus, Dr. Gardner had arranged for a symposium on women to be included as an official session of the convention. Her panel was entitled, "What Can the Behavioral Sciences Do to Change the World So That Women Who Want to Participate Are Not Regarded As and Are Not in Fact Deviates?" The panel was composed of Dr. Wilma Scott Heide, chairwoman of NOW's Board of Directors; Dr. Kathryn Clarenbach, head of the Wisconsin State Commission on the Status of Women, and a founder of NOW; and Dorothy Haener, of the United Auto Workers Women's Department, also a founder of NOW. Two other feminist symposia were presented during the convention although they were not listed in the program: "Woman as Subject" and "Woman as Scientist and Subject."

A number of factors contributed to the formation of the Association for Women in Psychology (which, from its inception was an independent organization, not a caucus within APA): the extensive discussion generated by the symposia themselves; the existence of sex-segregated employment advertisements in the APA convention bulletin (violating both federal law and the APA constitution);[4] and the specific instance of a woman being refused two jobs during the convention week because of her sex (one function of the convention is to act as an informal employment agency). The women confronted APA with the illegality of listing sexual preferences in "want-ads" and finally forced the organization to close the offending recruitment booths. In addition the women set up their own booth with a sign—"If you find any sex discrimination, see us here." At the same time, three petitions were circulated demanding that APA accredit only those psychology departments which did not practice sex discrimination; that APA investigate its own practices of sex discrimination and report its findings at the next convention; and that APA support abortion as a basic civil right of women. By the end of the convention the Association for Women in Psychology was formed.

---

[4] The existence of the sex-preference employment advertisements became the basis of a formal complaint filed on April 27, 1970, against APA by Women's Equity Action League under Executive Order 11375.

AWP continued organizing during the following year, and presented fourteen symposia on women at the 1970 APA convention as well as 51 resolutions and demands. AWP also requested that women's rights be the official theme of the convention since it was the 50th anniversary of suffrage, but they were turned down. Three of AWP's 51 demands were approved: an APA-funded task force report on the status of women to be presented at the 1971 convention; free child care to be provided at the 1971 convention; and a "strengthening" of APA policy against discrimination on the part of employers using APA placement facilities.

Like other professionally-organized women's groups, AWP attacked the "woman question" on two fronts: in this case, the status of women psychologists within the professional ranks, and the image of women in psychological and psychiatric theory. With regard to the latter, at the 1970 convention, AWP demanded $1 million reparations from APA for damage done to women by psychologists who have, according to feminists, viewed women's psychological problems from the vantage point of "sexist" psychological theories.

A 1968 paper by psychologist Dr. Naomi Weisstein addressed itself to the relationship between psychology and women. " 'Kinder, Kuche, Kirche' As Scientific Law: Psychology Constructs the Female" states in part:

Psychologists have set about describing the true natures of women with an enthusiasm and absolute certainty which is rather disquieting. Bruno Bettelheim of the University of Chicago tells us [1965] that:

"We must start with the realization that as much as women want to be good scientists or engineers, they want first and foremost to be womanly companions of men and to be mothers."

Erik Erikson of Harvard University [states that a woman's]

". . . somatic design harbors an *inner space* designed to bear the offspring of chosen men, and with it, a biological, psychological and ethical commitment to take care of human infancy" [1964]. . . .[5]

The first reason for psychology's failure to understand

---

[5] *Sisterhood*, p. 206.

what people are and how they act, is that clinicians and psychiatrists, who are generally the theoreticians on those matters, have essentially made up myths without any evidence to support these myths; the second reason for psychology's failure is that personality theory has looked for inner traits when it should have been looking at social context.[6] . . . In brief, the usefulness of present psychology with regard to women, is simply a special case of the general conclusion: one must understand social expectations about women if one is going to characterize the behavior of women.[7]

To begin combatting these effects of "sexism" in psychology, AWP has published a roster of feminist therapists and counselors, as well as a list of the "most blatantly sexist" university psychology departments.

The fourth women's group in a professional association was formed in December, 1969, within the *Modern Language Association*, the largest (29,000 members) and one of the oldest academic societies. At MLA's 1969 convention a Commission on the Status of Women was formed to make a study of the status of women in the profession. (The Modern Language Association includes scholars and teachers of English, linguistics, foreign languages and literature.) The Commission reported at the 1970 convention that in U.S. colleges women make up half the English and foreign language lecturers, and 46 percent of the instructors. Among full professors, only 18 percent are women, most at institutions of low prestige. Florence Howe, chairwoman of the Commission stated, "The figures are particularly striking when you realize that English and foreign languages are in many ways female professions. Fifty-five percent of our graduate students are women, and an even higher proportion of our undergraduate majors."[8] Yet according to the study, only about eight percent of faculty members who teach Ph.D. candidates are women. According to Chairwoman Howe, the meaning of these figures is clear: "You can study here, but you can't work here."[9]

---

[6] *Ibid.*, p. 209.
[7] *Ibid.*, p. 219.
[8] "Study Shows Discrimination Against Women Professors," Modern Language Association press release, New York, December 27, 1970, unpaginated.
[9] *Ibid.*

In addition to the study, the Commission began to function as a clearing-house for information on curriculum developments in the women's studies programs across the country. In the fall of 1970 the Commission put together *Female Studies II,* a collection of syllabi and bibliographies for feminist humanities courses taught at 66 colleges and universities that fall.[1] In December, 1970, Florence Howe, Chairwoman of the Commission, was elected second vice president of the Modern Language Association, an office which makes her president automatically in 1973. (A Women's Caucus for Modern Languages was formed at the same time as the Commission, some say as a "conservative" balance to the liberal, feminist Commission.)

By 1970 sufficient momentum had been generated by women academicians so that feminist caucuses were formed in the fields of American Studies, Economics, History and Library Science. By the time of the 1971 annual meetings nearly every professional association had a woman's caucus, commission, or committee. In many cases these groups had the financial as well as moral support of the parent association. In others the women met with hostile resistance. Although various associations have passed resolutions on "women's issues," in most cases these have not yet been translated into official policy or action.

Law

FEMINIST ACTIVITY within the legal profession has manifested itself in two areas of concern—the rights of women under the law; and the rights of women lawyers.

Although some of the traditional professional legal associations have set up "committees on the status of women lawyers," as of mid-1971 none had a militant feminist caucus analogous to those previously discussed. One explanation for the lack of militancy within legal associations like the American Bar Association is the refusal of many young, activist lawyers (male and female) to join these "establishment" organizations. Moreover, the prevailing view among "establishment" women lawyers is,

---

[1] *Female Studies I,* a compilation of courses offered in the behavioral and social sciences, was put together by Sheila Tobias of Wesleyan University.

"That some discrimination exists against women in our profession I cannot deny, but I do not believe in making a big issue of women's rights."[2] Activist women lawyers, on the other hand, frequently cite the available statistics to publicly dramatize the degree of "some discrimination against women":[3]

> —women make up only three percent of the nation's lawyers;
> —of 2708 lawyers employed by 40 top law firms in six major cities, only 186 were women (1966 survey);
> —of 2500 teaching positions in law schools, only 53 percent of such full-time positions are held by women in 45 out of the 144 accredited law schools;
> —out of nearly 9700 judgeships in the United States, only 200 are held by women.

The reluctance of women lawyers to speak up on their own behalf was perhaps most evident in 1969 when the National Association of Women Lawyers declined to participate in a joint survey on the status of women in the legal profession and in law schools.[4]

Despite the general reluctance of women lawyers to address themselves to women's issues, there is an increasing number of feminist lawyers speaking and writing about women and the law. A woman lawyer testifying at government hearings on sex discrimination described the conflict among women within the profession:

> Female attorneys, in advising other members of their sex as to the best way of handling sex discrimination, subscribe to two distinct and violently conflicting schools of thought. One group advises open conflict—the other the diplomatic use of tactical weapons and a graceful retreat if necessary. . . . The "fighters" see the "diplomats" as

---

[2] Arlyss Spense, quoted in *Student Lawyer Journal,* November, 1970, p. 18. It should be remembered that among the founders of NOW and some of the other early women's rights organizations there were some dynamic and successful women lawyers. Their energy at that time, however, was directed toward the broad spectrum of women's rights rather than the more limited spectrum of discrimination within the legal profession itself.
[3] Margaret Laurance, "Statement submitted by the National Association of Women Lawyers," *Green Hearings,* pp. 1120–1128.
[4] National Association of Women Lawyers has since formed a Committee on the Status of Women.

cowardly and damaging to members of their own sex. "Sex discrimination exists in the legal field because women themselves have been unwilling to break down its barriers," charges a dynamic female attorney in private practice.[5]

One of the earliest "fighter" attempts to break down the barriers occurred in November, 1968, with the publication of an article in *Trial* magazine, a predominantly male journal. In it, Doris Sassower, a lawyer and women's rights activist, used the minuscule number of women lawyers who have risen to judgeships as the most telling symbol of the discrimination against female attorneys. She divided the blame fairly equally among three areas of the legal profession: law firms for relegating women lawyers to the lower-paying and less-prestigious jobs (estate and trust work with no client contact or opportunity to go to trial); law schools for neither hiring women law professors nor recruiting or encouraging women law students; and women lawyers themselves for accepting the *status quo*. The following February, the National Conference of Bar Presidents invited Sassower to present her views on the subject at their annual conference. (The New York Women's Bar Association, of which she was president, would not allow her to speak on behalf of the Association, but only as an individual.)

Since 1969, a considerable number of feminist articles have appeared in law journals, and a great many legal bodies have been addressed by activist women lawyers about the second-class status of women in the profession. That the American Bar Association formed a Committee on Women's Rights in 1970 does not impress feminists as a major breakthrough. They believe it will be used to raise ABA's public image more than to raise the status of women in the profession.

The most visible changes regarding women within the legal profession have occurred on law school campuses, where there now exists a tremendous amount of organized and militant feminist pressure. Indeed, one young woman lawyer has commented that every law school in the country with women students must now have an active feminist group. Moreover, she theorized that a great many women presently in law school decided to get

---

[5] Beatrice Dinerman, "Sex Discrimination in the Legal Profession," *American Bar Association Journal*, October, 1969, reprinted in *Green Hearings*, p. 1132.

their law degrees because of their previous involvement in the women's movement, which "sensitized" them to the need for legal aid and legal reform on behalf of women in general.[6] Many of these women students, however, appear to be much more interested in how they, as women lawyers, can use the legal system to liberate all women, rather than how the women's liberation movement can upgrade their status within the legal profession.

Perhaps the major campaign of feminist law students, and indeed of most feminist lawyers, is to press law schools, and thereby the legal profession, into making women's rights a law specialty. They argue that since it was the law schools which, to all intents and purposes, created the specialties of civil rights and race relations, it is also within their power to do the same for sex discrimination. Feminist lawyers argue that the rapidly increasing number of suits of sex discrimination being brought under Title VII, Equal Pay Act, Executive Order 11375, and various state and local laws, have created a pressing need for a large group of lawyers well versed in those areas. They also point to the myriad state laws which they maintain discriminate against women—property rights, labor laws, abortion laws, tax laws, marriage and divorce laws—and to the need for these laws to be studied and challenged by lawyers well trained in the subject. Some feminist lawyers, although advocates of a women's law specialty, speculate dryly that once there is money to be made in that field, male lawyers will undoubtedly try to take it over.

Although substantial curriculum changes have yet to be made, strong feminist pressures have resulted in the creation of some individual courses on Women and the Law. The first such course, planned and taught by feminist lawyer Diane Schulder, was offered on a non-credit basis at the University of Pennsylvania in the spring of 1969. The course covered the areas of law considered most discriminatory against women and included an analysis of the various Supreme Court decisions affecting women. By the fall of 1969, enough pressure had been created by women law students at New York University to have Schulder teach the course there as a credit seminar. In addition, the women at NYU Law School formed the Women's Rights Committee which,

---

[6] Interview, Ann Marie Boylan, editor, *Women's Rights Law Reporter*, March, 1971.

among other things, sponsored a National Conference of Women Law Students the following spring. Over one hundred women from seventeen law schools across the country attended and testified at length about their personal experiences of discrimination at their respective law schools. The women also discussed the need for courses on sex discrimination in the law. (The National Conference became an annual event and the second one, held in April, 1971, in Chicago, was attended by women from nearly every law school in the country.)

By the fall of 1970, another handful of law schools, among them Yale, Georgetown, and George Washington, were offering women's courses. Many feminists believe that within five years every law school in the country will have introduced women's rights into its curriculum. In 1971, three law journals—Hastings (California), Valparaiso (Indiana), and Rutgers (New Jersey)— each devoted an entire issue to women and the law, "a remarkable occurrence considering the male prejudice built into the law and the legal profession."[7]

The first issue of a publication created specifically to aid lawyers already working in the field of women's rights appeared in 1971. *Women's Rights Law Reporter* described itself as a "new weapon for women lawyers" and added in its statement of purpose:

> There is now no law reporter dealing solely, or even in large part with the changing legal condition of women in various areas of the law. . . . By its coverage of decisions from all over the country [*The Women's Rights Law Reporter*] will provide lawyers with the firm legal documentation they need if they are to use the results of another action for their clients' benefit.

The *Reporter* will also include theoretical papers, reprints of articles of interest to women's rights lawyers, and information about women's caucuses and women's law courses.[8]

---

[7] Boylan, interview, April, 1971.

[8] In February, 1971, interest in the relationship between women and the law extended well beyond the boundaries of the legal profession. That month's issue of *McCall's* magazine, read by over seven million people each month, carried a state-by-state guide of the legal rights of women. The charts were captioned "The Geography of Inequality," and the first sentence accompanying the one about laws affecting married women stated, "In most states of the Union, the most sacrificial act a woman can perform is to get married." P. 90.

In addition to pressing for the inclusion of women's rights courses in curriculums, there are several other demands of law school women's caucuses: that law schools actively recruit women law students; that they actively recruit and hire women law professors; that placement services stop cooperating with law firms that discriminate against women, i.e., firms that flatly refuse to hire women, demand personal data from them during interviews (e.g., when do they plan to marry and have children), or relegate them to lower-paying and less-prestigious kinds of jobs. The Law Women's Caucus at the University of Chicago Law School took legal action in this area. In February, 1970, the group filed a complaint with EEOC against the law school's placement office for allowing firms that discriminate to use its services. By mid-1971 court action had not yet been initiated by the women because after a series of meetings between EEOC and the University, the University agreed it would bar any firm that obviously and blatantly discriminated against women. In April, 1970, the University of Michigan Law School barred by unanimous faculty vote one large New York-Washington firm from using the law school placement office because of charges against the firm of sex discrimination. A similar action occurred at Berkeley.

In April, 1970, the Association of American Law Schools, which represents all the accredited law schools in the country, formed the Committee on Women in Legal Education. Many activist women lawyers see the establishment of the Committee as a sign of progress. An attempt to set up a similar committee had been defeated in 1969 because of the "demands" of prior issues. That it was created in 1970 is credited almost entirely to the pressure exerted on the Association by numerous women lawyers along with the combined efforts of many of the law school women's caucuses. Although the Committee's mandate is broad, its first report will concentrate on the status of women in law schools, both as students and professors. Feminists are hopeful that the Committee will issue some far-reaching recommendations to combat sex discrimination in law schools. Some are fearful, however, that the Committee will be reluctant to be as forceful as necessary, because of alleged threats by member law schools to resign from AALS rather than accept such recommendations.

In addition to the increasing involvement of female law students in women's issues, in 1971 practicing feminist lawyers took a variety of steps to combat sex discrimination within the profession. In March of that year, a formal charge of sex discrimination was brought by the Legal Task Force of Professional Women's Caucus against every law school in the country receiving federal funds. The class action was based in part on preliminary figures gathered by the AALS Committee, which indicated that from 1966 to 1970 the number of women law students had only increased by an average of three percent. Moreover, for approximately one-third of the law schools, the percentage of women had decreased. Also in the spring of 1971, several women's rights groups undertook fundraising campaigns to finance sex discrimination cases. In addition, a number of feminist lawyers began to discuss the possibilities of organizing law firms to specialize in women's rights.

Medicine

THE MUSHROOM GROWTH of the women's movement during its early years did not produce considerable feminist activity within the medical profession. Although many feminists railed against the profession in general for its conservative stand on abortion, the "chauvinistic" and often "sadistic" treatment of women patients on the part of male doctors, etc., only rarely did any accusations come from women doctors themselves. Even more rarely did women doctors complain of the barriers against women in the profession. It has been suggested that women physicians (seven percent of the U.S. total) are extremely reluctant to speak out on their own behalf for two reasons: one stems from a feeling of superiority—"I made it, and if other women can't, they just haven't got what it takes"; the second results from a fear of losing whatever degree of status and equality has been achieved. The few feminists within the profession argue that recent studies of the nation's medical schools prove irrevocably that strong discrimination exists against women applying to medical schools. For example, a 1968 Women's Bureau Fact Sheet[9] notes that the number of women applicants to medical schools in-

---

[9] "Facts on Prospective and Practicing Women in Medicine," *U.S. Department of Labor, Women's Bureau, 1968,* reprinted in *Green Hearings,* pp. 523ff.

creased over three hundred percent between 1930 and 1966, while the number of male applicants increased only 29 percent; yet, according to the study, the proportion of women accepted by medical schools during this period has decreased and that of men risen. The comment of medical school admissions officers to these statistics is that they do not show discrimination because the percentage of women and the percentage of men accepted out of total applicants from each group is roughly the same, i.e., about 50 percent of women applicants are accepted as are about 50 percent of men applicants. Advocates of women's rights dismiss this "equal rejection" theory because:

> . . . it is unfair to reject half the women just as are rejected half the men. There is a far smaller number of women applying; for example, 1,000 women applying in one year compared to 13,000 men applying. Yet they reject half of those 1,000 women equally as they do half of the 13,000 men, because they are women. This is unfair. Sex is a qualification that should not be considered. It places women in a disadvantageous category.[1]

Another study, sponsored by the National Institute of Mental Health,[2] found that prejudice against women physicians was a "significant factor" contributing to the lower percentage of women doctors in the United States. Dr. Harold Kaplan, author of the study, noted that this prejudice manifested itself not only against women applicants to medical school, but against women who were already in medical schools. On the basis of a questionnaire, to which 95 percent of the medical schools in the United States and Canada responded, Dr. Kaplan concluded that there does exist great

> . . . resistance to making adequate provisions for women once they are in school (e.g., if they marry and have children) and encounter problems unique to women (e.g., childbirth and the care of children). Schools may refuse to provide any time off for childbirth, or insist upon rigid adherence to work or night schedules—

---

[1] Dr. Frances Norris, testimony, *Green Hearings*, p. 513.
[2] Dr. Harold Kaplan, "Women Physicians: The More Effective Recruitment and Utilization of Their Talents and the Resistance to It—A Seven Year Study," reprinted in *Green Hearings*, p. 559.

whereas minor modifications in these areas might allow a student who is a mother to successfully perform both.[3]

The significantly larger proportions of women physicians in other countries (75 percent in the USSR, 24 percent in England), where flexible provisions are made for women medical students, prompted Dr. Kaplan, feminists, and others to view the "backwardness" in attitude on the part of American medical educators as "startling, disturbing and troublesome."[4] They argue further that the failure to make provisions for potential women doctors is particularly lamentable at a time of general health care crisis and the tremendous shortage of doctors. Activists cite U.S. Public Health figures which indicate that the United States will need 400,000 physicians in 1975—almost 100,000 more than exist today.

In October, 1970, the above-mentioned statistics served as the basis of a formal charge of sex discrimination filed against every medical school in the country. Women's Equity Action League (WEAL) filed a class action complaint under Executive Order 11375 upon learning that U.S. medical schools receive more than half their annual expenditures from federal funds. These funds, it might be added, are awarded primarily by HEW which is, at the same time, the compliance agency for discrimination complaints filed under the Order. In May, a medical study group report recommended "a sweeping national program to increase the number of blacks and other minority-group students in the nation's medical schools."[5] That no mention was made of increasing the number of women in the nation's medical schools was quickly pointed out by women activists. Moreover, Dr. Bernice Sandler, Chairman of WEAL's contract compliance committee, noted that by 1971 some medical schools had begun to increase their places for blacks, but only with a corresponding decrease of places for women.

According to Dr. Frances Norris, the growth of the women's movement has elicited a backlash reaction from the medical community rather than heightened sensitivity. She points to two incidents in particular to support her argument: 1) In 1968

---

[3] *Ibid.*, p. 562.
[4] *Ibid.*, p. 561.
[5] Harold M. Schmeck, Jr., "Increase is Urged in Black Doctors, Study Lists Steps to Widen Recruitment for Schools," *New York Times,* May 17, 1970, reprinted in *Green Hearings,* p. 575.

the only women's medical school in the country, Women's Medical College in Pennsylvania, changed its status to coeducational,
with a future goal of a 50–50 ratio of men to women. The
Alumnae Association protested the change, arguing that unless
the school doubles its enrollment in the future, the few existing
openings to train women doctors will be markedly reduced. The
Association also noted that 73 percent of the women at the
Women's Medical College had been rejected by other medical
schools. Dr. Glen R. Leymaster, the president and dean of the
college at that time, commented two years later:

> If you say "want more" women in medicine, then I can
> answer. If you say "need more," I don't quite know what
> the need is. Who says we need them? There's a shortage
> of places in medical school. If an effort were successful
> to get more women, it would mean that more men could
> not get in.[6]

2) For many years the *Journal of the American Medical Association* in its annual education round-up issue listed by sex the
number of applicants accepted by medical schools. In the 1970–
71 round-up issue, no sex-breakdown of the statistics was included. According to Dr. Norris, AMA concealment of this information proves not only the medical schools' guilt, but their
unwillingness to change their policy of discrimination against
women. "Both the AMA and the Association of American Medical
Colleges, which is responsible for accrediting medical schools,
have been informed over and over of the sex bias on the part of
medical schools, but they have refused to take any action. In fact,
their attitude seems to be one of strong re-entrenchment."[7]

Some feminists attack male prejudice against women doctors
even more directly:

> A few years back, I was severely criticized by a surgeon
> who did not know me and did not know whether I was a
> good or bad surgeon. He stated flatly that a woman is not
> capable of doing surgery. So I went and found him, and I
> said, "Doctor, I want to watch you operate. I want to see

---

[6] Quoted in "Women MD's Join the Fight," *Medical World News,* October
23, 1970, p. 26. Dr. Leymaster is presently director of the AMA's Advisory
Committee on Undergraduate Medical Education.
[7] Interview, March, 1971.

what part of your anatomy you use in performing surgery that I as a woman am not equipped with."[8]

Though feminist activism among women doctors has been
limited, the medical profession itself has come under severe feminist attack as a system designed to make rich doctors richer,
most often at the expense (literal and psychic) of women. The
long list of allegations includes:

—generally condescending and chauvinistic treatment of
women by male doctors, reinforced by the lack of women
doctors;
—sexual liberties taken by doctors while examining women
patients;
—complete lack of preventive medical care for poor women
and children;
—haphazard preventive health care for middle and upper-
middle class women;
—restricting every phase of the practice of medicine to
licensed physicians and refusing to train paramedicals to
perform simple medical procedures that do not require
eight years of medical training; for instance, pregnancy
tests, preventive check ups, early abortions;
—lack of effort to educate women of all classes about female
physiology and simple health care procedures for themselves and their children;
—great numbers of unwarranted breast removals and hys-
terectomies, considered the most extreme examples of
medical male chauvinism.

The last item particularly angers feminists as well as many
women doctors. One woman doctor, a surgical pathologist, insists that there exist "kinder, less debilitating and less expensive
means of ridding women of breast cancer, but that the male surgeons will not look into them." According to surgeon William
Nolen, the reason is:

That's the way we've treated the disease for fifty years;
therefore, it must be the best way to treat it. We've continued to believe that, even though with this extensive

---

[8] Dr. Mildred E. Ward, quoted in *Medical World News*, p. 24.

and somewhat mutilating operation our cure rate in 1970 is the same as it was in 1930. . . . No one [until very recently] had ever made a serious attempt to find out whether a lesser operation might not be just as effective.[9]

Dr. Nolen argues further that not only should attempts be made to find other remedies, at least for some kinds of breast cancer, but that women patients have the right to know all the possible options, as well as the right to join in the decision-making process of which treatment is best for them. Other surgeons have remarked that they rarely hesitate to remove a breast or take out an ovary, but they do think twice about removing a testicle.[1] "Said one of them, wryly: 'No ovary is good enough to leave in, and no testicle is bad enough to take out.' "[2] The lack of women surgeons is felt to be the major reason for these sex-oriented attitudes.

Gynecology and obstetrics have been particularly singled out by feminists as medical specialties that should be turned over to women. They maintain that this exclusively female area of medicine has become almost totally under the control of men. An article in *Medical World News* on women and medicine discussed complaints of women, noting in particular ". . . that ubiquitous grievance heard whenever women discuss doctors—the unnecessarily rough pelvic exam, with the too-hot or too-cold speculum. 'How is a man to understand how that speculum feels in the vagina?' asks Dr. [Violet] Stephenson."[3] Feminists also complain of being rendered totally dependent on doctors during childbirth:

> The obstetrician . . . rather than the woman herself, becomes the expert in this most intimate area of her life. The obstetrician holds the key, almost literally, to her body. . . . She is the passive witness to her own act of giving birth, bought off possibly by a few breathing exercises she is allowed to perform.[4]

[9] Dr. William Nolen, "The Operation Women Fear Most," *McCall's*, April, 1971, p. 52.
[1] "Women MD's Join the Fight," *Medical World News*, p. 24.
[2] *Loc. cit.*
[3] *Ibid.*, p. 25.
[4] Anne Treseder, *Obstetrics in the Wrong Hands*, Association to Repeal Abortion Laws reprint, August 26, 1970, p. 1.

There is a small groundswell of feminist opinion urging the reinstatement of midwives to help combat "male control" of childbirth. Activists argue that the core of the problem is education:

> Women are capable of absorbing and understanding more information about their physiology than they receive from Kotex "introduction-to-menstruation" films, high school "family life" classes, and patronizing gynecologists. The more ignorance the woman has about her body, the more dependent she is upon her (usually male) doctor.[5]

To counter what they regard as the abuses of the medical profession, some women's liberation groups have organized health care collectives in a number of cities. Most often these collectives direct their efforts to aiding poor women and children with the long-range aim, of dispensing free health care. Some of the collectives have organized health seminars offering free courses on female physiology, simple health care procedures, sex education, contraceptive methods and abortion information. In addition, elevating the status of women working in health-related fields often becomes part of the collective's program, and members attempt to organize hospital and community clinic personnel.

One health care collective was founded on the following premise:

> Women, more than men, need and use health care, especially preventive care, for themselves and their children. Since women and young families have relatively low incomes, they can't afford to pay for adequate care. The only health system that can fully meet women's needs is a health system that gives care on the basis of need, not on ability to pay, a health care system fully oriented towards prevention.

> Since women use the health care system during their active healthy years, unlike men who go to doctors only when they are sick or old, women are more likely to engage in an active struggle for change in health care. Those in power, doctors and health administrators and

[5] *Ibid.*, p. 2.

the executives of insurance, drug and health industries which all profit off the health system, will not change unless they are forced to do so.

A strong women's health movement—an alliance of patients and health workers—could be an important force for change—could begin to initiate the demand for free and complete health care as the right of every citizen.[6]

Municipal Government

THE FIRST KNOWN feminist group of municipal employees was formed in November, 1969. Susan Harman, a New York City employee actively involved in the women's movement, organized a small group of her colleagues into *Women in City Government United*. The idea of a feminist-oriented activist group within municipal ranks had its origins in the mayoral campaign the previous month:

> . . . women campaigners felt they were being discriminated against by the Administration they had just helped to elect. During the campaign Mayor [John V.] Lindsay issued a position paper on women in which among other things he fully supported equal opportunity for women in all level positions and establishment of day care centers for women who need them. We decided to take him up on this even though he has tried to forget about it.[7]

The most obvious manifestation of discrimination was the salary differential between men and women. According to an early member of WCGU, male campaigners who joined the Administration were called aides and paid $11,000 a year; women were called administrative assistants and paid $8,500.

Shortly after the election, the Mayor announced "Talent Search," a project designed to find the best possible people for the

---

[6] "Women and Health Care" by Women's Health Collective, New York City, reprinted from *Rat*, no date.
[7] Judith Layzer and Susan Bennetti, "Sisters Recall . . . ," *The Unionist*, January 22, 1971, p. 5.

sixty-one high-level appointments he had to fill, and which was to include ". . . an active search for qualified women to serve in top and middle level positions in City government."[8] WCGU's first action was to draw up a list of eighty non-City employed women (including many black and Puerto Ricans) they deemed to be qualified for any of the over $15,000 a year positions. A petition urging Lindsay to fulfill his promise to hire more women was signed by fifty City women from the Commissioner level down and was included with the list. According to WCGU only three of the sixty-one appointments made over the subsequent months went to women. (Eleanor Holmes Norton, appointed Human Rights Commissioner, was on the WCGU list.)

In May, 1970, WCGU presented another petition to the Mayor, signed by 187 female employees, reminding him of two City executive orders which did not include women and older people in their discriminatory bans. Executive Order 41, passed during the Wagner Administration, required the City to give equal treatment to all in the hiring of municipal employees "regardless of race, creed, color or national origin." Executive Order 71, issued in 1968, sets forth the same policy for City contractors as well as making it a condition for contract approval. WCGU asked that the words "sex" and "age" be added to each order. On August 24, 1970, two days before the national women's strike, Mayor Lindsay "with political cunning"[9] fulfilled the request. Six months later, however, the order regarding City hiring had not been implemented, causing a WCGU member to dub it the "Vanishing Order," and write in a union publication distributed to many of the municipal employees:

Have you ever heard of . . . the executive order that Mayor Lindsay signed on August 24 which was intended to end discrimination based on age or sex in City employ- ment . . . ? Most people haven't, mainly because the agency chiefs have failed to distribute the order, and because the City Commission on Human Rights along with the City Personnel Department have failed to act on its mandate. . . . Lindsay and his "conspirators," have conveniently not let any woman know of her right to file

---

[8] Emily Greenspan, "City Hall Women Organize to End Sex Discrimina- tion," *New York Feminist,* a special edition published by the *Manhattan Tribune,* April 5, 1970.
[9] Layzer and Bennetti, *loc. cit.*

and get *action* on a complaint to the tune of about $3000
(that's roughly how much *less* women earn than men
for doing the same type of work). . . . There continues
to be *no action* on this anti-discrimination measure, but
much discrimination and exploitation.[1]

Early in 1970, the Administration offered to sponsor a series
of hearings the following June on the status of women. The hearings were put off until September after WCGU suggested that an
in-depth study on women in the City employ would make the
hearings more valuable. The study was made and the hearings
were held from September 21–25, 1970, by the Human Rights
Commission headed by Eleanor Holmes Norton. The witnesses
included Betty Friedan, Dr. Mary Keyserling, former head of the
Federal Women's Bureau; Dr. Jo-Ann Evans Gardner, founder
of the Association for Women in Psychology, as well as representatives from various other fields—law, education, sociology, social
welfare, and women's liberation groups. Although the hearings
were the first ever held by a municipal government, little new or
surprising information came out of them. In fact, WCGU felt
that the "educational" premise on which Commissioner Norton
had based the hearings was useless. They maintained that by
September, 1970, what was needed were specific recommendations for reform based on the already available statistics, not
another recitation of those statistics.
    Like most of the other occupationally-organized feminist
groups, Women in City Government United eschews working
only toward elevating the status of women within the higher
administration ranks. They have also been active at every level
of employment and have spent a good deal of time meeting with
the City's union leaders toward this end. "While the vast array
of unions . . . claim to fully represent all their members, the
benefits negotiated for female members are often minimal."[2]
After many months of meeting with union leaders, WCGU believes it has been recognized, tentatively at least, as a bargaining
force for the rights of women union members. Some WCGU
members feel this is the group's most significant accomplishment. In January, 1971, District Council 37, representing nearly
100,000 non-uniformed City employees, agreed to send out a
questionnaire (formulated by but not attributed to WCGU) to

---

[1] *Loc. cit.*
[2] Greenspan, *Manhattan Tribune*, April 5, 1970.

survey the members' interest in and need for City or union-sponsored child care centers. Also in January, 1971, the municipal Labor Committee, representing all the City unions in negotiations involving health insurance coverage, agreed to add to its list of health insurance demands the extension of abortion coverage to all women regardless of marital status. That the Committee would even agree to negotiate with the City on this matter can be considered noteworthy since the membership represented is largely male and predominantly Catholic.

Other activities of WCGU include a proposal for a design for part-time employment; information sheets informing City employees of various ways and bases for filing complaints about sex discrimination; and a column in *The Unionist,* the bi-weekly house newspaper of the Social Services Employees Union distributed to approximately 16,000 people.

The Arts

FEMINIST ACTIVITY in the arts—painting, sculpture, theater, dance and music—has become increasingly evident. By mid-1971 activists had written numerous articles about the absence of women in most of these fields, about the general lack of encouragement given to "creative" women, and about the manner in which women have been portrayed by playwrights and artists throughout the centuries. Feminists have also staged protests to dramatize these issues and, in some cases, formed groups to produce feminist theater, art, dance, music. Some of these groups are composed of women professionally active in the arts; others have been formed on an amateur "collective" basis.

The earliest known feminist activities in the arts were organized in New York City by women in the art and theater worlds. Although women in all the other fields, as well as in many other cities, have now become active, these early actions served a "consciousness raising" function. Moreover, they are prototypical of the kinds of activities in all of the fields.

PAINTING AND SCULPTURE

In 1969, politically active artists in New York City organized the Art Workers Coalition to protest the alleged discriminatory practices of the "powerful museum-gallery pantheon" as well as to speak out against the Vietnam War and other federal government policies. *Women Artists for Revolution* began as a caucus in the Coalition but became an autonomous group a few months later "when we saw that the rights for women artists always ended up at the bottom of the Coalition's list of demands."[3] WAR began with a politico orientation, but slowly became more feminist.

The group's long-range goal is straightforward—that 50 percent of the artists exhibited by every New York Gallery and museum be women and 50 percent of the art school teachers in the city be women. (Although women comprise 60 to 80 percent of New York art students, it is estimated that they constitute less than 10 percent of the professional artists and art teachers.) To achieve some degree of numerical equality, however, is perhaps even more difficult than in other professions because so many decisions about an artist's ability are based on personal aesthetics. Art critic Lucy Lippard pointed out how hard it is to prove sex discrimination when a gallery owner says he rejected a woman artist's work purely because he thinks "she's a lousy artist." On the other hand one art professor remarked, "that art is male, that aesthetic values are in masculine terms, [and] that no one could possibly understand a work of art outside of its cultural environment."[4] The psychology of aesthetics—"art is supposed to be above sex"—plus the enormous amount of time and energy needed to even attempt a career as an artist have deterred many women artists from joining feminist activities. Nonetheless, WAR, and later groups, have been able to attract many sympathizers and have organized some public actions.

The first and the most highly publicized was a confrontation with New York's Whitney Museum of American Art. In the spring of 1970, WAR began demanding that 50 percent of the works exhibited in the Museum's biannual sculpture show the following December be by women. The Whitney was singled out for protest because its Annual show purports to be a yearly "survey" of the entire contemporary American art scene (alternating each year between painting and sculpture). WAR was joined in the fall by the Ad Hoc Women's Committee (made up largely of women sculptors and art critics) and the two groups

---

[3] Juliet Gordon, founding member of WAR, interview, July, 1970.
[4] Sarah Saporta, "The Status of Women in Art," report to the Conference of Professional and Academic Women, April 11, 1970, p. 1. Reprinted by K.N.O.W., Inc.

increased their pressure on the Whitney. They drew up and presented to the museum's selection committee a list of one hundred women artists whose work the Ad Hoc Committee felt was worthy of recognition. A free advertisement was donated to WAR and the Ad Hoc Committee by the prestigious *Art Forum* magazine. The advertisement, which appeared in the December, 1970, issue, was designed by the women's groups and stated their demand of 50 percent representation in the Annual. The Museum conceded that the continued pressure had had some effect, noting that 22 percent of the sculptors represented in the 1970 Annual were women, as opposed to the usual 5–10 percent of previous years. The campaign against the Whitney also included some "zap" actions. Whitney letterhead was pilfered and used to send out a fake press release stating that 50 percent of the works shown would be by women. On the day of the Annual's opening, December 12, eggs with the message "50 percent" were found all over the museum's staircases. Picket lines were thrown up at the invitational opening, a sit-in was staged around an enormous piece of sculpture, and tickets to the opening were forged and given out to friends and protesters. The women continued to picket the Whitney every Saturday during the run of the Annual, December 12–February 17, 1970–71.

Feminist pressure was also considered responsible for the creation of a second show at the Whitney, mounted to coincide with the Annual. "The Permanent Collection—Women Artists" exhibited the works of 52 artists from the Whitney's permanent collection. (Out of 3000 permanent Whitney artists, 450 are women). The show itself was not acclaimed by critics, patrons or feminists. Although most feminists approved the idea of the show, they criticized it on the basis that most of the artists exhibited were minor ones, and of the major artists, only minor works were shown.

Direct and indirect feminist activity, organized by feminist artist groups, has brought results in other areas of the art world:

—The January, 1971, issue of *Art News* was devoted entirely to "Women's Liberation, Women Artists, and Art History." The articles covered a range of topics, including "Why Have There Been No Great Women Artists," "Sexual Art-Politics," "Moving Out, Moving Up," "Women Without Pathos." The authors were art historians, critics, and well-known women artists.

—An application was submitted to the New York State Council on the Arts for a grant to set up a women's art center.

—Women's groups are investigating the possibility of filing suit against New York art schools for not hiring women art professors. One possible ground for the suit is that art schools receive substantial state and municipal funds.

—Women are also looking into the possibility of suing galleries and museums, also recipients of state and municipal money, for not giving women equal attention in selecting the works of new artists. The most commonly-used process by which galleries and museums select new works is the "studio visit." Whenever an artist feels ready to show his or her work invitations are sent out to galleries, museums and critics to visit the artist's studio. Feminists are compiling statistics to prove that, traditionally, there has been a far smaller response on the part of the selection committees to the invitations of women artists than to those of men.

—Activists have also conducted a series of meetings with museum and gallery officials to protest the absence of women from their ranks.

—The number of art critics (men and women) who have become sympathetic to the feminist cause has increased, and they keep the subject of women in the art world in the public arena via newspapers and magazine articles, and speaking engagements.

As in other occupations, however, the biggest barrier to women artists, according to many, is that they simply are not taken seriously as artists—not by themselves or in museum and gallery circles. According to one feminist:

The work of a woman artist is thought of as an ornamental attraction, a feminine pastime, of no consequence, not to be confused with *real* art, the profoundly serious contributions made to our culture, which will live in immortality, etc.—which is men's work.[5]

---

[5] Saporta, p. 1.

THEATER

There are a growing number of feminist theater groups around the country—on college and university campuses as well as in various cities. Most often these groups perform on an *ad hoc* basis and primarily at women's movement events. Although as yet there is no widespread feminist activity within the "professional" theater, some early events received significant public attention and, again, served a "consciousness raising" function.

In the fall of 1968, Anselma dell'Olio, an actress and active in the women's movement since the end of 1966, staged a satirical cabaret of feminist material. The first performance of this *New Feminist Theater* was on March 21, 1969, at the Redstockings abortion hearings in New York City. The reviews included a short play which by a sex-reversal raised the issues of abortion and childbearing; a male character who awakened to find that a uterus containing a fetus had been implanted in his body is unable to obtain help. The playlet written by Myrna Lamb was entitled "But What Have You Done for Me Lately?" In the following months the cabaret material was expanded and the New Feminist Theater performed in an off-Broadway theater for the remainder of the spring. Enough attention was engendered to warrant coverage by *The New York Times*. The May 18 theater section carried a lengthy feature article extensively praising the group for taking a truly critical view of the "prevailing thought system," and for suggesting that society needs "adjusting," not the individual. The article also described one of the skits:

> "The Middle Voice" by Gerry Beirne, has a baritone and a soprano preparing to exercise their charms on the unknown singer who is to do a motet with them. The baritone, swaggering, expects a woman. The soprano, mixing a mince with an aggressive wiggle, awaits a man since the part might be sung by either. When a charming creature whose sex it is impossible to guess arrives, they are both frustrated, unable to relate to another being on a purely human level.[6]

The group's reputation grew, primarily within the women's movement, and it spent the summer and fall touring eastern college

---

[6] *New York Times*, May 18, 1969, theater section, p. 5.

campuses, performing in one of New York's underground
theaters, and at various feminist functions such as the Congress
to United Women in November, 1969. Fearful of becoming an
"intra-movement thing" or nothing more than "agitprop" theater,
dell'Olio disbanded the group until a feminist cabaret suitable for
the general public could be put together. By the spring of 1970,
"A Cabaret of Sexual Politics" was completed and the search for
a producer had begun.

The second feminist theatrical event of note was the production of Myrna Lamb's musical play, "The Mod Donna" by the
New York Shakespeare Festival Public Theater. It opened on April
24, 1970, and ran through June 7. Both audience and critical reaction were sharply divided. One critic attacked the "logic" of the
plot as "neither masculine nor feminine, just dangerous."[7]
Another wrote that the play was not a "lecture against sex, but a
powerful statement against what has happened to sex (and to
human relationships as a whole) in a society in which people
are taught that the supreme goal in one's life should be winning
over other people."[8]

In December, 1970, a number of women—several actresses,
a poet, and two directors—formed a consciousness raising
theater group with a plan to develop new theatrical techniques,
styles, and content. This non-commercial group calls itself *New
York Tea Party;* one of the founders said the idea for its formation came out of the women's realization that, through the ages,
the theater had been created, written, produced, directed and,
during some periods of history, acted exclusively by men. Moreover, although there are great dramatic roles for women, they
are few in number. Standard acting exercises are done each
week, but, according to the women, imposing a feminist point of
view often changes the meaning of the exercise: for example,
an improvisation may center around a mother who has lost two
sons in Vietnam; by using a feminist frame of reference, the
women say that the action moves in a very different direction
than it would if a more traditional motivation were used.

Although none of these "feminist theatrical events" was designed to create substantially more or better jobs for actresses,
women directors, playwrights or technicians, the feminists in-

---

[7] "Upfront," *International Socialist Review,* July–August, 1970, p. 2.
[8] *Loc. cit.*

volved hoped to raise the consciousness of both theater people themselves and of the theater-going public to feminist issues.

· · ·

The long-term impact of all the occupationally-oriented feminist groups is difficult to predict. It can be noted, however, that their emergence represents the first time professional women have organized themselves *as women* on a large scale. Since professional groups often exercise some degree of political influence, the existence of these women's groups may well bring about significant changes in the traditional structure of social institutions and work patterns.

11

The Church

ALTHOUGH NOT as widely publicized as "secular" women's liberation activities, feminist actions within the confines of organized religion have become an almost daily occurrence. Women activists in the church include theology professors and students, biblical scholars, ministers, nuns, lay administrators, heads of women's divisions of various denominations, and parishioners. Like their secular counterparts, these activists run the gamut from "women's rightists," who see feminism in terms of better jobs and salaries for women within the church structure, to "radical feminists," who have called that entire structure into question by challenging the most basic tenets of the Judaeo-Christian tradition. All, however, would agree that:

> ... at this point in history the Church is in the somewhat comical position of applauding women's legal, professional, and political emancipation in secular society while keeping them in the basement of its own edifice.[1]

One feminist in the church observed that after generations of listening to the church preach about "equality of all people," women in the church now want to "cash in their chips."[2] It must be noted at the outset, however, that the women who are challenging church doctrine and practices are to a person deeply

---

[1] Mary Daly, "Toward Partnership in the Church," *Voices of the New Feminism*, ed. Mary Lou Thompson (Boston: Beacon Press, 1970), pp. 146–147.
[2] Sarah Bentley Doely, staff member Church Women United, December, 1970.

committed to the belief that the church is an important social institution worth reforming. Moreover, feminists within the church believe that they may be the only ones who can carry the idea of "women's liberation" to the average "middle-American" woman. "She's highly suspicious of women's liberation in general, but she'll often listen to a church woman—even when she's preaching the same message."[3]

Origins of Feminist Activity

WITHIN THE Catholic Church, the first stirrings of the current wave of feminist agitation began at the Second Vatican Council (1962–1965), during which time nearly every facet of Catholic doctrine was questioned. During the two years of meetings some particularly noteworthy events occurred regarding women.

First, several scholarly petitions were presented to the Council Fathers urging a reassessment of the theological and professional status of women in the Catholic Church in light of contemporary scientific, sociological and scholastic information. These petitions were prepared by respected theologians from a number of different countries.

Second, several events at the meetings specifically involving women attracted public attention. Two in particular were widely reported. In one case, economist Barbara Ward was prohibited from reading her paper at Vatican II because she was a woman. In consequence, the paper was presented by a man. In the second instance, two women journalists were barred from attending Council Masses, an occurrence which provoked outrage from their male colleagues and resulted in a strongly-worded petition from them in support of the women. Subsequently, women journalists were allowed to attend Council Masses. One, however, was prevented from approaching the altar railing to receive Holy Communion.

Third, there were several progressive statements by Pope John and in the Vatican II Pastoral Constitution which recognized the low social status of women. For example, the Constitu-

---

[3] Patricia Kepler, Task Force on Women, United Presbyterian Church, U.S.A., interview, January, 1971.

tion noted that women had been ". . . denied the right and freedom to choose a husband, to embrace a state of life, or to acquire
an education or cultural benefits equal to those recognized for
men."[4]

All these events prompted extensive discussion in the Catholic press about the status of women, which has since snowballed
into a significant feminist movement within the intellectual
spheres of the Church. Of all the religious communities the most
radical analysis and militant actions about the "woman question"
have come from Catholics.

In the Protestant Church, although a few denominations have
granted women full religious rights for more than a century, a
formal "women's rights" movement within Protestantism has
existed for barely a quarter of a century. It had its beginnings in
1948 when the World Council of Churches was formed. In
1950, after two years of persistent pressure from an international
group of church women, the Council authorized the Commission
on the Life and Work of Women in the Church to study the status
of women in the Council's member churches. As a result of the
Council's work, over the years many denominations have granted
women the right to ordination; in addition, several added provisions to their constitutions stipulating that a specific percentage
of governing board members be women.

It is the existence of the new women's movement, however,
that has had a most dramatic effect on activist church women,
who have since become much more militant in their demands
for equality in the church. In December, 1969, the women's
liberation movement made its "formal entry" into the Protestant/
Orthodox (Greek, Russian) community. A women's caucus
was founded at the General Assembly meeting of the National
Council of Churches, a 200-member ecumenical body representing 33 American denominations. The caucus presented a fact-
and-statistic-filled statement regarding the status of women in
religious life. It read in part:

> We begin our statement with an affirmation of support
> for the movement to liberate women in the United States
> . . . especially for [those who have] chosen to gather into
> *the church.* . . . We will not be able to create a new

---

[4] Vatican II Pastoral Constitution, quoted from Mary Daly, *The Church
and the Second Sex* (New York and Evanston: Harper & Row, 1968), p. 78.
See also *Pacem in Terris* encyclical of 11 April, 1963, n. 41.

church and a new society until and unless women are full participants. . . .

Nowhere is the situation of women better illustrated than in our male-dominated and male-oriented churches. The church, both in its theology and in its institutional forms, is a reflection of culture. It has shown no propensity to transcend culture as regards the status of women, although it knows it ought. Indeed, the church has too often maintained anachronistic attitudes and practices long after other societal institutions have begun to shift. . . .

In 1950 when the NCC was organized in Cleveland, Ohio, only 5 out of 82 members of the General Board were women. That was 6 percent. . . . Nineteen years later in 1969, out of approximately 200 members of the General Board, 11—or barely 6 percent—are women. . . . Were a visitor from outer space to visit the Assembly and were that visitor told that it was a body representative of the churches in the United States, that visitor would naturally conclude that the churches are composed of white-skinned male clergy over 40. . . . As the Council is called to re-examine functions and roles, indeed the very nature of the church in mission, it simply must deal with women. You will be sick of this theme, but we will not stop raising it.[5]

Within the Jewish religious community there has been a noticeable lack of organized feminist activity in any of its three main branches—Orthodox, Conservative or Reform. There is no single or simple explanation for the absence of a feminist movement in so overtly a male-oriented and male-dominated structure as Judaism, but several overlapping theories have been suggested.

A good portion of feminist attack within the Christian religious community is against the symbolic image of women as articulated by Christian theology. A parallel "theological" or "symbolic" image of woman does not exist in Jewish teachings. For example, Judaism has no Doctrine of Original Sin which blames woman's sexuality for the Fall of Man; nor is there a Jewish

---

[5] Statement of Women's Caucus, December, 1969. It should be noted that at this meeting, for the first time in the history of the National Council of Churches, a woman, Dr. Cynthia Wedel, was elected president of the Council.

woman who symbolically combines virginity and motherhood as does Christianity's Mary.

Another explanation is that women play a special role in traditional Jewish daily life. Although barred (until the advent of Reform Judaism) from performing many of the religious rites, women were given well-defined and important religious duties to perform in the home. Thus, many argue that the Jewish woman has historically had a significant part to play in religious life. Feminists, on the other hand, argue that the religious importance attached to women's duties in the home represent nothing more than the bestowing of religious sanction on the generally prevailing assumption that woman's proper place is in the home.

A third explanation for the lack of feminist activity within the contemporary Jewish community is related to the minority and oppressed status of all Jews: the desire and need to present a "united front" to a hostile outside world precludes any thought of independent and/or devisive action on the part of women.

Although there has been no organized feminist activity within Judaism, there has been some discussion about the rights of women. It must be noted, however, that many of the advocates for women's rights sharply reject any association with the women's movement. For example, Sally Priesand, who will be ordained in June, 1972, as Reform Judaism's first woman rabbi, argues that she is not a supporter of women's liberation:

> I don't need it. But I do think the feminist movement is important because it is time for us to overcome psychological and emotional objections. We must fulfill our potential as creative individuals.[6]

The National Federation of Temple Sisterhoods, the women's "arm" of Reform Judaism, issued a statement in April, 1970, calling for greater recognition of women in all levels of Reform Judaism. The statement included lists of statistics which document that although men and women have always had the same religious rights in Reform Judaism, this equality ". . . has been honored far more in word than in fact."[7] The Federation denied, however, that its call for women's equality was predicated

---

[6] *New York Times*, April 13, 1971.
[7] Resolution, National Federation of Temple Sisterhoods, April, 1970. Unpaginated.

... on feminist activism ... [or] on leadership for its own sake. Rather, we firmly believe that in these days of crisis when the institutions, beliefs and values of religion are on trial for their relevance to the complex world of today, men and women together, both individually and through their organizations, have an equal, vital responsibility.[8]

Dr. Trude Weiss-Rosmarin, editor of the Orthodox publication *The Jewish Spectator,* published an editorial in the October, 1970, issue entitled, "The Unfreedom of Jewish Women." In it she railed against Orthodox Jewish law arguing that it is *"male-*made and it protects the rights and advantages of men."[9] Moreover, she argued that Jewish law is particularly degrading to women by making them legally the possessions of their husbands, and maintained that these areas of religious family law must be changed. She attacked feminists, however, and advocated a separate but equal status for women: "The real challenge of Women's Liberation is not taking women out of the home but emancipating *the home-maker* as *home-maker* and *house wife* by bestowing *dignity* upon her work instead of derogating it, as most men and 'creative women' do."[1]

Feminist Issues

FEMINIST ACTIVITIES within the Christian community most often fall into three categories: 1) challenging the theological view of women; 2) challenging the religious laws and/or customs which bar women from ordination; 3) demanding that the professional status and salaries of women in the church be upgraded.

THEOLOGICAL VIEW OF WOMEN

The assault made by "secular" radical feminists on traditional sex roles has caused radical feminists within the church to re-

---

[8] *Ibid.*
[9] *The Jewish Spectator,* October, 1970, p. 5.
[1] *Ibid.,* p. 3.

examine the traditional roles of women as expressed by theological doctrine. Since the Judaeo-Christian tradition is a primary source of Western thought and culture, it is argued that the Western view of women and the social institutions which reflect and reinforce that view have been shaped in large part by this tradition. The most obvious examples of church influence can be found in the prevailing attitudes toward sex, marriage, divorce, contraception and abortion—attitudes formed almost entirely by religious doctrine. (Christian doctrine has been particularly influential in these areas for it has equated sexual activity with sin.) Feminists in the church argue, however, that these "visible" examples of religious influence over secular thought constitute only the tip of an iceberg of subtle and insidious ideas about men and women which are directly attributable to theology. Although many of these ideas did not originate in theological doctrine, feminists blame theology for its active role in their perpetuation. They argue that theologians, as "symbolic" not "scientific" thinkers (until the contemporary era of biblical scholarship), infused ancient myths and assumptions about woman's nature with "divine authority." These assumptions were thus deemed part of "God's plan" and therefore immutable. Feminists in the church contend that while responsible theologians and biblical scholars have reinterpreted in a contemporary light past "immutable" truths—slavery, for instance, or the divine right of kings—they still accept as immutable the theological assumptions about men and women. Feminists argue further that these assumptions reflect centuries of "male-only" thinking—theologians having always been male. Thus, the basic assumptions in theological doctrine that feminists are challenging

—that God is male

—that woman's subordination to man is divinely ordained

—that woman by nature is either "evil" or "pure" as symbolically incarnated in Eve and Mary

—that "God's plan" for women was revealed through St. Paul

all reflect this "male-thinking."

God is male: It is implicit throughout the Old Testament that God is not male or female, or male and female, but uniquely divine. However, centuries of male church leadership, male interpretation of the Scriptures, and the use of the male pronoun to refer to God, have given rise to the popular conception that God is male. Dr. Mary Daly, a Catholic theologian, writes, "Of course, no theologian or biblical scholar believes that God literally belongs to the male sex."[2] She notes, however, a certain confusion about this point, and cites as an example a respected male theologian's explanation of the "supra-sexuality" of God:

> We have already noticed that in the Mesopotamian myths sex was as primeval as nature itself. The Hebrews could not accept this view, for there was no sex in the God they worshipped. God is, of course, masculine, but not in the sense of sexual distinction, and the Hebrew found it necessary to state expressly, in the form of a story, that sex was introduced into the world by the creative Deity, who is above sex as he is above all things which he made.[3]

Feminists note further that the belief that the church is properly "male" has been reinforced by referring to the Christian Trinity only in masculine terms—God the Father, God the Son, God the Holy Ghost. Contemporary feminist theologians are not questioning the use of the masculine pronoun for Jesus, obviously, but they have begun to dispute the continuing use of the same pronouns to refer to God and the Holy Ghost. It should be noted also that there are feminists who argue that the assumption that God, *the* Supreme Being, is male is the quintessence of sexism. They are not, however, suggesting that God should be seen as female, since this would merely replace one form of sexism with another.

Woman's subordination to man is Divinely Ordained: Some feminists note that the popular conception that God is male implies a secondary, somewhat simplistic assumption that woman, who can never be male, is by definition a lesser being than man. They note that until the age of modern biblical scholarship, most theologians believed and taught that:

> The order of creation established the supraordination of men and the subordination of women, rooted in fixed sexual roles throughout the historical process. These sexual

---

[2] Daly, *The Church and the Second Sex*, p. 138.
[3] John L. McKenzie, *The Two-Edged Sword: An Interpretation of the Old Testament*, pp. 93–94. Quoted from Daly, *The Church and the Second Sex*, p. 139.

roles are not understood culturally or sociologically, but as rooted in the Law and, therefore, ontological and inevitable at any period of history.[4]

The "divine proof" of women's subordination to man is found in the creation story, Genesis 2:18-23. This story states that God created Eve (woman) from one of Adam's ribs[5] for the purpose of being Adam's (man's) "helper." Throughout the ages, little emphasis has been placed on the other creation story found in Genesis 1:26-27, written several centuries after the first. In the second version, no mention is made of a time lag between the creation of man and woman, nor is there any mention of one sex being a "helper" for the other:

> Then God said, "Let us make man in our image, after our likeness; and let them have dominion over the fish of the sea, and over the birds of the air, and over the cattle, and over all the earth, and over every creeping thing that creeps upon the earth." So God created man in his own image, in the image of God he created him; male and female he created them.[6]

The general acceptance by contemporary theologians of this latter version as proof of the absolute equality of male and female in God's eye has not, according to feminists, erased the damage done to the image of women by the theological stress on the "Adam's rib" version for thousands of years.

Woman by nature is either "evil" or "pure":   Feminists argue that theology offers only two images of woman which define both her nature and behavior: Eve—the first transgressor, who is responsible for the fall of man; and Mary—the unattainable ideal combining virginity and motherhood, and also the "model of perfect obedience." One female biblical scholar laments that:

> Otherwise reliable scholars traditionally neglect Biblical women, and what meaning their stories have for their

---

[4] Peggy Ann Way, "An Authority of Possibility for Women in the Church," *Women's Liberation and the Church,* ed. Sarah Bentley Doely (New York: Association Press, 1970), p. 79.

[5] In 1892, Elizabeth Cady Stanton, in an essay in *The Woman's Bible,* referred to Eve's creation from one of Adam's ribs as "a petty surgical operation."

[6] All biblical quotations from Revised Standard Version.

time or ours. Lacking a reasonably complete and objective survey of women's contribution to the Hebrew-Christian tradition, we keep drawing our illustrative material from the same few female characters and the stylized concept of them as "very, very good" or "very, very horrid." But the women we read about in the Bible were *people* (even as you and I). They had their virtues, their faults, their conflicts, their disappointments, their aspirations, their love, their faith. It is as *people* that we should like to know them, and though many interesting details of their lives have been lost in the telling and retelling (usually by male priests and editors) over a good many centuries, much remains to be revealed by an objective survey based on the disciplines of Biblical scholarship.[7]

Feminists reason further that by lifting only the Eve-Mary images from the Bible and infusing them with "divine authority," Christianity has made it impossible for women in general to be viewed as anything but *symbolic* representations of male ideas about sex: sexual evilness, i.e., the temptress; sexual purity, i.e., the virgin; sexual procreativity, i.e., the mother. Moreover, these simplistic representations have been rendered even more immutable throughout the ages because theologians have enveloped them in a veil of "feminine mystery." This interpretation of *woman,* known as the "eternal feminine" or "eternal woman" has been strongly criticized by many scholars and philosophers besides feminists for its neat avoidance of dealing with *women* as flesh and blood human beings. One woman Catholic theologian adds another thought:

Subtly flattering to the male is the invariable tendency of the Eternal Woman school to describe woman strictly within the categories of virgin, bride, and mother, thus considering her strictly in terms of sexual relationship, whether in a negative or a positive sense. It would not occur to such writers to apply this reductive system to the male, compressing his whole being into categories of "virgin, husband, and father."[8]

---

[7] Elsie Thomas Culver, *Women in the World of Religion* (Garden City, New York: Doubleday & Company, Inc., 1967), p. 13.
[8] Daly, *The Church and the Second Sex,* p. 111.

It should be noted that although the Eternal Feminine view of women is most clearly expressed in Catholicism, its effects are to be found throughout all Christian thought.

"God's plan" for women was revealed through St. Paul: Paul's statements about the inferior status of women have been theologically interpreted over the centuries as "divine proof" that women are by nature inferior, and are therefore to be proscribed from certain spheres of life, both within the church and without. The most commonly-used Pauline statements (quoted by clergymen with "relish," according to some women) "to keep women in their place" are:

> . . . any woman who prays or prophesies with her head unveiled dishonors her head—it is the same as if her head were shaven. For if a woman will not veil herself, then she should cut off her hair; but if it is disgraceful for a woman to be shorn or shaven, let her wear a veil. For a man ought not to cover his head, since he is the image and glory of God; but woman is the glory of man. (For man was not made from woman, but woman from man. Neither was man created for woman, but woman for man.) That is why a woman ought to have a veil on her head . . . (I Cor. 11:5-10).

> Wives, be subject to your husband, as to the Lord. For the husband is the head of the wife as Christ is the head of the church, his body, and is himself its Savior. As the church is subject to Christ, so let wives also be subject in everything to their husbands (Ephesians 5:22-24).

> . . . also that women should adorn themselves modestly and sensibly in seemly apparel, not with braided hair or gold or pearls or costly attire but by good deeds, as befits women who profess religion. Let a woman learn in silence with all submissiveness. I permit no woman to teach or to have authority over men; she is to keep silent. For Adam was formed first, then Eve; and Adam was not deceived, but the woman was deceived and became a transgressor. Yet woman will be saved through bearing children, if she continues in faith and love and holiness, with modesty (I Timothy 2:9-15).

Most modern biblical experts argue that Paul was describing the social and political condition of women at his time, as well as looking for theological justification for that condition. Moreover,

> We now know it is important to understand that Paul was greatly preoccupied with *order* in society and in Christian assemblies in particular. In modern parlance, it seemed necessary to sustain a good "image" of the Church. Thus it appeared to him an important consideration that women should not have too predominant a place in Christian assemblies, that they should not "speak" too much or unveil their heads. This would have caused scandal and ridicule of the new sect, which already had to face accusations of immorality and effeminacy.[9]

Thus, few responsible contemporary theologians use the Pauline statements as a current guide for the role of women in the church or the world. Some of them argue that, taken as a whole and in historical context, Paul's writings, although anti-feminist, are basically pro-humanist: several of his statements, they believe, transcend the contemporary political and social realities of the early Christian church. For example, following immediately the statement, "neither man was created for woman, but woman for man" comes:

> Nevertheless, in the Lord woman is not independent of man nor man of woman; for as woman was made from man, so man is now born of woman. And all things are from God (I Cor. 11:11-12).

Another example:

> For as many of you as were baptized into Christ have put on Christ. There is neither Jew nor Greek, there is neither slave nor free, there is neither male nor female; for you are all one in Christ Jesus (Galatians 3:27-28).

Feminists in the church argue that although many of Paul's teachings regarding women may transcend the literal and symbolic interpretation historically given them, the emphasis placed

---

[9] *Ibid.*, p. 38.

on the anti-woman themes of the Bible over the centuries, to the exclusion of the transcendental ones, has so marked woman with a subordinate status that the image may be in fact irreversible.

According to many feminists in the church, the centuries of "male-only" interpretation of the Scriptures is reflected not only in the Western view of men and women *per se,* but also in the entire Western construct of morality and ethics. As noted previously, the most obvious manifestations of this can be seen in the traditional code of sexual morality. Had women over the centuries been able to contribute "female thinking" to the formulation of sexual attitudes, feminists argue that the concepts of sex, marriage, and the family would undoubtedly be radically different.

In the broader areas of ethics and morality, some feminists in the church have suggested that the theological concept of sin itself reflects a *male* interpretation of the "human condition." In this light, one woman theologian discussed the "sin of pride":

> . . . major theological emphasis upon pride as the condition for human sin reflects the traditional nature of male existence as embodying aggressiveness and power. False pride and the temptation to misuse power thus create the masculine condition for sinfulness, and the theological plea is for greater humility and less confidence in one's own resources. The situation is different for women. The nature of feminine existence has traditionally been more passive and self-denying. Yet the theological plea has emphasized even greater humility and self-abnegation. Few —if any—have recognized that *too little pride, rather than too much pride, may be the condition of feminine sinfulness.*[1]

This heightened consciousness of the androcentricity of traditional theology has caused many feminists in the church to maintain that until theology is fully re-examined, the status and image of women (both within the church and without) will never be altered. Indeed, some of them contend that "breaking out of the male framework of theology" should be *the* goal of activist women in the church.

There is some evidence that a move in that direction has begun. In Boston in May, 1970, an ecumenical group of women

---

[1] Quoted anonymously from Margaret Sittler Ermarth, *Adam's Fractured Rib* (Philadelphia: Fortress Press, 1970), p. 32.

convened the National Conference on the Role of Women in Theological Education to discuss feminist issues in the church. The conference resulted in a formal proposal to set up an Institute on Women funded and sponsored by the various theological schools in the Boston area. A central component of the Institute would be support of *theological* research on women. In the spring of 1971, Alverno College in Milwaukee invited a number of women theologians to a week-long conference on theology and women. In addition, various seminaries across the country have organized speakers bureaus, women's centers, and consciousness raising sessions to address the issue of women in the church in general and women in theology in particular. Berkeley, Drew Seminary in New Jersey, Union Theological Seminary in New York and the half-dozen schools of theology in Chicago were some of the first to become active in these areas. Moreover, paralleling the demand for women's studies programs at secular colleges and universities, women students at theological schools and seminaries have also begun to demand women's courses.

ORDINATION OF WOMEN

Women are barred by canon law from the priesthood of the Roman Catholic Church. Atlhough 30 of the 33 largest Protestant and Orthodox denominations ordain women,[2] women ministers make up only a minuscule percentage of American Protestant clergy. Moreover, when Protestant women are ordained, they rarely preside over significant pastorates. Reform Judaism will not have its first woman rabbi until June, 1972, although there are no religious laws barring ordination. (Orthodox and Conservative Jewish law prohibits women rabbis.)

The issue of ordaining women has become a rallying point for Christian feminists for both practical and symbolic reasons. In the "practical" realm there are perhaps three primary reasons why feminists feel women should be ordained.

First, the all-male clergy traditionally has been the theological interpreters and teachers of scripture, church doctrine, morality and ethics. Women clergy are vital in order to reassess and counterbalance these historically "male" interpretations and teachings.

Second, the clergy determines church policy (lay governing

---

[2] Protestant denominations which do not ordain women (as of mid-1971): Reform, Lutheran-Missouri Synod and Episcopal. At the Episcopal 1970 annual meeting, ordination was vetoed on a parliamentary technicality.

boards and executive councils notwithstanding) through its decision-making powers on such matters as where and how church funds will be allocated, what new curriculums will be taught in church schools and seminaries, what will be the church's handling of such political issues as its tax-exempt status, church schools, abortion and contraception. Decisions on all of these questions are made by the clergy who function as "chairmen of the board," "marketing directors," and "ad-men" of the church "corporation." Women in the clergy would put women into policy-making positions enabling them to help shape the decisions that affect women's as well as men's lives.

Third, men have traditionally had their choice whether to serve the church via the laity or the ministry. Women should be given the same choice. Thus, they should not be relegated to the laity either by *de jure* or *de facto* discrimination.

Symbolically, the issue of ordination is important to feminists for several other reasons.

First, the ordination of women (by changing either church law or "hallowed" church tradition) would serve as the symbolic affirmation that the doctrine of "supraordination of man and subordination of woman" had finally been transcended. Feminists feel that the door has already been opened to this eventuality by the vast number of contemporary theologians (including Catholics) who see no *theological* justification whatever for barring women from the clergy.[3] Ordaining women would also, symbolically at least, purge the church of the "eternal feminine" interpretation of women and force it to transform its image of women from mysterious and mystical creatures into people.

Second, preponderance of male clergy serves to reinforce the symbolic male-female relationship within the church structure: the man's role is to "lead" the church and shape its destiny, the woman's is to "serve" the church no matter what its destiny. The woman's role in this relationship (paid or volunteer) manifests itself in many ways according to feminists: the minister's wife, the Catholic nun, the legions of volunteer women on "flower and music" committees, the women Sunday School teachers, etc. A large number of women clergy would begin to visibly challenge the assumption that leader/follower is the only acceptable male/female relationship within the church structure. It is the poten-

---

[3] In April, 1971, one officially sponsored in-depth study on the American priesthood found no theological reason for barring women from the Catholic priesthood.

tial threat to the "comfortable" leader/follower relationship that seems to elicit the loudest response from those opposed to ordaining women—"But that's not her role!" One woman theology professor remarked, "It's all right if women come to Church with a cake in their hands, but if they come with an idea in their heads, they're not welcome."[4] Even those women already ordained apparently are presumed to have a particular "woman's place":

> . . . I resented the fact that when I would go to a new Presbytery, it was immediately assumed that here they had a recruit for the Children's Work Committee. And I *resented* the *resentment* I experienced when I would say that under no circumstances was I suited to serving on Children's Work. It would be implied that a woman who would thus reject little children must necessarily be a bad woman, or at least an unnatural one. In vain did I protest that I actually *like* little children—that, in fact, some of my best *friends* are children, but that my objection to being on the Children's Work Committee arose from my ignorance of how to teach little folk. It seemed obvious to me that most of my male colleagues would have been better at this than I. They, at least, were parents![5]

According to feminists in the church, there is another "symbolically" important reason why women should be ordained: clergymen have always been considered to have a more "direct line" to God than anyone else; women clergy would contradict the generally-accepted assumption that this relationship to God can only be attained by one sex. Finally, the symbolic image of the clergy in a local community is often one of not only spiritual and moral leadership, but also of intellectual leadership. The ordination of women would force parishioners to question the assumption that only men are capable of such leadership.

Feminists hope that by pressing for ordination, they can change what they see as the church's hypocritical stance which, on the one hand, applauds the political, legal and economic elevation of women in the "outside" world, but, on the other, bars them from elevation within its own hierarchy. Stated in another

---

[4] Dr. Elizabeth Farians, *New York Times,* May 17, 1970.
[5] Norma Ramsey Jones, "Women in the Ministry," *Women's Liberation and the Church,* p. 62.

way—the church appears to accept, at least in theory, women's demands for higher status in the church's *lay* organizations, but views their demands for entrance into the clerical hierarchy as an entirely different matter. The "entirely different matter" argument is used not only by the male hierarchy, but also by many lay women employed by the church. These women will pressure for higher salaries and higher-level jobs for church women, but often seem to fear that the achievement of these limited goals will be jeopardized by insisting on ordination as well. Others simply do not see ordination as a "rights" issue. Still others insist that they are sincerely satisfied by serving the church within the confines of the laity. "But I wouldn't *want* to be ordained," is often heard when the subject comes up. The radical feminists within the church reject this limited approach to equality for they argue there can be *no* equality until women are permitted to enter the clergy as freely and frequently as men. They somewhat condescendingly refer to the above-mentioned lay women as the "women's rightists" of church feminism.

It must be noted in conclusion that at the same time that women are pressing for ordination (either to be granted that right, or be allowed to really use the right that is already theirs on paper), the whole concept of ordination itself is being challenged by other reformers within the church. Alternate forms of ministry are being heatedly debated, as is the more basic question of what being "ordained" has to do with "serving God." Also under fire is the concept that the organizational structure of the church must be based on a hierarchical principle. For the moment, however, church feminists are operating under the assumption that the clerical hierarchy will remain for some time to come; accordingly, they are demanding that women be admitted to it on an equal basis with men.

Professional Status of Women in the Church

For the most part, women's rights activities in the church mirror women's rights activities outside the church and, similarly, tend to attract middle-aged and "moderate" women. Notwithstanding their moderate goals, however, the pressure these women have been able to create is considerable. They are demanding more equitable salaries, more women in decision-making positions, and more women voting members on church governing boards.

A 1969 employment study conducted by the National Council

of Churches surveyed the boards and agencies of 65 denominations and concluded that the status of women employed by the church is no better, and perhaps worse, than that of their secular counterparts. A total of 1558 professional and executive positions were surveyed; 25 percent of them were held by women. The results of the survey showed that 43.2 percent of the women received salaries under $10,000, whereas only 16.1 percent of the men employed received under $10,000. As the salary and job level rose, the percentage of women dropped markedly. The survey also noted that answers to opinion questions ". . . reflect adherence to the rhetoric of equality of opportunity for women and men, on the one hand, and the factual conditions of considerable discrimination, on the other."[6] Two major contributing factors to the dearth of women executives appear to be the preference for *clergy* in high-level positions and upper-echelon jobs, and the channeling of women into certain areas of church work —Education Director, Music Director, Church Secretary, Church School Teacher, etc.—jobs not designed for upward mobility.

For the most part women are found in high executive jobs only in women's divisions of various denominations. Some of these divisions have achieved a significant degree of power within their respective church organizations, even though most of them were formed a century or so ago as the "auxiliary" or "support troops" of the church. Until very recently, the goal of most women's divisions was to be absorbed and integrated into the main church structure, a goal that was achieved by several of them. The advent of the women's liberation movement, however, has resulted in a marked interest in "separatism" on the part of women's divisions. One of the strongest statements to this effect was made by the Women's Division of the Board of Missions of the United Methodist Church, perhaps the most powerful and richest of all the women's divisions. Their 1969 statement reads in part:

> Where organized women's groups have been removed
> from a visible policy-making and power-sharing role, the
> following things tend to occur:

---

[6] Earl D. C. Brewer, Ph.D., *A Study of Employment of Women in Professional or Executive Positions in the Churches at a National Level.* Paper presented at a Consultation on the Recruiting, Training, and Employing of Women Professional Church Workers, February, 1969, p. 3.

a. Male chauvinism increases;
b. The status of women declines. . . .

For the sake of the whole, as well as for ourselves, we
believe that our denomination needs to maintain an organized women's group which exercises real power. Otherwise, women will have to reorganize later under more
difficult circumstances.[7]

Women's Rights Organizations
Within the Church

FOLLOWING are descriptions of a number of feminist groups
within the church. Some of them are independently organized,
others are formally attached to their respective church bodies.
Some were formed expressly to work for women's equality within
the church, while others have worked for general social reform
for years, and only recently have begun to equate social reform
with women's rights. In addition to on-going groups, *ad hoc* committees have been organized for specific actions or projects.

Perhaps the only cross-denominational feminist group devot-
ing all its energies to the question of women in the church is the
Ecumenical Task Force on Women and Religion, one of the
many task forces established by the National Organization for
Women. It was formed in the spring of 1967 and has issued a
number of general statements on women in the church, as well
as statements on specific issues such as birth control and ordination. The Task Force is headed by Dr. Elizabeth Farians, a
Catholic theologian, and long-time women's rights activist. Task
Force members have testified at Equal Rights Amendment hearings and also participated in some "guerrilla" actions. One such
action, touched off by the publication of a new Roman Catholic
Missal, received a fair amount of public attention. According to
the Missal women would be allowed (for the first time) to participate in some liturgical roles previously open only to men. The
Task Force viewed the new Vatican ruling as more degrading to

---

[7] Statement, Women's Division of Board of Missions, United Methodist
Church, 1969. Reprinted in *Women's Liberation and the Church*, pp. 107ff.

women than the old one because "it gives with one hand takes away with other."[8] On April 19, 1970 a group from the Task Force burned the particular portion of the Missal which granted women the opportunity to be lectors at Mass because of the restrictions attached to the new ruling. A woman could read the lesson only if a man were not available, and a woman lector had to stand outside the altar area (a male lector is not barred from the altar area). The Task Force looked upon the rule as "discriminatory and insulting to American Women."[9] The women sent the charred Missal ashes to John Cardinal Dearden, president of the American Bishops, who was holding a Bishops' meeting in San Francisco at the time. The package was tied with a pink ribbon, signed "Woman," and accompanied by a poem entitled "Pink and Ash."

CATHOLIC GROUPS

St. Joan's Alliance, an independent group of Catholic lay women, was first organized in England during the suffrage movement. When the vote was won the organization continued to work for *civic* equality for women. In 1963, as a result of Pope John's *Pacem in Terris* and some proposals made during Vatican II, the Alliance shifted its emphasis from equality for women in the secular world to equality for women within the Catholic Church, and became the pioneer in this effort. The American branch of the Alliance was formed in 1965 and began a campaign for women's rights within the Catholic Church in this country. The group's most active campaign centers around the issue of ordination. Any "mini-concessions" that the church grants women short of ordination are considered "insulting, because they simply reinforce in modern terms the church's position that women are too inferior to be given all the same rights as men."[1]

National Coalition of American Nuns was formed in July, 1969, "to speak out on human rights and social justice," and was the first activist group to be organized by American nuns. Composed of nearly 2000 radical nuns (about two percent of all American nuns) from various orders, the Coalition directs its

---

[8] Elizabeth Farians, reported in *Catholic Star Herald,* Camden, N.J., February 7, 1969.
[9] Press release, April 19, 1970.
[1] Frances McGillicuddy, president, St. Joan's Alliance, interview, March, 1971.

energies to a number of issues—welfare rights, race relations, peace, and complete equality for women in secular and church life. A statement issued at the time of the group's formation reads in part:

> We protest any domination of our institutions by priests, no matter what their hierarchical status. We defend ourselves against those who would interfere with the internal administration and/or renewal that we alone must and can evolve in our religious community.[2]

The Coalition was called "diabolical" by a nun in St. Louis, and "a highly significant event in American Church history," by Dr. Mary Daly, a Catholic theologian.[3] In July, 1970, the Coalition issued a statement calling for "ordination for any qualified woman who so desires . . . [since] there is no theological, sociological or biological reason for denying ordination to women."[4]

Joint Committee of Organizations Concerned with the Status of Women in the Church is an *ad hoc* umbrella organization headed by Dr. Elizabeth Farians and composed of various Catholic women's groups, which issues policy statements and plans actions around the "woman question" in the Catholic Church. With a long-range goal of complete equality, the Joint Committee is pressuring for the creation of an official Office of Women's Affairs, within the U.S. Catholic Conference. The purpose of the Office, which would be funded by the Church but run by women, would be to study issues and problems of women in the Church and educate the Church hierarchy to these problems. However,

> Men have spoken for women so long in the Church that it's difficult to even communicate the idea that we are capable of self-determination. . . . The Bishops want to speak for us, to relay our complaints from one group of men to another.[5]

The *National Council of Catholic Women,* the "official" lay women's organization of the Catholic Church and traditionally

---

[2] National Coalition of American Nuns, Statement of Purpose.
[3] "Justice and the National Coalition of American Nuns," *Trans-Sister,* November, 1969, p. 4.
[4] "National Coalition of American Nuns Asks for Ordination of Women," *Trans-Sister,* November, 1970, p. 7.
[5] Dr. Elizabeth Farians, quoted in "Women Seeking Bigger Role in Churches," *U.S. News & World Report,* January 18, 1971, p. 25.

conservative on the issue of women's rights, recommended in 1970 that women be considered equally for all liturgical duties not requiring ordination. As noted previously, the more militant groups view this position as a "cop-out," arguing that full participation of women in lay organizations is meaningless if they are still barred from the official church hierarchy, i.e., the priesthood.

PROTESTANT DENOMINATIONS

The *Unitarian-Universalist Women's Federation* was formed in 1963 after the merger of the two denominations. Of all the caucuses and groups in Protestantism concerned with women's rights, the Federation is the most militant. The Unitarians have almost always been in the vanguard of social reform (along with the Quakers); indeed some of its members were the vanguard of the first feminist movement in this country—Susan B. Anthony, Elizabeth Cady Stanton, Lucretia Mott, Lucy Stone.

The Federation's continuous flow of literature designed to alert church members to feminist issues is sprinkled with radical terminology—for example, "God is a sex symbol—male." The Federation lobbies hard for federal and local legislation to ensure equality for women, the Equal Rights Amendment, abortion law repeal; and sponsors various research projects. The major 1970 project was the publication of an anthology of feminist writings, *Voices of the New Feminism.* The book was edited by Mary Lou Thompson and includes pieces by Dr. Mary Daly, Betty Friedan, Elizabeth Koontz, Roxanne Dunbar, Martha Griffiths, and others.

On July 4, 1970, the Federation introduced a resolution to the annual meeting of the Unitarian-Universalist Church calling for equal rights and opportunities for women in secular *and* church life. The resolution asked that the Unitarian-Universalist Church utilize women in important positions including the ministry, noting that there are ten women and 874 men ministers within the denomination. The Assembly passed the resolution with only one dissenting male vote.

Church Women United, connected with the National Council of Churches, is comprised of women from various Protestant and Orthodox denominations. In November, 1969, the group formed a "Commission on Women in Today's World." The Commission members were instrumental in the formation of the National Council's Women's Caucus the following month. Since that time, Church Women United staff members have concerned themselves with women's issues. They have already established numerous groups of church women across the country interested in the subject. "We're trying to find out how we can involve the average church woman into thinking in terms of 'self-determination.' "[6] CWU also serves as a communications link among staff women of various denominations around the country who wish to exchange information about their respective women's liberation projects. On another front, CWU has considered the possibility of withholding funds from other kinds of projects unless women have a voice in the manner in which the funds will be used. The State of Washington chapter of CWU *publicly* threatened to withhold funds from the Washington Migrant Ministry unless women were given a voice in how the money was to be allocated.

The *Board of Missions, Women's Division, United Methodist Church* is one of the richest and most powerful of all the denominational women's divisions. The advent of the women's movement resulted in a reassessment of goals, and in 1970–71 the Division appropriated $25,000 for women's liberation projects:

—A study "Sex Role Stereotyping in the United Methodist Nursery Curriculum" was made ". . . to discover what was being taught by the curriculum about sex roles. . . . The study revealed blatant sexual stereotyping of behavior, emotions, abilities, occupations and life style on almost every page. . . . [The] curriculum is immersed in the sex-role caste system and, therefore, is particularly limiting for girls, which is then contrary to good principles of education and to the Gospel."[7]
—Seed money was provided for various theological projects undertaken by women at seminaries across the country.
—A small grant was given to female seminary students in Chicago to set up a women's center to be used by the seven seminaries and one divinity school in the area.
—Consciousness raising sessions have been organized within church groups and seminaries.

[6] Sarah Bentley Doely, staff member Church Women United, interview, December, 1970.
[7] Miriam Crist and Tilda Norberg, "Sex Role Stereotyping in the United Methodist Nursery Curriculum," preliminary report, 1970. Reprinted in *Women's Liberation and the Church*, pp. 119ff.

Moreover, the Women's Division voted to keep itself a separate Division within the Board of Missions.

In addition to the foregoing women's groups, two Protestant denominations have made official studies on the status of women. The United Presbyterian Church in the U.S.A. appointed an official Task Force on Women at its 1969 General Assembly meeting. The Task Force is making a three-year study on the status of women in society and the church. Their first preliminary report, delivered to the 1970 General Assembly meeting, concluded that although there are no "constitutional provisions restricting the full participation of women in all the offices and ministries of the church . . . *de facto* discrimination against women does exist at all levels in the church."[8] The report noted in particular that women comprise only 15.7 percent of church elders although they make up 57 percent of church membership. Moreover, though the Presbyterian clergy has been open to women since 1956, women make up only one-half of one percent of Presbyterian ministers. It might be noted that at the 1971 General Assembly meeting, for the first time in the organization's 183 year history, a woman, Lois H. Stair, was elected Assembly moderator.

The American Baptist Convention's executive staff women prepared a study in October, 1970, on the status of professional women in their denomination. It found that although the American Baptist Convention has been ordaining women for 80 years, the few women ministers had always been relegated to insignificant pastorates. The report concluded—predictably—that:

> . . . although American Baptists have been among the leaders in opening opportunities to women, a study of the record of the past 12 years shows that in professional leadership opportunities the American Baptist Convention has been retreating to tokenism.[9]

.   .   .

Theological assumptions about the "inherent nature" and "appropriate behavior" of women have historically been the products of a male-dominated religious hierarchy. Since these theological assumptions have informed secular social values as

---

[8] *Report of the Task Force on Women and the Standing Committee on Women*, p. 8.
[9] *Retreat to Tokenism*, October, 1970, p. 1.

well, feminist activity within the church, if sufficiently radical, may well cause repercussions far beyond the confines of the church structure. It must be noted, however, that some feminists (most often outside the church) argue that precisely because theological doctrine is so firmly rooted in thousands of years of tradition, the church may well be the most difficult (if not an impossible) institution to change.

Conclusion

A DECADE HAS PASSED since the President's Commission on the Status of Women first addressed itself to women's issues. Although feminism and the women's movement have since received considerable mass media coverage (by 1970, 80 percent of all Americans had heard and/or read about the women's movement), there are still many people who do not yet view the movement as both serious and political. In fact, the women's movement that has emerged during these ten years is serious, political, and could potentially change society more profoundly than any other movement for social change.

All political movements emerge from a growing discontent with the social system, its values and premises of organization, and articulate that discontent in the form of a political critique. This critique analyzes and challenges the established power relationships and institutions in society and offers a generally-formulated goal that provides the philosophical criteria for defining the necessary and appropriate actions to reach that goal.

In these terms the feminist movement must be considered a political movement. In the 1960's as women grew progressively dissatisfied and angry with the social and political inequities between males and females, they began to perceive themselves not merely as individuals with "personal problems," but as an oppressed *political* class whose condition was a natural—logical —outgrowth of historically-rooted and generally-prevailing assumptions about men and women. Feminists have defined this ideological system as *sexism*—the rigid prescriptions about "appropriate" behavior patterns and social roles defined solely on the basis of sex. Thus, the goal of the feminist movement is the complete elimination of this sex-role system. This goal provides the philosophical basis for all feminist political action.

In at least two respects the women's movement is a unique political movement. First, it has, to all intents and purposes, redefined the very meaning of politics. Since the sex-role system underlies all social institutions and social relationships, questions and issues which have never before been considered political are now being defined in that light; e.g., dress codes, the institution of marriage, the concept of motherhood, sexual behavior, etc. Second, since in feminist analysis the sex-role system is at the core of women's oppression, for the first time women are defining themselves as a political group that includes all women irrespective of race, national, socio-economic, religious, distinctions. It might be noted that in the history of social movements this is the only time men have not been included in the definition of the oppressed.

Each major branch of the women's movement—women's rights and women's liberation—from its own perspective is working toward the elimination of the sex-role system: by external reform of social institutions and internal raising of consciousness, respectively. Thus, any action from lobbying for the Equal Rights Amendment to establishing small groups to talk both personally and analytically about the nature of women's oppression is deemed appropriate if it challenges sex-role stereotyping. Not only are all such actions "appropriate," but for the women's movement to progress toward its stated goal both external and internal approaches on each issue are essential. For instance, it is necessary to enact and enforce anti-sex discrimination labor laws in order to eliminate the concept of "men's work" and "women's work" from the legal code. It is equally necessary, however, to raise the consciousness of individuals so that they themselves no longer think stereotypically: men are doctors; women, nurses; men are breadwinners; women, housekeepers; men are doers; women, mothers. Thus, the women's movement must remain multi-issued and multi-tactical if it is to confront all forms of sex-role stereotyping. Moreover, in this way it can remain flexible enough to meet new needs and new situations as they arise. Nonetheless, it is often assumed that the most "important" activity of the women's movement has been accomplished by women's rights groups. It should be noted that a definition of specific actions is perhaps more difficult for the radical branch of the movement than for women's rights groups. There is no such thing as a "myth of job equality." Statistics that prove job discrimination, wage disparities, etc., are solid enough foundation around which to structure activity. It is far less easy to define a plan of action to overcome the assumption that woman "by nature" is totally fulfilled through marriage and motherhood. Moreover, it must be emphasized that much of the philosophical analysis of radical feminist groups has provided the ideological framework in which moderate feminist actions have been undertaken.

Since the emergence of the women's movement a considerable degree of cross-fertilization between the two branches has occurred. For the most part, however, it has been unstructured, accidental, and even unconscious. The movement now has grown sufficiently strong in both numbers and ideological definition for there to be conscious and deliberate exchange between the two branches in order to most systematically confront the sex-role system in all its manifestations. In addition, for each branch to increase its effectiveness it must begin to broaden its own perspective by incorporating some of the ideas of the other. Thus, if most moderate and conservative feminists focus exclusively on reforming laws and official practices without recognizing the importance of issues and ideas raised by radical feminists, they run the risk of confusing short-range activities with the long-range goal of completely eliminating the sex-role system. By the same token, if many radical feminists become mired in introspection, they face the danger of never transforming their new insights and analyses into actions to effectuate specific changes.

Although the women's movement has grown enormously since its inception, and there has occurred as well a general "raising of consciousness" to women's issues, the feminist movement, like all political movements, is confronted with the kinds of problems virtually inherent in the building of a political movement: establishing viable organizational structures, defining short-term goals and tactics, creating adequate and effective means of communication among women within the movement as well as establishing lines of communication to non-movement women, avoiding the dangers of ideological factionalism and inter-group hostilities, etc. Because of these internal problems the movement is in a state of organizational and ideological flux. It must be remembered, however, that the uniqueness and newness of feminist thought—questioning and confronting ideas, practices, and assumptions never before analyzed in political terms —has generated an enormous amount of energy, creativity, and commitment on the part of activist women—"tools" necessary not only to break new ground, but to solve the intra-movement problems as well.

The feminist movement has emerged during a time of general social dislocation, rapid and virtually unchecked technological innovation, and widespread attacks on the traditional power structure and established institutions. Precisely because feminism, however, challenges the most basic assumptions about the nature of men and women that underlie all value systems and institutions, it may well inspire social change more fundamental and radical than any other political movement.

Chronology

THIS CHRONOLOGY can serve as an overview of a political process—the development of the current feminist movement in the United States. The events, issues and activities listed are representative of the entire spectrum of the women's movement and illustrative of its mushroom growth.

1961

January: Eighty-seventh Congress convenes with seventeen women members—fifteen in House, two in Senate. Highest number of women members in Congress history.

December 14:   President John F. Kennedy establishes President's Commission on the Status of Women. First such Commission in U.S. history, and first time since passage of suffrage amendment federal government formally addresses itself to "women's issues." Eleanor Roosevelt, chairwoman; seven study committees set up.

1962

July 20:   President Kennedy issues directive reversing traditional interpretation of 1870 federal law used over the years to bar women from high-level civil service jobs. (1870 law finally repealed in 1965.)

November 6:   After elections, thirteen women members of Congress—eleven in House, two in Senate.

1963

February: Publication of *The Feminine Mystique* by Betty
                      Friedan; delineation of social pressures—psycho-
                      logical, educational, media, etc.—on women in
                      America. Becomes best-seller.

June 10:   Equal Pay Act passed requiring equal pay for men
                      and women with same jobs. Act amends 1938 Fair
                      Labor Standards Act.

October 11:   President's Commission on the Status of Women
                      completes study begun in 1961 and issues report
                      American Women which includes twenty-four major
                      recommendations to combat sex discrimination.
                      (The Commission's existence and its report created
                      the political and psychological framework for the
                      growth of the current women's rights movement.)

November 1:   Acting on Commission's recommendations, Presi-
                      dent Kennedy establishes Interdepartmental Com-
                      mittee on the Status of Women (composed of gov-
                      ernment officials) and Citizens' Advisory Council on
                      the Status of Women (composed of private citi-
                      zens).

1964

February 8:   After heated debate, House of Representatives votes
                      to add "sex" to discriminatory bans of race, color,
                      religion, and national origin in Title VII of Civil
                      Rights Bill.

Spring: *Daedalus,* Journal of the American Academy of Arts
                      and Sciences, devotes entire spring issue to "The
                      Woman in America." One of the earliest "academic
                      forums" on the nature and role of women.

June 12–13:   First National Conference of State Commissions on
                      the Status of Women, sponsored by Citizens' Ad-
                      visory Council and Interdepartmental Committee on
                      the Status of Women. Twenty-four State Commis-
                      sions represented by 73 delegates. Eight states with-
                      out State Commissions also send delegates.

July 2:   Congress enacts 1964 Civil Rights Act including
                      Title VII, the equal employment opportunities sec-
                      tion with the ban on sex discrimination.

September 12:   Senate Judiciary Subcommittee on Constitutional Amendments reports favorably on Equal Rights Amendment (ERA).

November 3:   After elections, Congress includes twelve women members—ten in House, two in Senate.

No date: At Student Non-Violent Coordinating Committee staff meeting, Ruby Doris Smith Robinson presents paper on the position of women in the organization. Elicits comment from SNCC leader Stokely Carmichael, "The only position for women in SNCC is prone." Although paper dismissed by civil rights activists, it signals the stirrings of resentment among women participants.

1965

February 21:   St. Joan's Alliance, British-based Catholic lay women's organization, establishes U.S. branch to campaign for women's equality in the Catholic Church.

June 7:   U.S. Supreme Court in *Griswold v. State of Connecticut* strikes down restrictive Connecticut law on contraceptives.

July 28–30:   Second National Conference of State Commissions on the Status of Women. Attended by 322 participants representing 44 State Commissions. The six remaining states also send representatives.

August: At White House Conference on Equal Opportunity, sex provision of Title VII dubbed "bunny law" when question arises whether Playboy Clubs have to hire male bunnies. Women's rights activists decry ridicule, but name sticks.

October 1:   Citizens' Advisory Council issues first policy paper. Recommends that Equal Employment Opportunity Commission (EEOC) narrowly interpret *bona fide occupational qualification* (*bfoq*) clause of Title VII; also urges EEOC eliminate separate male-female "help wanted" listings in newspapers.

December: At Students for a Democratic Society (SDS) conference, discussion of "women's issue" elicits "storms of ridicule and verbal abuse."

December 2:   EEOC issues first set of guidelines on state protective legislation. State laws can be interpreted as *bfoq* exception to Title VII, provided employer acts in "good faith" and that laws effectively protect rather than discriminate against women. EEOC does not define what constitutes "protection" or "discrimination."

No date: Casey Hayden and Mary King, women active in SNCC, write paper on role of women in the movement. Paper attacked by male radicals. Later published as two-part article, "Sex and Caste," *Liberation,* April, December, 1966.

1966

February 7:   In *White v. Crook* three-judge federal court declares Alabama law excluding women from state juries unconstitutional.

April: Publication of study by Dr. William H. Masters and Virginia E. Johnson, *Human Sexual Response.* Massive 12-year clinical study on physiology of sex.

April 22:   EEOC issues guidelines expressly permitting separate male-female "help wanted" columns in newspapers, in contradistinction to recommendations of Citizens' Advisory Council and women's organizations.

May 9:   Sarah Lawrence College president Dr. Esther Raushenbush and Radcliffe College president Dr. Mary Bunting charge American universities fail to recognize that many college-trained women want both families and careers.

June 28–29:   Twenty-eight women found National Organization for Women (NOW) while meeting at Third National Conference of State Commissions on the Status of Women. First militant feminist organization since 19th century women's rights movement.

August 19:   EEOC issues another set of guidelines regarding Title VII-state protective legislation conflict. Commission states it has no authority to rule on issue; courts will have to resolve conflict.

October 29:   National Organization for Women formally announces incorporation at Washington, D.C. press conference.

November 8:   After elections, eleven women members in Congress
               —ten in House, one in Senate.

December: NOW petitions EEOC to hold public hearings on sex
               provisions of Title VII. (Hearings finally held May,
               1967.)

No date: At SDS convention, women demand plank on
               women's liberation; harassed and thrown out of
               convention.

1967

April: First-known "bootleg" women's liberation child care
               center, organized in New York City, run on volun-
               teer and cooperative basis.

April 25:   Colorado becomes first state to reform its 19th cen-
               tury abortion law.

May: EEOC holds public hearings on sex provisions of
               Title VII. Hearings result of pressure from women's
               rights activists.

August: In Chicago, formation of first known independent
               radical women's group (not caucus within any other
               political organization). Later called Westside Group.

August 30:   NOW pickets *New York Times* protesting its policy
               of separate male-female "help wanted" columns.

August 31–
September 4:   National Conference for a New Politics (NCNP),
               nationwide meeting of new left groups, held in
               Chicago. Strong women's rights plank ignored. As a
               result, Chicago women's group begins to meet regu-
               larly.

October 13:   President Lyndon B. Johnson signs Executive Order
               11375 (amending EO 11246) prohibiting sex dis-
               crimination in federal employment and by federal
               contractors and subcontractors.

October 13:   Federal Women's Program established by Civil Serv-
               ice Commission to implement portion of EO 11375
               banning sex discrimination in federal employment.

October 20:   National Federation of Business and Professional
               Women's Clubs (BPW), with membership of 170,-

000, charges both subtle and overt discrimination against women in many fields; cites state protective labor laws as major cause.

End October–
early
November: Radical women's group in New York (later called New York Radical Women) formed. An important "seed bed" group of radical branch of women's movement: individual members and later breakaway groups were among first to formulate much of theory and analysis generally accepted by movement today.

November 8:   President Johnson signs public law removing restriction that prohibits women in armed services from attaining rank higher than colonel.

November 18:   At NOW's second national conference, resolution adopted demanding repeal of abortion laws and laws restricting access to contraceptive methods and information. First time national women's organization supports abortion law repeal. Passage of resolution precipitates resignations from group.

December 14:   NOW organizes National Day of Demonstration Against EEOC. Sets up picket lines in cities with EEOC offices.

1968

January 15:   In Washington, D.C., a coalition of women's peace groups (5000 women), called the Jeanette Rankin Brigade, demonstrates against the Vietnam war at opening of Congress. New York Radical Women stage a "Burial of Traditional Womanhood"—the first public action radical women undertake to "raise the consciousness" of other women to women's issues. First use of slogan "sisterhood is powerful."

February 15:   NOW files formal suit against EEOC to "force it to comply with its own governmental rules."

February 21:   EEOC issues another set of guidelines regarding Title VII-state protective legislation. Commission will determine on a case-by-case basis whether a particular state law is discriminatory and therefore superseded by Title VII.

February 28:   *U.S. ex. rel. v. Robinson.* Federal District Court strikes down Connecticut statute requiring longer prison sentences for women than for men as unconstitutional.

March:
First independent radical women's newsletter: *Voice of the Women's Liberation Movement,* written and published in Chicago. By 1971, there were over a hundred women's movement journals, newsletters and newspapers throughout the country.

April:
Citizens' Advisory Council issues four task force reports: Health and Welfare; Social Security and Taxes; Labor Standards; Family Law and Policy. Family Law and Policy report recommends repeal of abortion laws.

April:
Twelve Trans World Airlines stewardesses file complaint with EEOC against airline for sex discrimination. Allege that TWA maintains two classifications for flight cabin attendants: purser and hostess; both do same duties but men (pursers) receive from $2500 to $3500 more a year.

April 29:
At University of Washington (Seattle) annual Men's Day, appearance of Playboy bunny protested by radical women as "an exhibition of womanhood just as a body."

June:
Publication of first radical feminist journal, *Notes From the First Year*—a collection of writings and reports on radical feminism.

June:
Publication of one of the earliest radical feminist position papers: *Toward A Female Liberation Movement* (called *The Florida Paper*) by Beverly Jones and Judith Brown.

June 20–22:
National Conference of State Commissions on the Status of Women. 450 participants attend.

July 1:
In *Commonwealth v. Daniels,* Pennsylvania Supreme Court voids State's Muncy Law which required longer prison sentences for women than for men convicted of the same crime.

August:
Women's Conference in Sandy Springs, Md. First attempt to bring together radical women from different parts of the country to discuss "women's liberation."

August 9:
EEOC issues guidelines expressly forbidding separate male-female "want-ad" listings.

September: Formation of Federally Employed Women (FEW).
                  First organized effort of government women to press
                  for equal rights.

September 7:   Group of about 200 radical women stage "guerrilla"
                  actions at Miss America contest in Atlantic City to
                  protest contest as "boob girlie show." "Bra-burning"
                  story started here, although no bras burned.

September 20:   American Newspaper Publishers Association sues
                  EEOC arguing that Commission's guidelines on sex-
                  segregated "want-ad" listings do not have force of
                  law and Commission should be enjoined from en-
                  forcing them.

October 17:   Nine NOW members (New York Chapter) leave the
                  organization to form "October 17th Movement,"
                  later called The Feminists. One of the first groups
                  to formulate radical feminist theory.

October 26:   Dr. Naomi Weisstein delivers paper, " 'Kinder,
                  Küche, Kirche' As Scientific Law: Psychology Con-
                  structs the Female," at American Studies Associa-
                  tion Meeting, Davis campus, University of Cali-
                  fornia. Paper widely distributed in the women's
                  movement.

October 31:   Formation of WITCH (Witches International Con-
                  spiracy from Hell), a group of radical women in
                  New York City. Perform yippie-style street theater
                  actions. First action: "hexing" and "spooking" the
                  New York Stock Exchange. Other WITCH covens
                  periodically emerge around country to perform *ad
                  hoc* actions.

November 5:   After elections, eleven women members in Congress
                  ten in House, one in Senate. Women members of
                  House of Representatives are 2.3% of total House
                  (435 members) whereas, according to 1968 Census
                  Bureau statistics, women make up 53.3% of voting
                  age population.

                  First Negro woman, Shirley Chisholm, elected to
                  House of Representatives (D., N.Y.) Rep. Chisholm
                  commented at a later date, "In the political world I
                  have been far oftener discriminated against because
                  I am a woman than because I am black. When I de-
                  cided to run for Congress I knew I would encounter
                  both anti-black and anti-feminist sentiments. What
                  surprised me was the much greater virulence of the
                  sex discrimination."

November 22: In *Rosenfeld v. Southern Pacific*, federal district court rules Title VII supersedes California laws which restrict women from working overtime and from lifting weights in excess of prescribed limit. Case considered landmark by women's rights advocates. (Southern Pacific appealing the decision.)

November 28–30: Over 200 women from 37 states and Canada convene in Chicago for first national women's liberation conference. First time radical women have a sense of a "national" movement. (Several working papers distributed that have influenced the thought and organizational development of the radical feminist movement.)

December: Formation of Human Rights for Women, Inc. (HRW) in Washington, D.C. First tax-exempt legal defense organization established to work solely in the area of sex discrimination.

December 1: New York City newspapers discontinue sex-segregated "want-ads" (as per EEOC guidelines) because of charges filed with New York Fair Employment Practices Commission. Similar decisions in other cities.

December 1: Women's Equity Action League (WEAL) incorporated in Cleveland, Ohio. Organization to direct its activities to combat sex discrimination in employment, education, and *de facto* tax inequities. WEAL considered responsible for legitimizing issue of sex discrimination in field of education.

1969

January: President Richard M. Nixon appoints Elizabeth Koontz to head Women's Bureau. During her directorship Bureau becomes more directly involved in women's movement. For example, in June, 1970, it reverses its traditional position of opposition to Equal Rights Amendment and advocates Amendment passage.

January: Formation of New Yorkers for Abortion Law Repeal (NYALR). First abortion law repeal group based entirely on radical feminist analysis of the abortion issue.

January: Firing of University of Chicago sociology Assistant Professor Marlene Dixon (allegedly because of her "radical" teachings and the fact that she was a woman) precipitates first public action of Chicago's women's liberation group. Along with other campus radical groups, women demonstrate against firing.

January 20:   Radical left groups organize counter-inaugural activities at Nixon inauguration. While some women activists speak about women's issues and attack "male chauvinism," they are booed off stage. Event moves radical women a step further toward creating an autonomous women's movement.

February: New group, Redstockings, formed in New York City. Formalized concept of "consciousness raising" as political ideology, intra-group technique and organizational tactic.

February 5:   Ten Grinnell College (Iowa) students, male and female, stage "nude-in" to protest speaking appearance of *Playboy* magazine representative. Charge magazine demeans women.

February 13:   Members of Redstockings break up New York State legislative hearings on abortion reform, protesting panel of witnesses that includes fourteen men and one nun. Group also demands complete repeal, not reform, of abortion laws.

February 14:   Simultaneous St. Valentine's Day demonstrations in New York and San Francisco to protest Bridal Fair shows (expo exhibits by involved companies) as "commercial exploitation" of women. Yippie-style street theater tactics.

March 4:   In *Weeks v. Southern Bell Telephone & Telegraph Co.*, U.S. Court of Appeals (Fifth Circuit) rules company weight-lifting rule for women not a *bfoq* exception to Title VII. Women's rights advocates consider decision landmark. On April 24, 1971, two years after Court ruling, Weeks awarded $31,000 in back pay for job she had been denied.

March 21:   Redstockings hold "public hearings" in New York on abortion. Before audience of over 300, women recount individual abortion experiences. Perhaps earliest use of "speak out" as political tactic. (Equivalent to peace movement's "teach-ins" on Vietnam.)

Spring: First accredited women's study course in spring curriculum, Cornell University, N.Y. Somewhat informal colloquium on nature of the female personality from behavioral science perspective. By Spring, 1970, course formally titled "Evolution of the Female Personality." Extensive syllabus compiled. Over 200 enrolled students, 100 auditing. (By 1971 over 100 colleges and universities had women's studies courses.)

First women's law course, "Women and the Law," offered spring semester, University of Pennsylvania; non-credit.

May: United Presbyterian Church in the U.S.A. appoints official Task Force on Women to make three-year study on women in society and in church.

May: New Feminist Theater has Spring run in a New York off-Broadway theater. Series of satiric sketches draws praise from *New York Times* reviewer for taking critical view of "prevailing thought system" and for suggesting *society* needs "adjusting," not *individuals.*

May: First two University administrations—University of California at Berkeley, University of Chicago—to appoint task forces on the status of women to survey each university's admission, hiring, and promotion policies.

May 6–7: Chairwomen of State Commissions on the Status of Women meet with Director of Women's Bureau Elizabeth Koontz to establish Interstate Association of the Commissions on the Status of Women. Mrs. Richard Nixon tells Commissioners she does not "feel there's any discrimination against women."

June: Publication of Boston group's "Bread and Roses" position paper. One of earliest attempts to draw sharp distinctions among different philosophies and tactics of radical women's groups. "Bread and Roses" position is socialist in orientation.

July: National Coalition of American Nuns founded to support civil rights and anti-war movements, and to pressure for women's equality within Catholic Church.

July: Publication of Redstockings Manifesto. First clearly "feminist" paper (as distinct from "Bread and Roses"). Women's issues paramount: "We identify with all women. . . . We repudiate all economic, racial, educational or status privileges that divide us from other women."

August 4–6:   Public hearings on proposed Department of Labor sex discrimination guidelines issued to implement Executive Order 11375. Hearings direct result of pressure from women's rights organizations.

August 8:   President Nixon signs Executive Order 11478 prohibiting sex discrimination in federal employment. No substantial change from Johnson's EO 11375.

August 19:   EEOC issues another set of guidelines stating that state protective labor laws which apply only to women are in direct violation of Title VII of the 1964 Civil Rights Act.

Fall: First known feminist FM radio program begins on WBAI in New York City. Half hour broadcast, "Womankind: Discussion and Commentary from the Feminist Community." News events and roundtable discussions of women's issues.

Fall: Columbia University (N.Y.) Women's Liberation group publishes lengthy report on status of women faculty at Columbia. Data reveals that 24 percent of all doctoral degrees are awarded to women (highest in nation); however, percentage of women professors with tenure is only 2 percent.

September: First accredited women's law course taught at New York University Law School.

September: Highly-acclaimed children's television program, "Sesame Street," receives sharp feminist criticism for its "stereotypical portrayal" of girls and women. As result of protest, some changes made by "Sesame Street" producers.

September: Formation of first three feminist caucuses within professional associations: American Sociological Association, American Political Science Association, American Psychological Association. At ASA meeting, Dr. Alice Rossi presents nationwide survey "Status of Women in Graduate Departments of Sociology, 1968–69." Data reveals women comprise 33 percent of graduate students in sociology but only 4 percent of professors in field. (By end of 1971, nearly every professional association had activist women's caucus or "official commission" to study status of women.)

September 23: Radical group, The Feminists, pickets New York City Marriage License Bureau to protest institution of marriage as both demeaning and oppressive to women.

September 26: In *Bowe et. al. v. Colgate-Palmolive Co. et. al.,* U.S. Court of Appeals (Seventh Circuit) rules that company weight-lifting restriction does not qualify as *bfoq* exception to Title VII. Moreover, weight-lifting requirement ruled invalid if applied only to women.

October 1: President Nixon announces formation of Task Force on Women's Rights and Responsibilities to study current status of women and to make recommendations to combat sex discrimination.

November: First known women's organization of municipal employees formed to combat sex discrimination in a city government: Women in City Government United (New York).

November: Church Women United, inter-denominational group, forms Commission on Women in Today's World to evaluate status of women in church and society.

November 21–23: First Congress to Unite Women. A coalition conference of over 500 feminists holds northeast regional meeting in New York City. Closed to men and media. Group issues platform advocating abortion law repeal, passage of Equal Rights Amendment, etc. Workshop reports and conference resolutions represent fusion of moderate and radical feminist interests. (Similar conferences held in Chicago and San Francisco.)

December: Formation of women's caucus in National Council of Churches. Caucus states, "Nowhere is the situation of women better illustrated than in our male-dominated and male-oriented churches."

December: New York City Junior High School student sues Board of Education on grounds she was denied opportunity to take metal shopwork class.

December: Modern Languages Association, largest academic society, establishes Commission on the Status of Women to study role of women in the field.

December 5:   New militant radical feminist action group, New
                   York Radical Feminists, formed. Perhaps earliest
                   attempt to formalize organizational and theoretical
                   bases, and tactical approaches necessary for the de-
                   velopment of a radical feminist movement.

December 15:   *A Matter of Simple Justice,* report by Nixon Task
                   Force on Women's Rights and Responsibilities trans-
                   mitted to President. Not released publicly until June
                   9, 1970, allegedly because of militant tone of report.

1970

January 14:   During Senate Subcommittee hearings on oral con-
                   traception small group of women activists disrupt
                   proceedings. Protest fact that most witnesses are
                   doctors (male) not women, and that women are
                   being used as "guinea pigs" to test pill.

January
23–24:   Three hundred and fifty people attend midwest
                   women's liberation conference sponsored by Univer-
                   sity of Kentucky women's liberation group. Tone of
                   conference militant and anticapitalist.

January 26:   Women staff take over New York radical under-
                   ground paper, *Rat.* Only male-run underground
                   paper permanently taken over by women. "Coup"
                   widely known throughout radical movement.

January 29:   NOW president Betty Friedan and Rep. Patsy Mink
                   (D., Hawaii) testify against Supreme Court nom-
                   inee Harrold G. Carswell at Senate hearings on
                   grounds he is "insensitive" to women's rights and
                   aspirations. First time women's rights issue raised
                   against Supreme Court nominee.

January 31:   Women's Equity Action League (WEAL) files for-
                   mal charges of sex discrimination against Univer-
                   sity of Maryland under Executive Order 11375.
                   First time Executive Order used to combat sex dis-
                   crimination in education. By end 1971, over 300
                   individual colleges and universities so charged by
                   various women's groups.

February 13:   Women's Bureau releases *1969 Handbook on
                   Women Workers.* Largest compendium to date of
                   data and statistical analysis of women's status in the
                   labor market. Called by one feminist, ". . . the only

book of graphs and statistics guaranteed to raise a woman reader's blood pressure."

February 17:   During Senate hearings on constitutional amendment to enfranchise 18-year-olds, chairwoman of the Board of Directors of NOW, Wilma Scott Heide, and about twenty women disrupt proceedings and demand Senate hearings be scheduled on Equal Rights Amendment. ERA hearings subsequently held May, 1970.

February 21:   Yale Alumni Day luncheon disrupted by 40 women undergraduates protesting the "token number" of women students at Yale. Request that ratio of men to women in each class be 700 men to 300 women. President Kingman Brewster, Jr. rejects request noting that one reason for graduating 1000 men each year is "nostalgia of the alumni."

March: Hawaii becomes first state to change its abortion law to one based on repeal as opposed to reform arguments. Some restrictions limiting "abortion on request" remain.

March 7:   In Wisconsin Rapids, Wis. first statewide AFL-CIO women's conference ever held. About 200 women from many unions convene to discuss women's status in the unions. Conference takes stand endorsing Equal Rights Amendment (national AFL-CIO opposes it) and opposing state protective legislation.

March 16:   Forty-six editorial staff women of *Newsweek* magazine file formal charges of sex discrimination against the magazine. Settlement between women and magazine reached August 26, 1970.

March 18:   Two hundred women stage an 11-hour sit-in at *Ladies' Home Journal* protesting image of women portrayed by women's magazines and the status of women working in the field. *Journal* agrees to allow women to put out women's liberation supplement to August, 1970, issue.

March 25:   NOW files formal charge of sex discrimination under EO 11375 against Harvard University. During subsequent government compliance review more than $3 million in pending government contracts held up for two weeks until university agrees to disclose to investigators personnel information regarding its women employees and students.

March 30:   Colonel Jeanne Holm, Director of Women in the Air
                    Force, and Dr. Hester Turner, Chairman, Defense
                    Advisory Committee on Women in the Services,
                    publicly deplore treatment of women in the armed
                    services.

Spring: New York University Law School Women's Rights
                    Committee sponsors first National Conference of
                    Women Law Students. Over 100 women from 17
                    law schools participate in discussions and work-
                    shops on women and the law.

Spring: American Association of University Professors re-
                    activates after 40-year hiatus its Committee W to
                    act as watchdog over college and university policies
                    regarding women.

April: Alaska liberalizes its abortion law. New law similar
                    to Hawaii's.

April: Association of American Law Schools establishes
                    Committee on Women in Legal Education to study
                    status of women in law schools and to recommend
                    action to combat sex discrimination.

April: Publication of the radical feminist journal, *Notes
                    From the Second Year*. Over 100 pages of analytical
                    papers, manifestos, personal statements, many of
                    which have become movement "classics."

April: University of Michigan Law School bars large New
                    York-Washington, D.C. law firm from on-campus
                    recruiting because firm discriminates on basis of
                    sex. Similar action occurs at University of California
                    (Berkeley) law school.

April 11:   Over 300 women from various academic and profes-
                    sional fields convene in New York City to attend
                    workshops and meetings on the status of women in
                    various professions. Papers analyze status of women
                    in law, architecture, engineering, library science,
                    etc. Plans made for establishment of permanent
                    organization, Professional Women's Caucus, to carry
                    out conference recommendations and maintain lines
                    of communication with women's caucuses in pro-
                    fessional associations.

April 15:   Nine women invade Columbia Broadcasting Sys-
                    tem's annual stockholders' meeting in San Francisco
                    charging CBS and media in general with downgrad-

ing and distorting role of women in commercials and programming.

April 18: New York City Women's Center opens as meeting place and information center for women's movement activists in New York. Similar women's centers open in cities, towns and on college campuses throughout the country.

April 19: In Detroit, Michigan NOW's Ecumenical Task Force on Women and Religion stage demonstration to burn Roman Catholic missal to protest Church's discrimination treatment of women. Group sends ashes to President of the National Conference of Bishops.

April 23: A group of women and their children stage protest rally at Washington University (St. Louis, Mo.). Demands include turning ROTC building into day-care center.

April 24: Feminist play, "The Mod Donna," by Myrna Lamb, opens at New York Shakespeare Festival Public Theatre. Play runs through June 7.

April 25: At its national convention, United Auto Workers endorses Equal Rights Amendment. First major national union to do so.

April 30: At Democratic Party's Committee on National Priorities, Rep. Patsy Mink urges women's rights be given high priority. Dr. Edgar F. Berman argues women are incapable of holding important decision-making jobs because menstrual cycle and menopause subject them to "raging hormonal influences." Feminist protest Berman's position. Berman resigns from Committee.

May: National Conference on Role of Women in Theological Education sponsored in Boston, Mass. by ecumenical group of women theologians and students.

May 4: 147 editorial staff women of Time, Inc. file formal charges of sex discrimination with New York State Division of Human Rights against the corporation's four magazines—*Time, Life, Fortune, Sports Illustrated.* Settlement reached February 6, 1971.

May 5–7: Senate Subcommittee on Constitutional Amendments holds hearings on the Equal Rights Amendment. First Senate ERA hearings since 1956.

May 16–17:   First Southern California Congress to Unite Women.

May 25:   WEAL files charges of sex discrimination under EO
                  11375 against entire college and university system
                  of the state of Florida.

June: Feminists on Children's Media (New Jersey-New
                  York coalition) release in-depth survey on the por-
                  trayal of girls and women in children's grade school
                  textbooks and trade books. Of 1000 trade books sur-
                  veyed only 200 considered "non-sexist."

June 1:   WEAL files charges of sex discrimination under EO
                  11375 against entire college and university system
                  of the state of California.

June 3:   Editor of the *Washington Post* issues staff memo-
                  randum on guidelines for reporting about women
                  and women's issues. Memorandum includes stipula-
                  tion that reporters avoid words such as "brunette,"
                  "cute," "divorcee," etc., unless same kinds of words
                  also used about men.

June 7:   Biennial conference of American Civil Liberties
                  Union adopts strong policy recommendation sup-
                  porting women's rights.

June 9:   Department of Labor issues guidelines designed to
                  eliminate sex discrimination in jobs under federal
                  contract. Women's groups protest guidelines because
                  no goals or timetables established.

June 9:   Public release of Nixon Task Force report, *A Matter
                  of Simple Justice*. (Report originally submitted to
                  the President December, 1969.)

June 11:   Rep. Martha Griffiths (D., Mich.), longtime women's
                  rights advocate, in a political coup employs rarely
                  used parliamentary tactic, the discharge petition, to
                  force Equal Rights Amendment out of House Ju-
                  diciary Committee to floor of House. ERA had been
                  held in Committee since 1948.

June 11–13:   Women's Bureau (Department of Labor) holds
                  fiftieth anniversary conference, "American Women
                  at the Crossroads: Directions for the Future." More
                  than 1000 women representing spectrum of women's
                  movement groups convene in Washington, D.C. to
                  discuss women's issues. Occasion used to announce

Department of Labor's support of Equal Rights Amendment, a reversal of its traditional stand.

June 21–25:   At American Medical Association convention in Chicago, dissenting groups allowed to present views. Among many radical groups protesting AMA's generally conservative stance, Chicago women's groups stage skits about medical treatment of women in general and about AMA position on abortion in particular.

June 23:   WEAL files charges of sex discrimination against entire university system of the State of New York (SUNY).

June 25:   NOW files blanket complaint of sex discrimination under EO 11375 against 1300 major U.S. corporations.

June 28:   National Association for the Advancement of Colored People adopts women's rights platform at its annual convention.

June–July: House Special Subcommittee on Education holds seven days of hearings on sex discrimination in education. First such hearings in U.S. history. Results in 1250 pages of testimony including reports, surveys, individual and group statements, statistically documenting status and role of women in all fields (not limited to education).

July: New York State liberalizes its abortion law. Of the first three new state abortion laws (Hawaii and Alaska), New York's is least restrictive. Shortly after passage, conservative forces launch campaign to reinstitute old law.

July 4:   Strong women's rights resolution passed by delegates of the Unitarian Universalist Association at its annual meeting. Resolution includes support of the Equal Rights Amendment.

July 20:   Department of Justice files first suit of sex discrimination under Title VII of 1964 Civil Rights Act. Suit against Libby-Owens, United Glass and Ceramic Workers of North America (Ohio). Settled by consent decree December 7, 1970.

July 21:   New York City passes bill banning sex discrimination in public accommodations. Earliest known law of this type in major U.S. city.

July 25–26:   Northwest regional Women's Liberation Conference
                   convenes in Eugene, Oregon.

August: National Conference of Commissioners on Uniform
                   State Laws draft uniform Marriage and Divorce Act
                   based on premise that marriage is partnership of
                   equals. Word "spouse" replaces prior references to
                   "husband" or "wife."

August: American Federation of Teachers passes resolution
                   at annual conference to examine traditional his-
                   tory text book portrayal of early feminist and suf-
                   fragist movement and to make recommendations for
                   changes.

August: At YWCA national convention in Houston, Texas,
                   organization announces formation of National
                   Women's Resource Center to realize an organiza-
                   tional priority of mobilizing "our full power as a
                   movement to revolutionize society's expectations of
                   women and their own self-perception."

August: As result of March 18 sit-in, *Ladies' Home Journal*
                   includes feminist supplement in August issue. Sup-
                   plement conceived and written by several demon-
                   stration participants.

August 10:   Group of feminists stage demonstration at Statue of
                   Liberty. Women march, sing and picket for women's
                   equality. String large banner—"Women of the World
                   Unite"—across the statue.

August 10:   House of Representatives passes Equal Rights
                   Amendment by a vote of 352 to 15. Marks first
                   action by full House since Amendment's introduc-
                   tion in 1923.

August 26:   Nationwide Women's Strike for Equality. Mass
                   demonstration commemorating fiftieth anniversary
                   of passage of women's suffrage amendment. Three
                   central Strike Day demands: equal opportunity in
                   employment and education; free abortion on de-
                   mand; twenty-four-hour child care centers. Tens of
                   thousands of women (individuals and moderate
                   and radical groups) participate in demonstrations
                   in cities and towns around the country. Largest pro-
                   test for women's equality in U.S. history.

September: NOW and Princeton University co-sponsor nursery
                   school in Princeton, N.J. First known licensed nur-
                   sery school operated by feminists.

September:	First multi-course accredited women's studies program begins at San Diego State University: ten courses on issues dealing with women.
September:	Seattle High School girl sues State of Washington Board of Education for discrimination against girls by requiring them (but not boys) to take Home Economics courses as prerequisite for graduation.
September:	New York City school teacher applies for child care leave to share child-rearing responsibilities with wife. Application based on city school system's maternity and child care leave policy. Application turned down by school principal and district superintendent. (By mid-April, 1971, Board of Education had not yet responded.) Board spokesman indicates refusal of application on grounds that requests are "granted only to people who give birth and then stay home to take care of the child; the two things—maternity and child care—can't be divided into separate parts." Teacher's wife argues city is "arbitrarily prescribing what our roles as mother and father should be." Couple intend to go to court if appeals fail.
September 9–15:	In response to House passage of Equal Rights Amendment, Senate Judiciary Committee holds hearings on House-passed version and a substitute motion introduced by ERA opponent Senator Sam Ervin (D., N.C.)
September 10:	Twelve TWA stewardesses file multi-million-dollar suit against TWA on grounds of sex discrimination stemming from April, 1968, complaint to EEOC.
September 15:	Release of "inside study" (anonymously authored) "Sexism on Capitol Hill." Report documents discrimination against women on Congressional staffs; e.g., of the 990 Senate staffers paid $12,000 to $31,000, nearly three-fourths are men.
September 28:	Woman air force captain files federal court suit charging "blatantly inequitable sex discrimination" in military regulations which prohibit service women (not service men) from having personal custody of minor children.
October:	American Baptist Convention receives report prepared by a group of executive staff women accusing

Convention of "retreat to tokenism" in its utilization of women within the Church structure.

October:

At its annual meeting, the Board of Missions, Women's Division of the United Methodist Church appropriates $15,000 for women's liberation projects. An additional $10,000 later appropriated in April, 1971, for similar projects.

October 5:

WEAL files class action complaint under EO 11375 against every U.S. medical school on charges of sex discrimination. Suit based on data showing that women comprise only 9 percent of U.S. doctors; also that women applicants to medical schools increased 300 percent over past forty years but women accepted into medical schools decreased during same period.

October 13:

WEAL files suit against entire Montgomery County, Md. school system under EO 11375 for sex discrimination in hiring, promotion and benefits.

November:

Male teacher refused request for "maternity" leave by City College of New York. Legal case for couple to argue deprivation of constitutional rights to privacy, liberty and equal protection of the law.

November:

American Film Institute of Washington, D.C. sponsors one-month program on "Women's Liberation and the Cinema," featuring ten well-known Hollywood films, followed by discussions of the portrayal of women in the films.

November 3:

After elections, thirteen women members of Congress—twelve in House, one in Senate. Largest number since 1960. As distinct from traditional pattern, none of the women who ran for Congress this year were widows trying to fill seats vacated by deaths of husbands.

November 22:

First woman Lutheran pastor ordained. Lutheran Church of America (largest of U.S. Lutheran branches) paved way previous summer by substituting word "person" for "man" in its ordination qualifications.

November 29:

Study presented at medical conference in conjunction with AMA clinical convention reveals results from 16-month experiment during which girls played on co-ed varsity teams in non-contact sports at 100 high schools throughout New York State. According to study little evidence of physical, psychological or social harm to either girls or their male team-mates and opponents.

December: At the decennial White House Conference on Children, NOW organizes strong feminist caucus to introduce feminist issues into discussions of child rearing and education.

December: In Kirkland, Washington, woman has maiden name legally reinstated in Superior Court, arguing that her married name "implies possession by another human being."

December: Little, Brown Publishing Co. signs agreement to give female employees same treatment as men in hiring, training and promotion practices. Agreement followed six months of negotiations with company's women employees. Original complaint filed by women copy editors with Massachusetts Commission Against Discrimination.

December 3: Announcement of first all-women's professional tennis tour. Resulted from suspension of women players by U.S. Lawn Tennis Association when women had protested inequality with male pros over prize money.

December 7: EEOC seeks to block American Telephone and Telegraph Co. rate increase on grounds its operating companies engage in "pervasive system-wide, and blatantly unlawful" discrimination in employment of women, blacks and Spanish-surnamed Americans.

December 8: Women's National Press Club votes to admit men. Changes name to The Press Club of Washington.

December 12: Women artists protest opening of New York's Whitney Museum 1970 Sculpture Annual for not giving women sculptors equal representation with men sculptors.

December 14: National Press Club, Washington, D.C. traditional "male stronghold," votes to admit women members.

1971

January: Goucher College (Maryland) offers course for women only titled "Nuts and Bolts in Contemporary

Society." Students learn small appliance repair, carpentry, plumbing, electronics, etc.

January 11:   U.S. Court of Appeals (Ninth Circuit) rules that a "substantial constitutional issue" is involved in the case of *Mengelkoch v. Industrial Welfare Commission of California.* Velma Mengelkoch had argued that the California state protective laws for women violated women's constitutional rights under the 14th Amendment. Case remanded to district court. Decision expected Fall, 1971.

January 24:   New York Radical Feminists hold "Speak-out on Rape." Women testify about experiences with assailants, and analyze traditionally-accepted social, legal, and psychological assumptions about rape.

January 25:   U.S. Supreme Court hands down first decision on sex discrimination under Title VII (*Phillips v. Martin-Marietta*). Rules company cannot refuse to hire mothers with small children unless same policy applies to fathers with small children. Feminists protest section of ruling which states that responsibilities of motherhood (not fatherhood) might constitute *bfoq* exception under Title VII.

February 17:   New York Board of Education votes to allow high school girls and boys to compete in non-contact sports, basing decision on 16-month experiment of co-ed sports participation at 100 high schools throughout New York State.

February 27:   Two women members, Maryland House of Delegates, introduce bill to legalize three-year marriage contract with option to renew. Contract would incorporate agreements on alimony, property settlements, and legal fees should marriage terminate at end of three years.

March: As result of class action suit filed by Michigan women's rights group, FOCUS, under EO 11375, University of Michigan becomes first university to incorporate an affirmative action plan for hiring and promotion of women, including goals and timetables. Over $400,000 in federal contracts had been withheld from university pending adoption of satisfactory affirmative action program to improve status of women.

March 8:   Women's liberation group occupies Harvard University building demanding child care facilities, a women's center, and Harvard-sponsored low-income housing. Occupation lasts ten days.

March 10: Radical feminist Ti-Grace Atkinson, while addressing an audience of over 800 at Catholic University (Washington, D.C.), is physically attacked by Patricia Buckley Bozell, managing editor of conservative Catholic monthly, *Triumph* and sister of columnist William Buckley and Sen. James Buckley (Con-Rep., N.Y.). Her attempt to strike Atkinson is in reaction to latter's critique of Catholic doctrine regarding women.

March 13: About 35 members of Journalists for Professional Equality picket Gridiron Club (Washington, D.C.) because of its policy of excluding women members. Pickets say they represent about 250 members of the Washington press corps.

March 24: House subcommittee opens hearings on Equal Rights Amendment. First such hearings in House since 1948. ERA reported out of committee favorably, April.

March 25: Ten members of the House of Representatives introduce most comprehensive child care development bill to date, to provide adequate nutritional, educational, health and day care services for pre-school children.

March 26: Professional Women's Caucus files class action sex discrimination suit against every law school in the country receiving federal funds. Suit based in part on preliminary statistical findings of Association of American Law Schools Committee on Women in Legal Education.

March 27: Pennsylvania Court rules that Pittsburgh daily newspapers must run "help wanted" columns under single classification, not separate male-female classifications. Case result of formal complaint filed by Pittsburgh NOW chapter with Pittsburgh Human Rights Commission, October 9, 1969.

April 1: Boy Scouts of America announces its Explorer Scout Division (scouts between ages of 15 and 20) will begin to admit girls.

April 3: President Nixon announces in public statement his opposition to abortion at any time during pregnancy. Position based on "personal and religious beliefs."

Several days earlier Sen. Edmund Muskie (D., Maine), Catholic, in television interview had drawn distinction between contraception, which he supports, and abortion, which he opposes, stating "It's the very nature of motherhood . . . to shield and protect life, not to destroy it."

April 17:   As follow-up to "Speak-out" in January, New York Radical Feminists hold day-long Workshop on Rape to discuss social, legal, psychological aspects of rape.

April 21:   Supreme Court in first decision on constitutionality of abortion laws upholds District of Columbia's abortion statute (*U.S. v. Vuitch*) and declares it "not unconstitutionally vague."

May 3:   Supreme Court agrees to consider whether two states' abortion laws violate the constitutional rights of women by denying them the right to decide whether or not they will have children. (Texas: *Roe v. Wade;* Georgia: *Doe v. Bolton.*) First time Supreme Court will consider the constitutional issue with regard to abortion.

May 14:   First time in 150-year history of U.S. Senate girls appointed as Senate pages. Rules Committee took six months to approve idea of female pages.

May 13–14:   Urban Research Corporation sponsors conference, "Equal Pay and Promotion: Corporate Affirmative Action Programs for Women Employees." Includes corporate presentations by Polaroid and General Electric as well as panels on "What the Government Will Require," and "What Women's Groups Have in Mind." Designed for corporate personnel executives.

June 13:   U.S. Office of Education Summer Institute begins month-long program, "Crisis: Women in Higher Education" for college administrators and faculty.

June 18–20:   First Interstate Association of the Commissions on the Status of Women convenes in St. Louis, Mo. One purpose of Association to develop coalition of women's groups, regardless of style and ideological differences to work on specific women's issues.

July 10:   As part of drive to put more women in positions of real political power, over 200 women organize the National Women's Political Caucus in Washington,

D.C. Board of directors includes Reps. Bella Abzug (D., N.Y.) and Shirley Chisholm (D., N.Y.), Betty Friedan, Gloria Steinem.

Fall: Stoughton High School, Stoughton, Wis. offers one of the first known high school courses in country on history of women in America. Part of new social studies curriculum of elective courses.

Addenda

1971

December: Coalition of New York feminists hold conference on prostitution. Some of the workshops cover prostitution and the law, the so-called "victimless crime theory," other manifestations of "prostitution" in a sexist society, etc.

December 4: Labor Department issues Revised Order No. 4 outlining requirements for affirmative action programs for federal government contractors and subcontractors (E011375). Revised order result of two years pressure by feminist groups to extend policy of establishing goals and timetables for women.

December 9: President Nixon vetoes comprehensive child care bill sought by broad coalition of feminists and child care advocates. Bill would have authorized $2 billion for establishment of nationwide network of child care centers.

1972

March 22: Equal Rights Amendment passed by Congress. First introduced in 1923, the 49-year struggle ended with Senate passage (84 to 8) in March following October passage in House (354 to 23). Ratification by 38 states required for formal adoption. (As of August 1972, 20 states had ratified the Amendment.)

March 24: Equal Employment Opportunity Act of 1972 passed extending enforcement powers of EEOC. Commission can now directly sue employer in federal courts for noncompliance with civil rights laws. For first

REBIRTH OF FEMINISM

time, EEOC's authority extended to educational institutions. Bill does not grant cease and desist powers as demanded by activist groups.

May 1:

New York Chapter of NOW, concluding year-and-a-half study of WABC-TV programming, files petition with FCC to deny station's license renewal. NOW charges ABC affiliate with "massive violations of FCC fairness doctrine." (As result of earlier NOW petition, in February, FCC had extended its anti-discrimination requirements to women.)

June 23:

Education Amendments of 1972 prohibit discrimination in all federally assisted educational programs with some exceptions. Exemptions include admission policies to elementary and secondary schools, and all matters pertaining to private undergraduate schools. Law does not apply to all vocational schools. Amendments extended Equal Pay Act to cover administrative, professional and executive employees.

July 10–13:

As result of delegate selection reforms, Democratic National Convention in Miami opened to women, youth and minorities. Women constitute 34 percent of delegation, and form sizeable voting block. For first time a woman, Shirley Chisholm, runs as candidate for party's presidential nomination.

Historical Documents

1848—Seneca Falls Convention

DECLARATION OF SENTIMENTS

When, in the course of human events, it becomes necessary for one portion of the family of man to assume among the people of the earth a position different from that which they have hitherto occupied, but one to which the laws of nature and of nature's God entitle them, a decent respect to the opinions of mankind requires that they should declare the causes that impel them to such a course.

We hold these truths to be self-evident: that all men and women are created equal; that they are endowed by their Creator with certain inalienable rights; that among these are life, liberty, and the pursuit of happiness; that to secure these rights governments are instituted, deriving their just powers from the consent of the governed. Whenever any form of government becomes destructive of these ends, it is the right of those who suffer from it to refuse allegiance to it, and to insist upon the institution of a new government, laying its foundation on such principles, and organizing its powers in such form, as to them shall seem most likely to effect their safety and happiness. Prudence indeed, will dictate that governments long established should not be changed for light and transient causes; and accordingly all experience hath shown that mankind are more disposed to suffer, while evils are sufferable, than to right themselves by abolishing the forms to which they were accustomed. But when a long train of abuses and usurpations, pursuing invariably the same object evinces a design to reduce them under absolute despotism, it is their duty to throw off such government, and to provide new guards for their future security. Such has been the patient sufferance of the women under this government, and such is now the necessity which constrains them to demand the equal station to which they are entitled.

The history of mankind is a history of repeated injuries and usurpations on the part of man toward woman, having in direct object the establishment of an absolute tyranny over her. To prove this, let facts be submitted to a candid world.

He has never permitted her to exercise her inalienable right to the elective franchise.

He has compelled her to submit to laws, in the formation of which she had no voice.

He has withheld from her rights which are given to the most ignorant and degraded men—both natives and foreigners.

Having deprived her of this first right of a citizen, the elective franchise, thereby leaving her without representation in the halls of legislation, he has oppressed her on all sides.

He has made her, if married, in the eye of the law, civilly dead.

He has taken from her all right in property, even to the wages she earns.

He has made her, morally, an irresponsible being, as she can commit many crimes with impunity, provided they be done in the presence of her husband. In the covenant of marriage, she is compelled to promise obedience to her husband, he becoming, to all intents and purposes, her master—the law giving him power to deprive her of her liberty, and to administer chastisement.

He has so framed the laws of divorce, as to what shall be the proper causes, and in case of separation, to whom the guardianship of the children shall be given, as to be wholly regardless of the happiness of women—the law, in all cases, going upon a false supposition of the supremacy of man, and giving all power into his hands.

After depriving her of all rights as a married woman, if single and the owner of property, he has taxed her to support a government which recognizes her only when her property can be made profitable to it.

He has monopolized nearly all the profitable employments, and from those she is permitted to follow, she receives but a scanty remuneration. He closes against all her the avenues to wealth and distinction which he considers most honorable to himself. As a teacher of theology, medicine, or law, she is not known.

He has denied her the facilities for obtaining a thorough education, all colleges being closed against her.

He allows her in Church, as well as State, but a subordinate position, claiming Apostolic authority for her exclusion from the ministry, and, with some exceptions, from any public participation in the affairs of the Church.

He has created a false public sentiment by giving to the world a different code of morals for men and women, by which moral delinquencies which exclude women from society, are not only tolerated, but deemed of little account in man.

He has usurped the prerogative of Jehovah himself, claiming it as his right to assign for her a sphere of action, when that belongs to her conscience and to her God.

He has endeavored, in every way that he could, to destroy her confidence in her own powers, to lessen her self-respect, and to make her willing to lead a dependent and abject life.

Now, in view of this entire disfranchisement of one-half the people of this country, their social and religious degradation—in view of the unjust laws above mentioned, and because women do feel themselves aggrieved, oppressed, and fraudulently deprived of their most sacred rights, we insist that they have immediate admission to all the rights and privileges which belong to them as citizens of the United States.

In entering upon the great work before us, we anticipate no small amount of misconception, misrepresentation, and ridicule; but we shall use every instrumentality within our power to effect our object. We shall employ agents, circulate tracts, petition the State and National legislatures, and endeavor to enlist the pulpit and the press in our behalf. We hope this Convention will be followed by a series of Conventions embracing every part of the country.

RESOLUTIONS

WHEREAS, The great precept of nature is conceded to be, that "man shall pursue his own true and substantial happiness." Blackstone in his Commentaries remarks, that this law of Nature being coeval with mankind, and dictated by God himself, is of course superior in obligation to any other. It is binding over all the globe, in all countries and at all times; no human laws are of any validity if contrary to this, and such of them as are valid, derive all their force, and all their validity, and all their authority, mediately and immediately, from this original; therefore,

Resolved, That such laws as conflict, in any way, with the true and substantial happiness of women, are contrary to the great precept of nature and of no validity, for this is "superior in obligation to any other."

Resolved, That all laws which prevent woman from occupying such a station in society as her conscience shall dictate, or which place her in a position inferior to that of man, are contrary to the great precept of nature, and therefore of no force or authority.

Resolved, That woman is man's equal—was intended to be so by the Creator, and the highest good of the race demands that she should be recognized as such.

Resolved, That the women of this country ought to be enlightened in regard to the laws under which they live, that they may no longer publish their degradation by declaring themselves satisfied with their present position, nor their ignorance, by asserting that they have all the rights they want.

Resolved, That inasmuch as man, while claiming for himself intellectual superiority, does accord to woman moral superiority, it is pre-eminently his duty to encourage her to speak and teach, as she has an opportunity, in all religious assemblies.

Resolved, That the same amount of virtue, delicacy, and refinement of behavior that is required of woman in the social state, should also be required of man, and the same transgressions should be visited with equal severity on both man and woman.

Resolved, That the objection of indelicacy and impropriety, which is so often brought against woman when she addresses a public audience, comes with a very ill-grace from those who encourage, by their attendance, her appearance on the stage, in the concert, or in feats of the circus.

Resolved, That woman has too long rested satisfied in the circumscribed limits which corrupt customs and a perverted application of the Scriptures have marked out for her, and that it is time she should move in the enlarged sphere which her great Creator has assigned her.

Resolved, That it is the duty of the women of this country to secure to themselves their sacred right to the elective franchise.

Resolved, That the equality of human rights results necessarily from the fact of the identity of the race in capabilities and responsibilities.

Resolved, therefore, That, being invested by the Creator with the same capabilities, and the same consciousness of responsibility for their exercise, it is demonstrably the right and duty of women, equally with man, to promote every righteous cause by every righteous means; and especially in regard to the great subjects of morals and religion, it is self-evidently her right to participate with her brother in teaching them, both in private and in public, by writing and by speaking, by any instrumentalities proper to be used, and in any assemblies proper to be held; and this being a self-evident truth growing out of the divinely implanted principles of human nature, any custom or authority adverse to it, whether modern or wearing the hoary sanction of antiquity, is to be regarded as a self-evident falsehood, and at war with mankind.

At the last session Lucretia Mott offered and spoke to the following resolution:

Resolved, That the speedy success of our cause depends upon the

zealous and untiring efforts of both men and women, for the overthrow of the monopoly of the pulpit, and for the securing to woman
an equal participation with men in the various trades, professions,
and commerce.

1963—President's Commission on the Status of Women[1]

RECOMMENDATIONS

Education and Counseling
  Means of acquiring or continuing education must be available to
every adult at whatever point he or she broke off traditional formal
schooling. The structure of adult education must be drastically revised. It must provide practicable and accessible opportunities, developed with regard for the needs of women, to complete elementary
and secondary school and to continue education beyond high school.
Vocational training, adapted to the nation's growing requirement for
skilled and highly educated manpower, should be included at all of
these educational levels. Where needed and appropriate, financial
support should be provided by local, state, and federal governments
and by private groups and foundations.
  In a democracy offering broad and everchanging choices, where
ultimate decisions are made by individuals, skilled counseling is an
essential part of education. Public and private agencies should join
in strengthening counseling resources. States and school districts
should raise their standards for state employment service counselors
and school guidance counselors. Institutions offering counseling education should provide both course content and ample supervised
experience in the counseling of females as well as males, adults as
well as adolescents.
  The education of girls and women for their responsibilities in
home and community should be thoroughly re-examined with a view
to discovering more effective approaches, with experimentation in
content and timing, and under auspices including school systems,
private organizations, and the mass media.

Home and Community
  For the benefit of children, mothers, and society, child-care serv-
ices should be available for children of families at all economic levels.
Proper standards of child care must be maintained, whether services

---

[1] Commission established by John F. Kennedy, December 14, 1961.

are in homes or in centers. Costs should be met by fees scaled to parents' ability to pay, contributions from voluntary agencies, and public appropriations.

Tax deductions for child-care expenses of working mothers should be kept commensurate with the median income of couples when both husband and wife are engaged in substantial employment. The present limitation on their joint income, above which deductions are not allowable, should be raised. Additional deductions, of lesser amounts, should be allowed for children beyond the first. The 11-year age limit for child-care deductions should be raised.

Family services under public and private auspices to help families avoid or overcome breakdown or dependency and establish a soundly based homelife, and professionally supervised homemaker services to meet emergency or other special needs should be strengthened, extended, or established where lacking.

Community programs under public and private auspices should make comprehensive provisions for health and rehabilitation services, including easily accessible maternal and child health services, accompanied by education to encourage their use.

Volunteers' services should be made more effective through coordinated and imaginative planning among agencies and organizations for recruitment, training, placement, and supervision, and their numbers augmented through tapping the large reservoir of additional potential among youth, retired people, members of minority groups, and women not now in volunteer activities.

Women in Employment

Equal opportunity for women in hiring, training, and promotion should be the governing principle in private employment. An Executive order should state this principle and advance its application to work done under federal contracts.

At present, federal systems of manpower utilization discourage part-time employment. Many able women, including highly trained professionals, who are not free for full-time employment, can work part time. The Civil Service Commission and the Bureau of the Budget should facilitate the imaginative and prudent use of such personnel throughout the government service.

Labor Standards

The federal Fair Labor Standards Act, including premium pay for overtime, should be extended to employment subject to federal jurisdiction but now uncovered, such as work in hotels, motels, restaurants, and laundries, in additional retail establishments, in agriculture, and in nonprofit organizations.

State legislation, applicable to both men and women, should be enacted, or strengthened and extended to all types of employment, to provide minimum-wage levels approximating the minimum under federal law and to require premium pay at the rate of at least time and a half for overtime.

The normal workday and workweek at this moment of history should be not more than 8 hours a day and 40 hours a week. The best way to discourage excessive hours for all workers is by broad and effective minimum-wage coverage, both federal and state, providing overtime of at least time and a half the regular rate for all hours in excess of 8 a day or 40 a week.

Until such time as this goal is attained, state legislation limiting maximum hours of work for women should be maintained, strengthened, and expanded. Provisions for flexibility under proper safeguards should allow additional hours of work when there is a demonstrated need. During this interim period, efforts should continuously and simultaneously be made to require premium rates of pay for all hours in excess of 8 a day or 40 a week.

State laws should establish the principle of equal pay for comparable work.

State laws should protect the right of all workers to join unions of their own choosing and to bargain collectively.

Security of Basic Income

A widow's benefit under the federal old-age insurance system should be equal to the amount that her husband would have received at the same age had he lived. This objective should be approached as rapidly as may be financially feasible.

The coverage of the unemployment-insurance system should be extended. Small establishments and nonprofit organizations should be covered now through federal action, and state and local government employees through state action. Practicable means of covering at least some household workers and agricultural workers should be actively explored.

Paid maternity leave or comparable insurance benefits should be provided for women workers; employers, unions, and governments should explore the best means of accomplishing this purpose.

Women Under the Law

Early and definitive court pronouncement, particularly by the United States Supreme Court, is urgently needed with regard to the validity under the Fifth and Fourteenth Amendments of laws and official practices discriminating against women, to the end that the principle of equality become firmly established in constitutional doctrine.

Accordingly, interested groups should give high priority to bringing under court review cases involving laws and practices which discriminate against women.

The United States should assert leadership, particularly in the United Nations, in securing equality of rights for women as part of the effort to define and assure human rights; should participate actively in the formulation of international declarations, principles, and conventions to improve the status of women throughout the world; and should demonstrate its sincere concern for women's equal rights by becoming a party to appropriate conventions.

Appropriate action, including enactment of legislation where necessary, should be taken to achieve equal jury service in the states.

State legislatures, and other groups concerned with the improvement of state statutes affecting family law and personal and property rights of married women, including the National Conference of Commissioners on Uniform State Laws, the Council of State Governments, the American Law Institute, and state Commissions on the Status of Women, should move to eliminate laws which impose legal disabilities on women.

Women as Citizens

Women should be encouraged to seek elective and appointive posts at local, state, and national levels and in all three branches of government.

Public office should be held according to ability, experience, and effort, without special preferences or discriminations based on sex. Increasing consideration should continually be given to the appointment of women of demonstrated ability and political sensitivity to policy-making positions.

Continuing Leadership

To further the objectives proposed in this report, an Executive order should:

1. Designate a Cabinet officer to be responsible for assuring that the resources and activities of the federal government bearing upon the Commission's recommendations are directed to carrying them out, and for making periodic progress reports to the President.

2. Designate the heads of other agencies involved in those activities to serve, under the chairmanship of the designated Cabinet officer, as an interdepartmental committee to assure proper coordination and action.

3. Establish a citizens committee, advisory to the interdepartmental committee and with its secretariat from the designated Cabinet officer, to meet periodically to evaluate progress made, provide counsel, and serve as a means for suggesting and stimulating action.

MEMBERS OF THE COMMISSION

The names of the men and women appointed to the Commission, and the posts they occupied at the time of their appointment, were:

Eleanor Roosevelt, *Chairman (deceased)*

Esther Peterson, *Executive Vice Chairman*, Assistant Secretary of Labor

Dr. Richard A. Lester, *Vice Chairman*, Chairman, Department of Economics, Princeton University.

The Attorney General, Honorable Robert F. Kennedy

The Secretary of Agriculture, Honorable Orville L. Freeman

The Secretary of Commerce, Honorable Luther H. Hodges

The Secretary of Labor, Honorable Arthur J. Goldberg, Honorable W. Willard Wirtz

The Secretary of Health, Education, and Welfare, Honorable Abraham A. Ribicoff, Honorable Anthony L. Celebrezze

Honorable George D. Aiken, United States Senate

Honorable Maurine B. Neuberger, United States Senate

Honorable Edith Green, United States House of Representatives

Honorable Jessica M. Weis *(deceased)*, United States House of Representatives

The Chairman of the Civil Service Commission, Honorable John W. Macy, Jr.

Macon Boddy, Henrietta, Tex.

Dr. Mary I. Bunting, President, Radcliffe College

Mary E. Callahan, Member, Executive Board, International Union of Electrical, Radio and Machine Workers

Dr. Henry David, President, New School for Social Research

Dorothy Height, President, National Council of Negro Women, Inc.

Margaret Hickey, Public Affairs Editor, *Ladies' Home Journal*

Viola H. Hymes, President, National Council of Jewish Women, Inc.

Margaret J. Mealey, Executive Director, National Council of Catholic Women

Norman E. Nicholson, Administrative Assistant, Kaiser Industries Corp., Oakland, Calif.

Marguerite Rawalt, Attorney; past president: Federal Bar Association, National Association of Women Lawyers, National Federation of Business and Professional Women's Clubs, Inc.

William F. Schnitzler, Secretary-Treasurer, American Federation of Labor and Congress of Industrial Organizations

Dr. Caroline F. Ware, Vienna, Va.

Dr. Cynthia C. Wedel, Assistant General Secretary for Program, National Council of the Churches of Christ in the United States of America

438

1969-MEMBERS OF THE TASK FORCE
ON WOMEN'S RIGHTS AND RESPONSIBILITIES[1]

VIRGINIA R. ALLAN
Executive Vice President
Cahalan Drug Stores, Inc.
Wyandotte, Michigan

HON. ELIZABETH ATHANASAKOS
Municipal Court Judge
and Practicing Attorney
Fort Lauderdale, Florida

DOROTHY HAENER
International Representative
Women's Department, UAW
Detroit, Michigan

ANN R. BLACKHAM
President
Ann R. Blackham & Company
Winchester, Massachusetts

LADDIE F. HUTAR
President
Public Affairs Service
Associates, Inc.
Chicago, Illinois

P. DEE BOERSMA
Student Gov't. Leader
Graduate Student
Ohio State University
Columbus, Ohio

KATHERINE B. MASSENBURG
Chairman
Maryland Commission on the
Status of Women
Baltimore, Maryland

EVELYN CUNNINGHAM
Director, Women's Unit
Office of the Governor
New York, New York

WILLIAM C. MERCER
Vice President,
Personnel Relations
American Telephone &
Telegraph Co.
New York, New York

SISTER ANN IDA GANNON,
B.V.M.
President
Mundelein College
Chicago, Illinois

DR. ALAN SIMPSON
President
Vassar College
Poughkeepsie, New York

VERA GLASER
Correspondent
Knight Newspapers
Washington, D.C.

EVELYN E. WHITLOW
Attorney at Law
Los Angeles, California

[1] Task Force established by Richard M. Nixon, October 1, 1969.

1968—National Organization for Women (NOW) Bill of Rights

I   Equal Rights Constitutional Amendment
II Enforce Law Banning Sex Discrimination in Employment
III Maternity Leave Rights in Employment and in Social Security Benefits
IV Tax Deduction for Home and Child Care Expenses for Working Parents
V   Child Care Centers
VI Equal and Unsegregated Education
VII Equal Job Training Opportunities and Allowances for Women in Poverty
VIII The Right of Women to Control Their Reproductive Lives

WE DEMAND:

I. That the United States Congress immediately pass the Equal Rights Amendment to the Constitution to provide that "Equality of rights under the law shall not be denied or abridged by the United States or by any State on account of sex," and that such then be immediately ratified by the several States.

II. That equal employment opportunity be guaranteed to all women, as well as men, by insisting that the Equal Employment Opportunity Commission enforces the prohibitions against sex discrimination in employment under Title VII of the Civil Rights Act of 1964 with the same vigor as it enforces the prohibitions against racial discrimination.

III. That women be protected by law to ensure their rights to return to their jobs within a reasonable time after childbirth without loss of seniority or other accrued benefits, and be paid maternity leave as a form of social security and/or employee benefit.

IV. Immediate revision of tax laws to permit the deduction of home and child care expenses for working parents.

V. That child care facilities be established by law on the same basis as parks, libraries, and public schools, adequate to the needs of children from the pre-school years through adolescence, as a community resource to be used by all citizens from all income levels.

VI. That the right of women to be educated to their full potential equally with men be secured by Federal and State Legislation, elim-

inating all discrimination and segregation by sex, written and un-
written, at all levels of education, including colleges, graduate and
professional schools, loans and fellowships, and Federal and State
training programs such as the Job Corps.

VII. The right of women in poverty to secure job training, housing,
and family allowances on equal terms with men, but without prejudice to a parent's right to remain at home to care for his or her
children; revision of welfare legislation and poverty programs which
deny women dignity, privacy and self-respect.

VIII. The right of women to control their own reproductive lives by
removing from penal codes laws limiting access to contraceptive information and devices and laws governing abortion.

1969—Politics of the Ego:
A Manifesto for
New York Radical Feminists

RADICAL FEMINISM recognizes the oppression of women as a fundamental political oppression wherein women are categorized as an
inferior class based upon their sex. It is the aim of radical feminism
to organize politically to destroy this sex class system.

As radical feminists we recognize that we are engaged in a power
struggle with men, and that the agent of our oppression is man insofar as he identifies with and carries out the supremacy privileges of
the male role. For while we realize that the liberation of women will
ultimately mean the liberation of men from their destructive role as
oppressor, we have no illusion that men will welcome this liberation
without a struggle.

Radical feminism is political because it recognizes that a group
of individuals (men) have organized together for power over women,
and that they have set up institutions throughout society to maintain
this power.

A political power institution is set up for a purpose. We believe
that the purpose of male chauvinism is primarily to obtain psychological ego satisfaction, and that only secondarily does this manifest
itself in economic relationships. For this reason we do not believe that
capitalism, or any other economic system, is the cause of female
oppression, nor do we believe that female oppression will disappear
as a result of a purely economic revolution. The political oppression

of women has its own class dynamic; and that dynamic must be understood in terms previously called "non-political"—namely the politics of the ego.*

Thus the purpose of the male power group is to fulfill a need. That need is psychological, and derives from the supremacist assumptions of the male identity—namely that the male ego identity be sustained through its ability to have power over the female ego. Man establishes his "manhood" in direct proportion to his ability to have his ego override woman's, and derives his strength and self-esteem through this process. This male need, though destructive, is in that sense impersonal. It is not out of a desire to hurt the woman that he dominates and destroys her; it is out of a need for a sense of power that he necessarily must destroy her ego and make it subservient to his. Hostility to women is a secondary effect; to the degree that he is not fulfilling his own assumptions of male power he hates women for not complying. Similarly, a man's failure to establish himself supreme among other males (as for example a poor white male) may make him channel his hostility into his relationship with women, since they are one of the few political groups available to him for reassertion.

As women we are living in a male power structure, and our roles become necessarily a function of men. The services we supply are services to the male ego. We are rewarded according to how well we perform these services. Our skill—our profession—is our ability to be feminine—that is, dainty, sweet, passive, helpless, ever-giving and sexy. In other words, everything to help reassure man that he is primary. If we perform successfully, our skills are rewarded. We "marry well"; we are treated with benevolent paternalism, we are deemed successful women, and may even make the "women's pages."

If we do not choose to perform these ego services, but instead assert ourselves as primary to ourselves, we are denied the necessary access to alternatives wherein we can manifest our self-assertion. Decision-making positions in the various job fields are closed to us; politics (left, right or liberal) are barred in other than auxiliary roles; our created efforts are *a priori* judged not serious because we are females; our day-to-day lives are judged failures because we have not become "real women."

The rejection is economic in that women's work is underpaid. It is emotional in that we are cut off from human relationships because we choose to reject the submissive female role. We are trapped in an alien system, just as the worker under capitalism is forced to sell his economic services in a system which is set up against his self-interest.

---

*ego: We are using the classical definition rather than the Freudian: that is, the sense of individual self as distinct from others.

Sexual Institutions

The oppression of women is manifested in particular institutions, constructed and maintained to keep women in their place. Among these are the institutions of marriage, motherhood, love, and sexual intercourse (the family unit is incorporated by the above). Through these institutions the woman is taught to confuse her biological sexual differences with her total human potential. Biology is destiny, she is told. Because she has childbearing capacity, she is told that motherhood and child rearing is her function, not her option. Because she has childbearing capacity she is told that it is her function to marry and have the man economically maintain her and make the decisions. Because she has the physical capacity for sexual intercourse, she is told that sexual intercourse too is her function, rather than just a voluntary act which she may engage in as an expression of her general humanity.

In each case *her* sexual difference is rationalized to trap her within it, while the male sexual difference is rationalized to imply an access to all areas of human activity.

Love, in the context of an oppressive male-female relationship, becomes an emotional cement to justify the dominant-submissive relationship. The man "loves" the woman who fulfills her submissive ego-boosting role. The woman "loves" the man she is submitting to— that is, after all, why she "lives for him." LOVE, magical and systematically unanalyzed, becomes the emotional rationale for the submission of one ego to the other. And it is deemed every woman's natural function to love.

Radical feminism believes that the popularized version of love has thus been used politically to cloud and justify an oppressive relationship between men and women, and that in reality there can be no genuine love until the need to *control* the growth of another is replaced by the love *for* the growth of another.

Learning to Become Feminine

The process of training women for their female role begins as far back as birth, when a boy child is preferred over a girl child. In her early years, when the basic patterns of her identity are being established, it is reinforced in her that her female role is not a choice but a fact. Her future will be spent performing the same basic functions as her mother and women before her. Her life is already determined. She is not given the choice of exploring activity toys. Her brothers play astronaut, doctor, scientist, race-car driver. She plays little homemaker, future mother (dolls), and nurse (doctor's helper). Her brothers are given activity toys; the world is their future. She is given service toys. Already she is learning that her future will be the maintenance of others. Her ego is repressed at all times to conform with this future submissiveness. She must dress prettily and be clean;

speak politely; seek approval; please. Her brothers are allowed to fight, get dirty, be aggressive and be self-assertive.

As she goes through school she learns that subjects which teach mastery and control over the world, such as science and math, are male subjects; while subjects which teach appearance, maintenance, or sentiment, such as home economics or literature, are female subjects. School counselors will recommend nursing for girls, while they will encourage boys to be doctors. Most of the best colleges will accept only a token sprinkling of women (quota system), regardless of academic abilities.

By the time she is of marrying age she has been prepared on two levels. One, she will realize that alternatives to the traditional female role are prohibitive; and two, she will herself have accepted on some levels the assumptions about her female role.

Internalization

It is not only through denying women human alternatives that men are able to maintain their positions of power. It is politically necessary for any oppressive group to convince the oppressed that they are in fact inferior, and therefore deserve their situation. For it is precisely through the destruction of women's egos that they are robbed of their ability to resist.

For the sake of our own liberation, we must learn to overcome this damage to ourselves through internalization. We must begin to destroy the notion that we are indeed only servants to the male ego, and must begin to reverse the systematic crushing of women's egos by constructing alternative selves that are healthy, independent and self-assertive. We must, in short, help each other to transfer the ultimate power of judgment about the value of our lives from men to ourselves.

It remains for us as women to fully develop a new dialectic of sex class—an analysis of the way in which sexual identity and institutions reinforce one another.

Charts and
Tables

Source: All charts marked (*) are from *1969 Handbook on Women Workers*, Women's Bureau, U.S. Department of Labor. All charts marked (**) are from *The Underutilization of Women Workers*, Women's Bureau, U.S. Department of Labor, 1970.

WOMEN IN THE LABOR FORCE, SELECTED YEARS, 1890–1968*

(Women 16 years of age and over)

Date	Number	As percent of all workers	As percent of woman population
HIGHLIGHTS[1]			
1968 (annual average)	29,204,000	37.1	41.6
1965	25,831,000	35.0	38.8
1960	22,985,000	33.3	37.4
1955	19,987,000	31.2	34.8
1950	17,882,000	29.1	33.0
1947	16,150,000	27.6	30.9
1945	19,290,000	36.1	38.1
1940	13,783,000	25.4	28.9
LONG-TERM TRENDS[2]			
1930	10,396,000	21.9	23.6
1920	8,229,000	20.4	22.7
1900	4,999,000	18.1	20.0
1890	3,704,000	17.0	18.2

[1] Civilian labor force.
[2] Decennial census figures cover those 14 years of age and over in the total labor force.

WOMEN'S EMPLOYMENT HAS INCREASED FASTER THAN MEN'S*

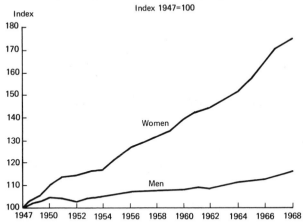

(Relative Growth of the Labor Force, by Sex, 1947-68[1])

Index 1947=100

[1] Annual averages.

MOST WOMEN WHO WORK ARE MARRIED*

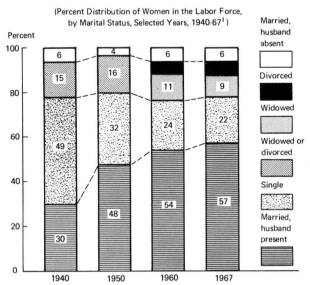

(Percent Distribution of Women in the Labor Force, by Marital Status, Selected Years, 1940-67[1])

Data cover March of each year and are for women 14 years of age and over except 1967 which are for 16 and over.

MOTHERS ARE MORE LIKELY TO WORK TODAY THAN EVER BEFORE *

(Labor Force Participation Rates of Mothers, by Age of Children,
Selected Years, 1948-67[1])

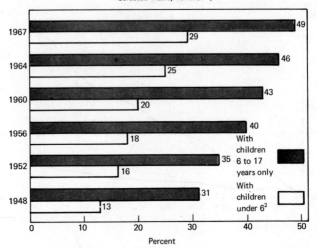

[1] Data cover March of each year except for April 1948 and 1952 and are for women
14 years of age and over except 1967 which are for 16 and over.

[2] May also have older children.

THE EARNINGS GAP BETWEEN WOMEN AND MEN REMAINS WIDE**

(Median Wage or Salary Income of Year-Round Full-Time[1] Workers, by Sex, 1957-68[2])

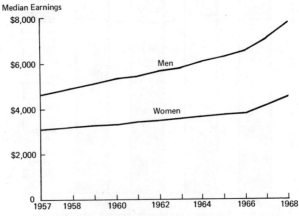

[1] 50 to 52 weeks a year, 35 hours or more a week.

[2] Data for 1967 and 1968 are not strictly comparable with prior years since they
include earnings of self-employed persons.

WOMEN ARE 3 TIMES AS LIKELY AS MEN TO EARN LESS THAN $5,000 FOR YEAR-ROUND FULL-TIME[1] WORK**

(Year-Round Full-Time Workers, by Total Money Earnings and Sex, 1968)

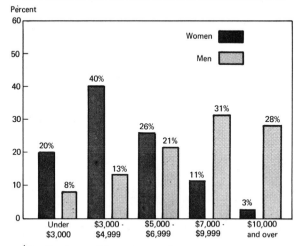

[1] 50 to 52 weeks a year, 35 hours or more a week.

INCIDENCE OF POVERTY IS HIGH IN FAMILIES HEADED BY A WOMAN WORKER**

(Percent of Families Living in Poverty in 1968 Whose Head Worked During Year, by Sex and Race)

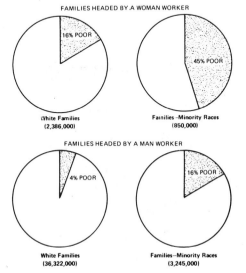

MILLIONS OF WOMEN ARE IN
LOW-PAID OCCUPATIONS **

(Year-Round Full-Time[1] Women Workers, by Selected
Occupations and Median Wage or Salary Income, 1968)

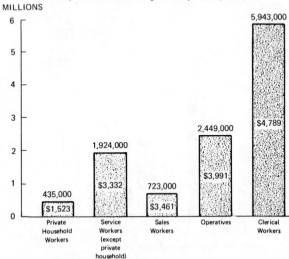

[1] 50 to 52 weeks a year, 35 hours or more a week.

STARTING SALARIES OF COLLEGE GRADUATES ARE LOWER
FOR WOMEN THAN FOR MEN **

(Average Monthly Starting Salaries of Women and Men With Bachelor's Degrees, 1970)

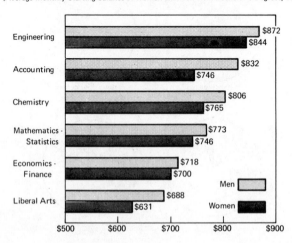

MANY WOMEN WORKERS ARE UNDERUTILIZED IN RELATION TO THEIR EDUCATIONAL ACHIEVEMENT**

(Women With 1 or More Years of College Employed in the Less Skilled Occupations, 1969)

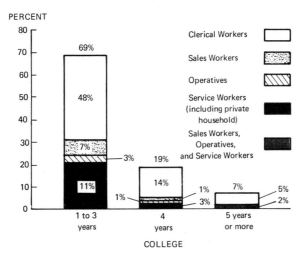

WOMEN ARE INADEQUATELY REPRESENTED IN LEADING PROFESSIONS**

(Women as Percent of Total Employed, Selected Professions)

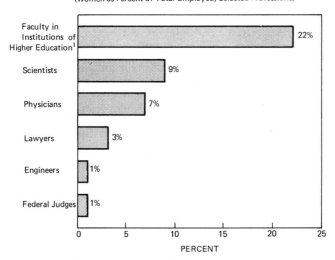

[1] Includes other professional staff.

A Selected Bibliography on Women

Compiled and Annotated by Lucinda Cisler

The selection that follows represents a wide spectrum of thinking and writing about women and about the issues that most strongly affect them. It is limited almost entirely to American titles, and reflects both traditional and feminist philosophies. It includes entries for sources cited in the text of this book. The ten categories into which it is divided, and the annotations that accompany most of the entries, are meant to serve as guides to the reader. An asterisk (*) denotes availability in paperback. Where price and address information is shown, it was as accurate as could be assured as of June, 1971.

1 GENERAL WORKS: BOOKS, ARTICLES, AND SPECIAL ISSUES OF PERIODICALS

Adams, Elsie, and Mary Louise Briscoe, eds. *Up Against the Wall, Mother.* . . . Beverly Hills (Calif.): Glencoe, 1971. Extensive and generally excellent anthology (prose, poetry, fiction, non-fiction) of both traditional and feminist views of women.

Altbach, Edith Hoshino, ed. *From Feminism to Liberation.* Cambridge, Mass.: Schenckman, 1971. Anthology containing some of the articles from *Radical America*'s issue on women (February, 1970), as well as new pieces from various sources.

Anderson, Mary. *Woman at Work.* Minneapolis: University of Minnesota, 1951. The story of the Women's Bureau, and of its first director, Anderson.

* Aries, Philippe. *Centuries of Childhood: A Social History of Family Life.* New York: Knopf, 1962. One of his theses is that the very concepts of "childhood" and "adolescence" are relatively modern ones; complex and thorough.

* Beard, Mary. *Woman as Force in History.* New York: Macmillan, 1946. The historian traces women's role through a study of law, and argues that in many respects women's position under American law is a Blackstone-derived distortion of their ancient rights in equity law.

* de Beauvoir, Simone. *The Second Sex.* New York: Knopf, 1953.

Classic examination of biological, historical, political, literary, and sexual assumptions about women. See also her other works, both fiction and non-fiction.

* Bernard, Jessie. *Academic Women.* University Park: Pennsylvania State University, 1964. Women as scholars and college teachers.
* Bird, Caroline. *Born Female: The High Cost of Keeping Women Down.* New York: McKay, 1968, Revised 1970. A lively overview; focuses on women's economic and employment position.
* Brecher, Ruth and Edward. *An Analysis of Human Sexual Response.* Boston: Little, Brown, 1966. An excellent popularization of the content of Masters and Johnson's *Human Sexual Response* (*q.v.*, Section 1). Also includes several important essays by others, especially a 50-page history of the concept of female orgasm.
* Brenton, Myron. *The American Male.* New York: Coward, 1966. Posits that sex-role stereotypes and fears about "masculinity" and "femininity" have a baleful effect on both sexes.
* Briffault, Robert. *The Mothers: The Matriarchal Theory of Social Origins.* New York: Macmillan, 1927. Abridged version: Universal Library paperbound. The theory and conclusions are highly influential—and still hotly debated.
* Brown, Helen Gurley. *Sex and the Single Girl.* New York: Bernard Geis, 1962. The editor of *Cosmopolitan* tells how the single girl can catch a man. Author's model of the "liberated woman" is not to be confused with women's liberation.
Bullough, Vern L. *The History of Prostitution.* New Hyde Park, N.Y.: University, 1964.
* Cade, Toni, ed. *The Black Woman: An Anthology.* New York: New American Library, 1970. A Signet book.
Callahan, Sidney. *The Illusion of Eve.* New York: Sheed and Ward, 1965. A modern Catholic woman views the concept of the female.
* Carson, Josephine. *Silent Voices: The Southern Negro Woman Today.* New York: Delacorte, 1969. Perceptive interviews with Southern black women from a variety of backgrounds; insights into the civil rights movement from black women's point of view.
Chisholm, Shirley. *Unbossed and Unbought.* New York: Houghton Mifflin, 1970. Autobiography of the first black Congresswoman.
* Cooke, Joanne, and Charlotte Bunch-Weeks, eds. *The New Women, a Motive Anthology on Women's Liberation.* Indianapolis: Bobbs-Merrill, 1970. Book version of "On the Liberation of Women" (Motive, 1969, *q.v.*, Section 7a).
Culver, Elsie Thomas. *Women in the World of Religion: From Pagan Priestesses to Ecumenical Delegates.* Garden City, N.Y.: Doubleday, 1967.
Daly, Mary. *The Church and the Second Sex.* New York: Harper and Row, 1968. By a feminist Catholic theologian.
"Dating, Mating and Sex." New York: Triangle, 1970. A *Seventeen* magazine In-Depth Study. Surveys attitudes of teenaged girls and their parents.
Davidson, Sara. "The Girls on the Bandwagon." *McCall's.* August, 1970. Perceptive picture of the women who devote their lives to serving national political figures [male].

Dexter, Elisabeth A. *Career Women of America, 1776–1840.* Frances-town, N.H.: Marshall Jones, 1950.

Dinerman, Beatrice. "Women in Architecture." *Architectural Forum.* December, 1969. Mixture of statistics with personal testimony from the women who make up one in 200 people in this profession.

Doely, Sarah Bentley, ed. *Women's Liberation and the Church.* New York: Association, 1970. Anthology, primarily of writings by Protestant women.

Edmiston, Susan. "The Psychology of Day Care." *New York.* 4:14 (April 5, 1971). Who argues for child care services, and why.

Efron, Edith. "Is Television Making a Mockery of the American Woman?" *TV Guide.* August 8, 1970. What the women's movement and various of its activists say about TV advertising, content, and employment patterns.

* Ejlerson, Mette, trans. Marianne Kold Madsen. *I Accuse.* London: Universal-Tandem, 1969; New York: Award, 1969. Outspoken Scandinavian best-seller, in which a woman describes female sexuality and dissects male-created ideas about its nature.

* Engels, Friedrich. *Origin of Family, Private Property, and the State* (1884). Reprinted, New York: International, n.d. Presents the theory that the institution of the family gave rise to and perpetuates the economic *status quo.*

* Epstein, Cynthia Fuchs. *Woman's Place: Options and Limits in Professional Careers.* Berkeley: University of California, 1970. Analytic, factual picture of employment problems.

"Equal Rights for Women: A Symposium on the Proposed Constitutional Amendment." *Harvard Civil Rights-Civil Liberties Law Review.* 6:2 (March, 1971). Six articles on the Equal Rights Amendment by such legal authorities as Pauli Murray, Paul Freund, Norman Dorsen, and Thomas Emerson.

Ermarth, Margaret Sittler. *Adam's Fractured Rib.* Philadelphia: Fortress, 1970. Commissioned by the Lutheran Church in America. Author surveys role of women in Catholic and Protestant church, touching on such subjects as ordination and "male backlash."

* Figes, Eva. *Patriarchal Attitudes.* New York: Stein and Day, 1970. Women in Revolt Series. Past and present place of women and projections for future. See especially analysis of Rousseau's attitudes: inconsistent with his *Social Contract.*

* Firestone, Shulamith. *The Dialectic of Sex: The Case for Feminist Revolution.* New York: Morrow, 1970. Historical, political, cultural analysis of nature and source of women's oppression; by long-time active feminist.

* Flexner, Eleanor. *Century of Struggle.* Cambridge: Harvard, 1959. Exhaustive description and analysis of the suffrage and women's rights movement through 1920; a basic work.

* Friedan, Betty. *The Feminine Mystique.* New York: Norton, 1963. Helped spark modern women's movement. See especially her analysis of the media and popularized Freud and anthropology.

Ginzberg, Eli, and Marie Yohalem. *Educated American Women: Self-Portraits.* New York: Columbia, 1966. Women describe their own lives and the conflicts some perceive between society's demands and their own aspirations.

Gornick, Vivian, and Barbara K. Moran, eds. *Woman in Sexist Society.* New York: Basic, 1971. Anthology.

Gray, Madeline. *The Normal Woman.* New York: Scribner's, 1967. Primary value in illuminating data on history of the medical treatment—and mistreatment—of women.

Greer, Germaine. *The Female Eunuch.* New York: McGraw-Hill, 1971. Personal view of female liberation. Serious inaccuracies about current U.S. movement.

Gruberg, Martin. *Women in American Politics: An Assessment and Sourcebook.* Oshkosh, Wisconsin: Academia Press, 1968. Pessimistic view of women's role in mainstream U.S. political activity since 1920, with focus on 1964. Useful bibliography.

Hacker, Helen. "Women as a Minority Group." *Social Forces.* 30 (October, 1951). Includes famous black/female analogy table; treats social distance, marginality, class and caste, etc.

Hartman, Sylvia. "Should Wives Work?" *McCall's.* February, 1969. Feminist's down-to-earth exposition of idea that most men just don't *want* any of the dirty work of "homemaking."

Hawes, Elizabeth. *Fashion is Spinach.* New York: Random, 1938. Designer's forthright discussion of sensible, pleasing clothing— as opposed to fashion.

* Hays, H. R. *The Dangerous Sex: The Myth of Feminine Evil.* New York: Putnam, 1964. Exciting, literate, historical and cross-cultural account of man's fear of woman—especially her genitalia —and of how he has institutionalized that fear.

* Herschberger, Ruth. *Adam's Rib.* New York: Pellegrini and Cudahy, 1948; Harper and Row, 1970. Witty challenge to many assumptions about women, particularly their sexuality. Especially perceptive on semantics of sexual terminology and biology; pre-Kinsey.

Irwin, Inez Haynes. *Up Hill With Banners Flying: The Story of the Woman's Party.* Penobscot, Maine: Traversity Press, 1964. Official, first-hand, post-1912 history; this party kept alive Equal Rights Amendment battle, almost alone, for over 40 years.

* Kanowitz, Leo. *Women and the Law: The Unfinished Revolution.* Albuquerque: University of New Mexico, 1969. Deals with legal aspects of employment, rape, abortion, prostitution, divorce, rights of single and married women, etc. (Since 1969, author's views on Equal Rights Amendment have changed from doubtful to positive.)

* Kinsey, Alfred C., Wardell B. Pomeroy, Clyde E. Martin, and Paul H. Gebhard. *Sexual Behavior in the Human Female.* Philadelphia: Saunders, 1953. Still of great interest. Attitude toward female sexuality displays at least as much feminism as do Masters and Johnson.

Klein, Viola. *The Feminine Character: History of an Ideology.* New York: International Universities, 1946, 1948. Important intellectual history of the idea of "feminine character" and how early

studies in biology, psychology, and social science helped form
that concept.

Komarovsky, Mirra. *Blue Collar Marriage*. New York: Random, 1964.
————. *Women in the Modern World*. Boston: Little, Brown, 1953.
Cultural stresses on educated women are given special attention.
Komisar, Lucy. *The New Feminism*. New York: Franklin Watts,
1971. Aimed at teenage readers.
————. "Violence and the Masculine Mystique." *Washington
Monthly*. July, 1970. Author argues rigid sex roles are major
determinant of war and interpersonal aggression.
Kraditor, Aileen S. *Ideas of the Woman Suffrage Movement, 1890–
1920*. New York: Columbia University, 1965. Key intellectual his-
tory of the movement, especially of split between older and
younger suffragists.
Lake, Alice. "The Day Care Business." *McCall's*. November, 1970.
Details dangers of franchised day care centers.
Leijon, Anna-Greta. *Swedish Women—Swedish Men*. Stockholm:
Swedish Institute for Cultural Relations with Foreign Countries,
1968. Lively account of institutionalized and informal efforts—
successes as well as failures—in altering Swedish sex-role stereo-
types. $2.25, New Yorker Book Shop, 250 West 89 Street, New
York City, 10024.
* Lewis, Oscar. *La Vida*. New York: Vintage, 1965. See for his de-
tailed portraits of poor Latin women in Puerto Rico and New York
City.
Ludovici, L. J. *The Final Inequality*. New York: Norton, 1965. History
and analysis of the misogyny implicit and explicit in religion.
Lynes, Russell. *The Domesticated Americans*. New York: Harper and
Row, 1957, 1963. Popular, informative work on evolution of the
American house; always set in context of culture, society and
family structure.
Mailer, Norman. *The Prisoner of Sex*. Boston: Little, Brown, 1971.
Critique of feminist writings; author ends up prisoner of his own
assumptions about the mystical meanings of sexuality and repro-
duction.
Masters, William H., M.D., and Virginia Johnson. *Human Sexual Re-
sponse*. Boston: Little, Brown, 1966. Key study focusing on em-
pirical observations of physiology of sexual functioning; deliber-
ately couched in heavily medical terms. Cf. Brecher and Brecher,
Section 1.
* Mattfeld, Jacquelyn A., and Carol G. Van Aken, eds. *Women and
the Scientific Professions*. Cambridge: M.I.T., 1965. An M.I.T.
Symposium. See especially contributions of Alice Rossi and Jessie
Bernard.
* Mead, Margaret. *Male and Female*. New York: Morrow, 1949.
Stresses biologically-based cultural "complementarity" of sex
roles. Had subtle but strong influence on contemporary American
society.
* ————. *Sex and Temperament in Three Primitive Societies*. New
York: Peter Smith, 1935. Important early work in comparative

anthropology showing that culture ultimately determines the meaning of sex roles. More feminist than most of her later writings.

Mead, Margaret, and Frances Balgley Kaplan, eds. *American Women: Report of the President's Commission on the Status of Women and Other Publications of the Commission.* New York: Scribner's, 1965. Commission report; condensed committee reports; introduction and epilogue by Mead.

Merriam, Eve. *After Nora Slammed the Door.* Cleveland: World, 1962. Incisive, ironic critique—using prose, poetry, parables—on general topic of women's current dilemma.

Millett, Kate. *Sexual Politics.* Garden City: Doubleday, 1970. Historical, cultural analysis of sexism; literary criticism of D. H. Lawrence, Henry Miller, Norman Mailer, Jean Genêt, especially as their work illuminates the dynamics of power expressed in sexual relations.

* Mitchell, Juliet. "The Longest Revolution." *New Left Review.* 40 (November–December, 1966). Study arguing that role of women has never been properly dealt with throughout history of socialist movements.

* Montagu, Ashley. *The Natural Superiority of Women.* New York: Macmillan, 1962. As title indicates, his biologically-deterministic outlook is hardly feminist.

* Morgan, Robin, ed. *Sisterhood is Powerful.* New York: Random, 1970. Compendium of diverse writings by women's liberation adherents: psychology, law, education, birth control, etc., plus songs, aphorisms; unacknowledged bibliography.

Murray, Pauli, and Mary Eastwood. "Jane Crow and the Law: Sex Discrimination and Title VIII." *George Washington Law Review.* 34:2 (1965). Review of women's legal status, especially in employment. Presents very broad interpretation of how 14th Amendment could be used to achieve legal equality for women.

Myrdal, Alva, and Viola Klein. *Women's Two Roles: Home and Work.* London: Routledge and Kegan Paul, 1956. Advocates women's rights to work outside home but still assigns her chief responsibility for work within it. Very influential in the fifties.

* Myrdal, Gunnar. *An American Dilemma.* New York: Harper, 1941, 1944. Two volumes. The classic Appendix 5, "A Parallel to the Negro Problem," is on women.

* McCarthy, Mary. *On the Contrary: Articles of Belief, 1946–1961.* Revised edition. New York: Noonday, 1951, 1962. Collection of essays including critiques of Lundberg and Farnham (*q.v.,* Section 2) and of the influence of women's magazines. See other works, both essays and fiction.

* McLuhan, H. Marshall. *The Mechanical Bride.* Boston: Beacon, 1951. Early diagnosis of how advertising and media manipulate consumers and play on sexual fears. Many contemporary visual examples.

Newcomer, Mabel. *A Century of Higher Education for American Women.* New York: Harper, 1959. Details contemporary lack of progress—and actual decline—in many areas.

Nolan, Dr. William. "The Operation Women Fear Most." *McCalls.* April, 1971. Argues for research on more humane, less debilitating, treatment for breast cancer.

Nye, F. Ivan, and Lois Wladis Hoffman, eds. *The Employed Mother in America.* New York: Rand McNally, 1963. Key compendium of research findings, most disproving old theories that working mothers are ogres.

O'Neill, William. *Everyone Was Brave: The Rise and Fall of Feminism in America.* Chicago: Quadrangle, 1969. Author sees "Sexual Revolution," marriage, and family as obstacles to further emancipation after suffrage. His concept of "social feminism" does not question sex roles but refers to almost any pursuit women engaged in outside the home.

Pomeroy, Wardell B. *Girls and Sex.* New York: Delacorte, 1969. Sensible book for young girls, with straightforward information and no moralizing. Advocates masturbation as healthy and positive. His 1968 *Boys and Sex* is somewhat more explicitly feminist.

* Rainwater, Lee, Richard P. Coleman, and Gerald Handel. *Workingman's Wife: Her Personality, World, and Lifestyle.* New York: Oceana, 1959. Bleak, revealing portrait of blue-collar women: their concepts of themselves, their men, their world.

* Reed, Evelyn. *Problems of Women's Liberation: A Marxist Approach.* New York: Pathfinder, 1969; revised and enlarged, 1970. Collected articles.

Rossi, Alice S. "Status of Women in Graduate Departments of Sociology, 1968–69." *The American Sociologist.* 5:1 (February, 1970). "Structural analysis" of a problem for which political solutions are now being sought.

* Roszak, Betty and Theodore, eds. *Masculine Feminine: Readings in Sexual Mythology and the Liberation of Women.* New York: Harper and Row, 1971.

Ruderman, Florence. *Child Care and Working Mothers: A Study of Arrangements Made for Daytime Care of Children.* New York: Child Welfare League of America, 1968. Study of maternal employment and child-care arrangements of working women in 7 American cities.

Scott, Anne Firor. *The Southern Lady from Pedestal to Politics.* Chicago: University of Chicago, 1970.

* Sherwin, Robert Veit. *Compatible Divorce.* New York: Crown, 1968. Lawyer gives practical, detailed advice on how to cut the legal bonds with minimum pain to all. Focus on people with money and relative youth.

* Stambler, Sookie, ed. *Women's Liberation: Blueprint for the Future.* New York: Ace, 1970. Anthology.

* Tanner, Leslie B., ed. *Voices from Women's Liberation.* New York: New American Library, 1971. Writings from early and current feminist movements.

* Taves, Isabella. *Women Alone.* New York: Funk and Wagnalls, 1968. Aimed at divorcee and widow, but illuminating for all women who seek self-reliance.

Thompson, Mary Lou, ed. *Voices of the New Feminism.* Boston: Beacon, 1970. Collection of new and reprinted essays. Sponsored by the Unitarian Universalist Women's Federation.

* Tiger, Lionel. *Men in Groups.* New York: Random, 1969. Author's thesis rests upon physical and biological determinism: concludes that what has been is right.

* Veblen, Thorstein. *The Theory of the Leisure Class.* New York: Macmillan, 1899. Classic analysis of women as vehicles of "conspicuous consumption." See also section on women's position at turn of the century.

* Ware, Cellestine. *Woman Power: The Movement for Women's Liberation.* New York: Tower, 1970. A woman in the movement details the origins of the new feminism; New York focus. Includes long chapter on relation of black women to feminist movement.

Welter, Barbara. "The Cult of True Womanhood, 1820–1860." *American Quarterly.* 18 (Summer 1966, part 1). Examines 19th-century version of the "feminine mystique."

White, James J. "Women in the Law." *Michigan Law Review.* 65 (April, 1967). Placement officers, deans, employers, students, on discrimination in legal profession.

* "The Woman in America." *Daedalus.* 93:2 (Spring 1964). See especially articles by Rossi, Degler, Riesman, Erikson, McClelland. Published in book form by Beacon Press, 1965; Robert Jay Lifton, ed.

* *The Woman Question: Selections from the Writings of Karl Marx, Frederick Engels, V. I. Lenin, Joseph Stalin.* New York: International, 1951.

"Women and the Law." *Valparaiso Law Review.* 5:2 (1971). Symposium issue; includes articles on various aspects of the law, many by active feminists.

"Women's Legal Rights in 50 States." *McCall's.* 98:5 (February, 1971). State-by-state graphic guide to various aspects of women's legal status. Some factual errors, especially in abortion law.

Woodward, Helen. *The Lady Persuaders.* New York: Astor-Honor, 1960. History of over 100 years of women's magazines; their important influence on women and society.

* Woolf, Virginia. *A Room of One's Own.* New York: Harcourt, Brace, 1929. Eloquent plea for women's economic independence as a prerequisite for real accomplishment. (See also her fiction and other essays.)

2 PSYCHOLOGY AND PSYCHIATRY

Bem, Daryl J., ed. *Beliefs, Attitudes, and Human Affairs.* Belmont, California: Brooks/Cole, 1970. Includes "Case Study of a Nonconscious Ideology: Training the Woman to Know Her Place," by Sandra L. and Daryl J. Bem.

* Bettelheim, Bruno. *Symbolic Wounds*. New York: Collier, 1962. Examines ritual meaning assigned to sex differences in various cultures.
Deutsch, Helene. *The Psychology of Women*. New York: Grune and Stratton, 1944. 2 volumes. Argues that to be "adult," a female must be narcissistic, masochistic, and passive.
Erikson, Erik H. "Inner and Outer Space: Reflections on Womanhood." In "The Woman in America," *q.v.*, Section 1.
* Freud, Sigmund, trans. A. A. Brill; introduction by H. M. Ruitenbeck. *Three Contributions to the Theory of Sex* (1910). New York: Dutton.
Goldberg, Philip. "Are Women Prejudiced Against Women?" *Trans/Action*. April, 1968. Yes, says this study of college students' attitudes toward scholarly authority.
Horner, Matina, *et al. The Feminine Personality in Conflict*. Belmont, California: Brooks/Cole, 1971. Studies of sex-role and other stresses on modern woman. Includes expanded version, "Fail: Bright Women."
Horney, Karen. *New Ways in Psychoanalysis*. New York: Norton, 1939. The chapter "Feminine Psychology" is a mature development of ideas explored in her early papers; presents rejoinder to penis-envy theory.
* Lundberg, Ferdinand, and Marynia F. Farnham. *Modern Woman: The Lost Sex*. New York: Harper, 1947. Anti-feminist and heavily psychoanalytic. Received much popular attention upon publication.
Maccoby, Eleanor, ed. *The Development of Sex Differences*. Stanford: Stanford University, 1966. Review of psychological literature, much based upon unquestioned acceptance of many traditional assumptions about women. Extensive bibliography.
Maslow, Abraham H. "Self-Actualizing People: A Study of Psychological Health." *Self: Explorations in Personal Growth*. Edited by Clark E. Moustakas. New York: Harper, 1956. Sets forth an influential and fruitful ideal of the mature personality. See especially observations on how healthy people perceive sex roles.
Money, John, ed. *Sex Research, New Developments*. New York: Holt, Rinehart, and Winston, 1965. By a leading researcher in gender-learning; finds that culture, not biology, is ultimate determinant of sex-role identity.
* Sampson, Ronald V. *The Psychology of Power*. New York: Pantheon, 1965. Traces patterns of dominance-and-submission from their roots in the family—between men and women—to the violent international culmination: war.
Seidenberg, Robert. *Marriage in Life and Literature*. New York: Philosophical Library, 1970. Marriage itself may be the real source of "marital problems," and not the people who enter into it, says this psychiatrist, who has been active in NOW. Sources range from clinical material to fiction; his critique, from the rigid legal contract to the uses of power.
Sherman, Julia A. "Problem of Sex Differences in Space Perception

and Aspects of Intellectual Functioning." *Psychological Review.* 74:4 (July, 1967). Apparent "inferiority" of women in analytic reasoning and mathematics explained in critique of the literature, especially of Maccoby (*q.v.*, Section 2).

Stoller, Robert J. *Sex and Gender: On the Development of Masculinity and Femininity.* New York: Science, 1968. Important research study of interplay between culture and biology in establishment of gender identity, and of cross-sex gender aberrations.

Weisstein, Naomi. "'Kinder, Küche, Kirche' as Scientific Law: Psychology Constructs the Female." Paper read at the Davis, California, meeting of the American Studies Association, October 26, 1968. Reprinted in *Sisterhood Is Powerful* (R. Morgan, ed.).

3 REPRODUCTION AND ITS CONTROL

* Bing, Elisabeth. *Six Practical Lessons for an Easier Childbirth.* New York: Grosset and Dunlap, 1967. By prominent instructor in Lamaze method of prepared childbirth.

Bumpass, Larry, and Charles Westoff. "The Perfect Contraceptive Population: Extent and Implications of Unwanted Fertility in the United States." *Science.* 169 (September 4, 1970). The extent: tremendous; major implication: if people were really allowed to use every means to limit their own fertility, U.S. population levels would begin to stabilize.

Clapp, James. *Abortion Legislation in New York State: What Really Happened, and What Can Be Learned From It.* August, 1970. Cautionary article on the 1970 New York law; why and how other states should not copy it. Shows vital link between legislation and litigation. 15¢ from New Yorkers for Abortion Law Repeal (*q.v.*, Sections 7B and 9).

* Doctor X. *The Abortionist.* As told to Lucy Freeman. Garden City: Doubleday, 1962. Revised edition, New York: Grove, 1970. Autobiography of famous abortion specialist, an M.D. who has provided illegal help for thousands of women.

Etzioni, Amitai. "Sex Control, Science, and Society." *Science.* September 13, 1968. Speculates in a somewhat limited manner on the social results of the coming capacity for prenatal sex-choice.

* Gebhard, Paul H., Wardell Pomeroy, Clyde Martin, and Cornelia Christenson. *Pregnancy, Birth and Abortion.* New York: Harper, 1958. Kinsey Institute study of 7000 women. Still important for detailed facts.

Hardin, Garrett. "Abortion—or Compulsory Pregnancy?" *Journal of Marriage and the Family.* 30:2 (May, 1968). Also in *Population, Evolution, and Birth Control*, Hardin, ed., San Francisco: Freeman, 1969. Reverse phrasing of usual question about what is "justifiable." Likens forced childbearing to rape; and argues for women's absolute right to decide to abort. Highly influential.

————. "The History and Future of Birth Control." *Perspectives in Biology and Medicine.* 10:1 (Autumn 1966). See especially his prescient remarks on the probability that an abortifacient will be the future major "contraceptive."

* Himes, Norman E. *A Medical History of Contraception.* Baltimore: Williams and Wilkins, 1936; revised edition, New York: Schocken, 1970. Exhaustive account, from 1850 B.C. to 1962 A.D.

Kennedy, David M. *Birth Control in America: The Career of Margaret Sanger.* New Haven: Yale University, 1970. Covers 1912–1945. Sets movement and Sanger's career in contemporary social and intellectual context, but presents a condescending interpretation of Sanger's feminism, social idealism, and anticlericalism. Chapter 8 details intra-movement disputes over contraception legislation in the 1920's; closely parallels current disputes within the abortion movement. Has fine bibliographic essay.

* Kennedy, Florynce, and Diane B. Schulder. *Abortion Rap.* New York: McGraw-Hill, 1971. Taken from eloquent testimony offered by women, their champions, and their opponents in 1970 class actions challenging New York abortion law. By two of the attorneys involved. Includes section on political role of religious anti-abortion lobbyists.

* Lader, Lawrence. *Abortion.* Indianapolis: Bobbs-Merrill, 1966. Best general work available to date; readable, but now rather dated.

Lucas, Roy. "Federal Constitutional Limitations on the Enforcement and Administration of State Abortion Statutes." *North Carolina Law Review.* 46:4 (June, 1968). Strong logical demonstration of unconstitutionality of abortion laws. Good references; rather feminist, except for treatment of late-abortion issue.

* Maginnis, Patricia T., and Lana Clarke Phelan. *The Abortion Handbook for Responsible Women.* North Hollywood: Contact, 1969. By two abortion activists. Sardonic, graphic descriptions of how to beat the system—and a call to change it entirely.

Rainwater, Lee, *et al. Family Design: Marital Sexuality, Family Size, and Contraception.* Chicago: Aldin, 1965. Important comparison of contraceptive and sexual attitudes and practices of middle- and lower-class couples; see especially for relationship of these to various kinds of marital power structures. Limited by failure to discuss abortion.

Rollin, Betty. "Motherhood: Who Needs It?" *Look.* September 22, 1970. Iconoclastic look at some of our most sacred, unexamined theories about "maternal instinct," marriage, population growth, "feminine fulfillment," etc. Attacks social pressures, not mothers themselves.

Vaughan, Paul. *The Pill on Trial.* New York: Coward-McCann, 1970. Detailed, fair investigative report on the pros and cons of oral contraceptives, their history, and their social impact.

* Wood, H. Curtis, Jr., and William S. Ruben. *Sex Without Babies.* New York: Lancer, 1971. Revised edition. Popular, factual treatment of voluntary sterilization as method of birth control.

4 LITERATURE AND LITERARY CRITICISM

Aristophanes. *The Women at Demeter's Festival* (411 B.C.). Women conspire to ruin Euripides because of his misogyny. See other works.

Austen, Jane. *Pride and Prejudice* (1813). Aside from many other qualities, this novel is a devastating critique of the economic function of marriage. See also her other novels and the volume *Early Works*.

* Brontë, Charlotte. See all works.

* Brontë, Emily. See all works.

* Eliot, George. *The Mill on the Floss* (1860). Autobiographical novel of great Victorian woman rebel (Marian Evans). See other novels.

* Ellmann, Mary. *Thinking About Women*. New York: Harcourt, Brace, and World, 1968. Feminist literary criticism; subtle, incisive, devastatingly witty examinations of Mailer *et al.*

* Fiedler, Leslie. *Love and Death in the American Novel*. Revised edition. New York: Dell, 1967. One issue he considers is the continuing dearth of realistic female characters in American literature, and deep-seated reasons for this lack.

Fisher, Elizabeth. "The Second Sex, Junior Division." *The New York Times Book Review*. May 24, 1970. Surveys portrayal of females in children's books.

Ibsen, Henrik. *A Doll's House* (1879). A 19th-century wife "withdraws consent to oppression." See other works.

* Lamb, Myrna. *The Mod Donna and Scyklon Z: Plays of Women's Liberation*. New York: Pathfinder, 1970. Includes play on abortion, "But What Have You Done For Me Lately?" in which a man is unwillingly pregnant.

* Lessing, Doris. *The Golden Notebook*. New York: Ballantine, 1968. Novel about a woman alone with her child in postwar London; important insights into her attempts to achieve independence, and her experience with the Left. See also other works.

* Lewis, Sinclair. *Main Street: The Story of Carol Kennicott*. New York: Harcourt, 1920. Classic portrait of a midwestern woman with ambitions beyond what she can attain. See other works.

* Moore, Brian. *The Lonely Passion of Judith Hearne*. Boston: Little Brown, 1955. Sensitive portrait of a single woman in a world which ridicules and rejects the single woman.

Parker, Dorothy. *The Collected Poetry of Dorothy Parker*. New York: Modern Library, 1944.

————. *The Collected Stories of Dorothy Parker*. New York: Modern Library, 1942.

Plath, Sylvia. *The Bell Jar*. New York: Harper and Row, 1971. A poet's sensitive and more-or-less autobiographical novel.

* Katharine M. Rogers. *The Troublesome Helpmate: A History of Misogyny in Literature*. Seattle: University of Washington, 1966.

* Stead, Christina. *The Man Who Loved Children* (1940). New York: Holt, Rinehart, and Winston, 1965. Striking novel of a family in prewar Washington, D.C., and its gradual destruction by internal stresses.

5 WORKS BY AND BIOGRAPHIES OF
   EARLY FEMINISTS (to 1920)

Anthony, Susan B., Elizabeth Cady Stanton, Matilda Joslin Gage, and Ida Husted Harper. *The History of Woman Suffrage.* Volumes 1–4 —New York: Fowler and Wells, 1881–1902. Volumes 5–6—New York: National American Woman Suffrage Association, 1922. (Six volumes—New York: Arno and The New York Times, 1969.) The famous history written by suffrage leaders; includes memoirs, letters, newspaper articles, speeches, reports, etc.
* Bernard, Jacqueline. *Journey Toward Freedom: The Story of Sojourner Truth.* New York: Norton, 1967. Biography of an ex-slave woman. Especially directed toward young people.
Dell, Floyd. *Women as World Builders: Studies in Modern Feminism.* Chicago, 1913. Biographies of E. Pankhurst, Gilman, Schreiner, Goldman, and others.
Gilman, Charlotte Perkins. *The Man-made World: Or, Our Androcentric Culture* (1911). New York: Source Book, 1971.
* ———. *Women and Economics* (1898). New York: Harper, 1966 (Carl N. Degler, ed. and introduction). Classic exposition of thesis that evolution of the human species suffers from effects of women's economic dependence upon men. Influence of Darwinism on Gilman is strong.
Goldman, Emma. *Living My Life* (1931). New York: Dover. 2 volumes. An early anarchist and birth-control advocate.
Grimké, Angelina. *Appeal to the Christian Women of the South* (1836). New York: Arno, 1969.
Grimké, Sarah M. *Letters on the Equality of the Sexes and the Condition of Woman* (1838). New York: Source Book, 1970.
* Kraditor, Aileen S., ed. *Up From the Pedestal: Selected Documents in the History of American Feminism.* Chicago: Quadrangle, 1968.
Lerner, Gerda. *The Grimké Sisters from South Carolina: Rebels Against Slavery.* Boston: Houghton Mifflin, 1967. Excellent study of early abolitionist-feminist family and its social milieu.
Lutz, Alma. *Created Equal.* New York: John Day, 1940. The biography of Elizabeth Cady Stanton.
———. *Emma Willard, Pioneer Educator of American Women.* Boston: Beacon, 1964.
———. *Susan B. Anthony.* Boston: Beacon, 1959.
* Mill, John Stuart and Harriet Taylor Mill. *Essays on Sex Equality.* Edited and with introductory essay by Alice S. Rossi. Chicago:

University of Chicago, 1971. Rossi describes how the Mills' contemporaries and later scholars have denigrated Harriet Taylor Mill's part in their common intellectual life and work. Includes "On the Subjection of Women" (1869).

Stanton, Elizabeth Cady. *Eight Years and More (1815–1897): Reminiscences of Elizabeth Cady Stanton* (1898). New York: Source Book, 1970.

——, Parker Pillsbury, Laura C. Bullard, and W. T. Clarke, eds. *The Revolution* (1868–1872). 8 volumes of the magazine. New York: Source Book, 1971.

——, *et al. The Woman's Bible.* New York: European, 1895, 1898. Two parts. A feminist exigesis of both testaments.

Stevens, Doris. *Jailed for Freedom.* New York: Boni and Liveright, 1920. Includes account of suffragists' incarceration in Occoquam prison; author was among them.

* Wollstonecraft, Mary. *A Vindication of the Rights of Women* (1792). 18th-century feminist classic, by a woman who tried to live what she preached.

6 ARTICLES ABOUT THE CURRENT WOMEN'S MOVEMENT

Brownmiller, Susan. "Sisterhood Is Powerful." *The New York Times Magazine.* March 15, 1970. An inside view of some New York City groups by a member of New York Radical Feminists.

Conley, Madelyn. "Do Black Women Need the Women's Lib?" *Essence.* August, 1970. Interviews with black women indicate that the answer to this question and its reciprocal can be positive.

Davidson, Sara. "Militants for Women's Rights." *Life.* December 12, 1969. Sensitive, personal account of some groups in the movement; focuses on New York.

Dudar, Helen. "Women's Lib: The War on 'Sexism'." *Newsweek.* March 23, 1970. The author's own emerging feelings are the most interesting element in her coverage of the current movement.

"Five Passionate Feminists." *McCall's.* July, 1970. Edited from taped interveiws with Judy Stein, Anne Koedt, James Clapp, Ellen Willis and Mrs. Malcolm Peabody.

Freeman, Jo. "The New Feminists." *Nation.* 208:8 (February 24, 1969). Description of current movement by one of its earliest activists.

Gornick, Vivian. "Women's Liberation: The Next Great Moment in History Is Theirs." *Village Voice.* November 27, 1969. Sympathetic, personal account of some aspects of current movement. Several factual errors.

Hinckle, Warren and Marianne. "A History of the Rise of the Unusual Movement for Women Power in the United States 1961–1968." *Ramparts.* February, 1968. Women activists criticized tone and content as both patronizing and inaccurate. One of the first magazine articles on current movement.

Lear, Martha Weinman. "The Second Feminist Wave: What Do These Women Want?" *The New York Times Magazine*. March 10, 1968. Very early and rather ambivalent description of current movement and of some of the people involved in it.

Lyon, Lilla. "The March of TIME's Women." *New York*. 4:8 (February 22, 1971). Detailed description of women editorial employees' suit against Time, Inc.

Steinem, Gloria. "What it would be like if women win." *Time*. August 31, 1970. Essay describing a future without sexism.

"A Woman's Place." Special supplement to *The Atlantic*. March, 1970. Articles by people within and without feminist movement, including Catherine Drinker Bowen, Benjamin DeMott, Elizabeth Janeway, Sandie North, Alice Rossi, Diane Schulder.

"Women re Women." Special section of *Mademoiselle*. February, 1970. Uneven collection of articles. Worthy of special mention: those by Hortense Calisher, Amy Gross, Elizabeth Hardwick, Rebecca West.

"Women MD's Join the Fight." *Medical World News*. 11:43 (October 23, 1970).

YWCA Magazine. Special issue on women's movement. 65:1 (January, 1971). Emphasizes class and race issues.

7 WRITINGS FROM THE CURRENT WOMEN'S MOVEMENT (for books, see Section 1)

Since women's movement groups and their locations, publications, and prices change, or even disappear without notice a special effort was made to select relatively stable sources for literature and information. When corresponding with those listed: include a return address on envelope; include proper payment or send a first-class postage stamp for prompt response.

7A—*Pamphlets, journals, articles, special issues:*

Allen, Pam. *Free Space: A Perspective on the Small Group in Women's Liberation*. New York: Times Change, 1970. Handbook for women in, or wanting to form, a small group.

Bird, Caroline. "What's Television Doing for 50.9% of Americans." *TV Guide*. February 27, 1971.

Cornell Conference on Women (January 22–25, 1969). 100-page edited transcript of panels on many aspects of women's situation; Sheila Tobias *et al.*, eds. $2.00 from KNOW, Inc. (*q.v.*, Section 9).

Feelings. July, 1970. By a group of New York feminists. Mostly litterary, but also includes piece about women's oppression in clerical jobs. $1.00 from Feelings, 243 Baltic Street, Brooklyn, N.Y. 11201.

Freeman, Jo. "The Building of the Gilded Cage." Describes mechanisms of social control over women, with emphasis on law and socialization. Extensive documentation. Reprinted in "Green Hearings" (U.S. Congress, House, 1970; *q.v.*, Section 10). Also reprinted in *Notes From the Third Year.*

————. "The Revolution Is Happening in Our Minds." *College and University Business.* February, 1970.

Gainesville [Fla.], Women's Liberation. Softbound collection of original and reprinted literature. $1.00 from Gainesville WL, Box 13248, University Station, Gainesville, Fla. 32601.

Hayden, Casey, *et al.* "Sex and Caste." *Liberation.* Part I: April, 1966; Part II: December, 1966. Early exchange about relation of women to contemporary radical movements.

How Harvard Rules Women. June, 1970. 80-page collection of articles edited by female members of the New University Conference. 75¢ from NUC, 14 Glenwood Avenue, Cambridge, Mass. 02139.

Jones, Beverly, and Judith Brown. *Toward a Female Liberation Movement.* 1968. "Known as "the Florida paper." 40 pages. 30¢ from Everywoman Bookstore (*q.v.*, Section 9).

Kempton, Sally. "Cutting Loose: A Private View of the Women's Uprising." *Esquire.* July, 1970.

Leviathan. "Women Unite" issue. 2:1 (May, 1970). 60¢ from Leviathan, 968 Valencia Street, San Francisco, Calif. 94110.

National Organization for Women: New York Chapter. Education Committee (Kate Millett, *et al.*) *Token Learning: A Study of Women's Higher Education in America.* Fall 1968. 57 pages. Out of print.

"The New Feminism." *Ladies' Home Journal.* August, 1970. Supplement touching on many topics; written by group of women who took part in March, 1970, *Ladies' Home Journal* sit-in.

"On the Liberation of Women." Special issue of *Motive.* 29:6–7 (March–April, 1969). Striking graphics; poetry and articles by many movement women.

Professional Women's Caucus. "Sixteen Reports on the Status of Women in the Professions." Presented at founding conference of PWC, April 11, 1970. $2.00 from KNOW, Inc. (*q.v.*, Section 9).

Radical America. Special issue on Women's Liberation. February, 1970. 75¢ from Radical America, 1237 Spaight St., Madison, Wis. 53703.

The Radical Therapist. Special issue on women, edited by Judith Brown. 1:3 (August–September, 1970). Reprints various women's movement articles and manifestos. $1.00 from The Radical Therapist, Box 1215, Minot, N.D. 58701.

United Presbyterian Church in the U.S.A. Task Force on Women and the Standing Committee on Women. "Report of the Task Force . . . [to the] 182nd General Assembly . . ." and "Presentation Made by the Task Force on Women to Introduce its Report. . . ." May 25, 1970. Discrimination in society and in the church, with a program to combat it. 50¢ from Women's Program, Board of Chris-

tian Education, United Presbyterian Church, 730 Witherspoon
Building, Philadelphia, Pa. 19107.
Weisstein, Naomi. " 'Kinder, Küche, Kirche' as Scientific Law: Psychology Constructs the Female." *q.v.* Section 2.
Willis, Ellen. "Up From Radicalism: A Feminist Journal." *US* #2.
New York: Bantam, 1969. A personal account of the author's
move from radical left politics into the women's movement.
Women's Liberation on Child Care. 1970. Articles on theory and practical problems, including piece on how a male-staffed center is
working. 30 pages. 75¢ from Women's Union Child Care Collective, c/o Women's Liberation Center of New York (*q.v.*, Section
9).

7B   *Periodicals and Other Periodic Mailings:*

Ain't I a Woman? Midwest newspaper of women's liberation. $4.00
for 24 copies, from Iowa City WLF Publications Collective, Box
1169, Iowa City, Iowa 52240.
The Alliance Link. Newsletter of the Equal Rights Alliance. For subscription data send stamped envelope to Equal Rights Alliance,
5256 Fairmount, Downers Grove, Ill. 60515.
Aphra. Feminist literary quarterly. $1.00 a copy, or $3.50 for 4
issues, from Aphra, Box 355, Springtown, Pa. 18081.
Everywoman. Newspaper. $6.00 per year (26 issues, US subscrip-
tion), or $15.00 for institutions, from Everywoman, 1043B West
Washington Boulevard, Venice, Calif. 90291.
FEW's News and Views. Newsletter of Federally Employed Women,
Inc. $3.00 per year, from FEW, Suite 487, National Press Build-
ing, Washington, D.C. 20004.
Feminist Studies. Analytic quarterly of original papers, notes and re-
views. $2.00 per copy, from Feminist Studies, 606 W. 116 St.,
New York City 10027.
Human Rights for Women, Inc. Bulletins on their activities in re-
search, litigation, and other areas. $3.00 to HRW, Box 7402,
Benjamin Franklin Station, Washington, D.C. 20044.
KNOW News Service. Bulletins on single topics. $3.00 per year from
KNOW, Inc., Box 10197, Pittsburgh, Pa. 15232.
The Ladder. Bimonthly magazine, "published since 1956 by Lesbians
and directed to ALL women seeking full human dignity." $1.00 for
sample back issue (Aug.–Sept. 1970 issue includes "The Woman-
Identified Woman" by Brown, Hart, *et al.*); $7.50 per year from
The Ladder, Box 5025, Washington Station, Reno, Nev. 89503.
The New Broom. A monthly legislative newsletter for Massachusetts
women. $6.00 per year from The New Broom, Box 341, Prudential
Center Station, Boston, Mass. 02199.
New Yorkers for Abortion Law Repeal. Monthly mailings on contraception and abortion topics of national relevance. $5.00 per year
from NYALR, Box 240, Planetarium Station, New York City
10024.

A Journal of Female Liberation (*No More Fun and Games*). Theoretical and literary writings; published irregularly. Current issue: $1.00 from Cell 16, 16 Lexington Avenue, Cambridge, Mass. 02138.

Notes from the Second Year: Women's Liberation—Major Writings of the Radical Feminists. April, 1970. 126 pages. Included are, "The BITCH Manifesto" (Joreen), "The Politics of Housework" (P. Mainardi), "The Myth of the Vaginal Orgasm" (A. Koedt), "Female Liberation as the Basis for Social Revolution" (R. Dunbar), "Abortion Law Repeal (sort of): a Warning to Women" (L. Cisler), and ,manifestos from Redstockings, New York Radical Feminists, and The Feminists. $1.50 a copy from Notes, Box AA, Old Chelsea Station, New York City 10011.

Notes from the Third Year: Radical Feminism. 1971. $1.50 a copy from Notes, Box AA, Old Chelsea Station, New York City 10011.

NOW Acts. National publication of NOW (National Organization for Women). Issued about 6 times a year. $1 a copy; subscription free to NOW members; others, $5.00 per year from NOW, 1957 East 73 St., Chicago, Ill. 60649. Source for information about local chapters, many of these newsletters may be subscribed to by nonmembers.

Off Our Backs. Newspaper. 25¢ a copy; $6.00 per year; $15.00 for businesses, schools, institutions, from Off Our Backs, Box 4859, Cleveland Park Station, Washington, D.C. 20008.

The Pedestal. Monthly newspaper. Single issue 25¢; $2.50 per year; $10.00 for institutions, libraries, universities, from Vancouver Women's Caucus, 511 Carrall St., Vancouver, B.C., Canada.

Rat. Newspaper published by a women's collective. $6.00 per year from Rat, 241 East 14 St., New York City 10009.

Skirting the Capitol. Newsletter about legislation and women (California focus). $15.00 per year, from Box 4569, Sacramento, Calif. 95825.

The Spokeswoman. Monthly newsletter on women's status and the women's movement. $6.00 per year from Urban Research Corporation, 5464 South Shore Dr., Chicago, Ill. 60615.

Up From Under. Magazine, directed toward working-class women. 60¢ a copy; $3.00 per year, from Up From Under, 339 Lafayette St., New York City 10003.

WEAL Word Watcher. Newsletter of Women's Equity Action League. For subscription information: WEAL, Box 30142, Midpoint P.O., Middleburg Heights, Ohio 44130.

The Woman Activist. Monthly newsletter: focus on federal legislation and Equal Rights Amendment. $5.00 per year from 2310 Barbour Rd., Falls Church, Va. 22043.

Woman's World. Newspaper edited by women from the former New York Redstockings group. $3.00 per year from Box 949, Radio City Station, New York City 10019.

Women: A Journal of Liberation. Quarterly. $1.00 a copy; $4.00 per year; $5.00 for institutions, from 3028 Greenmount Ave., Baltimore, Md. 21218.

The Women's Page. Newspaper. $2.00 for 6 months, from Box 14145, San Francisco, Calif. 94114.

Women's Rights Law Reporter. Journal. $1.00 a copy, from Women's Rights Law Reporter, 180 University Avenue, Newark, N.J. 07102.

8 BIBLIOGRAPHIES AND SYLLABI

Cisler, Lucinda. *Women: a Bibliography.* New York: Cisler, 1968, 1969, 1970. Annotated, categorized reading list, periodically revised and enlarged. Sixth Edition (1970): over 900 entries. Order from Lucinda Cisler, P.O. Box 240, New York City 10024 (prepaid orders and U.S. funds only): 50¢ a copy; 10/$4.50; 30/$12.00; 100/$30 (prices include postage *only* for third-class or book-rate to U.S. points; one copy weighs 2 oz.)

Damon, Gene, and Lee Stuart. *The Lesbian in Literature: a Bibliography.* $2.25 from The Ladder, Box 5025, Washington Station, Reno, Nev. 89503.

Ditzion, Sidney. *Marriage, Morals, and Sex in America: A History of Ideas.* New York: Bookman, 1953; Octagon, 1970. Bibliographic essay; see especially treatment of interrelation between social and sexual reform movements and 19th-century feminist movement.

Farians, Elizabeth J. *Selected Bibliography on Women and Religion.* Revised. Extensive reading list of articles and news stories, 1965–1971, by feminist Catholic theologian. 75¢ from the compiler, 6125 Webbland Place, Cincinnati, Ohio 45213.

Female Studies I: A Collection of College Syllabi and Reading Lists. 1970. Sheila Tobias, compiler. $2.50 from KNOW, Inc. (*q.v.,* Section 9).

Female Studies II. 1971. Florence Howe, compiler. $4.00 from KNOW, Inc. (*q.v.,* Section 9).

Feminists on Children's Media. *Little Miss Muffet Fights Back: Recommended Non-Sexist Books About Girls for Young Readers.* New York: Feminists on Children's Media, 1971. Annotated listing of about 200 works of fiction and non-fiction for children 3–15. Single copies: 35¢ and a self-addressed, stamped (16¢) business envelope, from publisher, Box 4315, Grand Central Station, New York City 10017.

Hughes, Marija M. *The Sexual Barrier: Legal and Economic Aspects of Employment.* September, 1970, revision. About 500 entries, 1959–1970. $5.00 from compiler, 2422 Fox Plaza, San Francisco, Calif. 94102.

Nower, Joyce. *Selected Bibliography of Women Writers.* San Diego: mimeo., 1970. 17 pages; international coverage. 50¢ from Joyce Nower, Center for Women's Studies, San Diego State College, San Diego, Calif.

Spiegel, Jeanne. *Sex Role Concepts: How Women and Men See Themselves and Each Other.* Washington, D.C.: Business and Professional Women's Foundation, 1969. Selected, annotated, non-evaluative bibliography, 1959–1969; includes books, pamphlets, reports, theses, articles, and microfilm. One of a series of BPW bibliographies; others include *Continuing Education for Women* (1967) and *Working Mothers* (1968). Single copies free (50¢ each in bulk) from BPW Foundation, 2012 Massachusetts Ave., N.W., Washington, D.C. 10036.

9 Sources for Original Material and Reprints

Association for the Study of Abortion, 120 West 57 St., New York City 10019. Source for several dozen reprints and texts of judicial opinions. Newsletter; reprint list—revised quarterly.

Day Care and Child Development Council of America, Inc., 1426 H St., N.W., Washington, D.C. 20005. Newsletter and various useful reprints and publications on this issue; maintains a record of relevant legislation.

Everywoman Bookstore, 1043B West Washington Blvd., Venice, Calif. 90291. Distribution source for many books by and about women as well as specifically women's liberation materials. Current catalog: 10¢ plus stamp.

The Feminists, 120 Liberty St., New York City 10006. 15–20 papers by The Feminists, on theory, group history, and goals: $2.00. For current literature list, send stamped envelope.

KNOW, Inc., Box 10197, Pittsburgh, Pa. 15232. Reprints many periodical articles on women's issues, especially in psychology and education. For current list of publications, send stamped envelope.

National Woman's Party, 144 Constitution Ave., Washington, D.C. 20002. Send stamped envelope for list of available materials; focus on Equal Rights Amendment.

New England Free Press, 791 Tremont St., Boston, Mass. 02118. General source for reprints on various issues, including many from women's movement. Write for current literature list.

New York Radical Feminists, Box 621, Old Chelsea Station, New York City 10011. "An Introduction to the New York Radical Feminists." Principles, programs, and ideas for starting groups; includes complete current NYRF literature list. Send 10¢ and stamped business envelope.

New Yorkers for Abortion Law Repeal, Box 240, Planetarium Station, New York City 10024. Source for variety of original feminist literature and factual information, on both contraception and abortion issues. 50¢ for sample packet.

Society for Humane Abortion, Inc., Box 1862, San Francisco, Calif. 94101. Send stamped envelope for list of reprints and original publications; quarterly newsletter.

Women's Bureau, U.S. Department of Labor, Washington, D.C. 20210. Source for many valuable publications, especially in areas

of economics, law, and education. Send for *Leaflet #10,* a list of current publications; also *Know Your Rights,* a summary of legal rights of American women.
Women's Heritage Series, 838 Fifteenth St., Santa Monica, Calif. 90403. Publishes and distributes variety of original materials. For list of offerings, send 10¢ and stamp.
Women's History Research Center, 2325 Oak St., Berkeley, Calif. 94708. Send 10¢ and stamped envelope for list of items available: synopsis of women in history, running catalogue of extensive Center library, women's song-book, back issues of SPAZM newsletter, etc.
Women's Liberation Center of New York, 36 West 22 St., New York City 10010. Distributes original materials and reprints; send two 8-cent stamps for list.

10   U.S. GOVERNMENT PUBLICATIONS

Citizens' Advisory Council on the Status of Women. "The Proposed Equal Rights Amendment to the United States Constitution." Memorandum, 1970. Single copies from Department of Labor, Washington, D.C. 20210.
President's Commission on the Status of Women. *American Women.* The report of the Kennedy-appointed commission. 1963. (Also available, Reports of the Committees; Report on Four Consultants.) From Department of Labor, Washington, D.C. 20210.
President's Task Force on Women's Rights and Responsibilities. *A Matter of Simple Justice.* Report of findings and recommendations of Nixon task force. 1970. Single copies free from Department of Labor, Washington, D.C. 20210.
U.S. Congress. House. Committee on Education and Labor. Special Subcommittee on Education. *Discrimination Against Women.* Hearings, 91st Congress, Second Session, on Section 805 of H.R. 16098. Washington, D.C., 1970. 2 volumes. "Green hearings." Massive compendium of status reports, testimony, and feminist articles. Available from any Member of Congress.
————. ————. Committee on the Judiciary. Subcommittee #4. Hearings, 92nd Congress, First Session, on H.J. Res. 208, the Equal Rights Amendment, and H.R. 916, the "Women's Equality Act." Washington, D.C., 1971.
————. Senate. Committee on the Judiciary. Subcommittee on Constitutional Amendments. *The "Equal Rights" Amendment.* Hearings, 91st Congress, Second Session, on S.J. Res. 61. Washington, D.C., 1970.
————. ————. ————. *Equal Rights 1970.* Hearings, 91st Congress, Second Session, on S.J. Res. 61 and S.J. Res. 231. Washington, D.C., 1970.
Women's Bureau, U.S. Department of Labor. *Handbook on Women*

Workers. 1969. Valuable source for many facts and statistics. Periodically revised. Single copies free from Women's Bureau, Washington, D.C. 20210.
————. Interdepartmental Committee and Citizens' Advisory Council on the Status of Women. *American Women 1963–68.* 1968. Progress Report.
————. ————. Reports of the Task Forces to Citizens' Advisory Council. 1968. Family Law and Policy; Health and Welfare; Labor Standards; Social Insurance and Taxes. Abortion law repeal, child-care provisions, and major tax reforms were some of the recommendations.

SELECTED ADDENDA *(as of August 1972)*

* Cohen, Susan. *The Liberated Couple.* New York: Lancer, 1971. Popularized exposition of feminist ideas.
Frankfort, Ellen. *Vaginal Politics.* New York: Quadrangle, 1972. Collection of articles on health issues, primarily from author's *Village Voice* column.
* Freeman, Jo. "The Women's Liberation Movement: Its Origins, Structure, and Ideas." Published in *Family, Marriage and the Struggle of the Sexes* (Hans Peter Dreitzel, ed.) New York: Macmillan, 1972.
Janeway, Elizabeth. *Man's World, Woman's Place: A Study in Social Mythology.* New York: Morrow, 1971.
Koedt, Anne, Ellen Levine and Anita Rapone, eds. *Radical Feminism.* New York: Quadrangle, 1972. Antholgy of contemporary writings, drawn chiefly from the journal *Notes.*
* Levine, Ellen. *All She Needs. . . .* New York: Quadrangle, 1972. Satirical feminist drawings.
Majority Report. Monthly newspaper of feminism in the New York area. $3.00 for 10 issues, from *MR,* 89–19 171st St., Jamaica, New York 11432.
Mitchell, Juliet. *Woman's Estate.* New York: Pantheon, 1972. Expansion of earlier essays placing women's movement in Marxist/socialist context.
Morgan, Elaine. *The Descent of Woman.* New York: Stein & Day, 1972. A fresh look at the evolution of the species.
Ms. New mass-circulation feminist monthly magazine. $9.00 per year, from *Ms.,* 370 Lexington Avenue, New York City 10017.
* Schneir, Miriam, ed. *Feminism: The Essential Historical Writings.* New York: Random, 1972. A selective anthology.
Shulman, Alix Kates. *Memoirs of an Ex-Prom Queen.* New York: Knopf, 1972. Novel by a movement activist.
* Strainchamps, Ethel, ed. *The Media Papers.* New York: Quadrangle, 1972. What it's like for women in the media, as told anonymously by more than 60 women who have worked in the field.

INDEX

Abolition Movement, 2, 3, 5, 8, 14
abortion, 26, 187, 188, 228n., 246, 265, 278–302
 "Abortion Laws The Cruel Fraud," 291n.
 actions, 410, 419
 AMA, 290, 419
 Assoc. for Study of, 281n., 284
 Catholic Church, 281, 290, 291–92
 Citizen's Council, 26, 279n., 407
 Conference for Repeal, 221n.
 Congress to Unite Women, 150
 counseling-referral services, 284, 290, 299–302
 court decisions on, 280, 284, 285–86n., 294, 426
 division on, 188–89, 190, 278, 279, 288–89
 fees, 300–301
 laws, 279–81, 283, 284, 285
  reasons for repeal, 281–82, 283–84
 Nixon on, 292–93, 294, 425
 NOW, 89, 279, 295, 299, 406
 NYC, 365
 political actions, 294–99, 410
 "quickening," 279, 281, 288
 Redstockings, 136, 296–97, 298, 369, 410
 Reform/Repeal Movement, 282–94
  organizations, 290–91, 393
   ARAL, 284, 295–96, 299, 360n., 361n.
   NYALR, 150, 279n., 287n., 296, 409
  reform states, 284, 405
  repeal qualifications, 286–88
  repeal states, 285–86, 415, 416, 419
 The Feminists, 143
 theological positions, 281
 UAW, 106
 viability, 288
 woman's right to, 289
 women's liberation, 92, 278–79, 286–92, 294–302
 women's strike, 93, 299
 YWCA, 291, 295
Abzug, Rep. Bella, 427
"Academic Women, The Status of," 326n.
actions, 245–46
 see also media; abortion; childcare; education; professions; church; tactics
Adam's Fractured Rib, 384n.
Adam's rib, 12, 380
Adam's Rib, 172n., 173n., 174n., 175n., 179n., 182–84
Advertising Age, 262n.

agricultural labor, 29, 69
Agriculture, U.S. Dep't of, 41, 312n.
Air Force, U.S., Director of Women, 210
Alaska, 285–86, 416
alimony, 26, 64, 66, 67
Allan, Virginia, 49, 80
Allen, Pam, 115, 121n.
Allred v. Heaton, 61n.
Altbach, Edith Hoshine, 287n.
Alverno College, Milwaukee, 385
"AMA Abortion Position Liberalized," 290n.
Amatniek, Kathie, 118
American Assoc. of University Professors, (AAUP), 325, 416
American Assoc. of University Women, (AAUW), 318n.
American Baptist Convention, 395, 421–22
American Bar Association, 349, 351
American Civil Liberties Union (ACLU), 101, 418
American Council on Education, 317
American Federation of Teachers, 333, 420
American Film Institute of Washington, D.C., 252, 422
American Journal of Sociology, 344
American Law Institute, 282, 283, 284, 285, 290
American Library Association, 335
American Medical Assoc. (AMA), 358
 on abortion, 290, 419
 coed sports, 422–23
 Convention, 298, 419
American Medical News, 290n.
American Newspaper Publishers Assoc. 43, 408
American Political Science Assoc., 344–45, 412
 see also professional women
American Political Science Review, 345
American Psychological Assoc., 340, 346, 347
American Sociological Assoc., 342, 343, 344, 412
American Sociological Review, 344
American Sociologist, The, 317n., 343n., 344n.
American Studies Assoc., 173n., 408
American Telephone and Telegraph Co., 423
American Woman Suffrage Assoc., 10, 11, 12
American Women, 18, 20, 21, 22n., 23n., 24, 25n., 402
Anderson, Mary, 79n.

Anthony, Rep. Daniel, 54
Anthony, Susan B., 3n., 5, 9, 10, 11, 12, 13, 54, 227, 342, 393
"Anthony Amendment," 13
anti-feminism, 8, 12, 195, 216, 226–42, 306
"Anything You Can Do . . .", 221n.
"Are Women Prejudiced Against Women?," 201n.
Art Forum, 367
Art News, 367
Art Workers Coalition, 365–66
Arts, The, 365–71
  Painting and Sculpture, 365–68, 423
  Theater, 162, 299, 369–71, 411
Associated Press, 339n.
Atkinson, Ti-Grace, 90, 91, 101, 143, 145, 147, 154n., 196n., 207n., 425
Atlantic Monthly, 258
Austen, Jane, 205n.
"Authority of Possibility for Women in The Church, An," 380n.
Authors' Guild, 334
Ayre Directory of Newspapers, 248n.

Background on Federal Action Toward Equal Opportunity for Women, 45n., 46n.
Baird, Bill, 284, 299
Baltimore, Md., 271, 332, 337
Baltimore Sun, 333
Bartl, Joan, 335
Baxandall, Rosalyn, 308n., 310, 312n.
Bay of Pigs, 174, 175
Bayh, Sen. Birch, 55–56
Beauvoir, Simone de, 175, 178n., 192–93, 197, 198n., 206, 209, 210n., 213, 214, 215n., 220, 323
Beirne, Gerry, 369
Belair, Felix, Jr., 217n.
Beliefs, Attitudes and Human Affairs, 176n.
Bem, S. L. and D. J., 176, 185n., 199n., 205, 206
Bennetti, Susan, 362n., 363n., 364n.
Berger, Caruthers, 101
Berman, Edgar, 174, 175, 417
Best Word Book Ever, 200
Bettelheim, Bruno, 181, 347
bfoq (*bona fide* occupational qualification), 31–32, 34–35, 36–37, 38, 41, 45, 46, 68, 404, 410, 413, 424
Bible, The, 380, 382, 383
Bill of Rights for Women, 88
biological differences, 76, 170, 171–93
  biology, 172–76, 417
  morality, 184–86
  politics of, 192–93
  primate studies, 172–74
  psychology, 176–84
  sex hormones, 174–76
  technology, 186–91
Bird, Caroline, 30n., 31, 34n., 64, 83n., 266, 304
Bird, Joan, 151

birth control, 390, 414
Bill of Rights, 88, 89
blacks, 188–89, 190
  Citizens' Council, 26
  information, 187
  moral issue, 185
  NYALR, 296
Bitch Declaration of Independence, 233
"Bitch Manifesto, The," 210n., 233–235
black liberation, 148–49, 188
Black Panther women, 151, 254
black power, 116
black studies, 326
Black Woman, The: An Anthology, 149n., 190n.
blacks, 50, 82, 260, 263, 270
  birth control, 188–89, 190
  civil rights movement, 108, 110, 111, 116
  CORE, 110
  federal employment, 99
  in films, 252
  NAACP, 110
  NCNP Conference, 112
  slavery, 2, 5
  SNCC, 110, 111
  women, 20, 71, 75, 148–49, 190
  Women's Bureau, 53
  see also racism; Constitutional Amendments
Blackwell, Elizabeth, 342
Blaisdell, Virginia, 218n.
Block, Rita, 341
Bloomer, Amelia, 8
Booth, Heather, 112
bona fide occupational qualification, *see bfoq*
Born Female, 30n., 304
Boston, 164, 171, 276, 292n., 384, 385
Boston Female Anti-Slavery Society, 3
Boston Female Liberation, 150, 151, 271n.
Bowe v. Colgate-Palmolive Co., 37, 86, 86n., 101, 106, 413
Boy Scouts of America, 425
Boyer, Elizabeth, 95, 96, 98n.
Boylan, Ann Marie, 352n., 353n.
Bozell, Patricia Buckley, 425
"bra-burning," 123, 136, 229–30, 266, 408
Bradlee, Benjamin, 263
Bradwell v. the State, 71, 71n.
"Brainwashing and Women," 140
Bram, Joseph, 223
Bread and Roses, 276
"Bread and Roses," 148n., 411
Brewer, Earl, D. C., 389n.
Brewster, Kingman, Jr., 415
Bridal Fair Exposition, 128–29, 410
Brown, Judith, 111n., 142n., 407
Brownmiller, Susan, 179n.
Brush v. San Francisco Newspaper Printing Co., 43
"Building of the Gilded Cage, The," 198–99, 203n., 226n., 227n.
"bunny law," 34, 403

Bunting, Mary, 404
"Burial of Traditional Womanhood,
    The," 117–18, 406
Burns, Arthur, 48–49
Burris, Carol, 306n., 314n.
Business and Professional Women's
    Clubs, National Federation of
    BPW), 18n., 49, 78, 79–81, 82,
    405–06
"But What Have You Done for Me
    Lately?", 369

"Caberet of Sexual Politics, A," 370
Cade, Toni, 149n., 190
Cadwell, Franchellie, 248
Cahalan, William, 298
Calhoun, Susan Kennedy, 210n.
California, 215, 272, 418
    conference on abortion, 291n.
    state university system, 97, 320, 418
    University of (Berkeley), 308, 325,
        343, 354, 385, 411, 416
    University of (Davis), 173n., 408
Caprio, Frank S., 178n.
Carbine, Pat, 265
Carlo, Charles de, 208
Carmichael, Stokely, 110, 403
Carswell, G. Harrold, 87, 414
Carter, John Mack, 255, 256, 257
"Case Study of a Nonconscious Ide-
    ology:", 176n.
Cassirer, Ernst, 216n.
castrating, 239
Catholic Church, see Church, The
Catholic Star Herald, 391n.
Catt, Carrie Chapman, 13, 14
Cavett, Dick, 229
CBS, 248–49, 262, 416–17
    News poll, 269n., 340n.
Cell 16, 164–65, 271
Celler, Rep. Emanuel, 19, 55
Center for Radical Research, 112
Century of Struggle, 2, 191
Chicago, 119, 130, 150, 165, 270, 312,
    385, 410
    University of, 112, 115, 308, 323–24,
        325, 347, 354, 409, 411
child care, 67, 265, 303–15
    books on, 265, 306n., 308, 333–37,
        418
    centers
        academia, 308, 324
        "bootleg," 309, 309n., 310, 405
        city/union, 365
        conventions, 344, 347
        day, 24, 101, 305, 306, 313, 417
        funds, 303, 304, 309n., 309–10, 312,
            427
        industrial, 256, 314–15
        licensing, 303, 304, 309, 310, 312
        national, 51, 87, 88, 92, 95, 106,
            150, 313
        NOW/Princeton, 307–308, 420
        resistance to, 304, 315, 427
        SFU Co-op, 309, 311
        tax deduction, 24, 88, 312

    Women's Liberation, 309, 311–12
    custody, 7, 22, 64, 67
    federal level, 312–14, 423, 427
    goals, 306
    "Head Start," 303
    illegitimate children, 26
    lobby groups, 312
    NOW, 87, 88, 92, 93, 95, 213–14,
        305n., 307–08, 313, 420, 423
    rearing, 17, 19, 22, 24, 66–67, 76, 85,
        95, 199–200, 210, 305, 306, 313,
        421, 423
    sexism, 306, 313
    television, 250–51, 313, 412
    White House Conference, 306n., 313,
        423
    Women's Strike, 93, 420
"Children Are Only Little People,"
    306n.
Children's Book Council, 334, 335
Chisholm, Rep. Shirley, 75, 408, 427
chivalry, 215, 216–18
Chronicle of Higher Education, 321n.
Chronology, 401–27
church, the, 3, 4, 8, 10, 12, 86, 181, 246,
    336, 372–96
    Catholic, 90
        abortion, 281, 290, 291–92
        missal action, 390–91, 417
        Second Vatican Council, 373–74
    Clergy Consultation Service, 284,
        299, 301
    equality in, 12, 372, 374, 376, 377,
        380, 390, 392, 393, 422
    Eternal Woman, 381–82, 386
        Eve-Mary symbolism, 378, 380–81,
            382
    feminist organization in, 390–96
    issues
        ordination, 385–88, 390, 391, 392,
            422
        professional status, 388–90, 421–22
        theological, 3, 4, 12–13, 377–85, 395
    Jewish, 375–77
    Protestant/orthodox, 374, 393
        conferences on women, 385, 417
        women's status, 373n., 395, 411
    Saint Paul, 378, 382–83
    seminaries, 385, 394
Church and the Second Sex, The, 374n.,
    379n., 381n., 383n.
Church Women United, 290, 372n.,
    393–94, 413
Cisler, Lucinda, 102, 285n., 287n.,
    288n., 289n.
Citizens' Advisory Council on Status of
    Women, 24–27, 28, 41, 48, 55, 62n.,
    81, 82, 279n., 402, 403, 404, 407
"City Hall Women Organize to End Sex
    Discrimination," 363n.
Civil and Political Rights Committee,
    20, 22, 33n., 80, 82
civil disobedience, 295
Civil Rights Act (1964), 21, 25, 29n.,
    30, 31, 40, 41, 68, 264, 285, 319,
    339n., 402

See also Equal Employment Opportunity Commission; Title VI; Title VII
Civil Rights Commission, U.S., 319
Civil Rights movement, 108, 110, 111, 115–16
Civil Service Act (1957), 59n.
Civil Service Commission, 41, 47, 86, 405, 406
Federal Women's Program, 47–48
FEW, 98–100
Civil War, 9
Clarenbach, Kathryn, 83, 83n., 84, 85, 346
Clark, Ramsey, 86
Clergy Consultation Service, 284, 299, 301
College and University Business, 133n.
colleges, women's, 2n., 208
Columbia University, 208, 257, 308, 309, 320, 323
Women's Liberation, 241, 412
Commentary, 218n.
Commerce, U.S. Department of, 41
Commission on the Legal Status of Women, 19, 55
Commission on the Status of Women (MLA), 348, 413
Commission on Uniform State Laws, 22n., 67, 291, 420
Commission on Women in Today's World, 393, 413
Commonwealth v. Jane Daniels, 60n., 407
Communications Workers Union, 98
Congregationalist Ministers, Council of, 3
Congress, U.S.; 31n., 51, 57, 248, 421
Abortion Bill, 285
child care centers, 312–13, 425
ERA, 18
House, 19, 54, 55, 56, 57, 97, 418
Senate, 56–57, 76, 403, 415, 417, 420, 421
girl pages, 426
sex discrimination, 41–42, 47, 51, 217, 230–31, 238, 316–17, 319, 419, 421
the Pill, 414
Title VII, 30–31, 402
Woman's Party, 79
woman's suffrage, 13, 14
women in, 401, 403, 405, 408, 422
See also Civil Rights Act; Green Hearings
Congress to Unite Women, 102, 150–52, 159–60, 162, 239, 370, 413, 418
Congressional Digest, 66n.
Congressional Quarterly, 56n.
Congressional Record, 31n., 41n., 62n., 71n., 75n., 77n., 82n.
Congressional Union, 13
Connecticut College, 328–29
Conroy, Catherine, 83n.
consciousness raising, 102, 118, 125–26, 131–32, 133, 136–39, 140–41, 143,

152, 155, 157, 160, 169, 237, 275, 326, 329, 330–31, 341, 365, 369, 370–71, 385, 394, 398, 406, 410
Constitution, U.S., 281n.
5th Amendment, 23, 62, 69, 73, 285
13th Amendment, 9, 10n.
14th Amendment, 9, 10n., 11, 14, 23, 40, 59n., 69, 70, 72, 73, 75, 82, 285
15th Amendment, 10, 70
19th Amendment, 11, 13, 14, 17, 78
women's rights, 9, 10, 22, 40, 69–70
Constitution, U.S.
See also Equal Rights Amendment
contraception. *See* birth control
Cook, Sen. Marlow C., 63
Cooney, Joan, 250, 251
"Cooperative Nurseries," 308n.
CORE, 110
Cornell Conference on Women, 237n., 324
Cornell University, 324, 326, 327, 410
Cosmopolitan, 250, 251, 265
courts, the, 68, 86
For court cases, See Industry; Landmark Decisions; Marriage; State Legislation; Supreme Court; Title VII; *specific cases*
Crist, Miriam, 394n.
Critic, The, 13n.
"Critique of Sexual Politics," 235n.
"Critique of the Miss America Protest, A," 123n., 124n.
Culver, Elsie Thomas, 381n.
Curtis, Sen. Charles, 54
Cushing, Richard Cardinal, 292n.
"Cutting Loose," 195n.

Daedalus, 178n., 402
Daily News, 123
Dale, Patt, 329n.
Daly, Mary, 372n., 374n., 379, 392, 393
Damon, Gene, 240n.
Dating, Mating and Sex, 330n.
Daughters of Bilitis, 150, 241
David Frost Show, The, 293n.
Davis, Caroline, 105, 106
Day Care and Child Development Council, 315n.
"Day Care Business, The," 315n.
day care centers, *See* child care
Dearden, John Cardinal, 391
Declaration of Sentiments (1848), 5–6
Decter, Midge, 218n.
Defense, U.S. Dep't of, 41, 44
Defense Management Journal, 210n.
Dellinger, David, 134
Democratic Party, 18, 19, 55, 174, 417, 427
demonstrations, 13, 42–43, 87, 117, 118, 123, 128, 136, 143, 255–57, 258–59, 267, 296, 298, 299, 323, 366–68, 369, 407, 408, 410, 414, 415, 416, 417, 419, 420, 424
Dennis, Rep. David W., 61–62
Detroit Free Press, 298n.

Detroit Women's Liberation Coalition, 298
Dialectic of Sex, The, 176–77, 182n., 187, 188n., 189, 190n., 192n., 204n., 209n., 219n.
Dinerman, Beatrice, 351n.
Divine Sanction, 3, 71
"Divisiveness and Self-Destruction in the Women's Movement," 162–63
Dixon, Marlene, 112n., 132n., 308, 323–24, 339n., 409–10
Doe v. Bolton, 285, 426
Doely, Sarah Bentley, 372n., 380n., 394n.
domestic labor, 29, 69
Dorson, Norman, 75n.
double standard, 10, 216
"Double Standard of Justice, The," 59n.
Douglass, Frederick, 7
"Down With Love," 203
draft resistance, 112
Drew Seminary, 385
Dudar, Helen, 259n.
Due to Circumstances Beyond Our Control, 249
Dunbar, Roxanne, 393
Dunlap, Carol, 175
Dvorkin, Connie, 332n.
Dwyer, Rep. Florence, 48

East, Catherine, 26, 82
Eastland, Sen. James, 116
Eastwood, Mary, 26, 59n., 69n., 82, 83n., 101
economic status of women, 153
    family law, 22, 64–67, 73
    job opportunities, 322–29, 338
    social security & taxes, 22, 24, 88, 312
    wages and salaries, 68, 79, 102, 204–05, 217, 256, 317–18, 338
    WEAL, 96
    See also Equal Pay Act
Ecumenical Task Force on Women and Religion, 390–91, 417
Edelsberg, Herman, 34
Edmiston, Susan, 304n.
Education, 20, 23, 39, 93, 316–37
    action, 246, 323–24, 334–37, 409–10, 414, 415, 418, 419, 422, 424, 425, 427
    boards of, 331, 332, 333, 413, 421, 424
    books, 265, 308, 332–37, 342, 420
    career counseling, 318, 324
    Congressional hearings, 316–17, 319
    discrimination, 47, 73, 87, 88, 92, 96, 207, 210, 317, 320, 321, 326, 331, 409, 412, 414
    elementary, 333–36, 418
    EO 11375, 319–20, 321, 322, 414
    ERA, 60–61
    graduate schools, 317, 318, 342–43
        law, 98, 103, 320, 325, 351, 352–53, 355, 411, 412, 416, 425
        medical, 97, 320, 355–59, 422
    "Head Start," 303

high schools, 329–33, 427
    coed sports, 422–23, 424
higher, 2, 265, 317–18, 321–29, 412
    hiring and promotion, 47, 96, 321, 348, 411, 412, 424
    nepotism rule, 321, 324
    salaries, 28–29, 102, 317–18
    women's status, 308, 317, 325
    women's studies, 324–25, 326–27, 328, 410–11, 421, 423–24
maternity leave, 321, 422
nursery schools, 336
OFCC, 46, 96–97, 322
Title VII, 30, 319
toys, 337
women's movement, 80, 86, 96, 316–18, 320, 322–37, 409, 412, 414
    See also Professional Women
Education Committee, 20
Efrom, Edith, 250n.
"Electra Rewired," 275
elitism, 156–57, 158, 159, 160–61, 257, 258, 339, 340
Ellison, Sylvia, 101
Embree, Alice, 248n., 249n.
Emerson, Thomas, 70n.
employment, 21, 34, 68, 86, 87, 88, 92, 93, 96, 97, 106, 403
    See also education; Equal Employment Opportunity Commission; Equal Pay Act; Equal Rights Amendment; executive orders; federal employment; media; Title VII
Employment Service, U.S., 30
Epstein, Cynthia Fuchs, 340n.
Equal Employment Opportunity Commission, 25, 31, 34, 51, 52, 253, 354, 421, 427
    ANPA suit, 43, 408
    A.T.&T., 423
    Commissioners, 82, 83, 84, 85n., 86, 87
    guidelines 1965–69, 35, 43, 84, 106, 404, 406, 412
    Justice Dep't, 39–40
    Newsweek, 259
    NOW, 42–43, 84, 86–87, 405, 406
    protective legislation hearings, 35, 106
    Supreme Court, 38
    See also "Want-ad" controversy
Equal Pay Act (1963), 21, 28–29, 30, 51, 79, 81, 319, 339n., 352, 402, 427
Equal Rights Amendment, 54–77, 68, 69–77, 79
    Congress, 18, 19, 54, 403, 417, 421, 427
    Ervin substitute, 56, 57, 421
    Hayden rider, 55, 56
    Hearings, 97, 415
        Hearings 1, 60n., 61n., 63n., 64n., 65n., 66n., 67n., 106n., 107n., 169n.
        Hearings 2, 56n., 58n., 68n., 70n., 73n., 74n., 75n., 76n.
        Hearings 3, 55n.

laws affected, 59–67, 406–407
legal equality, 58, 79
opposition to, 19, 20, 22, 23, 55, 56–57, 58, 68, 106, 264, 415
party platforms, 18, 55
policy papers, 27
public education, 60–61
support for, 53, 78–79, 80, 88, 97, 101, 106–107, 136, 150, 390, 393, 409, 415, 417, 419, 427
Eric Clearing House on Higher Education, 326n.
Erikson, Erik, 177–78, 208, 347
Ermath, Margaret Sittler, 384n.
Ervin, Sen. Sam D., 56–57, 66, 75, 76n., 421
Esquire, 195, 228
Establishment, The, 8, 92, 95, 254, 258, 267, 268, 269, 272, 349
Etiquette, 216n.
Everywoman, 189n., 224n.
Executive Order 41, 363
Executive Order 71, 363
Executive Order 10980, 18n.
Executive Order 11246, 44, 405
Executive Order 11375, 21n., 44–48, 51, 96, 97, 99, 319–20, 321, 322, 346, 352, 357, 405, 412, 414, 415, 418, 419, 422, 424, 427
Executive Order 11478, 48, 412

"Fail: Bright Women," 201
Fair Labor Standards Act (1938), 28, 29, 402
family, 24, 64–67, 73, 86, 211, 214–15, 266
See also child care; motherhood; society; sexism
Family Circle, 265
family law and policy, 26, 67n., 279n., 407
Farians, Elizabeth, 387n., 390, 391n., 392
Farnham, Marynia, 219n.
Fauri, Fedele, 320
Fear of Being a Woman, The, 186n.
Federal Communications Commission, 264–65
Federal Contractors and Sub-Contractors, 21, 44–47, 405, 424
federal employment, 79
workforce, 21, 47n., 47–48, 99, 401
Executive Order 11375, 47, 99, 405
FEW, 98
Federal Employment Committee, 20, 21, 25n.
federal government, 22, 31, 80
See also Congress, U.S.; Equal Rights Amendment, Laws; Title VII; *Specific Department*
Federal Women's Program, 47–48, 99
Federally Employed Women (FEW), 98–101, 405, 408
Female Studies I, 327n., 349n.

Female Studies II, 349
"Feminine Mistake, The," 228
feminine mystique, 17, 18–19, 102, 248, 318
Feminine Mystique, The, 17, 82, 206n., 228, 248n., 323, 402
feminism, 94, 95, 108, 136, 142, 148, 151, 169, 196, 397–400
resistance to, 170, 187, 226–42, 289
See also Equal Rights Amendment; feminists; sexism; society; women's liberation; *Specific issue or organization*
feminist analysis, 14, 120, 122, 130, 131, 139, 141, 143, 145, 151, 169–93, 207, 216–217, 218, 222, 242, 289, 305, 339, 341, 398
feminist critique, 14, 141, 144, 169, 181, 194–215, 216–42, 317, 397–99
feminist philosophy, 14, 87, 120, 170, 372–73, 398, 399
feminist movement, 107, 108–09, 397–400
feminist-politico split, *See* politico-feminist positions
Feminist Press, 337
feminists, 79, 82, 84, 87, 89, 95, 107, 109, 114–15, 116, 118–19, 121–22, 124, 125, 128, 129–30, 131, 133, 138, 139, 141, 142, 148–49, 150, 169–70, 189, 213, 235, 236, 255–58, 267–68, 268n., 289, 309, 316–17, 322–37, 339, 341, 372–73
Feminists, The, 90, 136, 143–47, 151, 152, 153, 154, 160, 238–39, 255, 408, 413
Manifesto, 238n.
Feminists on Children's Media, 334, 335–36, 418
Fields, Daisy, 98, 99, 100n.
"51 Percent Minority, The," 54n.
films, *See* Media, Mass
Finer, June, 287n.
Finkbine, Sherri, 283n.
Firestone, Shulamith, 113, 115, 117n., 136, 152, 176–77, 178n., 187–88, 189, 209, 215n., 228n., 250n., 267n.
Fisher, Elizabeth, 200, 221n., 334n.
"Five Passionate Feminists," 200n.
Flexner, Eleanor, 2n., 7, 9, 10, 14n., 191n.
Florida Paper, The, 111n., 202n., 214n., 215n., 407
Florida State University, 320, 418
FOCUS, 320, 424
Foloway, Betty, 307
Fortune, 260, 417
Free Space, 121n., 141n.
Freed, Betty, 308n.
"Freedom is a Long Time Comin'," 218n.
Freeman, Jo, 109n., 112n., 113, 115, 125n., 133n., 137n., 158n., 198, 203n., 226n., 270
Freud, Sigmund, 176–77, 178, 180
Freund, Paul, 73, 73n., 74

Friedan, Betty, 17, 81, 82, 83, 84, 85, 86, 87, 89, 91, 92, 93, 206n., 221, 228, 235n., 237, 240, 248, 265, 279n., 323, 364, 393, 402, 414, 427
Friendly, Fred, 248–49
Fritchey, Clayton, 174n.
From Feminism to Liberation, 287n.
"Fucked-Up in America," 222n.

Gage, Matilda Joslyn, 3n., 5
Gardner, Jo-Ann Evans, 102, 250, 251, 346, 364
Gay Liberation Movement, 93, 240
"Genocide? Women Re-Examine Abortion Demands," 189
Gilman, Charlotte Perkins, 342
Glaser, Vera, 48, 49
Goesaert v. Cleary, 72
Goldberg, Philip, 201
Goldman, Peter, 259n.
"Goodbye to All That," 273–74
Gordon, Juliette, 366n.
Goucher College, 328, 423
Graham, Richard, 82, 83, 85, 85n.
Green, Rep. Edith, 30, 77, 197, 223n., 230–31, 238, 316, 319, 322
Green Hearings, 100n., 176n., 191n., 192n., 195n., 198n., 199n., 201n., 205n., 206n., 207n., 208, 210n., 213n., 217n., 223n., 225n., 229n., 231n., 238n., 317n., 318n., 320, 350n., 351n., 355n., 356n., 357n.
Greenspan, Emily, 363n., 364n.
Griffiths, Rep. Martha, 31n., 41–42, 56, 82, 83, 97, 393, 418
Grimké, Angelina & Sarah, 2–3, 4, 342
Grinnell College, 324, 410
Grinnell Herald Register, 324n.
Griswold v. Connecticut, 74, 403
Group, The, 326
Gruenwald v. Gardner, 62
Guardian, 134
Gutwillig, Jacqueline, 26, 27

Hadden, Briton, 261
Haener, Dorothy, 83n., 106, 346
Halberstam, Michael T., 288n.
Hall, Robert E., 287n.
Handbook on Women Workers, 1969, 53, 414–15
Hanisch, Carol, 116, 123, 124n., 159n., 228n.
Hansen, Pat, 121
"Hard Knocks," 116n.
Harman, Susan, 362
Harper, Ida Husted, 3n.
Harper's, 221n., 224n.
Harris, Ann Sutherland, 191n., 207, 208
Harvard University, 308, 320, 327, 347, 415, 424–25
Hawaii, 174, 285–86, 415
Hayden, Casey, 111, 125, 404
Hayden, Sen. Carl, 55, 56
"Head Start," 303

Health, Education and Welfare, U.S. Dep't of (HEW), 41, 44, 47, 51, 320, 321n., 357
Health and Welfare, 26, 407
Heaton v. Bristol, 61n.
Heckler, Rep. Margaret, 48
Heide, Wilma Scott, 56, 70n., 76, 306n., 314n., 346, 415
Hepburn, Katherine, 252
Hernandez, Aileen, 31, 63, 82, 85n., 93, 94
Herschberger, Ruth, 172n., 173, 178–79, 182, 223
heterosexuals, 181, 240
Hickey, Margaret, 25, 26
High School Women's Liberation Coalition, 330–31
"History of The Equality Issue," 90n.
History of Woman Suffrage, 3, 4, 8n., 9, 10n., 184, 185
Hodgson, James D., 46
Holm, Jeanne M., 210, 416
Home and Community Committee, 20
homemaking, 17, 19, 22, 24, 56, 59, 62, 66–67, 76, 205–207, 228, 248
homosexuals, 93, 181, 240
Horner, Matina, 201
Howe, Florence, 348, 349
Hoyt v. Florida, 59n., 62
Human Rights Commission (NYC), 364
Human Rights for Women (HRW), 36, 101–02, 409
   Mengelkoch case, 40, 86n., 101, 424
Human Sexual Response, 179, 404
humor, 231
Humphrey, Hubert H., 174
hunger strikes, 13

"I Love Lucy," 248
Ideas of The Woman Suffrage Movement, 1890–1920, The, 13n.
Illinois, 275
   See also Chicago
"Increase is Urged in Black Doctors," 357n.
Indians, Amreican, 252
industry, 70, 426
   abortion-referral services, 301
   child care centers, 256, 314–15
   court cases, 36–39
   NOW, 36–39, 87, 419
   WEAL, 98
"In Memoriam: Avenge Norma Jean Baker!" 215
"Inequality, The Geography of," 185n., 265, 353n.
infiltration, 163–65
"Inner and Outer Space," 177–78
Institute on Women, 385
Intercollegiate Association of Women Students, 63, 325
Interdepartmental Committee on the Status of Women, 25, 41, 402
International Socialist Review, 370n.

"Introduction: The Women's Revolution," 112n.
"Is Television Making a Mockery of the American Woman?" 250n.
issues *See* abortion; *bfoq;* biological differences; child care, the church; constitutional amendments; economic status; education; Equal Rights Amendment; laws; lesbianism; marriage; motherhood; media; professional women; sex discrimination; sexism; slavery; society; suffrage; temperance; third world women; "want-ad" controversy; working women
It Ain't Me Babe, 215, 272–73
"It's Not Only Up to Mom," 308n.

Jacobson, L., 181
"Jane Crow and The Law," 82
Jeanette Rankin Brigade, 117, 118, 119 267, 268, 406
Jewish Spectator, The, 377
job training opportunities, 88, 303
Johns Hopkins University, 343
Johnson, Lyndon B., 25, 26, 44, 55, 86, 405, 406, 412
Johnson, Virginia, 179, 180, 404
Jones, Beverly, 111n., 407
Jones, Norma Ramsey, 387n.
Joreen, 54n., 210., 233
Journal of Female Liberation, A, 164–65, 271
Journal of The American Medical Association, 358
Journalists for Professional Equity, 425
Judaism, 375–77
Judson Memorial Church, 284
jury service, 22, 59–60, 73, 404
Justice, U.S. Dep't. of, 31, 44, 86 and women's rights, 39–40
"Justice and The National Coalition of American Nuns," 392n.

Kanowitz, Leo, 65, 73, 77, 211, 212n.
Kaplan, Harold, 356, 357
Kayden, Xandra, 47n.
Kearon, Pamela, 238n.
Kempton, Sally, 195n.
Kennedy, Florynce, 292
Kennedy, John F., 18, 19, 20, 24, 25n., 28, 47n., 55, 174, 175, 401
Kennedy, Robert F., 47n.
Kennedy Commission *see* President's Commission on the Status of Women
Kepler, Patricia, 373n.
Keyserling, Mary, 364
Kilian, Melody, 306n., 309n., 311n.
" 'Kinder, Küche, Kirche' as Scientific Law," 172, 173n., 176, 180, 347–48, 408
King, Mary, 111, 125, 404
Kinsey, Alfred, 178

Klotzburger, Kay, 345n.
K.N.O.W. Inc. News Service, 94n., 272, 327n., 366n.
Koedt, Anne, 110n., 131, 152, 153n., 154n., 178, 188n., 200n., 201, 208n., 220, 221, 221n., 222, 239n., 240
Komisar, Lucy, 192n., 225n., 252n., 259n.
Koontz, Elizabeth B., 49, 53, 339n., 393, 409, 411
Kraditor, Aileen S., 13n.
KSAN-FM, 276

labor
Commission recommendations, 21, 28
Equal Rights Amendment, 20, 68–69
labor market, 20, 28, 53, 247
laws affecting, 22, 28, 32–33, 34, 73
lobby, 19
standards, 21, 22, 26, 407
Labor, U.S. Dep't. of, 29, 30, 51–52, 204
child care centers, 312n.
ERA, 53, 56, 419
Laws on Sex Discrimination in Employment, 41n.
OFCC, 44, 45, 46, 49, 96, 97
Order No. 4, 45–46, 427
Salary gap, 318
Secretary of, 41, 45, 46, 96
See also Women's Bureau
labor unions, 39, 56
AFL–CIO, 106, 415
and WCGU, 364–65
Communications Workers, 98
discrimination in, 97–98
publishing, 253–54
U.A.W., 69, 83, 88, 105–07, 417
Women's Bureau, 52
Labov, William, 223
Lader, Lawrence, 280n., 282n., 292n.
"Ladies Felt at Home at the Journal," 257n.
Ladies' Home Journal, 25n., 139n., 253, 254, 255–58, 314, 415, 420
"Ladies' Home Journal 2," 257n.
Lake, Alice, 315n.
Lamb, Myrna, 369, 370, 417
landmark decisions, 101
Mengelkoch, 40, 86n., 101, 424
Muller v. Oregon, 32–33, 40, 72–73
Rosenfeld v. Southern Pacific, 36, 101, 409
Weeks v. Southern Bell, 36–37, 410
language, institution of, 215, 222–25, 229–30, 313–14
Language and Society, 223
Lanham Act, 303
Laurance, Margaret, 350n.
law firms, 351, 354, 416
law journals, 353
law schools, 98, 103, 320, 325, 351, 352–53, 354, 355, 411, 412, 416, 425

Law Women's Caucus, 354
Lawrenson, Helen, 228
laws, 10, 20, 28
    alimony, 26
    child custody, 22
    criminal, 60, 406–07
    jury service, 22
    labor, 22, 32–33
    marriage, 22, 64–67, 211–12
    property rights, 22, 26, 211
    Selective Service, 61–64, 73
    sex discrimination, 28, 29
    Social Security, 22
    State Protective Legislation, 22, 23,
        32–34
    See also Abortion; Civil Rights Act;
    Equal Pay Act; Equal Rights Amend-
    ment; Title VII
Lawyers, Assoc. of American Women,
    66n., 67n.
Layzer, Judith, 362n., 363n., 364n.
League of Women Voters, 82
Lear, Martha Weinman, 200n.
"Least of These, The," 240n.
Lefkowitz, Louis J., 260
Leone, Vivian, 257n.
"Lesbian Issue and Women's Lib, The,"
    241n.
lesbianism, 91, 93, 94, 232, 239–42, 266
"Let's Draft Women Too," 64, 64n.
"Letter from the Publisher, A," 261
"Letters on The Equality of the Sexes,"
    4
Leviathan, 148n.
Levine, Jay, 251n.
Leymaster, Glen R., 358
Liberated Guardian, 189n.
"Liberated Woman, The," 218n.
Liberation, 111n., 404
Liberation News Service, 274
Life, 260, 417
Lilith, 271
Lily, The, 8
Lindsay, John V., 362–64
Lippard, Lucy, 366
Little Miss Muffet Fights Back, 336n.
lobby groups, 18n., 26, 42–43, 44, 57,
    78–79, 87, 96, 98, 217, 295, 312,
    393
Lollipop Power, 336–37
Look, 185n.
love, 154, 203–204
Loy, Myrna, 252
Lucas, Roy, 281n., 292n.
Luce, Henry, 261
Lundberg, Ferdinand, 219n.
Lutz, Alma, 227n.
Lyon, Lilla, 261n.

McAfee, Kathy, 148n.
McCall's, 185, 200n., 208n., 239n., 265,
    315n., 353n., 360n.
McCarthy, Mary, 219n., 326
McGillicuddy, Frances, 391n.

McKenzie, John L., 379n.
Macy, John, Jr., 86
Madar, Olga, 106
Mademoiselle, 258
magazines See media, mass; specific
    magazine
Maginnis, Patricia, 284, 295, 299, 300n.
Mailer, Norman, 221n., 224n.
Mainardi, Pat, 206
male chauvinism, 33, 153, 229
"Male Mystique, The," 251–52
"Manglish," 224
man-hating, 116, 235–39, 266
Manhattan Tribune, 257n., 363n., 364n.
Mann, Nancy, 222n.
Mannes, Marya, 281n.
"March of Time's Women, The," 261n.
marriage, 10
    "Bitch Manifesto," 234
    Citizens' Council, 26
    Commission on, 22–23, 67n.
    court decisions, 212
    economics of, 22, 67, 204–05
    ERA, 64–67
    institution of, 4, 95, 144, 210–11, 213,
        214, 226, 399, 413
    law and, 64–67, 211-12
        Uniform Marriage and Divorce
            Act, 22n., 67, 420
    love and, 203–04
    NOW on, 85, 95, 213
    social role in, 204–07
    sexual revolution, 218–22
    surname, 212, 212–13n., 423
    The Feminists, 144–45, 413
    3-year contract, 424
Marshall, Justice Thurgood, 38–39
Maryland, 321, 422, 424
    University of, 47, 96, 320, 414
Masters, William H., 179, 180, 404
Maternity Benefits, Job Related, 27n.
maternity leave, 27, 88, 321, 421, 422
Matter of Simple Justice, A, 45n., 49–50,
    414, 418
May, Rep. Catherine, 48
media, feminist
    FM Radio, 275–76, 412
    KNOW, 94n., 272
    Liberation News Service, 274
    publications, 8, 10, 110n., 147, 164–
        65, 215, 250n., 252, 270–71, 272–
        74, 407
    speakers' bureau, 274–75
media, mass
    actions against, 247, 248, 249, 250n.,
        251, 253n., 254, 255–57, 258–59,
        260, 262, 263–65, 267, 268, 415,
        427
    coverage, 112, 122–24, 136; 147, 150,
        266–70
        Miss America protest, 123, 408
    films, 198, 252
    image of women, 20, 85, 86, 87, 123,
        198, 225, 247–52, 254, 262, 264,
        265, 266–67
    journalism, 253, 264, 373

press, 8, 93, 250, 265, 267, 374
  conferences, 94n, 150, 241, 287n.,
    404
  publishing, 253–54, 333, 335, 336, 423
  radio, 253, 275–76, 412
  sexism quotient, 258
  television, 229, 250–51, 253, 262–63,
    264–65, 313, 412, 427
  underground, 254
  use of ridicule, 229–30, 231
  woman's status in, 252–66
  women's journals, 248, 253, 256, 265,
    415
  see also newspapers
"Media Images I," 248n.
Media Projects, 254
"Media Strategy," 266n.
Media Women, 253n., 254–58
Medical World News, 358n., 360
medicine, 291, 300, 359–62
  medical schools, 97, 320, 355–56, 357,
    358, 422
*Memorandum—Job Related Maternity
  Benefits,* 27n.
"Memorandum of Understanding,"
  259–60
*Memorandum on the Equal Rights
  Amendment,* 62n., 63n.
Mengelkoch, Velma, 40, 424
  v. Industrial Welfare Comm., 40,
    86n., 101, 424
"Mental Health of American Women,
  The," 210n.
Meyer, Marie, 324
Miami Herald, 49
Michigan, University of, 201, 320–21,
  354, 416, 424
"Middle Voice, The," 369
Mikva, Rep. Abner, 51
Millett, Kate, 102, 176n., 177n., 178,
  192n., 193n., 195n., 208, 215n.,
  216n., 219n., 241, 242, 265
*Mills v. Commonwealth of Pennsyl-
  vania,* 280n.
"Miniskirt Caucus, The," 268
Mink, Rep. Patsy, 174, 414, 417
"Minor Mystry, A," 178
Miss America Protest, 123–25, 159,
  229, 408
"Mister Rogers' Neighborhood," 251
M.I.T., 97, 327
Mobilization for Peace, 133, 410
"Mod Donna, The," 370, 417
Model Penal Code, 282, 283, 290
Modern Language Association, 348–49,
  413
Modern Woman, The Lost Sex, 219n.
Monroe, Marilyn, 215, 252
Moody, Howard, 284, 299
Morgan, Robin, 273
motherhood, 17, 18, 24, 52, 56, 185,
  205, 207–10, 293, 304
  as *bfoq* exception, 38, 74
  biological determinism, 88, 89, 192,
    207
  child care, 303–305

institution of, 209, 399
  maternity leave, 27, 88, 321, 421, 422
  protective legislation, 33, 52
  See also economic status; working
    women
"Motherhood, Some Views on the
  Institution of," 188n.
"Motherhood—Who Needs It?" 185n.,
  207
Mott, Lucretia, 5, 393
Muller v. Oregon, 32–33, 40, 72–73
municipal government, 362–65
Murray, Pauli, 82, 83n., 228–29
music, rock, 276n.
Muskie, Sen. Edmund, 292, 293, 426
Myth of The State, 216n.
"Myth of the Vaginal Orgasm, The,"
  119, 130, 131, 179, 220, 240

NAACP, 110, 419
National Abortion Act, 285n.
National American Woman Suffrage
  Association, 12, 13
National Association for Repeal of
  Abortion Laws, 295n.
National Association of Women
  Lawyers, 350
National Coalition of American Nuns,
  391–92, 411
National Conference for a New Politics,
  112–14, 405
National Conference of Bar Presidents,
  351
National Conference of Catholic
  Bishops, 291, 391, 417
National Conference of Women Law
  Students, 353, 416
National Conference on the Role of
  Women in Theological Education,
  385, 417
National Council of Churches, 374, 375,
  388–89, 393, 413
National Day of Demonstration Against
  EEOC, 42–43, 87, 406
National Eductaion Assocaition, 53,
  317, 318
National Federation of Temple Sister-
  hoods, 376, 377n.
National Institutes of Mental Health,
  356
National Manpower Council, 19
National Observer, 87n.
National Organization for Women
  (NOW), 31n., 63, 76, 81–95, 106,
  143, 145, 150, 217, 221n., 241,
  248, 255, 305n., 320, 342, 346,
  350n., 404, 408, 414, 415
  abortion, 88, 89
  accomplishments, 95
  and EEOC, 42–43, 86–87, 405, 406
  and women's liberation, 91–92
  Bill of Rights, 88, 279, 439
  child care centers, 87, 88, 92, 93, 95,
    213–14, 305n., 307–08, 313, 420,
    423

National Organization for Women
    (*cont.*)
  conferences, 84–85, 88, 90, 94, 406
  court cases, 36, 86, 419
  education, 322, 325
  ERA, 56, 95
  Labor Dep't., 46
  lesbianism, 93, 94
  media actions, 42, 248, 264–65, 334,
    405
  membership, 90, 91, 93, 95
  purpose, 85–86, 87, 91–92, 221
  resolutions, 213
  tactics, 42–43, 86–87
  task forces, 86, 295, 390, 417
  "want-ads," 42, 84, 86
  Women's Strike, 87, 92–93, 136, 249,
    263, 269, 299, 420
National Reformer, 8
National Woman Suffrage Association,
    10, 11, 12
National Woman's Party, 18n., 54,
    78–79, 81
National Women's Political Caucus,
    426–27
National Women's Resource Center,
    104
Negroes *See* blacks
Neuberger, Maurine, 26
New Broadside, The, 210n., 264n.
New England Free Press, 222n.
"New Feminism, The," 256
New Feminist Theater, 162, 369–370,
    411
New Jersey, 332, 334
  State University, 320
new left movement, 68, 108, 110, 111,
    112, 114–15, 120, 129, 130, 132–33,
    134, 158, 165, 236
New Republic, The, 320n.
New York, 218n., 260n., 261n., 304n.
New York City, 102, 128, 129, 143,
    144, 150, 164, 239, 241, 252n., 258,
    271, 273, 275, 284, 296, 306n., 309,
    312, 330, 331, 332, 334, 362–67,
    369, 405, 409, 410, 412, 413, 419,
    421
New York Fair Employment Practices
    Commission, 409
New York Feminist, 363n.
New York Free Press, 221n.
New York Post, 174n., 212–13n., 250,
    259n.
New York Radical Feminists, 136,
    138n., 152–57, 188, 196, 213, 214,
    221, 377, 378, 414
  Manifesto, 152, 153, 154
  Organizing Principles, 152, 154, 155,
    236n., 269n.
  rape, 157, 424, 426
New York Radical Women, 115, 117,
    118–19, 123, 125–26, 129, 132,
    133–34, 135, 143, 406, 408, 410
  See also radical women; *specific
    group*
New York Shakespeare Festival Public

Theater, 370, 417
New York State, 332, 422–23
  abortion law repeal, 285–86, 419
  Division of Human Rights, 260, 262,
    417
  Supreme Court, 301
  University, 320, 419
New York Stock Exchange, 126
New York Tea Party, 370
New York Times, The, 3n., 34, 46n.,
    57n., 92n., 179n., 198n., 200n.,
    217n., 241n., 287n., 292n., 296n.,
    301n., 315n., 327n., 328n., 333n.,
    357n., 376n., 387n.
  NOW's complaint, 42, 405
  on abortion, 293
  on ERA, 263–64
  on New Feminist Theater, 369, 411
  on women's studies, 327
New York University Law School, 325,
    352–43, 412, 416
New York Women's Bar Association,
    351
New Yorkers for Abortion Law Repeal
    (NYALR), 150, 279n., 287n., 296,
    409
*New York's Abortion Law. What About
    It?* 287n.,
Newell, Barbara, 321
newspapers, 49–50, 221n., 222n., 253
  court cases, 43
  editorial attacks, 8, 34, 74, 264
  NOW courage, 93, 94
  underground, 254, 270–71, 273, 274,
    414
  women's, 10, 147, 164–65, 215, 250n.,
    252, 271–73, 277, 407
  women's movement, 250, 263–64, 265
  See also "want-ad controversy";
    specific newspapers
Newsweek, 255n., 259–60, 265n., 415
Nixon, Pat, 55, 411
Nixon, Richard M., 26, 48, 51, 55, 133,
    217, 409, 412
  on abortion, 292–93, 294, 425
  counter-inaugural action, 133–35, 410
  education bill, 319
  State of Union, 48, 49, 52
  Task Force on Women's Rights, 45,
    48–52, 413
No More Fun and Games, 164–165, 271
Nolen, William, 359–60
Norberg, Tilda, 394n.
Norris, Frances, 356n., 357
North, Sandie, 255, 257
North Carolina, 336
  University of, 60–61
North Carolina Law Review, 281n.
Norton, Eleanor Holmes, 363, 364
Notes from the First Year, 110n., 117n.,
    118n., 119, 179, 219, 228n., 267,
    271, 407
Notes from the Second Year, 116n.,
    123n., 131n., 132n., 133n., 137n.,
    138n., 140n., 143n., 154n., 155n.,
    158, 159n., 179, 179–80n., 196n.,

202n., 204n., 206n., 207n., 210n.,
220n., 221n., 233n., 235n., 236n.,
237n., 238n., 239n., 240n., 269n.,
287n., 288n., 416
"Notes of a Radical Lesbian," 240n.
"N.O.W.—How It Began," 81n.
"NOW Takes on the Networks," 264n.

Oberlin College, 2
Obstetrics in The Wrong Hands, 360n.,
361n.
October 17th Movement, The, *See*
Feminists, The
Off Our Backs, 250n.
Office of Education, U.S., 426
Office of Federal Contract Compliance
(OFCC), *See* Labor, U.S. Dep't. of
Office of Women's Affairs, U.S., 392
Olio, Anselma dell', 162–63, 369, 370
Omnibus Post-Secondary Education
Act, 319
"On Abortion and Abortion Law . . .
A Warning," 287n.
"On the Condition of Women in The
United States," 4
On the Contrary, 219n.
"On Women's Liberation," 112n.
One, Varda, 224, 225n.
"Operation Women Fear Most, The,"
360n.
Order No. 4, 45–46
"Organizing Principles of the New
York Radical Feminists," 154n.
orgasm, vaginal, 178–79, 180, 219–22
"Our Revolution is Unique," 279

Pacem in Terris, 374n., 391
Pacifica Foundation, Inc., 275
Packwood, Sen. Robert, 285n.
Paley, William S., 262
Parents' Aid Society, 284, 299, 301
Paul, Alice, 13, 78, 79
peace movement, 108, 112, 113, 115,
117
Pennsylvania, University of, 325, 352
"Persistence of the Suffering Woman,
The," 218
Peterson, Esther, 19, 20
Phelan, Lana Clarke, 291n.
Phillips, Ida, 37, 38
Phillips, Lynn, 189n.
Phillips v. Martin-Marietta Corp., 37,
38–39, 73, 87, 87n., 101, 424
Piartney, Lynn, 268n.
"Pigeons," 198n.
pill, the, 190, 414
Pittsburgh Visitor, 8
Planned Parenthood, 290, 301
Playboy, 324, 327, 410
Playboy bunny, 323, 407
Playboy Clubs, 34, 403
"Playboy Fucked Up," 324n.
political science, 344–46, 412

politico-feminist positions, 109, 114–15,
116, 118–19, 121–22, 125, 126, 129,
130, 132, 133, 143, 148, 149, 151,
153, 158, 165, 170, 189, 215n., 221,
222, 236–37, 254, 255–58, 268–69,
276, 309, 339, 366
politics
confrontations, 109–110, 111
feminist view, 397–99
Democratic party, 18, 19, 55, 174,
417, 427
labor in, 20
of President's Commission, 19
Republican party, 9, 18, 55
woman's movement, 9
"Politics of Housework, The," 206
"Politics of the Ego," 152–54, 196,
203n., 236, 440–43
Pope John XXIII, 391
pornography, 274, 275
"Position of Women in SNCC, The,"
110
"Position Paper on the Woman
Question," 323n.
Post, Emily, 216
President's Commission on the Status
of Women, The, 18–24, 54, 81, 82,
105, 397, 401
areas of study, 20
assumptions of, 24
BPW on, 80
ERA, 19, 22, 23, 55
instructions to, 20
members of, 20, 21
report and recommendations, 18,
20–21, 24, 26, 28, 402, 433–37
President's Task Force on Women's
Rights and Responsibilities, 45,
48–52, 413, 438
A Matter of Simple Justice, 45n.,
49–50, 414, 418
BPW on, 80
ERA, 55
recommendations, 51, 53, 101
press clubs, 265, 423, 425
Pressman, Sonia, 102, 229n.
Pride and Prejudice, 205n.
Priesand, Sally, 376
Princeton University, 307, 420
"Prisoner of Sex," 221n.
Private Employment Committee, 20, 105
Professional and Academic Women,
Conference of, 366n.
professional women, 11, 28–29, 217,
339–71, 373
conferences, 252n., 366n.
in education, 316–37, 342, 348–49,
414
in law, 101–02, 349–55
as lawyers, 68, 70, 71, 72, 95,
101–02, 150, 230, 292, 341,
349–51, 352–54
in medicine, 340, 341–42, 346–48,
355–59, 364
in the arts, 365–71
in the church, 388–90, 393, 394

in media, 252–66
journalists, 261, 268, 270, 373
legislative exemptions, 319, 339
municipal employees, 362, 363
political science, 342, 344–46
sociology, 317, 342–44
tactics, 340–41
  See also specific profession
Professional Women's Caucus, 102–103,
    320, 342n., 355, 416, 425
"Program For Feminist 'Consciousness-
    Raising,' A," 131
property rights, 7, 22, 64, 65, 67, 211
prostitution, 10, 427
Protective Labor Legislation Committee,
    20
"pro-woman" line, 137, 139–40, 141,
    142, 153, 154, 158, 161–63
Psychology, Assoc. for Women in, 340,
    346–47, 364, 412
"Psychology of Day Care, The," 304n.
psychology of oppression, 42, 43–44, 86,
    137–38, 139, 142, 154, 170, 188,
    194–215, 218–21, 227, 341, 368
Psychology Today, 201n.
public accommodations, 87, 419
public hearings
  abortion, 136, 296–97, 369, 410
  ERA, 56, 57
  sex discrimination, 45, 86, 87, 405,
    412
  Title VII and State protective
    legislation, 35, 106
  "want-ads," 42, 86, 404
Pygmalion in the Classroom, 181n.

"Questions I Should Have Answered
    Better," 232

Rabkin, Richard, 185n.
racial discrimination, 9, 14, 21, 41, 45,
    46, 70, 82, 99
racism, 104–105, 116, 135, 136, 148,
    149, 160, 195, 260
"Racism and Sexism," 105n.
Radcliffe College, 2n., 404
Radical America, 112n.
radical feminism, 143, 152, 235,
    240–41, 289, 408
"Radical Feminism," 196n.
Radical Therapist, The, 140n., 142
radical women, 122, 123, 267, 273, 309,
    311, 341, 372
  Chicago, 112–15, 119, 270
  Miss America, 123–25
  New Orleans, 124–25
  San Francisco, 120–21, 128
  Seattle, 119–20
  Washington, 118, 119, 123, 133–34
  See also specific group
Radicalesbians, 241
radical-politico issues, 188, 236n.,
    255–58, 268–69
radicals
  abolitionists, 2, 3, 5, 8, 14

men, 2, 5, 9, 110, 111, 112, 113, 114,
    116, 120, 129, 133–34, 135–36, 273
radio *see* media
"Radio Free Chicago," 276
Rainone, Nanette, 275
Ramparts, 267–68
Random House, 333
Random House Dictionary, 195n.
Rankin, Jeanette, 117n.
rape, 157, 424, 426
Rappaport, Nathan, 143
Rat, 147, 257, 273–74, 362n., 414
Raushenbush, Esther, 404
Rawalt, Marguerite, 23, 26, 55n., 60n.,
    65n., 70–71, 80, 86
"Realities of Abortion," 287n.
recommendations and guidelines, 20–21,
    28, 35, 43, 46, 50–51
Redbook, 288n.
Redstockings, 136–42, 143, 146, 150,
    152, 153, 160, 255, 296, 297, 410
  Manifesto 137, 138, 139–40, 411–12
Reid, Rep. Charlotte, 48
*Report on Sexism in Children's
    Literature,* 335n., 336n.
*Report of the Committee on Civil and
    Political Rights,* 33n.
"Report . . . on the Status of Women,"
    25n.
Republican party, 9, 18, 55
Resolution on Abortion, 290n.
Retreat to Tokenism, 395n.
Revolution, The, 10–11
"Revolution is Happening in our Minds,
    The," 133n.
Rheingold, Joseph, 186
ridicule
  and *bfoq,* 34, 403
  and NOW, 89
  as resistance, 228–32
  Civil Service Comm., 99
  of women's liberation, 110–12, 114,
    117, 124, 133–34, 410
  of women's rights, 9
Rivera, Alice de, 331
Roberts, Sylvia, 217, 230–31
Robinson, Ruby Doris Smith, 110, 403
Rockefeller, Nelson, 292, 294
Roe v. Wade, 285, 426
Rollin, Betty, 185n., 207n.
Roosevelt, Eleanor, 20, 80, 401
Rosenfeld v. Southern Pacific, 36, 101,
    409
Rosenthal, A. M., 263
Rosenthal, R., 181
Ross, Jean, 318n.
Ross, Nancy, L., 174n.
Rossi, Alice, 26, 317n., 328, 342–43,
    344, 412
Roth, Joan Levine, 337

Sade, Janine, 90n., 145n.
St. Joan's Alliance, 391, 403
St. Paul, 378, 382–83
Salisbury Evening Post, 74

Salzman-Webb, Marilyn, 266n.
San Diego State College, 327, 421
San Francisco, 262, 276, 295, 300n.,
 391, 416
 University, 309, 311
San Francisco Chronicle, 263
Sandler, Bernice, 47n., 61n., 97, 322,
 357
Sandy Springs, Md., 122, 130, 271, 407
Saporta, Sarah, 366n., 368n.
Sarachild, Kathie, 131, 270n.
Sarah Lawrence College, 208, 404
Sassower, Doris, 102, 351
Saturday Evening Post, 64n.
Scarry, Richard, 200
Schlossberg, Stephen, 106
Schmeck, Harold M., Jr., 357n.
Schulder, Diane, 292, 352
Scott, Ann, 195n.
SCUM (Society for Cutting Up Men),
 91
Seattle, Wash., 119–20, 213n., 215n.,
 271, 308, 331, 407, 421
"Second Sex, Junior Division, The,"
 200n., 334n.
Second Sex, The, 175, 193n., 197n.,
 198n., 206n., 323
Seelye, John, 218
Selective Service Laws, 61–64, 73
Seneca County Courier, 5
Seneca Falls Convention, 5–7, 13, 54,
 78, 429–33
"Sesame Street," 250–51, 313, 412
Seventeen, 251, 330
"Sex and Caste," 111, 125, 404
sex discrimination, 9, 10, 11, 21, 25, 27,
 28, 29, 33, 34, 35, 197, 263, 346n.
 408
 and Congress, 41–42, 47, 51, 217,
  230–31, 238, 316–17, 319, 419, 421
 Constitutional Amendments, 9, 10,
  22, 40, 69–70
 ERA, 54–77
 court cases, 38–39, 419
 executive orders, 44, 51, 96, 99
 federal policy and law, 18–54, 79,
  319, 339, 405
 OFCC, 44–45, 96, 322, 412
 in education, 96–97, 316–37, 418, 419,
  422
 in government, 99, 362, 363–64
 in professions, 339, 346, 350–51, 353
 publishing, 253–54, 423
  Newsweek, 259
  Time, Inc., 260, 417
 state laws and, 105, 185, 352
 Task Force letter, 50
 U.A.W., 105
"Sex Discrimination in the Legal
 Profession," 351n.
sexism, 104, 135, 138, 141, 142, 149,
 182, 195, 196, 216, 398
 children's books, 265, 334–36
 identity, 4, 64, 124, 197–203, 204,
  212, 215, 250, 251, 306
 image, 86, 151, 154, 201–202

 language, 222–25
 relationships, 137, 142, 197–215
 see also sex-role system; society
Sexism in Children's Books, 334
"Sexism on Capitol Hill," 421
"sex-plus" theory, 38, 424
sex-role system, 6, 18, 89, 122, 135,
 138, 141, 143–44, 150, 152,
 170–222, 344
 children, 306, 313, 333, 412
 feminists on, 122, 236, 398
 man-hating, 235–39
 stereotypes, 25, 125, 197–200, 216,
  231, 233, 247–49, 398
 See also sexism; society
*Sex Role Stereotyping in Elementary
 School Readers,* 334n., 335n.
"Sex-role Stereotyping in the United
 Methodist Nursery School Curricu-
 lum," 336, 394
Sexual Politics, 176n., 177n., 178n.,
 192n., 193n., 195n., 265
sexual revolution, the, 196, 215, 218–22
Sexually Adequate Female, The, 178n.
Shain, Charles E., 329n.
Shanahan, Eileen, 57n.
Shearer, Lloyd, 175
Shelley, Martha, 240n.
Shevlin, Lorna, 337n.
Shuler, Nettie Rogers, 14n.
Shultz, George P., 96–97
Sisterhood is Powerful, 54, 112n., 118,
 128n., 148n., 173n., 240n., 248n.,
 249n., 253n., 285n., 289n., 332n.,
 347n., 348n., 406
"Sisterhood is Powerful," 179n.
"Sisters Recall . . . ," 362n.
slavery, 2, 3, 5, 9
Smith, Rep. Howard, 30
SNCC, 110, 111, 403
Social Policy, 235n.
social security, 22, 79, 88, 213–14
 and taxes, 20, 26, 51, 407
Socialist Workers Party, 120, 163–65
society, organization of, 6, 14, 18, 23,
 24, 33, 50, 85, 378, 384
 and law, 211–12
 biological differences, 171–93
 business forces, 248–49
 child rearing, 199–200
 chivalry, 216–18
 class structure, 18, 58, 70–71, 74,
  90–91, 132, 137, 149, 152, 204n.,
  397
 family, 214–15
 language, 223–25
 marriage, 204–207, 211–13
 political oppression, 196, 397
 separate but equal, 185, 377
 social institutions, 194–211, 398
 third world, 148–49
 woman's options, 207–208, 209, 210,
  240, 242
Society for Humane Abortion, 289n.,
 290n., 295
Sociolinguistics, 223

Sociologists for Women in Society, 344
sociology, 317, 342–44, 412
Solanas, Valerie, 91
Southard, Helen, 103n., 104n.
speakers' bureaus, 98, 101, 274–75, 385
Spense, Arlyss, 350n.
Spokeswoman, The, 264n., 328n.
sports, 422–23, 424
Sports Illustrated, 260, 417
Stair, Lois H., 395
Stanford University, 325n.
Stanton, Elizabeth Cady, 3n., 5, 7, 8, 9,
    10, 12, 13, 342, 383, 393
Stanton-Anthony Brigade, 150, 156, 157
State, U.S. Dept. of, 41
"State Abortion Statutes, Constitutional
    Limitations on," 281n.
State legislation, 14, 22, 23, 26, 32–34,
    56–57, 67, 69
    See also Equal Rights Amendment;
    Title VII
*Status of Women, Second Annual
    Report,* 25n.
Status of Women, State Commissions on
    the, 24, 25, 55, 80, 81, 82, 336,
    346, 411, 426
    conferences, 82–84, 106, 402, 403,
    404, 407
"Status of Women in Art, The," 366n.
"Status of Women in . . . Sociology,"
    317n., 343, 412
Steinem, Gloria, 169n., 215n., 229, 427
Stephenson, Malvina, 48
Stephenson, Violet, 360
stewardesses, airline, 38, 86, 407, 421
Stone, Lucy, 3, 10, 342, 393
student activism, 108–109, 110, 111, 270
Student Lawyer Journal, 350n.
Students for a Democratic Society, 111,
    112, 115, 120, 125, 403, 405
*Study of Employment of Women . . .
    in the Churches,* 389n.
"Study Shows Discrimination Against
    Women Professors," 348n.
"Suburban Scene, The," 332n.
Sudsofloppen, 120–21, 141n.
suffrage, woman's, 1, 2, 7, 10–14, 77–78,
    92, 420
Supreme Court, The
    abortion cases, 285, 285–86n., 426
    case decisions, 11n., 32–33, 38–39,
    40, 71, 72–73, 101, 424
    college admissions, 61n.
    14th Amendment, 11, 61n., 71–72
    jury selection, 59
    right to privacy, 74, 403
    protective legislation, 32–33
    "sex-plus" theory, 38, 424
    women's rights, 22–23, 69–77, 101
    working hours, 40
Susan B. Anthony, 227n.
Sutherland, Elizabeth, 228n.
"Suzie Cream Cheese Collective," 276

tactics, 245
    pressure, 13, 42–43, 86–87

protest, 123, 126–27, 128–29, 133,
    144, 267, 410, 419
    Women's Strike, 92–93
*Takahashi v. Fish and Game
    Commission,* 72
Tanner, Leslie B., 233n.
Taubman, Bryna, 250
Tax, Meredith, 202n., 204n.
television, *see* media
Temperance Movement, 11
Theater, 299, 369–71
    New Feminist, 162, 369–70, 411
    New York Tea Party, 370
"Them and Me," 236–37
third world, 111, 148, 189
Thompson, Mary Lou, 372n., 393
Time, 241, 260, 261, 417
Time, Inc., 260–62, 417
Title VI, 319
Title VII, 21n., 29n., 81, 82, 85n., 352,
    402, 405, 424
    court cases, 35–40, 73, 86, 409
    exemptions, 30, 319
    occupational qualification, 31–32
    policy paper, 25
    powers, 31
    State protective legislation, 34–36, 53,
    68, 406
    U.A.W., 106
    "want-ad" controversy, 40–44
To Benefit Women at Work, 52n.
Tobias, Sheila, 326–27, 349n.
Tokenism, Retreat to, 395n.
"Tokenism and the Pseudo-Radical
    Cop-out," 237n.
Tomasson, Verna, 257n., 258n.
Tonka Toys, 337
Toward a Female Liberation Movement,
    111n., 202n., 241n., 251n., 407
Toward Human Abortion, 289n.
"Toward Partnership in the Church,"
    372n.
toys, 308, 337
Transaction, 201n.
Transportation, U.S. Department of,
    217
Trans-Sister, 392n.
Treseder, Anne, 360n., 361n.
Trial, 351
"Trials of Lois Lane, The," 253n.
Triumph, 425
Truax v. Raich, 72
Truth, Sojourner, 191
Turner, Hester, 416
TV Guide, 248n., 250n., 266
TWA, 407, 421
Two-Edged Sword, The, 379n.
"Tyranny of the Orgasm, The," 219n.

Una, The, 8
underground communications, 254, 270,
    272, 275
"Unfinished Business," 285n.
"Unfreedom of Jewish Women, The,"
    377

Uniform Marriage and Divorce Act, 67, 420
Union Theological Seminary, 385
Unionist, The, 362n., 365
unisex, 142
Unitarian-Universalist Church, 393, 419
United Auto Workers, 69, 83, 88, 105, 106, 417
  Women's Department, 105–107, 346
United Methodist Church, Board of Missions, Women's Division, 389, 390n., 394–95, 422
United Nations Charter, 80
United Presbyterian Church, 373n., 395, 411
Up From Radicalism, 134n., 135n., 297n., 298n.
"Upfront," 370n.
US #2, 134n.
U.S. ex rel. Robinson v. York, 60n., 406–407
U.S. News and World Report, 392n.
U.S. v. Libbey-Owens et al., 39, 419
U.S. v. St. Clair, 62n.
U.S. v. Vuitch, 101, 285–86, 426

Valparaiso Law Review, 59n
Van Gelder, Lindsy, 250, 253n.
Variety, 262–63
Vatican Council II, 373, 391
"Verbal Systems and Women's Status," 300n.
Vietnam War, 117–18, 126, 133, 248, 366, 406, 410
View From the Bottom, 218n.
Virginia, University of, 61
Vive la Différence, 217
Voice of the Women's Liberation Movement, 115, 271, 407
Voices From Women's Liberation, 233n.
Voices of The New Feminism, 372n., 393
Volpe, John, 217
voting, *see* suffrage

Waite, Mary Abbott, 105n.
"want-ad" controversy, 26, 35, 40–44, 82–83, 84, 86, 346, 403, 404, 405, 407, 408, 409, 425
Ward, Barbara, 373
Ward, Mildred E., 359n.
Ware Cellestine, 128n., 149n.
Warhol, Andy, 91
Washington, 331, 394, 423
  University of, 120, 308, 323, 407
Washington, D.C., 82, 96, 118, 406, 422, 425, 426
  press corps, 265, 423, 425
Washington Evening Star, 263
Washington Migrant Ministry, 394
Washington Post, 174n., 175, 215n., 225, 252n., 263, 418

Washington Square Methodist Church, 241, 297
Way, Peggy Ann, 380n.
WBAI-FM, 275, 412
WBCN, 276
WEAW-FM, 275–76
Webb, Michael, 252
Webster's Academic Dictionary, 224
Webster's New Collegiate Dictionary, 224n.
Wedel, Cynthia, 375n.
WEEI, 276
Weeks, Lorena, 37, 410
Weeks v. Southern Bell Telephone and Telegraph Co., 36–37, 410
Weiss-Rosmarin, Trude, 377
Weisstein, Naomi, 112, 172, 173, 176, 180–81, 347, 408
Westinghouse Broadcasting Co., 293n.
Westside group, 115, 405
"What Every Young Girl Should Ask," 330–31
"What's Television Doing for 50.9% of Americans?," 266n.
White House, The, 48, 49
  Conference on Children, 306n., 313, 423
  Conference on Equal Employment Opportunity, 34, 106, 403
White v. Crook, 59n., 404
Whitney Museum of American Art, 366–67, 423
"Why Feminists Want Child Care," 305n.
"Why Men Maintain the Myth," 179, 220
"Why We Came Together," 121
Willard, Emma, 2
Williams v. McNair, 61n.
Willis, Ellen, 134n., 135n., 136, 297n., 298n.
WITCH, 126–30, 408
WITCH Resurrectus, 150
Wolfgang, Myra, 68n.
Wollstonecraft, Mary, 342
"Woman and Her Mind," 202n., 204n.
Woman at Work, 79n.
"Woman in America, The," 402
"Woman Power," 267
Woman Power: The Movement For Women's Liberation, 128n., 149n.
Woman Question, The, 215n.
Woman Suffrage and Politics, 14n.
"Womankind," 275, 412
Womanpower, 19
"Womanpower Problem, The," 320n.
Woman's Advocate, 8
Woman's Bible, The, 12, 13, 380n.
Woman's Day, 264
Woman's Party, 13
Woman's Place, 340n.
Woman's Rights Conventions, 5–8
women, freedom of, 2, 3, 5, 196, 228, 305
Women: A Journal of Liberation, 266n., 271, 324n., 333n.

"Women and Future Manpower Needs,"
    210n.
"Women and Health Care," 362n.
Women and the Law, 65n., 66n., 211
"Women and the Left," 134n.
"Women Are Asked to Lobby Against
    Drunken Drivers," 217n.
women artists, 366–67
"Women Freeing the Men, Too," 215n.
women in armed services, 406, 416, 421
Women in City Government United,
    362, 363, 364, 413
Women in Legal Education, Committee
    on, 354, 416, 425
"Women in Medicine, Facts on," 355n.
women in poverty, 20, 71, 86, 87, 88,
    301, 303, 311, 359, 361
Women in the Church, Joint Committee
    on, 392
Women in the Media, 252, 259n.
"Women in the Ministry," 387n.
"Women in the Radical Movement,"
    110n.
Women in the World of Religion, 381n.
"Women MD's Join the Fight," 358n.,
    360n.
"Women of the World Unite," 228n.
"Women Physicians . . . A Seven Year
    Study, 356n.
"Women Rap about Sex," 119, 219
"Women Seeking Bigger Role in
    Churches," 392n.
Women Speaking, 81n., 84n.
Women United, 107
Women's Action Program, 47n.
Women's Bureau, 19, 28, 32, 41n., 52–
    54, 79, 84, 339n., 355n., 364, 409
    50th anniversary conference, 46, 49,
        55, 418–19
    1969 Handbook, 53, 414–15
women's caucuses, 102–03, 112, 113–14,
    125, 313n., 320, 340, 342n., 343,
    344–46, 349, 352–53, 354, 355,
    366, 374–75, 393, 403, 405, 412–13,
    416, 425
women's centers, 164, 256n., 385, 394,
    417
Women's Equity Act, 51
Women's Equity Action League
    (WEAL), 43, 47, 95–98, 322,
    346n., 409
    Fact Sheets, 317n., 318n.
    higher education, 96–97, 320, 357,
        414, 418, 419, 422
    membership, 96
    secondary education, 321n., 422
Women's Health Collective, 362n.
Women's Liberaiton and the Church,
    380n., 387n., 390n., 394n.
"Women's Liberation and the Cinema,"
    252, 422
Women's Liberation Front, 262
women's liberation movement, 90, 96,
    329, 377
    anti-leadership ethic, 90, 145, 159

background, 109–114
black women, 148–50
class structure, 90–91, 137, 149, 152,
    204n., 397
conferences and workshops, 53, 106,
    115, 130–33, 150, 157, 160, 409,
    414, 420, 426
early groups, 114–122
"elitism," 156–57, 158, 160–61
infiltration, 163–65
Its Origins, Structures and Ideas,
    109n,. 112n., 125n., 126n., 137n.,
    158n.
membership, 108, 123–35, 146, 155
"pro-woman" line, 137, 139–40, 141,
    142, 153, 154, 158, 161–63
progression, 135, 145, 147–48, 157–65,
    398–400
"women's issues," 112, 113, 114, 115,
    116, 118, 119, 121, 125, 130, 150,
    278–302, 303–15, 316, 338–39
"zap action," 124, 136, 295, 296–98,
    340, 367
    See also tactics; *specific group, issue*
Women's Radical Action Project, 115
women's rights movement, 17–107
    constitutional rights, 22–23, 40, 69–
        76
    federal policy and law, 18–54, 79
    organizations, 78–107
    President's Commission, 18–24, 54,
        81, 82, 105, 397, 401
    President's Task Force, 48–52
    See also *specific issue, organization*
Women's Rights Law Reporter, 352n.,
    353
Women's Strike, 87, 92–93, 136, 249,
    263, 269, 299, 420
Women's Strike Coalition, 294
Wood, Myrna, 148n.
Wood, Sally Medora, 232
working women, 17–18, 20, 21, 28–29,
    33, 52, 53, 78, 148, 265, 338–39
    court cases, 36–40
    ERA, 68–69
    hours, 32–33, 40, 68, 72, 105
World Anti-Slavery Convention, 5
World Council of Churches, 374
Wright, Frances, 2

Yick Wo v. Hopkins, 72
Young Socialist Alliance, 163–65
YWCA (Young Women's Christian
    Association), 79, 103–105
    abortion, 291, 299
    Magazine, 104, 105n.
    teenage survey, 329–30
    Women's Resource Center, 104, 420

"zap action," 124, 127, 129, 136, 295,
    296–98, 340, 367
Zwerdling, Daniel, 320n., 321n.